Trees of
Eastern
North
America

Princeton Field Guides

Rooted in field experience and scientific study, Princeton's guides to animals and plants are the authority for professional scientists and amateur naturalists alike. **Princeton Field Guides** present this information in a compact format carefully designed for easy use in the field. The guides illustrate every species in color and provide detailed information on identification, distribution, and biology.

Birds of the Dominican Republic and Haiti, by Steven Latta, Christopher Rimmer, Allan Keith, James Wiley, Herbert Raffaele, Kent McFarland, and Eladio Fernandez

Birds of the West Indies, by Herbert Raffaele, James Wiley, Orlando Garrido, Allan Keith, and Janis Raffaele

Caterpillars of Eastern North America: A Guide to Identification and Natural History, by David L. Wagner

Common Mosses of the Northeast and Appalachians, by Karl B. McKnight, Joseph Rohrer, Kirsten McKnight Ward, and Warren Perdrizet

Dragonflies and Damselflies of the East, by Dennis Paulson

Dragonflies and Damselflies of the West, by Dennis Paulson

Mammals of North America, Second Edition, by Roland W. Kays and Don E. Wilson

Nests, Eggs, and Nestlings of North American Birds, Second Edition, by Paul J. Baicich and Colin J. O. Harrison

Trees of Eastern North America, by Gil Nelson, Christopher J. Earle, and Richard Spellenberg, Illustrations by David More, Edited by Amy K. Hughes

Trees of Western North America, by Richard Spellenberg, Christopher J. Earle, and Gil Nelson, Illustrations by David More, Edited by Amy K. Hughes

Trees of Panama and Costa Rica, by Richard Condit, Rolando Pérez, and Nefertaris Daguerre

Gil Nelson, Christopher J. Earle, and Richard Spellenberg

ILLUSTRATIONS BY DAVID MORE

Edited by Amy K. Hughes

Trees of Eastern North America

Princeton University Press

Princeton and Oxford

Published by Princeton University Press, 41 William Street, Princeton, New
Jersey 08540

In the United Kingdom: Princeton University Press, 6 Oxford Street, Woodstock,
Oxfordshire OX20 1TW

press.princeton.edu

ISBN 978-0-691-14590-7
ISBN (pbk.) 978-0-691-14591-4

Library of Congress Control Number: 2013945913

British Library Cataloging-in-Publication Data is available

This book has been composed in Minion Pro

Printed on acid-free paper. ∞

Edited and designed by D & N Publishing, Baydon, Wiltshire, UK

Printed in China

10 9 8 7 6 5 4 3 2 1

CONTENTS

■ ABOUT THIS BOOK

This guide presents the trees that grow without the aid of human cultivation in the eastern portion of North America north of Mexico. For the purpose of this book, we have chosen the 100th meridian as the division between East and West. In the United States this meridian defines the eastern border of the Texas panhandle, extends northward across the central portion of the Great Plains, and in Canada lies slightly east of the borders between Saskatchewan and Manitoba, and Northwest Territories and Nunavut. Southward, in Texas, there is a notable difference in the species composition of the woody vegetation that lies east or west of a dividing line that continues south from the panhandle's eastern border to Abilene, then curves eastward near the eastern edge of the Edwards Plateau, passing through Austin and ending at Corpus Christi on the Gulf of Mexico.

NATIVE AND INTRODUCED

We indicate in the tree descriptions whether a species is native or introduced to the region covered by this book. Most are "native," meaning they were already in North America before Europeans came to the New World. Since then many trees have been introduced as ornamentals, to provide food, browse, or wood products, or for erosion control or windbreaks. Some of these trees are naturalized: They are reproducing and persisting as populations without the aid of horticultural practice. A few prominent cultivated street and garden trees are also included.

This guide covers the eastern United States and Canada as indicated on the map.

TAXONOMIC ORGANIZATION AND SEQUENCE OF SPECIES

Species are arranged in the book in a manner that reflects the general relationships among species and, at the same time, provides a sequence convenient for the user. The first part of the book covers gymnosperms (conifers and their relatives); the larger group of trees called angiosperms (flowering plants) follows, first with the monocotyledons (monocots; essentially the palms), then the dicotyledons (dicots). See "Gymnosperms and Angiosperms" for more on these groups. Within the gymnosperms, the monocots, and the dicots, the trees are organized into families, within each family into its genera (singular, genus), and within each genus the species that occur in the East. Families, genera, and species are generally presented in alphabetic order, except in cases where juxtaposition of similar species is helpful for identification.

NAMES

We use up-to-date scientific names, drawn from the *Flora of North America North of Mexico* (www.efloras.org), the USDA PLANTS Database (www.plants.usda.gov), and recently published technical literature. We use a unique scientific name for each species. We also provide at least one, and often several, common names, some of them regional (see "Taxonomy and Names," below).

DESCRIPTIONS

Each family, genus, and species has its own description, except when a genus has only one species in the East; in such a case there is only one inclusive genus and species description. Family and genus descriptions describe the group and provide some information on how the plants are used, their ecology, and, sometimes, problems of classification.

Species descriptions begin with common and scientific names, including alternative names ("A.K.A."), if any. For all native species (and many introduced) we provide a "Quick ID," a short statement describing how to recognize quickly that particular species. A more detailed description follows, providing information on habit (the plant's growth form), bark, twigs, foliage, flowers, and fruit. Descriptions vary in length depending on our assessment of the cultural or ecological importance of the tree as well as the extent of its geographic distribution. We indicate whether the species is native or introduced, and describe the usual flowering period, elevation and general habitat, and geographic distribution. When applicable, we explain how to distinguish the species from similar, usually closely related species. For nearly all native and some introduced species we provide a thumbnail map showing the general geographic range of the species in North America north of Mexico.

■ TAXONOMY AND NAMES

Taxonomy defines groups of organisms, gives names to the groups, and arranges them in a hierarchy, thereby producing a classification. It is the oldest of biological sciences, originating in descriptions of organisms in nature. Modern classifications use many lines of evidence, including morphology, chemistry, and DNA-based data, to classify organisms according to their evolutionary relationships. At the higher levels of the hierarchy, those relationships are still unclear; in this book we use the traditional names angiosperms, gymnosperms, monocots, and dicots. At the lower levels of the hierarchy, we use the formal ranks of family, genus, and species, which form a useful framework for identification.

It is useful to be able to recognize plant families; knowing their characteristics makes identification easier and can give one some familiarity with local plants in any part of the world. Families are collections of genera that share a common ancestor. New interpretations, often reached through DNA analysis, are producing ongoing changes in our understanding of some traditional plant families. The former maple family (Aceraceae), for example, does not appear in this book; maples (genus *Acer*) are now placed within the soapberry family (Sapindaceae). For the most part, we have adopted new family alignments, but in a few cases where it helps identification, we have maintained traditional families. We explain the newer, often tentative, classification whether we adopt it or not.

SPECIES NAMES

As strange as it may seem, the precise definition of a plant species has been argued for decades. For our use, it is a group of populations that persists in nature, sufficiently distinct to bear a name. Most species have one or more common names, but common names differ among the world's many languages, as well as regionally, and often do not indicate relationships among species. Furthermore, one species may have several common names, or several species may have the same common name. The two-part scientific name assigned to each species applies to only one species. It distinguishes by name one species from another, indicates some degree of relationship, allows international communication

about organisms, and affords ready information retrieval from references. Scientific names inform us, for example, that Live Oak (*Quercus virginiana*) and Water Oak (*Quercus nigra*) are related, both being in the genus *Quercus*; but that Eastern Poison-oak (*Toxicodendron pubescens*) and the she-oaks (species of *Casuarina*) are not related to one another or to *Quercus*, despite being called "oaks."

The scientific name is a Latinized name, Latin being the primary language of science in the 18th century, when the system was devised. It is a two-part name, or binomial, composed of a genus name followed by a specific epithet. The binomial, together with the author's name, is the complete scientific name for a plant. The first part is a noun, referring to a kind of plant (sumac, oak). The specific epithet is usually an adjective that describes the species or commemorates a person. *Rhus glabra*, the scientific name for Smooth Sumac, provides an example: *Rhus* derives from an ancient Greek name for sumac; *glabra*, derived from the Latin for "bald," refers to the absence of hairs on plant parts. The names or abbreviations that follow the binomial indicate the author or authors (also called the authority or authorities) who named and described the plant. *Rhus glabra* is followed by "L.," for Carolus Linnaeus, the Swedish botanist who is credited with developing the binomial system 260 years ago. When a named species is later understood to belong to a different genus, the specific epithet may be moved from one genus to another. The name of the author who first named the plant is placed in parentheses, followed by the author who moved the name to a different genus. How names are applied and moved about is regulated by a set of rules, the *International Code of Nomenclature for algae, fungi, and plants* (www.iapt-taxon.org).

■ GYMNOSPERMS AND ANGIOSPERMS

Two great groups of land plants bear ovules, which when fertilized produce seeds. The seed has an outer protective layer that surrounds a nutritive tissue, the *endosperm*, to be used by the germinating embryo that developed from the fertilization of an egg within the ovule. The seed plants are traditionally divided into angiosperms and gymnosperms. We retain those terms in this book.

The conifers and their allies, the Ginkgo, cycads, and gnetophytes, comprise the *gymnosperms*, a term derived from the Greek words for "naked seeds." The ovules of these plants are not protected within a closed ovary, as they are in the angiosperms, but are borne directly on structures that expose them to the environment at the time of pollination, although the ovules are often protected to some degree by overlapping scales. Technically, the endosperm in gymnosperms has a different origin than that of the angiosperms, that difference further helping to distinguish the two groups. Most gymnosperms are pollinated by wind, but many cycads are pollinated by insects. In conifers and gnetophytes, as in angiosperms, the pollen grain grows a pollen tube that conveys sperm to, or even within, the ovule, where the egg is fertilized. In Ginkgo and the cycads, however, fertilization occurs when motile sperm swim from the pollen grain into the ovule.

While there is considerable ongoing scientific debate about how closely related the groups within the gymnosperms are, it is clear that the gymnosperms were formerly a highly diverse group, of which only a comparatively few families have survived to the present.

The other group of seed plants is the *angiosperms*, a term derived from Greek words meaning "vessel" and "seed," referring to a plant with seeds borne within an enclosure. Angiosperms evolved from gymnosperms around 200 million years ago, when a leaflike, ovule-bearing structure in a seed fern closed around its ovules (which when fertilized develop into seeds), producing a carpel. The flower, characteristic of angiosperms, became an organized reproductive structure consisting of carpels, stamens, petals, and sepals. The *carpel* is the fundamental unit of the *pistil*, the pollen-receiving, seed-producing part of the flower. There are two types of pistils: those composed of a single carpel (a simple pistil); and those composed of two or more carpels joined together (a compound pistil). One can usually determine the number of carpels in a pistil by counting the number of chambers (or locules), but because chamber walls are sometimes incomplete or absent in a compound pistil, the number of branches on the stigma (the pollen receptor at the tip of the pistil) is also usually a reliable indicator; two or more branches suggest a compound pistil. The diagram above illustrates the evolution of the carpel from an ovule-bearing leaf, and the development of a compound pistil from a fusion of several carpels. Two other features that distinguish angiosperms from gymnosperms are the seed-bearing closed fruits, and the way the endosperm develops.

Angiosperms are divided into the Monocotyledoneae, or monocots, and Dicotyledoneae, the dicots. The names refer to the number of embryonic, often nutrient-storing leaves in the embryo within the seed: *monocots* typically have one, whereas *dicots*

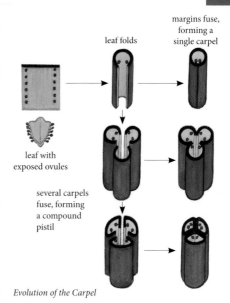

Evolution of the Carpel

typically have two. In addition, monocots usually have flowers with parts in multiples of three and leaves with a number of conspicuous parallel veins. Dicots usually have flowers with parts in multiples of four or five, and net-veined leaves with main veins branching in a pinnate or palmate pattern, interconnected by a conspicuous net of minor veins.

■ TREE BIOLOGY

There is no scientific difference between a tree and a shrub, although in general conversation a tree is understood to have a single woody stem (a trunk) and a well-defined crown of branches. In this book we include such plants, large and small, along with a number of plants generally taller than a human that may be thought of as shrubs, often growing with multiple woody trunks.

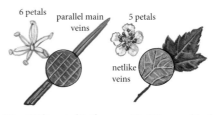

Monocot Flower and Leaf   *Dicot Flower and Leaf*

TREE GROWTH

A tree's growth may be seasonal, in the temperate zone beginning in the spring and ceasing in the fall. In some areas growth begins during the wet season and ceases during the dry period, and in the subtropical zone it continues throughout the year. At the tip of every twig and every root is a tiny patch of cells (the *apical meristem*) that divide, rapidly at the onset of the growing season and usually not at all during dormant periods. These divisions produce new cells behind the tip that enlarge, mature, and perform specific functions, at the same time adding length to the twig or root. The rate and direction of growth determines the shape of the crown of the tree. If the apical meristem on the main stem divides more rapidly than those at the tips of branches, the tree will be conical, as in firs and spruces. If all the meristems divide at the same rate, and branches spread equally, the crown will be round. The shape of the crown is often useful in the identification of open-grown trees, but is less useful in identifying forest-grown trees.

As a twig or young root matures, a new set of dividing cells forms beneath its outer layer. This is a continuation of a cylindrical layer of dividing cells (the *vascular cambium*) that extends throughout the tree beneath the bark of the branches, trunk, and roots. Cells of this layer divide inward and outward. New cells produced inward mature into water-conducting cells and other cells of the wood; those produced outward mature into cells that conduct sugar produced in the leaves and into cells of the bark. As new wood cells are added by the cambium, the wood increases in volume, and the cambium and bark are stretched. The bark becomes fissured and cracked as it stretches and dies, producing patterns helpful in tree identification. The dead outer layer protects the inner living tissue from insects, fungi, fire, abrasions, and other hazards.

TRUNK AND CROWN

Above ground, a tree has a trunk from which grows an array of branches and leaves that form the *crown*. We describe, in general terms, crown shapes of trees growing in the open under moderate conditions. Local conditions, however, can influence the shape of the crown. In a crowded forest the crowns of trees may be narrow, the shaded lower branches may be small or lost, and the upper branches may grow toward the light. Wind, salt spray, abrasion by windblown ice or sand, lightning, fire, and other environmental influences can injure or deform a tree's crown. On high windswept ridges, wind-blown ice crystals may kill exposed

foliage, producing a forest of low, gnarled trees called *krummholz* (German for "crooked wood").

The *trunk* is the branch-free portion between the roots and the crown. In our descriptions we usually give its diameter, measured at a height of about 1.3 m. In some cases, as in arid regions, tree trunks may be very short; for those the diameter is estimated at about the midpoint between the ground and the first branches. When we describe a tree as having more than one trunk, it means the trunk divides at a height lower than 1.3 m, often at ground level.

BARK

Bark is the outer protective covering of the branches, trunk, and roots. It varies among species from paper-thin to very thick. As a tree increases in girth, the bark is stretched, producing patterns of cracks, ridges, and flat areas that are often characteristic of a species. Large vertical cracks are often called *fissures*, smaller ones *cracks*, and short cracks or crosshatching may be called *checks*. Closely adjacent fissures have *ridges* between them; when they are farther apart the intervening space may form *plates*. Bark may be papery, fibrous, corky, or hard and woody. The elements may wear bark away very slowly, and it may become thick and deeply fissured. Thinner bark may continually shed its outer layers in long shaggy strips, flaking scales, or in paperlike sheets. We describe the bark of most species, and illustrate its features.

TWIGS AND BUDS

Buds are composed of tiny patches of cells ready to divide and are usually covered by protective scales. A *terminal bud* forms at the tip of a twig each year as growth ceases. It is usually covered by external scales that protect dormant cells (the apical meristem) that are ready to divide and produce new tissue the next growing season. When growth begins, the bud scales fall away from the terminal bud, leaving *bud-scale scars* on the twig that mark the point as the beginning of that season's growth. A *twig* is the portion at the tip of a branch system produced by the current year's growth—that is, the part between the terminal bud and the bud-scale scars left from the previous year's terminal bud. One may determine the age of a young branch by counting the rings of bud-scale scars produced each year along the branch.

Terminal buds form at the tips of the twigs; *lateral buds* form in the *axils* of leaves along a twig; *false terminal buds* are lateral buds that appear to be at the tip of the twig but are slightly offset. When buds become active and begin to grow, they may

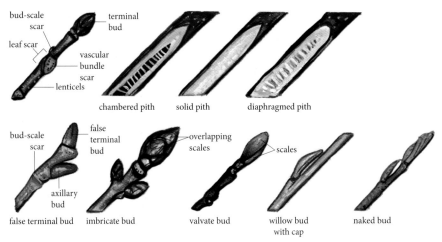

bud-scale scar · terminal bud · leaf scar · vascular bundle scar · lenticels · chambered pith · solid pith · diaphragmed pith

bud-scale scar · false terminal bud · overlapping scales · scales · axillary bud

false terminal bud · imbricate bud · valvate bud · willow bud with cap · naked bud

Twigs and Buds

give rise to a new twig with its new leaves, a flower, a flower cluster, or a cone.

The protective bud scales may be *imbricate*, overlapping like shingles; *valvate*, meeting only at their edges like a clamshell; or may consist of a *cap* formed by a single scale. If there are no scales at all, the bud is said to be *naked*. Buds and their scales may be covered by protective gummy or sticky substances, hairs, or minute glands.

Twigs provide many clues to the identification of a tree, useful in summer or winter. The place on a twig where leaves attach is the *node* (see "Leaf Arrangement," p. 12). When the leaf falls, the twig bears a distinctively shaped *leaf scar*. Within the scar is a pattern of several small points where *vascular bundles* entered the leaf; the number of these *bundle scars* can provide identification clues (see "Winter Twigs of Selected Eastern Trees," p. 20). Twigs usually have a distinctive color, and the surface may have noticeable *lenticels*, patches of loose, usually pale, corky cells, varying from small dots to short dashes or even long lines. The twig surface may be hairless, variably hairy, or glandular, the glands stalked or not (see "Hairs, Glands, Wax, and Resin," p. 15), or it may be winged or thorny (see "Thorns, Spines, and Prickles," p. 14). In cross section, a twig may vary from cylindric to angled (if four-angled, it is often described as "square"); in some cases the pattern or color of the twig's *pith*, or interior tissue, is important. In a number of trees we mention *short shoots*, twigs that grow very slowly and are much shorter than the faster-growing main branch; the short shoots may bear

leaves or fruits (described and illustrated in "Leaf Arrangement," p. 12).

LEAVES

Photosynthesis, the process by which sugars are produced from water and carbon dioxide using light energy from the sun, occurs in green tissues of plants. By this mode plants produce their "food," and ultimately provide support for almost all life on Earth. The complex chemical processes of photosynthesis operate best at different temperatures in different species, but always require sufficient water for cells to function. Leaves must neither dry out nor overheat, and their shapes, lobing, and divisions help cope with these limitations. Each leaf has a lifetime during which it is productive, after which it falls. The presence or absence of leaves and their many shapes and arrangements provide important characters for tree identification.

Trees that are never barren of leaves are *evergreen*. Their leaves persist on the tree for one or more years, and new leaves are borne before old leaves drop. Most conifers and many kinds of angiosperm trees are evergreen. *Deciduous* trees are without leaves for part of the year. Many drop their leaves before the cold season; others may be *drought deciduous*, dropping leaves during the dry season. In either case, leaves are dropped when they can no longer function. In species of the cypress family (Cupressaceae), entire twigs die and fall with all of their attached leaves, usually after three to four years in evergreen species, and seasonally in the deciduous Baldcypress and other species.

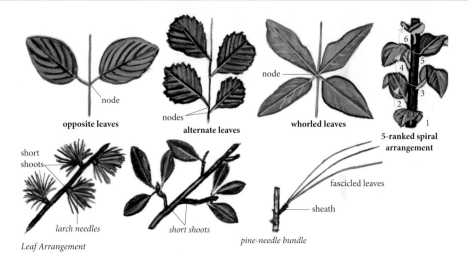

node

opposite leaves

nodes

alternate leaves

node

whorled leaves

6
5
4
3
2
1

5-ranked spiral
arrangement

short
shoots

larch needles

short shoots

fascicled leaves

sheath

pine-needle bundle

Leaf Arrangement

LEAF ARRANGEMENT The arrangement of leaves on the twig is helpful in identification. Leaves are *opposite* when two are attached on either side of a node. When three or more are attached at a node, the leaves are *whorled*. When only one leaf occurs at a node, they are *alternate*. (On leafless twigs, the leaf scars indicate the arrangement.) Alternate leaves show a *spiral* arrangement along the twig (illustrated above), discernible by tracing a line up or down a twig from one node to the next. The illustration shows a *five-ranked* spiral, with the first five leaves tracing a spiral around the twig, and the sixth positioned directly above the first. Leaves may bend or twist upon their petioles to reach for maximum light, in some species orienting on opposite sides of the twig in the same plane. Such leaves are *two-ranked*. In some conifers, such as firs, the arrangement of the needles on the shoot can look very different in sun foliage (sometimes resembling a toothbrush or bottlebrush) and shade foliage (which may appear two-ranked), even though the needles are actually spirally arranged. Some leaves grow in close clusters or bundles, called *fascicles*, usually from short shoots. The *pine-needle bundle* is a short shoot genetically programmed to grow only so long, to produce needles—often a certain number for the species—and then to stop growing and after a few seasons to drop as a unit.

PARTS OF A LEAF Leaves vary in shape and size. A *simple* leaf has an undivided blade of leaf tissue. The leaf blade may be cleft or lobed, sometimes deeply, but not separated into leaflets, as in a *compound leaf*, discussed below. A common kind of simple leaf in dicots consists of a stalklike *petiole* and an expanded, flat *blade*. If leaves have a petiole, they are *petiolate*; if the petiole is absent and the blade attaches directly to the twig, the leaf is *sessile*. At the base of the petiole is often a pair of *stipules*; these may be small green leaflike structures, or may be a different color or modified into scales, bristles, or spines (called *stipular spines*). Conifer leaves are often scalelike or needlelike. Scalelike leaves are short, thick, and often closely appressed to the twig. Needlelike leaves are much longer than wide and divergent from the twig.

The edge of the leaf blade is the *margin*, the features of which are often important. Margins may be *entire*, that is smooth and not incised or toothed; they may be *toothed* and have fine or coarse, sharp or blunt, bristle- or gland-tipped teeth; or they may be *scalloped* or more deeply cleft and thus *lobed*. The lobes can be round-tipped or pointed. Lobed leaves may be *pinnately lobed*, with a feather-like shape, as seen in many oaks; or *palmately* lobed, roughly hand-shaped, like most maples.

Leaves of monocots have *parallel veins* that run the length of the blade; additionally, tiny veins connect adjacent parallel main veins, often like rungs of a ladder. Most dicot leaves are *net-veined*, with tiny veins forming netlike interconnections between major veins, which usually form a prominent pinnate or palmate pattern. (Monocot and dicot venation is illustrated on p. 9.) A pinnately veined leaf has a *midvein*, or *midrib*, and several prominent *lateral veins* branching from it. Palmately veined leaves have several main veins originating from

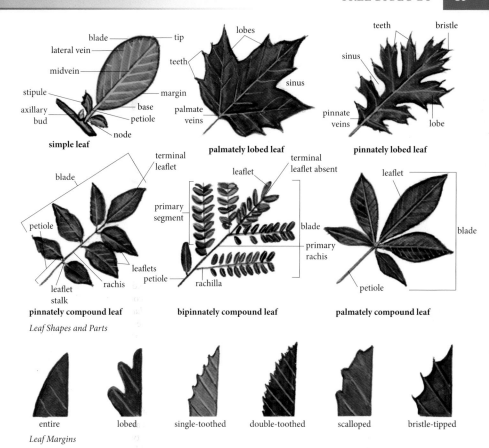

Leaf Shapes and Parts

| blade | tip | lobes | teeth | bristle |

simple leaf   **palmately lobed leaf**   **pinnately lobed leaf**

pinnately compound leaf   **bipinnately compound leaf**   **palmately compound leaf**

entire   lobed   single-toothed   double-toothed   scalloped   bristle-tipped

Leaf Margins

the same point at the base of the leaf. Veins may be relatively inconspicuous or, especially on the lower surface, may be raised well above the surface, often in a prominent netlike pattern.

COMPOUND LEAVES In a compound leaf the blade is divided to the midrib, which is then called the *rachis*. The blade is in the form of individual divisions called *leaflets*. If the leaflets are aligned along two sides of the rachis like the sides of a feather, the leaf is *pinnately compound*. If the divisions all join at the tip of the petiole, in the pattern of a hand with spreading fingers, the leaf is *palmately compound*. A palmately compound leaf has no rachis. Pinnately compound leaves may be *odd-pinnate* (with an odd number of leaflets because a terminal leaflet is present) or *even-pinnate* (terminal leaflet absent). The leaflets may be opposite one another or may be alternate on the rachis.

A compound leaf may be divided more than once; this is particularly common in pinnately compound leaves. If there is one more set of divisions—that is, the leaflets themselves are divided into leaflets—the leaf is *bipinnate*; if there is yet another division the leaf is *tripinnate*. In a bipinnate leaf, each divided section branching from the rachis has its own, secondary axis, called a *rachilla*, bearing leaflets; in this book we call the unit formed by the rachilla and its leaflets a *primary segment*. A tripinnate leaf has, in addition, secondary segments. Compound leaves often show pronounced responses to environmental conditions, with the leaflets orienting to the sun, folding together when it is hot and dry, or folding at night.

A compound leaf may resemble a spray of simple leaves: The presence of an axillary bud at the base of the petiole is a clue that a given stem is a twig with many small leaves rather than the rachis of a compound leaf. Buds do not occur in the axils of leaflets on a compound leaf.

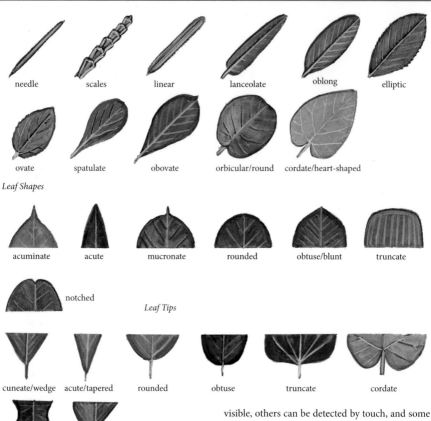

needle   scales   linear   lanceolate   oblong   elliptic

ovate   spatulate   obovate   orbicular/round   cordate/heart-shaped

Leaf Shapes

acuminate   acute   mucronate   rounded   obtuse/blunt   truncate

notched

Leaf Tips

cuneate/wedge   acute/tapered   rounded   obtuse   truncate   cordate

auriculate/eared   asymmetrical   *Leaf Bases*

SHAPES OF SIMPLE LEAVES
Simple leaves range in shape from the needlelike and scalelike leaves of many conifers, to linear to circular blades. In addition, the shape of the leaf tip or apex and the leaf base can vary. Where water is sufficient, leaves may have considerable surface area to capture sunlight. In drier situations they may be needlelike, the reduced surface area helping to reduce evaporation and conserve water. The shape of the leaf blade helps with identification, although on any one tree, leaves in the sun may differ in shape and lobing from those in the shade, and leaves on rapidly growing shoots are often larger than those elsewhere.

SURFACE FEATURES OF PLANT PARTS
It is often useful to examine features on the surfaces of leaves, twigs, and buds. Some features are visible, others can be detected by touch, and some can be seen only with a hand lens or other form of magnification.

STOMATA A leaf's surface is interspersed with *stomata* (singular, *stoma*), microscopic pores through which carbon dioxide, oxygen, and water vapor move from the surrounding air to the interior of the leaf and vice versa; the stomata open or close to help control the flow of atmospheric gases and the moisture content of the leaf cells. In many conifers, the stomata form conspicuous whitish lines on the surface of the leaf, and the size, position and number of these lines can be important features in identification.

THORNS, SPINES, AND PRICKLES Sharp-tipped thorns, spines, and prickles provide protection to plants (plants with such protrusions are often described as "armed"). They are also useful in identification. *Thorns* are sharp-tipped twigs, sometimes very stout, occasionally branched. *Spines*, such as those in cacti or in many species

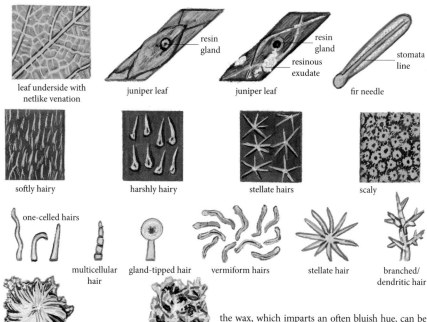

leaf underside with netlike venation

juniper leaf — resin gland

juniper leaf — resin gland, resinous exudate

fir needle — stomata line

softly hairy

harshly hairy

stellate hairs

scaly

one-celled hairs

multicellular hair

gland-tipped hair

vermiform hairs

stellate hair

branched/ dendritic hair

peltate/shield-like hair

malpighian/ T-shaped hair

wax scales

Leaf Surface Features

of the bean family (Fabaceae), are modified leaves. *Prickles* are small, sharp-pointed growths arising from the surface tissue of the plant; the sharp barbs on the cone of Virginia Pine and "thorns" on a rose are examples of prickles. *Bristles* (or awns) are minute hairlike extensions, such as those that tip the leaf lobes of some red oaks.

HAIRS, GLANDS, WAX, AND RESIN Leaves, twigs, fruits, and other plant parts may be *hairless* (*glabrous*) or *hairy* (*pubescent*). The hairs, which in plants are called *trichomes*, take many forms and colors, visible with magnification. Hairs may be unicellular or multicellular. Some have a sticky gland at the tip, while other glands lie directly on the leaf surface. *Vermiform* hairs are wormlike; *stellate* hairs are star-shaped; *dendritic* hairs branch like a tree; *peltate* hairs are somewhat shield-shaped with the attaching stalk at the center of the lower surface; and *malpighian* hairs are T-shaped.

When surfaces of leaves, twigs, or fruits are coated in a waxy substance they are described as *glaucous*;

the wax, which imparts an often bluish hue, can be rubbed off, exposing the darker surface (as in a blueberry). Pale hairs and wax reflect light, reducing heating of the surface beneath; wax is also impervious to water. Hairs, glands, and resins also help to protect plants from insect or large-animal herbivory. Some leaves are varnished with resin. The scalelike leaves of some conifers have a diagnostic gland that may or may not bear a drop of resin or whitish exudate and can be an important identification character.

TREE REPRODUCTION

Trees produce *pollen*, which bears the sperm, and *ovules*, which contain the egg and receive the sperm. The parts of the tree that produce these structures are often called male and female. In gymnosperms the ovules are borne in ovulate cones or occasionally develop singly at the end of a stalk; all gymnosperms covered in this book produce pollen in small, short-lived pollen cones. In angiosperms the reproductive structure is the flower; pollen is produced in the stamens, and the ovule(s) is contained in the pistil. Pollen is usually carried by wind, insects, or birds.

The basic flower is *bisexual*, containing both "male" stamens and a "female" pistil. In some species, stamens and pistils occur in different flowers, each sex separate and the flowers thus *unisexual*. Male unisexual flowers are described as *staminate*, female flowers as *pistillate*. Gymnosperms do not produce

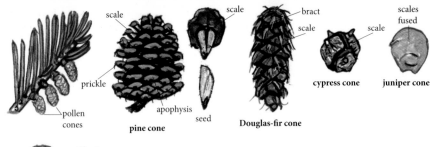

scale

prickle

pollen
cones

pine cone

apophysis

seed

scale

Douglas-fir cone

bract

scale

scale

cypress cone

scales
fused

juniper cone

aril

seeds

yew ovulate structure

Gymnosperm Cones and Seeds

flowers; instead they have unisexual *pollen cones* (male) and *ovulate cones*, or *seed cones* (female).

Unisexual flowers or cones may be distributed in several ways. Species that have both male and female structures (whether bisexual flowers or both male and female unisexual cones or flowers) on the same individual are *monoecious* ("one house"). If the male and female reproductive structures occur on separate plants, each plant having only-male or only-female cones or flowers, the plants are *dioecious* ("two houses"). In some species, bisexual and unisexual flowers may be intermixed on the same plant.

GYMNOSPERM REPRODUCTIVE STRUCTURES Gymnosperms produce ovules that are not included in a vessel-like structure akin to the angiosperm pistil. Most gymnosperm species in this book are monoecious, each plant bearing both pollen cones and ovulate cones; a few are dioecious. Pollen cones in most of the plants covered here are small, fragile, and short-lived (a few trees retain pollen cones for a year or more after releasing the pollen). A pollen cone consists of a central axis and few to many scales, each of which has two to several sacs where pollen forms. When pollen is released, it is carried by wind to the ovules. For a brief period the ovules are exposed to the external environment, and pollen reaches the receptive ovule, delivering the sperm.

The mature ovule-bearing reproductive structures are highly varied in gymnosperms. Ginkgo produces two naked ovules at the end of a long stalk, usually only one maturing. The seed that develops has a fleshy outer coat and a hard inner coat. In *Taxus* and *Torreya* the cone is reduced to a few tiny bracts, above which are one or two

naked ovules, usually only one maturing. The hard external covering of the seed is partially or wholly surrounded by a fleshy or leathery *aril*.

Conifers (all other gymnosperms in this book) have ovules borne in well-defined cones with multiple woody or fleshy *scales*. On the upper side of each scale lies one to several ovules, from which the seeds develop. In many species the seeds are winged. After cones mature, which may take from one to three years, they may either disintegrate into their component scales, fall whole from the tree after seed dispersal, or remain on the tree either with or without seeds.

Ovulate cones differ from species to species and vary in persistence (lasting for a season or several years), providing many characters useful in identification. The cone has from two to more than 100 scales arranged around a central axis. The scales are separated from each other by a highly modified infertile leaf called a *bract*, which may or may not be visible on the surface of the cone. In some conifers, including the families Araucariaceae and Cupressaceae, the bracts and fertile scales are fused; in *Juniperus* species the fused scales form the fleshy or juicy "berry." In other groups, including the Pinaceae, the bracts and fertile scales are separate, and the bracts may be *exserted* from between the fertile scales and thus visible. The cones of most *Pinus* species take two years to mature; the intervening period of dormancy results in the formation of a thickening, called an *apophysis*, at the tip of each scale. Apophyses vary among species with regard to size, shape, color, and the presence or absence of a prickle at the extreme end; these characters are useful in identification.

ANGIOSPERM FLOWERS In their complexity, the flowers and fruits of angiosperm trees provide many characters useful in identification. A *complete flower* consists of four whorls of parts (beginning from the bottom, or outside): the *calyx*, *corolla*, *stamens*, and *pistil* or pistils. (*Incomplete* flowers lack one or more of these whorls of parts.) The calyx

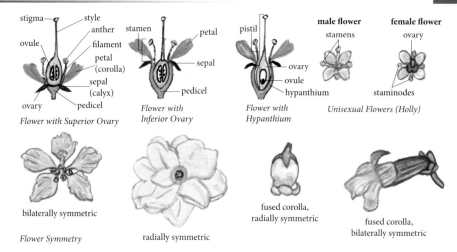

Flower with Superior Ovary

Flower with Inferior Ovary

Flower with Hypanthium

Unisexual Flowers (Holly)

bilaterally symmetric

radially symmetric

Flower Symmetry

fused corolla, radially symmetric

fused corolla, bilaterally symmetric

consists of *sepals*, usually flat green parts that protect the flower bud. The corolla consists of *petals*, often flat and colorful, which attract pollinators. Undifferentiated sepals and petals are often referred to as *tepals*. Stamens may be few or many, each consisting of a stalk (*filament*) with a pollen-bearing sac (*anther*) at its tip. The center of the flower may have one or more pistils, each consisting of an *ovary* that contains an *ovule* or several to many ovules. The ovary has one or more *styles*, each tipped with a pollen-receiving *stigma*. The pollen grain produces a tubular extension that grows through the style and places sperm at the opening of an ovule. Parts may be large, elaborate, and showy in flowers pollinated by insects or animals, or they may be tiny or even missing in flowers adapted for wind pollination. In trees, the tiny flowers are often unisexual.

Flowers that have the symmetry of a wheel when viewed from the top, their parts radiating equally in all directions, are *radially symmetric*. If the parts are oriented so that the flower can be divided only in one way to produce two equal halves, the flower is *bilaterally symmetric*. Any of the whorled parts of the flower (sepals, petals, stamens, pistils) may be fused to one another. This is particularly noticeable when the petals join to form a tube, funnel, bowl, or flask-shaped structure. Parts of adjacent series may also fuse together. For example, the bases of the sepals, petals, and stamens may all fuse into a cup that surrounds the ovary, forming a *hypanthium*, as in the rose family (Rosaceae).

Features of the pistil are important for plant identification. If all the flower parts attach at the base of the pistil, the ovary is said to be *superior*; if they attach at the top of the pistil, the ovary is *inferior*. The pistil may have one or several stigmas, and one to several chambers, both clues to the number of carpels in the pistil (see "Gymnosperms and Angiosperms," pp. 8–9 , for a discussion and illustration of the carpel). A *simple pistil* consists of a single carpel; it always has one chamber. A *compound pistil* consists of two or more fused carpels. If carpel walls remain in place, then the number of chambers suggests the number of carpels. If carpel walls have disappeared, the compound pistil may be one-chambered; the number of stigmas on the

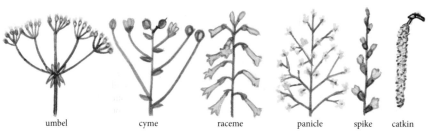

umbel   cyme   raceme   panicle   spike   catkin

Flower Clusters

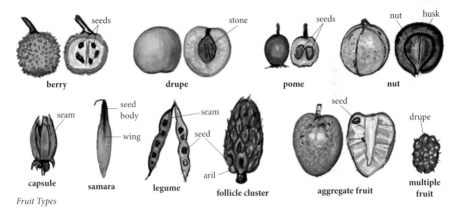

Fruit Types

pistil will often indicate the number of carpels. These variations in simple and compound pistils result in the different types of fruits.

The positions of flowers, and the manner in which they are held, can be important in identification. Flowers may be *terminal* on the stem, growing from its tip, or they may arise from *axillary* buds, at the junction where a leaf meets the twig. They may be single or occur in large or small clusters or *inflorescences*, many of which have technical names. Large, multibranched arrays are called *panicles*; tight, long, narrow arrays in which the flowers lack stalks are *spikes*; loose, narrow, elongate arrays with stalked flowers are *racemes*. *Catkins* are small, tightly packed clusters of highly reduced unisexual flowers.

ANGIOSPERM FRUITS The angiosperm fruit— the plant's seed-containing reproductive body— takes many forms and is so varied that a plethora of terms has been developed; we avoid the more technical ones as much as possible.

Many fruits are dry at maturity, and may or may not split open to release the seeds. A fruit that opens is said to be *dehiscent*; a fruit that does not is *indehiscent*. An indehiscent one-seeded fruit with a hard outer wall is a *nut*; an *achene* is also one-seeded, with a hard outer wall like a nut, but it is tiny. A hard, dry fruit with one or more wings, such as that of a maple, is a *samara*. A dry, more or less thin-walled, long and narrow, usually splitting fruit is often called a *pod*, a non-technical term that may refer to a follicle or a legume. The individual fruits of magnolia, which derive from a simple pistil, are dry, and split along one side, are *follicles*; the structure in which the magnolia's follicles are produced is a *folliculum*. A bean pod, also derived from a simple pistil and dry, splits along two sides and is

technically a *legume*. A fruit that is dry and splits but is derived from a compound pistil is a *capsule*. Capsules may have one or several chambers.

There are also many kinds of fleshy fruits. The term *berry*, in its technical sense, refers to a fleshy fruit with few to many seeds within. A *drupe* has an outer skin over a fleshy layer, and an innermost hard, bony layer (the "pit" or stone) that surrounds usually one seed; some drupes have several stones. The fruit of the apple is a *pome*, in which the hypanthium has become thick and fleshy and joined to the (inferior) ovary. Individual fruits of adjacent flowers may join together as a unit, as in the mulberry or fig; these are called *multiple fruits*. In an *aggregate fruit* adjacent ovaries of a single flower, joined or not, form the single structure we call the fruit. A blackberry and a strawberry are examples.

■ FOREST STRUCTURE

The study of how trees are distributed on the landscape is part of forest ecology, a topic much too large to be covered in this book. There are, however, some ecological and geographical concepts that appear throughout this book in the discussions of habitat and plant associations. These include the geographical provinces in which plants occur and the way in which these provinces are influenced by climate, soil composition, elevation, and topography. Disturbances, such as fire, are also important. This is especially true for southern pine forests dominated by Longleaf Pine or Slash Pine. In these forests natural and prescribed fire play a determinative role in maintaining forest structure and the composition of ground cover vegetation by retarding the encroachment of woody vegetation and exposing mineral soil to seed germination.

Three commonly mentioned eastern regions are the coastal plains, Piedmont, and mountains. The coastal plain of the eastern United States stretches from coastal New Jersey southward, throughout Florida and west to eastern Texas. The Piedmont lies between the coastal plain and the eastern mountains, and extends from northern New Jersey to east-central Alabama. The Piedmont and coastal plain are divided for part of their extent by the fall line, a comparatively narrow sandy upland that serves as an ecotonal transition between the two. The Appalachian Mountains, which include the highest elevations in the eastern U.S., lie generally northwest and west of the Piedmont, extending from the Chic-Choc Mountains of eastern Quebec province southwestward through northern Georgia into northeastern Alabama. West of the Appalachians, our region is dominated by plains and plateaus, including the Great Plains, the Interior Low Plateaus, and the Ozark Plateau. Some trees occur in more than one of these geographic provinces; others are restricted to only one. Knowing the geographic province in which a tree naturally occurs can help distinguish it from similar species that grow in other provinces; this is especially true for some of the oaks.

Our habitat descriptions use several terms to describe climate: Arid, mesic, humid, and wet describe a range of increasing moisture availability; and arctic, alpine, boreal, montane, temperate, subtropical, and tropical describe increasing temperature, which may be due to either reduced latitude or reduced elevation. Ecologists have long remarked on this correspondence between latitude and elevation, whereby trees seen on mountaintops are often the same species (or at least the same genera) that can otherwise be found only far to the north; Red Spruce and American Mountain Ash are examples. Climates that are highly seasonal, with hot summers and cold winters, are called continental because they are most commonly found in the interior of the continent; climates with cool summers and mild winters are called maritime, occurring in areas downwind of oceans.

Topography affects the distribution of trees. In North America, mountain slopes facing south are warmer and drier than adjacent north-facing slopes, and the vegetation reflects this. Trees reach the limits of their tolerance to cold in the high mountains and in the far north, and in such severe environments they are often reduced in size, sometimes appearing stunted or as shrubs.

The distribution of trees is also related to water availability. Wetland vegetation occurs where there is too much water; the plants are shallowly rooted or have special adaptations to deal with saturated soils. Mesic vegetation occurs where plants are seldom limited by insufficient water, usually due to both ample rainfall and adequate soil water, such as in many parts of the southern Appalachians. Xeric (dry) forests and woodlands occur in semiarid climates or in places where the soil retains moisture poorly, as in the central Florida scrub. Riparian forests or woodlands occur on the margins of freshwater bodies, or sometimes along seasonal streams.

Chemistry of the soil is also important. Acid soils, often derived from igneous rock or decaying vegetation, may have different associations of trees than do basic soils, which are often derived from sedimentary dolomite, limestone, or ancient coral reefs, all high in carbonates. Habitats with basic soils are often referred to as calcareous in our descriptions. Some areas have rock types rich in heavy metals, such as serpentine, which is so nutrient-poor and chemically different from "normal" soils that very few plants can grow upon it.

■ LEAF AND TWIG KEYS

The leaf keys that follow are designed to help the user with leaf in hand locate a species match inside the book. The Key to the Gymnosperms by Leaf Type (p. 25) shows a representative leaf or twig for each type of gymnosperm likely to be encountered growing naturally in eastern North America. The Key to Selected Angiosperms by Leaf Shape (p. 26) includes an array of angiosperm leaves grouped by leaf type, shape, proportions, arrangement on the twig, and details of the leaf margin. Each leaf shown represents its species, which is named in the caption, or its genus or occasionally a larger group of related species. Flip to the page noted, and compare your leaf in hand to the representative species and to its fellow genus and family members. The keys are not drawn to scale: Leaves that are very small may be adjacent to leaves that are very large; instead, the keys emphasize length/width proportions, margins, lobing, and, in compound leaves, the nature of the leaflets.

Preceding the leaf keys the reader will find Winter Twigs of Selected Eastern Trees (p. 20). This key shows the details of the twigs of more than 150 species of eastern North American trees. The illustrations and the groupings highlight features that are visible on the species's twigs when the tree is leafless, including features of the buds and the leaf scars. The captions give the species name and the page number on which a full account can be found.

WINTER TWIGS OF SELECTED EASTERN TREES

LEAF SCARS OPPOSITE
Terminal Bud Present
1 bundle scar

Hearts-a-bustin' (Celastraceae), p. 194

Eastern Wahoo (Celastraceae), p. 194

Pygmy Fringetree (Oleaceae), p. 451

Eastern Swampprivet (Oleaceae), p. 452

Yellow Buckeye (Sapindaceae), p. 632

Red Buckeye (Sapindaceae), p. 636

Painted Buckeye (Sapindaceae), p. 636

3 bundle scars, terminal bud stalked, spherical

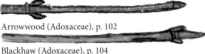

Flowering Dogwood (Cornaceae), p. 214

3 bundle scars, lateral buds appressed

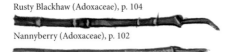

Arrowwood (Adoxaceae), p. 102

Blackhaw (Adoxaceae), p. 104

Rusty Blackhaw (Adoxaceae), p. 104

Nannyberry (Adoxaceae), p. 102

Possumhaw (Adoxaceae), p. 102

Maples: 3 bundle scars

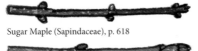

Sugar Maple (Sapindaceae), p. 618

Red Maple (Sapindaceae), p. 624

Maples: 3 bundle scars (cont.)

Striped Maple (Sapindaceae), p. 622

Boxelder (Sapindaceae), p. 626

Numerous bundle scars

White Ash (Oleaceae), p. 454

Green Ash (Oleaceae), p. 458

Carolina Ash (Oleaceae), p. 456

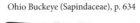

Yellow Buckeye (Sapindaceae), p. 632

Ohio Buckeye (Sapindaceae), p. 634

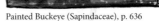

Red Buckeye (Sapindaceae), p. 636

Painted Buckeye (Sapindaceae), p. 636

Terminal Bud Absent
1 bundle scar

Lilac Chastetree (Verbenaceae), p. 694

5 bundle scars

American Elderberry (Adoxaceae), p. 100

Red Elderberry (Adoxaceae), p. 100
Numerous bundle scars

Southern Catalpa (Bignoniaceae), p. 166

Princesstree (Paulowniaceae), p. 466
Twigs piercing at tip

European Buckthorn (Rhamnaceae), p. 480
Others without terminal bud

Katsura Tree (Cercidiphyllaceae), p. 202

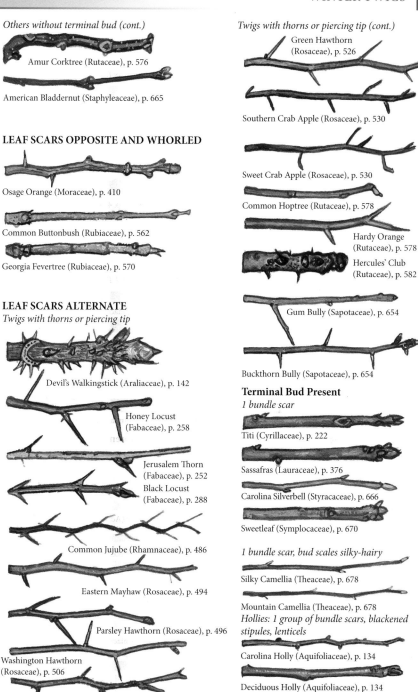

Others without terminal bud (cont.)

Amur Corktree (Rutaceae), p. 576

American Bladdernut (Staphyleaceae), p. 665

LEAF SCARS OPPOSITE AND WHORLED

Osage Orange (Moraceae), p. 410

Common Buttonbush (Rubiaceae), p. 562

Georgia Fevertree (Rubiaceae), p. 570

LEAF SCARS ALTERNATE
Twigs with thorns or piercing tip

Devil's Walkingstick (Araliaceae), p. 142

Honey Locust
(Fabaceae), p. 258

Jerusalem Thorn
(Fabaceae), p. 252
Black Locust
(Fabaceae), p. 288

Common Jujube (Rhamnaceae), p. 486

Eastern Mayhaw (Rosaceae), p. 494

Parsley Hawthorn (Rosaceae), p. 496

Washington Hawthorn
(Rosaceae), p. 506

Littlehip Hawthorn
(Rosaceae), p. 514

Twigs with thorns or piercing tip (cont.)

Green Hawthorn
(Rosaceae), p. 526

Southern Crab Apple (Rosaceae), p. 530

Sweet Crab Apple (Rosaceae), p. 530

Common Hoptree (Rutaceae), p. 578

Hardy Orange
(Rutaceae), p. 578
Hercules' Club
(Rutaceae), p. 582

Gum Bully (Sapotaceae), p. 654

Buckthorn Bully (Sapotaceae), p. 654

Terminal Bud Present
1 bundle scar

Titi (Cyrillaceae), p. 222

Sassafras (Lauraceae), p. 376

Carolina Silverbell (Styracaceae), p. 666

Sweetleaf (Symplocaceae), p. 670

1 bundle scar, bud scales silky-hairy

Silky Camellia (Theaceae), p. 678

Mountain Camellia (Theaceae), p. 678
*Hollies: 1 group of bundle scars, blackened
stipules, lenticels*

Carolina Holly (Aquifoliaceae), p. 134

Deciduous Holly (Aquifoliaceae), p. 134

Sarvis Holly (Aquifoliaceae), p. 138

Hollies (cont.)

Mountain Holly (Aquifoliaceae), p. 138

Common Winterberry (Aquifoliaceae), p. 140

3 bundle scars

Sweetgum (Altingiaceae), p. 106

American Smoketree (Anacardiaceae), p. 108

Alternateleaf Dogwood (Cornaceae), p. 220

Black Walnut (Juglandaceae), p. 354

Northern Spicebush (Lauraceae), p. 370

Sour Gum (Nyssaceae), p. 448

Black Gum (Nyssaceae), p. 448

Water Tupelo (Nyssaceae), p. 446

Carolina Buckthorn (Rhamnaceae), p. 480

Glossy Buckthorn (Rhamnaceae), p. 478

Eastern Cottonwood (Salicaceae), p. 590

Balsam Poplar (Salicaceae), p. 588

Swamp Cottonwood (Salicaceae), p. 592

Bigtooth Aspen (Salicaceae), p. 592

Lombardy Poplar (Salicaceae), p. 590

Quaking Aspen (Salicaceae), p. 594

Numerous bundle scars

American Mountain Ash (Rosaceae), p. 558

Numerous bundle scars (cont.)

Poison Sumac (Anacardiaceae), p. 116

Common Pawpaw (Annonaceae), p. 120

Bundle scars scattered, twig bitter/aromatic

Black Cherry (Rosaceae), p. 546

Chokecherry (Rosaceae), p. 544

Pin Cherry (Rosaceae), p. 546

Magnolias: Twig stout, rings of stipule scars below bud

Tuliptree (Magnoliaceae), p. 380

Cucumber-tree (Magnoliaceae), p. 382

Bigleaf Magnolia (Magnoliaceae), p. 386

Fraser Magnolia (Magnoliaceae), p. 382

Umbrella Magnolia (Magnoliaceae), p. 386

Terminal bud naked

American Witch-hazel (Hamamelidaceae), p. 350

Hickories: Bundle scars in 3 U-shaped clusters

Water Hickory (Juglandaceae), p. 358

Pecan (Juglandaceae), p. 358

Bitternut Hickory (Juglandaceae), p. 360

Mockernut Hickory (Juglandaceae), p. 364

Pignut Hickory (Juglandaceae), p. 362

Shagbark Hickory (Juglandaceae), p. 366

Beech: Buds lance- or cigar-shaped

American Beech (Fagaceae), p. 300

Oaks: Buds clustered near tip of twig

White Oak (Fagaceae), p. 303

Bluff Oak (Fagaceae), p. 304

Swamp White Oak (Fagaceae), p. 308

Bur Oak (Fagaceae), p. 310

Overcup Oak (Fagaceae), p. 312

Post Oak (Fagaceae), p. 312

Chestnut Oak (Fagaceae), p. 320

Swamp Chestnut Oak (Fagaceae), p. 320

Chinkapin Oak (Fagaceae), p. 322

Northern Red Oak (Fagaceae), p. 326

Black Oak (Fagaceae), p. 326

Scarlet Oak (Fagaceae), p. 328

Pin Oak (Fagaceae), p. 330

Shumard Oak (Fagaceae), p. 330

Southern Red Oak (Fagaceae), p. 334

Cherrybark Oak (Fagaceae), p. 332

Turkey Oak (Fagaceae), p. 334

Texas Red Oak (Fagaceae), p. 336

Darlington Oak (Fagaceae), p. 340

Willow Oak (Fagaceae), p. 342

Water Oak (Fagaceae), p. 344

Blackjack Oak (Fagaceae), p. 346

Terminal Bud Absent
1 bundle scar, may have pseudoterminal bud

Sweet Birch (Betulaceae), p. 154

Yellow Birch (Betulaceae), p. 152

River Birch (Betulaceae), p. 156

Paper Birch (Betulaceae), p. 154

Water Birch (Betulaceae), p. 158

American Hornbeam (Betulaceae), p. 162

Eastern Hophornbeam (Betulaceae), p. 164

Common Persimmon (Ebenaceae), p. 224

Sourwood (Ericaceae), p. 230

Chinese Tallow (Euphorbiaceae), p. 246

Two-wing Silverbell (Styracaceae), p. 667

American Snowbell (Styracaceae), p. 668

American Plum
(Rosaceae), p. 538

Canada Plum (Rosaceae), p. 540

Hog Plum (Rosaceae), p. 542

3 bundle scars, leaf scars V-shaped

Peachleaf Willow (Salicaceae), p. 598

Bebb Willow (Salicaceae), p. 602

Black Willow (Salicaceae), p. 604

3 bundle scars, leaf scars V-shaped (cont.)

Carolina Willow (Salicaceae), p. 606

Missouri River Willow (Salicaceae), p. 608

Balsam Willow (Salicaceae), p. 610

Shining Willow (Salicaceae), p. 612

Laurel Willow (Salicaceae), p. 612

Sandbar Willow (Salicaceae), p. 614

2–9 bundle scars, may have pseudoterminal bud

Eastern Redbud (Fabaceae), p. 256

Kentucky Coffeetree (Fabaceae), p. 260

Silktree (Fabaceae), p. 270

Kentucky Yellowwood (Fabaceae), p. 280

Chinaberry-tree (Meliaceae), p. 404

American Sycamore (Platanaceae), p. 470

Florida Soapberry (Sapindaceae), p. 644

Numerous bundle scars, may have pseudoterminal bud

Smooth Sumac (Anacardiaceae), p. 112

Winged Sumac (Anacardiaceae), p. 114

Staghorn Sumac (Anacardiaceae), p. 112

American Basswood (Malvaceae), p. 396

Red Mulberry (Moraceae), p. 406

Tree-of-heaven (Simaroubaceae), p. 659

Lateral buds stalked

Hazel Alder (Betulaceae), p. 148

Seaside Alder (Betulaceae), p. 150

Elms: Leaf scars 2-ranked, 3+ bundle scars depressed

Planertree (Ulmaceae), p. 682

Winged Elm (Ulmaceae), p. 684

American Elm (Ulmaceae), p. 684

Cedar Elm (Ulmaceae), p. 686

Slippery Elm (Ulmaceae), p. 686

September Elm (Ulmaceae), p. 688

Rock Elm (Ulmaceae), p. 688

KEY TO THE GYMNOSPERMS BY LEAF TYPE

LEAVES BROAD, FAN-SHAPED

Ginkgo, p. 35

LEAVES SCALELIKE
Irregularly Branching Twigs, Small Berry-like Cones

Junipers, pp. 40–46

Long, Ropy Twigs

Giant Sequoia, p. 48

deciduous

Pond Cypress, p. 48

leaves shorten toward branch tips
see also Cook Pine, p. 36

Norfolk Island Pine, p. 36

Twigs Forming Fans or Sprays

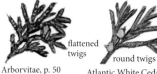

flattened twigs

Arborvitae, p. 50

round twigs

Atlantic White Cedar, p. 38

LEAVES NEEDLELIKE
Needles 2-ranked, Deciduous, Falling with Branchlet

shoots opposite on twig

Dawn Redwood, p. 46

shoots alternate on twig

Baldcypress, p. 48

Needles 2-ranked, Evergreen

leaves wide, varying lengths

Bunya Pine, p. 36

leaf with raised midrib

Yews, pp. 78–79

very sharp tips!

Florida Torreya, p. 79

shade-grown foliage is 2-ranked

Firs, pp. 51–55

leaf with central groove

Eastern Hemlock, p. 76

Needles Solitary, Spirally Inserted

broad leaves with sharp tips

Monkey-puzzle Tree, p. 36

sharp, incurved needles

Cryptomeria, p. 40

may appear roughly 2-ranked

China Fir, p. 40

very prickly leaves

Common Juniper, p. 46

upright cones, blunt leaves

Firs, pp. 51–55

hanging cones, leaves with sharp tips

Spruces, pp. 56–61

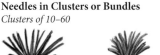

cones have 3-pointed bracts

Douglas-fir, p. 60

twigs smooth (no hairs)

Carolina Hemlock, p. 76

Needles in Clusters or Bundles
Clusters of 10–60

evergreen

Cedars, p. 54

deciduous

Tamarack, p. 56

Pines, pp. 62–75

Bundles of 2–5

2-needled pines, pp. 62–75

3-needled pines, pp. 66–72

5 needles

Eastern White Pine, p. 62

KEY TO SELECTED ANGIOSPERM TREES BY LEAF SHAPE

LEAVES NEEDLELIKE OR SCALELIKE

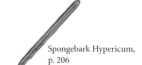 Spongebark Hypericum, p. 206

 Australian-pine, p. 190

 Canary Island Tamarisk, p. 674

SIMPLE LEAVES, MARGINS ENTIRE
Leaves Whorled

 Deviltree, p. 122

 Lipstick Tree, p. 124

 Common Buttonbush, p. 562

 Scarletbush, p. 568

Leaves Opposite

 Long Key Locustberry, p. 391

 White Indigoberry, p. 570

 West Indian False Box, p. 198

 Darlingplum, p. 484

 Chinese Privet, p. 462

 Pomegranate, p. 475

 Pale Lidflower, p. 426

 Long-stalked Stopper, p. 438

 White Stopper, p. 432

 Boxleaf Stopper, p. 432

 Twinberry, p. 438

 Caribbean Princewood, p. 564

 Leadwood, p. 484

 Blolly, p. 444

 White Mangrove, p. 209

 Tetrazygia, p. 402

 Black Mangrove, p. 98

Glossy Privet, p. 462

Wild Olive, p. 464

 Japanese Tree Lilac, p. 466

 Spiny Fiddlewood, p. 692

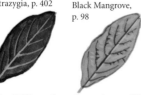 Possumhaw, p. 102

 Flowering Dogwood, p. 214

 Seven-year Apple, p. 564

 Guava, p. 440

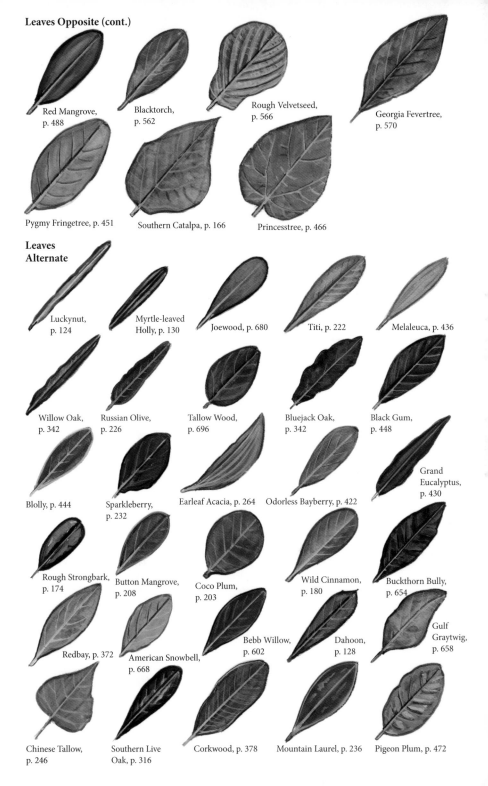

Leaves Opposite (cont.)

Red Mangrove, p. 488

Blacktorch, p. 562

Rough Velvetseed, p. 566

Georgia Fevertree, p. 570

Pygmy Fringetree, p. 451

Southern Catalpa, p. 166

Princesstree, p. 466

Leaves Alternate

Luckynut, p. 124

Myrtle-leaved Holly, p. 130

Joewood, p. 680

Titi, p. 222

Melaleuca, p. 436

Willow Oak, p. 342

Russian Olive, p. 226

Tallow Wood, p. 696

Bluejack Oak, p. 342

Black Gum, p. 448

Blolly, p. 444

Sparkleberry, p. 232

Earleaf Acacia, p. 264

Odorless Bayberry, p. 422

Grand Eucalyptus, p. 430

Rough Strongbark, p. 174

Button Mangrove, p. 208

Coco Plum, p. 203

Wild Cinnamon, p. 180

Buckthorn Bully, p. 654

Redbay, p. 372

American Snowbell, p. 668

Bebb Willow, p. 602

Dahoon, p. 128

Gulf Graytwig, p. 658

Chinese Tallow, p. 246

Southern Live Oak, p. 316

Corkwood, p. 378

Mountain Laurel, p. 236

Pigeon Plum, p. 472

Leaves Alternate (cont.)

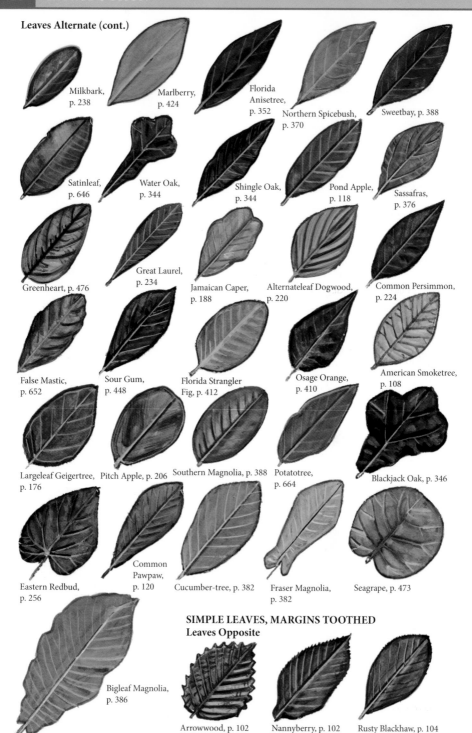

Milkbark, p. 238

Marlberry, p. 424

Florida Anisetree, p. 352

Northern Spicebush, p. 370

Sweetbay, p. 388

Satinleaf, p. 646

Water Oak, p. 344

Shingle Oak, p. 344

Pond Apple, p. 118

Sassafras, p. 376

Greenheart, p. 476

Great Laurel, p. 234

Jamaican Caper, p. 188

Alternateleaf Dogwood, p. 220

Common Persimmon, p. 224

False Mastic, p. 652

Sour Gum, p. 448

Florida Strangler Fig, p. 412

Osage Orange, p. 410

American Smoketree, p. 108

Largeleaf Geigertree, p. 176

Pitch Apple, p. 206

Southern Magnolia, p. 388

Potatotree, p. 664

Blackjack Oak, p. 346

Eastern Redbud, p. 256

Common Pawpaw, p. 120

Cucumber-tree, p. 382

Fraser Magnolia, p. 382

Seagrape, p. 473

Bigleaf Magnolia, p. 386

SIMPLE LEAVES, MARGINS TOOTHED
Leaves Opposite

Arrowwood, p. 102

Nannyberry, p. 102

Rusty Blackhaw, p. 104

Leaves Opposite (cont.)

Walter's Viburnum, p. 104

Katsura Tree, p. 202

Eastern Swampprivet, p. 452

European Buckthorn, p. 480

Leaves Alternate, Teeth Sharp or Distinct

Sandbar Willow, p. 614

Saltbush, p. 146

Black Willow, p. 604

Wax Myrtle, p. 420

Eastern Mayhaw, p. 494

Cockspur Hawthorn, p. 508

River Birch, p. 156

Gray Birch, p. 156

Planertree, p. 682

American Elm, p. 684

Florida Trema, p. 186

Common Winterberry, p. 140

American Holly, p. 126

Peachleaf Willow, p. 598

Washington Hawthorn, p. 506

Downy Serviceberry, p. 490

Manchineel, p. 240

American Hornbeam, p. 162

Hophornbeam, p. 164

Eastern Wahoo, p. 194

Black Cherry, p. 546

American Plum, p. 538

Common Hackberry, p. 184

Carolina Buckthorn, p. 480

American Beech, p. 300

Hazel Alder, p. 148

Sweet Birch, p. 154

Citron, p. 574

Sweet Crab Apple, p. 530

Silky Camellia, p. 678

Leaves Alternate, Margins Toothed (cont.)

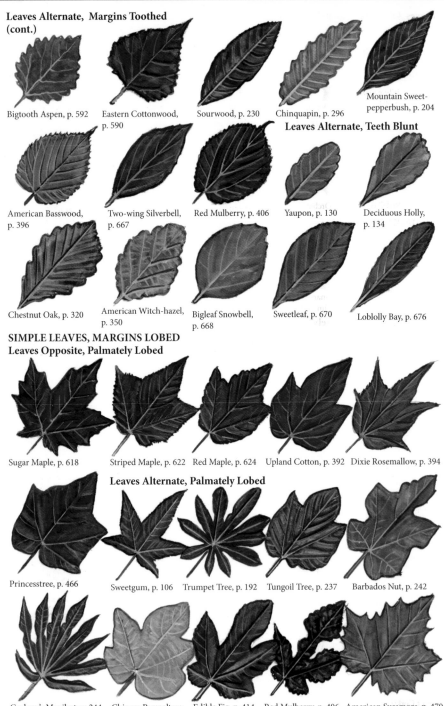

Bigtooth Aspen, p. 592

Eastern Cottonwood, p. 590

Sourwood, p. 230

Chinquapin, p. 296

Mountain Sweet-pepperbush, p. 204

Leaves Alternate, Teeth Blunt

American Basswood, p. 396

Two-wing Silverbell, p. 667

Red Mulberry, p. 406

Yaupon, p. 130

Deciduous Holly, p. 134

Chestnut Oak, p. 320

American Witch-hazel, p. 350

Bigleaf Snowball, p. 668

Sweetleaf, p. 670

Loblolly Bay, p. 676

SIMPLE LEAVES, MARGINS LOBED
Leaves Opposite, Palmately Lobed

Sugar Maple, p. 618

Striped Maple, p. 622

Red Maple, p. 624

Upland Cotton, p. 392

Dixie Rosemallow, p. 394

Leaves Alternate, Palmately Lobed

Princesstree, p. 466

Sweetgum, p. 106

Trumpet Tree, p. 192

Tungoil Tree, p. 237

Barbados Nut, p. 242

Graham's Manihot, p. 244

Chinese Parasoltree, p. 400

Edible Fig, p. 414

Red Mulberry, p. 406

American Sycamore, p. 470

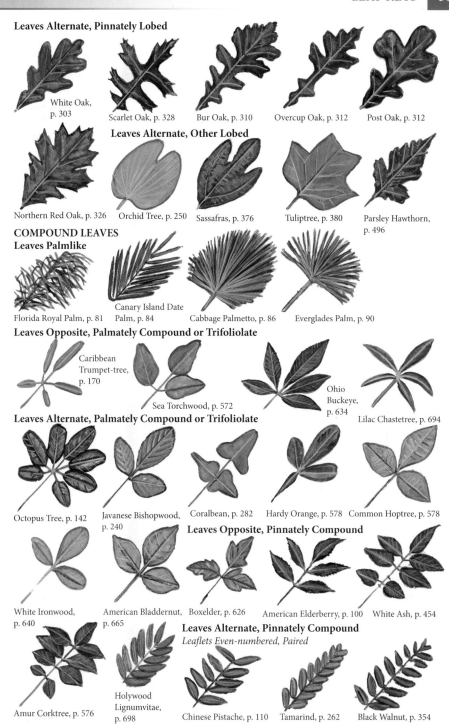

Leaves Alternate, Pinnately Lobed

White Oak, p. 303

Scarlet Oak, p. 328

Bur Oak, p. 310

Overcup Oak, p. 312

Post Oak, p. 312

Leaves Alternate, Other Lobed

Northern Red Oak, p. 326

Orchid Tree, p. 250

Sassafras, p. 376

Tuliptree, p. 380

Parsley Hawthorn, p. 496

COMPOUND LEAVES
Leaves Palmlike

Florida Royal Palm, p. 81

Canary Island Date Palm, p. 84

Cabbage Palmetto, p. 86

Everglades Palm, p. 90

Leaves Opposite, Palmately Compound or Trifoliolate

Caribbean Trumpet-tree, p. 170

Sea Torchwood, p. 572

Ohio Buckeye, p. 634

Lilac Chastetree, p. 694

Leaves Alternate, Palmately Compound or Trifoliolate

Octopus Tree, p. 142

Javanese Bishopwood, p. 240

Coralbean, p. 282

Hardy Orange, p. 578

Common Hoptree, p. 578

Leaves Opposite, Pinnately Compound

White Ironwood, p. 640

American Bladdernut, p. 665

Boxelder, p. 626

American Elderberry, p. 100

White Ash, p. 454

Leaves Alternate, Pinnately Compound
Leaflets Even-numbered, Paired

Amur Corktree, p. 576

Holywood Lignumvitae, p. 698

Chinese Pistache, p. 110

Tamarind, p. 262

Black Walnut, p. 354

Leaves Alternate, Pinnately Compound (cont.)

Leaflets even-numbered, paired (cont.)

West Indian
Mahogany,
p. 404

Inkwood, p. 640

Florida Soapberry, p. 644

Tree-of-heaven, p. 659

Leaflets even-numbered, opposite and alternate

Carrotwood,
p. 638

Wingleaf
Soapberry, p. 646

Paradisetree, p. 660

Leaflets Odd-numbered, in Lateral Pairs

Florida Poisontree,
p. 110

Smooth Sumac, p. 112

Winged Sumac, p. 114

Poison Sumac, p. 116

Gumbo Limbo,
p. 178

Yellow Necklacepod,
p. 284

Black Locust, p. 288

Water Hickory, p. 358

Pignut Hickory, p. 362

Mockernut Hickory,
p. 364

Silktree, p. 270

American
Mountain
Ash, p. 558

Hercules' Club,
p. 582

Lime Pricklyash,
p. 584

Florida Toadwood,
p. 638

Leaflets odd-numbered, opposite and alternate

Kentucky
Yellowwood, p. 280

Indian Rosewood,
p. 282

Mexican Alvaradoa,
p. 468

Florida Bitterbush,
p. 468

Chinese Box, p. 576

Leaves Alternate, Bipinnately or Tripinnately Compound

Devil's Walkingstick, p. 144

Pride-of-Barbados, p. 252

Jerusalem Thorn, p. 252

Royal Poinciana, p. 256

Water Locust, p. 258

Kentucky Coffeetree, p. 260

Sweet Acacia, p. 266

Silktree, p. 270

Chinaberry-tree, p. 404

Horseradish-tree, p. 418

Goldenrain Tree, p. 642

All gymnosperms are woody plants. Their seeds do not develop within a closed ovary, as those of the angiosperms do, but are exposed during fertilization and thereafter, in most cases, develop within a closed vegetative structure. Most gymnosperms contain aromatic resins in their wood, foliage, and reproductive structures. These resins serve several purposes, among them to discourage herbivory and fungal attack. Most species have tough evergreen foliage, simple or pinnate, with linear leaves or with broader leaves that have simple parallel venation.

Gymnosperms include the conifers, ginkgo, cycads, and gnetophytes. The only cycad native to our area is the **Coontie** (*Zamia pumila* L.), a small shrub native to Fla. and se. Ga. that bears a crown of sharp-edged pinnate fronds, each 20–100 cm long. The Coontie, like most cycads, is often mistaken for a palm, but it bears its seeds in cones. The only gnetophyte in e. North America is **Clap-weed** (*Ephedra antisyphilitica* Berland. ex C.A. Meyer), which grows as a shrub to 1 m tall in Tex. and Okla. at the extreme w. edge of our area. Species of *Ephedra* occur through much of the Northern Hemisphere and have a long history of medicinal use.

■ CONIFERS

The conifers are an ecologically and economically important group of about 650 species worldwide. They are usually classified into 6 families, of which the largest are the pine, podocarp, and cypress families, each containing more than 130 species. The araucaria, yew, and umbrella pine families are much smaller, totaling about 70 species. Of the families treated in this book, it appears that the pine family evolved first, then the araucarias, umbrella pine, cypresses, and yews.

Conifers are fundamentally distinguished from flowering plants by their reproductive structures, their wood, and their resins. Superficially, they are also generally distinguishable by their seed cones, growth form, and foliage. The cones are generally spherical to cylindrical, composed of few to many woody scales, but in junipers and the yew family the seeds are within fleshy green or red "berries." The conifer growth form generally features a single erect trunk, often with a uniform branching pattern. The foliage (and often the wood) of most conifers is aromatic with resins, is frequently in the shape of needles that are often more than 10 times longer than wide, and is usually evergreen.

Worldwide, the conifers have great ecological importance, dominating forest landscapes throughout much of the temperate and most of the boreal climate zones. The pine and cypress families are well represented in e. North America, and we also have 3 native yews. From Ky. northward, conifers primarily occur in the mountains or otherwise on harsh, rocky or boggy sites, but farther south they are also an important component of lowland and coastal ecosystems, where pine forests and baldcypress swamps cover vast swaths of landscape.

Coontie

Clap-weed

GINKGOACEAE: GINKGO FAMILY

This family includes a single species, which now survives in the wild in only a small area in sw. China. Ginkgo is a common ornamental in North America. Trees are dioecious.

GINKGO *Ginkgo biloba* L.
A.K.A. MAIDENHAIR TREE

QUICK ID The Ginkgo's fan-shaped leaves are unlike those of any other tree. The woody pegs covering the branches identify it in the winter.

Deciduous tree, usually with a single straight trunk, up to 30 m tall and 100 cm diam.; crown rounded or irregular. **BARK** Gray, with short, irregular furrows. **TWIG** Gray, bearing stubby, woody short shoots protruding up to 1 cm from the branch at regular intervals, each bearing a cluster of leaves and often a pollen cone or seed. **LEAF** Slightly leathery, fan-shaped, with a pattern of radiating veins (not seen in any other tree). Blade 5–10 cm broad, light green, turning golden and falling each winter. **POLLEN CONE** Borne on short shoots, catkin-like. **SEED** Naked, usually only 1, developing from a pair of ovules situated at the tip of a slender stalk borne on short shoots, appearing plum-like, almond-shaped, yellow to orange, about 2.5 cm long, the outer coating softening and giving off a foul odor when ripe.

HABITAT/RANGE Introduced; native to China. A common ornamental in temperate climates; there are unconfirmed reports of naturalization in the ne. U.S.

Notes: Millions of years ago members of the ginkgo family were common around the world, but they now occur in the wild in only a small area in sw. China. The name, meaning "silver seed," is from Chinese. Various tissues of the plant are toxic or are used medicinally, primarily in naturopathic and Chinese traditional medicine. Apart from being attractive landscape trees in general, Ginkgos are very resistant to air pollution and are commonly planted in cities. Female plants are undesirable, due to the unpleasant odor given off by the ripe seeds. The oldest and one of the largest Ginkgos in North America was planted in 1789 and can be seen at Longwood Gardens in Pa.; its trunk exceeds 4 m in girth.

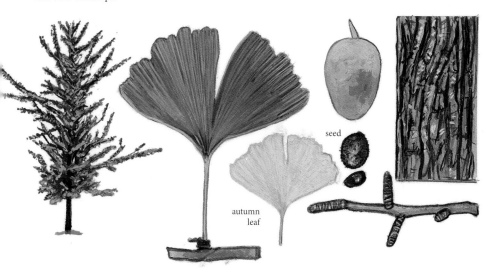

seed

autumn leaf

Ginkgo

ARAUCARIACEAE: ARAUCARIA FAMILY

The Araucariaceae includes 3 genera and 40 species native to Southeast Asia, Australia, Oceania, and South America. Several species are ornamentals in North America.

■ *ARAUCARIA:* ARAUCARIAS

Araucaria, the principal genus of trees in the Araucaria family, is native to the Southern Hemisphere and includes 19 species. Four species are popular ornamentals in warmer areas of the e. U.S., mainly on the Atlantic and Gulf coastal plains from S.C. to Tex. They are tall evergreen trees with a single straight trunk covered in uniform whorls of branches emerging at nearly right angles from the trunk, the branches cloaked in a dense sheath of needle-shaped to triangular leaves. **BARK** Rough, dark gray, horizontally ridged. **LEAF** Evergreen, multi-veined, spirally arranged on twigs, branches, and even the trunk. **POLLEN CONE** Large; the largest of any conifer. **SEED CONE** Dense and heavy, disintegrating before or soon after falling. The seeds are very tasty, widely eaten within these species' native ranges.

BUNYA PINE *Araucaria bidwillii* Hook.

LEAF Flat, spirally inserted on the branch, about 5 cm long, less than 1 cm wide at the base, stiff, with a sharp point. **CONES** Pollen cone 10–20 cm long; seed cone up to 30 cm long, weighing up to 5 kg.

MONKEY-PUZZLE TREE *Araucaria araucana* (Molina) K. Koch

LEAF Flat, triangular, spirally inserted on the branch, 3–5 cm long, 8–25 mm wide at the base, stiff, with a sharp point. **CONES** Pollen cone 10–20 cm long; seed cone up to 20 cm long.

COOK PINE *Araucaria columnaris* (J.R. Forst.) Hook.

LEAF Scalelike, blunt, 4–7 mm long, curved toward the branch and covering it on all surfaces. **CONES** Pollen cone 5–10 cm long; seed cone to 15 cm long.

NORFOLK ISLAND PINE *Araucaria heterophylla* (Salisb.) Franco

LEAF Scalelike, blunt, 4–7 mm long, curved toward the branch and covering it on all surfaces. **CONES** Pollen cone 3.5–5 cm long; seed cone up to 15 cm long. *Notes:* Very locally naturalized in s. Fla.

Bunya Pine

seed

leaves

cone

cone scale

Monkey-puzzle Tree

leaf

leaves

cone

seed

cone scale

cone scale

seed

leaves

Cook Pine

cone

cone scale

seed

Norfolk Island Pine

young leaves

cone

cone

CUPRESSACEAE: CYPRESS FAMILY

The cypress family includes about 140 species divided into about 30 genera, scattered across all continents except Antarctica. E. North America is home to 8 native species, all of which are competitively successful on physically stressful sites, such as swamps, bogs, cliffs, seashores, frequently burned areas, dry prairies, limestone, and dark forest understories. Many species in the family are widely planted as ornamental trees and shrubs.

Cypresses are trees and shrubs, monoecious or dioecious, deciduous or evergreen. **BARK** For all the species in our area bark is reddish, brown, or gray, and fibrous, peeling off in long, thin strips. **LEAF** Generally of 2 types: simple scalelike leaves that cover the twig; or needlelike leaves that may either cover the twig, or be flattened and 2-ranked. In all of our species only 1 type of leaf is predominant on mature trees. The twigs are shed, usually after 1–5 years, along with their attached leaves. **SEED CONE** Small and woody in most species, but junipers produce small, round, more or less fleshy cones, with cone scales fused at maturity, the structure resembling a berry. Most species have fragrant and very rot-resistant wood.

Many genera contain only a single species, and the family is a modern relic of a group that was once far more widespread and successful. The **Umbrella Pine** (*Sciadopitys verticillata* [Thunb.] Siebold & Zucc.) was formerly assigned to the cypress family but is now the sole species in its own family, Sciadopityaceae. Native to Japan, it is planted as an ornamental tree in North America. It is usually seen as a small tree with soft, fibrous bark and fleshy, pliable, needlelike leaves, 6–13 cm long, borne in whorls of 10–30 at nodes along the twig.

LEYLAND CYPRESS *Cupressus* × *leylandii* A.B. Jacks. & Dallim.

Usually a tree. **BARK** Fibrous, gray. **TWIG** Flattened, forming flattened sprays. **LEAF** Scalelike, 1.5–2.5 mm long, lacking conspicuous glands; underside waxy, with white X-shaped marks of stomata. **SEED CONE** Many cultivars are sterile; seed cones, when present, are globose, 1.5–2 cm diam., slightly waxy, composed of 4 pairs of woody scales. *Notes:* This plant, which arose in cultivation as a hybrid of Alaska Yellow Cedar (*C. nootkatensis* D. Don) and Monterey Cypress (*C. macrocarpa* Hartw.), is one of the most popular and diverse ornamental conifers, with dozens of named cultivars. There is great variability in its size and appearance.

ATLANTIC WHITE CEDAR *Chamaecyparis thyoides* (L.) Britton, Sterns & Poggenb.

A.K.A. POST CEDAR, SWAMP CEDAR

QUICK ID A usually small cedar with irregular roundish cones, favoring swampy habitats; stomata form a white X on the scalelike leaf underside.

Monoecious evergreen tree up to 37 m tall, 150 cm diam., usually with a single straight trunk and spire-shaped crown. **BARK** At first flaky, on older trees red-brown, often furrowed into a long spiral, peeling in thin strips. **TWIG** Forming flattened, fan-shaped sprays. **LEAF** Scalelike, overlapping slightly, to 2 mm long, often with a small, circular resin gland; stomata form a white X on the lower surface. **SEED CONE** Roundish but usually irregular, 4–9 mm wide and long

ATLANTIC WHITE CEDAR

Umbrella
Pine

cone

pollen
cones

Leyland
Cypress

cone

cone

immature
cone

Atlantic White Cedar

Port Orford
Cedar

cone

when mature, glaucous, blue-purple to red-brown, not very resinous, composed of 6–8 woody scales. Cones mature and open in 1 year. Seed 1 or 2 per scale, 2–3 mm long, with a narrow wing.

HABITAT/RANGE Native. Mostly grows in bogs and swamps or on highly acid soils, forming pure stands within forests dominated by other species, 0–500 m; along the Atlantic coastal plain from Maine to S.C. and along the Gulf coastal plain from nw. Fla. to Miss.

SIMILAR SPECIES Arborvitae (*Thuja occidentalis*) has strongly flattened twigs in flattened,

fan-shaped sprays. **Port Orford Cedar** (*Chamaecyparis lawsoniana* [A. Murray] Parl.), a popular ornamental in the East, is very similar to Atlantic White Cedar, but with round cones more than 8 mm diam. See also Chinese Arborvitae (*Platycladus orientalis*).

Notes: The species has become a popular ornamental, with more than 30 described forms and cultivars. It was logged heavily in the 20th century; the wood is light and very decay-resistant. Some trees on the Gulf coastal plain have been assigned to subsp. *henryae* (Li H.L.) E. Murray; these include the largest known trees in the species.

CHINESE ARBORVITAE *Platycladus orientalis* (L.) Franco

Very popular ornamental owing to its tolerance for cold. It has rhomboid leaves that are overlapped by boat-shaped, ridged lateral leaves; the ripe seed cones are 1.5–2.5 cm long, 1–1.8 cm wide.

CRYPTOMERIA *Cryptomeria japonica* (Thunb. ex L.) D. Don
A.K.A. SUGI, JAPANESE CEDAR

QUICK ID Ornamental tree with short, sharp, incurved needles that are unique to this species and the rare Taiwania (see "Similar Species").

Monoecious evergreen ornamental tree, up to 20 m tall and 80 cm diam., with a conical crown. **BARK** Red-brown to dark gray, fibrous, peeling in strips. **TWIG** Pendulous, green in 1st year, turning brown. **LEAF** Needlelike, 3–12 mm long, rigid, straight to strongly incurved, sharp, spirally arranged. **SEED CONE** Brown, round with an apical point, 1–2 cm diam., nodding, borne at tips of twigs in groups of 1–6.

HABITAT/RANGE Introduced; native to China and Japan; widely introduced as an ornamental in e. North America, where it grows best in regions with warm, moist summers.

SIMILAR SPECIES The similar and related Taiwania (*Taiwania cryptomerioides* Hayata) has needles that bear a broad blue-white band of stomata along the side.

Notes: One of the world's great trees, Cryptomeria grows to more than 300 cm diam. in its native range and can attain ages of more than 1,700 years. It is revered in Japanese culture.

CHINA FIR *Cunninghamia lanceolata* (Lamb.) Hook.
A.K.A. CUNNINGHAMIA

QUICK ID Distinguished by long, stiff, sharp-pointed leaves and oval cones of leathery, sharp-pointed bracts at twig tips.

Monoecious evergreen tree, to 30 m tall and 70 cm diam. (larger in its native range), with an irregularly cylindrical crown. **BARK** Dark gray to red-brown,

longitudinally fissured, exposing aromatic inner bark. **TWIG** Covered by dead leaves behind 2 or 3 years' growth of living leaves. **LEAF** Needlelike, glossy deep green, with stomata on both surfaces, stiff, straight or slightly curved, 3–6.5 cm; spirally inserted on twig but, especially on shade foliage, often spreading in 2 poorly defined ranks. **SEED CONE** Ovoid, red-brown at maturity, 1.8–4.5 cm, composed of glossy, leathery sharp-pointed bracts; borne at twig tips in groups of 1–4.

HABITAT/RANGE Introduced; native to Southeast Asia. An uncommon but very distinctive ornamental that grows well in most of e. North America.

Notes: In China, this is an important timber tree. Although sometimes called "China Fir," it is a member of the cypress family.

◼ *JUNIPERUS*: JUNIPERS

Worldwide, the junipers include about 50 species of trees and shrubs that dominate vast areas of semiarid woodland in Europe, Asia, Africa, and North America. They have the widest elevation range of any group of conifers, occurring from sea-level to more than 4,800 m elevation (in the e. Himalayas). Five species are native in e. North America, in highly varied habitats.

Dioecious (in our region), evergreen shrubs and trees with 1 to several trunks and a pyramidal, rounded, or irregular crown. **BARK** Fibrous, gray to red, peeling in longitudinal strips. **TWIG** 0.6–2.5 mm diam. **LEAF** Most seedlings bear sharp needles, up to 10 mm long, jutting out from the twig. Four of our 5 species, when they grow to sapling size, lose most or all of their needle leaves and grow leaves shaped like small overlapping scales, 1–3 mm long and about as wide, that cover the twig. Important characteristics of these scale leaves include their size, the shape of the tip, and the presence of resinous secretions from a gland on the leaf. **SEED CONE** Resembles a small, hard berry, up to 10 mm diam., usually green when immature and from blue to black (in one case red), often with a glaucous (pale blue, waxy) bloom when mature; containing 1–3 seeds. Seeds mature in 3–18 months.

Because they come wrapped in a berrylike cone, the seeds of junipers are distributed across the landscape by birds, instead of by the wind, as in all other trees of the cypress family. One may encounter many other species and cultivars in

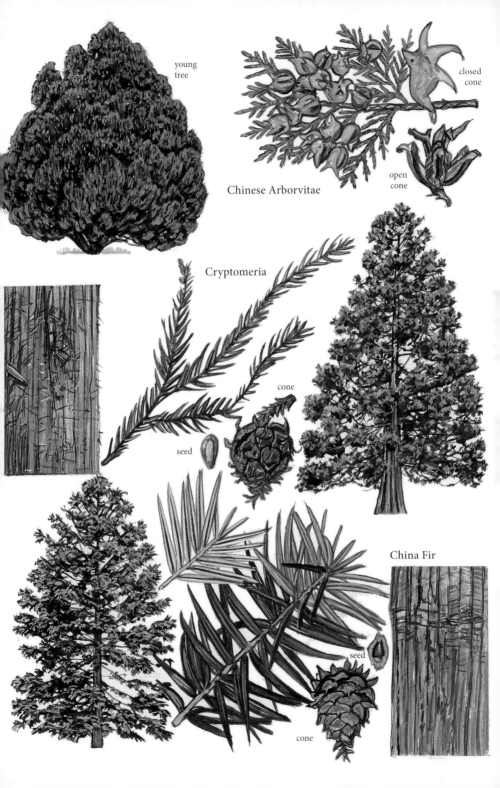

young
tree

closed
cone

open
cone

Chinese Arborvitae

Cryptomeria

cone

seed

China Fir

seed

cone

horticultural use. Ornamental trees that appear to be junipers but have round woody cones generally represent species of cypress (*Cupressus*), which is not native in the East. **Italian Cypress** (*Cupressus sempervirens* L.) is a common ornamental.

Italian Cypress

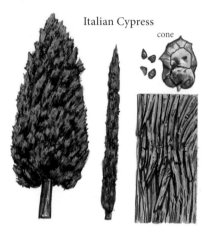

cone

with a conspicuous gland that does not show a resinous exudate; tip obtuse to acute. Needlelike leaves, 3–6 mm long, are mostly borne on young plants or on shaded foliage. **SEED CONE** 3–6 mm diam., green, maturing dark blue with a glaucous bloom, containing 1 or 2 seeds, each 1.5–4 mm diam.

HABITAT/RANGE Native. The most widespread conifer in our region, often growing on calcareous soils, typically in open areas and woodlands, and less commonly in forest interior settings, 0–1,070 m; in all eastern states and as far north as s. Ont. and Que.

Notes: This is the largest and most tree-like of our junipers, and is one of the longest-lived of our e. North American conifers, known to reach an age of 795 years. Its aromatic wood is widely used to line closets and chests. The species includes 2 varieties that hybridize extensively: Var. *virginiana* is widespread; Coastal Redcedar (var. *silicicola* [Small] E. Murray) occurs in coastal areas from N.C. to Tex.

EASTERN REDCEDAR *Juniperus virginiana* L.
A.K.A. PENCIL CEDAR, SOUTHERN JUNIPER, GENÉVRIER ROUGE DE L'AMÉRIQUE

QUICK ID The wide distribution in many habitats, including forest settings, and the dark blue, glaucous cones containing 1 or 2 seeds, 1.5–4 mm diam., serve to distinguish this species from our other native junipers.

Tree to 30 m tall and to 100 cm diam. A usually single trunk and a conical to globular crown. **BARK** Smooth when young, becoming fibrous and brown with increasing age, peeling in thin strips. **TWIG** Generally erect but sometimes lax, 3- or 4-sided, 0.6–2.0 mm diam. **LEAF** Primarily scalelike, 1–3 mm long, overlapping by more than ¼ of their length,

ROCKY MOUNTAIN JUNIPER *Juniperus scopulorum* Sarg.

QUICK ID Similar to Eastern Redcedar, but cones bear 2 seeds, 4–5 mm diam., each (vs. 1 or 2 seeds, less than 4 mm diam.), and the scalelike leaves barely overlap.

Tree to 15 m tall and 100 cm diam., with 1 to several short trunks and a conical to rounded or irregular crown. **BARK** Red-brown to dark brown, weathering gray, peeling in long strips. **TWIG** Spreading, erect to drooping, 0.8–1.2 mm thick. **LEAF** Almost all scalelike, 1–2 mm long, with conspicuous large glands that often bear a droplet of clear or whitish exudate. **SEED CONE** Attached at twig tips, blue-black at maturity, variably glaucous, 6–8 mm diam., with 2 seeds, each 4–5 mm diam.

HABITAT/RANGE Native. Widespread in the West; entering our area mainly in w. Dakotas, along waterways or on steep, north-facing slopes.

Notes: Rocky Mountain Juniper hybridizes with Eastern Redcedar. Hybrids appear intermediate between the 2 species.

EASTERN REDCEDAR

ROCKY MOUNTAIN JUNIPER

cone

juvenile leaves

Eastern Redcedar

cone

Rocky Mountain Juniper

MOUNTAIN CEDAR *Juniperus ashei* J. Buchholz
A.K.A. ASHE JUNIPER, ENEBRO DE MONTE

QUICK ID A juniper of c. Tex. with large, dark blue seed cones, and a raised gland on the needlelike leaves.

Shrub or small tree to 15 m tall, 30–50 cm diam., usually with a short single trunk, and an open, rounded or irregular crown. **BARK** Pink, turning gray and flaky, later brown and fibrous, finally turning gray and peeling in thin strips. **TWIG** Stiff, 1–1.3 mm thick. **LEAF** Mostly scalelike, in alternating pairs, keeled, with 2 bands of stomata; some needlelike leaves, each bearing a raised gland that resembles a small pimple, without visible resin. **SEED CONE** 6–10 mm diam., pink, maturing dark blue, usually glaucous, resinous, with 1 or 2 seeds.

HABITAT/RANGE Native. Occurs in open woodland with various types of oak and occasionally piñon pine at 150–1,550 m; found primarily in Tex. hill country, with small populations in Mo., Ark., Okla., and nw. Mexico.

Notes: Some authorities recognize 2 varieties. The cone of var. *ashei*, of Mo., Ark., Okla., and Tex. east of the Pecos River, is 9–10 mm diam. and contains 1 seed; var. *ovata* R.P. Adams, which occurs in the Mexican state of Coahuila and in Tex. west of the Pecos River, has cones mostly 6 mm diam. bearing 2 seeds.

REDBERRY JUNIPER *Juniperus pinchotii* Sudw.
A.K.A. PINCHOT JUNIPER, TEXAS JUNIPER, ENEBRO DE FRUTO ROJO

QUICK ID Seed cones are copper-colored when ripe. On trees without ripe cones, the ability to resprout from a cut stump, non-overlapping scalelike leaves, and non-resinous wood distinguish this species from our other junipers.

Shrub or small tree up to 6 m tall, with stems to 30 cm diam. Usually multistemmed and highly branched, often resprouting from the cut stump; crown irregular. **BARK** At first smooth, becoming flaky, later fibrous, pale gray, peeling in strips. **TWIG** Stiff, 1–2 mm thick, round or weakly quadrangular. **LEAF** In alternating whorls of 3, both needlelike and scalelike, but the latter predominate. Scalelike leaves 1–2 mm long, with an acute tip, not overlapping or overlapping only slightly; many bear ruptured glands that emit an aromatic white resin. **SEED CONE** 6–8 mm diam., copper to copper-red, juicy, sweet (not resinous), mostly with 1 seed.

HABITAT/RANGE Native. Mostly found on soils derived from limestone or gypsum, at 300–1,000 m; grows from Nuevo León, Mexico, to Okla., primarily at the western limits of our area.

Notes: Unlike most conifers, Redberry Juniper trees will sprout from the stump after a fire or after cutting, disturbances that kill other junipers. This species and Mountain Cedar were used by Native Americans as sources of both food and fuel. The mature cones are edible and sweeter than other juniper cones, and the wood makes a fine charcoal, though unlike that of most species in the cypress family, it is not rot-resistant. Cattle grazing, which exposes bare ground, and fire suppression, which favors woodland over grassland, have allowed Redberry Juniper to expand its range at the expense of native prairie species. It has flourished since European-American settlement and is now widely regarded as a weed.

MOUNTAIN CEDAR

REDBERRY JUNIPER

cone

Mountain Cedar

cone

Redberry Juniper

COMMON JUNIPER *Juniperus communis* L.
A.K.A. GROUND JUNIPER, SAVIN JUNIPER, GENÉVRIER COMMUN

QUICK ID The low, shrubby growth habit and the complete absence of scalelike leaves easily distinguish this species from all other junipers in North America.

Shrub, usually, or rarely a small tree to 6 m tall; usually multistemmed, decumbent, but sometimes upright and rarely single-stemmed. **BARK** Brown, weathering gray, fibrous and peeling off in thin strips. **TWIG** Spreading or ascending, 4-sided, diam. 1 mm or more. **LEAF** In alternating whorls of 3, needlelike, curved forward slightly, 8–15 mm long. **SEED CONE** Round, 6–9 mm diam., containing 3 seeds.

HABITAT/RANGE Native. Found usually in association with other conifers such as spruces or Jack Pine, on rocky or otherwise poor sites, often in high mountains, sometimes in peat bogs, 0–2,800 m. In our region, occurs from Nunavut southward to S.C.

Notes: Common Juniper is the most widespread conifer species in the world, found across much of temperate and boreal Europe, Asia, and n. North America. The species almost disappeared from e. North America during the last ice-age; fossils of that time are known only from the s. Appalachian Mountains. The species expanded to its current range as the climate warmed and the ice melted. The cones of this species give gin its flavor, and the word "gin" comes from the Dutch name for juniper. Our plants represent subsp. *depressa* (Pursh) Franco, and as that name suggests, rarely grow as erect trees but more often as spreading shrubs. Common Juniper is a widespread ornamental shrub, and can be distinguished from most other ornamental junipers by the absence of scalelike leaves.

DAWN REDWOOD *Metasequoia glyptostroboides* Hu & W.C. Cheng
A.K.A. WATER FIR

QUICK ID Closely resembles native Baldcypress (*Taxodium distichum*) but lacks "knees," the trunk usually becomes gnarled and lumpy, and the round cones are composed of 20–30 (instead of 5–10) woody scales.

Monoecious, winter-deciduous tree up to 45 m tall and 200 cm diam., with a fluted or irregular trunk and pyramidal to irregular crown. **BARK** Dark red-brown, fissured, and peeling in long, thin strips. **TWIG** Red-brown, shallowly ridged. **LEAF** Needlelike, bright green, opposite on deciduous twigs, linear, flattened, 12 mm long, 1.6 mm wide (more uniform in proportion than those of Baldcypress). In autumn, the leaves and their twigs turn red-brown before falling. **SEED CONE** Round, 12–25 mm diam., with 20–30 woody scales; borne at twig tip, solitary, pendulous.

HABITAT/RANGE Introduced; native to China, now a popular ornamental in North America.

Notes: The species was discovered to botany in the 1940s and has enjoyed fame as a horticultural "living fossil" because it was known from fossil evidence before being discovered in the wild and appears to have changed very little over the intervening several million years.

COAST REDWOOD *Sequoia sempervirens* (D. Don) Endl.

Closely related to Giant Sequoia (*Sequoiadendron giganteum*), has leaves similar to Baldcypress (*Taxodium distichum*), dark reddish bark, and cones only 12–35 mm long. **HABITAT/RANGE** Native to Calif.; planted in the East.

COMMON JUNIPER

immature cone

leaf

Common Juniper

spreading form

autumn

immature cones

Dawn Redwood

new leaves

pollen cones

Coast Redwood

seed

cone

GIANT SEQUOIA *Sequoiadendron giganteum* (Lindl.) J. Buchholz
A.K.A. SIERRA REDWOOD, WELLINGTONIA

QUICK ID The scalelike leaves are longer and larger than those in other species of the cypress family; cultivated trees can usually be picked out from a distance by their great size and uniform conical crown.

Monoecious evergreen trees to 50 m tall and 3 m diam. (larger in native range), with a conical crown. **BARK** Red-brown, commonly more than 10 cm thick, fibrous, ridged, and furrowed. **TWIG** Covered by old leaves. **LEAF** Scalelike, 8–15 mm long, with stomata on both surfaces. **SEED CONE** Solitary at tips of twigs, ovoid, 4–9 cm long, remaining green and closed for many years.

HABITAT/RANGE Native to Calif.; widely planted in public parks in areas with temperate climates.

Notes: This is the world's largest tree and one of its best-loved ornamental conifers.

BALDCYPRESS *Taxodium distichum* (L.) Rich.
A.K.A. SWAMP CYPRESS, POND CYPRESS, AHUEHUETE

QUICK ID A tall, straight-trunked, broad-based deciduous cypress, often growing in or near water, sometimes surrounded by knobby wooden "knees" protruding from the ground. The shoots of the Pond Cypress variety look like thick strands of yarn.

Monoecious, deciduous or semideciduous tree to 40 m tall and 3 m diam., usually with a single straight trunk with a broad base, and often with brown, woody "knees" projecting up to 2 m from the ground nearby; crown pyramidal, flattening in old trees. **BARK** Light brown, turning gray, exfoliating in long, thin strips. **TWIG** Slender, green to light brown, each year's growth consisting of a single long shoot with multiple shorter lateral shoots. **LEAF** Needlelike; in Swamp Cypress (var. *distichum*) alternate, in 2 ranks, 10–17 mm long; in **Pond Cypress** (var. *imbricatum* [Nutt.] Croom) appressed to twig, 3–10 mm long; winter-deciduous in temperate areas, but lasting a year or more in subtropical areas; when deciduous, the leaves and their twigs turn red-brown before falling. **SEED CONE** Borne in small clusters along branchlet, oval, 2–3.5 cm diam., green and fleshy when young, at maturity brown and woody, with 5–10 seed scales.

HABITAT/RANGE Native. Low-lying, usually swampy areas, 0–530 m; c. and s. U.S., Mexico, and Guatemala; also a popular ornamental tree.

SIMILAR SPECIES Mexican Baldcypress (*T. distichum* var. *mucronatum* [Ten.] A. Henry) enters the U.S. in southernmost Tex. It is essentially identical to var. *distichum* except for having needles less than 10 mm long and seed cones mostly 14–25 mm diam. Dawn Redwood (*Metasequoia glyptostroboides*), a common ornamental within the range of Baldcypress, has shorter twigs with more uniform needles (mostly 12 mm long) and similar-sized cones with 20–30 woody scales.

Notes: This is one of the longest-living and largest trees to be found in our area. The wood is extremely decay-resistant. The "knees" are unique to this species, and it is the only native species in the cypress family that is deciduous. The knees seem to be an adaptation to flooded soil, but their function is not well understood.

BALDCYPRESS

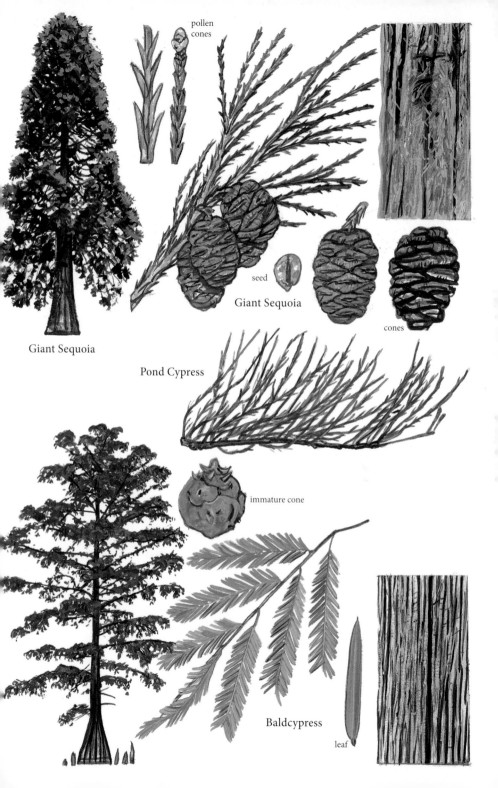

pollen cones

seed

Giant Sequoia

cones

Giant Sequoia

Pond Cypress

immature cone

Baldcypress

leaf

ARBORVITAE *Thuja occidentalis* L.
A.K.A. NORTHERN WHITE CEDAR, AMERICAN
ARBORVITAE, EASTERN ARBORVITAE, CEDRE BLANC

QUICK ID A native northern cypress with scale-like leaves, strongly flattened twigs in fan-shaped sprays, and a bilaterally symmetric cone.

Monoecious, evergreen tree to 25 m tall and 100 cm diam., with a single straight trunk and a conical crown. **BARK** Red-brown, turning gray with age, thin, fibrous, fissured, coming away in long, thin strips. **TWIG** Flattened in cross section and bearing foliage in flattened, fan-shaped sprays. **LEAF** Scalelike, flattened, 1–4 mm long, 1–2 mm wide, pointed, dull yellow-green on both upper and lower surfaces, with conspicuous glands on lateral leaves near twig tips. **POLLEN CONE** 1–2 mm long, reddish. **SEED CONE** Ovoid, 9–14 mm long, green maturing to brown, with 2 pairs of woody, fertile scales, each slightly longer than wide, and yielding a total of 8 seeds. Seed red-brown, 4–7 mm long (including wings).

HABITAT/RANGE Native. Grows on mostly limestone-derived soils, also in swamps, riparian areas, and on cliffs and talus, 0–900 m; common from Ont. to N.B. and in adjacent U.S. states; also in Appalachians south to N.C. and Tenn.

SIMILAR SPECIES Atlantic White Cedar (*Chamaecyparis thyoides*) has twigs round in cross section that form space-filling rather than flattened sprays of foliage. **Western Redcedar** (*Thuja plicata* Donn ex. D. Don), common ornamental in the East, is very similar to Arborvitae, except its twigs are not strongly flattened and its seed cones have 8 or more scales, the largest scales more than 1.5 times longer than wide. It is native to nw. U.S. and sw. Canada; planted in the East.

Notes: In 1536, an extract from the foliage of this tree saved the lives of Jacques Cartier and his crew, suffering from scurvy during their second voyage of discovery to Canada. They named it *arborvitae*, Latin for "tree of life," and brought it home with them—the first North American tree to be introduced to Europe. Since that time, more than 120 cultivars have been discovered and named, making this one of the most popular trees in horticulture. This is the longest-lived tree of e. North America, its longevity estimated at up to 1,890 years.

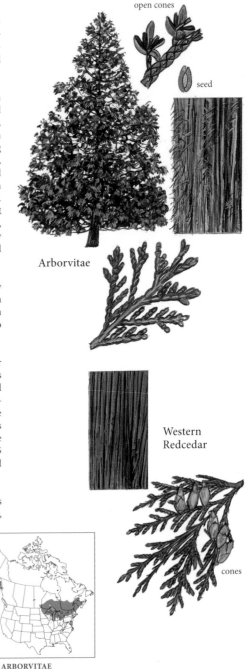

open cones

seed

Arborvitae

Western
Redcedar

cones

ARBORVITAE

PINACEAE: PINE FAMILY

Pinaceae is the largest conifer family, with about 235 species in 11 genera; 24 species in 5 genera are native to, or widely naturalized in, e. North America. Native eastern species occur in almost all forested habitats but are most widespread in the southern pine forests that cover the Atlantic and Gulf coastal plains and extend several hundred miles inland, and in the vast boreal forests that reach from the arctic tree-line southward from Man. to Maine.

Species in our region are all monoecious trees. **BARK** Highly variable. **TWIG** In firs (*Abies*), the branch pattern is very regular, with a single terminal and 2 lateral shoots produced each year at the tip of most active branches. This geometric regularity of form is only a little less common in spruces (*Picea*) and larches (*Larix*), is rather unusual in pines (*Pinus*), and is not found in hemlocks (*Tsuga*). **LEAF** Simple needle, shed singly, or in bundles of 2–5 needles in pines. **SEED CONE** Usually woody, comprised of many scales, maturing in 2–3 years in pines, 1 year in the other genera, then opening and shedding seeds upon maturity. In some species cones are serotinous, remaining closed usually until opened by the heat of a fire. Seeds are winged and dispersed by wind.

Among gymnosperms, only the ginkgo family is thought to be older. Worldwide, species of the pine family are more widely distributed, ecologically important, and economically valuable than those of any other tree family. Many of our species are valued for their timber, and their distribution has been heavily modified by forestry plantings. The distribution of some species has been greatly reduced by human factors such as air pollution and introduced diseases. Many species are popular ornamentals within or outside their native range.

■ *ABIES*: FIRS

There are more than 50 species of firs, distributed through much of the Northern Hemisphere. Firs have a low tolerance for fire and a high tolerance for shade, and live in regions that have snow cover for many months each year. In the East they are native to Canada and the northern tier of states, extending down the Appalachian Mountains to Ga., at elevations from sea-level to nearly 2,000 m. They usually occur in closed-canopy conifer-dominated forests, and are also found near the alpine timberline in woodlands, sometimes as shrubs. Firs can be distinguished from other Pinaceae genera by the often spire-shaped crown, resin blisters on the bark, and the erect (rather than pendent) cones located near the top of the tree, disintegrating when ripe and leaving a woody spike.

Single-trunked evergreen trees with a conical crown, often flattened in old trees. Branching is regular, with a whorl of branches usually produced every year. **BARK** Smooth and thin on young trees, bearing resin blisters; in age often thick and furrowed or flaky. **LEAF** Needlelike, simple, linear, with 2 white stomatal bands on lower surface, rounded or notched at the tip, persisting 5 or more years, spirally arranged but often appearing 2-ranked and twisted at the base; leaving a smooth scar on the twig after falling. Foliage formed in full sun is often thicker and stiffer than foliage formed in the shade. **POLLEN CONE** Usually borne lower on tree than seed cones, solitary, hanging from branchlets, resembling a catkin. **SEED CONE** Borne erect on year-old twigs, usually in upper crown, ovoid to cylindric, resinous, maturing in 1 season, the cone scales falling apart on maturity to leave an erect central "spike," called an axil, which persists on the branch for several years.

FRASER FIR *Abies fraseri* (Pursh) Poir.
A.K.A SOUTHERN BALSAM FIR, SAPIN DE FRASER

QUICK ID The only native fir in the s. Appalachians; recognized by its twigs being covered by short red hairs and its cones with many visible bracts.

Tree to 15 m tall and 50 cm diam. **BARK** Gray, becoming flaky with age. **TWIG** Yellowish brown, slightly grooved or smooth, with a dense cover of red hairs. **LEAF** Needle 1–2 cm long, 2–2.2 mm wide, dark green, the tip varying from notched to pointed, stomata mostly on lower surface, in 2 greenish-white bands. **POLLEN CONE** Numerous on lower side of branchlets, pendent, 8–10 mm long, yellow and red when mature. **SEED CONE** 3.5–6 cm long and 2.5–4 cm wide when mature, purple-brown, with pale bracts sticking out between the scales and bent downward.

HABITAT/RANGE Native. Montane forests, usually on north-facing slopes in mixed stands with Red Spruce, from 1,200 m to the mountain summits (approaching 2,000 m); s. Appalachians, in Tenn., N.C., and Va.

SIMILAR SPECIES Fraser Fir grows with Red Spruce (*Picea rubens*), which has less prominent white stomatal bands on the lower surface of the leaf and hanging cones that fall from the tree intact at maturity.

Notes: This species is declining and threatened due to an introduced insect pest, Balsam Wooly Adelgid (*Adelges piceae*), which has killed millions of trees and continues to cause severe damage. Fraser Fir is a popular Christmas tree.

BALSAM FIR *Abies balsamea* (L.) Mill.
A.K.A. CANADA BALSAM, SAPIN BAUMIER

QUICK ID The only fir native in the East north of Va.; recognized by its hairless twigs and cones with no visible bracts.

Tree to 25 m tall and 100 cm diam. **BARK** Gray, splitting into shallow blocks with age. **TWIG** Yellowish green, smooth, with sparse, short gray hairs; dormant buds 4.5–5.5 mm long. **LEAF** Needle, 1.5–2.5 cm long, 2 mm wide, dark green, the tip varying from notched to pointed, stomata mostly on lower surface, in 2 greenish-white bands on either side of the midrib. **POLLEN CONE** Numerous, pendent along the twig, 4–6 mm long, yellow and purple when mature. **SEED CONE** 4–7 cm long and 2–3 cm wide when mature, purple turning brown, with bracts hidden under the scales or just the tips sticking out.

HABITAT/RANGE Native. Mixed conifer forests and broadleaf–conifer northern forests, 0–1,200 m; Alta. to Nfld., south to northern tier of states from Minn. to Maine, and southward to n. Pa. and Va.

SIMILAR SPECIES Balsam Fir is closely related to Fraser Fir. A hybrid, Canaan Fir (*Abies* × *phanerolepis* Fernald), has been described from where their ranges overlap in Va. and W.Va.; in most characters it is like the Balsam Fir as described here, but its cones have long, protruding bracts that are bent downward, similar to those of Fraser Fir.

Notes: Balsam Fir is usually found in mixed conifer forests with species of spruce, Eastern Hemlock, and Jack Pine; it also grows with aspens, birches, maples, and beech species characteristic of northern forest. It is highly shade-tolerant, not fire-tolerant, and usually short-lived; the oldest tree recorded was less than 250 years old. A traditional Christmas tree in e. North America, it is widely farmed for that use. Its timber is exploited for pulp, and the tree is also the source of a resin called Canada balsam that was formerly widely used in medicine, optics, and microscopy but has now largely been replaced by synthetics.

FRASER FIR

BALSAM FIR

cone

Fraser Fir

leaf

seed

Balsam Fir

twig

cone

leaf

seed

Ornamental Firs

Many firs are planted ornamentally in e. North America, but the most common are the 2 native species, Fraser and Balsam, described above, and White Fir, Korean Fir, and Caucasian Fir. In the n. part of our region, where Balsam Fir is native, all of these firs do well. Moving to warmer climates, the Balsam Fir is less commonly planted, but the others remain popular, and Fraser Fir, especially, is widely planted outside its native range. Firs are rarely seen in the warmest areas (Gulf and s. Atlantic coasts); those that do grow there usually represent unusual species from hot places like Spain, Mexico, or s. China. White Fir and Caucasian Fir are popular Christmas trees in the e. U.S.

WHITE FIR *Abies concolor* (Gordon & Glendinning) Hildebrand

A w. U.S. native, available in many cultivars. **TWIG** Slender, smooth, yellowish green. **LEAF** Needle, 4–6 cm long and 2–3 mm wide (smaller in some cultivars). **POLLEN CONE** 1.2–2 cm long, hanging below the shoot. **SEED CONE** 7–12 cm long, green, maturing to light brown, bracts between scales not visible.

KOREAN FIR *Abies koreana* E.H. Wilson

Korean Fir has a pyramidal crown and is widely planted for its cones, which many people think are the loveliest of any fir, and because it grows relatively slowly. **TWIG** Yellowish green, shallowly grooved. **LEAF** Needle, 1–2 cm long and 2 mm wide. **POLLEN CONE** 1 cm long, clustered around the shoot. **SEED CONE** 4–7 cm long, blue, maturing purple-brown, with very conspicuous bracts that are bent downward.

CAUCASIAN FIR *Abies nordmanniana* (Steven) Spach

Caucasian Fir has a pyramidal crown and grows quickly to a large size. **TWIG** Olive-brown, ridged, grooved. **LEAF** Needle, 2–3 cm long and 1.5–2.5 mm wide. **POLLEN CONE** 1–2 cm long, crowded together, hanging from the shoot. **SEED CONE** 12–16 cm long, often crowded together, with visible bracts that are bent downward.

■ CEDRUS: CEDARS

The genus includes 2 species of evergreen trees native to mountains south and east of the Mediterranean and to the w. Himalayas, at 1,000–3,000 m, in habitats ranging from dry open woodland to wet closed-canopy forest. The needles grow in tufts from stubby "short shoots," an arrangement seen only on cedars and larches (*Larix*), which are deciduous North American natives.

Large trees, crown conical, becoming flatter and wider with age; branches forming nearly horizontal sprays, giving the crown a layer-cake appearance. **BARK** Dark gray-brown, fissured or breaking up into irregular blocks. **TWIG** 2 types of shoots: long shoots that elongate and form twigs; and short shoots that appear as stubs on the sides of the long shoots and produce leaves. **LEAF** Needle, pliable, 5–40 mm long, in tufts of 15–45 at ends of short shoots. **POLLEN CONE** 3–8 cm long, abundant, producing clouds of pollen when ripe. **SEED CONE** 5–12.5 cm long, oval to egg-shaped, brown when ripe, disintegrating completely while on the tree, shedding seeds 10–15 mm long with an attached wing 10–20 mm long.

Both cedars are popular ornamentals and lovely landscaping trees; full-size cultivars can grow very large, up to 30 m tall and 100 cm diam. Cedar of Lebanon is available in an array of strangely shaped cultivars.

DEODAR CEDAR *Cedrus deodara* (Lamb.) G. Don

TWIG 1st-year twig densely pubescent. **LEAF** More than 2.5 cm long, not or very slightly glaucous. **POLLEN CONE** More than 5 cm long, maturing and spreading pollen in autumn. **SEED CONE** Matures in autumn, disintegrating in early winter. **HABITAT/ RANGE** Introduced, native to the Himalayas; reported to be naturalized in N.C., S.C., and Ga.

CEDAR OF LEBANON *Cedrus libani* A. Rich.

TWIG 1st-year twig hairless or nearly so. **LEAF** Usually less than 2.5 cm long, weakly or strongly glaucous, depending on cultivar. **POLLEN CONE** Less than 5 cm long, maturing and spreading pollen in summer. **SEED CONE** Matures in late summer to autumn, disintegrating through winter. **HABITAT/ RANGE** Introduced from s. Mediterranean (Morocco to Lebanon); widely planted in e. U.S.

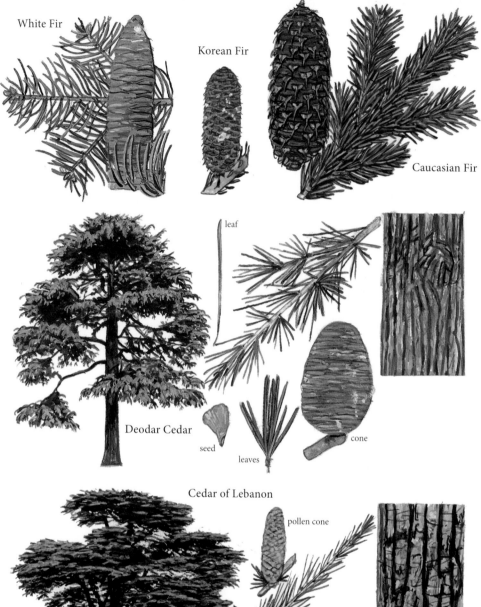

White Fir

Korean Fir

Caucasian Fir

Deodar Cedar

leaf

seed

leaves

cone

Cedar of Lebanon

pollen cone

cone scale

cone

seeds

■ *LARIX*: LARCHES

Larches occur in mountains and at temperate to polar latitudes; the northernmost trees in the world are larches. Three species are native to North America; 1 native and 1 introduced species are found in our range. Many larches are popular ornamentals valued mostly for their golden fall foliage.

Deciduous trees with sparse, open crowns. **TWIG** 2 types of shoots: long shoots that elongate and form twigs; and short shoots (several millimeters long), prominent on twigs 2 years old or more, bearing leaves and cones. **LEAF** Deciduous needle, in tufts of 10–60 on short shoots or borne singly on 1st-year long shoots. **SEED CONE** Erect, ovoid, initially brilliant red or violet, turning green and then brown with age, maturing and shedding winged seeds in 1 season but often persisting on the twig for several years; scales thin, tough and leathery.

TAMARACK *Larix laricina* (Du Roi) K. Koch
A.K.A. AMERICAN LARCH, MÉLÈZE LARICIN

QUICK ID A deciduous conifer with needles in tufts on short shoots and very small seed cones.

Deciduous tree, to 30 m tall and 80 cm diam., with an ovoid or conical crown. **BARK** Gray, smooth, becoming reddish brown and scaly, weathering to gray. **TWIG** Slender, flexible, orange-brown, hairless, with stubby short shoots on sides. **LEAF** Needlelike, 2–3 cm long, pliable, light green at first, darker in summer, turning yellow and falling in autumn, in tufts of 15–25 on short shoots. **POLLEN CONE** Spherical, 3–4 mm diam., borne on short shoots. **SEED CONE** 1–2 cm long, spherical or ovoid, usually red at first, maturing yellow-brown, borne upright on short shoots, usually on curved stalks 2–5 mm long. Cones fall after maturity or remain attached for 1 or 2 years longer.

HABITAT/RANGE Native. One of the most widely distributed conifers in the world, common from Alaska to Nfld., and southward in the East mainly along the northern tier of states; in e. North America it grows at elevations of 0–1,200 m.

Notes: In U.S., Tamarack grows mostly on acid soils with other

TAMARACK

northern conifers such as spruces, Balsam Fir, and Jack Pine, often with Yellow Birch or Balsam Poplar, sometimes in swamps; farther north, reaching to the arctic tree-line, it is abundant on well-drained uplands and often forms extensive pure stands.

EUROPEAN LARCH *Larix decidua* Mill.

The most common ornamental larch in e. North America. It differs from Tamarack primarily in having much larger cones, usually 4–5 cm long. **HABITAT/RANGE** Introduced; reported as naturalized in various, mostly northern, states and in the eastern provinces.

European Larch

■ *PICEA*: SPRUCES

The spruce genus contains 33 species and occurs throughout the Northern Hemisphere, mostly in mountains and at high latitudes. In e. North America there are 3 native and 1 naturalized species, only 2 of which, Red Spruce and Norway Spruce, occur south of the northern tier states. They are conifers with sharp bottlebrush-like needles and abundant cones with flexible scales and no visible bracts.

Evergreen trees; crown broadly conical to spirelike, usually with a single erect leader; branches mostly in whorls. **BARK** Gray to red-brown, thin and scaly, sometimes with resin blisters, thickening with age. **TWIG** Rough with persistent peg-like leaf bases. **LEAF** Needle, 4-angled in cross section, stiff, usually sharp-pointed, sometimes blunt, with stomata on all surfaces. Spirally arranged on twig, persisting for up to 10 years, leaving a rough stub on the twig after falling. **POLLEN CONE** Single or in groups, oblong, yellow to purple.

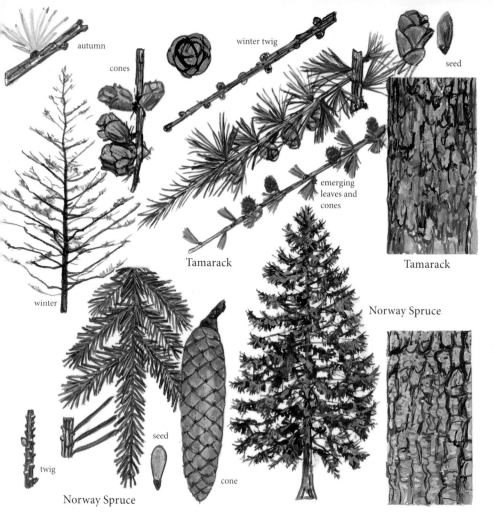

autumn

cones

winter twig

seed

emerging
leaves and
cones

Tamarack

Tamarack

Norway Spruce

winter

twig

seed

cone

Norway Spruce

SEED CONE Borne mostly on upper branches, pendent, ovoid to cylindric, green to purple, maturing to pale to dark brown; scales flexible, bracts not visible; seeds winged. Cones usually shed at maturity.

NORWAY SPRUCE *Picea abies* (L.) Karst.
A.K.A. EPICÉA COMMUN

QUICKID A spruce with very long cones, to 16 cm.

Tree to 40–50 m tall and 100–150 cm diam.; crown conical. **BARK** Orange-brown, finely flaking, becoming gray-brown, scaly on old trees. **TWIG** Orange-brown, usually smooth, often strongly drooping. **LEAF** Needle, 1–2.5 cm long, rigid,

light to dark green, blunt-tipped. **POLLEN CONE** 10–15 mm long, yellow. **SEED CONE** 12–16 cm long, cylindric with a conical tip; scales diamond-shaped, widest near middle, stiff, leathery, upper margin ragged to toothed, apex extending 6–10 mm beyond seed-wing impression.

HABITAT/RANGE Introduced; native to Europe. Cultivated in North America and reported as naturalized in all states and provinces east and north from Minn., Ill., Ky., and N.C., as well as locally in Ga. and Tenn.

Notes: This is one of the most widely distributed conifers in the world. There are many cultivated forms of this popular ornamental tree, some of them quite unusual in form and coloration.

WHITE SPRUCE *Picea glauca* (Moench) Voss

A.K.A. SKUNK SPRUCE, EPINETTE BLANCHE

QUICK ID A spruce with sharp-pointed blue-green waxy needles and cones to 6 cm long.

Tree to 30 m tall and 100 cm diam., with rows of horizontal branches forming a conical crown. **BARK** Gray-brown, reddish in fissures, flaky. **TWIG** Pinkish brown, hairless, slender, rough with peg-like leaf bases. **LEAF** Needle, 12–19 mm long, stiff, waxy, blue-green, sharp-pointed, giving off a skunky odor when crushed. **POLLEN CONE** 10–20 mm long, red. **SEED CONE** Solitary, hanging near ends of twigs, 3–6 cm long, cylindric, green or violet, ripening to light brown; scales thin, flexible, with a rounded, untoothed upper margin; seed 2–4 mm long, with a 5–8 mm wing.

HABITAT/RANGE Native. Abundant in the boreal forest, 0–1,500 m; from Alaska to Nfld., in e. North America from the low Arctic south to northern tier of states; outlying population in Black Hills of S.D.

Notes: White Spruce usually occurs on upland sites in pure stands or with Tamarack, Jack Pine, Red Pine, Balsam Fir, Black Spruce, Red Spruce, Paper Birch, Quaking Aspen, or Balsam Poplar. It mostly grows in uniform-age stands regenerated after destruction by fire or insect attack. The Black Hills trees are sometimes assigned to var. *densata* Bailey. Native peoples used White Spruce in at least 166 different recorded ways, including for medicine, food, structures, implements, and spiritual purposes. Today, it is the most economically important timber tree in the boreal forest, its wood used in musical instruments and for construction. Within its range, it is also a popular ornamental tree. Trees up to 688 years old have been found. It is the provincial tree of Man., and the Black Hills variety is the state tree of S.D.

BLACK SPRUCE *Picea mariana* (MILL.) BRITTON, STERNS & POGGENB.

A.K.A. BOG SPRUCE, EPINETTE NOIRE

QUICK ID A small northern spruce with short, blunt needles and very small cones.

Tree to 30 m tall and 50 cm diam., with a spire-like crown often topped by a "knot" of dense branches. **BARK** Gray-brown, thin, and scaly. **TWIG** Yellow-brown, with a dense cover of short hairs, rough with peg-like leaf bases. **LEAF** Needle, 0.8–1.5 cm long, rigid, blue-green, covered with wax that tends to wear away with time, usually blunt-tipped. **POLLEN CONE** 10–15 mm long, red-brown. **SEED CONE** 1.5–3 cm long, short-ovoid to ovoid, dark purple, ripening red-brown, scales thin, woody, brittle, with minutely toothed upper margin; seed 2–3 mm long, with a 2–5 mm wing. Cones often serotinous.

HABITAT/RANGE Native. Bogs and other wet areas at 0–1,600 m, throughout the boreal forest from the northern tier of states to the Arctic tree line and from lowland forest to the alpine zone.

Notes: Abundant in pure stands on the wettest sites, Black Spruce frequently covers bogs and other peatlands with a nearly continuous forest and an understory dominated by various mosses and lichens; it also grows with a variety of other trees, especially Tamarack, White Spruce, and Paper Birch, on slightly better sites. This little spruce is extremely well adapted to fire, easily killed by a burn but in the aftermath spreading its seeds widely over the fresh, mineral-laden seedbed. In consequence, it is one of the most common trees in the northern forest, often forming nearly pure stands that cover very large areas. Exploited mainly for pulp—and also a major source of wood for chopsticks—it is an economically important timber tree in the boreal forest. It occasionally hybridizes with Red Spruce, but the hybrids show low vigor.

WHITE SPRUCE

BLACK SPRUCE

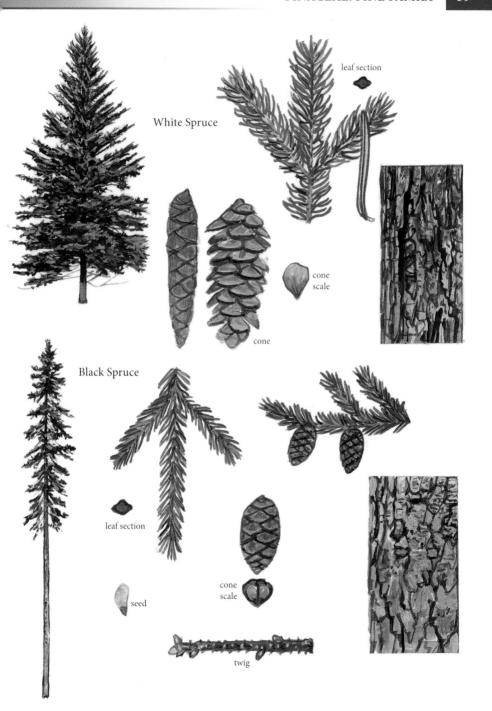

White Spruce

leaf section

cone scale

cone

Black Spruce

leaf section

seed

cone scale

twig

RED SPRUCE *Picea rubens* Sarg.
A.K.A. EPINETTE ROUGE

QUICK ID A spruce of upland sites with medium-small cones and without waxy foliage.

Tree to 40 m tall and 100 cm diam., with a broadly conical crown. **BARK** Gray-brown to reddish brown, flaky, furrowed on large trees. **TWIG** Stout, yellow-brown, hairy in grooves between peg-like leaf bases. **LEAF** Needle, 10–16 mm long, yellow-green to dark green, not waxy, sharp-pointed. **POLLEN CONE** 15–25 mm long, red. **SEED CONE** 2.3–4.5 cm long, ovoid, purplish green ripening to glossy orange-brown; scales thin, woody, brittle, with smooth to irregularly toothed margin; seed 2–3.5 mm long, with 4–8 mm wing.

HABITAT/RANGE Native. Areas with a cool, moist climate, from sea-level (in the north) to 2,000 m (in N.C.); lower Ont. and N.Y. to N.S. and along the Appalachians south to Tenn. and N.C.

Notes: Common associates of Red Spruce include Balsam Fir, Black Spruce, Eastern White Pine, Eastern Hemlock, Aspen, Paper Birch, and Sugar Maple. In the s. Appalachians it forms spruce–fir forests with Fraser Fir. Although Red Spruce and Black Spruce are closely related and sometimes hybridize, their ecology is very different. Red Spruce has a more southerly distribution, commonly regenerates in the forest understory, occurs on upland sites, and is not well adapted to fire. Native peoples used the peeled roots of Red Spruce for lacing and the pitch for waterproofing, and early settlers used the fresh green buds to flavor beer (a practice since revived by a few craft breweries). As a timber tree, it is used for paper-making, for construction lumber, and for stringed instruments. Air pollution, including both acid rain and nitrogen deposition, has been linked to extensive dieback of spruce–fir forests in the Appalachians.

Ornamental Spruces and Douglas-fir

Several spruces are planted ornamentally in e. North America; the most common are Norway Spruce (described above), Oriental Spruce, and 2 species native to w. North America, Engelmann Spruce and Blue Spruce. Specimens of both Engelmann Spruce and Blue Spruce can have green to very blue (glaucous) foliage, and glaucous cultivars of Engelmann Spruce are often sold under the name "Blue Spruce." The ornamental spruces do well in cold climates and are among the most cold-tolerant of trees. In warm climates spruces tend to suffer from various insect pests. Douglas-fir, the premier timber tree of w. North America, is also a common eastern ornamental conifer.

ORIENTAL SPRUCE *Picea orientalis* (L.) Link

Commonly a large tree with a conical crown. **LEAF** Needle, glossy green, less than 1 cm long. **SEED CONE** 5–9 cm long.

BLUE SPRUCE *Picea pungens* Engelm.

LEAF Needle, green to very glaucous, very sharp and stiff, 1.5–3 cm long, directed forward along the shoot. **SEED CONE** 5–8 cm long, pointed.

ENGELMANN SPRUCE *Picea engelmannii* Parry ex Engelm.

LEAF Needle, green to very glaucous, pointed but less sharp and set at a greater angle (usually more than 60 degrees) to the twig than those of Blue Spruce. **SEED CONE** Smaller (3–6 cm long) and less pointed than Blue Spruce cone.

DOUGLAS-FIR *Pseudotsuga menziesii* (Mirb.) Franco

A large tree. **LEAF** Needle, similar to those of spruces but flexible and not sharply pointed. **SEED CONE** 4–10 cm long, with prominent 3-pointed bracts protruding from between the scales.

RED SPRUCE

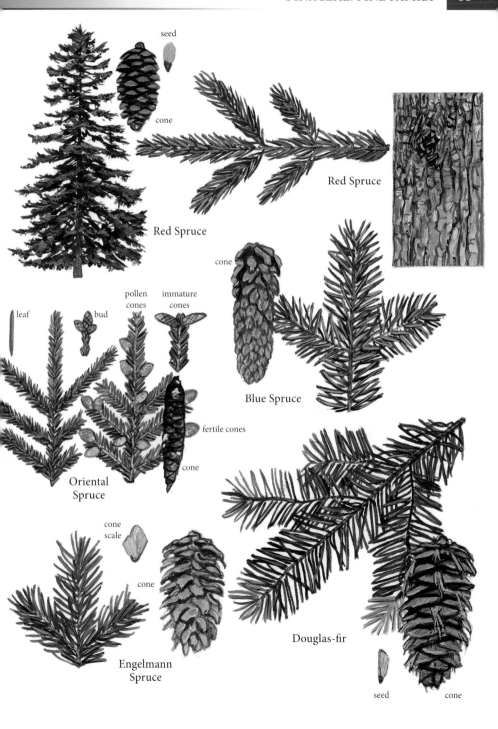

seed

cone

Red Spruce

Red Spruce

cone

Blue Spruce

leaf

bud

pollen cones

immature cones

fertile cones

cone

Oriental Spruce

cone scale

cone

Engelmann Spruce

Douglas-fir

seed

cone

■ *PINUS*: PINES

Pines occur throughout the Northern Hemisphere and are the most widely planted trees in the Southern Hemisphere. Found throughout the forested portions of e. North America, they are especially common on the coastal plains from N.J. to Tex., and in uplands of the s. U.S. They are distinguished from other Pinaceae genera by their needle-shaped leaves occurring in bundles of 2–5.

Evergreen trees, usually with rounded or irregular crowns and spreading, ascending branches with most foliage borne in rounded clumps near the branch ends. Plants with bundles of 2 or 3 needles and stiff, woody cone scales are called hard pines, while those with 5 needles and pliable cone scales are called soft or white pines. **BARK** Scaly, or with layered plates separated by furrows. **TWIG** Stout, smooth in soft pines, scaly in hard pines. **LEAF** On mature plants typically 2–5 needles bound together in a bundle clasped at the base in a papery sheath that usually wears shorter with age and may fall off in 5-needle pines. **POLLEN CONE** Small and numerous, cylindric to conical, in a dense cluster around the base of the current year's growth. **SEED CONE** Solitary to few. Scales numerous; the exposed, thickened tip of each cone scale (the apophysis) is often important for identification; 2 winged seeds form at base of each cone scale. Cones mature in 2 growing seasons, and are sometimes serotinous.

Pinus is the most economically important tree genus in the world. Archeological investigations show that pines have fed, sheltered, and kept humans warm since before the dawn of history, and they continue to be the mainstay of timber production in modern North America. "Pine" is the popular name for conifers, and a great many trees not in *Pinus* are referred to as such. A number of species are referred to as "southern yellow pine" commercially, including Virginia Pine, Pitch Pine, Loblolly Pine, Longleaf Pine, Slash Pine, and Shortleaf Pine.

EASTERN WHITE PINE *Pinus strobus* L.
A.K.A. WEYMOUTH PINE

QUICK ID The only 5-needle pine native to e. North America.

Tree to 56 m tall and 180 cm diam., with a conical crown of upswept branches that becomes cylindric or irregular with age. **BARK** Gray-brown, with deep furrows and broad ridges of purple-tinged, scaly plates. **TWIG** Smooth, slender, pale red-brown. **LEAF** Needle, 6–10 cm long, 0.7–1 mm wide, straight, slightly twisted, pliable, light green, in bundles of 5 held in sheath 1–1.5 cm long that drops away soon after needle maturity. **POLLEN CONE** Ellipsoid, 10–15 mm long, yellow, numerous. **SEED CONE** Clustered, pendent, ellipsoid-cylindric, 8–20 cm long, pale brown, with a 2–3 cm stalk and pliable scales; typically falling soon after maturity. Seed 5–6 mm long, with a 18–25 mm wing.

HABITAT/RANGE Native. Usually in mesic closed-canopy forests, in pure stands or mixed with a variety of conifers and hardwoods, 0–1,500 m; in Canada from Man. to Nfld; in the U.S. from Minn. to Maine and south to Ark. and Ga.

SIMILAR SPECIES Several other 5-needle pines are planted as ornamentals in the East; they are easily distinguished from Eastern White Pine by their seed cones. Globular cones, or cones wider than long, typically belong to the piñon pines (various species). Narrow cones 6–8 cm long belong to Japanese White Pine (*Pinus parviflora* Siebold & Zucc.). Cones 11–15 cm long and 5–8 cm wide with slightly leathery scales identify Chinese White Pine (*P. armandii* Franch.). Large cones (more than 20 cm long) characterize several species, with Western White Pine (*P. monticola* Douglas ex D. Don) the most common.

Notes: Eastern White Pine was a valued source of naval stores in the 1700s, used for ships' masts, and large tracts were once reserved for exploitation by the Royal Navy. The tallest and, but for Baldcypress (*Taxodium distichum*), the largest of our eastern conifers, it is also a very popular ornamental tree, widely planted in both North America and Europe.

JACK PINE *Pinus banksiana* Lamb.
A.K.A. BLACKJACK PINE, PIN GRIS

QUICK ID A scrubby northern pine with short needles in bundles of 2 and very small cones.

Tree to 27 m tall and 60 cm diam. but often small and spindly; trunk straight or crooked, crown rounded or irregular, often with some dead branches. **BARK** Scaly, orange-brown. **TWIG** Slender, reddish when young, aging gray-brown and rough. **LEAF** Needle 2–5 cm long, 1–1.5 mm wide, twisted, yellow-green, in bundles of 2 held in a sheath 3–6 mm long. **POLLEN CONE** 10–15 mm long, yellow to orange-brown, in small clusters.

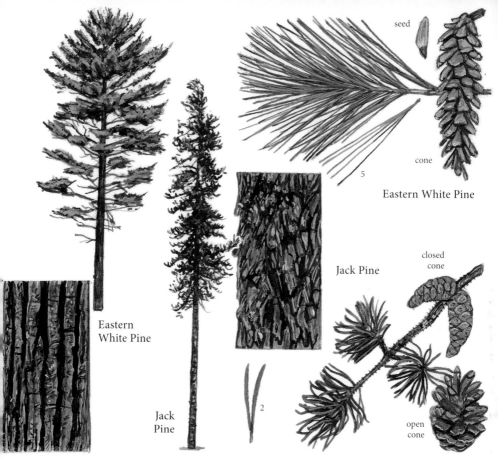

seed

cone

Eastern White Pine

closed cone

Jack Pine

5

Eastern White Pine

open cone

Jack Pine

2

SEED CONE In whorls of 1–4 at intervals on twigs, curved, asymmetric, and pointing forward along twigs, 3–5.5 cm long, light brown, sessile or short-stalked, scale thickened at tip, with an easily broken prickle. Cones shed seeds soon after maturity or are serotinous.

HABITAT/RANGE Native. Often on thin, poor, or dry sandy soils, often with Paper Birch, Quaking Aspen, or Black Spruce; at the southern limits of its range, it can occur in more productive forests dominated by species like Red Pine, Red Maple, and various oaks; from sea-level to 1,250 m; from Minn. to Maine, extending north to the arctic tree-line from N.W.T. to Nunavut.

Notes: Jack Pine rarely reaches 150 years of age, and the oldest tree known was less than 250 years old. It is superbly adapted to fire; its cones open and shed seeds soon after a burn, and the young trees produce cones at an early age. Although usually regarded as a homely little tree, rarely planted as an ornamental, it is nonetheless the most widespread Canadian pine and an important timber tree. The seeds are eaten by rodents and birds, and the tree also supports a wide variety of insects.

EASTERN WHITE PINE

JACK PINE

VIRGINIA PINE *Pinus virginiana* Mill.
A.K.A. SCRUB PINE, SPRUCE PINE, JERSEY PINE

QUICK ID A pine with twisted needles 4–8 cm long in bundles of 2, and cones with a thin, stiff prickle that remain on the tree several years after opening.

Tree to 18 m tall and 50 cm diam., with a single straight or crooked trunk and an irregular crown of long, spreading branches. **BARK** At first smooth, then reddish and scaly, finally gray-brown, thick, and shaggy. **TWIG** Slender, reddish or purplish, aging red-brown to gray, rough. **LEAF** Needle, 4–8 cm long, 1–1.5 mm wide, twisted, green, in bundles of 2 held in a sheath 4–10 mm long. **POLLEN CONE** 10–20 mm long, red-brown, turning yellow. **SEED CONE** Solitary and in pairs, borne throughout the crown, symmetric, narrowly ovoid, 4–7 cm long, red-brown, nearly sessile or on stalks to 1 cm long; scales rigid, with strong purple-red or purple-brown border on the outer surface and a thin, stiff prickle. Cones open when mature and persist several years before falling.

HABITAT/RANGE Native. Usually found on dry upland soils, rarely on limestone, often with oaks or other pines such as Shortleaf, Loblolly, or Pitch; 0–900 m, from Miss. north and east through the central-eastern states to N.Y.; naturalized in Ont.

Notes: Virginia Pine is often a successful colonist in abandoned agricultural fields. With its thin bark and shallow roots it is easily killed by fire, but it also reseeds soon afterward, and requires periodic fire to maintain its dominance over shade-tolerant broadleaf trees. It is used for lumber, pulpwood, and Christmas trees, and for foresting former coal strip mines. Although it can be attractive in its habitat, Virginia Pine is seldom grown as an ornamental.

RED PINE *Pinus resinosa* Aiton
A.K.A. NORWAY PINE, PIN ROUGE

QUICK ID The longest-leaved (12–16 cm) 2-needle pine in the northerly part of our area.

Tree to 37 m tall and 150 cm diam., with a straight trunk and a narrowly rounded crown. **BARK** Light red-brown, furrowed and cross-checked into irregularly rectangular, scaly plates. **TWIG** Up to 1 cm thick, usually 4–6 mm, pliable, orange- to red-brown, aging darker brown, rough. **LEAF** Needle, 12–16 cm long, straight or slightly twisted, breaking cleanly when bent, deep yellow-green, in bundles of 2 held in a sheath 10–25 mm long. **POLLEN CONE** 15 mm long, red to dark purple. **SEED CONE** Solitary or in pairs, symmetric, nearly globose when open, 3.5–6 cm long, light red-brown, nearly sessile, scales without a prickle. Cones open at maturity and fall soon after.

HABITAT/RANGE Native. Occurs on sandy soils and the margins of swamps, chiefly in the mixed conifer and deciduous hardwood forest that lies just south of the boreal forest, often growing with Jack Pine, Eastern White Pine, aspens, and cottonwoods; 200–1,300 m, from Minn. and Ont. to Pa. and Nfld.

Notes: Red Pine trees up to 500 years old have been found. For a time in the 19th century, logging of this species was the economic mainstay of the Great Lakes region, and it is called Norway Pine in Minn. after the homeland of the men who logged it. The destruction of native forests in that time was so complete that pre-settlement Red Pine forests are now quite rare. The tree's native habitat is ice age sand dunes, and it is planted to stabilize dune soils and to create shelterbelts to protect farmland from wind erosion, as well as for timber production. Several cultivars exist and are planted as ornamentals.

VIRGINIA PINE

RED PINE

Virginia Pine

cone

seeds

Red Pine

cone

seed

2

PITCH PINE *Pinus rigida* Mill.
A.K.A. PIN RIGIDE

QUICK ID A 3-needle pine with adventitious branches and broadly ovoid cones in clusters.

Tree to 31 m tall and 90 cm diam., with a straight or crooked trunk and a rounded or irregular crown containing dead branches. **BARK** Red-brown, deeply furrowed, with long, irregularly rectangular, flat, scaly ridges; often sprouting adventitious branches (uncommon in pines). **TWIG** Stout, orange-brown, aging darker brown, rough. **LEAF** Needle, 5–10 cm long, 1–1.5 mm wide, straight, twisted, stiff, sharp, deep to pale yellow-green, in bundles of 3 (rarely up to 5) held in a sheath 9–12 mm long. **POLLEN CONE** 20 mm long, yellow. **SEED CONE** Often clustered, symmetric, broadly ovoid when open, 3–9 cm long, light red-brown, sessile to short-stalked, scales stiff, with a slender, downcurved prickle. Cones variably serotinous, remaining on tree for many years.

HABITAT/RANGE Native. Upland or lowland sites on infertile, often thin or sandy, dry to boggy soils; at 0–1,400 m (higher elevations at southerly latitudes), from Ga. to Maine and Que.

Notes: This is the dominant tree of the pine barrens of N.J. Elsewhere, it is a codominant species in forests of Virginia Pine, Table Mountain Pine, Eastern White Pine, Atlantic White Cedar, and many types of oak. Owing to its ability to resprout, this pine can survive fires that kill all the green foliage, and can regrow from a cut stump. The wood is rich in resins that make it very decay-resistant. Historically, it was a preferred timber for shipbuilding, mine props, and railway ties, and the wood was distilled to produce pitch. The species remains ecologically important as a dominant forest tree, and the seeds are a winter forage source for wildlife.

SAND PINE *Pinus clausa* (CHAPM. EX ENGELM.) SARG.
A.K.A. SCRUB PINE, SANDHILL PINE

QUICK ID A pine with short needles, small cones, and scrubby growth form, found in sandy Fla. habitats.

Tree to 21 m tall and 50 cm diam., single trunk or multitrunked, much branched; crown rounded or irregular. **BARK** Smooth, becoming red-brown and broken into plates. **TWIG** Slender, violet- to red-brown. **LEAF** Needle, 6–9 cm long, 1 mm wide, in bundles of 2 held in a sheath 3–5 mm long. **POLLEN CONE** 10 mm long, brownish yellow. **SEED CONE** In whorls of 1–3, symmetric, 3–8 cm long, red-brown, scales tapering to a sharp tip with a weak, easily broken prickle. Cones variably serotinous, remaining on the tree for many years.

HABITAT/RANGE Native. Grows as the dominant tree over an understory of evergreen shrub oaks and small palms on sandy coastal sites and inland sand ridges; 0–60 m, Fla. and extreme s. Ala. Sometimes planted for timber production and naturalized in Miss., Ga., and N.C.

SIMILAR SPECIES Sand Pine resembles Spruce Pine, which grows in a very different habitat—mainly se. coastal plain broadleaf woodlands.

Notes: Sand Pine is the dominant tree in critically endangered sand scrub ecosystems that provide habitat for many threatened or endangered wildlife species.

SAND PINE

PITCH PINE

3

cone

Pitch Pine

cone

2

Sand Pine

TABLE MOUNTAIN PINE *Pinus pungens* Lamb.
A.K.A. HICKORY PINE, MOUNTAIN PINE

QUICK ID A pine with long-persisting cones over 6 cm long, the cone scales bearing a stout, curved, sharp claw.

Tree to 12 m tall and 60 cm diam., trunk straight to crooked, often with dead branches; crown irregularly rounded or flattened. **BARK** Red- to gray-brown, irregularly checked into scaly plates. **TWIG** Slender, orange- to yellow-brown, aging darker brown, rough. **LEAF** Needle, 3–6 cm long, 1–1.5 mm wide, twisted, deep yellow-green, in bundles of 2 held in a sheath 5–10 mm long. **POLLEN CONE** 15 mm long, yellow. **SEED CONE** Mostly in whorls, asymmetric, downcurved, broadly ovoid, 6–10 cm long, pale red-brown, nearly sessile or on stalk to 1 cm long, scales bearing a stout, curved, sharp claw. Cones variably serotinous, remaining some years before falling.

HABITAT/RANGE Native. Dry, mostly sandy or shale-laden uplands, at 500–1,350 m, from Pa. and N.J. south in the Appalachian Mountains and associated foothills to n. Ga.

TABLE MOUNTAIN PINE

LOBLOLLY PINE

LOBLOLLY PINE *Pinus taeda* L.
A.K.A. OLDFIELD PINE, BULL PINE

QUICK ID A large, fairly long-needled pine, with cones bearing a stout, sharp prickle.

Tree to 46 m tall and 160 cm diam., usually straight-trunked, with a rounded crown. **BARK** Red-brown, forming rectangular scaly plates. **TWIG** To 1 cm thick, yellow-brown, darker with age, rough. **LEAF** Needle, 12–18 cm long, 1–2 mm wide, slightly twisted, pliable, deep yellow-green, in bundles of 3 (sometimes 2) held in a sheath 10–25 mm long. **POLLEN CONE** 20–40 mm long, yellow to yellow-brown. **SEED CONE** Solitary or in small clusters at ends of branches, symmetric, narrowly ovoid when open, 6–12 cm long, dull yellow-brown, sessile or nearly so, scales with a stout, sharp prickle. Cones shed seeds and fall soon after maturity.

HABITAT/RANGE Native. Grows in moist, productive lowland forests and near swamps, or sometimes in dry uplands; 0–700 m, from Tex. to Fla. and northeast to N.J.

SIMILAR SPECIES Ponderosa Pine (*Pinus ponderosa* Douglas ex C. Lawson) resembles Loblolly Pine but has slightly shorter needles and slightly smaller cones, and barely enters e. North America in nc. Neb.

Notes: "Loblolly" is an old word for a small closed-basin swamp. This tree is the largest hard pine in e. North America. Common associates include a variety of pines and oaks. Bastard Pine (often named as *Pinus* × *sondereggeri*), the natural hybrid between Loblolly Pine and Longleaf Pine, is recorded in Tex., La., and N.C. The trees have intermediate characteristics, but unlike Longleaf Pine, have no seedling grass stage, and the cones have a sharp prickle like Loblolly (but not Longleaf). Loblolly has been widely planted outside its native range and is now the most economically important timber species in the se. U.S. It is also widely planted for timber production in other countries.

Table Mountain Pine

cone

seed

2

Ponderosa
Pine

cone

Loblolly Pine

cone

3

POND PINE *Pinus serotina* Michx.
A.K.A. MARSH PINE, POCOSIN PINE

QUICK ID A pine of swampy habitats, with adventitious branches, needles 15–20 cm long, mostly in bundles of 3, tufted at branch ends, and persistent conical cones that are often wider than long.

Tree to 21 m tall and 60 cm diam., with a straight or crooked trunk and a sparse, broadly rounded crown. **BARK** Red-brown, irregularly furrowed into rectangular, flat, scaly plates; sometimes bearing adventitious sprouts. **TWIG** Yellow-orange, darkening with age, stout. **LEAF** Needle, 15–20 cm long, 1.3–1.5 mm wide, slightly twisted, straight, yellow-green, in bundles of 3 (to 5 in adventitious branches) held in a sheath 10–20 mm long, in tufts at branch tips. **POLLEN CONE** To 30 mm long, yellow-brown. **SEED CONE** In clusters along branches, often in whorls, symmetric, broadly ovoid (often wider than long), 5–8 cm long, pale red-brown, sessile or on stalk to 1 cm long, scale with a short, weak prickle. Cones variably serotinous, retained for many years.

HABITAT/RANGE Native. Grows in sandy flats with a high water table, and in and along the edges of swamps, often with Slash Pine or Baldcypress, in areas with a dense understory of tall shrubs, at 0–200 m, from Ala. along the Atlantic coastal plain to N.J.

Notes: Pond Pine is closely related to Pitch Pine, with which it shares the unusual ability to produce adventitious shoots. It usually does this after injury, for instance when scorched in a fire. Although it is very well adapted to fire, it can nonetheless persist for a long time in the absence of fire, although it will eventually give way to more shade-tolerant Atlantic White Cedar. Pond Pine is not a common ornamental tree, nor is it an economically important timber tree, though its resinous and often crooked wood is sometimes used for pulp. Its main importance is ecological, adding to the diversity of wetland habitats within its range.

SPRUCE PINE *Pinus glabra* Walter
A.K.A. CEDAR PINE, WALTER PINE

QUICK ID A gray-barked pine that usually grows in broadleaf forests lacking other conifers.

Tree to 30 m tall and 100 cm diam., with a straight or crooked trunk and a pyramidal to rounded crown. **BARK** Unusual for a pine, resembling bark of a hardwood: smooth, gray, later becoming fissured and cross-checked into elongate, irregular, scaly plates. **TWIG** Slender, purple-red to red-brown, aging gray and smooth. **LEAVES** Needle, 4–8 cm long, 0.7–1.2 mm wide, slightly twisted, dark green, in bundle of 2 held in sheath 5–10 mm long. **POLLEN CONE** 10–15 mm long, purple-brown. **SEED CONE** Solitary and in pairs on twigs, nearly symmetric, ovoid-cylindric when open, 3.5–7 cm long, red-brown, aging gray, on stalk 1–10 mm long. Cone scales slightly thickened and raised at edges, bearing a small, weak, incurved prickle. Cones shed seeds at maturity and fall 1–2 years later.

HABITAT/RANGE Native. Widespread on acidic, sandy loam soils and moist woodlands in the Atlantic and Gulf coastal plains, at 0–150 m, from S.C. south to n. Fla. and west to far e. La.

SIMILAR SPECIES The shoots and leaves resemble those of Shortleaf Pine, but the cones are less prickly and leaves are a deeper green.

Notes: Spruce Pine wood is of poor quality and is not useful as timber. The tree, although attractive, is seldom used in horticulture. This pine is mostly of interest for its unusual ecology as a dominant species in the broadleaf floodplain forest. It is one of the only shade-tolerant pines, establishing in the shade of broadleaf trees such as magnolias, hickories, beech, and oaks, and surviving by growing taller than them. It sometimes grows with Loblolly Pine. It is one of the few pines that is easily killed by, and not adapted to, fire.

POND PINE   SPRUCE PINE

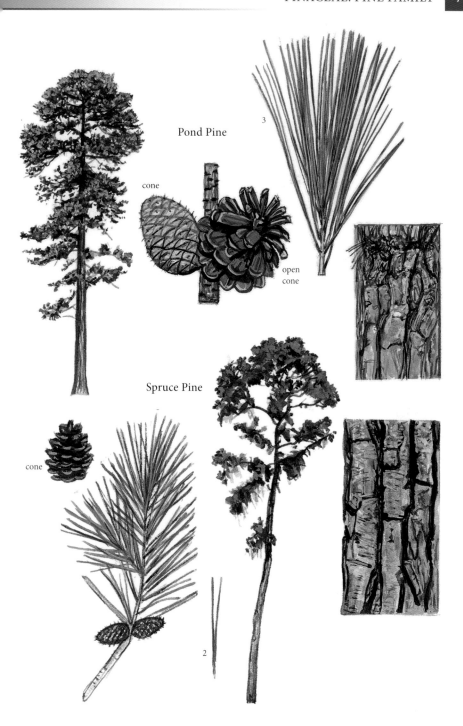

Pond Pine

cone

open cone

3

Spruce Pine

cone

2

LONGLEAF PINE *Pinus palustris* Mill.

QUICK ID A fine, tall forest tree with the longest needles of any pine in the world and the largest cones of any e. North American pine.

Tree to 47 m tall and 120 cm diam., with a straight trunk and a rounded or flattened crown. **BARK** Orange-brown, with rectangular, scaly plates. **TWIG** Up to 2 cm thick, orange-brown, darkening with age, rough; tuft of foliage forms a ball at end of branch. **LEAF** Needle, 20–45 cm long, about 1.5 mm wide, slightly twisted, yellow-green, in bundles of 3 held in a sheath 2–2.5 cm long. Foliage lives only about 2 years, and the fallen needles usually form a thick carpet on the forest floor. **POLLEN CONE** Cylindric, 30–80 mm long, purple. **SEED CONE** Solitary or paired toward twig tips, symmetric, cylindric when open, 15–25 cm long, dull brown, sessile, scales with a short, stiff prickle. Cones shed seeds at maturity and soon fall.

HABITAT/RANGE Native. Mostly on dry sandy uplands and sandhills, also on clayey soils, 0–700 m, se. Va., south and west along coastal plains to e. Tex.

Notes: Longleaf Pine once formed an almost continuous coastal plain forest from Va. to Tex., but in historic times that forest has been almost all cut and either put to nonforest use or replanted with other pine species, so that pure Longleaf Pine stands are now found mostly in isolated parks and preserves. Longleaf Pine is wonderfully adapted to fire; in the absence of fire suppression, the fallen needle layer burns off at intervals of a few years, clearing the understory without harming the mature trees. The subterranean stem is unharmed by fire and can quickly resprout a new crop of leaves in the aftermath of a light burn. The seedlings have a "grass stage," in which they look like bunchgrasses. Longleaf is the most important tree species for the endangered Red-cockaded Woodpecker (*Picoides borealis*), providing nesting and foraging habitat.

SLASH PINE *Pinus elliottii* Engelm.
A.K.A. SWAMP PINE

QUICK ID A long-needled pine, native only in lowlands of the Deep South, with cones 9–18 cm long bearing a short, stout prickle.

Tree to 30 m tall and 80 cm diam., with a straight or contorted trunk and a rounded or flattened crown. **BARK** Orange-brown, irregularly furrowed into large, quadrangular, flaky plates. **TWIG** About 1 cm thick, orange-brown, aging darker brown, rough. **LEAF** Needle, 15–20 cm long, 1.2–1.5 mm wide, slightly twisted, pliable, yellow- to blue-green, in bundles of 2 (var. *densa*) or 3 held in a sheath 1–2 cm long. **POLLEN CONE** 30–40 mm long, purplish. **SEED CONE** Single or in pairs, symmetric, ovoid when open, 9–18 cm long, light brown, on stalk up to 3 cm long, scales with a short, stout prickle. Cones shed seeds upon maturity and fall in the next year.

HABITAT/RANGE Native. Grows mostly on sandy, wet but not saturated soils, such as sandy islands in large swamps, where it often forms pure stands; 0–150 m, s. coastal plains of extreme se. La. east to Fla. and north to S.C.

SIMILAR SPECIES Very similar to Loblolly Pine, but with longer needles and native only in lowlands of the Deep South.

Notes: Slash Pine is highly fire adapted, both tolerant of fire and able to establish rapidly after fire. The Slash Pine flatwoods habitat features pines over a palmetto-shrub layer with a rich herb understory. It is also found with various oaks, Eastern Redcedar, and Baldcypress. South Florida Slash Pine (var. *densa* Little & K.W. Dorman) has needles in bundles of 2, and the seedlings develop a "grass stage," in which they resemble bunchgrass for several years. Slash Pine is widely planted for pulp and pole production, and the species is used in what little turpentine production still occurs. Plantations can be seen in many parts of the s. U.S.

LONGLEAF PINE

SLASH PINE

Longleaf Pine

young sapling

cone

seed

3

Slash Pine

2/3

seed

cone

SHORTLEAF PINE *Pinus echinata* Mill.
A.K.A. SHORTSTRAW PINE

QUICK ID A pine of typical form, but with resin pockets in the bark, short needles, and small cones in large numbers that remain on the tree for several years.

Tree to 40 m tall and 120 cm diam., usually with a single straight trunk and a rounded or conical open crown. **BARK** Red-brown, scaly, composed of plates with scattered resin pockets. **TWIG** Slender (about 5 mm thick), greenish brown to red-brown, aging to gray, rough, and cracking over time. **LEAF** Needle, 7–11 cm long, 1 mm wide, straight, slightly twisted, gray- to yellow-green, most in bundles of 2 held in a sheath 5–10 mm long. **POLLEN CONE** 15–20 mm long, yellow-green to purple-green. **SEED CONE** Solitary or clustered, widely distributed throughout the crown, symmetric, ovoid when open, 4–6 cm long, red-brown, aging gray, on very short stalks, scales with a stout, sharp prickle of variable length. Cones persist up to several years after maturity before falling.

HABITAT/RANGE Native. Grows on highly varied soil types on relatively dry uplands, 150–600 m; Tex. to Mo.; east to Fla. and north to N.Y.

Notes: Shortleaf Pine is fire resistant, surviving moderate burns and seeding in after severe ones; trees up to about 30 years old may resprout from the base after a fire. In the absence of fire, it is typically succeeded by hardwoods, especially oaks. It can form pure stands, especially as a colonist species on abandoned farmlands, but may also be accompanied by other pines such as Longleaf Pine, Loblolly Pine, or Virginia Pine. This important commercial species produces a better wood than most pines, suitable for fine uses such as furniture and cabinetry. It is sometimes planted in parks or along roadways, but is generally not a popular ornamental.

SHORTLEAF PINE

SCOTS PINE *Pinus sylvestris* L.
A.K.A. SCOTCH PINE

QUICK ID An ornamental pine with orange-red bark and fairly short blue-green needles in 2s.

Tree to 25 m tall and 70 cm diam., with a straight trunk and highly variable crown. **BARK** Thin, flaking, orange-red, with age becoming thick, scaly-plated and gray-brown. **TWIG** Slender, green initially, becoming gray-buff by the end of the 1st summer. **LEAF** Needle, 4–6 cm long, 1.5–2 mm wide, always glaucous (the only 2-leaved hard pine with blue-green or gray-green leaves), longest on vigorous young trees, shorter on old trees, in bundles of 2 held in a sheath 5–8 mm long. **POLLEN CONE** 8–12 mm long, yellow or pink. **SEED CONE** Conical, symmetric, 3–6 cm long, gray-buff to gray-green, scales with a very small prickle. Cones fall soon after seed is shed.

HABITAT/RANGE Introduced. Scots Pine has the largest natural distribution of any pine in the world, from Scotland to Siberia; it is widely naturalized in ne. U.S. and e. Canada and is a very popular ornamental.

AUSTRIAN PINE *Pinus nigra* J.F. Arnold
A.K.A. EUROPEAN BLACK PINE

QUICK ID A pine with thick, stiff needles and largish cones borne in whorls.

Tree to 45 m tall and 150 cm diam., with a straight trunk and a conical crown that becomes flat-topped with age. **BARK** Platy, gray-brown. **TWIG** Green, becoming orange-brown, densely leaved. **LEAF** Needle, 8–15 cm long, 1.5–2 mm thick, often slightly twisted, stiff, dark green, in bundles of 2. **POLLEN CONE** 10–15 mm long, yellow. **SEED CONE** In whorls near branch ends, symmetric, 5–10 cm long, scales rounded, with a small, fragile prickle. Cones often fall soon after seed is shed.

HABITAT/RANGE Introduced. Austrian Pine is one of the premier timber trees of Europe; it is naturalized in the ne. U.S. and se. Canada, though to a lesser extent than Scots Pine, and is likewise a very popular ornamental.

cone

seed

Shortleaf Pine

2

3

Shortleaf
Pine

seed

cone

2

Scots Pine

Scots Pine

Austrian Pine

cone

Austrian Pine

2

■ *TSUGA*: HEMLOCKS

There are 7 hemlock species worldwide, found in North America and East Asia. The 2 species native to our area grow in generally moist forest on good soils, in pure stands or with a wide variety of other conifers and hardwoods. They are shade-tolerant trees, able to establish under a forest canopy, and slowly grow to become canopy-dominant trees.

Hemlocks are monoecious evergreen trees, usually with a straight single trunk; branches are produced throughout the growing season; the crown is topped by a single drooping leader. **BARK** Rough, scaly, longitudinally fissured. **LEAF** Needle, spirally arranged on twig but usually appearing 2-ranked, flattened, upper surface shiny, stomata in 2 whitish bands on lower surface. **POLLEN CONE** Solitary, nearly globular. **SEED CONE** Solitary, erect at pollination but soon becoming pendulous, bracts hidden within the seed scales.

The common name "hemlock" was given because the crushed foliage smells a bit like the poisonous herb hemlock (*Conium* species), native to Europe. The genus name, *Tsuga*, is the common Japanese name for hemlock, and is also the common name in most countries where there are no native hemlocks. Both of our native species are now experiencing catastrophic dieback as a result of infestation by Hemlock Woolly Adelgid (*Adelges tsugae*), an insect pest introduced to North America from Asia in 1924. Unless some way of controlling this pest is found, hemlock may soon be a rare tree, confined mostly to gardens and arboreta.

EASTERN HEMLOCK *Tsuga canadensis* (L.) Carrière
A.K.A. Pruche du Canada

QUICK ID Evergreen tree with small brown cones; the twigs are covered with fine, short hairs; the strongly 2-ranked leaves have minutely toothed edges.

Tree to 30 m tall and 150 cm diam., with a drooping leader atop a broadly conical crown that grows cylindric with age. **BARK** Brown to dark gray, scaly, fissured. **TWIG** Yellow-brown, with a dense covering of very short, fine hairs. **LEAF** Needle, 8–15 mm long, mostly 2-ranked, flattened, blunt-tipped, with rows of tiny teeth along the edges; upper surface shiny green with a central groove, the lower with 2 wide stomatal bands. **POLLEN CONE** Numerous, 3–5 mm long, yellow. **SEED CONE** Numerous on outer branches, hanging by slender peduncle, ovoid, 15–25 mm long, 10–18 mm wide when open, light brown, with thin, papery scales.

HABITAT/RANGE Native. Closed-canopy forest on relatively moist upland sites, primarily in mountains, often with pines or various hardwoods, at 600–1,800 m, in all provinces eastward from Ont., except Nfld., and all states eastward from Minn. to Ala., except Fla.

Notes: Before the introduction of Hemlock Woolly Adelgid, the Eastern Hemlock was an important timber tree.

EASTERN HEMLOCK

CAROLINA HEMLOCK *Tsuga caroliniana* Engelm.

QUICK ID A hemlock with smooth twigs (or with a few short, dark hairs), and needles that are not 2-ranked on branches in full sun and that do not have minutely toothed edges.

Tree to 30 m tall and 150 cm diam., generally very similar to Eastern Hemlock except as follows: **TWIG** Light brown, smooth or thinly covered with

CAROLINA HEMLOCK

cone

seed

leaf

Eastern Hemlock

cone

Carolina Hemlock

short, dark hairs. **LEAF** Needle, 10–20 mm long, mostly spreading in all directions from twig, flat but slightly downcurled, margins smooth. **SEED CONE** Ovoid to oblong, 2.5–4 cm long, 1.5–2.5 cm wide, the scales spreading widely as the cone dries.

HABITAT/RANGE Native. Mostly found on sites with shallow, nutrient-poor soils and a low risk of fire; grows in mixed hardwood–conifer stands, often with Eastern Hemlock, commonly with a rhododendron understory; 600–1,500 m, sw. Va., e. Tenn., w. N.C., and w. S.C. to nw. Ga.

Notes: Although an attractive tree, Carolina Hemlock has little commercial value and is rarely grown ornamentally.

TAXACEAE: YEW FAMILY

A family of 6 genera and 28 species, with 2 genera and 3 species in e. North America. Globally, the family is found throughout much of the Northern Hemisphere and farther south in Indonesia. In our area, 2 species are confined to a tiny range in Fla. and a 3rd occurs in e. Canada and ne. U.S.

Dioecious or monoecious evergreen trees and shrubs, often multistemmed. **BARK** Scaly or fissured, usually reddish. **LEAF** Simple, alternate needle, appearing 2-ranked; unlike other conifers, crushed leaves do not smell resinous. **SEED CONE** Naked at end of a short stalk, partially or completely covered by a fleshy aril, resembling small green or red berries, usually only 1 ovule of 2 developing. The seeds of trees in the yew family are mostly dispersed by birds.

■ *TAXUS*: YEWS

The 7 species of yews are primarily trees or shrubs of the forest understory; 3 species are native to North America, with 2 native and 1 introduced species in our range.

Dioecious or monoecious trees or shrubs, commonly in the forest understory, with an irregular crown of ascending to drooping branches. **TWIG** Alternate, green to orange, turning brown with age. **LEAF** Appearing 2-ranked, yellowish to bronze-green, flexible, soft-pointed, with 2 broad whitish stomatal bands on the underside. **SEED CONE** Orange to red fleshy aril enclosing a single brown seed.

Many yew populations were decimated in the late 20th century when it was found that they contain taxol, which has proved effective against breast, ovarian, and other cancers. Today, taxol is artificially produced.

fleshy aril green, maturing orange or red, partially enclosing a single seed 3–4 mm long.

HABITAT/RANGE Native. An understory shrub primarily in late-successional forests; also locally in bogs, swamps, and rocky places; 0–1,500 m; from Wis. east to Va., north to Man. and east to Nfld.

SIMILAR SPECIES English Yew (*Taxus baccata* L.) is a very similar tree-size plant, usually single-stemmed, grown as an ornamental; various cultivars show different habits and foliage colors. English Yew is reportedly naturalized in some areas of the ne. U.S., but is usually seen as a planted tree or large shrub.

Notes: All parts of the plant except the fleshy red aril are at least mildly poisonous, but nonetheless it was used by native peoples to treat a wide variety of ailments.

CANADA YEW *Taxus canadensis*
Marshall
A.K.A. L'IF DU CANADA

QUICK ID A shrubby yew of the northeastern and Canadian forests.

Usually monoecious, spreading shrub to 2 m tall. **BARK** Reddish, very thin. **TWIG** Round, ridged, orange, turning brown. **LEAF** Needlelike, 10–25 mm long, 1–2.4 mm wide, dark green to yellow-green, with a raised midrib on both upper and lower surfaces. **POLLEN CONE** Solitary, 2–3 mm long, yellow. **SEED CONE** Solitary, on underside of shoot,

FLORIDA YEW *Taxus floridana* Nutt. ex
Chapm.

QUICK ID The only yew native to Fla.; very rare.

Dioecious shrub or small tree to 10 m tall and 38 cm diam., with an irregular crown. **BARK** Purple-brown, smooth, becoming thin-scaly. **TWIG** Round, ridged, orangish, turning brown. **LEAF** Needlelike, pliable, 15–25 mm long, 1–2 mm wide, slightly falcate; upper surface dark green; lower surface light green, with 2 whitish bands of stomata. **POLLEN CONE** Solitary along

CANADA YEW

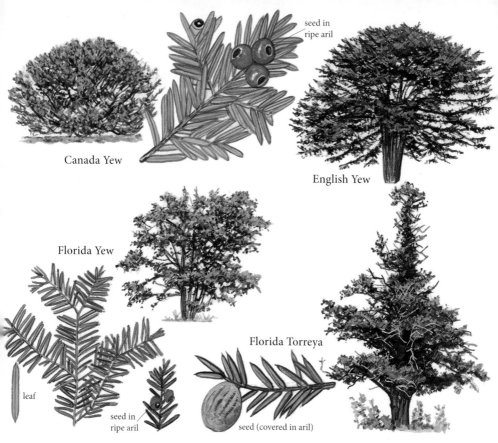

Canada Yew

English Yew

Florida Yew

Florida Torreya

leaf

seed in
ripe aril

seed (covered in aril)

seed in
ripe aril

shoots, 2–3 mm diam., yellow. **SEED CONE** Solitary, on underside of shoot, a cup-shaped, berrylike fleshy aril, green, maturing orange or red, holding a single exposed seed 5–6 mm long; cone and seed together about 2 cm long and 1 cm diam.

HABITAT/RANGE Native. Moist, shaded ravines in hardwood forests at 15–30 m along the Apalachicola River, in Gadsden and Liberty counties, Fla., where it grows with Florida Torreya.

Notes: Florida Yew is classified as critically endangered, and is the rarest American conifer except for Florida Torreya.

FLORIDA TORREYA *Torreya taxifolia* Arn.
A.K.A. STINKING CEDAR, GOPHERWOOD

QUICK ID A small yew-like tree with whorled branches and very sharp-pointed leaves; seed cone resembles a green berry, 25–35 mm long.

Dioecious evergreen tree, ornamental specimens to 18 m tall and 80 cm diam., surviving wild trees much smaller. Open conical crown of whorled branches. **BARK** Pale brown to dark gray, irregularly fissured. **TWIG** Slender, grooved, green, turning yellowish brown. **LEAF** Needlelike, in 2 ranks, linear, 1.5–3.8 cm long, 2–3 mm wide, very sharp-pointed, abruptly wider at base, with twisted 1 mm petiole; emitting a fetid odor when crushed. **POLLEN CONE** On underside of lateral twigs, 5–6 mm long, pale yellow. **SEED CONE** In pairs, ovoid, aril dark green, streaked with purple when mature, 25–35 mm long, completely enclosing a single seed.

HABITAT/RANGE Native. On limestone bluffs, slopes, and moist ravines at 15–30 m, along a 64 km stretch of the Apalachicola River in sw. Ga. and nw. Fla.

Notes: Fewer than 1,000 wild plants remain of Florida Torreya, North America's most endangered conifer, and most are small stem sprouts from trees that are in the process of dying from a presumed fungal pathogen.

Angiosperms, the flowering plants, may be herbaceous or woody, large or small, with large showy flowers or tiny flowers that escape notice. Found almost throughout the world, they are absent from only the harshest environments. There are 250,000–400,000 species of angiosperms.

MONOCOTS

Monocotyledons (monocots for short) are a large group of the flowering plants (angiosperms) that includes the palms, agaves and yuccas, grasses, orchids, sedges, rushes, and lilies. Most monocots have parallel leaf veins (as opposed to netlike venation of the other major assemblage, the dicotyledons, or dicots) and the flower parts, such as sepals, petals, and stamens, are usually in multiples of 3 (rather than 4 or 5).

ARECACEAE: PALM FAMILY

The palms compose a large and distinctive family of shrubs and trees whose primary centers of distribution lie in South America, Central America, and Southeast Asia. About 190 genera and 2,500 species are known worldwide. Of the 29 species that occur in North America north of Mexico, not all of which become trees, 14 are native and 15 are introduced. Most North American species are restricted in range to s. Fla., s. Calif., and the Southwest.

Palms are evergreen trees or shrubs, or rarely vinelike, evolutionarily younger than the conifers but older than many dicots. They exhibit a unique morphology that usually renders a species immediately recognizable as a palm. **TRUNK** Palms produce neither true bark nor true wood, and the food- and water-conducting cells within their trunks are more or less intermixed, rather than neatly layered in a ring under the bark as in most dicots. The outer shell of the trunk is composed of living tissue that does not flake off as the bark does in most other trees. Hence, external injuries to a palm's trunk do not disappear as new bark is formed and old bark lost. Palms typically grow from the tip of the trunk, or apical meristem. If this tip is excessively damaged or is removed, the tree will die. As a result of this predominantly apical growth pattern, palms do not produce twigs, and branching is rare. The trunks of some palms are covered with leaf scars or with the remains of old leaf bases, which can be relatively small and appear as rings or horizontal knobs on the trunk, or can be large, with the remains of the lower portion of the petiole still evident (sometimes referred to as "boots"). **LEAF** Pinnate, palmate, or in some cases appearing palmate but with a very short midrib extending beyond the tip of the petiole (costapalmate); petiole sometimes with conspicuous piercing spines. **FLOWER** Bisexual or unisexual, when the latter on the same or separate plants; in clusters arising from leaf axils within or below the crown. Sepals and petals each number 3, stamens usually 6, and the ovary is superior and most often 3-chambered. **FRUIT** Usually a drupe or drupe-like.

Although palms are probably best known in the U.S. for their ornamental value, they are used in a wide array of products, including food, beverages, building materials, feeds, fertilizers, clothing, furniture, and an assortment of household items.

FLORIDA ROYAL PALM *Roystonea regia* (Kunth) O.F. Cook

QUICK ID A palm easily distinguished by the combination of large size, elongated crownshaft, concrete-like trunk, and arching crown of pinnate, dark green leaves.

Evergreen tree to about 30 m tall, 40 cm diam. Stately, erect, single trunk; crown vase-shaped or rounded, the numerous arching and ascending leaves densely clustered at the top of the trunk and subtended by a smooth, lustrous, medium green crownshaft to about 1.8 m long. **TRUNK** Medium gray, smooth or slightly roughened, the texture and color reminiscent of concrete; swollen at base, sometimes with a slight bulge at mid-trunk; uppermost portions and the entire trunk of young trees often encircled with prominent brown rings. **LEAF** Pinnate, to about 4 m long; petiole to about 20 cm long. Blade composed of numerous flaccid, pointed segments arranged in 4 rows and appearing to emanate at various angles from the central axis; upper surface lustrous dark green; segments 60–120 cm long. **FLOWER** Unisexual, with both sexes borne in the same arching inflorescence; petals 3, white or creamy white; sepals 3; inflorescence arising below the leaves. Year-round, mostly late winter to midsummer. **FRUIT** Drupe-like, rounded, blue or blue-black, usually single-seeded, about 1 cm diam.; matures year-round, mostly spring to autumn.

HABITAT/RANGE Native. Swamps, cypress wetlands, margins of subtropical hammocks; southernmost peninsular Fla., excluding Fla. Keys.

SIMILAR SPECIES Florida Cherry Palm (*Pseudophoenix sargentii*) is much smaller and has rings around the trunk, which Florida Royal Palm usually lacks.

Notes: Roystonea is a genus of 11 species, one of which occurs in North America.

FLORIDA ROYAL PALM

old tree   young tree   seed   fruit   base of trunk

Florida Royal Palm

FLORIDA CHERRY PALM
Pseudophoenix sargentii H. Wendl. ex Sarg.
A.K.A. BUCCANEER PALM, HOG PALM, SARGENT'S
CHERRY PALM

QUICK ID A palm distinguished by its pinnate leaves partly folded into a V shape and bright red fruit.

Evergreen tree, 4.5–7.5 m tall, to 30 cm diam. Erect, single trunk; crown spreading, the several arching or ascending, recurved fronds usually subtended by a smooth, sometimes bulging, gray or light green waxy crownshaft. **TRUNK** Gray-green or light gray, with numerous horizontal rings, especially on the upper part; often bulging at, or slightly above, midpoint. **LEAF** Pinnate, 2–3 m long; petiole about 60 cm long, lacking spines. Blade V-shaped in cross section; upper surface dark green or bluish green; segments stiff, to about 50 cm long. **FLOWER** Bisexual and unisexual, tiny; petals 3, yellow or greenish yellow; sepals 3; inflorescence arising from leaf axils, multibranched, 90–120 cm long. Year-round. **FRUIT** Rounded drupe, about 12 mm diam., green at first, becoming red at maturity. Year-round.

HABITAT/RANGE Native. Very rare, with natural populations remaining only on Elliott Key, off the coast of Miami, Fla.; cultivated or restored in coastal habitats elsewhere in s. Fla.

SIMILAR SPECIES Florida Royal Palm (*Roystonea regia*) is somewhat similar but larger, and its inflorescence is produced below, rather than within, the leaves.

Notes: Pseudophoenix is a genus of 4 species, one of which occurs in North America.

FLORIDA CHERRY PALM

■ *PHOENIX*: DATE PALMS

A genus of about 137 species, 2 introduced and established in North America, and at least 1 other species used horticulturally and potentially naturalized. **LEAF** Pinnate, with armed petiole. **FLOWER** Unisexual, in multibranched clusters, male and female on separate plants. **FRUIT** Fleshy, usually 1-seeded, berrylike or drupe-like fruits, with the tissue covering the seed paperlike.

SENEGAL DATE PALM *Phoenix reclinata* Jacq.
A.K.A AFRICAN DATE PALM

QUICK ID A palm identified by the combination of clump-forming habit and pinnate leaf with stout, sharp orange spines on the petiole.

Evergreen, thicket-forming small tree or large shrub 9–15 m tall, 10–18 cm diam. Arching, ascending, or leaning, usually with multiple trunks arising from a clustered base; crown of numerous, mostly drooping fronds. **TRUNK** Lower portion gray with rings or grooves; upper portion densely matted with fibrous leaf bases. **LEAF** Pinnate, 3–4.5 m long; petiole armed with stiff, sharp-tipped yellow-orange spines to about 9 cm long. Upper surface lustrous dark green; blade segments stiff, linear, 30–45 cm long, strongly V-shaped in cross section at base. **FLOWER** Unisexual; petals 3, cream-colored; sepals 3; inflorescence multibranched, arising from leaf axils within the crown and much shorter than the leaves. Spring. **FRUIT** Drupe-like, rounded or ellipsoid, 1–2 cm long, about 8 mm diam.; green at first, becoming orange, then coppery brown or blackish brown at maturity, in summer to autumn.

HABITAT/RANGE Introduced. Native to Africa and Madagascar; invasive in rock-land hammocks, coastal dunes, and disturbed sites of s. peninsular Fla.

SIMILAR SPECIES Jelly Palm (*Butia capitata*) and African Oil Palm (*Elaeis guineensis*) also have pinnate leaves with armed petioles, but lack the combination of these with a clump-forming habit.

fruit

old plant

young plant

Florida Cherry Palm

base of trunk

seeds

Senegal Date Palm

leaf base with
spines

CANARY ISLAND DATE PALM *Phoenix canariensis* Chabaud

QUICK ID A pinnate-leaved palm recognized by the combination of its stately crown and the diamond-shaped leaf scars that decorate the trunk.

Evergreen tree, 15–27 m tall, 55–90 cm diam. Stately, erect, single trunk; crown more or less rounded, with numerous overlapping and strongly drooping fronds. **TRUNK** Light brown, decorated with stout, closely set rings of horizontally elongated diamond-shaped leaf bases. **LEAF** Pinnate, 3–6 m long, V-shaped in cross section. Blade segments stiff, dark green, the lowermost modified into long orange spines. **FLOWER** Unisexual; petals 3, yellow; sepals 3; inflorescence multibranched, tinted orange, arising within the crown but clearly visible. Spring. **FRUIT** Drupe-like, ellipsoid, 2.4–2.7 cm long, 1.0–1.2 cm diam.; green at first, becoming reddish purple or orange at maturity, in summer to autumn.

HABITAT/RANGE Introduced. Native to Canary Is.; cultivated throughout Fla. but probably not naturalized (cultivated and naturalized in s. Calif., 0–1,000 m).

DATE PALM *Phoenix dactylifera* L.

Similar in form, frond, and size to Canary Island Date Palm but distinguished by its rougher trunk with old leaf bases less flattened. Evergreen tree, 21–27 m tall, typically not exceeding about 60 cm diam. **HABITAT/RANGE** Introduced; cultivated in Fla. (and Calif.) but probably not naturalized.

COCONUT PALM *Cocos nucifera* L.

QUICK ID A pinnate-leaved palm recognized by its leaning and arching form and distinctive fruit, the coconut.

Evergreen tree, 9–30 m tall, to about 30 cm diam. Erect, ascending, more often leaning, single trunk; crown spreading, the fronds arching, ascending, often moderately recurved. **TRUNK** Grayish white or tan, marked with darker, conspicuous horizontal rings; often swollen at the base. **LEAF** Pinnate, 2.5–7 m long; petiole 90–150 cm long. Blade segments usually in 4 rows, stiff on young leaves, becoming pendent on older leaves, to about 1.5 m long and 5 cm broad; upper surface dark green or yellow-green. **FLOWER** Unisexual, creamy yellow, 1.1–1.3 cm diam., petals and sepals 3; inflorescence arising from leaf axils within the crown, multi-branched and stiffly ascending; the woody bracts enveloping the inflorescence split into boat-shaped segments, often falling as, or after, the fruit develops. Year-round. **FRUIT** Three-angled, capsule-like, usually single-seeded, hard brown drupe exceeding 10 cm diam.; seed—commonly referred to as the coconut—large, hollow, with a hard, hairy shell and 3 spots at one end, filled with fluid. Year-round.

HABITAT/RANGE Pantropical, nativity uncertain, probably introduced to Fla. in the early 1800s; naturalized along the coastal strand, s. Fla., including Fla. Keys.

SIMILAR SPECIES The Queen Palm (*Syagrus romanzoffiana*) is similar but typically with an erect trunk, and the fruits are much smaller and fleshy.

Notes: This is the coconut of commerce and is an important crop in tropical and subtropical regions nearly worldwide. It is the source of a variety of food and cosmetic products, not the least of which is coconut oil, and its fibers are used to weave mats and rugs.

fruit

Canary
Island
Date
Palm

fruit

fruit
(dried)

seed

Date Palm

fruit
section

Coconut Palm

mature
fruit

immature fruit

seedling

QUEEN PALM *Syagrus romanzoffiana*
(Cham.) Glassman

QUICK ID A palm distinguished by the combination of an unarmed trunk, lack of a crownshaft, pinnate leaf segments spreading in 2 or 3 planes, and fleshy orange or yellow fruit.

Evergreen tree, 13–25 m tall, 25–50 cm diam. Erect, single trunk; crown spreading and drooping. **TRUNK** Light gray, more or less smooth near the base, sometimes ringed with the remains of leaf bases nearer the top, swollen and lacking a crownshaft below the leaves. **LEAF** Pinnate, 2–5 m long. Blade segments spreading in 2 or 3 planes, limp, drooping, medium or dark green, to about 1 m long. **FLOWER** Unisexual, white, both sexes borne in a single drooping, branched inflorescence to about 1.5 m long; inflorescence emerges from large, "woody," boat-shaped bract. Year-round. **FRUIT** Drupe-like, ovoid, about 2.5 cm long, orange or yellow at maturity. Year-round.

HABITAT/RANGE Introduced from South America; established in disturbed hammocks and considered an invasive species in s. Fla.

SIMILAR SPECIES The somewhat similar Coconut Palm (*Cocos nucifera*) bears the distinctive coconut fruit and a graceful leaning form. The trunk of Gru-gru Palm (*Acrocomia totai*) bears numerous black spines.

■ *SABAL*: SABAL PALMS

A genus of 16 species; 5 species are native to North America, only two of which grow to tree stature. **LEAF** The sabal palms are usually grouped with the fan- or palmate-leaved palms (as they are here), but the leaves are technically costapalmate: The petiole extends a short distance into the blade, forming a midrib and slightly modifying the palmate form so the blade usually folds upward (V-like) from the midrib. Most species in the genus bear threadlike fibers along the margins of the leaf segments. **FLOWER** Bisexual, creamy white, fragrant; petals and sepals 3; stamens 6. **FRUIT** More or less spheroid, fleshy or dryish, lustrous black berrylike drupe.

CABBAGE PALMETTO *Sabal palmetto*
(Walter) Lodd. ex Schult. & Schult. f.

QUICK ID A palm distinguished most easily by the circular, V-angled leaves with threadlike fibers along the margins of the segments.

Evergreen tree, 15–24 m tall, 20–35 cm diam. Erect, single trunk; crown rounded, the tips of the leaves often slightly drooping. **TRUNK** Brown or light brown, sometimes more or less smooth, more often moderately roughened or distinctly decorated with the crowded remains of old leaf bases (colloquially referred to as "boots"). **LEAF** Modified palmate; blade circular, 1–2 m broad; petiole to about 20 cm long, lacking spines or prickles, the tip extending for a short distance into the blade and giving rise to numerous closely clustered segments that often angle upward in a V shape from the axis. Upper surface lustrous green, lower surface gray-green. Blade segments 50–100 cm long, to about 4 cm broad, tapering to a divided tip, margins often bearing threadlike fibers. **FLOWER** Bisexual, tiny, about 3 mm long; petals 3, creamy white; sepals 3; inflorescence large, conspicuous, multibranched, 1–2.4 m long. Spring to summer. **FRUIT** Round or ellipsoid drupe to about 14 mm diam., green at first, becoming black at maturity; matures late summer to autumn.

HABITAT/RANGE Native. Maritime hammocks, margins of tidal marshes, beach swales, dunes, flatwoods, usually within about 120 km of the coast, to about 30 m; S.C. south to Fla. Keys, west to c. Fla. panhandle; introduced and established in La.

SIMILAR SPECIES Washington Fan Palm (*Washingtonia robusta*) is distinguished by its distinctive skirt of dead fronds, lacking in Cabbage Palmetto. Mexican Palmetto is more robust, has larger fruit, and differs in range.

CABBAGE PALMETTO

fruit
cluster

fruit

Queen Palm

seed

flowers

dried
fruit

fruit

Cabbage Palmetto

RIO GRANDE PALMETTO *Sabal mexicana* Mart.
A.K.A. MEXICAN PALMETTO

QUICK ID A palm of se. Tex. distinguished by the combination of its circular, V-angled leaves and drupes 1.5–1.9 cm diam.

Evergreen tree, 12–15 m tall, 20–35 cm diam. Erect, single stout trunk; crown rounded, the tips of the leaves drooping. **TRUNK** Brown or grayish brown, obscurely or strongly horizontally ribbed, sometimes roughened with the remains of old leaves. **LEAF** Modified palmate; blade circular, 1.5–1.8 m broad; petiole 90–120 cm long, lacking spines or prickles, the tip extending well into the blade and giving rise to numerous closely set segments that often angle upward in a V from the axis. Upper surface lustrous green, lower surface gray-green; blade segments 80–145 cm long, tapering to a divided tip, margins often bearing threadlike fibers. **FLOWER** Bisexual, 4–7 mm diam.; petals 3, creamy white; sepals 3; inflorescence multibranched, arching, 1.2–1.8 m long. Spring to summer. **FRUIT** Rounded black drupe, 1.5–1.9 cm diam.; matures late summer to autumn.

HABITAT/RANGE Native. Moist hammocks, floodplains, levees, riverbanks, swamps, 0–50 m; se. Tex. south to Central America.

SIMILAR SPECIES Cabbage Palmetto is closely similar but has smaller fruit and a less robust appearance.

RIO GRANDE PALMETTO

WASHINGTON FAN PALM
Washingtonia robusta H. Wendl.

QUICK ID A palmate-leaved palm easily identified by the combination of a shaggy skirt of dead leaves, armed petiole split at base, and fibers along margins of leaf segments.

Evergreen tree, 21–30 m tall, to about 80 cm diam. Erect, single slender trunk; crown rounded, usually subtended by a dense, shaggy skirt of dead leaves. **TRUNK** Gray, grayish white, or brownish, slightly roughened with residual leaf bases. **LEAF** Modified palmate; blade circular, 90–120 cm broad; petiole split at base, to about 1.2 m long and armed with slightly recurved reddish spines, the petiole tip extending into the leaf blade and giving rise to closely set segments. Blade segments 45–60 cm long, demonstrably drooping at the tip, margins bearing threadlike fibers. **FLOWER** Bisexual; petals 3, yellowish white; sepals 3; inflorescence multibranched, arising from leaf axils, arching, extending beyond the leaves. Spring to summer. **FRUIT** Rounded or ellipsoid black drupe, about 6 mm diam.; matures summer to autumn.

HABITAT/RANGE Introduced from Mexico. Widely cultivated in s. Fla., where it is considered an invasive species in disturbed hammocks; one of the most widely cultivated palms in s. Calif.

SIMILAR SPECIES The similar Cabbage Palmetto (*Sabal palmetto*) and Mexican Palmetto (*S. mexicana*) lack the combination of spines on the petiole and a shaggy skirt of dead leaves subtending the crown.

Notes: Washingtonia is a genus of 2 species; the other, California Fan Palm (*W. filifera* Wendl.), is native to the U.S. Southwest and into Mexico.

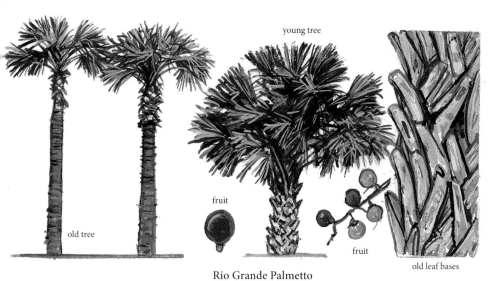

young tree

fruit

old tree

Rio Grande Palmetto

fruit

old leaf bases

dead leaves

fruit

seeds

petiole

Washington Fan Palm

EVERGLADES PALM *Acoelorrhaphe wrightii* (Griseb. & H. Wendl.) H. Wendl. ex Becc.
A.K.A. PAUROTIS PALM

QUICK ID The palmate leaves and clump-forming habit of Everglades Palm distinguish it from similar species.

Evergreen, clump-forming tree to about 12 m tall, less than 15 cm diam. Trunks numerous, very slender, ascending, usually arising from a central point and forming a dense cluster, especially when young. **TRUNK** Reddish brown, usually matted with the remains of old leaf bases. **LEAF** Palmate; blade circular, to about 90 cm broad; petiole orange-tinted, 20–90 cm long, armed with hooked orange spines to about 5 mm long. Upper surface lustrous, medium or dark green; lower surface silvery. Blade segments stiff, lanceolate, 30–45 cm long. **FLOWER** Bisexual, petals 3, yellowish-white; sepals 3; inflorescence arising from leaf axils, arching, multibranched, to about 90 cm long, usually longer than the leaves. Summer. **FRUIT** Rounded drupe, 5–8 mm diam.; reddish orange, maturing black in autumn.

HABITAT/RANGE Native. Restricted to swamp margins and hammocks of the Fla. Everglades; cultivated for ornament in s. Fla.

SIMILAR SPECIES Senegal Date Palm (*Phoenix reclinata*) is also clump-forming but has sharp spines on the petiole.

Notes: This is the only species in its genus. It is treated as threatened in Fla.

FLORIDA SILVER PALM *Coccothrinax argentata* (Jacq.) L.H. Bailey
A.K.A. BISCAYNE PALM, SEAMBERRY PALM, SILVERTOP PALM

QUICK ID A palm recognized by the combination of a purplish-black fruit and a palmate leaf that is conspicuously silvery on the lower surface and whose petiole is not split at the base.

Evergreen tree, usually not exceeding about 6 m tall or 15 cm diam. (potentially to about 9 m tall). Erect, single trunk, occasionally several trunks; crown rounded, with several drooping fronds. **TRUNK** Slender, gray, the upper part often matted with fibers. **LEAF** Palmate; blade circular, to about 60 cm broad; petiole 60–100 cm long, not split at the base. Upper surface lustrous green; lower surface conspicuously silvery white. Blade segments to about 2.5 cm broad, lanceolate, flexible, tapering to an elongated tip. **FLOWER** Bisexual, yellowish white; inflorescence multibranched, arising at the top of the crown, often curving downward. Spring. **FRUIT** Round drupe, 1–2 cm diam., purplish black at maturity, in summer to autumn.

HABITAT/RANGE Native. Coastal hammocks, rocky pinelands; s. Fla. and Fla. Keys.

SIMILAR SPECIES Key Thatch Palm (*Leucothrinax morrisii*) can be distinguished by the combination of white fruit, less deeply divided leaves, wider leaf segments, and the petiole split at the base.

Notes: In need of increased systematic study, *Coccothrinax* is a genus of as few as 14 to as many as 50 species native to the Caribbean Basin; 1 species occurs in North America.

EVERGLADES PALM

FLORIDA SILVER PALM

seed

fruit

petiole

Everglades Palm

immature fruit

Florida Silver Palm

KEY THATCH PALM *Leucothrinax morrisii* (H. Wendl.) C.E. Lewis & Zona
A.K.A. SILVER THATCH PALM, BRITTLE THATCH PALM, SMALL-FRUITED THATCH PALM

QUICK ID A palm distinguished by the combination of white fruit, palmate leaves that are silvery beneath, and a petiole split at the base.

Evergreen tree to about 7 m tall (potentially to 10 m) and about 20 cm diam. Erect, single trunk; crown rounded, central fronds mostly erect, lateral fronds often drooping. **TRUNK** Grayish or grayish white, with closely set rings. **LEAF** Palmate; blade more or less circular, 60–90 cm broad; petiole slender, 90–150 cm long, split at base. Upper surface lustrous dark green; lower surface whitish or silvery green. Blade segments lanceolate, 30–45 cm long, 3–4 cm broad. **FLOWER** Bisexual, 5–7 parts, creamy white; inflorescence multibranched, yellowish, conspicuous, arising through the split petiole base, 90–150 cm long, pendent. Spring. **FRUIT** Round white drupe, about 1.2 cm diam.; matures summer to autumn.

HABITAT/RANGE Native. Hammocks, rare in s. Fla., including Fla. Keys; also in West Indies.

SIMILAR SPECIES Florida Silver Palm (*Coccothrinax argentata*) can be distinguished by its nearly black fruit and its intact (not split) petiole. Florida Thatch Palm (*Thrinax radiata*) has a pale but not silvery lower surface of the leaf.

Notes: This species was formerly included within the genus *Thrinax*.

FLORIDA THATCH PALM *Thrinax radiata* Lodd. ex Schult. & Schult. f.

QUICK ID A palm recognized by the combination of a palmate leaf whose lower surface is pale but not silvery white, a split petiole base, and white fruit.

Evergreen tree, 9–15 m tall, about 13 cm diam. Erect, single trunk, rarely several; crown rounded. **TRUNK** More or less smooth, grayish white, with faint rings. **LEAF** Palmate; blade circular, about 90 cm broad; petiole slender, to about 90 cm long, split at the base. Upper surface of blade green with conspicuous yellowish midribs; lower surface paler, with minute whitish dots. Blade segments lanceolate, about 45 cm long, joined at the margins for about ½ their length, drooping at tip. **FLOWER** Bisexual, 5–7 parts, white; inflorescence pendent, 90–120 cm long, arising through the split petiole base. Spring. **FRUIT** Round white drupe, about 1.2 cm diam.; matures summer to autumn.

HABITAT/RANGE Native. Rare, in coastal thickets, usually in association with limestone; s. Fla. and Fla. Keys.

SIMILAR SPECIES The lower surface of the leaf is more silvery in Key Thatch Palm (*Leucothrinax morrisii*).

KEY THATCH PALM

FLORIDA THATCH PALM

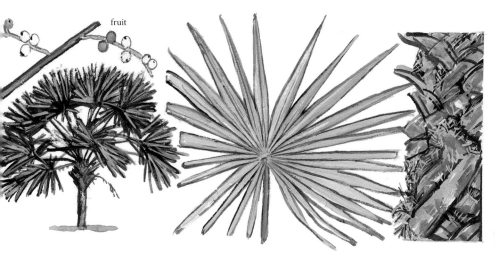

fruit

Key Thatch Palm

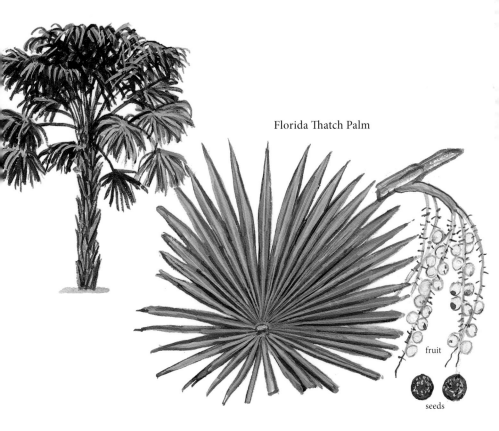

Florida Thatch Palm

fruit

seeds

Other Introduced Palms

These palms have been introduced to, and naturalized in, s. Fla.

SOLITARY FISHTAIL PALM *Caryota urens* L.

A.K.A. JAGGERY PALM

Erect, single-trunked palm; can exceed 12 m tall in its native India, but usually much shorter in Fla. It has fan-shaped leaves with jagged margins, in shape reminiscent of a fish tail. **HABITAT/RANGE** Introduced from India, cultivated in s. Fla. **SIMILAR SPECIES** Burmese Fishtail Palm (*C. mitis* Lour.), also cultivated in s. Fla., is smaller and occurs with clustering, multiple trunks.

CHINESE FAN PALM *Livistona chinensis* (Jacq.) R. Br. ex Mart.

A.K.A. FOUNTAIN PALM

Erect, single-trunked, palmately leaved palm. The petiole is armed with spines and its tip extends into the leaf blade, much like the tip of the spineless petiole of Cabbage Palmetto (*Sabal palmetto*). **HABITAT/RANGE** Introduced from China and Japan. Naturalized in s. Fla., where it is considered an invasive species. **SIMILAR SPECIES** Footstool Palm (*L. rotundifolia* [Lam.] Mart.) is also cultivated but rarely naturalized in s. Fla.; its petiole is armed but does not extend into the leaf blade.

ALEXANDER PALM *Ptychosperma elegans* (R. Br.) Blume

Small, single-trunked tree to about 12 m tall and 10 cm diam. Its crown is open and spreading, with relatively few fronds, and its trunk is ringed with the remains of old leaf scars. The leaves are green above, gray beneath, and have 5 or more longitudinal pleats. **HABITAT/RANGE** Native to Australia, naturalized in Fla. **SIMILAR SPECIES** Macarthur's Palm (*P. macarthurii* (H. Wendl. ex J.H. Veitch) H. Wendl. ex Hook. f.) usually has multiple trunks, and its leaves lack pleats.

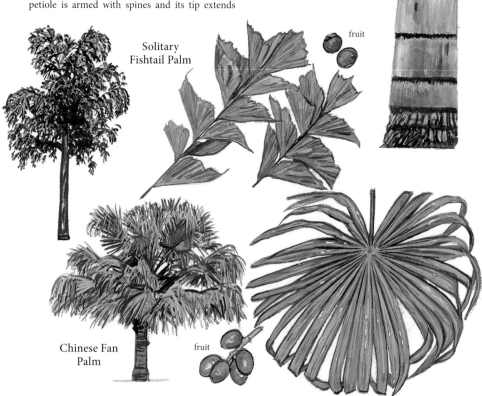

Solitary
Fishtail Palm

fruit

Chinese Fan
Palm

fruit

BAMBOO PALM *Chamaedorea seifrizii*
Burret

Small tree, usually with numerous slender, clustering trunks. It is recognized by the combination of its red fruit, green crownshaft, and spineless petioles that are about ¼–⅓ as long as the leaf blade. **HABITAT/RANGE** Native to Mexico and Central America; planted for ornament and naturalized in s. Fla. *Notes:* As many as 100 species of bamboo palms are known, many of which are grown in North America as houseplants and in subtropical gardens.

fruit

fruit

Alexander Palm

Macarthur's Palm

seed

fruit

Macarthur's Palm

fruit

Bamboo Palm

fruit

GRU-GRU PALM *Acrocomia totai* Mart.

Erect, single-trunked palm with numerous black spines along the trunk. Leaves to about 4 m long, pinnate, with mostly opposite segments and numerous needlelike spines along the rachis. **HABITAT/RANGE** Introduced from Central and South America; rarely naturalized in s. Fla.

JELLY PALM *Butia capitata* (Mart.) Becc.
A.K.A. WIND PALM, PINDO PALM

Grows upright, with a short, stocky trunk, to about 6 m tall and 50 cm diam. The trunk is often covered with the bases of fallen leaves but becomes smooth as the leaf bases are shed. Leaves are bluish gray or grayish green, pinnate, and strongly recurved, the tips often nearly reaching the ground. **HABITAT/RANGE** Widely planted in the southeastern coastal plains and sparsely naturalized in N.C., S.C., Ga., and Fla.

ARECA PALM *Dypsis lutescens*
(H. Wend.) Beentje & J. Dransf.

Usually a vase-shaped, multitrunked, unarmed, clump-forming palm with a gracefully spreading crown, and main trunk usually less than 15 cm diam. The trunk is usually encircled with old leaf bases, which usually produce a yellowish crownshaft. Leaves pinnate, 2–2.5 m long, segments 50–70 cm long and about 4 cm broad; petiole and midrib usually yellowish. Fruit an ellipsoid yellow drupe. **HABITAT/RANGE** Naturalized and potentially invasive in s. Fla.

AFRICAN OIL PALM *Elaeis guineensis*
Jacq.

Medium-sized palm with a stout, erect trunk, often roughened with the bases of fallen leaves. The massive crown has numerous pinnately divided leaves, these 3–8 m long with up to 120 lanceolate segments. The petiole is lined near the base with hard, piercing spines. The fruit is an oily orange-yellow to blackish drupe, about 4 cm long. **HABITAT/ RANGE** Native to tropical Africa and naturalized in s. Fla. *Notes:* The viciously armed petioles, very long fronds, stout trunk, and massive crown are useful in identification.

base of leaves

fruit

fruit section

trunk

Gru-gru Palm

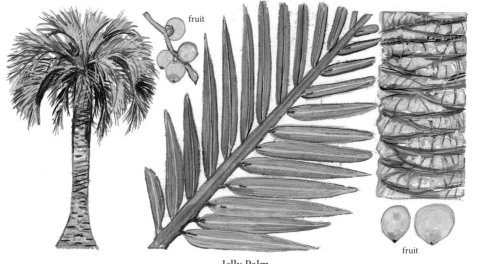

fruit

fruit

Jelly Palm

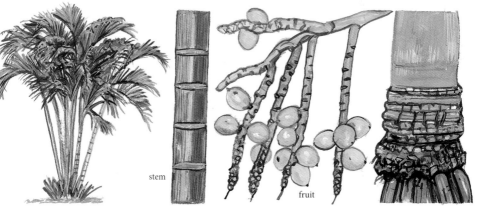

stem

fruit

Areca Palm

base of trunk

African Oil Palm

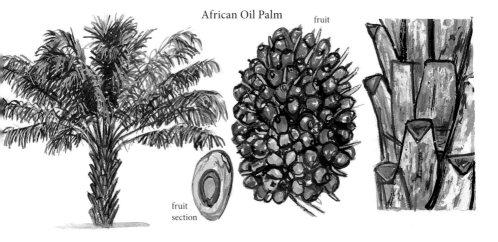

fruit

fruit
section

DICOTS

Dicotyledons (dicots for short) are a very large assemblage of the flowering plants (angiosperms). Dicots usually lack the parallel leaf veins seen in the monocots (the other major group), displaying instead netlike venation, and the flower parts (sepals, petals, stamens, etc.) are usually in multiples of 4 or 5.

ACANTHACEAE: ACANTHUS FAMILY

The acanthus family includes about 3,500 mostly herbaceous species and a much smaller number of woody shrubs, trees, and vines. As treated here, the family has only a single arborescent species, of the genus *Avicennia*, in the East. Traditionally, *Avicennia* has been placed in either the monotypic black mangrove family (Avicenniaceae) or the vervain family (Verbenaceae), but recent molecular and genetic studies suggest it is better placed within the Acanthaceae. *Avicennia* includes 8 species of woody shrubs distributed in tropical and subtropical coastal and estuarine habitats throughout the world.

BLACK MANGROVE *Avicennia germinans* (L.) L.

QUICK ID A coastline tree distinguished by the combination of flat, pod-like fruit, grayish leaves with evident salt crystals, and numerous breathing roots.

Evergreen shrub or small tree to about 10 m tall (potentially to 25 m tall in the American tropics) and 30 cm diam. Erect, single short trunk or multiple trunks; crown dense, rounded, branching near the ground. Numerous conspicuous pneumatophores (upright breathing roots) usually form dense thickets below the tree. **BARK** Smooth on young trees, becoming scaly and fissured with age; gray or dark brown, immediate inner bark bright orange or yellow. **TWIG** Gray or brown, finely hairy (especially when young), enlarged and ringed at the nodes. **LEAF** Opposite, simple, thick, leathery; elliptic or oblanceolate, tapering to a blunt point at the base and tip, margins entire. Upper surface grayish green or yellowish green, moderately lustrous; lower surface densely gray-hairy; excreted salt crystals usually evident on 1 or both surfaces. Blade 5–12 cm long, 2–4 cm broad; petiole 3–12 mm long, grooved. **FLOWER** 1.2–2 cm long, white; petals 5, hairy, partially united at base to form a short tube. Year-round. **FRUIT** Flat, lustrous green or gray-green asymmetrical pod, to 2 cm long and 1.2 cm broad, narrowing to a pointed tip. Year-round.

HABITAT/RANGE Native. Low-energy coastlines, usually where salt content is high, 0–10 m; s. Fla. and Fla. Keys north to nw. Fla., also coastal Tex.; likely reaching tree stature only along coastlines of southernmost Fla.

SIMILAR SPECIES Other mangroves, in the families Combretaceae and Rhizophoraceae, can be confused with Black Mangrove but none has the flat, pod-like fruit.

Notes: All mangroves are halophytic, or adapted to survive in extremely salty conditions. Black Mangrove absorbs saltwater into its tissues, then expels the salt through special glands on its leaves. Excreted salt crystals are often visible on the leaf surfaces.

BLACK MANGROVE

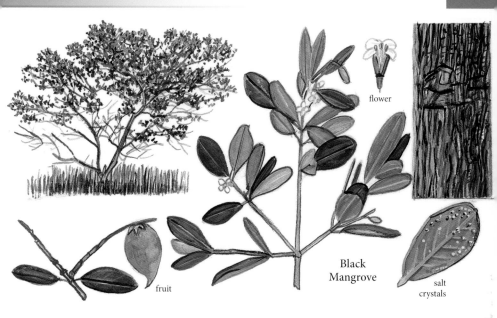

flower

Black
Mangrove

fruit

salt
crystals

ADOXACEAE: MOSCHATEL FAMILY

The moschatel family includes 4 or 5 genera and 220–245 species, distributed mostly in temperate and tropical montane zones of the Northern Hemisphere; 3 genera and about 29 species occur in the East. Deciduous shrubs or small trees, less frequently vines and herbs. **LEAF** Opposite, either simple or compound. **FLOWER** Bisexual, radially symmetric, usually borne in showy, often flat-topped or convex cymes. **FRUIT** Berrylike drupe with 1–5 stones, the stones compressed and single-seeded.

Some members of the family—including all of those treated here—have been included within Caprifoliaceae, which is distinguished from Adoxaceae by its bilateral flowers and elongated style. Many members of this family, especially species of *Viburnum*, are widely used in gardening and landscaping for their attractive inflorescences. The flowers are pollinated by bees, wasps, and flies; the fleshy fruits are attractive to wildlife; and the seeds are usually dispersed by birds.

■ *SAMBUCUS*: ELDERBERRIES

A genus of about 10 species distributed in temperate and subtropical regions; 2 species are native to North America. Deciduous shrubs, small trees, or herbs, the shrubs and trees usually with very soft wood and conspicuous pith; branches usually have raised, vertically elongated lenticels.

LEAF Opposite, compound, usually pinnate, sometimes bipinnate, with the lower leaflets also divided; leaflets lanceolate or ovate, margins distinctly toothed. **FLOWER** Small, white, petals 3–5, stamens 5. **FRUIT** Round, lustrous red or black berrylike drupe with 3–5 stones. Danewort (*S. ebulus* L.), a herbaceous species native to Europe and Asia, is reportedly naturalized in the ne. U.S.

AMERICAN ELDERBERRY *Sambucus nigra* L. subsp. *canadensis* (L.) R. Bolli
A.K.A. BLACK ELDERBERRY

QUICK ID A shrubby tree, often in colonies, recognized by its combination of opposite, pinnately compound leaves and large clusters of small white flowers followed by lustrous black fruit.

Deciduous, fast-growing shrub or very small tree to about 6 m tall, 20 cm diam., often forming colonies via aggressive underground runners. Erect or arching, single trunk or multiple; crown ascending and spreading, somewhat flat-topped. **BARK** Grayish brown, smooth, with prominent lenticels; becoming roughened with age. **TWIG** Stout, brownish or greenish, with conspicuous warty lenticels; pith thick, white. **LEAF** Opposite, usually pinnately compound, sometimes bipinnate, blade 15–25 cm long; petiole 3–10 cm long. Leaflets 5–7, each 5–15 cm long, 2–6 cm broad; stalk 0–10 mm long; margins coarsely toothed. Upper surface dark green, with short hairs along the veins and sometimes on the blade tissue; lower surface paler green, usually hairless except along the veins. **FLOWER** White, small, about 3–5 mm diam.; petals 5, spreading; stamens 5; pistil 1; produced in large, showy, flat-topped terminal inflorescences to about 40 cm across. Spring. **FRUIT** Lustrous, juicy black 3–5-stoned berrylike drupe, 4–6 mm diam.; matures mid- to late summer.

HABITAT/RANGE Native. Roadsides, wetland and woodland margins, ditches, often aggressively colonizing wet clearings, 0–1,600 m; throughout the East.

SIMILAR SPECIES Red Elderberry has red fruit. Boxelder (*Acer negundo*, Sapindaceae) and ashes (*Fraxinus*, Oleaceae), which also have opposite, compound leaves, could be confused with American Elderberry, but both lack the fleshy fruits.

Notes: Foliage and twigs give off a rank odor when crushed.

RED ELDERBERRY *Sambucus racemosa* L.

QUICK ID The opposite, compound leaves and red fruit are usually enough to identify this shrub or small tree.

Deciduous, fast-growing shrub or small tree, 2.5–6 m tall, to 15 cm diam. Erect or leaning, single trunk or multiple; crown narrow, branches ascending. **BARK** Gray to reddish brown, with prominent lenticels. **TWIG** Stout but soft, with a large spongy pith. **LEAF** Opposite, pinnately compound, blade 15–30 cm long; petiole 5–8 cm long. Leaflets 5–7, each 6–16 cm long, 2–4 cm broad; stalk 0–5 mm long; margins toothed. Upper surface lustrous, dark or medium green, hairless; lower surface paler. **FLOWER** White, produced in elongated upright clusters about 10 cm across. Spring. **FRUIT** Several-stoned, usually red drupe, 4–6 mm diam.; matures midsummer.

HABITAT/RANGE Native. Moist to wet woodlands and wetland margins; widespread in the East, from Man. and Nfld. south to N.C., Tenn., and n. Ga.

SIMILAR SPECIES American Elderberry is distinguished by the black, rather than red, fruit. Red-fruited sumacs (*Rhus*, Anacardiaceae) have alternate, pinnately compound leaves.

■ *VIBURNUM*: VIBURNUMS

A genus of 175–200 species distributed in north temperate and tropical montane zones; there are 26 species in North America, 16 native and 10 introduced. Of the native viburnums, 14 occur in the East.

Deciduous or evergreen trees or shrubs. **LEAF** Opposite, simple, margins often toothed, sometimes entire. **FLOWER** Usually white or creamy white (rarely reddish or pinkish), petals and stamens 5, style short or absent, the 3 stigmas usually sessile at the summit of the ovary; usually produced in a showy, flat-topped terminal cluster of successive 3-flowered units, the terminal flower of each cluster opening first and arresting

AMERICAN ELDERBERRY

RED ELDERBERRY

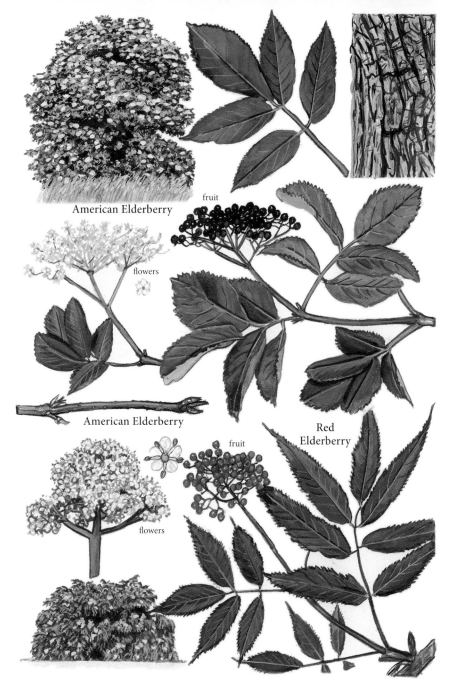

American Elderberry

fruit

flowers

American Elderberry

Red Elderberry

flowers

fruit

further elongation of the cluster's axis (cyme). **FRUIT** Dark blue, purplish, black, coppery, or red drupe with a flattened stone containing 1 seed. Viburnums are potentially confused with dogwoods (Cornaceae), which also have opposite leaves, but dogwood leaves have entire margins and a few pairs of prominent, arching parallel veins, and the flowers have 4 petals.

ARROWWOOD *Viburnum dentatum* L.
A.K.A. SOUTHERN ARROWWOOD

QUICK ID A shrub or small tree recognized by the combination of opposite, coarsely toothed leaves and showy inflorescences followed by blue-black drupes.

Deciduous shrub or small tree, usually not exceeding about 3 m tall, 1–4 cm diam. Vase-shaped or ascending, usually shrubby, with several trunks or branches from the base, rarely a single trunk and treelike. **BARK** Grayish brown or reddish. **TWIG** Brown, usually shaggy-hairy. **LEAF** Opposite, simple, ovate or broadly lanceolate; base rounded, heart-shaped, or somewhat flattened; tip bluntly or sharply pointed; margins distinctly and coarsely toothed, the teeth blunt or sharp-pointed, comparatively large. Upper surface smooth or rough, hairy, the lateral veins angling, approximately parallel, usually terminating at the tip of a marginal tooth; lower surface paler, hairy. Blade 3–15 cm long, 2–10 cm broad; petiole 1–3 cm long, hairless or shaggy-hairy. **FLOWER** White, 5–8 mm diam., produced in numerous conspicuous flat-topped inflorescences, 4–10 cm across. Early summer. **FRUIT** Ellipsoid or rounded blue-black drupe, 5–8 mm long; matures late summer to autumn.

HABITAT/RANGE Native. Moist or dry woodlands, river- and stream banks, flatwoods, margins of bogs, 0–1,450 m; widespread in the East, from Maine and Iowa south to n. Fla. and e. Tex.

NANNYBERRY *Viburnum lentago* L.
A.K.A. SHEEPBERRY

QUICK ID An erect shrub or small tree recognized by the combination of wetland habitat, opposite, finely toothed leaves, tiny creamy-white flowers, and bluish-black drupes.

Deciduous tall shrub or small tree, 5–10 m tall, 10–20 cm diam. Erect or ascending, usually with several slender, crooked trunks; crown rounded, irregular, open, with few arching, crooked branches. **BARK** Grayish brown when young, becoming reddish and broken into small plates or scales. **TWIG** Green and hairy at first, becoming reddish brown and hairless, with rounded lenticels. **LEAF** Opposite, simple, ovate, elliptic, or nearly round; base rounded or wedge-shaped; tip abruptly tapering to an elongated point; margins finely and sharply toothed, the teeth incurved and callous-tipped. Upper surface lustrous, green or yellowish green; lower surface paler, with tiny black or brown dots. Blade 5–10 cm long, 2–5 cm broad; petiole 1–3 cm long, grooved, frequently winged. **FLOWER** Creamy white, produced in numerous showy, branched, flat-topped clusters, 5–10 cm across. Late spring to early summer. **FRUIT** Ellipsoid bluish-black drupe, 8–15 mm long; matures early autumn.

HABITAT/RANGE Native. Floodplains, stream banks, swamp and lake margins, 0–800 m; N.B. and Que. west to Sask., and south to N.C. and Colo.

SIMILAR SPECIES Arrowwood differs from other viburnums in having distinctly coarsely toothed, rather than finely toothed, leaf margins.

POSSUMHAW *Viburnum nudum* L.

QUICK ID A shrub or small tree recognized by the combination of opposite, mostly lanceolate or elliptic leaves with entire or finely toothed margins and showy, flat-topped inflorescences and conspicuous whitish, pinkish, or deep blue fruit.

Deciduous shrub or small tree to about 6 m tall, typically 1–5 cm diam., potentially larger. Erect or ascending, usually with multiple trunks, rarely a single trunk; crown spreading, rounded. **BARK**

ARROWWOOD   NANNYBERRY   POSSUMHAW

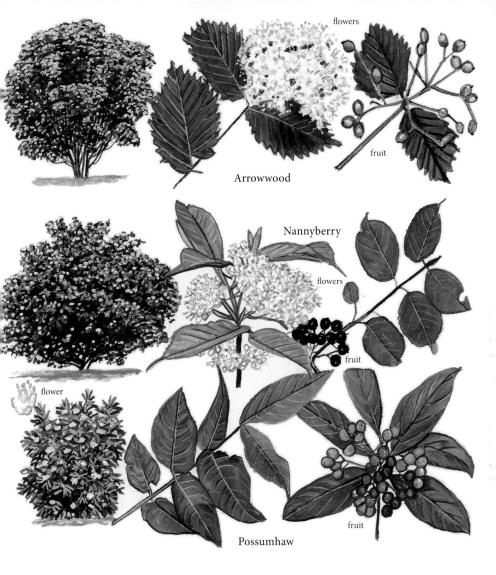

flowers

fruit

Arrowwood

Nannyberry

flowers

fruit

flower

fruit

fruit

Possumhaw

Brown, with pale lenticels. **TWIG** Sparsely or densely scaly, becoming warty. **LEAF** Opposite, simple, narrowly elliptic, broadly lanceolate, or narrowly ovate, sometimes widest above the middle; base rounded or wedge-shaped; tip abruptly narrowed to a short point; margins mostly entire, occasionally finely toothed, sometimes slightly rolled under. Upper surface dark green, lustrous, sometimes marked with tiny glandular dots; lower surface paler, with numerous glandular dots, especially when young. Blade 10–15 cm long, 3.5–5 cm broad; petiole 5–20 cm long, winged. **FLOWER** White, produced in flat-topped cymes about 15 cm across. Early

summer. **FRUIT** Ellipsoid drupe, 6–10 mm long, changing from whitish or pink to deep blue at maturity; matures late summer to early autumn.

HABITAT/RANGE Native. Swamps and swamp margins, bogs, wet woodlands, 0–600 m; widespread across the East, from Nfld. west to Ont. and Mich., and south to Fla. and e. Tex.

SIMILAR SPECIES The native shrub Withe-rod (*V. cassinoides* Ashe) is similar, but the main stalk of its fruit cluster is 5–17 mm long, compared to 10–50 mm long in Possumhaw.

BLACKHAW *Viburnum prunifolium* L.

QUICKID A large shrub or small tree recognized by the combination of opposite, finely toothed leaves that lack spots beneath, a petiole lacking rusty hairs, blocky bark, and a stalkless inflorescence.

Deciduous large shrub or small tree to about 10 m tall, 25 cm diam. Erect or ascending, single trunk or multiple, usually branched from near the base. **BARK** Reddish brown, broken into small, thick, squarish plates. **TWIG** Slender, reddish brown or yellowish brown, ridged, stiff, sometimes rusty-scaly. **LEAF** Opposite, simple, elliptic to obovate, sometimes nearly circular; base rounded or wedge-shaped; tip blunt or long-pointed; margins finely toothed, the teeth incurved. Upper surface dull, dark green, hairless; lower surface duller, hairless, often rusty-scaly along the midvein. Blade 2–10 cm long, 1–5 cm broad; petiole to about 1 cm long. **FLOWER** White, produced in a flat-topped, stalkless inflorescence. Mid- to late spring. **FRUIT** Ellipsoid or ovoid black or dark blue drupe, 9–14 mm long; matures summer to autumn.

HABITAT/RANGE Native. Moist woods, rich hillsides and slopes, thickets, roadsides, 0–600 m; widespread in the East, N.Y., Mich., and Iowa south to n. Ga. and e. Tex.

SIMILAR SPECIES Rusty Blackhaw can be distinguished by its rusty petiole hairs, and Nannyberry by the dots on the leaf undersurface.

RUSTY BLACKHAW *Viburnum rufidulum* Raf.

QUICKID A viburnum distinguished by the combination of checkered, dark, blocky bark and opposite, lustrous, finely toothed leaves with rusty-hairy petioles.

Deciduous large shrub or small tree to 9 m tall, 40 cm diam. Erect or shrublike, mostly with a single trunk, usually not suckering. **BARK** Dark brown to nearly black, broken into small, thick, squarish plates. **TWIG** Rusty-hairy, becoming grayish, with raised lenticels. **LEAF** Opposite, simple, oval or broadly elliptic, sometimes widest above the middle; tip blunt, short-pointed, or occasionally notched; base wedge-shaped or rounded; margins finely toothed. Upper surface lustrous, dark green; lower surface paler, with varying amounts of rusty hairs, especially along the veins. Blade 4–8 cm long, 3–6 cm broad, sometimes as broad as long; petiole about 8 mm long, rusty-hairy, winged. **FLOWER** Creamy white, produced in a flat-topped inflorescence 5–10 cm across. Spring. **FRUIT** Ellipsoid or rounded drupe, dark blue or purple and glaucous, 1–1.5 cm long; matures summer.

HABITAT/RANGE Native. Well-drained upland woods, 0–750 m; widespread in the East, from Va. and Ohio, west to Kans., and south to n. Fla. and Tex.

SIMILAR SPECIES The bark of Flowering Dogwood (*Cornus florida*, Cornaceae) is similar, but the leaf margins are entire and the flower clusters are subtended by large white bracts.

WALTER'S VIBURNUM *Viburnum obovatum* Walter
A.K.A. SMALL-LEAF ARROWWOOD

QUICKID The opposite, simple, obovate, bluntly toothed leaves are usually enough to identify this viburnum.

Deciduous or evergreen shrub or small tree to about 9 m tall, 15 cm diam. Erect, leaning, or ascending, single trunk or multiple; crown spreading and irregularly branched, branches often bearing

BLACKHAW

RUSTY BLACKHAW

WALTER'S VIBURNUM

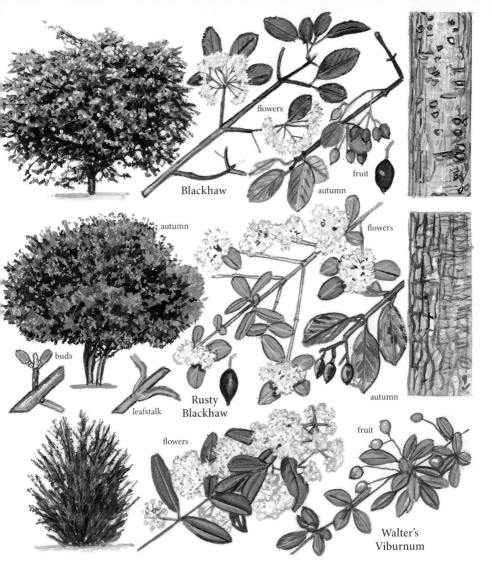

flowers

fruit

Blackhaw

autumn

autumn

flowers

buds

leafstalk

Rusty
Blackhaw

autumn

fruit

flowers

Walter's
Viburnum

short, stiff twigs. **TWIG** Scaly, often winged during the 1st year. **LEAF** Opposite, simple, oblanceolate or spatulate, distinctly widest above the middle; base wedge-shaped; tip bluntly pointed; margins irregularly and bluntly toothed or less often entire. Upper surface medium or dark green; lower surface copiously brown-dotted. Blade 2–5 cm long, 1–3 cm broad; petiole 0–6 mm long, winged. **FLOWER** Creamy white, individually tiny, produced in showy clusters 4–6 cm across. Late winter to spring. **FRUIT** More or less laterally flattened drupe, 6–10 mm long, changing from green to red to black; matures late summer to autumn.

HABITAT/RANGE Native. Moist hammocks, wet woods, floodplains, stream banks, often where limestone is present, to about 200 m; southeastern coastal plains, S.C., Ga., Fla., Ala.

SIMILAR SPECIES The similar Deciduous Holly (*Ilex decidua*, Aquifoliaceae) can be distinguished by its alternate (though often closely set) rather than opposite leaves.

Notes: Walter's Viburnum has become popular in cultivation, with numerous forms and horticultural selections.

SIEBOLD'S ARROWWOOD *Viburnum sieboldii* Miq.
A.K.A. SIEBOLD VIBURNUM

QUICK ID A viburnum recognized by the combination of opposite leaves with veins deeply impressed above and raised beneath, and red fruit stalks.

Deciduous shrub or small tree, 3–6 m tall, to about 30 cm diam. Erect, single trunk or multiple; crown open, rounded, with stiff, erect branches. **BARK** Gray, checkered and blocky, with prominent lenticels. **LEAF** Opposite, simple, narrowly elliptic, lanceolate, or oval; base tapering or wedge-shaped; tip abruptly pointed; margins bluntly toothed. Upper surface lustrous, dark green, the lateral veins parallel, impressed, conspicuous; lower surface paler, veins raised. Blade 7–20 cm long, 5–10 cm broad; petiole 1–1.5 cm long. Foliage sometimes turns reddish purple in autumn. **FLOWER** Creamy white, produced in abundant flat-topped clusters, each 7–15 cm across. Late spring to early summer. **FRUIT** Ovoid drupe, 7–13 mm long, red at first, turning black, produced in a red-stalked fruiting cluster; matures late summer to early autumn.

HABITAT/RANGE Introduced from Asia. Established along the mid-Atlantic seaboard, Mass. and N.Y., south to Va.

ALTINGIACEAE: SWEETGUM FAMILY

A small family of temperate or tropical deciduous trees and shrubs distributed in North and Central America, Southeast Asia, and Turkey. It includes 2 genera and about 13 species, 1 species native to North America. **LEAF** Alternate, simple, usually palmately lobed, with conspicuous stipules borne on the base of the petiole. **FLOWER** Individually inconspicuous, lacking petals and sepals, unisexual, male and female flowers borne on the same tree, and female flowers clustered in a distinctive ball-like head. **FRUIT** Round, stalked cluster formed of numerous capsules.

The sweetgum family has long been included with the witch-hazels in the Hamamelidaceae, but is distinguished from them by its spirally arranged (rather than 2-ranked leaves), stipules borne on (rather than adjacent to) the petiole, unisexual flowers lacking petals and sepals, and globose fruiting heads.

SWEETGUM *Liquidambar styraciflua* L.

QUICK ID The palmately lobed, star-shaped leaves and the spiky fruiting balls are both diagnostic.

Deciduous tree to about 40 m tall and 1.5 m diam. Erect, single trunk, usually clear of branches on the lower half at maturity, especially when forest-grown; crown rounded, broadly cylindric, or pyramidal. **BARK** Grayish or greenish gray, finely to moderately fissured, sometimes with corky outgrowths. **TWIG** Greenish, finely hairy, often slightly angled, often developing corky wings or outgrowths. **LEAF** Alternate, simple, palmately 5- to 7-lobed, nearly star-shaped; base usually flattened; tips of lobes pointed; margins toothed. Upper surface lustrous green, hairless, lower surface paler, hairy at least in the lower vein axils. Blade 6–12 cm long, 10–18 cm broad; petiole 3–10 cm long, slender and flexuous, as long as, or longer than, the blade, the petiole of developing leaves with a pair of stipules 8–10 cm long on the upper side. In autumn, turning yellow, red, maroon, or deep blackish purple. **FLOWER** Sepals and petals absent; male flowers greenish yellow, produced in oblong 3–6 cm clusters at the tip of the branch; female flowers pale green, produced in a ball-like,

SWEETGUM

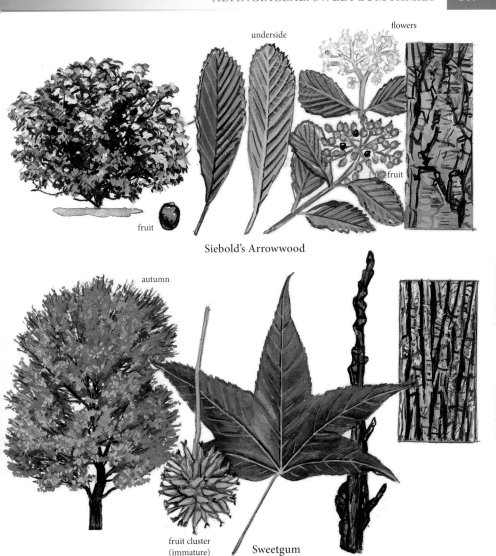

flowers

underside

fruit

fruit

Siebold's Arrowwood

autumn

fruit cluster
(immature)

Sweetgum

dangling cluster. **FRUIT** Infructescence of numerous capsules consolidated into a "spiny" ball, about 3 cm diam., the "spines" formed from the coalesced stigmal tips of numerous stiff, persistent styles.

HABITAT/RANGE Native. Rich woods, slopes, fields, urban and residential landscapes, disturbed sites, low woods, hammocks, swamp margins, floodplains, 0–800 m; widespread in the East, from Md. south to c. Fla., and west to s. Ill., e. Okla., and e. Tex.

SIMILAR SPECIES Japanese Maple (*Acer palmatum*, Sapindaceae) is sometimes mistaken for Sweetgum, but the fruit is a paired samara rather than a spiky ball. American Sycamore (*Platanus occidentalis*, Platanaceae) also has ball-like flower and fruit clusters, but they are not spiky.

Notes: An important and commercially valuable eastern tree. The genus name is derived from the combination of "liquid" and "amber," a reference to the sweet-smelling yellowish sap.

ANACARDIACEAE: CASHEW FAMILY

The cashew family includes about 600 species distributed worldwide in warm temperate to tropical regions; approximately 10 genera and 30 species are native to, or naturalized in, the U.S. Tubular resin ducts occur in the twigs, bark, and larger veins of the leaves, and often also in the flowers and fruits. This resin imparts a spicy odor that ranges from pleasant to obnoxious; in sensitive individuals it also may cause contact dermatitis when the plant is touched, or result in severe irritation of mucous membranes or even anaphylaxis if ingested.

Evergreen or deciduous vines, subshrubs, shrubs, or trees. **LEAF** Alternate, pinnately compound or simple by reduction and therefore unifoliolate; thin and flexible or thick and leathery. In pinnately compound leaves the rachis (midrib) is often winged. **FLOWER** Usually small, whitish to greenish, radially symmetric; functionally unisexual and borne on separate plants, or bisexual and unisexual intermixed (plants then polygamodioecious). Each flower usually has 5 petals and sepals, and 5–10 stamens and/or a single ovary with 1–3 styles. At the base of the flower is a small, thick disk. Flowers occur in small to large, sometimes extensively branched, terminal or axillary racemes or panicles. **FRUIT** Usually a small to large drupe with resinous flesh.

Members of the family produce some economically important fruits and nuts, among them mango (genus *Mangifera*), pistachio (*Pistacia*), and cashew (*Anacardium*). Several species have become aggressive, troublesome weeds that displace other vegetation. Poison Oak, Poison Ivy, and Poison Sumac (*Toxicodendron*) are widespread creeping or treelike members of the family, appreciated for their brilliant fall color but notorious for causing contact dermatitis in many people.

■ *COTINUS*: SMOKETREES

A small genus of 5 species distributed in Europe, Asia, and North America. It is composed of shrubs or small trees with alternate unifoliolate leaves, yellow wood, pungent sap, and hairy inflorescences that are often nearly devoid of fruit.

AMERICAN SMOKETREE *Cotinus obovatus* Raf.
A.K.A. CHITTAM-WOOD

QUICK ID A small tree easily identified by the distinctive shape of its alternate, broadly elliptic or obovate leaves and plumelike flower clusters, with individual flower stalks hairy and purplish.

Deciduous large shrub or small tree, 10–30 m tall, to 48 cm diam. Erect or vase-shaped, usually with multiple trunks, sometimes developing a single dominant trunk with age; crown rounded, dense, branches spreading and often drooping with age;

wood yellow. **BARK** Scaly, strongly aromatic when crushed. **TWIG** Covered with a whitish bloom when young, eventually becoming brown, with whitish corky lenticels; terminal buds to about 6 mm long, with sharp-pointed scales. **LEAF** Alternate, unifoliolate, thin, obovate to broadly elliptic-obovate, rounded at base and tip, margins entire. Upper surface dark green, hairless; lower surface paler, with silky hairs at first, becoming sparsely hairy at maturity. Blade 10–17 cm long, 5–9 cm broad; petiole 1.5–6 cm long. Autumn foliage brilliant orange or scarlet. **FLOWER** Unisexual (rarely

AMERICAN SMOKETREE

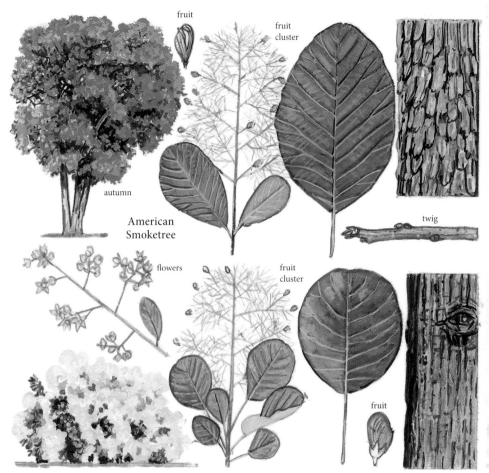

fruit

fruit cluster

autumn

American Smoketree

flowers

fruit cluster

twig

fruit

European Smoketree

bisexual), male and female flowers borne on separate trees; about 3 mm diam., numerous, yellowish white or greenish white, sepals and petals 5; produced in lax terminal panicles averaging 10–20 cm long. Spring. **FRUIT** Dry, 1-seeded drupe, 3–6 mm long, rarely or scarcely produced; fruiting panicles usually to about 20 cm long, usually mostly empty of fruits, their hairy stalks giving the tree its "smoky" appearance.

HABITAT/RANGE Native. Dry, open woods, usually where limestone is present; rare and scattered, c. Tex., e. Okla., Ark., Mo., ne. Ala., nw. Ga., s. Tenn.

Notes: Although seen in cultivation less often than European Smoketree, American Smoketree is increasing in popularity as a garden plant.

EUROPEAN SMOKETREE *Cotinus coggygria* Scop.
A.K.A WIG TREE

Usually a large shrub to about 5 m tall, similar to its American counterpart. The hairy stalks of the typically empty or nearly empty fruiting panicles impart a "smoky" purplish effect. **HABITAT/ RANGE** Introduced. Commonly used ornamentally in the East; naturalized mostly north of the range of American Smoketree, from Ill., Ohio, and Md. north to Ont. and Vt., but sometimes cultivated in the South.

FLORIDA POISONTREE *Metopium toxiferum* (L.) Krug & Urb.
A.K.A. POISONWOOD

QUICKID No other tree of subtropical s. Fla. has the combination of alternate, pinnately compound leaves with blackish spots and orange and reddish bark.

Evergreen tree to about 14 m tall, 30 cm diam. Erect, single trunk; crown spreading, irregular. **BARK** Thin, smooth; inner bark orange; outer bark reddish brown, splotchy, with blackish spots of exuded poisonous sap; bark on mature trunks usually splitting into large scaly plates. **LEAF** Alternate, pinnately compound, blade to about 20 cm long, petiole to about 15 cm long. Leaflets 3–7, usually 5, each 2–8 cm long, 1.5–5 cm broad; stalk 1.3–2 cm long; ovate, triangular, or nearly circular, bluntly pointed at the tip, margins entire. Upper surface dark or medium green, lustrous, usually with irregularly distributed blackish spots; lower surface paler. **FLOWER** Functionally unisexual, male and female borne on separate trees, individually inconspicuous, greenish yellow, petals and sepals 5, the sepals much shorter than the petals; produced in conspicuous, loose, long-stalked, branched clusters from the leaf axils. Spring. **FRUIT** Oblong orange-yellow drupe, 1–1.5 cm long; matures mostly in autumn.

HABITAT/RANGE Native. Tropical hammocks, often invading pinelands following fire but usually not persisting there; s. Fla., including Fla. Keys.

Notes: The sap that exudes from the bark and leaves can cause contact dermatitis similar to that caused by Poison Ivy (*Toxicodendron radicans* [L.] Kuntze) and Poison Oak (*T. pubescens* Mill.).

FLORIDA POISONTREE

MANGO *Mangifera indica* L.

QUICKID The combination of long leaves with conspicuous parallel veins and large, distinctive fruit is diagnostic.

Evergreen tree to about 15 m tall and about 1 m diam. Erect, single trunk; crown very dense, spreading, dark green. **BARK** Dark brown outside, yellowish brown inside, exuding a pinkish resin when bruised. **LEAF** Alternate, unifoliolate, lanceolate to narrowly long-elliptic, tapering to base and to the long-pointed tip, margins entire. Upper surface lustrous, dark green, hairless, veins conspicuous, straight, parallel, in 20–30 pairs; lower surface paler. Blade 10–25 cm long, 2–7 cm broad; petiole about 3 cm long and swollen at base. **FLOWER** Bisexual and functionally unisexual, greenish white, petals 5, about 5 mm long, sepals 5, about 2.5 mm long. Mostly late winter and spring. **FRUIT** Large, fleshy ovoid, pear-shaped, or irregularly shaped drupe, 5–15 cm long, green or yellow, often tinged red or pink; seed large, flattened, 6–9 cm long. The skin can cause contact dermatitis.

HABITAT/RANGE Introduced. Native to Asia; cultivated as a fruit crop and naturalized mostly in disturbed sites, s. Fla.

SIMILAR SPECIES Loquat (*Eriobotrya japonica*, Rosaceae) has somewhat similar leaves but is easily distinguished by its fruit, a whitish, yellow, or orange pome 3–4 cm long.

CHINESE PISTACHE *Pistacia chinensis* Bunge

Deciduous drought-tolerant tree, 7–12 m tall, with a rounded crown. **LEAF** Alternate, pinnately compound, usually with an even number of leaflets; similar to those of Winged Sumac (*Rhus copallinum*). **FRUIT** Small, laterally compressed red drupe, about 5 mm diam. **HABITAT/RANGE** Introduced from China; used ornamentally in s. U.S. from N.C. to Ga. and Ala., primarily for its easy cultivation and stunning autumn color. *Notes:* The genus *Pistacia* includes about 11 species, mostly from the Mediterranean region, and is best known for Pistachio (*P. vera* L.), grown commercially for its seeds. Only the American (or Mexican) Pistachio (*P. mexicana* Kunth) is native to North America, ranging primarily from s. Tex. south to Guatemala.

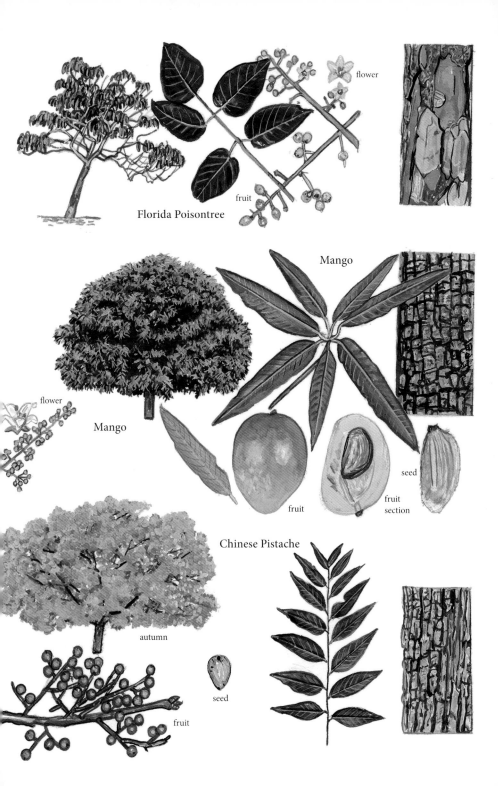

Florida Poisontree

flower

fruit

Mango

Mango

flower

fruit

fruit
section

seed

Chinese Pistache

autumn

seed

fruit

■ *RHUS*: SUMACS

The genus *Rhus* has between 30 and 250 species worldwide, depending on which classification is followed. The present tendency, followed here, is to divide this very large genus into smaller units as molecular genetic studies reveal relationships. About 15 species occur in North America, 14 native; at least 10 species occur in the East, several of which are typically shrubs.

Deciduous or evergreen shrubs or small trees widely distributed in the U.S., the deciduous species well known for red-orange to purplish autumn color. **LEAF** Alternate, unifoliolate or compound, the rachis sometimes winged, margins entire or toothed. **FLOWER** Bisexual or functionally unisexual, male and female borne on separate trees or intermixed with bisexual flowers on a single tree; small, radial, with 5 separate sepals, 5 separate whitish or pinkish petals, 5 stamens, and a 1-chambered, 1-ovuled ovary topped by 3 styles; produced in a terminal or axillary paniculate cyme. **FRUIT** Small, hairy or hairless, round or nearly round, often reddish drupe, the solitary seed borne on a small stalk that arises at the base of the ovary.

None of the species in the genus as it is presented here produces irritating oils similar to those of Poison Oak, Poison Sumac, or Poison Ivy, all once included in the genus *Rhus* but now in *Toxicodendron*. *Rhus* species are used as ornamentals for their lustrous evergreen leaves or colorful fall foliage and their bright reddish fruits. There is little other economic use. Birds eat and distribute the berries, which may partially contribute to the establishment of dense colonies of some species.

SMOOTH SUMAC *Rhus glabra* L.

QUICK ID A sumac easily distinguished by its hairless whitish twigs and hairless leaves with an unwinged rachis.

Deciduous shrub or tree to about 12 m tall, 18 cm diam. Erect, single trunk or multiple, often sprouting abundantly from the roots and creating dense colonies; crown spreading, irregular, usually sparsely branched. Branches thick, stocky, with large, conspicuously raised leaf scars. **BARK** Grayish, smooth, often splotchy; raised, warty lenticels usually conspicuous. **TWIG** With a whitish bloom and numerous raised lenticels, exuding a milky sap when crushed. **LEAF** Alternate, pinnately compound; blade 30–90 cm long, to about 30 cm broad; petiole

to about 15 cm long, hairless or essentially so; rachis not winged. Leaflets 9–31, each 5–15 cm long, 1–4 cm broad, stalkless, lanceolate, margins coarsely toothed. Upper surface bright green, hairless; lower surface grayish, hairless. Brilliant red in autumn. **FLOWER** Usually functionally unisexual, male and female typically on separate trees, about 6 mm diam., greenish white or yellowish green, petals 5, about 3 mm long, sepals 5, about 1 mm long; inflorescence a cone-shaped paniculate cyme 10–15 cm long. Spring. **FRUIT** Rounded red drupe, 3–4 mm diam., borne in conspicuous, narrow, cone-like terminal clusters; minutely hairy with short hairs to about 0.2 mm long; matures summer to autumn.

HABITAT/RANGE Native. Thickets, fencerows, woodland borders, old fields, roadsides, rights of way, disturbed sites, 20–1,350 m; throughout U.S. and Canada, south to nw. Fla.

SIMILAR SPECIES The similar Staghorn Sumac and Winged Sumac have hairy twigs, and Winged Sumac has a leaf with a winged rachis.

Notes: Mature leaflets often bear irregularly scattered purplish blotches on both surfaces, especially in late summer and autumn. This species produces excellent autumn color, both in its bright red leaves and in the fruit, which remains on the plant well after the leaves have fallen.

STAGHORN SUMAC *Rhus typhina* L.

QUICK ID A sumac recognized by its combination of alternate, pinnately compound leaves with an unwinged rachis, toothed leaflets, hairy twigs and petioles, and large cone-shaped clusters of red fruit.

Deciduous low shrub or tree, 9–15 m tall, 32 cm diam. Often a clonal shrub with numerous trunks, or sometimes erect with a single trunk. Crown dense, rounded, often flat-topped; the many-branched stems sometimes resemble antlers. **BARK** Thin, smooth, gray on young trees, becoming dark brown with horizontal lenticels, similar to bark of several cherries; bark of older trees sometimes separating into small blocky scales. **TWIG** Stout, densely hairy, with long hairs; exudes milky sap when broken. **LEAF** Alternate, pinnately compound; blade 20–60 cm long, to about 25 cm broad; rachis hairy, not winged. Leaflets 11–31, each 5–12 cm long, 1.5–3.5 cm broad, stalkless or nearly so, lanceolate

autumn

fruit

Smooth Sumac

fruit

flowers

Staghorn Sumac

or oblong, tapering to an elongated tip, margins toothed. Upper surface reddish-hairy on young blades, at first yellow-green, becoming dark green at maturity; lower surface paler, whitish, hairless except along the midvein. Scarlet or bright orange in autumn. **FLOWER** Unisexual or functionally so, male and female usually on separate trees, green or greenish white, petals and sepals 5; inflorescence a large terminal panicle, male panicle 20–30 cm long, female panicle to about 20 cm long. Early summer. **FRUIT** Small red drupe, 3–4 mm diam., hairy, borne in a terminal paniculate cyme, maturing in late summer and persisting throughout much of the winter.

HABITAT/RANGE Native. Old fields, fencerows, swamp margins, roadsides, often on sandy or rocky soils, 100–1,500 m; Ont., Que., and N.B. south to n. Ga. and n. Ala., west to Mo. and Minn.

SIMILAR SPECIES The similar Smooth Sumac can be distinguished by the hairless petioles and twigs. See also Northern Smooth Sumac.

SMOOTH SUMAC

STAGHORN SUMAC

NORTHERN SMOOTH SUMAC *Rhus ×*
pulvinata Greene

QUICK ID A sumac distinguished by moderately hairy twigs and fruit (as opposed to densely hairy or hairless).

A shrub considered by some to be a hybrid between Smooth Sumac and Staghorn Sumac. It has somewhat hairy twigs and fruit with hairs that appear intermediate between the purported parent species.

HABITAT/RANGE Native, a hybrid form, occurring mostly in the North, from about Man. and Minn. east to Maine and Va.

Northern Smooth Sumac

NORTHERN SMOOTH SUMAC

WINGED SUMAC *Rhus copallinum* L.
A.K.A. SHINING SUMAC

QUICK ID A sumac recognized by the alternate, pinnately compound leaves with a winged rachis, the wing more than 4 mm broad.

Deciduous shrub or small, slender tree to about 12 m tall and 20 cm diam. Erect, single trunk or often multiple trunks, often thicket-forming from the production of numerous root suckers. Crown open, ascending, branches slender. **BARK** Smooth, brown or reddish brown, with numerous lenticels. **TWIG** Stout, copiously shaggy-hairy, with tawny hairs. **LEAF** Alternate, pinnately compound; blade 10–30 cm long, to about 16 cm broad; conspicuously winged rachis, the wing more than 4 mm broad on at least some leaves; petiole 2–6 cm long. Leaflets 9–23, each 3–8 cm long, 1–3 cm broad, stalkless or nearly so, lanceolate or narrowly elliptic, margins usually entire, sometimes remotely toothed. Upper surface lustrous, dark green, hairless except along the major veins; lower surface duller, hairy. Red in autumn, especially following early-season cold fronts. **FLOWER** Unisexual or functionally so, male and female typically on separate trees, greenish white, petals and sepals 5, sepal about 1 mm long, petal about 3 mm long; inflorescence a terminal paniculate cyme 10–20 cm long. Spring to early summer. **FRUIT** Rounded, hairy, dull red drupe, 4–5 mm diam.; matures late summer to autumn and persists into winter.

HABITAT/RANGE Native. Roadsides, medians, residential shrub beds, old fields, freshly burned pinelands, fencerows, disturbed sites, often in sandy soils, 0–1,400 m; throughout e. U.S. and Canada, from Ont. and Maine south throughout Fla., west to Neb. and e. Tex.

SIMILAR SPECIES The winged rachis of Prairie Sumac does not exceed about 3.5 mm broad.

WINGED SUMAC

Winged Sumac

fruit

Prairie Sumac   autumn

fruit

PRAIRIE SUMAC *Rhus lanceolata* (A. Gray) Britton

QUICK ID A sumac with 9–21 forward-curved, unstalked leaflets, entering the East only in e. Tex. and Okla.

Deciduous large shrub or small tree to about 10 m tall, with a short, slender trunk. **LEAF** Pinnate, with a winged rachis and 9–21 stalkless leaflets with few or no marginal teeth.

HABITAT/RANGE Native; confined in the East largely to limestone and calcareous soils of e. Tex and e. Okla.; occurs west to N.M.

SIMILAR SPECIES Similar to and overlapping in range with Winged Sumac; distinguished by the wing of the rachis not exceeding about 3.5 mm broad.

PRAIRIE SUMAC

EVERGREEN SUMAC *Rhus virens* Lindh. ex A. Gray

QUICK ID An evergreen sumac with leathery leaves bearing only 3–9 leaflets.

Evergreen shrub or small tree to 5 m tall. Distinguished from other eastern sumacs by the leathery evergreen leaves with 9 or fewer leaflets. **LEAF** Pinnate, with 3–9 short-stalked leathery leaflets.

HABITAT/RANGE Native; dry hillsides, rocky slopes; restricted in the East to a few counties in e. Tex., extending west to s. N.M. and s. Ariz.

POISON SUMAC *Toxicodendron vernix* (L.) Kuntze

QUICK ID A tree of moist habitats recognized by its combination of alternate, pinnately compound leaves with 7–15 leaflets, axillary flower clusters, and whitish drupes.

Deciduous shrub or small, slender tree to about 7 m tall, 35 cm diam. Erect, single trunk or multiple; sap of the trunk watery, darkening to nearly black on exposure to air, strongly irritating to the skin of most people. Crown sparingly branched, open, irregular. **BARK** Smooth, medium or dark gray. **TWIG** Reddish brown and smooth at first, quickly becoming tan, with numerous closely spaced lenticels. **LEAF** Alternate, pinnately compound, blade 18–30 cm long, petiole 2–10 cm long. Leaflets 7–15, each 3.5–10 cm long, 2–5 cm broad; stalks to about 5 mm long, usually reddish or maroon; ovate or elliptic, tapering at base, narrowing to a point at tip, margins entire. Upper surface lustrous green, hairless; lower surface paler, usually hairy along the major veins. Orange or scarlet in autumn. **FLOWER** Functionally unisexual, male and female typically borne on separate trees; about

3 mm diam.; petals 5, erect, creamy white with purplish venation; stamens 5; inflorescence a drooping or arching, long-stalked panicle produced in the leaf axils simultaneously with the emerging leaves. Late spring. **FRUIT** Round whitish drupe, 5–6 mm diam., produced in open, long-stalked, hairy, drooping panicles; matures late summer.

HABITAT/RANGE Native. Swamps, pineland depressions, wet woods, bogs, to about 300 m, rarely higher; throughout the East, in Ont., Minn., and N.S., south to c. Fla. and west to e. Tex.

SIMILAR SPECIES The nonpoisonous sumacs can be distinguished by their red rather than whitish fruit, mostly in terminal clusters.

Notes: The genus *Toxicodendron* includes about 20 species of shrubs, small trees, and woody climbers, distributed in East Asia and North America. Leaves are alternate, unifoliolate, pinnately compound, or trifoliolate. All produce poisonous sap that may cause severe dermatitis in some people. Three species are native to North America—Poison Sumac, Poison Ivy (*T. radicans* [L.] Kuntze), and Poison Oak (*T. pubescens* Mill.).

BRAZILIAN PEPPER *Schinus terebinthifolius* Raddi

QUICK ID A shrub or tree recognized by its combination of alternate, pinnately compound leaves, hairless red fruit, and an aggressive, colony-producing growth habit.

Evergreen shrub or small tree to about 8 m tall, 20 cm diam. Erect or more often vase-shaped; often forming impenetrable thickets in c. and s. Fla. **BARK** Smooth, gray. **TWIG** Light brown, finely hairy when young, nearly hairless at maturity, with numerous conspicuous raised lenticels. **LEAF** Alternate, pinnately compound, blade 3–10 cm long, petiole 1–4 cm long, rachis narrowly winged. Leaflets 5–9 (rarely 11), 2–8 cm long, 1.5–2 cm broad, stalkless or nearly so, lanceolate or narrowly elliptic, bluntly rounded at the tip, margins bluntly toothed (rarely entire); imparting an aroma of turpentine when bruised. Upper surface lustrous, dark green, finely hairy; lower surface dull

EVERGREEN SUMAC

POISON SUMAC

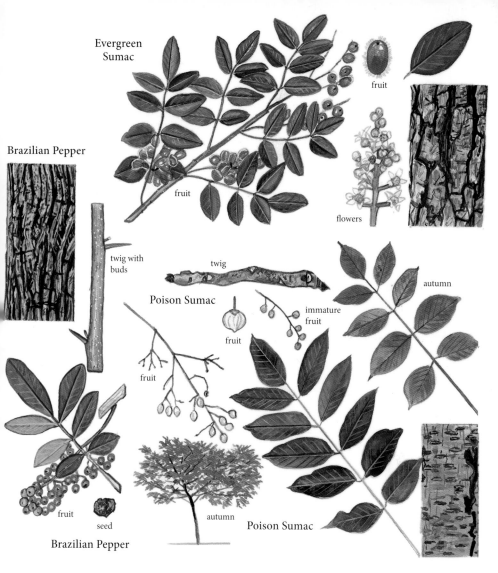

Evergreen Sumac

fruit

Brazilian Pepper

flowers

twig with buds

twig

Poison Sumac

immature fruit

fruit

autumn

fruit

fruit

fruit

seed

autumn

Poison Sumac

Brazilian Pepper

light green. **FLOWER** Functionally unisexual, male and female usually borne on separate plants, 3 mm diam., white; sepals 5, petals 5, stamens 10; pistil 1; inflorescence a panicle, usually emerging from the axils of the upper leaves, 3–8 cm long, on long stalks. Year-round. **FRUIT** Rounded, single-seeded, hairless red drupe, 6–8 mm diam., produced in abundance; matures year-round.

HABITAT/RANGE Introduced from South America. Disturbed sites, mesic and moist woodlands, pinelands, roadsides, margins of hammocks; c. and s. Fla., including Fla. Keys.

SIMILAR SPECIES The similar Winged Sumac (*Rhus copallinum*) can be distinguished by its more numerous leaflets (9–23) and hairy fruit.

Notes: This is one of Florida's most damaging invasive weeds. Originally cultivated for ornament, it now covers thousands of hectares in the lower peninsula, is the dominant roadside plant in some regions, and is reported increasingly in coastal regions of n. Fla. Sap from the bark and crushed leaves causes contact dermatitis in some people. *Schinus* is a genus of about 30 species, all native to South America.

ANNONACEAE: CUSTARD APPLE FAMILY

The Annonaceae is a family of about 128 genera and 2,300 species, distributed mostly in the tropics; 3 genera and 12 species occur in North America, most of which are woody shrubs. **LEAF** Alternate, simple, membranous or leathery, margins entire, short-petioled, lacking stipules. **FLOWER** Mostly bisexual, typically with 6 petals produced in 2 whorls of 3, and numerous pistils and stamens. **FRUIT** Distinctive aggregate of berries, with the seeds embedded within a plump, pulpy mesocarp and covered by a skinlike exocarp. In the custard apples (genus *Annona*), the berries are individually indistinguishable and fused into a single fleshy structure called a syncarp. In the pawpaws (genus *Asimina*), the berries are individually distinct, but joined at the base to form a cluster. This is an ancient family, closely related to the magnolias and laurels. Members of the family have little economic importance, except for some species of *Annona*, the fruits of which have been used for food in the tropics. Several of the North American species of *Asimina* are also grown for ornament, and at least one for fruit.

■ *ANNONA*: CUSTARD APPLES

A genus of about 110 species, distributed mostly in the New World tropics, with a few in North America and Africa. Evergreen or deciduous trees and shrubs, easily recognized by their fleshy, aggregate fruit. **BARK** Thin, often scaly or fissured. **LEAF** Alternate, simple, leathery or papery. **FLOWER** Creamy white or yellowish; petals 6 or 8, fleshy, produced in 2 series of 3 or 4; sepals 3 or 4, distinctly smaller than the petals, usually falling early. **FRUIT** Fleshy, ovoid or rounded syncarp (aggregate of fused berries), 1 per flower.

POND APPLE *Annona glabra* L.

QUICK ID No other tree in s. Fla. has the combination of swampy habitat, buttressed trunk, creamy-white flowers, and large yellowish fruit.

Evergreen or late deciduous, with leaves falling as new leaves develop; shrub or contorted tree to about 15 m tall, usually 20–45 cm diam., potentially to 1 m. Erect, single trunk or multiple, low branching; base of trunk often swollen and buttressed. Crown rounded, spreading, usually somewhat open in aspect, branches often curved upward and contorted. **BARK** Grayish brown or reddish brown, smooth at first, becoming roughened, slightly fissured, and fluted with age. **TWIG** Yellowish brown, becoming brown. **LEAF** Alternate, simple, usually in 2 ranks; thick, leathery, more or less heart-shaped, often folded upward from the midvein in a V shape, tapered or rounded at base, pointed at tip, margins entire. Upper surface lustrous green, hairless; lower surface paler, hairless. Blade 7.5–15 cm long, 3–7 cm broad; petiole 7–14 mm long. **FLOWER** Borne singly and appearing axillary, technically terminal and displaced by a new lateral shoot; 2.5–6 cm diam., petals 6, in 2 series of 3, thick, fleshy; outer petals creamy white, inner petals creamy white or yellowish white with a purplish or reddish blotch inside at the base. Spring. **FRUIT** Technically an aggregate of fused berries, superficially exteriorly apple-like; ovoid, 7–13 cm long, to 9 cm diam.; light green at first, becoming yellowish and brown-spotted; seeds numerous, rounded or flat. Usually maturing in autumn.

HABITAT/RANGE Native. Stream margins, sloughs, ponds, swamps, swampy hammocks, usually where fresh water stands much of the time; southernmost peninsular Fla. and Fla. Keys.

POND APPLE

fruit

flower

Pond Apple

fruit

flower

seeds

Sugar Apple

fruit

flower

SIMILAR SPECIES Florida Strangler Fig (*Ficus aurea*) and Shortleaf Fig (*Ficus citrifolia*, Moraceae) have somewhat similar leaves but without the V angle in the leaves; they can also be distinguished by their hidden flowers and fig fruit. See also Sugar Apple.

SUGAR APPLE *Annona squamosa* L.
A.K.A. Sweetsop

Evergreen or semideciduous shrub or small tree with an irregular crown of contorted branches that often droop at their tips. Distinguished among other tropical species of s. Fla. by its large, rounded, knobby fruit. **LEAF** 10–16 cm long, to about 6 cm broad, narrower than leaf of Pond Apple. **FRUIT** Aggregate of fused berries; more or less round, 6.5–10 cm diam., surface distinctly knobby and easily distinguished from that of Pond Apple. **HABITAT/ RANGE** Introduced from the American tropics and cultivated for its sweet fruit; naturalized in Fla. Keys.

Notes: The pulp of ripe fruit is sometimes eaten raw and has been used in the fabrication of beverages and sherbets.

■ *ASIMINA*: PAWPAWS

A genus of 8 species, mostly shrubs, all of which are confined to subtropical and warm temperate regions of e. North America; several occur only in Fla. and adjacent s. Ga. Common Pawpaw is the only species that is widespread.

FLAG PAWPAW *Asimina obovata* (Willd.) Nash

QUICK ID Distinguished by the combination of its deep-sand habitat, oval or obovate lustrous leaves, and conspicuously showy white flowers.

A large white-flowered shrub, rarely a very small tree. **FLOWER** Fragrant, 6–10 cm diam., petals and sepals 3.

HABITAT/RANGE Native; restricted in range to sandy scrub and other dry sites in c. Fla.

SMALL-FLOWER PAWPAW *Asimina parviflora* (Michx.) Dunal
a.k.a. SMALL-FRUITED PAWPAW

QUICK ID Distinguished by the combination of obovate leaves usually not exceeding about 15 cm long, and short-stalked to stalkless reddish flowers less than 2 cm diam., these hanging below the branch and often obscured from easy view.

Similar to Common Pawpaw but distinguished by smaller flowers, less than 2 cm diam., with shorter stalks (less than 1 cm); smaller fruit (6–7 cm diam.); and smaller leaves (averaging 6–15 cm long).

HABITAT/RANGE Native; throughout the southeastern coastal plains and Piedmont from N.C. south to Fla., west to e. Tex.

COMMON PAWPAW *Asimina triloba* (L.) Dunal
a.k.a. DOG-BANANA, INDIAN-BANANA

QUICK ID A small tree or shrub recognized by its combination of large leaves, dull red flowers, and oblong yellow-green berries.

Deciduous large shrub or small tree to about 14 m tall, 10–30 cm diam. Erect, usually single straight trunk; crown open, with slender, spreading branches. **BARK** Smooth or very slightly roughened, grayish brown, often splotched with circular patches of grayish-white lichens. **TWIG** Slender, reddish, rusty-hairy when young, becoming hairless; buds rusty-hairy. **LEAF** Alternate, simple, thin and pliable, oblong or obovate, widest toward the short-pointed tip, tapering at base, margins entire. Upper surface medium green, hairless; lower surface paler, rusty-hairy throughout at first, mostly along the veins with age. Blade 15–30 cm long, 8–14 cm broad; petiole 5–10 mm long. **FLOWER** 4–5 cm diam., petals 6, dull red, thickened; stalk at least 1 cm long. Mid-spring. **FRUIT** Aggregate of berries; each berry 5–15 cm long, oblong, greenish yellow; matures summer to early autumn.

HABITAT/RANGE Native. Floodplains, moist woods, bottomlands, often in association with alluvial soils, 10–790 m; from e. Nebr. east to N.Y., south to nw. Fla., and west to e. Tex.; largely confined to the Piedmont and northward, scattered in the southeastern coastal plains from nw. Fla. to e. Tex.

SIMILAR SPECIES Georgia Fevertree (*Pinckneya bracteata*, Rubiaceae) is superficially similar and occurs in similar habitats where the two overlap, but differs by its opposite leaves. Leaves of deciduous magnolias (Magnoliaceae) are similar to those of Common Pawpaw, but magnolias have a large terminal bud and conelike fruit. See also Small-flower Pawpaw and Flag Pawpaw.

COMMON PAWPAW

SMALL-FLOWER PAWPAW

FLAG PAWPAW

Flag Pawpaw

flowers

Small-flower
Pawpaw

flower

Small-flower
Pawpaw

fruit

seed

flowers

Common
Pawpaw

fruit

APOCYNACEAE: OLEANDER FAMILY

The oleander (or dogbane) family includes about 355 genera and 3,700 species of trees, shrubs, vines, and herbs. The woody members of the family are distributed primarily in the tropics and subtropics, the herbs primarily in temperate zones. Recent circumscriptions of the family include the milkweeds of the genus *Asclepias*, a mostly temperate genus of about 230 species, and several other genera that were once included within the Asclepiadaceae. This realignment added numerous temperate genera to the oleander family and increased the family's number of herbaceous species. About 15 species of trees and shrubs occur in the East, most of which are introduced in s. Fla.

LEAF Simple, usually opposite or whorled (occasionally alternate), with margins entire; twigs and leaf stalks exude a milky sap. **FLOWER** Bisexual, usually showy, radially symmetric, with 5 petals. The apical portion of the flower's style is usually expanded and highly modified, forming a head. **FRUIT** Follicle (a pod-like fruit splitting along 1 seam to release the seeds) or drupe, usually borne in pairs.

The family is well known for several ornamental species, many of which are widely planted and now naturalized in tropical and subtropical climes. These include the well-known southern landscape plant **Oleander** (*Nerium oleander* L.), as well as **Carissa** (*Carissa macrocarpa* [Eckl.] A. DC.), the frangipanis, and Luckynut. The native **Pearl Berry** or Tear Shrub (*Vallesia antillana* Woodson) is an endangered species, restricted in the U.S. to southernmost Fla. It is typically a shrub, rarely forming a small tree. Its nearly translucent white fruit and 5-petaled, star-shaped white flowers are distinctive.

DEVILTREE *Alstonia macrophylla* Wall. ex G. Don

QUICK ID An evergreen tree readily identified by its grayish trunk, large whorled leaves, tubular white flowers, and long, narrow fruit pods.

Evergreen fast-growing tree to about 20 m tall. Erect, single trunk; crown open, branches more or less ascending and spreading. **BARK** Smooth, gray. **TWIG** Smooth, gray; young twigs exuding milky sap when broken. **LEAF** Usually in whorls of 3 or 4, rarely opposite; simple, leathery, obovate or elliptic, usually widest near, or slightly above, the middle; base wedge-shaped; tip abruptly pointed; margins entire. Upper surface lustrous green, hairless; lower surface paler, hairy (at least when young). Blade 10–30 cm long, 4–14 cm broad; petiole 1–4 cm long. **FLOWER** 5–10 mm long, white, tubular, flaring into 5 narrow lobes; stalks exude milky sap when broken. Year-round. **FRUIT** Narrow brownish follicle, to about 45 cm long, less than 5 mm diam., borne in dangling clusters. Year-round.

HABITAT/RANGE Introduced, native to Malaysia and Asia. Cultivated, naturalized, and listed as an invasive species in s. Fla., where it grows mostly in hammocks, pinelands, and disturbed sites.

SIMILAR SPECIES Deviltree is one of two species of *Alstonia* naturalized in s. Fla. The similar Dita or White Cheesewood (*A. scholaris* [L.] R. Br.) usually has leaves 9–20 cm long, occurring 5–7 per whorl.

Oleander

flowers

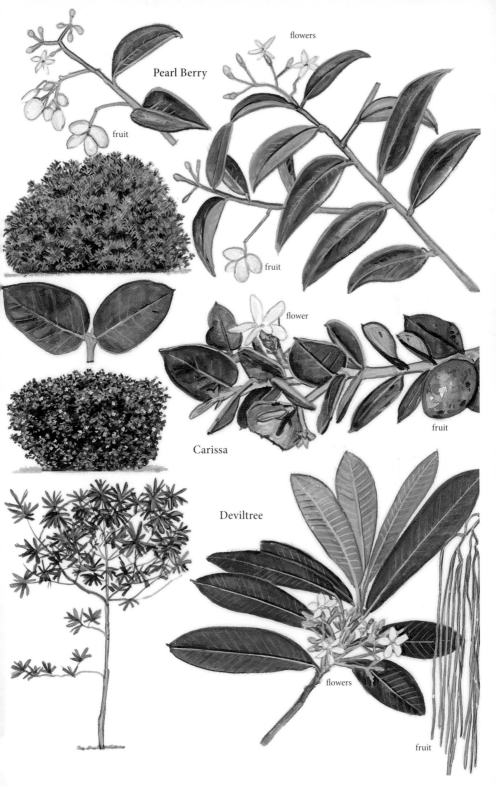

Pearl Berry

flowers

fruit

fruit

Carissa

flower

fruit

Deviltree

flowers

fruit

LIPSTICK TREE *Ochrosia elliptica* Labill.
A.K.A. ELLIPTIC YELLOWWOOD, BLOODHORN

QUICK ID A shrub or small tree easily distinguished by the bright red fruit and opposite or whorled, closely veined, lustrous green leathery leaves with margins entire.

Evergreen large shrub or small tree, 5–9 m tall. Erect, trunks usually several, sometimes single; crown dense, symmetric, more or less ellipsoid or ovoid, varying little from plant to plant. **BARK** Usually brown with grayish splotches, finely furrowed, somewhat scaly. **TWIG** Smooth or slightly roughened, exuding milky sap when broken. **LEAF** Opposite or in whorls of 3 or 4, simple, leathery, obovate, tapering to a more or less V-shaped base, tip rounded, margins entire. Upper surface dark lustrous green, veins numerous, conspicuous, finely parallel, forking at the tip and joining a conspicuous marginal vein; lower surface paler. Blade 8–20 cm long, 3–8 cm broad; petiole 1.5–2 cm long, exuding milky sap when broken. **FLOWER** About 1 cm long, white, tubular, lobes slightly twisted and overlapping at base. Autumn to winter. **FRUIT** Usually single-seeded, ellipsoid, lustrous, bright red waxy drupe, 5–6 cm long, 2–3 cm diam., with a pointed tip; poisonous. Maturing in late summer to autumn.

HABITAT/RANGE Introduced, native to Australia; cultivated and naturalized in s. Fla., including Fla. Keys.

FRANGIPANI *Plumeria obtusa* L
A.K.A. SINGAPORE GRAVEYARD FLOWER

Usually a large shrub; somewhat similar to Lipstick Tree. **FLOWER** White, usually with a yellow spot in the throat. **FRUIT** Paired, green, podlike. **HABITAT/RANGE** Introduced; cultivated in s. Fla. and naturalized in Fla. Keys.

LUCKYNUT *Thevetia peruviana* (Pers.) K. Schum.

QUICK ID Usually a shrub, recognized by its combination of linear leaves crowded near the branch tips and tubular pinkish or yellowish flowers.

Evergreen, usually a shrub, rarely a small tree, 5–8 m tall. **BARK** Grayish brown. **TWIG** Grayish brown, exuding milky sap when broken. **LEAF** Alternate or subopposite, often crowded near tips of branches; simple, linear, long-tapering to base and tip, margins entire. Upper surface lustrous, bright green, hairless, midvein evident, lateral veins obscure; lower surface paler. Blade 10–15 cm long, 0.5–1.2 cm broad; petiole to about 3 mm long. **FLOWER** 6–7 cm long, 4.5–5.5 cm diam.; corolla fragrant, tubular, flaring into 5 lobes at the apex; petals overlapping, yellow, salmon, or pinkish. **FRUIT** Rounded to laterally flattened and conspicuously angled drupe, yellow-green to reddish, often becoming blackish at maturity, 2.5–4 cm diam.

HABITAT/RANGE Introduced, native to Central America and Mexico; cultivated and escaped in c. and s. Fla.

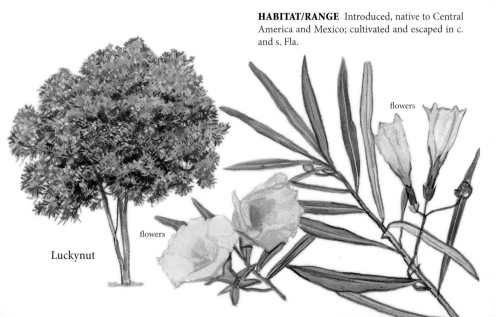

flowers

flowers

Luckynut

Lipstick Tree

flowers

immature fruit

fruit

Frangipani

flowers

fruit

AQUIFOLIACEAE: HOLLY FAMILY

The hollies constitute a collection of about 400 species of trees and shrubs distributed nearly worldwide. The family's 3 major centers of distribution include East Asia, South America, and, with somewhat fewer species, the se. U.S. Species also occur in Hawaii, Tahiti, the Canary Islands, the Azores, Europe, Africa, and Australia. Nineteen species and 1 natural hybrid are native to the U.S., and at least 4 commonly cultivated non-native species are naturalized here. As currently circumscribed, Aquifoliaceae includes the single genus *Ilex*. Previously, the family was considered to contain 3 additional genera, one of which, *Nemopanthus*, included two species in North America. Genetic analyses have, however, shown that the former genus *Nemopanthus* is deeply nested within the genus *Ilex*. In North America the hollies are essentially eastern in distribution; only 1 native species occurs naturally west of the 100th meridian.

■ *ILEX*: HOLLIES

Deciduous and evergreen trees and shrubs. **BARK** Gray or mottled gray, often marked with darker and lighter splotches; usually smooth, often with distinctive lenticels. **TWIG** Usually gray or brown, often bearing circular or elongated lenticels; deciduous species often produce short leafy shoots with leaves closely clustered at the tip and appearing whorled. **LEAF** Alternate, simple; margins usually toothed, rarely entire, teeth sometimes spine-tipped. **FLOWER** Functionally unisexual, usually male and female flowers on separate trees (sometimes with a few bisexual flowers intermingled, predominantly on cultivated plants). Female flowers typically have a plump, conspicuous, functional ovary surrounded by several obviously nonfunctional stamens (staminodes). Male flowers usually have conspicuous stamens with obvious pollen-filled anthers surrounding a more or less shriveled or diminutive ovary that in some species aborts and is not evident when the flower matures (reaches anthesis). Petal number varies by species; the flowers of some species produce predominately 3–5 petals and others predominately 5–9; petals greenish white, yellowish white, or creamy white, averaging about 5 mm wide at bloom time in most species. Flowers produced in clusters (fascicles, cymes, or panicles), or solitary in the leaf angles. **FRUIT** Round red, yellow, orange, or black multistoned drupe, often erroneously called a berry.

AMERICAN HOLLY *Ilex opaca* Aiton

QUICK ID An evergreen holly easily recognized by the lustrous, dark green leaves with spiny margins.

Evergreen, slow-growing, long-lived tree to 20 m tall, 75 cm diam. (usually not exceeding about 15 m tall and 60 cm diam. in n. part of range). Erect, single trunk; crown of open-grown trees pyramidal, symmetric, often branching close to the ground, branches spreading at more or less right angles to the trunk; crown of forest-grown trees less densely branched, more or less cylindric. **BARK** Essentially smooth, sometimes with warty outgrowths, light gray with dark gray splotches. **TWIG** Finely hairy at first, becoming hairless, brown, and roughened with conspicuous lenticels. **LEAF** Alternate, simple, stiff, oblong or elliptic, the apex spine-tipped; margins usually rolled downward, often with relatively large spine-tipped teeth, occasionally entire. Upper surface lustrous, dark green, hairless at maturity; lower surface duller, hairless or with short, fine hairs along midvein. Blade 3–12 cm long, 2–5.5 cm broad; petiole 5–10 mm long, finely hairy. **FLOWER** Male and female flowers borne on separate trees, male flowers mainly in clusters in the leaf axils and female flowers mostly between the leaves along developing stems; small, petals and sepals usually 4, petals creamy white. Spring. **FRUIT** Rounded, lustrous red (rarely yellow) drupe, 7–12 mm diam.; stones (or pyrenes) usually 4, ribbed, 6–8 mm long; matures autumn.

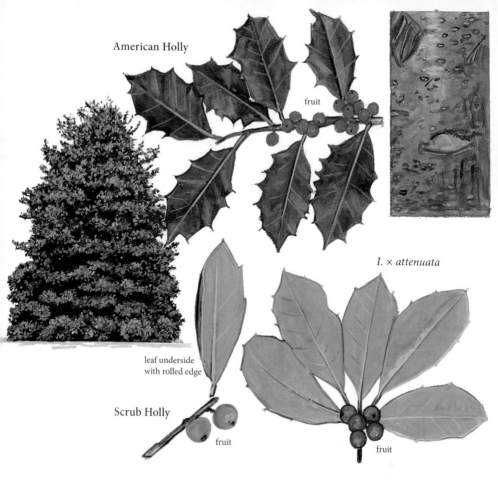

American Holly

fruit

I. × attenuata

leaf underside
with rolled edge

Scrub Holly

fruit

fruit

HABITAT/RANGE Native. Moist woodlands, rich slopes, margins of floodplain forests, often with calcareous soils, 10–1,500 m; N.Y. and Mass., south to Fla., west to se. Mo. and e. Tex.

SIMILAR SPECIES The similar **Scrub Holly** (*I. opaca* var. *arenicola* [Ashe] Ashe), a shrub or small tree endemic to the sand scrub of c. Fla., has smaller yellowish-green leaves with conspicuously downward-rolled margins. The often cultivated English Holly is rarely encountered in the wild; its leaves are shinier above and the female flowers are in clusters.

Notes: American Holly was likely among the first trees recognized by European colonists because of its similarity to English Holly. Although English Holly is widely cultivated in North America, American Holly is seldom cultivated in Europe. More than 100 named cultivars of American Holly are available in the garden trade. The species hybridizes naturally with Dahoon to produce *I.* × *attenuata* Ashe, a popular ornamental often sold under the cultivar names 'East Palatka', 'Savannah', and 'Foster 2'.

AMERICAN HOLLY

SCRUB HOLLY

ENGLISH HOLLY *Ilex aquifolium* L.

QUICKID A small evergreen holly recognized by its lustrous, dark green leaves with spiny, wavy margins; usually seen in cultivation, rarely naturalized or seen in the wild.

Evergreen shrub or small tree, 6–10 m tall (potentially to 25 m under ideal conditions), usually to about 40 cm diam. (potentially 80 cm). Erect, usually single trunk; crown more or less pyramidal or oval, with stiff, laterally spreading branches. **BARK** Gray, smooth when young, becoming horizontally wrinkled with shallow furrows at maturity. **TWIG** Greenish or purplish. **LEAF** Alternate, simple, stiff, frequently oval or elliptic, but variable in outline; margins wavy, spiny-toothed, potentially becoming nearly entire in the crowns of older trees. Upper surface lustrous, dark green; lower surface paler. Blade 2–8 cm long, 2–6 cm broad; petiole to about 5 mm long. **FLOWER** Creamy white, petals 4, the pistillate (female) flowers borne in umbel-like clusters of 1–8 or in short spurs. Late spring. **FRUIT** Round, 2–4-stoned reddish drupe, 6–10 mm diam.; matures autumn.

HABITAT/RANGE Introduced; native to the U.K. and continental Europe; frequently cultivated in North America; rarely naturalized.

SIMILAR SPECIES Trees encountered in the wild are likely to be American Holly, which has similar large spiny leaves, but they are duller on top, and the female flowers are borne singly, scattered on the twig. Three other introduced hollies are widely cultivated and occasionally naturalized in e. North America; Chinese Holly and Kurogane Holly are illustrated below. Japanese or Box-leaf Holly (*I. crenata* Thunb.) is typically an evergreen shrub that sometimes becomes arborescent in shaded woodlands. It has relatively small, bluntly toothed leaves, reminiscent of those of Yaupon, and black fruit.

CHINESE HOLLY *Ilex cornuta* Lindl. & Paxton
A.K.A. BURFORD HOLLY

Typically a densely foliaged shrub, rarely a small tree. **LEAF** Lustrous, dark green; 1 to many marginal spines. **HABITAT/ RANGE** Introduced; may be naturalized in Ala. and N.C.

KUROGANE HOLLY *Ilex rotunda* Thunb.

Small evergreen tree. **LEAF** Ovate or elliptic, 4–10 cm long, with entire margins. **HABITAT/ RANGE** Introduced; native to Japan and Korea; reported in Ga.

DAHOON *Ilex cassine* L.

QUICKID The only evergreen wetland holly bearing oblong or oblanceolate leaves with predominantly entire margins.

Evergreen tree, 5–20 m tall, 10–25 cm diam., often flowering and fruiting when of a low, shrubby stature. Erect, usually single trunk; crown vase-shaped, with strongly ascending branches. **BARK** Smooth, gray, often with darker gray splotches; becoming slightly darker with age. **TWIG** Light gray, sometimes hairless, more often shaggy-hairy or with short curly hairs. **LEAF** Alternate, simple, varying considerably in outline: oblong, oblanceolate, oval, elliptic, or nearly spatulate, usually widest above the middle, tapering evenly to the base; tip blunt or acute, usually with a short, abrupt point; margins usually entire, sometimes (most frequent from c. Fla. southward) with a few small, spreading teeth. Upper surface lustrous, medium green, usually hairless or slightly hairy along the midvein; lower surface paler, commonly hairy at least along the veins, sometimes sparsely hairy throughout or hairless. Blade 2–10 cm long, 1–4.5 cm broad; petiole 5–15 mm long. **FLOWER** Greenish white, petals 4. Spring. **FRUIT** Rounded, usually 4-stoned drupe, 6–9 mm diam., typically red, sometimes yellow or orange; matures autumn.

HABITAT/RANGE Native. Coastal wetlands, floodplains, cypress ponds and bays, margins of spring-fed streams, flatwood depressions, moist hammocks, 0–200 m; chiefly distributed in southeastern coastal plains, se. N.C. south throughout Fla., west to se. Tex.

DAHOON

SIMILAR SPECIES The Myrtle-leaved Holly is closely related to Dahoon and shares similar habitats but differs significantly in leaf size and shape (leaves of Myrtle-leaved Holly are smaller and narrower). Dahoon hybridizes with American Holly to produce the darker-leaved 'East Palatka' Holly (*I. × attenuata* Ashe).

fruit section

English Holly

fruit

flowers

♂

♀

stone

Chinese Holly

flowers

fruit

Kurogane Holly

fruit

♀ flower

Dahoon

fruit

fruit

fruit colour varies

MYRTLE-LEAVED HOLLY *Ilex myrtifolia* Walter
A.K.A. MYRTLE DAHOON

QUICK ID A small evergreen holly easily distinguished from other hollies by its short, narrow leaves.

Evergreen shrub or small tree, 5–8 m tall, typically to about 30 cm diam. Erect, often with multiple trunks; arborescent forms usually with a single trunk; crown dense, compact or openly spreading, the branches stiff, often ascending, the twigs and branchlets usually diverging at nearly right angles. **BARK** Smooth and gray at first, becoming slightly roughened and whitish gray with age, especially on single-trunked arborescent plants. **TWIG** Grayish and hairy at first, becoming hairless, finely roughened, and more or less waxy with age. **LEAF** Alternate, simple, stiff, narrowly lanceolate or nearly linear, abruptly narrowing at base and tip; tip with a short, abrupt point; margins entire or rarely with 1 or a few small teeth. Upper surface lustrous, dark green, hairless or finely hairy along midvein; lower surface paler, usually hairless, sometimes sparsely hairy; on both surfaces midvein evident, lateral veins obscure. Blade 5–30 mm long, 3–8 mm broad; petiole 1–3 mm long. **FLOWER** Creamy white, petals 4. Spring. **FRUIT** Rounded drupe, 5–8 mm diam., usually red or orange, rarely yellow; stones usually 4; matures autumn.

HABITAT/RANGE Native. Coastal wetlands, margins of cypress swamps, often forming large colonies along intermittent drainages and ephemeral pools of flatwoods, bogs, and savannas, 0–100 m; restricted in distribution to southeastern coastal plains, se. N.C. south to n. Fla., west to e. Tex., overlapping considerably with range of Dahoon.

SIMILAR SPECIES Yaupon can be similar but is distinguished by its leaf margins being bluntly toothed rather than mostly entire. The leaves of Dahoon are predominantly much longer than 3 cm.

Notes: Myrtle-leaved Holly is sometimes considered to be a variety of Dahoon. Apparent intermediates between these species are rare, and the two are easily distinguished in the wild. It is sometimes suggested that Myrtle-leaved Holly is one of the parents of *I. × attenuata* Ashe, which is here considered to be a hybrid of American Holly and Dahoon.

YAUPON *Ilex vomitoria* Aiton

QUICK ID An evergreen thicket-forming holly, easily recognized by its combination of small, bluntly toothed leaves and bright, lustrous red fruit.

Evergreen, typically a large shrub forming dense thickets, occasionally becoming a tree to about 10 m tall and 15 cm diam. Shrubby forms usually produce multiple trunks from the base; arborescent forms are often erect, with a single trunk; crown compact, irregular, often diffusely ascending, with somewhat contorted branches. **BARK** Pale gray, smooth. **TWIG** Densely or sparsely hairy at first, with age becoming hairless, finely roughened, and waxy. **LEAF** Alternate, simple, stiff, narrowly oval or elliptic, margins bluntly toothed. Upper surface lustrous, dark green, hairy along midvein at first, becoming hairless; lower surface paler, dull green, usually hairless. Blade 5–30 mm long, 5–25 mm broad; petiole 2–3 mm long. **FLOWER** Greenish white or creamy white, occasionally yellowish, petals 4. Spring. **FRUIT** Round, 4-stoned, lustrous, bright red drupe, 4–8 mm diam.; matures autumn to winter.

HABITAT/RANGE Native. Coastal dunes, maritime forests, swales, pine flatwoods, rich upland woods, sometimes in association with calcareous soils, 0–150 m; southeastern coastal plains, se. Va.

MYRTLE-LEAVED HOLLY

YAUPON

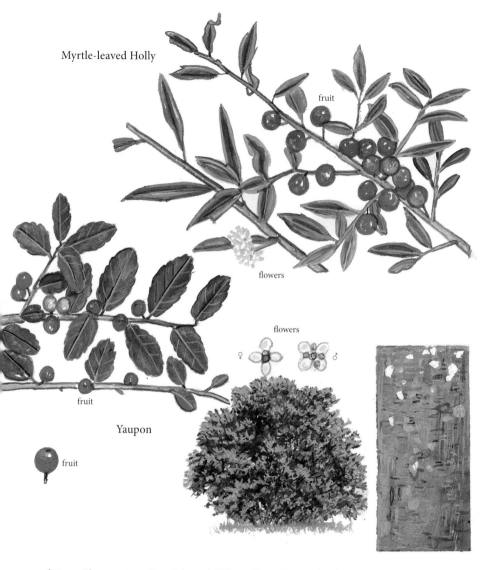

Myrtle-leaved Holly

fruit

flowers

flowers

♀ ♂

fruit

Yaupon

fruit

south to sc. Fla., west to e. Tex., Ark., and Okla. Frequently cultivated and now naturalized beyond its original range.

SIMILAR SPECIES Among *Ilex*, only Myrtle-leaved Holly is likely to be confused with this species, but it has leaves with margins entire. The leaves of Walter's Viburnum (*Viburnum obovatum*, Adoxaceae) are somewhat similar but are opposite and usually deciduous.

Notes: Yaupon has become an extremely popular and successful native garden and landscape plant. Numerous forms are recognized, many of which are propagated by cuttings and sold as one of several named cultivars. 'Pendula' and 'Folsom's Weeping' are among the more commonly seen arborescent forms, favored for their erect stature and conspicuously drooping branches.

LARGE GALLBERRY *Ilex coriacea*
(Pursh) Chap.

QUICK ID An evergreen shrub distinguished from other hollies by its combination of leaves with short bristlelike teeth, flowers with 5–9 petals, and black fruit.

Evergreen, usually a shrub, occasionally a small tree to about 7 m tall, 5 cm diam. Erect or vase-shaped, arborescent forms usually with a single trunk; crown open, pyramidal, major branches usually spreading at nearly right angles to the trunk. **BARK** Smooth, mottled light and dark gray. **TWIG** Brown and finely hairy when young, becoming grayish or tan and roughened with conspicuous lenticels. **LEAF** Alternate, simple, leathery and moderately stiff, elliptic or oval, margins usually with a few tiny bristlelike, widely spaced teeth, or sometimes entire. Upper surface lustrous dark green, finely hairy along the midvein; lower surface paler, hairless or finely hairy, usually with depressed glands in the surface. Blade 3.5–9 cm long, 1.5–4 cm broad; petiole 5–10 mm long. **FLOWER** Creamy white, petals 5–9. Spring. **FRUIT** Round or slightly vertically flattened, lustrous black drupe, 6–8 mm diam.; stones 5–9; matures autumn.

HABITAT/RANGE Native. Swamps, bogs, wet depressions in flatwoods, pine savannas, rich woodlands, 0–150 m; confined chiefly to the southeastern coastal plains, se. Va. south to c. Fla., west to e. Tex.

SIMILAR SPECIES The leaves of Shrub Gallberry (*I. glabra* [L.] A. Gray) are similar but easily distinguished by the marginal teeth, which are notchlike and confined to the tip of the blade, rather than bristlelike and extending nearly to the base of the blade.

TAWNYBERRY HOLLY *Ilex krugiana* Loes.
A.K.A. KRUG'S HOLLY

QUICK ID A small evergreen holly distinguished by leaves with wavy margins, fruit that turns black at the time of falling, and black fallen leaves.

Evergreen tree to about 10 m tall, 20 cm diam. Erect, single trunk. **BARK** Gray. **TWIG** Whitish, usually hairless, at least when mature; slightly roughened with lenticels. **LEAF** Alternate, simple, ovate or elliptic, often folded upward from midvein, rounded at base, tapering to an acute tip, margins usually entire, rarely toothed. Blade 5–9 cm long, 3–5 cm broad; petiole 1.0–2.2 cm long, subtended by minute black stipules. Leaf turns black after falling. **FLOWER** Functionally unisexual, greenish white, about 6 mm diam., petals 4, borne in clusters at the leaf axils. Early spring. **FRUIT** Round drupe, 4–7 mm diam., reddish yellow at first, becoming purplish or black just before or after falling; stones 4; matures summer.

HABITAT/RANGE Native. Subtropical hammocks, chiefly in the Everglades, southernmost Fla. peninsula.

SIMILAR SPECIES Dahoon is somewhat similar but its typically red (sometimes yellow or orange) mature fruit does not turn black at maturity. In s. Fla., West Indian Cherry (*Prunus myrtifolia*, Rosaceae) and Milkbark (*Drypetes diversifolia*, Euphorbiaceae) can appear similar, but neither has minute black stipules subtending the petiole.

LARGE GALLBERRY

TAWNYBERRY HOLLY

Large Gallberry

fruit

fruit

stone

Large Gallberry

flowers

new leaves

Tawnyberry Holly

fruit

CAROLINA HOLLY *Ilex ambigua*
(Michx.) Torr.
A.K.A. SAND HOLLY

QUICK ID A deciduous holly recognized by its combination of usually elliptic, obscurely toothed leaves to about 8 cm long, and multi-stoned red drupe.

Deciduous shrub or small tree to about 6 m tall and about 15 cm diam. Arborescent plants are typically erect with a single trunk and a more or less open, irregular crown of several spreading branches; shrubby forms are usually vase-shaped with multiple trunks. **BARK** Light gray with dark gray splotches. **TWIG** Green or brown, somewhat lustrous when new, with tan lenticels. **LEAF** Alternate, simple, variable in size and shape from plant to plant: oval, elliptic, or narrowly elliptic, usually widest near the middle, but sometimes widest slightly above or below the middle; rounded or acute at base; tip acute, bluntly acute, or abruptly tapered to a slender tip; margins bluntly and obscurely toothed, typically above the middle, or less often entire. Upper surface dull, yellow-green, hairless to finely hairy; lower surface paler, hairless or finely hairy. Blade 1.5–8 cm long, 1–5 cm broad; petiole 2–10 mm long. **FLOWER** Creamy white, petals 4–6; female with a plump ovary and usually 4 nonfunctional stamens (staminodes); male often lacking a rudimentary ovary at bloom time, which helps to distinguish this species from other deciduous hollies. Spring. **FRUIT** Round drupe, 4–7 mm diam., green at first, turning red at maturity; stones 4–6, creamy white, distinctly ribbed; matures late summer to autumn, usually falling with the leaves.

HABITAT/RANGE Native. Well-drained or moist woods, sand ridges, sandy hardwood hammocks, sandy old fields, 0–300 m; widely distributed in the Southeast, most common in the southeastern coastal plains, Va. and Ky., south to c. Fla., west to Ark., Okla., and e. Tex.

SIMILAR SPECIES Deciduous Holly is distinguished from Carolina Holly by its mostly spatulate to obovate leaves, which are often densely clustered near the tips of lateral twigs.

Notes: Some experts have treated larger-leaved forms of Carolina Holly as var. *monticola* or var. *montana*, distinguishing them by leaf length. Plants of the mountains with most leaves longer than about 8 cm are treated here as Mountain Holly.

DECIDUOUS HOLLY *Ilex decidua* Walter
A.K.A. POSSUMHAW HOLLY

QUICK ID A deciduous holly recognized by the combination of bluntly toothed, spatulate leaves, often clustered near the tips of lateral twigs, and multistoned reddish drupes on relatively short fruit stalks.

Deciduous shrub or small tree to 10 m tall and 30 cm diam. Ascending, leaning, or erect, often with a single trunk, sometimes with multiple trunks; crown of forest-grown trees open, branches few, spreading or ascending; crown of open-grown trees often cylindric and somewhat densely foliaged. **BARK** Grayish or grayish brown, smooth, becoming slightly roughened with age. **TWIG** Greenish at first, becoming greenish brown then gray, with conspicuous, rounded lenticels. **LEAF** Alternate, often produced in closely set clusters on short shoots and appearing whorled or opposite; simple, oblanceolate, spatulate, or obovate, usually distinctly widest toward the tip, with a long-tapering base, occasionally elliptic; margins obscurely or conspicuously bluntly toothed, each tooth tipped with a tiny gland. Upper surface dark green, hairless or sparsely hairy; lower surface moderately to

CAROLINA HOLLY

DECIDUOUS HOLLY

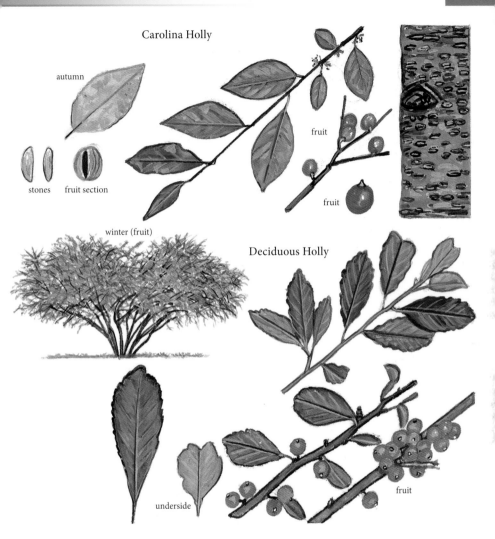

Carolina Holly

autumn

stones   fruit section

fruit

fruit

winter (fruit)

Deciduous Holly

underside

fruit

densely hairy, at least on the midvein. Blade 1–8 cm long, 1–4.5 cm broad; petiole 2–15 mm long, usually hairy. **FLOWER** Greenish white, petals 4–6, usually 5. Spring. **FRUIT** Round, multistoned drupe, 4–9 mm diam., varying red, yellow, or nearly orange, produced on stalks less than 1 cm long; matures autumn and usually persists into winter.

HABITAT/RANGE Native. Alluvial floodplains, bottoms, wet and moist woodlands, occasionally dry uplands, reaching its largest form in association with large river floodplains, 0–360 m; Md. south to c. Fla., west to Kans. and c. Tex.

SIMILAR SPECIES Carolina Holly can be distinguished by its predominantly elliptic rather than oblanceolate or spatulate leaves; and Georgia Holly by its fruit stalks, which are usually at least 1 cm long (less than 1 cm long in Deciduous Holly). Suwannee or Curtis's Holly (*I. decidua* var. *curtissii* Fernald or *I. curtissii* [Fernald] Small), considered endemic to the drainage basin of the Suwannee River in s. Ga. and n. Fla., has smaller leaves—usually not exceeding about 5 cm long and 1.5 cm broad—and smaller fruit, averaging 4–5 mm diam.

GEORGIA HOLLY *Ilex longipes* Chapm. ex Trel.

QUICK ID A shrub or small tree, readily distinguished from other deciduous hollies within its range by its longer flower and fruit stalks, usually exceeding 1 cm.

Deciduous shrub or small tree to about 8 m tall, usually not exceeding about 15 cm diam. Erect or somewhat arching, usually single trunk, sometimes several; crown openly branched, with several spreading and ascending branches. **BARK** Smooth, medium gray, often with darker gray splotches. **TWIG** Light to dark gray, sometimes yellowish, hairless; young branches usually green, sometimes reddish, gray, or brown. **LEAF** Alternate, often produced in closely set clusters on short shoots and appearing whorled or opposite; simple, narrowly or broadly oblanceolate, elliptic, or ovate, tip usually acute, base wedge-shaped, margins bluntly toothed, often hairy. Upper surface dark green or yellow-green, hairless; lower surface paler, sometimes with whitish hairs near the midrib, the hairs decreasing in abundance toward the blade margin. Blade 4–8 cm long, 1.5–4 cm broad; petiole usually 7–14 mm long, sometimes with a line of white hairs extending onto the leaf margin. **FLOWER** Greenish white, petals usually 4–5; flower stalk conspicuous, on female flowers usually exceeding or much exceeding 1 cm long, on male flowers usually exceeding 1.5 cm. Spring. **FRUIT** Round, multistoned, shiny red or orange drupe, 8–14 mm diam.; stalks averaging 1–2 cm long; matures autumn.

HABITAT/RANGE Native. Moist upland woods, sandy bluffs above floodplains, stream banks and adjacent bottomlands, usually in association with limestone, shale, or clay soils, 0–550 m; Piedmont and southeastern coastal plains, N.C. south to n. Fla., west to Ark. and e. Tex.

SIMILAR SPECIES Sometimes treated as a variety of Deciduous Holly, which is most easily distinguished by the much shorter flower and fruit stalks. See also Cuthbert's Holly and Long-stalked Holly.

CUTHBERT'S HOLLY *Ilex cuthbertii* Small

QUICK ID Distinguished from other deciduous hollies by having margins of sepals hairy, upper surface of leaf hairy throughout, and margins of at least some leaves entire.

Similar to, and sometimes considered a variety of, Georgia Holly. **LEAF** Upperside of blade hairy; the margins of at least some leaves entire.

HABITAT/RANGE Native; lower Piedmont and upper coastal plain, along the S.C. and Ga. border.

LONG-STALKED HOLLY *Ilex collina* Alexander

QUICK ID Recognized by the combination of its long fruit stalks (1–3 cm), comparatively large fruit that often equals or exceeds 1 cm diam., and mountainous habitat.

Small tree, 3–4 m tall. **LEAF** More or less ovate, usually widest at, or below, the middle. **FRUIT** Stalks 1–1.5 cm long.

HABITAT/RANGE Native, endemic to s. Appalachian Mountains, at 1,100–1,800 m elevation, in Va., W. Va., e. N.C. and w. Tenn.

GEORGIA HOLLY

CUTHBERT'S HOLLY

LONG-STALKED HOLLY

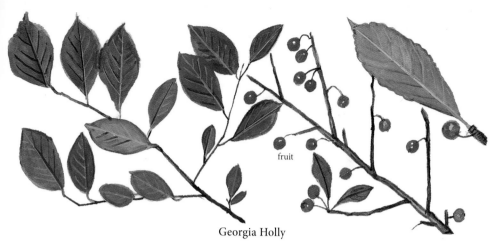

Georgia Holly

Cuthbert's Holly

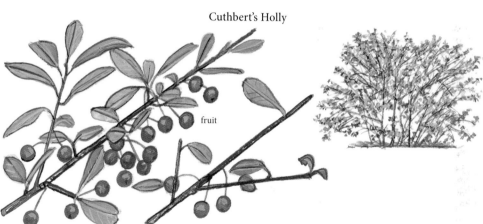

Long-stalked Holly

SARVIS HOLLY *Ilex amelanchier* M.A. Curtis in Chapman

QUICK ID The only deciduous wetland holly with netted venation clearly visible on the lower surface of the leaf blade.

Deciduous shrub or small tree to about 6 m tall and 13 cm diam. Erect, leaning, or ascending, single or multiple trunks; crown of tree-sized specimens spreading or ascending, sparsely branched. **BARK** Grayish brown, with raised, horizontally oriented, tan-colored corky lenticels. **TWIG** Grayish brown and hairy when young, becoming grayish, paler, and mostly hairless with age; lenticels on young twigs blackish at first, becoming buff-colored. **LEAF** Alternate, simple, oblong or ellipitic, with tip rounded or bluntly pointed, base rounded, margins finely toothed, the teeth appressed, sometimes appearing entire. Upper surface dull green, usually hairless at maturity; lower surface duller, with a covering of dense, shaggy hairs and distinctive net-like venation. Blade 5–9 cm long, 1.5–4.5 cm broad; petiole 3–15 mm long, usually hairy. **FLOWER** Greenish white or yellowish white, petals 4. Spring. **FRUIT** Rounded, multistoned, dull fluorescent red drupe, 5–10 mm diam.; matures late autumn.

HABITAT/RANGE Native. Floodplains of small creeks, moist to wet bottoms, cypress swamps, wetlands dominated by Atlantic White Cedar; southeastern coastal plains, N.C. south to nw. Fla., west to se. La.

SIMILAR SPECIES Deciduous Holly and Common Winterberry occur in similar habitats and can potentially be confused with Sarvis Holly, but neither has the distinctive netlike (reticulate) venation on the lower surface of the leaf.

MOUNTAIN HOLLY *Ilex montana* Torr. & A. Gray

QUICK ID A small deciduous tree, distinguished from other hollies by a combination of mountain habitat, many leaves exceeding 8 cm long, and stones with 4 or 5 ridges.

Deciduous, typically a small tree 10–15 m tall, to about 15 cm diam., sometimes shrubby. Usually erect, single trunk or occasionally multiple; crown open, broader than tall, with several laterally spreading branches. **BARK** Smooth, dark gray with lighter splotches. **TWIG** Gray, densely hairy or hairless, often producing short, abbreviated spur shoots. **LEAF** Alternate, simple, variable in shape, usually widest above the middle of the blade, varying to ovate or elliptic; tip most often acuminate (abruptly tapered to a slender point), sometimes acute or blunt; base often asymmetrical; margins singly toothed or doubly toothed. Upper surface medium green, hairless or sparsely hairy, especially on the veins; lower surface paler, hairless, hairy on the veins, or hairy throughout the surface. Blade usually 9–12 cm long, 3–6 cm broad; petiole 8–26 mm long. Foliage soft yellow in autumn. **FLOWER** Greenish white, petals 4–8. Spring to summer. **FRUIT** Round, multistoned, lustrous red or scarlet drupe, 6–11 mm diam.; stones conspicuously ridged; matures autumn.

HABITAT/RANGE Native. Rich mountain slopes, above 400 m; N.Y. and s. Mass., south to n. Ga. and n. Ala.

SIMILAR SPECIES Some experts believe Mountain Holly, with leaves averaging longer than 8 cm, to be a large-leaved variety of Carolina Holly, which has leaves less than 8 cm long. Common Winterberry and Smooth Winterberry have 6–8 stones that are smooth rather than ridged.

SARVIS HOLLY

MOUNTAIN HOLLY

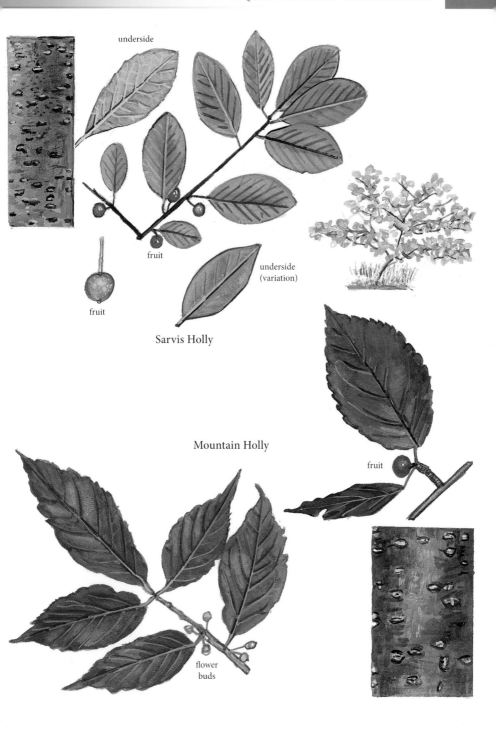

underside

fruit

fruit

underside
(variation)

Sarvis Holly

Mountain Holly

fruit

flower
buds

SMOOTH WINTERBERRY *Ilex laevigata* (Pursh) A. Gray

QUICK ID A holly recognized by the combination of bluntly toothed leaf margin, nutlets of the fruit smooth on the back, and margins of the sepals mostly hairless.

Similar to Mountain Holly. **FRUIT** Typically with 6–8 stones that are smooth on the back.

HABITAT/RANGE Native; a mostly coastal species ranging from Maine and N.Y. south to S.C.

CATBERRY *Ilex mucronata* (L.) M. Powell, V. Savolainen, & S. Andrews

QUICK ID Our only deciduous holly, with mostly entire-margined leaves and satiny-red fruit.

A deciduous shrub or very small tree to about 4 m tall, the crown to about 2 m broad.

HABITAT/RANGE Native; an uncommon species of high-elevation bogs and moist forests ranging from Nfld. west to Ont. and south to Md., W.Va., Ohio, Ind., and Ill.

Notes: Until recently, Catberry was included within the genus *Nemopanthus* and is still seen by the name *Nemopanthus mucronatus* (L.) Trel.

COMMON WINTERBERRY *Ilex verticillata* (L.) A. Gray

QUICK ID A deciduous holly recognized by the combination of typically wetland habitat, flowers with 5–8 petals, and fruit with nutlets that are smooth rather than ridged on the back.

Deciduous shrub or small tree to about 8 m tall and 15 cm diam. Erect or ascending, typically with a short trunk and several branches arising at or near the ground; crown dense, rounded. **BARK** Gray, dark gray, or brownish, smooth, or roughened with conspicuous warty lenticels. **TWIG** Greenish and usually hairy at first, turning gray or brown, sometimes becoming hairless; with circular tan lenticels. **LEAF** Alternate, simple, typically elliptic or oval, usually widest near the middle, rarely widest above the middle; tip abruptly or conspicuously tapered into a slender point; margins distinctly toothed. Upper surface dark green, sparsely hairy, often becoming hairless, the veins usually impressed and conspicuous; lower surface paler, hairless or finely hairy, more often hairy only along the veins. **FLOWER** White or greenish white, petals 5–8, sepals 5–8, hairy along the margins. Spring. **FRUIT** Round, bright red (rarely yellow) drupe, 5–7 mm diam.; stones 5 or 6, smooth on the back; matures autumn and persists well into winter, long after the leaves have fallen.

HABITAT/RANGE Native. Swamps, wet woods, seepage areas, wet stream margins, 10–700 m; Minn. east to Nfld., south to nw. Fla., west to La. and e. Tex.

SIMILAR SPECIES Smooth Winterberry has lighter green leaves, the veins on the upper surface of the leaf are not conspicuously impressed, and the sepals lack hairs along the margins.

Notes: Common Winterberry has become a popular landscape and garden plant, valued for its abundance of showy red fruits that persist well after the leaves have fallen.

SMOOTH WINTERBERRY

CATBERRY

COMMON WINTERBERRY

Smooth Winterberry

flowers

fruit

fruit

Catberry

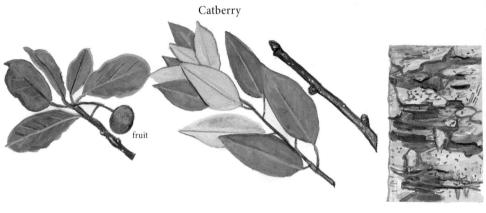

fruit

Common Winterberry

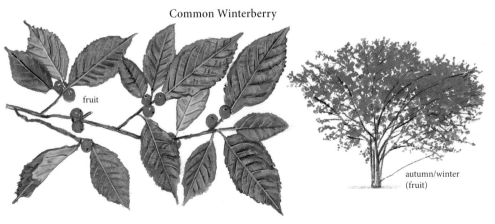

fruit

autumn/winter
(fruit)

ARALIACEAE: GINSENG FAMILY

The ginseng (or ivy) family includes about 43 genera and 1,450 species of trees, shrubs, woody vines, and a few herbs. The family is widespread and diverse in the tropics and subtropics, with fewer species in temperate regions. Devil's Walkingstick is the only tree-sized member of the family native to North America.

Plants of the family are evergreen or deciduous. Most species have secretory canals in their tissues that contain ethereal oils and resins and are aromatic when bruised or crushed. **LEAF** Usually alternate, often deeply lobed or compound, the petioles often subtended by a conspicuous stipule. **FLOWER** Unisexual or bisexual, borne in a terminal or axillary, usually conspicuous inflorescence. **FRUIT** Drupe or berry.

Several members of the family are economically important. Ginseng (*Panax* spp.) and Wild Sarsaparilla (*Aralia nudicaulis* L.) are used medicinally, and English Ivy (*Hedera helix* L.) and Octopus Tree are popular ornamentals.

OCTOPUS TREE *Schefflera actinophylla* (Endl.) Harms

A.K.A. SCHEFFLERA, UMBRELLATREE

QUICK ID An evergreen tree easily distinguished by a combination of large, palmately compound leaves and conspicuously radiating inflorescences.

Evergreen tree, 10–13 m tall, 20–35 cm diam. Erect or leaning, single trunk or multiple; crown spreading, often dense, sometimes forming an umbrella-like canopy on single-trunked trees. **BARK** Smooth, grayish green or green. **LEAF** Alternate, crowded at branch tips and sometimes appearing whorled; palmately compound, blade outline circular, to about 50 cm broad; petiole 20–45 cm long, subtended by a pair of conspicuous stipules. Leaflets 5–18, radiating from a central disk at the apex of the petiole, each 8–30 cm long, 4–12 cm broad, oblong or narrowly elliptic, margins entire. Upper surface lustrous green with a yellowish central vein; lower surface paler. **FLOWER** Red, 25 mm diam.; inflorescence a conspicuous terminal panicle of 10–20 narrow, elongated reddish to pinkish branches radiating from the apex of the stem, branches 60–120 cm long. Year-round. **FRUIT** Several-seeded purplish-red drupe, about 5 mm diam.; year-round.

HABITAT/RANGE Introduced from Australia; established and invasive in disturbed sites and tropical hammocks in s. Fla.

CASTOR ARALIA *Kalopanax septemlobus* (Thunb.) Koidz.

Deciduous tree to about 30 m tall, 1 m diam., trunk bearing numerous prickles. **LEAF** Alternate, palmately lobed, blade 9–25 cm broad, superficially similar in outline to Sweetgum (*Liquidambar styraciflua*, Altingiaceae). **FLOWER** White or yellowish green, in an inflorescence 18–25 cm long, 20–30 cm broad. **FRUIT** Spherical, slightly vertically flattened, dark blue drupe, 3–5 mm diam. **HABITAT/RANGE** Introduced from China; used ornamentally and sparsely naturalized in the East.

GERANIUM ARALIA *Polyscias guilfoylei* (W. Bull) L.H. Bailey

Evergreen shrub or small tree to about 5 m tall, lacking prickles. **LEAF** Alternate, pinnately compound (once or more), pungently aromatic when crushed. **FLOWER** Yellow, trumpet-shaped, in a compound terminal umbel to about 60 cm long. **HABITAT/RANGE** Introduced from Malaysia; cultivated for ornamental use, naturalized in Fla. Keys.

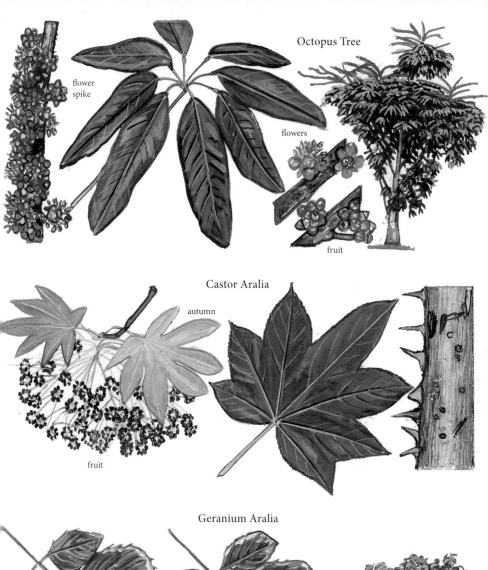

Octopus Tree

flower spike

flowers

fruit

Castor Aralia

autumn

fruit

Geranium Aralia

■ *ARALIA*: SARSAPARILLAS

A genus of about 40 species distributed primarily in China and Southeast Asia. Six species are native to North America, only one of which forms a tree. Deciduous shrubs or small trees, the trunk and leaves often armed with conspicuous prickles. **LEAF** Alternate, pinnately compound; petioles long, fused with the stipule at base. **FLOWER** Bisexual, petals 5; sepals 5, tiny; styles usually 5, sometimes 3; inflorescence a terminal or axillary, compound cyme or umbel. **FRUIT** Rounded, multistoned drupe with flattened seeds.

CHINESE ANGELICA TREE *Aralia chinensis* L.

A shrub or small tree, distinguished from native Devil's Walkingstick by the densely hairy lower surface of the leaflets. **HABITAT/RANGE** Introduced; sparingly naturalized in the East.

JAPANESE ANGELICA TREE *Aralia elata* (Miq.) Seem.

A shrub or small tree, similar to Devil's Walkingstick. **LEAF** The main lateral veins of the leaflets run directly to the teeth rather than repeatedly dividing before reaching the leaflet margin. **FLOWER** Inflorescence usually does not exceed about 40 cm long. **HABITAT/RANGE** Introduced; naturalized in the Northeast and Northwest.

DEVIL'S WALKINGSTICK *Aralia spinosa* L.

QUICKID The combination of prickly trunk, umbrella-like form, and large bipinnate or tripinnate leaves distinguishes Devil's Walkingstick.

Deciduous shrub or small tree to about 10 m tall, 12 cm diam.; main stem, branches, and sometimes the leaf axes bear sharp, stiff, straight or curved prickles. Erect, single trunk, often unbranched, or with a few ascending branches; branches and leaves spreading, clustered at or near the top of the main stem, the crown usually umbrella-like. **BARK** Brown, smooth or slightly roughened, bearing conspicuous prickles. **TWIG** Stout, prickly, often with large encircling leaf scars; terminal bud large, conical. **LEAF** Alternate, bipinnately or tripinnately compound, blade triangular, 30–120 cm long; petiole to about 30 cm long, expanded at base, partially fused with the stipule and clasping the stem. Leaflets numerous, 3–10 cm long, 1.5–8 cm broad, usually with a short stalk, usually ovate, margins toothed. Upper surface dark green; lower surface pale green, hairless or slightly hairy, veins repeatedly dividing and usually not reaching the margin. **FLOWER** White, tiny, petals and sepals 5, styles 5; inflorescence a large terminal compound panicle to about 1.2 m long, equally broad. Early summer. **FRUIT** Rounded, 5-stoned purplish, purplish-black, or lavender drupe, 5–8 mm diam.; matures autumn.

HABITAT/RANGE Native. Upland and lowland woods, margins of disturbed pinelands, thickets, shrubby bogs, 0–1,500 m; Maine south to c. Fla., west to se. Mo. and e. Tex.

SIMILAR SPECIES Two non-native tree-size species of *Aralia* are naturalized in North America: Japanese Angelica Tree and Chinese Angelica Tree, illustrated below.

DEVIL'S WALKINGSTICK

Chinese
Angelica Tree

flowers

fruit

Japanese
Angelica Tree

fruit

Japanese
Angelica
Tree

fruit

Devil's
Walkingstick

fruit

fruit

ASTERACEAE: ASTER FAMILY

The aster family (also called the Compositae, or composite family) is among the largest families of flowering plants, containing about 1,500 genera and 23,000 species distributed nearly worldwide. Nearly 420 genera and about 2,400 species occur in North America. The only tree species in the East is in the genus *Baccharis*, which contains 350–450 species (21 in North America), most of which are shrubs.

Most species of Asteraceae are herbaceous, a smaller number are woody shrubs, and even fewer are small trees. **LEAF** Alternate, simple, sometimes entire, usually coarsely and irregularly toothed. **FLOWER** The typical inflorescence, often called a "flower head," includes a central collection of tightly packed disk flowers surrounded by few to many petal-like ray or ligulate flowers, all subtended by a cuplike whorl of bracts called an involucre. The structure of the head varies among species, with some species lacking disk flowers and others lacking ray flowers; in some species the typical structure is not readily apparent. **FRUIT** Usually produced below the disk flowers; referred to colloquially as a seed, and sometimes botanically as an achene, but because the ovary is inferior it is technically a cypsela.

SALTBUSH *Baccharis halimifolia* L.
A.K.A. EASTERN BACCHARIS, GROUNDSEL TREE, SEA MYRTLE

QUICK ID The combination of toothed, thick, fan-shaped obovate leaves, the surfaces distinctly gland-dotted, and white cottony fruiting heads is distinctive.

Tardily deciduous or nearly evergreen vase-shaped shrub or small tree, to about 4 m tall, usually with multiple trunks. **LEAF** Alternate, simple, obovate, narrowed at the base, margins usually coarsely toothed; grayish green,

SALTBUSH

gland-dotted on both upper and lower surfaces. Blade 4–7 cm long, 1–4 cm broad. **FLOWER** Unisexual, the sexes borne on separate plants. Male inflorescences yellowish and compact; female flowers become whitish at maturity from the conspicuous, cottonlike tufts of bristles that provide buoyancy and aid in seed distribution.

HABITAT/RANGE Native; marshes, coastal swales, shores, from N.Y. south to Fla., west to e. Tex.; formerly perhaps confined to coastal areas, now common and weedy in disturbed sites and along roadsides well inland.

flowers

Saltbush

BETULACEAE: BIRCH FAMILY

This relatively small but well-known family includes 6 genera and 125–157 species, distributed primarily in cool temperate zones of the Northern Hemisphere. Five genera and 35 species occur in North America; 31 are native, 4 introduced. Taxonomically, the family is divided into 2 subfamilies: Betuloideae, which includes the North American alders (*Alnus*) and birches (*Betula*); and Coryloideae, with hornbeam (*Carpinus*), hazelnut (*Corylus*), and hophornbeams (*Ostrya*).

Plants of the family are monoecious, deciduous woody shrubs or trees. **BARK** Variable but usually distinctive, flaking in large plates or small platelets or smooth, varying from whitish to brown or bluish gray. **BUD** Lateral or near or at the twig tips, the scales clamlike and meeting at the edges (valvate) or overlapping. **LEAF** Alternate, simple, with margins usually double-toothed, occasionally lobed, sometimes nearly entire. **FLOWER** Typically borne in unisexual inflorescences, male and female on the same tree. Male flowers have 1–6 stamens (usually 2–4) and are usually produced in elongate, cylindric, often conspicuously dangling catkins. Female flowers typically have a single pistil and an inferior ovary of 2 or 3 parts, and are usually borne in shorter dangling or erect catkins or in tiny clusters. Individual flowers are tiny, with much-reduced sepals and petals, and are usually subtended by leaflike bracts. Catkin morphology is an aid to field identification. Most species flower in the spring, with or prior to leaf emergence, and are wind-pollinated. **FRUIT** Winged samaras, tiny nutlets (achenes), or nuts. The unique conelike fruiting structure of some species (*Alnus*, *Betula*) is also helpful for identification. Fruits are dispersed by wind, water, birds, or rodents and other small mammals.

The birch family is ancient, traceable to the upper Cretaceous (100–70 million years ago). It is commercially important for filberts and hazelnuts (*Corylus*), the production of timber and wood pulp (*Betula*, *Alnus*), land reclamation (*Alnus*), and ornamental uses (*Betula*, *Corylus*, *Carpinus*, *Ostyra*). The fruits of many species are consumed by birds.

■ *ALNUS*: ALDERS

A genus of about 25 species, 8 in North America, of which 3 are introduced. Six species occur in the East, 5 native. Deciduous shrubs or small trees, usually with several trunks. **BARK** Often waxy gray at first, usually with conspicuous horizontal orange or reddish-brown lenticels, remaining smooth or splitting with age to reveal reddish-brown inner bark. **TWIG** Green, brown, or purplish, 2-ranked or diffusely spreading, of uniform or variable length, hairy or not. **BUD** Usually stalked, sessile in some species, lateral or near the twig tip. **LEAF** Alternate, simple, thin or leathery; margins finely or coarsely toothed. **FLOWER** Male and female flowers borne in separate inflorescences on the same plant. Male flowers usually borne in conspicuous slender, elongate catkins; female flowers usually in short, inconspicuous catkins. **FRUIT** Tiny samara, concealed within an erect or pendulous, scaly, conelike fruiting structure similar in appearance to a tiny pine cone, the cone scales spreading at maturity to release the winged seeds. The woody cones persist on the plant for up to 2 years and are an important feature for distinguishing alders from birches.

Some North American *Alnus* species have been used medicinally by native peoples, others for wetland reclamation. Through interaction with bacteria, the roots fix atmospheric nitrogen, enriching the soil by helping to make nitrogen available to other plants.

HAZEL ALDER *Alnus serrulata* (Aiton) Willd.
A.K.A. SMOOTH ALDER

QUICK ID Recognized by the combination of lustrous obovate leaves with irregularly toothed margins, conspicuous clusters of dangling male catkins, and conelike fruiting structures.

Deciduous, typically a shrub, occasionally a small tree, to 10 m tall, 9 cm diam. Vase-shaped, usually with multiple trunks, rarely with a single low-branching main trunk; crown irregular, dense or open, usually with ascending branches. **BARK** Light gray or pale reddish brown, smooth. **TWIG** Smooth, with a waxy bloom and scattered raised lenticels. **LEAF** Alternate, simple, stiff, leathery, obovate, wedge-shaped at base; tip bluntly pointed, the midvein extending slightly beyond the leaf tip as a blunt point; margins irregularly toothed. Upper surface lustrous dark green, lateral veins impressed, conspicuous, parallel, each terminating at the tip of a marginal tooth; lower surface paler, veins raised. Blade 5–14 cm long, 2–8 cm broad; petiole 1–1.5 cm long, subtended at time of emergence by conspicuous stipules 6–10 mm long. **FLOWER** Male catkin 3–8.5 cm long, 5–6 mm diam., usually in dangling clusters of 3–5; female catkin stiffly erect, sticky, 5–10 mm long, about 2 mm diam., 1 or more at the base of the male catkin. Spring. **FRUIT** Tiny winged, obovate samara, borne in an egg-shaped or ellipsoid conelike fruiting structure averaging 1–2 cm long, 5–10 mm diam.; matures summer to autumn.

HABITAT/RANGE Native. Swamp borders, river swamps, stream banks, ditches, bogs, margins of sloughs, usually where water stands much of the time, 0–800 m; widespread in the East from N.S. and Que. south to n. Fla., west to e. Tex. and Okla.

SIMILAR SPECIES Seaside Alder flowers later, near the end of the growing season, and its female flowers and fruiting structures are usually solitary in the leaf axils along main stems. The leaves of Speckled Alder and European Alder have conspicuously double-toothed margins with distinct secondary teeth.

SPECKLED ALDER *Alnus incana* (L.) Moench **subsp.** *rugosa* (Du Roi) R.T. Clausen
A.K.A. TAG ALDER, SWAMP ALDER

QUICK ID Distinguished from other alders by the ovate or elliptic leaves with flat, coarsely double-toothed margins and an acute tip.

Deciduous, usually a shrub to about 9 m tall in the East, potentially to 25 m tall, 20 cm diam. in the West. Erect, single trunk or multiple; crown open, spreading. **BARK** Reddish or grayish brown, smooth, with prominent whitish lenticels. **LEAF** Alternate, simple, thick, ovate or elliptic, base wedge-shaped, tip acute or abruptly short-tapered; margins coarsely double-toothed, the teeth acute or blunt-tipped. Upper surface hairless or sparsely hairy; lower surface often whitish, hairy or not. Blade 5–10 cm long, to about 5 cm broad. **FLOWER** Male catkin 2–7 cm long, dangling in clusters of 2–4; female catkin erect, in clusters of 2–6. Spring, prior to leaf emergence. **FRUIT** Elliptic or obovate, winged samara; borne in an ovoid conelike fruiting structure, 1–2 cm long, to about 1.2 cm diam.; matures summer to early autumn.

HABITAT/RANGE Native. Stream banks, lake shores, bogs, swamps, wet roadsides; often colonizes wet areas, somewhat weedy and forming dense thickets, 0–800 m; Sask. to Nfld., south to Iowa and W.Va.

HAZEL ALDER

SPECKLED ALDER

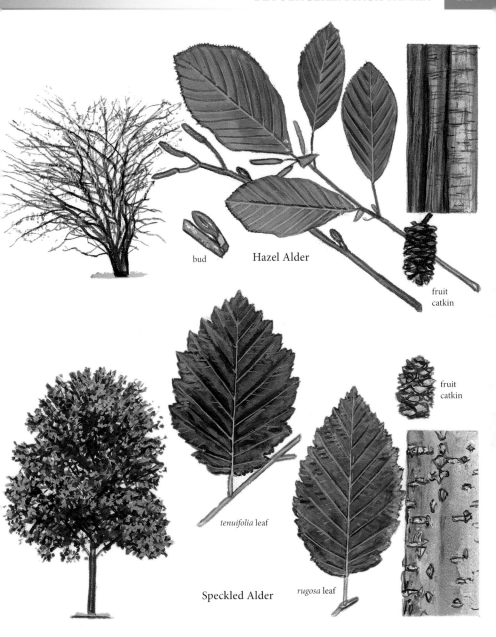

bud

Hazel Alder

fruit catkin

fruit catkin

tenuifolia leaf

Speckled Alder

rugosa leaf

SIMILAR SPECIES Two subspecies of *A. incana* occur in North America. The western subspecies (subsp. *tenuifolia* [Nutt.] Breitung) is typically arborescent at maturity, to about 12 m tall, and distinguished from the eastern subspecies (subsp. *rugosa*) by its papery leaves with blunt or rounded marginal teeth. The eastern subspecies intergrades with subsp. *tenuifolia* in the West and with Hazel Alder in the South.

SEASIDE ALDER *Alnus maritima*
(Marshall) Muhl. ex Nutt.

QUICKID Distinguished from other alders by its narrow leaves and autumn flowering.

Deciduous shrub or small tree to 10 m tall, 10–70 cm diam. Erect, single straight trunk; crown narrow, rounded. **BARK** Grayish brown or light brown, smooth. **LEAF** Alternate, simple, narrowly elliptic, oblong, or narrowly obovate, usually conspicuously longer than broad; margins toothed, the teeth not closely set. Blade 4.5–10 cm long, 2–5 cm broad. **FLOWER** Female flower produced in a solitary catkin in leaf axils; autumn.

HABITAT/RANGE Native; pond and stream margins, often in standing water, 0–100 m, restricted to 2 disjunct, widely separated locations: Del. and Md., and s. Okla.

SEASIDE ALDER

EUROPEAN ALDER *Alnus glutinosa* (L.)
Gaertn.
A.K.A. BLACK ALDER

QUICKID Distinguished from other alders by the sticky, more or less rounded leaves with a notched tip.

Deciduous tree, to 20 m tall, usually not exceeding about 50 cm diam., potentially to 100 cm diam. Erect, single trunk; crown narrowly oval or pyramidal and vertically elongate when open-grown, narrowly rounded and vertically shorter when forest-grown. **BARK** Dark brown, smooth, lustrous, becoming nearly black and shallowly fissured at maturity. **TWIG** Heavily resin-coated and sticky to touch, with obvious lenticels. **LEAF** Alternate,

simple, leathery, oval, obovate, or nearly round; base broadly wedge-shaped, tip usually with a rounded notch; margins double-toothed, the tips of the teeth sharp or rounded. Upper surface dark green; lower surface paler, hairless or sparsely hairy, especially on the veins; both surfaces resin-coated and sticky to touch, especially on young leaves. Blade 3–12 cm long, 3–11 cm broad; petiole 1–2 cm long. **FLOWER** Male catkin 8–16 cm long, in clusters of 2–5, reddish or brownish, anthers red; female catkin 3.5 mm long, reddish or brownish, in clusters of 2–5. Spring, prior to leaf emergence. **FRUIT** Narrowly winged or ridged samara, borne in an egg-shaped to nearly rounded conelike fruiting structure, 1.2–2.5 cm long, 1–1.5 cm diam.; matures summer to autumn.

HABITAT/RANGE Introduced from Europe, escaped from cultivation and established along stream banks, floodplains, and wetland borders, 0–200 m; sporadically distributed from Conn., Mass., and Pa., west to Iowa, Minn., and Ont.

SIMILAR SPECIES Hazel Alder and Speckled Alder overlap in range with European Alder; neither has rounded sticky leaves.

■ *BETULA*: BIRCHES

A genus of about 35 species, with 32 taxa (species, subspecies, or hybrids) in North America, 27 in the East, 23 native, 4 introduced.

Deciduous trees or shrubs, often with several trunks. **BARK** Dark brown to silvery white, usually smooth, often peeling into large or small plates; typically with conspicuous horizontal lenticels. **LEAF** Alternate, simple, usually ovate to triangular, varying to elliptic or nearly rounded; margins toothed or double-toothed (especially in tree forms). **FLOWER** Unisexual, male and female flowers in separate inflorescences on the same plant; male catkins slender, dangling, usually terminal on the branch; female catkins inconspicuous, mostly borne at the base of male catkins. **FRUIT** Two-winged samara, borne in a scaly, erect, semierect, or dangling, cylindric or conelike catkin. The samaras and subtending scales of dangling catkins usually fall simultaneously at maturity to leave a spindle-like central axis; samaras of erect catkins fall individually, the scales persisting.

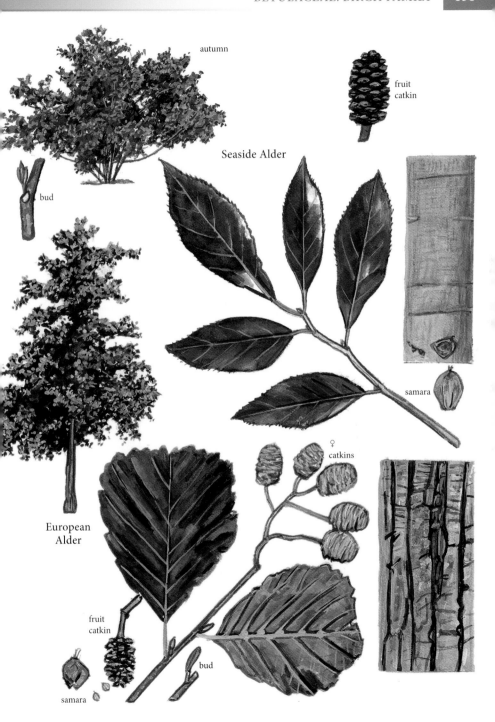

autumn

fruit
catkin

Seaside Alder

samara

bud

European
Alder

♀ catkins

fruit
catkin

bud

samara

YELLOW BIRCH *Betula alleghaniensis*
Britton

QUICKID Recognized by its combination of leaves with double-toothed margins, yellowish exfoliating bark, and wintergreen aroma of scraped twigs.

Deciduous tree to 30 m tall, 60–120 cm diam. Erect, single straight trunk; crown narrowly rounded. **BARK** Reddish brown on very young trees, soon becoming yellowish, or tan or grayish with a yellowish tint; lustrous, smooth, peeling and stripping in thin, mostly horizontal plates on young trees, developing thick, ragged brownish plates at maturity. **TWIG** Slender, densely hairy when young, becoming hairless or sparsely hairy, reddish brown, usually covered with resinous glands; exhibiting a wintergreen aroma when scratched or crushed. **LEAF** Alternate, simple, ovate tending toward oblong, usually widest and rounded at the base, tip abruptly tapered and pointed; margins coarsely double-toothed. Upper surface dull green, hairless; lower surface paler, yellowish green, hairy, especially along the veins. Blade 6–11 cm long, 3–5 cm broad; petiole 1.5–2.5 cm long, usually hairy. Turns yellow in autumn. **FLOWER** Male catkin slender, dangling, 2–7.5 cm long; female catkin erect or nearly so, 1.5–2 cm long. Spring, with leaf emergence. **FRUIT** Winged samara, borne in a scaly, sparsely to moderately hairy, erect egg-shaped fruiting structure, 1.5–3.5 cm long and resembling a tiny pine cone; matures summer to early autumn.

HABITAT/RANGE Native. Forested mountain slopes, stream banks, swampy woods, 0–2,000 m; Nfld. and Ont., south to n. Ga. and n. Ala.

SIMILAR SPECIES Sweet Birch can be distinguished from Yellow Birch by the bark seen on mature trunks, which is dark grayish brown to nearly black and not exfoliating, and by the scales of the conelike fruiting structures, which are mostly hairless.

MOUNTAIN PAPER BIRCH *Betula cordifolia* Regel
A.K.A. MOUNTAIN WHITE BIRCH, EASTERN PAPER BIRCH

QUICKID Recognized by the combination of whitish bark and leaves with a heart-shaped base, double-toothed margins, and 9 or more pairs of lateral veins.

Deciduous shrub or tree to about 25 m tall, 70 cm diam. Erect, single trunk or multiple; crown of forest-grown trees narrow, of open-grown trees broad and spreading with nearly horizontal branches. **BARK** Reddish brown when young, whitish or bronzy white at maturity and separating into thin layers that are copper-colored on the inner surface; readily peeling, giving the trunk a disheveled appearance; usually with distinctive horizontal lenticels, 2–7 cm long. **TWIG** Hairless or sparsely hairy, yellowish brown or dark brown with grayish lenticels and conspicuous warty resin glands. **LEAF** Alternate, simple, thin, pliable, ovate, the base often heart-shaped, tip abruptly tapered to a sharp point, margins coarsely double-toothed. Upper surface dull green, lateral veins in 9–12 pairs; lower surface usually sparsely to moderately hairy; both surfaces with resinous glands. Blade 6–12 cm long, 4–8 cm broad; petiole about 1 cm long. Turns yellow in autumn. **FLOWER** Male catkin 2–4 cm long, in clusters of 2–4; female catkin 1–2 cm long, usually dangling. Late spring. **FRUIT** Winged samara, borne in a dangling, scaly, cylindric fruiting structure, 3.5–5 cm long; matures summer to early autumn.

YELLOW BIRCH

MOUNTAIN PAPER BIRCH

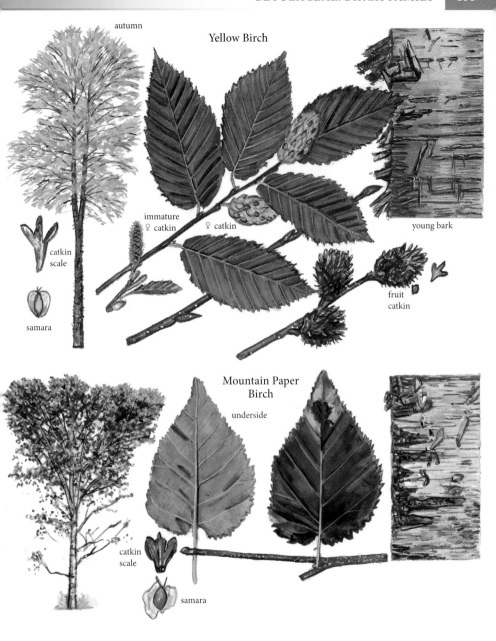

autumn

Yellow Birch

immature ♀ catkin

♀ catkin

young bark

catkin scale

samara

fruit catkin

Mountain Paper Birch

underside

catkin scale

samara

HABITAT/RANGE Native. Found in rich forests, rocky slopes, margins of depressions, often in cooler habitats, 800–2,000 m; Ont. and Nfld. south to Mich., Minn., and N.C.

SIMILAR SPECIES Considered by some to be a variety of Paper Birch, which can be distinguished from it by leaves with rounded or flattened rather than heart-shaped bases and usually fewer pairs of lateral veins.

SWEET BIRCH *Betula lenta* L.
A.K.A. CHERRY BIRCH

QUICK ID Recognized by a combination of leaves with finely and sharply toothed margins, dark brown to nearly black bark, wintergreen aroma of scraped twigs, and the scales of the conelike fruiting structures being mostly hairless.

Deciduous tree to 20 m tall, usually not exceeding about 1 m diam. Erect, single straight trunk; crown rounded. **BARK** Dark grayish brown to nearly black, smooth when young, becoming furrowed with age but not exfoliating. **TWIG** Hairless or sparsely hairy, usually covered with resinous glands, exhibiting the odor and taste of wintergreen when scratched or bruised. **LEAF** Alternate, simple, papery, ovate or somewhat oblong, base heart-shaped, tip tapering abruptly to a sharp point; margins finely and sharply toothed, sometimes obscurely double-toothed. Upper surface dark green, hairless; lower surface paler, usually lacking hairs on the blade tissue, sometimes hairy along the veins. Blade 5–15 cm long, 3–8 cm broad; petiole 1–2.5 cm long, stout, grooved. Turns yellow in autumn. **FLOWER** Male catkin reddish brown, 7–10 cm long; female catkin pale green, 1.5–2.5 m long. Late spring. **FRUIT** Winged samara, borne in a scaly, erect egg-shaped fruiting structure 2.5–3 cm long; matures late summer to autumn.

HABITAT/RANGE Native. Rich, well-drained soils of moist, cool forests, mountain slopes, northern and southern Appalachian hardwood forests, 0–1,500 m; N.Y. and Maine south to n. Ga. and n. Ala., disjunct to c. Miss.

SIMILAR SPECIES Yellow Birch can be distinguished from Sweet Birch by its yellowish exfoliating bark and by the sparsely or densely hairy scales of its conelike fruiting structures.

PAPER BIRCH *Betula papyrifera* Marshall
A.K.A. CANOE BIRCH, WHITE BIRCH

QUICK ID Recognized by the combination of creamy-white papery bark that exfoliates in thin, curly plates, orange inner bark, and leaves with double-toothed margins.

Deciduous fast-growing, shade-tolerant tree, usually 15–22 m tall, potentially to 30 m tall, 30–60 cm diam. Erect, usually a single trunk, sometimes 2 or more; crown of young trees compact, pyramidal or oval, with many slender branches; crown of mature trees broad and spreading, with few large branches. **BARK** Alternate, simple, smooth, thin, reddish brown on young trunks, becoming creamy white, exfoliating in thin, curly, horizontal plates to reveal orange inner bark; becoming dark brown or nearly black at the base of the trunk. **TWIG** Slender and dull red at first, becoming lustrous orange-brown; slightly or moderately hairy. **LEAF** Alternate, sometimes closely set in groups of 3 at the tips of short shoots on older branches; thick, stiff, ovate, with a rounded or flattened base and abruptly short-tapered tip; margins double-toothed. Upper surface dark green, 9 or fewer pairs of lateral veins; lower surface paler, sparsely to moderately hairy, covered with numerous resinous glands. Blade 5–10 cm long, 3–7 cm broad; petiole 1.5–2.5 cm long, stout, hairy or not. Turns yellow in autumn. **FLOWER** Male catkin 7–10 cm long, slender, dangling, brownish; female catkin 3–4 cm long, slender, dangling, greenish. Late spring. **FRUIT** Broadly winged samara, borne in a long-stalked, drooping fruiting structure, 3–4 cm long, the axis of which remains well into winter, long after the samaras have fallen; matures early autumn.

HABITAT/RANGE Native. Upland forest, cut-over or burned-over woodlands, lake and stream margins, swamps; tolerant of a wide range of soils and moisture regimes, varying from acidic to basic,

SWEET BIRCH

PAPER BIRCH

Sweet Birch

autumn

♀ catkin

♀ catkin

catkin scale

samara

immature ♀ catkin

♂ catkin

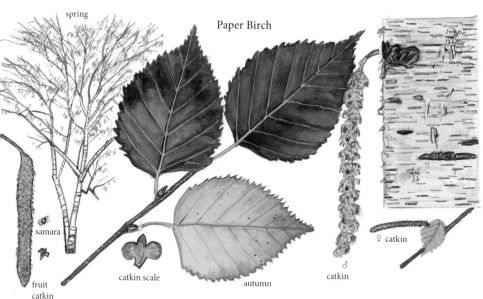

spring

Paper Birch

samara

fruit catkin

catkin scale

autumn

♀ catkin

♂ catkin

300–900 m; northernmost North America, Y.T. to Ore., east to Nfld. and Pa.; rare in n. Va.

SIMILAR SPECIES The leaves of Mountain Paper Birch are more often heart-shaped than flattened or rounded.

Notes: This is the birch used by Native Americans for the fabrication of the birch-bark canoe. The bark is high in oil content and waterproof. The papery layers are highly flammable.

GRAY BIRCH *Betula populifolia* Marshall

QUICK ID Distinguished by the triangular leaf with a flattened base, a conspicuously elongate tip, and double-toothed margins.

Deciduous tree to about 12 m tall and about 30 cm diam. Trunks usually several, curving or leaning, often clump-forming. **BARK** Reddish brown when young, becoming grayish or chalky white at maturity; smooth, tight, not exfoliating; often forming triangular black fungal patches immediately below the branches. **TWIG** Slender, dark brown, hairless to sparsely hairy, usually with numerous inconspicuous resin glands. **LEAF** Alternate, simple, thin, often pendulous, reminiscent of those of Quaking Aspen (*Populus tremuloides*, Salicaceae); triangular, with a flattened base, tip narrowly tapering to a conspicuously elongate point, margins conspicuously double-toothed. Upper surface rough, lustrous green, with 6–9 pairs of parallel lateral veins; lower surface paler, lustrous, hairless or sparsely hairy. Blade 3–10 cm long, 3–8 cm broad; petiole averaging about 2 cm long. Turns yellow or orange-yellow in autumn. **FLOWER** Male catkin solitary, cylindric, 6–10 cm long; female catkin 1–1.5 cm long. Late spring. **FRUIT** Winged samara, wings conspicuous, much broader than the body, borne in a narrow, bluntly pointed, erect or drooping fruiting structure, 1–2.5 cm long; matures summer to autumn.

HABITAT/RANGE Native. Moist or well-drained rocky or sandy forests, abandoned pastures, old fields; particularly important in natural reforestation of burned, cleared, and other disturbed sites, 100–600 m; N.B. south to Pa. and Del., sparingly to the mountains of Va. and N.C.

SIMILAR SPECIES The somewhat similar non-native European White Birch is distinguished from Gray Birch by its leaf with a wedge-shaped base and a short-tapering tip, bark peeling in long strands, and trunk that darkens to black near the base. Paper Birch often grows in association with Gray Birch and is distinguished by its peeling bark and abruptly short-tapered leaf tip. Hybrids between Gray Birch and Mountain Paper Birch are often referred to as Blue Birch; they exhibit leaves and fruiting structures similar to Gray Birch, and reddish young bark and coppery inner bark similar to Mountain Paper Birch.

RIVER BIRCH *Betula nigra* L.

QUICK ID Distinguished by the combination of peeling, curling bark, conelike fruiting structures, triangular leaves, and wetland habitat.

Deciduous, moderately to very fast-growing tree to about 35 m tall, 1 m diam.; often flowering and fruiting when of shrubby stature. Erect or leaning, often with multiple trunks; crown rounded, low-branched, and often moderately pendulous on open-grown trees; more narrowly rounded on forest-grown trees. **BARK** Pinkish tan to reddish brown or coppery brown, peeling and curling in thin horizontal plates, exposing yellowish inner bark; becomes darker with age. **TWIG** Slender, somewhat zigzag, reddish brown with tan lenticels, brittle and easily broken. **LEAF** Alternate, simple, more or less 2-ranked; papery, triangular to ovate, rarely elliptic; base broadly wedge-shaped to nearly flattened; tip bluntly pointed; margins inconspicuously double-toothed. Upper surface yellowish green or dark green, hairy at first, becoming nearly hairless; lower surface very hairy when new, eventually becoming hairy mostly along the veins. Blade 3–10 cm long, 1.5–5 cm broad; petiole 1–1.5 cm long, densely hairy, subtended at first by stipules 4–5 mm long, these falling quickly as the leaves mature. Turns dingy yellow, brownish yellow, or brown in autumn. **FLOWER** Male catkin in clusters of 1–3, dark brown, 5–7.5 cm long, developing in

GRAY BIRCH

RIVER BIRCH

Gray Birch

♀ catkin

underside

fruit catkin

catkin scale

samara

♂ catkin

River Birch

catkin scale

samara

late summer, maturing the following spring prior to the leaves or as they emerge; female catkin to about 1 cm long, green. Late spring. **FRUIT** Winged samara, typically borne in an erect conelike fruiting structure to about 3 cm long; matures early summer.

HABITAT/RANGE Native. Stream banks, river swamps, floodplains, usually where periodically inundated, 0–300 m; widespread in the East, from N.Y. and N.H. south to n. Fla., west to Wis., Iowa, Mo., Okla., and e. Tex.

SIMILAR SPECIES The bark of American Hornbeam (*Carpinus caroliniana*) is smooth, bluish gray, and does not peel. The bark of Eastern Hophornbeam (*Ostrya virginiana*) is scaly, but does not produce curly exfoliating plates.

MURRAY'S BIRCH *Betula murrayana*
B.V. Barnes & Dancik

QUICK ID Distinguished by a combination of its swampy habitat, narrowly winged samaras, reddish-brown bark, and ovate to elliptic leaves with 7–10 pairs of lateral veins and a pointed tip.

Deciduous tree 4–15 m tall, 5–20 cm diam. Erect, single trunk or multiple; crown open, rounded, with numerous slender, pendulous branches. **BARK** Thin, smooth, not exfoliating, dark red to reddish brown, lustrous, with conspicuous horizontally elongate lenticels. **TWIG** Greenish, becoming reddish brown or chestnut brown, sparsely hairy or hairless, covered with resinous glands, with the taste and aroma of wintergreen when crushed. **LEAF** Alternate, simple, sometimes in pairs on short shoots; oval or elliptic, base wedge-shaped, tip pointed, margins sharply but obscurely single- or double-toothed. Upper surface dark green; lower surface paler, sparsely hairy or hairless. Blade 5–11 cm long, 3–6 cm broad; petiole about 1.3 cm long. Turning yellow or greenish yellow in autumn. **FLOWER** Male catkin 4–7 cm long, slender, pendent; female catkin 2–3 cm long, erect. Late spring. **FRUIT** Narrowly winged samara, borne in an erect, oval fruiting structure, 2–4 cm long; matures autumn.

HABITAT/RANGE Native. Bogs and wet woods, usually in association with the Shrub Bog Birch, 0–300 m; se. Mich.

SIMILAR SPECIES This species is a purported derivative of *B.* × *purpusii* C.K. Schneid., a hybrid of Yellow Birch and Shrub Bog Birch (*B. pumila* L.), which has smooth, dark reddish-brown bark, leaves not exceeding about 5 cm long, and twigs with small, scattered glands. With the exception of its larger leaves, the features of Murray's Birch are intermediate between those of its parent species.

WATER BIRCH *Betula occidentalis* Hook.
A.K.A. WESTERN BIRCH, RIVER BIRCH, RED BIRCH, BROWN BIRCH, BLACK BIRCH

QUICK ID Recognized by its combination of purplish or brownish bark, small leaves with 4 or 5 pairs of veins, and reddish twigs.

Deciduous shrub or small tree to about 12 m tall, 10–35 cm diam. Erect, single trunk or multiple, sometimes clump-forming; crown narrowly oval, upright, the branches ascending, drooping at the tips. **BARK** Thin, smooth, with pale horizontal lenticels, dark reddish brown to bronze or purplish; not exfoliating. **TWIG** Slender, reddish brown, densely covered with resinous glands. **LEAF** Alternate, simple, thin, pendulous, ovate to more or less diamond-shaped, tip sharply or bluntly pointed, margins coarsely double-toothed. Upper surface deep green, often lustrous, resinous when young, usually with 4 or 5 pairs of lateral veins; lower surface paler, dotted with dark glands, hairy or not. Blade 4–6 cm long, 1–4.5 cm broad; petiole 5–20 mm long, hairy. **FLOWER** Male catkin 6 cm long, pendent; female catkin 2–4 cm long at maturity, pendent. Late spring. **FRUIT** Winged samara, the body about as wide as the wings, subtended by a hairy 3-lobed scale; matures autumn.

HABITAT/RANGE Native. Moist or wet areas, stream banks, lake shores, slopes, ridges, 100–3,000 m; chiefly western, entering the East to Man., Ont., and N.D.

SIMILAR SPECIES Paper Birch usually has larger leaves with 6–9 pairs of veins, and creamy-white exfoliating bark.

WATER BIRCH

MURRAY'S BIRCH

Murray's Birch

Water Birch

samara

♀ catkin

♂ catkin

catkin scale

RESIN BIRCH *Betula neoalaskana* Sarg.

QUICK ID Recognized by the combination of leaves with sharply double-toothed margins and a long-pointed tip, twigs with a dense covering of resinous glands, and mature bark pinkish to white.

Deciduous tree 6–15 m tall, 10–40 cm diam. **BARK** Dark reddish brown, becoming pinkish white to light reddish or white, peeling in papery sheets. **TWIG** Bright reddish brown, hairless, abundantly covered with resinous glands. **LEAF** Alternate, simple, oval or somewhat triangular, tip long-tapered to a fine point, margins sharply double-toothed. Upper surface lustrous, dark green, with 5–18 pairs of lateral veins; lower surface pale yellow-green, gland-dotted, hairy, especially along veins. Blade 3–8 cm long, 2–6 cm broad; petiole about 2 cm long. **FLOWER** Male catkin 2.5–4 cm long, greenish brown; female catkin cylindric, 1–3.5 cm long, drooping or spreading. Late spring. **FRUIT** Winged samara.

HABITAT/RANGE Native. Poorly drained sites, bog margins, 100–1,200 m; chiefly western, Alaska and B.C. east to Man. and Ont.

SIMILAR SPECIES The leaf tip of Paper Birch is abruptly short-tapered.

RESIN BIRCH

EUROPEAN WHITE BIRCH *Betula pendula* Roth
A.K.A. WEEPING BIRCH, SILVER BIRCH

QUICK ID The silvery-white bark that exfoliates in narrow strands and leaf blades that are sparsely hairy or hairless beneath help to distinguish this introduced birch.

Deciduous tree to about 25 m tall. Erect, with 1 or multiple trunks; crown broad, spreading, with pendulous branches. **BARK** Smooth, silvery or creamy white, exfoliating in long, horizontal strands. **TWIG** Reddish purple, hairless, with numerous resinous glands. **LEAF** Alternate, simple, ovate or triangular; base broadly wedge-shaped, rarely flattened; tip pointed; margins coarsely double-toothed. Upper surface dark green, with 5–8 pairs of lateral veins; lower surface paler, sparsely hairy or hairless, covered with numerous resinous glands. Blade 3–7 cm long, 2.5–5 cm broad; petiole 2–3 cm long. **FLOWER** Male catkin in groups of 2–4, slender, 4–9 cm long; female catkin pendulous, 2–4 cm long. Late spring. **FRUIT** Winged samara, the wings much broader than the body; matures autumn.

HABITAT/RANGE Introduced from Europe. Roadsides, bog margins, disturbed sites; established in the Northeast, in N.H., N.Y., Pa., Conn., Mass.; also Man. and Ont.

SIMILAR SPECIES Leaves of Gray Birch narrowly taper to an elongate point. Leaves of Paper Birch have an abruptly tapered tip and are lightly or densely hairy beneath.

DOWNY BIRCH *Betula pubescens* Ehrh.

QUICK ID Recognized by having leaves with finely toothed margins, grayish bark, and finely hairy grayish-brown twigs.

Deciduous shrub or tree to 20 m tall, 70 cm diam. Erect, usually single trunk; crown narrow, with ascending or spreading branches. **BARK** Smooth, dull grayish white, with dark horizontal lenticels. **TWIG** Gray-brown, finely hairy, usually with resinous glands. **LEAF** Alternate, simple, ovate, base rounded, flattened, or wedge-shaped; tip acutely pointed; margins finely or coarsely toothed. Upper surface dark green; lower surface hairy, at least along major veins. Blade 3–6 cm long, 2–6 cm broad; petiole 1–2.5 cm long, hairy. **FLOWER** Male and female catkins in separate drooping clusters, female catkin 2.5–3 cm long. **FRUIT** Winged samara, the wings slightly broader than the body, borne in a cylindric, dangling catkin; matures summer to early autumn.

HABITAT/RANGE Introduced from Europe. Moist roadsides, abandoned plantings, 0–200 m; sporadically established in the Northeast from Maine to Pa., west to Ind.

SIMILAR SPECIES European White Birch has warty and hairless twigs and silvery-white bark.

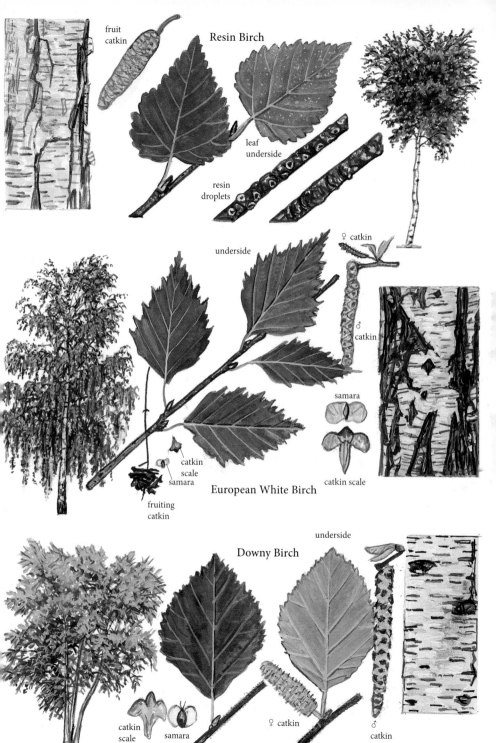

fruit
catkin

Resin Birch

leaf
underside

resin
droplets

underside

♀ catkin

♂ catkin

samara

catkin
scale

samara

catkin scale

European White Birch

fruiting
catkin

underside

Downy Birch

catkin
scale

samara

♀ catkin

♂
catkin

VIRGINIA ROUNDLEAF BIRCH *Betula uber* (Ashe) Fernald

QUICK ID Recognized by its leaves (it is the only birch in which they are rounded), the catkins and fruiting structures typical of the birch family, and wetland habitat.

Deciduous tree to 10 m tall. Erect, single trunk, often low-branching; crown narrow, with slender ascending or spreading branches. **BARK** Dark reddish brown to nearly black on young trees, becoming reddish brown; marked with elongate horizontal lenticels. **TWIG** Slender, reddish brown, with numerous lenticels; releases a wintergreen aroma when broken. **LEAF** Alternate, simple, ovate or broadly elliptic to more commonly nearly round; margins single- or double-toothed. Upper surface medium or dark green, with 2–6 pairs of lateral veins; lower surface paler, hairy or not, the hairs more prominent along the veins. Blade 2–5 cm long, 2–4 cm broad; petiole 5–10 mm long. **FLOWER** Male catkin 4–7 cm long, pendent, becoming yellow-green; female catkin erect, 2–3 cm long, light green. Spring. **FRUIT** Winged samara borne in a cylindric conelike fruiting structure, 1–1.5 cm long; matures autumn.

HABITAT/RANGE Native. Stream banks, floodplains, rich mesic forests, 500 m; very rare and known in the wild only from sw. Va.

■ *CARPINUS*: HORNBEAMS

A genus of about 25 species distributed mostly in the north temperate zone. A single species is native to North America, and another is introduced.

AMERICAN HORNBEAM *Carpinus caroliniana* Walter
A.K.A. BLUE BEECH, IRONWOOD

QUICK ID The combination of smooth, splotchy grayish bark and leaves with double-toothed margins distinguishes this species.

Deciduous tree, 8–25 m tall, 15–70 cm diam., shorter and sometimes shrubby in the North. Erect, with a single fluted and muscle-like trunk; trunk sometimes short

and low-branched; crown tight, rounded, more or less flat-topped, with fine branches and twigs that are especially evident in winter. **BARK** Bluish gray, thin, tight, mottled with lighter and darker splotches. **TWIG** Slender, pale green, and hairy at first, becoming lustrous grayish brown or reddish brown and nearly hairless; lateral buds ovoid, pressed against the twig. **LEAF** Alternate, simple, stiff, narrowly ovate or long-elliptic, base rounded, tip pointed, margins double-toothed. Upper surface dark green, veins conspicuously impressed; lower surface paler, hairy or not. Blade 3–12 cm long, 2–6 cm broad; petiole 3–7 mm long. **FLOWER** Unisexual, borne in separate catkins on the same tree; male catkin 2–4 cm long, pendent; female catkin 1–2.5 cm long. Spring. **FRUIT** Longitudinally ribbed brown nutlet, about 4 mm long, set within a conspicuous fruit cluster with several 3-lobed leaflike bracts with toothed margins, each bract subtending a small ribbed brownish nutlet; fruiting structure 2.5–12 cm long.

HABITAT/RANGE Native. Rich moist woods, moist bottoms, floodplains, stream banks, 0–200 m; widespread in the East, Maine to Fla., west to Minn. and e. Tex.

Notes: Two closely similar subspecies are recognized. The leaves of subsp. *caroliniana,* restricted mostly to the southeastern coastal plains, are predominantly shorter than 8 cm, and those of the more northerly subsp. *virginiana* (Marshall) Furlow mostly longer than 8 cm.

EUROPEAN HORNBEAM *Carpinus betulus* L.

Similar to American Hornbeam, but the 3-lobed bracts of the fruiting structure have entire margins. **HABITAT/RANGE** Introduced; cultivated in North America.

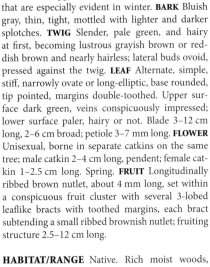

VIRGINIA ROUNDLEAF BIRCH   AMERICAN HORNBEAM

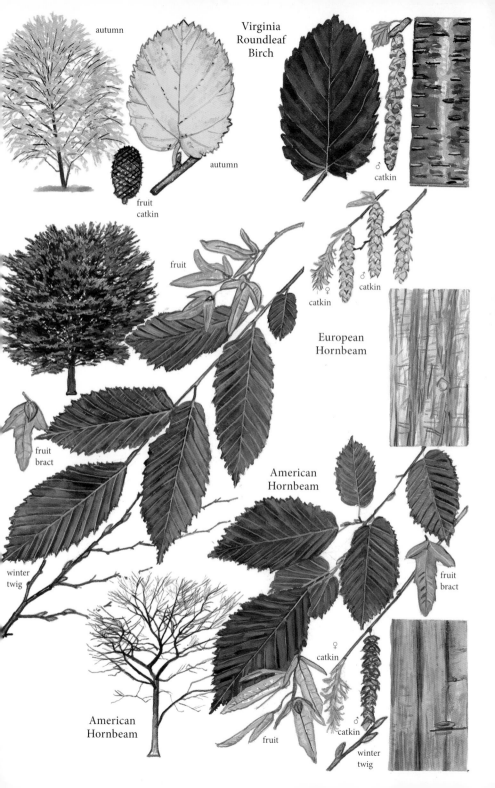

autumn

Virginia
Roundleaf
Birch

autumn

♂
catkin

fruit
catkin

fruit

♂
catkin

♀
catkin

European
Hornbeam

fruit
bract

American
Hornbeam

winter
twig

♀
catkin

American
Hornbeam

fruit

♂
catkin

fruit
bract

winter
twig

EASTERN HOPHORNBEAM *Ostrya virginiana* (Mill.) K. Koch
A.K.A. HOPHORNBEAM, IRONWOOD

QUICK ID **Easily recognized by the combination of leaves with double-toothed margins, reddish-brown shredding bark, and the hops-like fruiting cluster.**

Deciduous tree to about 22 m tall, 90 cm diam. Erect, single trunk, often low-branching, especially on young trees; crown broad, rounded or conical when open-grown, narrower and more compact when forest-grown. **BARK** Smooth and tight on very young trees, becoming reddish brown and shredding into narrow, often short, vertical strips. **TWIG** Slender, light brown, becoming lustrous reddish brown, moderately to densely hairy; lateral buds ovoid, yellowish green to greenish brown, usually diverging from the branch. **LEAF** Alternate, simple, narrowly ovate or elliptic, varying to oblong or broadly lanceolate; base rounded, heart-shaped, or wedge-shaped; tip abruptly tapered to a point; margins sharply and unevenly double-toothed. Upper surface dull yellowish green, hairy along the midvein and usually throughout; lower surface paler, sparsely to densely short-hairy throughout, especially along the veins. Blade 5–10 cm long, 2–5 cm broad; petiole 2–5 mm long. **FLOWER** Unisexual; male and female borne in separate catkins on the same tree; male catkin conspicuous, pendent, stalkless, 2–4 cm long; female catkin inconspicuous, softly silky-hairy, borne singly and erect at the tips of branchlets, 5–8 mm long. Late spring. **FRUIT** Small ovoid, ribbed nutlet, borne within a thin, papery, saclike bract; several sacs clustered together and overlapping in a hops-like fruiting cluster 4–5 cm long; matures autumn.

HABITAT/RANGE Native. Dry uplands, rich, well-drained woods, mesic slopes, 0–300 m; widespread in the East, N.B. and N.S. south to n. Fla., west to Man., Colo., and e. Tex.

SIMILAR SPECIES Potentially confused with American Hornbeam (*Carpinus caroliniana*), which is easily distinguished by the thin, tight gray bark mottled with lighter and darker splotches.

Notes: *Ostrya* is a genus of 5, mostly north temperate species, 3 native to North America, 1 in the East.

BEAKED HAZELNUT *Corylus cornuta* Marshall

QUICK ID **Recognized by the soft, bristly involucre surrounding the fruit, and distinguished from other *Corylus* by the softly hairy or hairless petiole and twigs.**

Deciduous, usually a shrub to about 2 m tall, rarely achieving the stature of a small tree to about 6 m tall. Erect-ascending, usually with several trunks or low branches from near the base. **BARK** Grayish brown, smooth. **TWIG** Slender, light brown, usually zigzag, hairless or sparsely hairy; buds 2-toned, darker at the base. **LEAF** Alternate, simple, ovate, oval, or narrowly elliptic; margins coarsely and irregularly double-toothed. Upper surface dark green, finely hairy; lower surface paler, hairy on the veins or hairless. Blade 5–12 cm long, 3–9 cm broad; petiole 5–10 mm long, hairless or moderately hairy. **FLOWER** Unisexual, male and female borne in separate catkins on the same tree; female flower ovoid, budlike, only the conspicuous red styles protruding. **FRUIT** Edible brown nut, about 12 mm diam., its tip with an elongate beak, enclosed within a bristly, husklike involucre; matures late summer.

HABITAT/RANGE Native. Roadsides, woodland margins, disturbed sites, thickets, 100–500 m; Nfld. south along the e. seaboard to n. Ala., n. Ga., and S.C., west across the upper Midwest from N.Y. to Iowa, and to Ore. and B.C.

EASTERN HOPHORNBEAM

BEAKED HAZELNUT

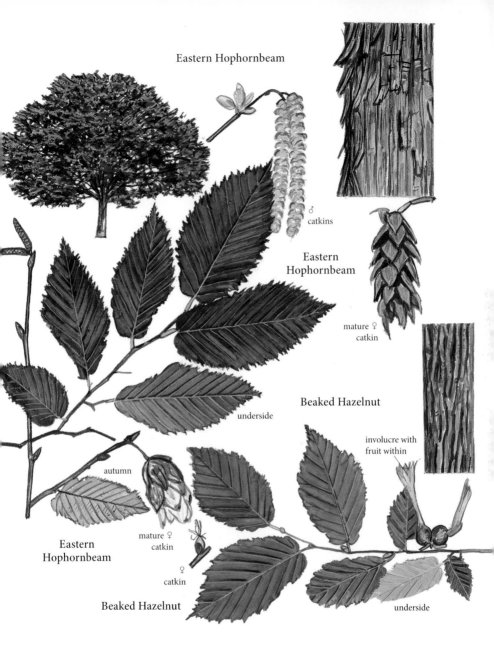

Eastern Hophornbeam

♂ catkins

Eastern
Hophornbeam

mature ♀
catkin

Beaked Hazelnut

underside

involucre with
fruit within

autumn

mature ♀
catkin

Eastern
Hophornbeam

♀
catkin

Beaked Hazelnut

underside

SIMILAR SPECIES American Hazel (*C. americana* Walter) is a widespread shrub in the East; it has bristly-hairy petioles and twigs.

Notes: Two subspecies are recognized. The western form, subsp. *californica* (A. DC.) E. Murray, is more often a small tree to about 15 m tall. It is distinguished by glandular hairs on the twigs and petioles, and leaves more or less rounded or broadly elliptic. The 2 subspecies do not overlap in range. *Corylus* is a small genus of about 15 species distributed in north temperate regions, 2 native to North America.

BIGNONIACEAE: BIGNONIA FAMILY

The bignonia family includes 104–110 genera and 800–860 species of deciduous or evergreen trees, shrubs, and high-climbing woody vines (lianas) distributed mainly in the tropics and subtropics. The family is especially diverse in South America. Numerous species are grown ornamentally in subtropical and warm temperate regions and are prized for their usually large, colorful, showy bell-shaped or tubular flowers. As many as 16 species in 13 genera occur in North America, 6 native and 10 introduced.

BARK Variable, grayish to reddish or brownish, smooth, furrowed, or scaly. **LEAF** Most members of the bignonia family have compound leaves, often opposite. **FLOWER** Bisexual, characterized by 4 fertile stamens and 1 nonfertile stamen (sometimes 2 fertile stamens and 3 nonfertile stamens), a superior ovary, and a single pistil with a 2-lobed stigma. **FRUIT** The fruits of many species are podlike structures that split along 1 side to release numerous seeds. These resemble legumes, the characteristic fruit of the bean family, which sometimes confounds identification (most beans have compound leaves as well).

■ *CATALPA*: CATALPAS

A genus of 9 species distributed in North America, the Greater Antilles, and East Asia; 3 occur in North America, 2 native. Deciduous trees, usually with a single erect trunk. **LEAF** Opposite or whorled, simple, heart-shaped, with 5 veins arising from the base of the blade; margins entire. Leaves are potentially confused with those of Princesstree (*Paulownia tomentosa*, Paulowniaceae), which is sometimes included within the Bignoniaceae. **FLOWER** Bisexual; usually white or pale yellow, purple-spotted in the throat or lower lip, petals 5, fused. **FRUIT** Narrow, elongate, many-seeded capsule that looks like a bean pod but splits along only 1 seam.

SOUTHERN CATALPA *Catalpa bignonioides* Walter

QUICK ID Recognized by the combination of large heart-shaped leaves that exhibit an offensive odor when crushed, distinctive flowers, and conspicuously elongate fruit pods that normally do not exceed about 1 cm diam.

Deciduous fast-growing tree, normally to about 15 m tall (potentially taller), to 1–1.5 m diam. Erect, single trunk; crown broad, rounded, with spreading branches. **BARK** Smooth at first, eventually becoming reddish brown and scaly. **TWIG** Pale orange or grayish, finely hairy or hairless;

lateral buds 2–5 mm long, reddish, with overlapping scales. **LEAF** Opposite or whorled, simple, thin to moderately thick; broad at heart-shaped, rounded, or nearly flattened base, tapering to a long-pointed tip; margins entire, sometimes wavy, rarely with 1 or 2 lateral lobes. Upper surface medium green or yellow-green, hairless; lower surface paler, hairy. Blade 10–30 cm long, 8–18 cm broad; petiole 7–29 cm long. **FLOWER** More or less bell-shaped, with 4 or 5 fused petals, white with conspicuous yellow and purple spots, 4–5 cm long, 3–5 cm diam.; fertile stamens 2, pistils 1; inflorescence pyramidal, produced at branch tips. Spring. **FRUIT** Slender, elongate podlike capsule, 10–40 cm long, to about 1 cm diam., splitting along one side to reveal numerous flat, winged seeds, the wings with tufts of hair at the tip; matures summer to autumn.

HABITAT/RANGE Native. Stream banks and riverbanks, margins of floodplains, 0–200 m; native to

SOUTHERN CATALPA

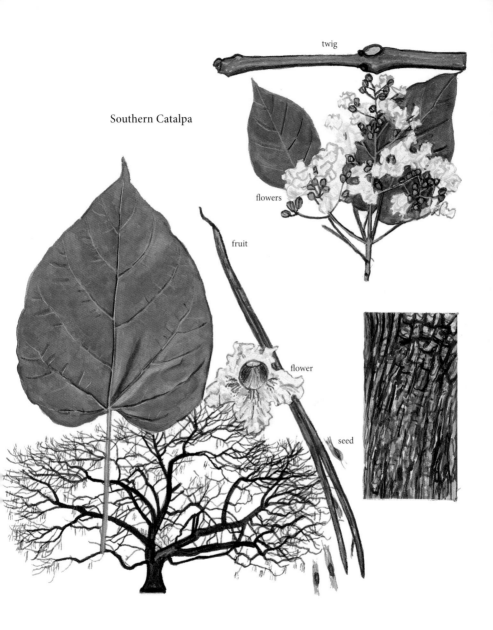

Southern Catalpa

twig

flowers

fruit

flower

seed

s. Ga., Ala., Miss., and nw. Fla.; widely planted and established throughout much of the East.

SIMILAR SPECIES Northern Catalpa can be distinguished by its larger flowers, broader fruit, and non-malodorous leaves.

CHINESE CATALPA *Catalpa ovata*
G. Don

Deciduous fast-growing tree, 15–30 m tall. Erect, single trunk; crown mostly vase-shaped on younger trees, becoming more or less irregularly oval or rounded, with low branches. **BARK** Gray to grayish-brown, narrowly and longitudinally fissured, with narrow ridges. **LEAF** Opposite, subopposite, or occasionally whorled, 3 to a node; simple; ovate; margins entire, usually 3-lobed; base heart-shaped. Light green, with 5–7 palmately arranged veins from the base; lower surface mostly hairless. Blade to about 25 cm broad and long; petiole 6–18 cm long. Turns yellow-green in autumn. **FLOWER** More or less bell-shaped, pale yellow, often with purple lines and spots in the throat, to about 25 mm long, 20 cm diam. Inflorescence an open panicle from the tips of the branches. Late spring, early summer. **FRUIT** A narrow, linear, podlike dangling capsule 20–30 cm long, 5–7 mm diam. Splitting to reveal ellipsoid seeds 6–8 mm long, to about 3 mm diam.; seeds hairy at the tips. Maturing late summer to early autumn.

HABITAT/RANGE Introduced from China. Cultivated and established from about Vt. south to Md. and W.Va., west to Ont., Minn., Nebr., and Mo. Potentially invasive.

SIMILAR SPECIES The flowers of Southern Catalpa and Northern Catalpa are white with yellow and purple markings and the lower surface of the leaf is usually hairy.

NORTHERN CATALPA *Catalpa speciosa*
(Warder) Warder ex Engelm.

QUICK ID Recognized by the combination of large, heart-shaped, non-malodorous leaves, distinctive flowers, and conspicuously elongate fruiting pod at least 1.5 cm diam.

Deciduous fast-growing tree, normally to about 30 m tall, 1 m diam. Erect, single trunk; crown narrow, rounded. **BARK** Becoming reddish brown, fissured, and scaly. **LEAF** Opposite, simple, moderately thick to nearly leathery; broad at heart-shaped or rounded base, tapering to a long-pointed tip; margins entire, rarely with 1–3 lobes. Upper surface dark green, hairless; lower surface paler, hairy. Blade 10–30 cm long, 8–18 cm broad; petiole averaging 10–16 cm long. **FLOWER** More or less bell-shaped, with 5 fused petals, white with conspicuous yellow and purple spots, 6–7 cm diam.; fertile stamens 2, pistils 1; inflorescence an open, few-flowered cluster at branch tips. Spring. **FRUIT** Slender, elongate podlike capsule, 25–60 cm long, 1.5–2 cm diam., splitting along 1 side at maturity to reveal numerous flat winged seeds, the wings with tufts of hair at the tip.

HABITAT/RANGE Native. Riverbanks and stream banks, bottomlands, roadsides, 50–200 m; probably native from s. Ill. and Ind. south to Ark. and Tenn.; widely planted and established throughout much of the East.

SIMILAR SPECIES Southern Catalpa is distinguished from Northern Catalpa by the unpleasant odor of its crushed leaves, smaller flowers, and a narrower fruit pod. Chinese Catalpa has pale yellow flowers with purple spots in the throat and roughened leaf surfaces.

NORTHERN CATALPA

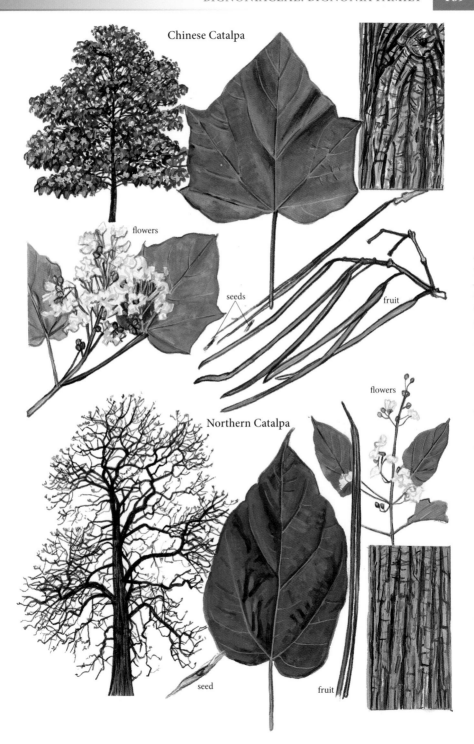

Chinese Catalpa

flowers

seeds

fruit

Northern Catalpa

flowers

seed

fruit

COMMON CALABASH TREE
Crescentia cujete L.

Evergreen tree, 6–20 m tall, to 20 cm diam. Erect, single trunk; crown spreading, irregular, open, with numerous branches. **BARK** Dark brown or gray, smooth at first, becoming scaly and fissured. **LEAF** Alternate, simple, closely clustered in bundles on short shoots, spatulate, elliptic, or oblanceolate, gradually tapering to a narrow base, tip short-pointed, margins entire. Blade 5–18 cm long, to about 5 cm broad; petiole absent or to about 1 cm, winged. **FLOWER** Strongly aromatic, bell-shaped; petals 5, the tips recurved, greenish white or greenish yellow, streaked with purple, to about 6 cm long; opens at night, falling by morning. Year-round. **FRUIT** Large capsule-like green berry with a hard "shell," to about 30 cm long, 10–20 cm diam. **HABITAT/RANGE** Introduced from tropical America; rarely seen, established in hammocks of extreme s. Fla.

BLACK CALABASH *Amphitecna latifolia* (Mill.) A.H. Gentry

QUICK ID A small evergreen tree of se. Fla., recognized by the large gourdlike fruit, short-pointed leaves, and bell-shaped flowers.

Evergreen tree, to about 6 m tall, 30 cm diam. Erect, single trunk; crown oval or irregularly rounded, dense, with numerous branches. **BARK** Rough, furrowed; inner bark light brown and slightly bitter to the taste. **TWIG** Stout, green or light gray. **LEAF** Alternate, simple, oval or obovate, usually conspicuously broadest above the middle; base wedge-shaped; tip rounded, slightly notched, or more often with a short point; margins entire. Upper surface lustrous, dark green with impressed veins, hairless; lower surface paler, with raised veins, hairless. Blade 9–20 cm long, 6–8 cm broad;

BLACK CALABASH

petiole 5–7 mm long, stout. **FLOWER** Creamy white or purplish, bell-shaped, to about 6 cm long, produced at the leaf node; fertile stamens 4, pistil 1, stigma 2-lobed. Year-round, but irregularly. **FRUIT** Capsule-like, dark green berry with a hard outer "shell," resembling a gourd, 5–12 cm long, 4–8 cm diam., with whitish pulp and numerous flattened, heart-shaped black seeds, 1 cm long. Year-round.

HABITAT/RANGE Native. Coastal hammocks, shell mounds; se. Fla.

SIMILAR SPECIES Common Calabash Tree (*Crescentia cujete*) can be distinguished by its larger fruit, clustered, less conspicuously alternate leaves, and short-pointed leaf tip.

■ *TABEBUIA*: TRUMPET-TREES

The genus *Tabebuia* includes about 100 species, none native but at least 10 cultivated in s. Fla. Species are easily recognized by their palmately compound leaves with long-stalked leaflets.

CARIBBEAN TRUMPET-TREE
Tabebuia aurea (Silva Manso) Benth. & Hook. f. ex S. Moore
A.K.A. SILVER TRUMPET, TREE OF GOLD

QUICK ID Recognized by the opposite, palmately compound leaves with long-stalked leaflets and the large trumpet-shaped yellow flowers.

Evergreen tree, 6–13 m tall. Erect, single trunk; crown narrow, open, with many irregular branches. **BARK** Gray to brownish gray, coarsely furrowed, with broad ridges at maturity. **LEAF** Opposite, palmately compound, blade 20–35 cm long and broad, petiole 10–18 cm long. Leaflets 5–7, oblong or narrowly elliptic, rounded at base and tip; leaflet blade 10–23 cm long, 2–5 cm broad; stalk 1.5–8 cm long. Upper surface silvery or grayish green; lower surface paler. **FLOWER** Trumpet-shaped, yellow, 5–9 cm long; tree very showy when in flower. Mid-spring. **FRUIT** Hard, elongate, dark brown podlike capsule to about 15 cm long, 2 cm diam.; matures summer to autumn.

HABITAT/RANGE Introduced from the West Indies, established in s. Fla.

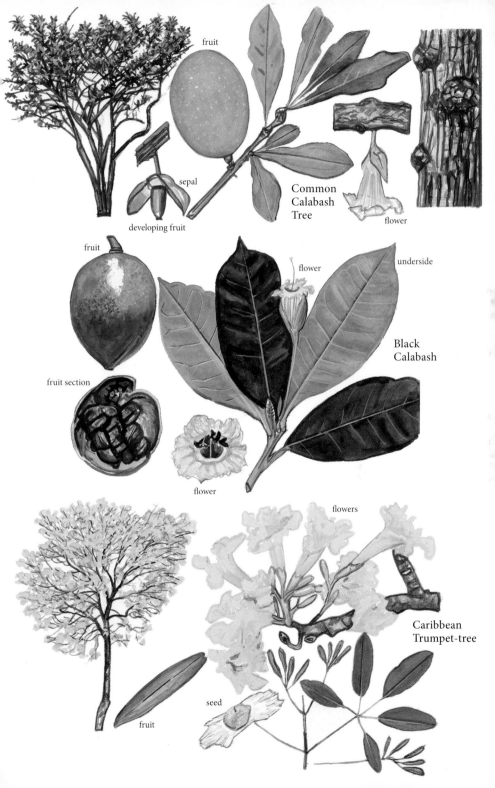

fruit

sepal

developing fruit

Common
Calabash
Tree

flower

fruit

flower

underside

Black
Calabash

fruit section

flower

flowers

Caribbean
Trumpet-tree

seed

fruit

WHITE CEDAR *Tabebuia heterophylla*
(DC.) Britton

Small to medium deciduous tree to about 13 m tall. **BARK** Smooth, becoming scaly. **LEAF** Opposite, palmately compound; blade to about 35 cm long and broad; petiole to about 25 cm long. Leaflets usually 5, sometimes fewer, oval or elliptic, rounded or blunt at the tip, margins entire; leaflet blade 5–30 cm long, 2–7 cm broad. **FLOWER** Pinkish, purplish, or whitish, bell- or funnel-shaped, 5–10 cm long; inflorescence an abundantly flowered terminal cluster. Year-round. **FRUIT** A slender, elongated, podlike capsule 7–15 cm long, about 8 mm diam., splitting to reveal numerous white-winged seeds.

HABITAT/RANGE Introduced; cultivated and naturalized in s. Fla. and Fla. Keys.

SIMILAR SPECIES Caribbean Trumpet Tree (*Tabebuia aurea*) has yellow flowers.

YELLOW TRUMPETBUSH *Tecoma stans* (L.) Juss. ex Kunth
A.K.A. YELLOW ELDER

QUICK ID Recognized by its bell-shaped, bright yellow flowers, elongate fruit pods, and pinnately compound leaves with coarsely toothed leaflets.

Evergreen or deciduous, usually a shrub, rarely a small tree 5–8 m tall. Erect, single trunk or multiple; crown of arborescent plants broad, dense, rounded. **BARK** Light gray, furrowed. **LEAF** Opposite, pinnately compound, blade 10–25 cm long, 7–13 cm broad, petiole to about 5 cm long. Leaflets 5–13, lanceolate or elliptic, margins toothed; leaflet blade 4–12 cm long, to about 4 cm broad. Upper surface dark green, veins impressed and conspicuous; lower surface paler. **FLOWER** Bright yellow, bell-shaped, about 5 cm long. Year-round. **FRUIT** Slender, elongate podlike capsule to 20 cm long, about 5 mm diam. Year-round.

HABITAT/RANGE Native to w. U.S., where it is typically a shrub; widely cultivated in Fla., but not native; most commonly a tree in Fla. Keys.

AFRICAN TULIPTREE *Spathodea campanulata* P. Beauv.

QUICK ID Easily recognized by the combination of opposite compound leaves, large, showy orange or orange-red flowers, and elongate capsule with papery brownish seeds.

Evergreen tree, 16–27 m tall, 20–45 cm diam. Erect, single main trunk, often buttressed at base; crown spreading, the branches ascending or sometimes somewhat drooping at the tips. **LEAF** Opposite or whorled, pinnately compound, with 9–17 elliptic or ovate leaflets, each 7–15 cm long. **FLOWER** Scarlet or orange-red, petals fused below, margins crinkly and golden outside, yellowish, streaked red inside; corolla about 10 cm long, bell- or cup-shaped. **FRUIT** Narrow, elongate 2-valved capsule, 15–30 cm long; splitting to reveal numerous papery seeds that are green at first but turn brown.

HABITAT/RANGE Introduced from tropical Africa; established in woodland margins and disturbed sites in s. Fla.

White Cedar

flowers

seed

fruit with seeds

Yellow Trumpetbush

flowers

fruit

African Tuliptree

fruit

flowers

fruit

seed

BLACK POUI *Jacaranda mimosifolia* D. Don

A.K.A. JACARANDA

A usually deciduous tree, 8–16 m tall, 20–30 cm diam. Erect, single trunk; crown open, spreading, more or less rounded. **BARK** Smooth, becoming roughened. **LEAF** Alternate, bipinnately compound, blade 23–45 cm long, to about 30 cm broad; petiole stout, to about 7 cm long. Leaflets numerous, 1.5 cm long. **FLOWER** Tubular, flaring at the apex, blue, to about 3.5 cm long, produced in a showy panicle, 30–45 cm long and 20 cm broad. Spring. **FRUIT** Winged, disk-like brown capsule to 6 cm long, 5 cm broad; matures spring to summer. **HABITAT/RANGE** Introduced from South America; established in s. Fla.

BORAGINACEAE: BORAGE FAMILY

The borage family is composed mostly of perennial, biennial, or annual herbs, with fewer numbers of trees, shrubs, and high-climbing woody vines. There are 134–156 genera and 2,500–2,650 species worldwide, distributed in temperate and tropical regions, with the greatest number of species centered in the Mediterranean region.

LEAF Alternate and simple. **FLOWER** Usually bisexual or functionally unisexual, with 5 petals, a tubular corolla that flares at the apex, 5 stamens, and a superior ovary. **FRUIT** In the woody species, often a drupe or drupelike, sometimes a nut.

Classification in the Boraginaceae is usually based on fruit morphology, especially with the herbaceous species, and the presence of fruit is often required for accurate identification. This is less true for the woody species, which can often be distinguished by a combination of leaves and flowers, especially in those species that occur in North America. Pollination is usually accomplished by bees, wasps, butterflies, and flies, but moths, beetles, bats, and birds have also been recorded.

◼ *BOURRERIA:* STRONGBARKS

A genus of about 50 species distributed in the warmer regions of the Americas; 3 species are native to North America, all restricted to s. Fla., including Fla. Keys. Two of our species are listed as endangered.

ROUGH STRONGBARK *Bourreria radula* (Poir.) G. Don

QUICKID A shrubby evergreen distinguished by a combination of hairy, dark green leaves, tubular white flowers, and red drupes.

Evergreen, typically a shrub, rarely a small tree to about 12 m tall, 17 cm diam. Erect or ascending, single trunk or multiple; crown dense, rounded, tips of branches often drooping. **BARK** Reddish brown, scaly. **LEAF** Alternate, simple, elliptic, margins entire. Upper surface lustrous dark green, hairy, the hairs stiff and rough to the touch; lower surface paler. Blade 2.5–6.5 cm long, 1.2–3.5 cm broad; petiole 2–7 mm long. **FLOWER** Bisexual, white, tubular, to about 11 mm long, with 5 flared petals. Year-round. **FRUIT** Rounded red drupe, 9–14 mm diam. Year-round.

HABITAT/RANGE Native. Tropical hammocks; very rare in the lower Fla. Keys.

SIMILAR SPECIES Bahama Strongbark can be distinguished from Rough Strongbark by the upper surface of the leaf being hairless rather than hairy and rough to the touch.

ROUGH STRONGBARK

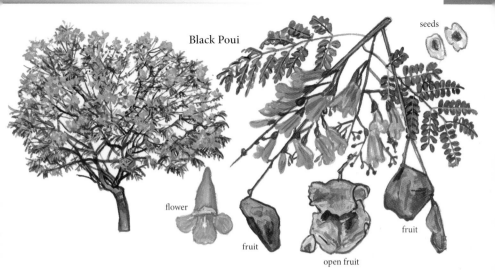

Black Poui

seeds

flower

fruit

open fruit

fruit

Smooth Strongbark

Rough Strongbark

flower

fruit

fruit

fruit

fruit

SMOOTH STRONGBARK *Bourreria cassinifolia* (A. Rich.) Griseb.

QUICK ID A strongbark distinguished by the hairy upper surface of the leaf, short petiole, and small fruit.

Evergreen shrub. Distinguished from Rough Strongbark by its very short petiole, usually not exceeding about 3 mm long, and its fruit not exceeding about 8 mm diam.

HABITAT/RANGE Native; s. Fla. and Fla. Keys.

SMOOTH STRONGBARK

BAHAMA STRONGBARK *Bourreria succulenta* Jacq.
A.K.A. BODYWOOD, STRONGBARK

QUICK ID An evergreen shrub or small tree distinguished by its funnel-shaped flowers, red fruit, and hairless leaves.

Evergreen shrub or small tree to about 12 m tall and about 20 cm diam. Erect or ascending, single trunk or multiple; crown dense. **BARK** Reddish brown. **LEAF** Alternate, simple, oval, tip abruptly pointed or often notched, margins entire. Upper surface yellow-green, hairless, with a conspicuous orange-yellow midrib; lower surface paler. Blade 6–12 cm long, 4–8 cm broad; petiole 3–15 mm long. **FLOWER** Bisexual, white, tubular or funnel-shaped, to about 1.3 cm diam.; petals 5, spreading at the apex of the corolla; produced in branched, flat-topped terminal clusters. Year-round. **FRUIT** Rounded red or orange drupe to about 12 mm diam. Year-round.

HABITAT/RANGE Native. Subtropical hammocks; s. Fla. and Fla. Keys.

BAHAMA STRONGBARK

■ *CORDIA*: CORDIAS OR MANJACKS

A genus of about 325 species distributed mostly in the American tropics. Seven species occur in North America, 5 native, 2 introduced; 4 of these occur in the East, including 2 shrubs of s. Fla. Deciduous or evergreen trees or shrubs. **LEAF** Usually alternate (rarely opposite), simple. Usually stiff, leathery, often hairy above and sometimes rough to the touch. **FLOWER** Bisexual or functionally unisexual, bell- or funnel-shaped; white, yellow, orange, or red; petals usually 5, varying 4–8; pistil with a twice-branched style, stigmas 4. **FRUIT** Usually a drupe, sometimes lacking a fleshy mesocarp, then more appropriately classed as a nut; stone with 1–4 seeds.

In addition to the species covered here, Anacahuita (*C. boissieri* A. DC.), a small tree of extreme s. Tex., is planted as far east as Corpus Christi and may be sparsely established in the East.

LARGELEAF GEIGERTREE *Cordia sebestena* L.
A.K.A. GEIGERTREE

QUICK ID Easily distinguished by the combination of the dense clusters of orange flowers and stiff, rough leaves.

Evergreen shrub or small tree, to about 9 m tall, about 12 cm diam. Erect, sometimes leaning, single trunk; crown rounded, dense. **BARK** Dark brown. **TWIG** Green, hairy. **LEAF** Alternate, simple, stiff, ovate or oval, often appearing tattered; base rounded or occasionally heart-shaped; tip pointed; margins entire or coarsely toothed near the tip. Upper surface dark green, lustrous or semi-lustrous, rough to the touch from the presence of short, stiff hairs, with 5–9 pairs of conspicuously impressed lateral veins; lower surface paler, hairy. Blade 10–25 cm long, 5–13 cm broad; petiole 1–3 cm long, stout. **FLOWER** Bisexual, orange or orange-red, corolla funnel-shaped, flaring at the apex into 5 or 6 lobes, 3–4 cm long, 3–3.5 cm diam.; stamens 5–7, about as long as the corolla, anthers 3–3.5 mm long, style about 2 cm long. Produced in dense, showy clusters year-round. **FRUIT** Hard, dry, fleshy drupe, 3–5 cm long, with 1–4 seeds, typically enclosed in the enlarged whitish or greenish-white calyx; matures mostly in summer but potentially year-round.

HABITAT/RANGE Likely introduced from the West Indies, questionably native to s. Fla.; s. Fla. and Fla. Keys.

SIMILAR SPECIES Fragrant Manjack has small, white flowers and hairless upper leaf surface.

LARGELEAF GEIGERTREE

fruit

fruit

Bahama Strongbark

flowers

flower

fruit

Largeleaf Geigertree

fruit

flowers

seed

FRAGRANT MANJACK *Cordia dichotoma* G. Forst.

QUICK ID Recognized by the combination of white flowers, pinkish fruit, and coarsely toothed leaves that are not hairy above.

Deciduous tree, 3–4 m tall (at least in North America). Erect or slightly leaning, single short, low-branching trunk; crown spreading, somewhat open. **BARK** Grayish brown, smooth, becoming finely furrowed or vertically wrinkled. **LEAF** Alternate, simple, leathery, ovate, oval, or broadly elliptic; base rounded or broadly wedge-shaped; tip blunt, bluntly pointed, or notched; margins coarsely toothed, especially toward the leaf tip. Upper surface hairless, with 4–6 pairs of conspicuous lateral veins, lower surface paler. Blade 6–15 cm long, 4–9 cm broad; petiole 3–5 cm long. **FLOWER** Bisexual and unisexual on the same plant, white, tubular, 5–6 mm long, produced in loose, leafy terminal clusters. Year-round. **FRUIT** Egg-shaped yellow, pinkish-yellow, or reddish drupe, to about 1.5 cm diam., with 1–4 seeds. Year-round.

HABITAT/RANGE Introduced from India, potentially invasive in se. Fla.

SIMILAR SPECIES Largeleaf Geigertree has larger orange to orange-red flowers, and the upper surface of the leaf is rough and hairy.

BURSERACEAE: TORCHWOOD FAMILY

The torchwood family, also sometimes called the gumbo limbo family, includes 17 genera and about 500 species of mostly tropical trees and shrubs. Only the genus *Bursera* occurs naturally in North America, and includes 1 species in the East and 2 in the West. Most members of the family have resinous sap, which has been used medicinally, for incense, and in the fabrication of an aromatic glue used in catching birds.

GUMBO LIMBO *Bursera simaruba* (L.) Sarg.
A.K.A. WEST INDIAN BIRCH

QUICK ID A tree of s. Fla., easily recognized by the combination of its compound leaves and coppery exfoliating bark.

Semideciduous tree, to about 20 m tall, 1 m diam., losing and quickly replacing its leaves in spring. Erect, single trunk; crown open, spreading, with several lateral branches. **BARK** Smooth, lustrous, reddish brown, often flaking off in curly plates; outer bark resinous, with the aroma of turpentine. **TWIG** Hairy. **LEAF** Alternate, pinnately compound, blade 15–20 cm long, 10–15 cm broad, petiole 3–8 cm long. Leaflets 3–9, ovate or oblong, strongly asymmetric, especially at base; tip acuminate, concavely tapering to a short point; margins entire; leaflet blade 6–7.5 cm long, 2–5 cm broad, stalk 3–8 mm long. Upper surface lustrous green, lower surface paler. **FLOWER** Unisexual and bisexual on the same tree; petals 3–5, creamy white or greenish; sepals 3–5; inflorescence an axillary cluster of racemes, produced at the base of new leaves and appearing terminal. Spring. **FRUIT** One-seeded ellipsoid drupe, about 1.5 cm long, 1 cm diam.; matures mostly in autumn to winter.

HABITAT/RANGE Native. Coastal and subtropical hammocks; s. peninsular Fla.

GUMBO LIMBO

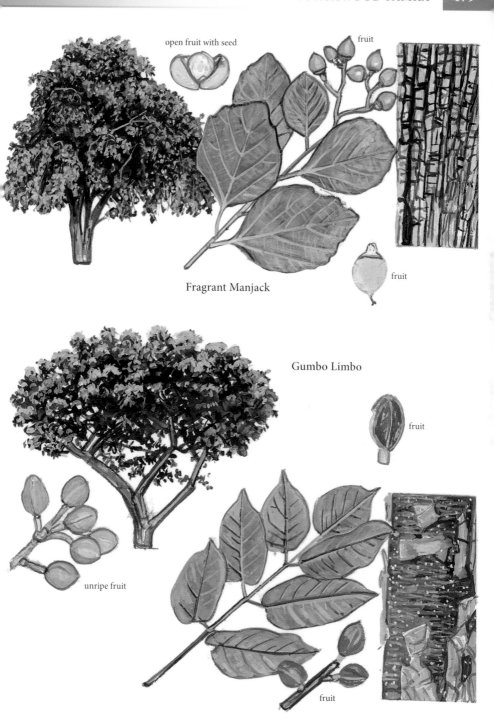

open fruit with seed

fruit

fruit

Fragrant Manjack

Gumbo Limbo

fruit

unripe fruit

fruit

CACTACEAE: CACTUS FAMILY

This is a family of mostly shrubs and subshrubs, but some species are erect and treelike. The family includes 125–130 genera and about 1,800 species worldwide; 23 arborescent species occur naturally in North America north of Mexico, 22 in the West and 1 in the East. Most species are characterized by succulent, spiny stems.

DEERING'S TREE CACTUS *Pilosocereus polygonus* (Lam.) Byles & G.D. Rowley
A.K.A. KEY TREE CACTUS, COLUMN CACTUS

QUICKID The only erect, single-trunked, tree-sized cactus to be encountered in s. Fla.

An erect, leafless, sparsely branched, cylindric cactus to about 7 m tall, 10 cm diam. Trunk succulent, with yellow spines, lower portion brown and appearing woody, upper portion green. **FLOWER** Bell-shaped, 5–6 cm long; petals 1–1.5 cm long; inner petals white, outer petals greenish; produced late afternoon and evening, wilting after sunrise. **FRUIT** Red drupe, about 5 cm long.

HABITAT/RANGE Native. Subtropical hammocks; rare and local in a few hammocks on Fla. Keys.

DEERING'S TREE CACTUS

CANELLACEAE: WILD CINNAMON FAMILY

This is a small family of about 6 genera and 15–20 species distributed primarily in the tropics, including the West Indies, Brazil, Venezuela, East Africa, and Madagascar. The single species native to North America is found in s. Fla.

Evergreen aromatic trees or prostrate shrubs. **LEAF** Alternate, simple. The leaf tissue contains oil cells, which are visible as small pellucid dots when held up to light (most easily seen with 10× magnification). These oil-bearing cells often impart a strong aroma and fiery taste to the leaf. **FLOWER** Bisexual, mostly with 5 petals, 3 persistent sepals, and 1 style. **FRUIT** Several-seeded berry.

WILD CINNAMON *Canella winterana* (L.) Gaertn.

QUICKID The combination of aromatic, obovate, dark green leaves and red flowers distinguishes Wild Cinnamon.

Evergreen shrub or small tree, 10–15 m tall, to about 20 cm diam. Erect, single trunk or multiple; crown dense, small, narrow, and more or less vertically elongate. **BARK** Grayish brown, becoming scaly and fissured at maturity; inner bark aromatic, with a cinnamon-like fragrance when crushed. **LEAF** Alternate, simple, obovate, rounded at the tip, tapering to a narrowed base; margins entire.

Upper surface dark, lustrous green, veins obscure, tissue with pellucid dots; lower surface paler. Blade 7–13 cm long, 1–5 cm broad; petiole 3–8 mm long,

WILD CINNAMON

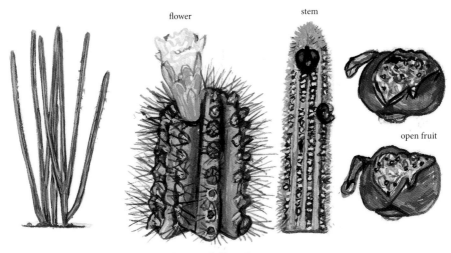

flower

stem

open fruit

Deering's Tree Cactus

Wild Cinnamon

flowers

seed

fruit

usually grooved on the upper surface. **FLOWER** Petals 5, deep red; sepals 3; pistil 1, becoming receptive before the anthers mature; stamens 10, united in a tight ring around the ovary. Midsummer. **FRUIT** Fleshy, bright red berry, about 1 cm diam.; matures autumn, often persisting into the following spring.

HABITAT/RANGE Native. Subtropical hammocks, especially coastal; southernmost Fla.

CANNABACEAE: HEMP FAMILY

The hemp family is a collection of 11 genera and about 180 species of shrubs, trees, herbs, and vines, primarily of temperate regions but extending into the tropics; 4 genera and 13 or 14 species occur in North America, 9 native; 8 occur in the East, 7 native. The hackberries (*Celtis*) and nettletrees (*Trema*) have long been included within the elm family (Ulmaceae), but recent molecular studies suggest that they should be included within Cannabaceae. Woody species of the family are characterized by their alternate, simple leaves with 3 primary veins from the base, unisexual and inconspicuous flowers, superior ovary, and drupe fruit.

Among the best-known members of the family is Marijuana (*Cannabis sativa* L.), a non-native species widely naturalized in the U.S. and Canada. *Cannabis* is a source of fiber and psychotropic drugs; another genus, *Humulus*, commonly known as hops, is used for flavoring beer; and species of *Celtis* are used ornamentally and for timber production.

■ *CELTIS*: HACKBERRIES

A genus of 70–100 species distributed nearly worldwide in all but the coldest regions, occurring from low to moderate elevations; 6 species occur in the East, one essentially a shrub.

Deciduous shrubs or trees. **BARK** Thick, gray, smooth, with raised, warty, corky protuberances often developing on older parts. **LEAF** Alternate, simple, harshly to softly hairy or hairless, the tip pointed, the base round or heart-shaped, often asymmetric; margins toothed or entire; 3 primary veins from the base of the blade, often these and sometimes smaller veins raised on the lower surface. **FLOWER** Usually functionally unisexual, a few bisexual, male and female on the same plant; tiny, greenish, borne singly or in small clusters; sepals 4 or 5, separate or slightly joined; petals absent; stamens 4 or 5, opposite the sepals; pistil 1, the ovary superior, 1-chambered. **FRUIT** Small drupe.

Hackberries and nettletrees can be distinguished from the elms (Ulmaceae), with which they were formerly grouped, by the lateral leaf veins curving toward the leaf tip as they approach the margin, flowers usually unisexual, and the drupe-like fruit with rounded seeds. Hackberries are an important source of food and cover for wildlife.

SUGARBERRY   *Celtis laevigata* Willd.
A.K.A. HACKBERRY, SOUTHERN SUGARBERRY

QUICKID Recognized by alternate, simple, evenly long-tapering leaves with margins mostly entire to irregularly toothed, and gray,

mostly smooth bark, roughened by wartlike corky outgrowths or ridges.

Deciduous tree to about 30 m tall, 1–2.4 m diam.; often flowering and fruiting when of small stature. Erect, single straight trunk; crown open, spreading, ascending to more or less rounded. **BARK** Gray, smooth at first, becoming marked with corky ridges or wartlike outgrowths, these often resulting from the excavations certain birds create to access the sweet sap and attract insects to the wounds. **TWIG** Slender, gray, hairy at first, buds very small. **LEAF** Alternate, simple, usually thin and papery, sometimes moderately thick, lanceolate or rarely ovate, often curved, moderately scythe-shaped; base rounded, flattened, or asymmetric; tip long-pointed, usually evenly long-tapered, rarely acute; margins entire, or regularly toothed near the base, or sometimes wavy or irregularly toothed throughout. Upper surface pale green, hairless, smooth or rough, veins conspicuous, curved toward the blade tip; lower surface pale green. Blade 3–15 cm long, 1.5–8 cm broad, usually well over 2 times longer than broad; petiole 5–15 mm long, slender, hairy. **FLOWER** Yellowish green, sepals 5, calyx deeply lobed, petals absent; male flowers solitary or in few-flowered clusters at the tips of elongating branches; female flowers usually in the leaf axils on developing shoots. Spring to autumn. **FRUIT** More or less rounded, 1-stoned brownish-orange or reddish drupe, 5–8 mm diam., stone nearly filling the fruit, pulp thin; matures autumn.

HABITAT/RANGE Native. Floodplains, bottomlands, rocky and alluvial soils along streams,

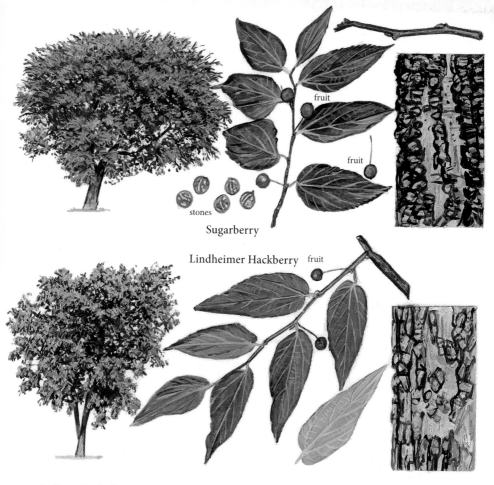

fruit

fruit

stones

Sugarberry

Lindheimer Hackberry   fruit

mixed woodlands along river bluffs, ravines, fields, disturbed sites, 0–300 m; Md. and Va. south to Fla., west to Kans., Okla., and Tex.

SIMILAR SPECIES Common Hackberry has leaves about 2 times longer than broad that are uniformly coarsely toothed from about mid-blade to the tip. See also Lindheimer Hackberry.

LINDHEIMER HACKBERRY *Celtis lindheimeri* Engelm. ex K. Koch

QUICK ID A hackberry recognized by having leaves that are densely white-hairy beneath.

Many-branched tree, to about 10 m tall and 15 cm diam. Similar to Sugarberry, it also has bark with warty outgrowths, but the leaves are densely white-hairy beneath and the fruit is usually light brown.

HABITAT/RANGE Native; endemic to brushlands and dry creek beds near San Antonio, Tex.

SUGARBERRY

LINDHEIMER HACKBERRY

COMMON HACKBERRY *Celtis occidentalis* L.
A.K.A. NORTHERN HACKBERRY, BEAVERWOOD

QUICK ID Recognized by the combination of alternate, simple leaves, 3–14 cm long, coarsely toothed from about mid-blade to the tip (margins entire toward the base of the blade), usually not exceeding about 2 times longer than broad, and the hard, rounded, 1-stoned drupe.

Deciduous tree, sometimes a shrub, to about 35 m tall, usually 25–40 cm diam., potentially to 1.5 m. Erect, single trunk; crown of open-grown trees low-branching, broad, rounded, with slender, horizontal, often zigzag branches; crown of forest-grown trees high-branching and narrower. **BARK** Light brown or silvery gray, divided into narrow ridges, often with wartlike corky outgrowths; becoming deeply furrowed on old trees. **TWIG** Slender, greenish, finely hairy, becoming lustrous reddish brown. **LEAF** Alternate, simple, thin, leathery, broadly ovate, ovate-lanceolate, or triangular; base usually strongly asymmetric; tip usually abruptly short- or long-pointed; margins entire at the base, coarsely and conspicuously toothed from about mid-blade to the tip. Upper surface light green or bluish green; lower surface paler, hairy on the veins; both surfaces usually rough to the touch. Blade 3–14 cm long, 1–9 cm broad, about 2 times longer than broad; petiole to about 2 mm long, hairy. **FLOWER** Greenish, tiny, sepals 5, petals absent; usually solitary in the axils of the upper leaves. Spring. **FRUIT** Ellipsoid or rounded, 1-stoned orange-red or dark purple drupe, 7–13 mm diam.; stone cream-colored; drupe matures autumn, shriveling and persisting through winter.

HABITAT/RANGE Native. Stream banks, floodplains, wooded hillsides, calcareous soils, often where moist, 0–1,800 m; s. Que., s. Ont., s. Man., and Maine, south to N.C., west through n. Ga. and Ala. to N.D., Wyo., Colo., Ark., n. Okla., and n. Tex.

SIMILAR SPECIES Sugarberry has evenly long-tapering, mostly lanceolate leaves well over 2 times longer than broad, and with entire or only partially and finely toothed margins.

NETLEAF HACKBERRY *Celtis reticulata* Torr.

QUICK ID Recognized by its leaves, which have 3 main veins, an asymmetric base, are harshly hairy above, and have veins forming a raised netlike pattern beneath.

Deciduous tree to 10 m tall, sometimes taller in moist situations, to about 30 cm diam., rarely larger. Trunk often crooked, low-branching; crown broad, irregular, with stout, ascending, crooked branches. **BARK** Gray and smooth when young, becoming thick, with wartlike corky protuberances. **TWIG** Red-brown, hairy, with pale lenticels, becoming gray and hairless. **LEAF** Alternate, simple, thick, ovate; base round or heart-shaped, usually asymmetric; tip narrowly sharp-pointed; margins usually entire, occasionally few-toothed. Upper surface dark green or gray-green, rough-hairy, with 3 main veins from the base; lower surface smooth or rough-hairy, with soft yellowish hairs along the veins, veins raised, conspicuously netlike. Blade usually 3–7 cm long, 2–4 cm broad; petiole 3–8 mm long. **FLOWER** Greenish, tiny, 1–4 in axils of young leaves. Late winter to spring. **FRUIT** Rounded lustrous yellowish, orange-red, red-brown, or reddish-black drupe, 7–10 mm diam.; pendent, from a slender stalk 1–1.5 cm long; matures autumn to winter.

HABITAT/RANGE Native. Canyons, riverbanks, washes, slopes, 300–2,000 m; chiefly western, extending into the East in Nebr., Okla., and Tex.

SIMILAR SPECIES Common Hackberry usually has larger, more consistently toothed leaves.

COMMON HACKBERRY

NETLEAF HACKBERRY

DWARF HACKBERRY

fruit

underside

twig

stone

Common Hackberry

leaf variation

twig

underside

fruit section

Netleaf Hackberry

fruit

DWARF HACKBERRY *Celtis tenuifolia*
Nutt.
A.K.A. GEORGIA HACKBERRY

Dwarf Hackberry

fruit

QUICK ID Recognized by the predominantly deltoid, dark dull green leaf to about 7 cm long with finely toothed margins, the upper surface sandpapery.

Shrub or small tree, to about 8 m tall and 30 cm diam., which some taxonomists include within Common Hackberry. **LEAF** Dark, dull green above, rough to the touch, and more sparingly toothed toward the tip.

HABITAT/RANGE Native; widespread across the East from Pa. and Mich., south to Fla., and west to e. Tex., Okla., and Nebr.

■ *TREMA*: NETTLETREES

A genus of about 15 species distributed in tropical and subtropical regions: Mexico, West Indies, Central and South America, Asia, and Africa; 3 species in the U.S., 2 native. Evergreen shrubs or trees, often spindly. **LEAF** Alternate, simple; ovate, lanceolate, or oblong; base rounded, often asymmetric; veins usually 3 from the leaf base; margins usually toothed. **FLOWER** Usually functionally unisexual, sometimes bisexual; whitish, pinkish, or greenish, sepals 5, petals absent. **FRUIT** Rounded, fleshy, 1-stoned drupe.

PAIN-IN-THE-BACK *Trema lamarckiana* (Schult.) Blume
A.K.A. LAMARCK'S TREMA, WEST INDIAN TREMA

QUICK ID A species of s. Fla. recognized by the oblong or lanceolate 2-ranked leaves with finely toothed margins, and the clusters of tiny flowers produced in the leaf axils.

Evergreen, usually a shrub not exceeding about 3 m tall, rarely a small tree to about 6 m tall, 25 cm diam. Erect or upright, single trunk or multiple; crown of numerous spreading, slightly zigzag branches. **BARK** Light brown, smooth or finely fissured, with numerous warty lenticels. **TWIG** Slender, green, becoming brown, usually covered with minute stiff whitish hairs. **LEAF** Alternate, simple, conspicuously 2-ranked, stiff, lanceolate, oblong, or elliptic; base rounded or slightly asymmetric; tip short-pointed; margins finely toothed. Upper surface dull, dark green, hairy, rough to the touch; lower surface pale green. Blade 2–5 cm long, not exceeding 2 cm broad; petiole 3–7 mm long, hairy. **FLOWER** Male and female on the same plant; about 2 mm diam., sepals 5, whitish or pinkish; produced in dense clusters in the leaf axils. **FRUIT** Egg-shaped reddish drupe, 2–3 mm long.

HABITAT/RANGE Native. Subtropical hammocks, shell middens; extreme s. Fla. and Fla. Keys. Treated as endangered in Fla.

SIMILAR SPECIES Florida Trema and African Elm have larger leaves.

FLORIDA TREMA *Trema micrantha* (L.) Blume
A.K.A. JAMAICAN NETTLETREE, NETTLETREE

QUICK ID Recognized by the alternate, simple, ovate or heart-shaped leaves, finely toothed, 2-ranked, and dull, dark green above, and the 1-seeded orange-red to yellow drupe.

Evergreen shrub or tree to about 12 m tall; to about 13 cm diam. in Fla., potentially to 30 cm diam. in the West Indies. Erect, single trunk; crown spreading, with horizontal branches often drooping near the tips. **BARK** Light brown, smoothish, often with rows of wartlike lenticels, sometimes becoming finely fissured. **TWIG** Green, hairy. **LEAF** Alternate, simple, conspicuously 2-ranked, long-ovate or broadly lanceolate; base rounded or heart-shaped, somewhat asymmetric; tip abruptly long-pointed; margins finely toothed. Upper surface dull, dark green above, hairy, rough; lower surface paler, softly hairy on the veins. Blade 5–10 cm long, 2.5–4.5 cm broad; petiole 5–10 mm long. **FLOWER** Male and female on the same plant; greenish yellow, sepals 5, petals absent, produced in crowded clusters, 1–2 cm diam., in the leaf axils. Potentially year-round. **FRUIT** Rounded, fleshy, 1-stoned yellow or orange drupe, 2–3 mm diam. Year-round.

HABITAT/RANGE Native. Margins and interior of subtropical hammocks, disturbed sites, pineland prairies, 0–100 m; s. peninsular Fla. and Fla. Keys.

SIMILAR SPECIES Pain-in-the-back has smaller, more or less oblong leaves. Similar to both is **African Elm** (*T. orientalis* (L.) Blume), distinguished by black fruit and leaves much longer than broad. Introduced from Asia and Africa, it is established in s. Fla., especially east of Lake Okeechobee.

PAIN-IN-THE-BACK   FLORIDA TREMA

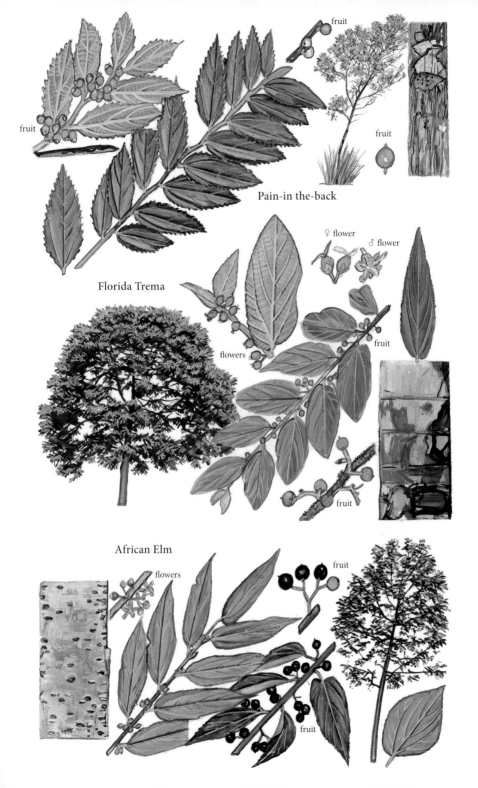

fruit

fruit

Pain-in the-back

fruit

fruit

♀ flower

♂ flower

Florida Trema

flowers

fruit

fruit

African Elm

flowers

fruit

fruit

CAPPARACEAE: CAPER FAMILY

This is a family of 16–28 genera and 480–650 species of mostly woody shrubs and trees (a few herbs and vines), distributed mainly in the tropics and warm temperate regions; 1–3 genera and 4 species occur in North America. Recent phylogenetic studies reduce the number of genera and species in this family to the lower numbers in these ranges. The flowers have stalked pistils that are raised above the receptacle and usually numerous stamens with long, conspicuous filaments.

■ *CAPPARIS*: CAPERS

A genus of about 250 species, 3 in North America. Two species are sometimes included in the genus *Quadrella*, including Jamaican Caper, treated here, and *Capparis incana* Kunth, a shrub of extreme s. Tex. Bay-leaved Caper is sometimes included within the genus *Cynophalla*.

JAMAICAN CAPER *Capparis jamaicensis* Jacq.

QUICK ID Recognized by the notched leaves with the lower surface densely covered with scales, and the fragrant nocturnal flowers with 18–30 stamens.

Evergreen shrub or small tree to about 6 m tall. **BARK** Reddish brown. **LEAF** Alternate, simple, leathery, ovate or elliptic; tip acute or concavely tapering to a short point (acuminate), often notched; margins entire. Lower surface densely covered with visible scales. Blade 5–15 cm long, 2.5–8 cm broad; petiole 6–21 mm long. **FLOWER** Bisexual, fragrant, nocturnal; petals 4, creamy white, varying to purple; sepals 4, reddish spots on the lower surface; stamens 18–30 in number, averaging about 40 mm long, filaments usually purple. **FRUIT** Narrow, long-stalked, elongate capsule, 20–38 cm long, with numerous seeds.

HABITAT/RANGE Native. Coastal hammocks and shell middens; s. peninsular Fla. and Fla. Keys.

SIMILAR SPECIES Bay-leaved Caper can be distinguished by its flowers having more numerous stamens and the lower surface of the leaf lacking scales.

BAY-LEAVED CAPER *Capparis flexuosa* (L.) L.
A.K.A. LIMBER CAPER

QUICK ID Recognized by the notched leaves and the fragrant flowers with more than 24 stamens.

Evergreen shrub or very small tree, potentially to 8 m tall, often with vinelike branches. **LEAF** Alternate, simple, leathery, elliptic to nearly linear; tip blunt or notched; margins entire. Upper surface lustrous, pale or dark green; lower surface paler. Blade 3–9 cm long, 2–5 cm broad; petiole 4–10 mm long. **FLOWER** Bisexual, fragrant, nocturnal; petals 4, white or yellowish; sepals 4; stamens usually much exceeding 24 in number, averaging 40–80 mm long, filaments usually white. **FRUIT** Elongate reddish-brown or yellowish capsule, 5–15 cm long.

HABITAT/RANGE Native. Coastal hammocks, shell middens; e. peninsular Fla. south to the Fla. Keys.

SIMILAR SPECIES Jamaican Caper is distinguished from Bay-leaved Caper by the flowers having comparatively fewer stamens and the dense covering of scales on the lower surface of the leaf.

JAMAICAN CAPER

BAY-LEAVED CAPER

Jamaican Caper

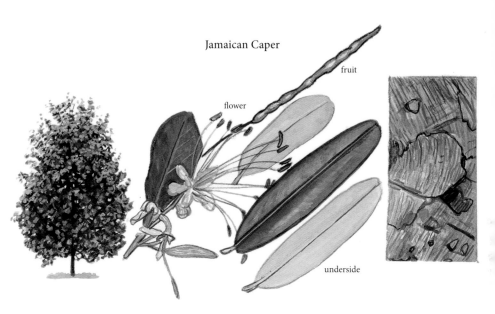

fruit

flower

underside

Bay-leaved Caper

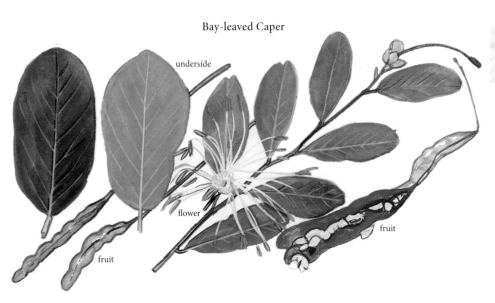

underside

flower

fruit

fruit

CASUARINACEAE: SHE-OAK FAMILY

The she-oak (or Casuarina or Beefwood) family includes 4 genera and about 90 species, distributed mostly in Southeast Asia, Malaysia, and Australia. A single genus, *Casuarina*, is represented in North America.

■ *CASUARINA*: SHE-OAKS

A genus of 17 species, 3 of which are naturalized in the s. half of Fla., native to Australia, Indonesia, and Asia, and recognized among Florida's most aggressive invasive species. All 3 species are commonly referred to as Australian-pine, a reference to the similarity of their branchlets to pine needles and the conelike shape of their small fruits. **LEAF** The true leaves are tiny and scalelike, and encircle the branchlets at regular intervals. The number of leaves per encircling whorl provides the primary means for distinguishing one species from another.

RIVER SHE-OAK *Casuarina cunninghamiana* Miq.

Evergreen tree, 15–35 m tall, with a single erect trunk, rarely suckering. **LEAF** Scalelike, 7–14 per whorl. **FLOWER** Unisexual, male and female on separate trees. **FRUIT** Conelike, usually less than 7 mm diam. **HABITAT/RANGE** Introduced; s. Fla.

GRAY SHE-OAK *Casuarina glauca* Sieber ex Spreng.
A.K.A. SUCKERING AUSTRALIAN-PINE

Evergreen tree, 8–20 m tall, often producing root suckers and forming small colonies. **LEAF** Scalelike, 10–14 per whorl. **FLOWER** Unisexual, male and female on separate trees. **FRUIT** Conelike, usually less than 1.3 cm diam. **HABITAT/RANGE** Introduced, s. Fla.

AUSTRALIAN-PINE *Casuarina equisetifolia* L.
A.K.A. HORSETAIL CASUARINA, BEACH SHE-OAK

QUICK ID Distinguished by the combination of shaggy crown, conifer-like appearance, and tiny, appressed, scalelike leaves in whorls of 6–8 encircling the needlelike branchlets.

Evergreen tree to 20 m tall, 1 m diam. Erect, single trunk; crown conical, medium green, shaggy, with distinctly drooping needlelike branchlets. **BARK** Brown or reddish brown, becoming shallowly furrowed and splitting into strips at maturity. **TWIG** Branchlet angular, green, flexible, drooping; the primary photosynthetic surface; conspicuous and often confused for pine needles. **LEAF** Tiny, scalelike, produced in whorls of 6–8 minute "teeth," each less than 1 mm long and appressed to the subtending needlelike branchlet (some experts refer to the whorl as teeth of the "leaf-sheath"). **FLOWER** Unisexual, male and female on the same tree; male flowers in more or less terminal spikes 1.2–4 cm long, female flowers in small rounded clusters on short lateral stalks. Inflorescences reddish. Predominately spring. **FRUIT** Rounded, conelike, about 1.2 cm diam., green, becoming brown, hard, "woody," the valves gaping at maturity to release a samara-like wind-dispersed seed; matures late summer to autumn.

HABITAT/RANGE Introduced in s. Fla. and naturalized from cultivation mostly in the southern peninsula, chiefly in the coastal zone, 0–50 m.

SIMILAR SPECIES River She-oak has 7–14 leaves per whorl, Gray She-oak has 10–14 leaves per whorl, and both produce male and female flowers on separate trees.

River She-oak

Gray She-oak

Australian-pine

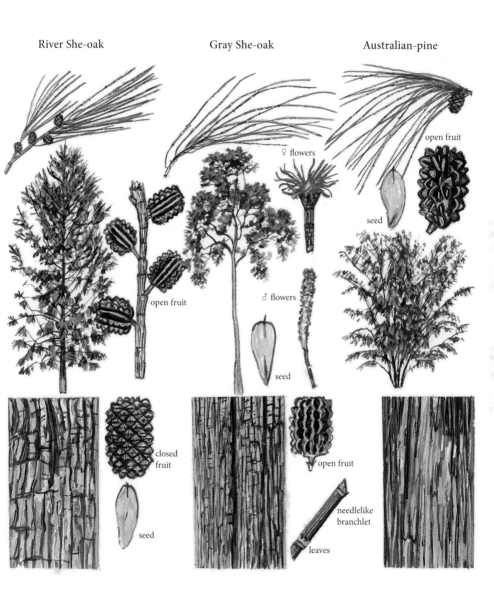

open fruit

♀ flowers

seed

open fruit

♂ flowers

seed

closed fruit

open fruit

seed

needlelike branchlet

leaves

CECROPIACEAE: CECROPIA FAMILY

This small family of 6 genera and 275 species of trees, shrubs, and woody vines is distributed mainly in tropical America. A single species is naturalized in s. Fla. Some modern taxonomists include the family within the much larger nettle family (Urticaceae), some species of which are noted for stinging hairs that irritate the skin when brushed.

TRUMPET TREE *Cecropia palmata* Willd.

QUICK ID Recognized by the deeply lobed, palmate, peltate leaves that are whitish beneath.

Deciduous or semi-evergreen fast-growing, short-lived tree to 15 m tall, 18 cm diam. Erect, single trunk; crown spreading, with few stout branches that arise high on the trunk. **BARK** Smooth, brown or brownish gray, usually ringed with narrow leaf scars at regular intervals of 5–10 cm. **LEAF** Alternate, simple, nearly circular, with 7–11 deep lobes, peltate, with the stout green petiole attached near the base of the blade. Upper surface medium or dark green, slightly roughened, hairless; lower surface with a conspicuous covering of whitish hairs. Blade 25–45 cm long, 15–40 cm broad; petiole 25–50 cm long, somewhat swollen at the base. **FLOWER** Unisexual, male and female on separate trees; male flowers tiny, crowded in several elongate, finger-like, pale yellow clusters, each cluster at the end of a stalk 5–8 cm long arising from near the base of the leaf; female flowers minute, borne in several stalkless grayish spikes that are clustered at the end of a stalk 5–8 cm long. Year-round. **FRUIT** Minute glossy whitish-yellow drupelet less than 4 mm long; produced in an elongate, narrowly cylindric fruiting structure; year-round.

HABITAT/RANGE Introduced from tropical America; escaped from cultivation and naturalized in rockland hammocks in s. Fla.; considered an invasive species in Fla.

Trumpet Tree

underside

fruiting structures

CELASTRACEAE: STAFF TREE FAMILY

This is a moderately sized family of about 98 genera and 1,221 species of trees, shrubs, and vines distributed largely in the tropics and subtropics; a few species, several of which are included here, occur in temperate regions. About 10 genera are native to North America, 5 of which include trees. The family is usually broadly circumscribed to include a large number of seemingly loosely related species but is considered by most experts to constitute a distinct evolutionary lineage.

LEAF Alternate or opposite and simple. **FLOWER** Unisexual or bisexual, usually small, often inconspicuous, radially symmetric, petals 4 or 5. **FRUIT** Drupes or capsules, the capsules typically containing several colorful seeds with a fleshy red or orange covering (aril). Pollination is effected by bees, flies, and beetles. Fruit is dispersed by birds. The family produces ornamental plants, oils, timber, dye; one species, khat, yields a narcotic alkaloid.

MAIDENBERRY *Crossopetalum rhacoma* Crantz

QUICK ID Distinguished in its s. Fla. range by the combination of mostly opposite (rarely alternate or whorled), thick, short-stalked leaves and long-stalked, bright red fruit.

A shrub, rarely a small, short-trunked tree to about 6 m tall. **LEAF** Opposite, rarely alternate or whorled, simple, obovate to spatulate, margins bluntly toothed; blade 1–4 cm long, 5–20 mm broad; petiole 1–3 mm long. **FLOWER** Green with reddish petals, to about 2 mm diam. **FRUIT** Round red or purplish-red drupe, 5–7 mm diam.

HABITAT/RANGE Native; pinelands, occasionally subtropical hammocks; southernmost Fla.

MAIDENBERRY

Maidenberry

flowers

fruit

■ *EUONYMUS*: SPINDLETREES

A genus of about 130 species distributed in Asia, Australasia, Europe, Madagascar, and North America; 13 species, 5 of them native, occur in North America; 12 species are found in the East, 4 of them native. The introduced species are often aggressive colonizers; at least one is recognized as invasive in the U.S.

Deciduous shrubs or small trees. **LEAF** Opposite, simple, often with a long petiole; margins finely toothed. **TWIG** Usually greenish and 4-angled. **FLOWER** Bisexual, small; petals 4 or 5, not fused, radially spreading; stamens inserted at the margins of a flattened, fleshy central disk. **FRUIT** Capsule, usually brightly colored, splitting to reveal several seeds enclosed within a brightly colored aril.

EASTERN WAHOO *Euonymus atropurpureus* Jacq.
A.K.A. BURNING BUSH

QUICK ID Recognized by the combination of opposite, finely toothed leaves, 4-angled green twigs, small purplish flowers, and 4-winged purplish fruit.

Deciduous shrub or small tree to about 8 m tall, 18 cm diam., often growing in small colonies of several to numerous plants. Erect, usually single trunk, often branching close to the ground; crown rounded. **BARK** Grayish green with reddish-brown streaks; smooth or slightly scaly. **TWIG** Green at first, becoming brown in the 2nd year; smooth, slightly or moderately winged or 4-angled, especially when young; usually with elongate buff-colored lenticels. **LEAF** Opposite, simple, elliptic, oval, or ovate, usually widest slightly below or at the middle; base rounded or wedge-shaped; tip abruptly or gradually tapered to an elongate point; margins finely toothed. Upper surface dull, light green, hairless; lower surface sparsely hairy. Turns red in autumn. Blade 5–12 cm

long, 2–5 cm broad; petiole 1–2 cm long. **FLOWER** About 10 mm diam.; sepals 4; petals 4, maroon or purplish, about 4 mm long, radially spreading. Spring. **FRUIT** Smooth, deeply 4-winged purplish or pinkish-purple capsule, 10–14 mm broad; seeds enclosed in a bright orange or reddish seed coat; capsule splits at maturity but barely if at all exposes the seeds until just before seed-fall; matures autumn.

HABITAT/RANGE Native. Margins of floodplains, stream banks, moist woodlands, 0–600 m; widespread throughout the East: Maine to Ont. and N.D. south to n. Fla. and e. Tex.; rare or uncommon south of the Carolinas, Tenn., Ark., and Okla.

SIMILAR SPECIES Hearts-a-bustin' has darker green leaves, whitish flowers, and round, knobby red fruit.

HEARTS-A-BUSTIN' *Euonymus americanus* L.
A.K.A. STRAWBERRY BUSH, BURSTING-HEART

QUICK ID Recognized by its opposite, sessile, finely toothed, dark green leaves; conspicuously stalked white flowers arising from the leaf axils; green stems; and knobby round reddish fruiting capsule.

Usually a multistemmed shrub, rarely achieving the form of a very small tree. Easily identified by the knobby red fruit. **LEAF** Margins finely toothed; blade to about 4 cm long, 2 cm broad; petiole 0–3 mm long. **FLOWER** Creamy white, petals 4, spreading radially. **FRUIT** Rounded, knobby capsule, splitting at maturity to reveal several red-coated seeds; matures autumn.

HABITAT/RANGE Native; moist woods, floodplains, 0–500 m, throughout much of the East, from N.Y. and Ill. southward.

EASTERN WAHOO

HEARTS-A-BUSTIN'

Eastern Wahoo

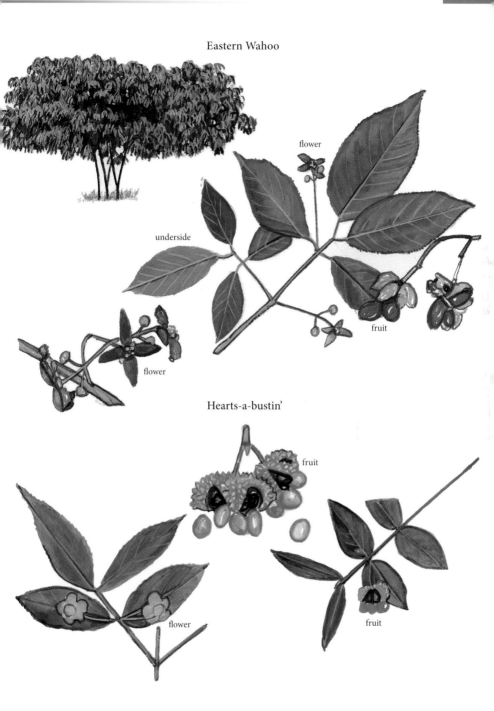

flower

underside

flower

fruit

fruit

Hearts-a-bustin'

fruit

flower

fruit

BURNINGBUSH *Euonymus alatus*
(Thunb.) Siebold

QUICK ID Recognized by the combination of winged stems, opposite leaves with short petioles, paired purplish fruits, and a bushy form.

Deciduous, usually a shrub, rarely a small tree to about 4 m tall. Usually with multiple trunks, often branching near the ground; crown broad, with ascending branches. **BARK** Light gray at first, becoming dark gray. **TWIG** Lime green, squarish, with 2 or 4 corky wings to about 5 mm broad, 1–2 mm thick. **LEAF** Opposite, simple, thin, obovate, elliptic, or oblong; base wedge-shaped or long-tapering; tip abruptly tapered to a short or extended point; margins finely and bluntly toothed. Upper surface medium or dark green, with 5–7 pairs of veins that curve forward near margin, the midvein whitish; lower surface lighter green. Turns crimson or purplish in autumn. Blade 2.5–10 cm long, 1–4 cm broad; petiole 0–4 mm long. **FLOWER** Greenish yellow, about 9 mm diam., petals 4, radially spreading. Spring. **FRUIT** Four-lobed reddish-brown or purplish capsule, 10–13 mm diam.; seed with a bright red coat; matures autumn to winter.

HABITAT/RANGE Introduced; established in shaded woodlands, roadsides; N.H. and Ont. south to Mo., Okla., and Ga.; considered an invasive species in the Southeast.

SIMILAR SPECIES Several non-native species of *Euonymus* have been introduced to the U.S., largely for ornament. In the absence of flowers or fruit, all could potentially be confused with the viburnums (Adoxaceae), which also have opposite leaves but can be distinguished by their brownish, as opposed to greenish, twigs.

WINTERBERRY EUONYMUS
Euonymus maackii Rupr.

QUICK ID Distinguished by opposite, variably shaped, long-tapering leaves, with marginal teeth numbering 6–8 per cm.

Deciduous shrub or small tree, 3–10 m tall, about 15 cm diam. Erect, single trunk or multiple. **BARK** Reddish brown, slightly roughened. **TWIG** Round

in cross section, stout, medium to light green. **LEAF** Opposite, simple, thin to slightly leathery, ovate, ovate-lanceolate, elliptic, or nearly circular; base rounded; tip abruptly tapered to an elongate point; margins finely toothed. Upper surface dark green, hairless; lower surface paler, hairless. Blade 6–11 cm long, 2–4 cm broad; petiole 1–2 cm long, slender. **FLOWER** White or greenish white, about 1 cm diam., petals 4, radially spreading. **FRUIT** Four-angled yellowish- or reddish-brown capsule, less than 1 cm long; splitting at maturity to reveal several red-coated seeds; matures autumn.

HABITAT/RANGE Introduced from Asia; sporadically established in Ill., S.C., Ga., and Fla.

SIMILAR SPECIES Some leaves are reminiscent in shape of those of Chinese Tallow (*Sapium sebiferum*, Euphorbiacae), which can be distinguished by its alternate leaves.

HAMILTON'S SPINDLETREE
Euonymus hamiltonianus (Wall.) Roxb.

QUICK ID Recognized by its opposite, comparatively long leaves, white flowers, and yellow- or red-brown 4-lobed capsule.

Deciduous shrub or small tree, 3–20 m tall, to 25 cm diam. Erect, single trunk or multiple; crown rounded. **BARK** Gray, roughened, furrowed, the furrows forming a crisscross pattern. **TWIG** Rounded in cross section, green or light green, stout. **LEAF** Opposite, simple, thin or moderately leathery, ovate or elliptic; base wedge-shaped or somewhat rounded; tip abruptly tapered to a short point; margins finely toothed, the teeth angling forward. Upper surface medium green, mid- and lateral veins distinct, yellowish green; lower surface paler. Blade 11–15 cm long, 3–7 cm broad; petiole 9–20 cm long, stout. **FLOWER** White, about 1 cm diam., petals 4, radially spreading. Spring. **FRUIT** Four-lobed yellow- or red-brown capsule, 10–13 cm diam.; seeds brown with an orange coat; matures autumn.

HABITAT/RANGE Introduced from Asia; sporadically naturalized in Pa., Mich., Ill., and Ind.

SIMILAR SPECIES The leaves of European Spindletree usually do not exceed about 9 cm long.

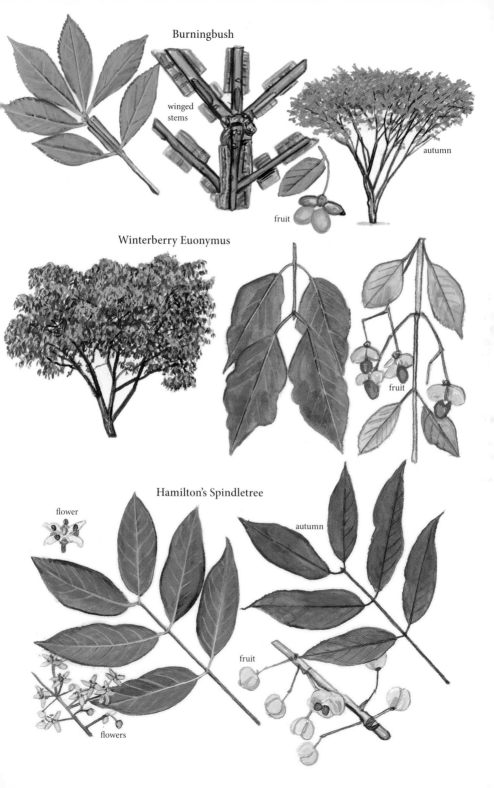

Burningbush

winged stems

fruit

autumn

Winterberry Euonymus

fruit

Hamilton's Spindletree

flower

autumn

fruit

flowers

EUROPEAN SPINDLETREE *Euonymus europaeus* L.

Deciduous shrub or small tree, 4–9 m tall, with a rounded crown. **LEAF** Margins toothed; blade 2–9 cm long, dull green above, hairless. Turns yellowish green or reddish purple in autumn. Similar in general respects to Hamilton's Spindletree, but with predominately shorter leaves. **HABITAT/ RANGE** Introduced from Europe, cultivated and naturalized in the East; Que. and Ont., sporadically south to N.C., Tenn., and n. Miss.

JAPANESE SPINDLETREE *Euonymus japonicus* Thunb.

Evergreen shrub or small tree, to 3 m tall, usually erect, with a single trunk. **LEAF** Margins toothed; blade averaging 5–10 cm long, 3–5 cm broad; petiole to about 1 cm long. **FLOWER** Green or yellowish, occasionally creamy white, nearly circular, 5–6 mm diam., petals 4; often has a vinegar-like aroma. **FRUIT** Pinkish- or red-brown capsule, 6–9 mm diam.; seeds dark brown with a red coat. **HABITAT/RANGE** Introduced from Japan; cultivated and sporadically naturalized in Ind., Va., N.C., Miss., La., and perhaps elsewhere.

WEST INDIAN FALSE BOX *Gyminda latifolia* (Sw.) Urb.
A.K.A. FALSE BOXWOOD, FALSEBOX

QUICKID Recognized by its combination of thickened, opposite, obovate leaves with a rounded and often bluntly toothed tip, and square twigs.

Evergreen shrub or small tree, to about 8 m tall, to about 15 cm diam. Erect, single trunk or multiple; crown dense, rounded. **BARK** Grayish brown

or reddish brown, flaking in thin, vertical strips. **TWIG** Four-angled, squared in cross section. **LEAF** Opposite, simple, somewhat thick, elliptic to obovate, usually widest above the middle; base often gradually tapering and more or less wedge-shaped; tip rounded, often bluntly toothed, occasionally notched; margins thickened, entire or bluntly toothed near the tip, occasionally rolled under. Surfaces light green. Blade 1.5–6 cm long, to about 3 cm broad; petiole to about 3 mm long. **FLOWER** Unisexual, male and female on separate trees; greenish white, about 4 mm diam., sepals and petals 4, stamens 4; male flowers with a vestigial, nonfunctional ovary; female flowers lacking vestigial stamens. All year except midwinter. **FRUIT** Rounded, 1- or 2-seeded, long-stalked black or dark blue drupe, 5–8 mm diam.; matures year-round.

HABITAT/RANGE Native. Subtropical hammocks; rare and restricted to a few locations in southernmost Fla. and Fla. Keys.

SIMILAR SPECIES Florida Mayten (*Maytenus phyllanthoides*) and Florida Boxwood (*Schaefferia frutescens*) have alternate leaves.

Notes: Gyminda is a genus of 3 species in tropical and subtropical America.

WEST INDIAN FALSE BOX

European Spindletree

autumn

fruit

flowers

fruit

Japanese Spindletree

flowers

fruit

underside

West Indian False Box

flowers

stem cross section

fruit

FLORIDA MAYTEN *Maytenus phyllanthoides* Benth.
A.K.A. MAYTEN, GUTTA-PERCHA MAYTEN

QUICK ID Recognized by its combination of thick, fleshy, obovate leaves that are often notched at the tip, small white flowers, and 3-angled fruit.

Evergreen shrub or small tree to about 7 m tall. Erect, single short trunk or multiple; crown dense, rounded. **BARK** Gray or gray-brown, smooth. **TWIG** Slender, pale gray. **LEAF** Alternate, simple, thick, fleshy, and leathery; oblong, elliptic, or more often obovate, usually widest above the middle, often notched near tip; base more or less acute; tip rounded, margins entire, usually wavy, minutely scaly or glandular. Upper and lower surfaces light green, dull; venation obscure. Blade 2–4 cm long, 1–2 cm broad; petiole 2–3 mm long. **FLOWER** Bisexual and unisexual on same or different trees; white, about 4 mm diam.; sepals and petals 5, stamens 5. Spring to summer. **FRUIT** Three-angled, egg-shaped capsule, 6–12 mm long; splitting into 3 parts, each containing a white seed embedded in a fleshy red aril; matures year-round.

HABITAT/RANGE Native. Coastal scrub, margins of hammocks; sw. peninsular Fla. and Fla. Keys.

SIMILAR SPECIES West Indian False Box (*Gyminda latifolia*) has opposite leaves; the leaves of Florida Boxwood (*Schaefferia frutescens*) are pointed, not notched, at the tip.

Notes: One of about 200 evergreen shrubs or trees in the genus *Maytenus*, distributed in tropical and warm temperate climes.

FLORIDA BOXWOOD *Schaefferia frutescens* Jacq.
A.K.A. YELLOWWOOD

QUICK ID Recognized by the combination of angled green young twigs, roughened grayish-white older twigs, hairless and stiff leaves with a pointed tip, and axillary fruit clusters that are present nearly year-round.

Evergreen shrub or small tree to about 10 m tall, to 13 cm diam. Erect, single trunk or multiple; vase-shaped, dense, with numerous slender, ascending branches. **BARK** Light brown or gray, slightly furrowed. **TWIG** Slender, green at first, becoming gray or whitish, sometimes with wart-like clusters of bud scales. **LEAF** Alternate, simple, leathery, stiff; elliptic or oval; base wedge-shaped; tip pointed; margins entire, often at least slightly rolled under. Upper surface lustrous yellow-green, hairless; lower surface paler, hairless. Blade 3–7 cm long, 1–2.5 cm broad; petiole 3–8 mm long. **FLOWER** Unisexual, male and female flowers borne on separate trees, white, about 3 mm diam., sepals and petals 4; male flowers with 4 stamens and a vestigial ovary; female flowers in axillary clusters, lacking vestigial stamens. Mainly spring, potentially year-round. **FRUIT** Rounded, fleshy, 1- or 2-seeded red or orange drupe, 5–8 mm diam.; matures year-round.

HABITAT/RANGE Native. Subtropical hammocks, southernmost Fla. and Fla. Keys.

SIMILAR SPECIES The leaves of Florida Mayten (*Maytenus phyllanthoides*) are notched at the tip.

Notes: *Schaefferia* is a genus of about 16 species of trees and shrubs distributed in the U.S., West Indies, Mexico, and Central and South America.

FLORIDA MAYTEN

FLORIDA BOXWOOD

Florida Mayten

Florida Boxwood

flower

flower

fruit

flower

fruit

underside

CERCIDIPHYLLACEAE: KATSURA TREE FAMILY

This small family includes a single genus with 2 species distributed in China and Japan; 1 species is cultivated for ornament in North America.

KATSURA TREE *Cercidiphyllum japonicum* Siebold & Zucc.

QUICK ID Readily identified by the opposite, heart-shaped leaves.

Deciduous tree, 10–20 m tall. Erect, single main trunk; crown pyramidal or ovoid, to about 10 m broad; sweetly aromatic in autumn. **BARK** Brown, shaggy, peeling and curling in thin strips. **TWIG** Hairless. **LEAF** Opposite, rarely sub-opposite or alternate on new shoots, simple; obovate, broadly elliptic, or nearly rounded, base heart-shaped, margins bluntly toothed. Upper surface reddish purple when new, green at maturity, hairless, venation palmate, prominent; lower surface hairless or hairy in the vein axils. Turns brilliant burnt orange in autumn. Blade of typical leaves 3.7–9 cm long, 5–8.3 cm broad (blades on leaves of elongate lateral shoots of the main branches often smaller); petiole 1.4–4.7 cm long. **FLOWER** Unisexual, produced on separate trees, green, male flowers with pink anthers 3–4 mm long, female flowers with 1 red stigma. Spring. **FRUIT** Curved brown or black pod (follicle), 10–18 mm long, 2–3 mm broad, borne in clusters.

HABITAT/RANGE Introduced from China and Japan; cultivated, naturalized in N.Y., Mass., Pa., and Ohio.

SIMILAR SPECIES The leaves of Eastern Red-bud (*Cercis canadensis*, Fabaceae) and several of the basswoods (*Tilia*, Malvaceae) are similar but are alternate rather than opposite.

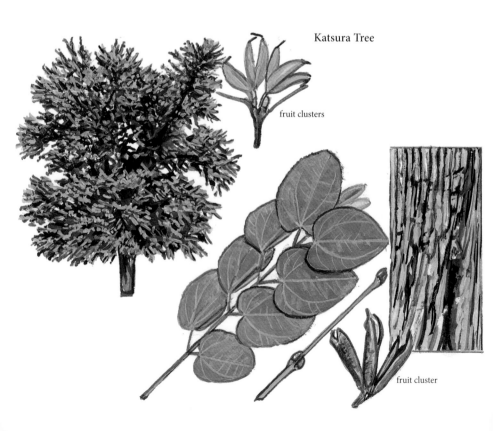

Katsura Tree

fruit clusters

fruit cluster

CHRYSOBALANACEAE: COCO PLUM FAMILY

This family includes 17 genera and about 460 species, distributed largely in tropical regions. Two genera, each represented by a single species, occur in North America, only 1 of them a tree. Gopher Apple (*Licania michauxii* Prance) is a low-growing shrub of the Southeast.

COCO PLUM *Chrysobalanus icaco* L.

QUICK ID The combination of 2-ranked circular leaves that appear to be borne along one side of the branch and the typically purple, fleshy fruit is diagnostic.

Evergreen large shrub or small bushy tree to about 5 m tall, 7–15 cm diam. Erect or more often leaning, usually with a single short trunk and numerous low branches; crown rounded, dense. **BARK** Thin, brownish. **TWIG** Reddish brown, hairless. **LEAF** Alternate, simple, thick, leathery; broadly elliptic, oval, obovate, or nearly circular; tip sometimes notched; margins entire. Upper surface dark lustrous green, hairless; lower surface duller, usually hairless. Blade 2–8 cm long, 1–6 cm broad; petiole to about 5 mm long, thickened, usually twisted so all leaves are oriented to same side of branch. **FLOWER** Bisexual, white, more or less bell-shaped, 5–7 mm long, petals and sepals 4 or 5, stamens about 20, style 1. Year-round. **FRUIT** Rounded or oval, drupelike, hairless, sweet-tasting, pulpy, with a dark purple, yellowish, or whitish skin, 1–4 cm diam., with a single bony seed; matures year-round.

HABITAT/RANGE Native. Hammocks, beaches, dunes, margins of cypress-dominated wetlands, usually near the coast, 0–10 m; s. Fla. and American tropics.

Notes: Coco Plum's seeds contain high levels of oils and are readily consumed by wildlife. In its native regions, the fruit has also been widely used as human food and is often canned, and reports suggest that the oily seeds have been strung on sticks and burned like candles.

COCO PLUM

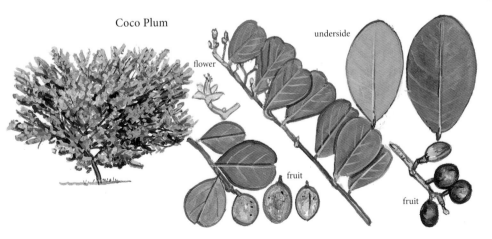

Coco Plum

flower

underside

fruit

fruit

CLETHRACEAE: WITCH ALDER FAMILY

A small family of 1 or 2 genera and up to about 75 species, 2 or 3 of which occur in North America. The family is closely related to heaths (Ericaceae) and titis (Cyrillaceae). Some experts include the tropical genus *Purdiaea*, distributed mostly in Cuba, within this family; others include only *Clethra*, assigning *Purdiaea* to Cyrillaceae.

MOUNTAIN SWEETPEPPERBUSH
Clethra acuminata Michx.
A.K.A. MOUNTAIN PEPPERBUSH, CINNAMON CLETHRA

QUICK ID Recognized by the combination of coarsely toothed, acuminate leaves, the elongate raceme of white flowers, and shredding and peeling bark.

Deciduous shrub, rarely a small tree to about 6 m tall. Erect, single short trunk or multiple. **BARK** Brownish or reddish brown, peeling and shredding into thin plates. **TWIG** Light brown or light reddish brown, with patches of star-shaped hairs and a single, prominent internodal ridge; terminal bud 3–6 mm long, yellowish, silky, larger than the lateral buds. **LEAF** Alternate, simple, often crowded near the tip of the twig, elliptic or lanceolate, tip acuminate (concavely tapered to an abrupt point); margins finely and distinctly toothed. Upper surface dark green, hairless; lower surface hairless or with a few star-shaped hairs. Blade 8–20 cm long, 5–9 cm broad; petiole 2–4.5 cm long. **FLOWER** Bisexual, white, 6–8 mm diam., petals and sepals 5; borne in a densely hairy, narrow, elongate raceme 8–20 cm long. Summer. **FRUIT** Ovoid 3-parted capsule about 5 mm diam.; splits at maturity to release numerous seeds; matures autumn.

HABITAT/RANGE Native. Moist mountain forests, 500–1,400 m; Pa. south to S.C., Ga., and Ala.

SIMILAR SPECIES 1 or 2 other species of *Clethra* occur in the Southeast, both of which are shrubs of the coastal plains. **Coastal Sweetpepperbush** (*C. alnifolia* L.) is distributed from N.S. south to Fla. and west to e. Tex. It occurs in pine–palmetto flatwoods, along swamp margins, in Atlantic White Cedar wetlands, and in dry woodlands, usually below 200 m, and is distinguished from Mountain Sweetpepperbush by distribution and habitat. Some experts recognize *C. tomentosa* Lam. as distinct from *C. alnifolia*, distinguishing it by its very hairy inflorescence.

MOUNTAIN SWEETPEPPERBUSH

COASTAL SWEETPEPPERBUSH

Mountain Sweetpepperbush

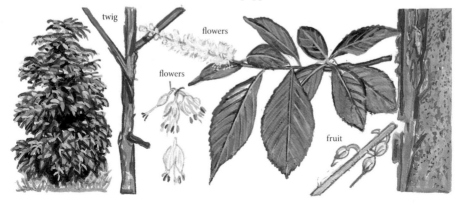

CLUSIACEAE: GARCINIA FAMILY

As treated here, the garcinia family includes about 36 genera and more than 1,600 species, only 3 of which occur in North America. Some experts treat the St.-John's-wort family (Hypericaceae; 9 genera, 560 species) and calophyllum family (Calophyllaceae; 13 genera, 460 species) as distinct, segregating them from a smaller garcinia family of about 14 genera and 595 species. Members of the broadly construed garcinia family are noted for the pockets of colored exudate (*Calophyllum*, *Clusia*) or resinous sap (*Hypericum*) within the leaf tissue.

SANTA MARIA *Calophyllum antillanum*
Britton
A.K.A. GALBA, ANTILLES CALOPHYLLUM

QUICK ID Recognized by its combination of oval leaves with numerous closely set parallel veins and deeply pitted, diamond-patterned bark.

Evergreen, salt-tolerant tree to about 12 m tall and 75 cm diam. in Fla., potentially taller in its native range. Erect, usually single trunk, sometimes with multiple low branches; crown dense, rounded, usually with large spreading branches. **BARK** Dark gray or nearly black; deeply ridged and furrowed, the ridges often crisscrossing and forming a diamond pattern. **LEAF** Opposite, simple, thick, stiff, elliptic or oval; tip rounded or notched; margins entire. Upper surface lustrous dark green, veins numerous, closely set, parallel, terminating at the margin; lower surface dull green. Blade 5–8 cm long, 3–6 cm broad; petiole 5–15 mm long. **FLOWER** Unisexual, about 2.5 cm diam., to 13 cm long, fragrant; corolla narrowly tubular below, flaring at the apex into 4 white lobes; male flowers with 40–50 stamens. **FRUIT** Rounded drupe, 2–2.5 cm long; yellowish or brown at maturity.

HABITAT/RANGE Introduced from the West Indies, cultivated and naturalized in s. Fla.; invades mangrove forests and inland hammocks.

SIMILAR SPECIES Alexandrian Laurel (*C. inophyllum* L.) is also naturalized in s. Fla. but is distinguished by its bisexual flowers with 200–300 stamens and fruit 2.5–4 cm long.

Santa Maria

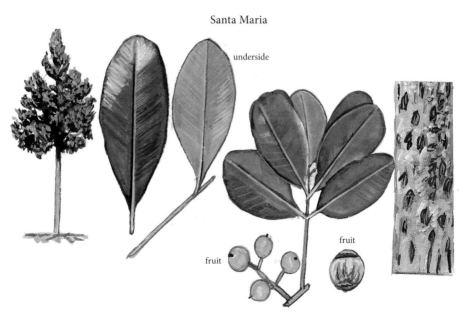

underside

fruit

fruit

fruit

PITCH APPLE *Clusia rosea* Jacq.
A.K.A. AUTOGRAPH TREE, BALSAM APPLE, SCOTCH ATTORNEY

QUICK ID Easily recognized in s. Fla. by the large, opposite, stiff, obovate leaves.

Evergreen shrub or tree to about 18 m tall, often much shorter, to about 20 cm diam. Erect, single trunk; crown dense, rounded. **BARK** Gray, smooth or slightly roughened. **LEAF** Opposite, simple, thick, very stiff; obovate and paddle-shaped; tip rounded, flat, or notched; margins entire, slightly rolled under. Upper surface dull grayish green; lower surface yellow-green. Blade 7–18 cm long, 5–13 cm broad; petiole about 1 cm long, grooved, pitted at base. **FLOWER** Bisexual, borne in short-stalked clusters of 1–3; petals 6–12, lustrous white, tinged with pink around a yellow center; sepals 6, circular, 1–1.5 cm broad. **FRUIT** Fleshy, rounded, 5–6 cm diam., brown at maturity, splitting to expose large red seeds.

HABITAT/RANGE Considered native to s. Fla. by some observers, non-native by others; hammocks, disturbed sites, widely cultivated but uncommon in natural areas.

SIMILAR SPECIES Seven-year Apple (*Genipa clusiifolia*, Rubiaceae) has similarly shaped leaves but the upper surface is dark, lustrous green.

PITCH APPLE

SPONGEBARK HYPERICUM
Hypericum chapmanii W.P. Adams
A.K.A. APALACHICOLA ST.-JOHN'S-WORT

QUICK ID The thick spongy bark of Spongebark Hypericum is diagnostic among members of the St.-John's-worts.

Evergreen, low shrub or small tree to about 4 m tall, 5–15 cm diam. Erect, single trunk; crown spreading, vertically flattened. **BARK** Brown or reddish brown, flaking and peeling in strips and plates; thick, spongy, 3–4 cm thick on old trunks and easily compressed when squeezed. **LEAF** Opposite or whorled, angling upward from the branch, simple, linear and needlelike; margins entire, strongly rolled under. Surfaces medium green. Blade 8–25 mm long, about 2 mm broad; petiole absent, the blade attaching directly to the branch and breaking away cleanly when pulled. **FLOWER** Bisexual, yellow, petals and sepals 5, stamens numerous; inflorescence usually a 3-flowered cluster. **FRUIT** Narrowly ovoid capsule, about 6 mm long, styles protruding from the apex; seeds numerous, less than 1 mm long.

HABITAT/RANGE Native. Wet pine flatwoods, margins of bogs, swamps, and cypress ponds, 0–30 m; endemic to the central portion of the Fla. panhandle.

SIMILAR SPECIES Numerous shrubby species of St.-John's-wort occur within the distribution of Spongebark Hypericum, none with spongy bark or a trunk diameter as large.

SPONGEBARK HYPERICUM

Pitch Apple

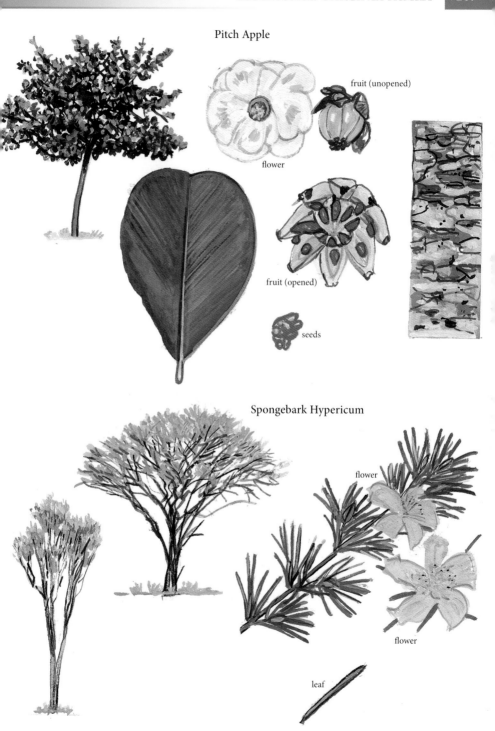

flower

fruit (unopened)

fruit (opened)

seeds

Spongebark Hypericum

flower

flower

leaf

COMBRETACEAE: WHITE MANGROVE FAMILY

This pantropical family includes 14–20 genera and 500–600 species; 5 genera and 8 species occur in continental North America, including 3 native trees, 4 introduced trees, and 1 introduced vine. The family's range in the U.S. is restricted entirely to s. Fla.

The family is best known in the U.S. for its two mangrove species, both of which are closely associated with saltwater shorelines. **LEAF** Usually alternate, occasionally opposite; simple. Many members of the family (including species of *Conocarpus* and *Terminalia*) produce small cavities or pouches along the veins on the lower surface of the leaves. These structures are often inhabited by mites, an apparent adaptation to protect the leaves from destruction by fungi or tiny herbivores. **FLOWER** In most species flowers have inferior ovaries and produce nectar that attracts insects, birds, or small mammals. **FRUIT** Drupelike and usually flattened, ribbed, or winged, with a single large seed.

BUTTON MANGROVE *Conocarpus erectus* L.
A.K.A. BUTTONWOOD

QUICK ID A mangrove easily identified by the clusters of buttonlike flower and fruit heads.

Evergreen shrub or tree, to 20 m tall, 38–139 cm diam. Erect, single trunk; crown dense, irregular, more or less rounded or cylindric. **BARK** Gray or brown, scaly, usually fissured, with broad ridges. **TWIG** Slender, usually winged, hairless or finely hairy, yellowish at first, becoming gray or brownish. **LEAF** Alternate, simple, leathery; elliptic, lanceolate, or oblanceolate, usually with a tiny sharp point at the tip; base usually with 2 glands near the point of attachment with the petiole; margins entire. Upper surface yellowish green; lower surface paler, hairless or silky-hairy, usually with tiny pockets in the vein axils. Blade 2–10 cm long, 1–4 cm broad; petiole 9–12 mm long. **FLOWER** Unisexual, male and female flowers on separate plants, tiny, greenish, sepals 5, petals absent, borne in branched clusters of dense, buttonlike heads. Spring to autumn. **FRUIT** Tiny, flattened, and scalelike, borne in a rounded conelike cluster that shatters on ripening; matures autumn to winter, with "cones" potentially present at any time of year.

HABITAT/RANGE Native. The margin landward of the mangrove zone, margins of coastal hammocks, transition zone between coastal and upland habitats; s. Fla.

SIMILAR SPECIES The leaves of Silver Buttonwood (*C. erectus* var. *sericeus* Griseb.), sometimes treated as a variety of Button Mangrove, are covered with silvery hairs that give the plant a silvery-gray appearance. Silver Buttonwood is popular in landscaping and is often seen in cultivation. *Lumnitzera racemosa* Willd., referred to as Black Mangrove, was introduced from the Old World tropics and is naturalized along saltwater shores in Miami-Dade County, Fla. It differs from Button Mangrove by its spikelike inflorescence and drupelike fruit; its leaves are widest toward the usually notched tip.

Notes: Although commonly referred to as a mangrove, Button Mangrove does not usually occur in the intensely salty environments favored by our native species, White Mangrove (*Laguncularia racemosa*), Red Mangrove (*Rhizophora mangle*, Rhizophoraceae), and Black Mangrove (*Avicennia germinans*, Acanthaceae), and usually does not form colonies as intensively.

BUTTON MANGROVE

WHITE MANGROVE

Button Mangrove

flowers

fruit

fruit

White Mangrove

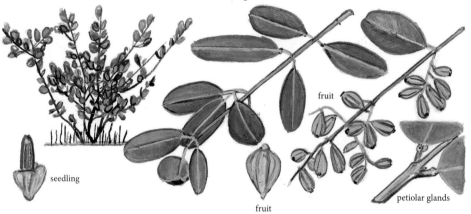

seedling

fruit

fruit

petiolar glands

WHITE MANGROVE *Laguncularia racemosa* (L.) C.F. Gaertn.

QUICK ID Recognized by the combination of oval leaves, glands on the petiole, ribbed fruit, and a saltwater habitat.

Evergreen shrub or tree, to about 18 m tall, 40 cm diam. Erect, single trunk; crown rounded or cylindric, often producing colonies along the landward margin of mangrove shorelines. **BARK** Reddish brown, dividing into long, scaly strips with age. **TWIG** Slender, hairless, reddish brown. **LEAF** Opposite, simple, thick, stiff, leathery, predominantly oval or broadly elliptic; base more or less rounded; tip often notched; margins entire. Upper surface dark green or grayish green, veins obscure; lower surface paler; both surfaces with excretory salt glands that produce visible salt crystals on the blade surface. Blade 2.5–8 cm long, 2.5–3 cm broad; petiole 9–12 mm long, with a conspicuous pair of wartlike glands near its attachment to the blade. **FLOWER** Bisexual or unisexual, the unisexual ones usually male; tiny, petals 5, greenish white, velvety-hairy, stamens usually 10. Spring to early summer. **FRUIT** Thick, flattened drupe, usually 10-ribbed, narrow at base, widening toward the tip; seeds often germinate while still attached to the tree, producing water-dispersed seedlings that root after becoming stranded along muddy shorelines. Drupe matures late summer to autumn.

HABITAT/RANGE Native. Saltwater shorelines, often in the zone washed by changing tides; s. Fla.

SIMILAR SPECIES Distinguished from Black Mangrove (*Avicennia germinans*, Acanthaceae) and Red Mangrove (*Rhizophora mangle*, Rhizophoraceae) by the more or less oval leaves and the ribbed fruit.

■ *BUCIDA*: BLACK OLIVES

A genus of 2 species distributed in the American tropics and subtropics; 2 species in s. Florida, 1 native. Evergreen shrubs or trees. **BARK** Gray or brown, scaly or flaking. **LEAF** Alternate, simple, leathery, margins entire, often clustered near the ends of twigs. **FLOWER** Small, borne in spikes, some unisexual, usually male, others bisexual; petals absent, stamens 10. **FRUIT** Small, slightly fleshy drupe, usually crowned by the calyx.

BLACK OLIVE *Bucida buceras* L.
A.K.A. OXHORN BUCIDA, GREGORYWOOD

QUICKID Recognized by the combination of leaves crowded at the tips of short shoots, dangling spikelike inflorescences, spiny branches, and the twisted galls that adorn the fruit.

Evergreen tree, to about 25 m tall, 80–112 cm diam. Erect, single trunk; crown broad, rounded, with horizontally spreading branches. **BARK** Dark brown, scaly, roughened. **TWIG** Brown or gray, with short shoots bearing closely crowded leaf scars at their tips. **LEAF** Alternate, but often closely clustered at tips of short shoots and appearing opposite or whorled; simple, obovate to elliptic, margins entire. Upper surface dark green; lower surface yellowish green. Blade 2.5–9 cm long, 1–5 cm broad; petiole 0–3 mm long, often subtended by a short, sharp spine. **FLOWER** Bisexual, small, greenish white, petals absent, sepals 5, stamens 10; borne in congested spikes dangling from the leaf axils. **FRUIT** Hard, dry, leathery, egg-shaped, 7–9 mm long; often deformed by twisted galls up to 10 cm long.

HABITAT/RANGE Introduced from the West Indies; cultivated and naturalized in hammocks in s. Fla. and Fla. Keys.

SIMILAR SPECIES The short shoots with closely crowded leaves are reminiscent of several of the deciduous hollies, which do not overlap in range with Black Olive.

SPINY BUCIDA *Bucida molinetii* (M. Gómez) Alwan & Stace
A.K.A. SPINY BLACK OLIVE

QUICKID Recognized by the flat-topped crown, spiny twigs and branches, and comparatively small leaves.

Evergreen, spiny shrub or small tree, to about 8 m tall, 20 cm diam. Erect, leaning, or contorted, usually single trunk; crown vertically flattened, laterally spreading, appearing flat-topped. **BARK** Gray and brownish, scaly and flaking, with shallow vertical and lateral fissures. **TWIG** Reddish brown or gray, conspicuously zigzag, spiny. **LEAF** Alternate, but closely set in short fascicles (bundles) and appearing whorled; simple, elliptic or obovate, tip often notched, margins entire. Upper surface dark, lustrous green; lower surface paler. Blade 1–2.5 cm long, to about 5 mm broad. **FLOWER** Bisexual, small, petals 5, greenish white; calyx bell-shaped, about 3 mm long, hairy inside; borne in densely flowered spikes. **FRUIT** Small, fleshy, egg-shaped, the remains of the stalked calyx creating a beaklike extension at the apex.

HABITAT/RANGE Native. Hammocks, possibly extirpated in the wild; Miami-Dade County, Fla.

SIMILAR SPECIES The tangled form and spiny branches are reminiscent of those of *Vachellia* species (Fabaceae), but *Vachellia* leaves are compound rather than simple.

SPINY BUCIDA

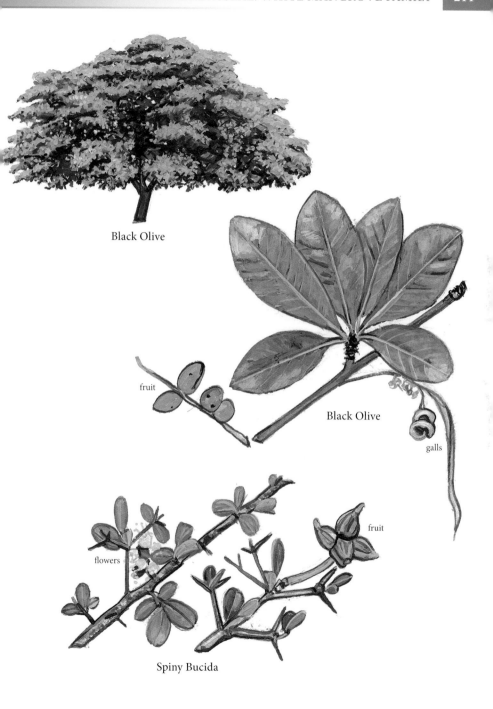

Black Olive

fruit

Black Olive

galls

flowers

fruit

Spiny Bucida

■ *TERMINALIA*: TROPICAL ALMONDS

A genus of about 150 species widely distributed throughout the tropics. Deciduous trees and shrubs, often very large, with a buttressed base. **BARK** Smooth, steel gray at first, in some species becoming brown, ridged, and scaly. **LEAF** Alternate, sometimes closely clustered, simple, leathery, tip rounded or concavely tapered to an abrupt point; margins entire. **FLOWER** Small, white or greenish white, lacking petals, borne in slender cylindric spikes, stamens 8 or 10. **FRUIT** Dry or fleshy drupe, sometimes with 2–5 wings or ridges.

WEST INDIAN ALMOND *Terminalia catappa* L.

A.K.A. TROPICAL ALMOND, SEA-ALMOND

QUICK ID The large whorled leaves that turn crimson in autumn are distinctive.

Deciduous tree, to about 25 m tall, to about 110 cm diam. Erect, single trunk, straight, sometimes becoming wider at the base; crown spreading, the branches borne in whorls and often drooping. **BARK** Smooth and steel gray when young, becoming scaly with age. **LEAF** Alternate, often crowded near tips of branches in an umbrella-like cluster; simple, leathery, obovate, narrowing at base; tip blunt or abruptly narrowing to a short point; margins entire, often wavy. Upper surface dark green, veins conspicuous; lower surface densely hairy and feltlike. Turns crimson just before falling in winter. Blade 10–40 cm long, to about 20 cm broad; petiole to about 1 cm long. **FLOWER** Bisexual and unisexual (the unisexual ones usually male), usually borne on a single elongate spike from the leaf axils, the bisexual flowers at the base of the spike, the male flowers near the tip; petals absent; sepals 5, greenish white; stamens 10. Early summer. **FRUIT** More or less flattened, fleshy, almond-shaped drupe, green at first, becoming yellowish, then red or blackish green when ripe, slightly or moderately winged, to about 5 cm long; matures autumn to winter.

HABITAT/RANGE Introduced from the West Indies; cultivated and naturalized in hammocks and the coastal zone of s. Fla. and Fla. Keys.

SIMILAR SPECIES Wild Almond (*T. arjuna* [Roxb. ex DC.] Wight & Arn.), also naturalized in s. Fla., is similar, but the leaves are more or less oblong or oval rather than distinctly obovate.

AUSTRALIAN ALMOND *Terminalia muelleri* Benth.

QUICK ID The closely crowded, obovate leaves and slender spikes of greenish-white flowers help distinguish this species.

Deciduous tree, to about 10 m tall, 25 cm diam. Erect, single trunk; crown spreading, with whorled and layered branches. **BARK** Dark gray, roughened by ridges and furrows. **LEAF** Alternate, but closely clustered at ends of branches and appearing whorled; simple, leathery, obovate, rounded or bluntly pointed at the tip. Upper surface dark or medium green; lower surface paler. Turns burgundy-red or crimson before falling. Blade 4–15 cm long, 3–8 cm broad; petiole 5–8 mm long. **FLOWER** Bisexual and unisexual (the unisexual ones usually male), usually borne from the leaf axils in a slender spike to 6 cm long, bisexual flowers at the base of the spike, male flowers near the tip; petals absent; sepals 5, greenish white; stamens 10. Spring to early summer. **FRUIT** Drupe to 2 cm long, green at first, becoming dark blue or purple; matures summer to autumn.

HABITAT/RANGE Introduced from Australia; cultivated, naturalized, and becoming invasive in hammocks and along the margins of mangrove swamps in s. Fla.

SIMILAR SPECIES The leaves of West Indian Almond are similar but on average longer and broader.

West Indian Almond

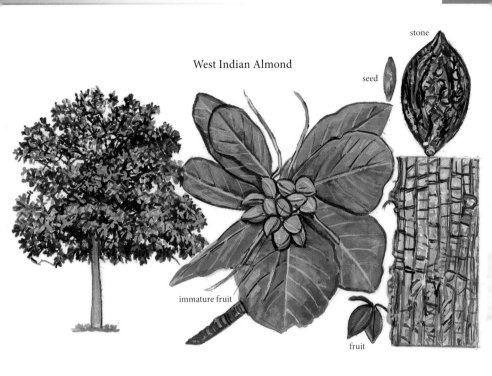

stone

seed

immature fruit

fruit

Australian Almond

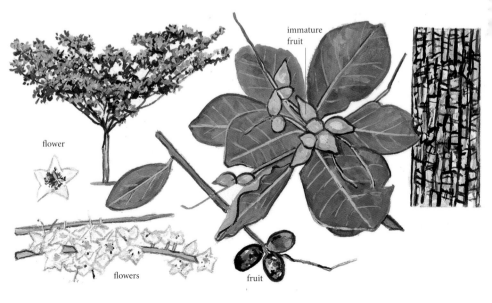

immature fruit

flower

flowers

fruit

CORNACEAE: DOGWOOD FAMILY

As treated here, the dogwoods constitute a small family of 1 or 2 genera and 55–76 species, distributed primarily in north temperate regions, with fewer species in tropical, subtropical, and boreal regions. About half of the species occur in China. The precise taxonomy of this family is controversial, and some experts recognize as many as 17 genera, including the North American tupelos (*Nyssa*), which we place in family Nyssaceae. With one exception, the dogwoods are easily distinguished from the tupelos by their opposite leaves. **FLOWERS** Bisexual or unisexual, with male and female flowers borne on the same plant; petals 4, stamens 4. **FRUIT** A drupe.

■ *CORNUS*: DOGWOODS

A genus of about 55 species distributed mostly in north temperate regions; 20 species and several hybrids occur in North America, 16 native.

Deciduous shrubs or trees, often with multiple trunks, at least 1 species low-growing and appearing herbaceous. **LEAF** Opposite, simple; margins entire or slightly wavy; pairs of arching veins, the tips of the veins paralleling the leaf margins. The leaf veins exude strands of stringy material when the leaves are transversely folded, creased, and gently pulled apart, a characteristic often referred to as the "*Cornus* test." **FLOWER** Bisexual, radially symmetric, petals 4, stamens 4, produced in loose or compact umbels or cymes, in some species the inflorescence subtended by large, conspicuous petal-like bracts, in other species by small, inconspicuous bracts; nectar-producing and pollinated by bees, flies, or beetles. **FRUIT** Colorful drupe; stones smooth or ribbed, 1- or 2-seeded.

A fungal disease known as dogwood anthracnose (caused by the fungus *Discula destructiva*) attacks Flowering and Pacific Dogwood.

FLOWERING DOGWOOD *Cornus florida* L.

QUICK ID Recognized by the blocky bark, opposite leaves with curving veins, and the large, creamy-white bracts subtending the cluster of small greenish flowers.

Deciduous, shallow-rooted tree to about 12 m tall and 50 cm diam. Erect, rarely slightly leaning or angling, a single short trunk; crown rounded. **BARK**

Grayish or nearly black, broken into small, regularly shaped scaly blocks. **TWIG** Minutely hairy at first, becoming hairless; usually green suffused with red throughout the 1st year, becoming brown; pith pale green at first, becoming white. **LEAF** Opposite, simple, ovate to narrowly or broadly elliptic, occasionally circular; base broadly wedge-shaped or rounded, sometimes asymmetric; tip usually abruptly tapered to a narrow point; margins entire. Upper surface medium or dark green, minutely hairy, with appressed hairs; lateral veins conspicuously curving, their tips paralleling the leaf margin; lower surface paler, grayish, minutely hairy on the tissue, often shaggy-hairy along the midvein. Turns burgundy to purplish in autumn. Blade 3–12 cm long, 2–7 cm broad; petiole 5–15 mm long, sparsely hairy. **FLOWER** Greenish yellow or yellow, tiny, compacted into a headlike cluster; the cluster subtended by 4 large, showy creamy-white petal-like bracts; bracts 3–5 cm long, usually widest above the middle, often notched at the tip. Spring. **FRUIT** Smooth, lustrous, bright red drupe, 8–14 mm long; matures late summer to autumn, produced in dense clusters that sometimes persist into winter.

HABITAT/RANGE Native. Understory of well-drained upland woods and mountain slopes, sometimes moist woodlands near rivers, 0–1,500 m; widespread in the East, Me. and Ont. south to c. peninsular Fla., west to Kans. and e. Tex.

SIMILAR SPECIES Rusty Blackhaw (*Viburnum rufidulum*, Adoxaceae) has similar bark but toothed leaves. All other native eastern dogwoods lack conspicuous bracts subtending the flowers; Kousa Dogwood has bracts with pointed tips and a knobby fruit cluster.

FLOWERING DOGWOOD

Flowering Dogwood

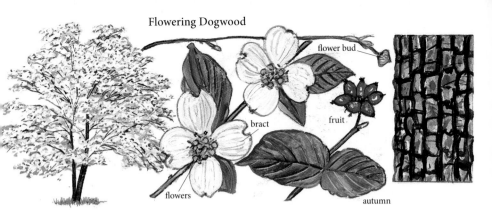

flower bud

bract

flowers

fruit

autumn

Roughleaf Dogwood

flowers

fruit

ROUGHLEAF DOGWOOD *Cornus drummondii* C.A. Mey.

A.K.A. CORNEL DOGWOOD, WHITE CORNEL

QUICK ID Recognized by the combination of white fruit and opposite leaves with the upper surface rough to the touch.

Deciduous shrub or small thicket-forming tree, 5–10 m tall. Erect, single trunk or multiple; crown rounded. **BARK** Grayish, narrowly ridged and fissured, with small scales. **TWIG** Mostly smooth (rarely rough); grayish, dark brown, or reddish brown; pith usually brown, varying to whitish. **LEAF** Opposite, simple, narrowly ovate, lanceolate, or narrowly elliptic; tip abruptly tapered to a moderately long point; margins entire. Upper surface medium or dark green, rough to the touch from short, stiff hairs; lower surface paler, conspicuously whitish-hairy. Turns coral or orange in autumn. Blade 3–12 cm long, 2–6 cm broad; petiole to 15 mm long. **FLOWER** Petals creamy white, 3.5–5.5 mm long, often with an unpleasant aroma; borne in a round-topped cluster to about 7.5 cm broad. Late spring to summer. **FRUIT** Round white drupe, 5–6 mm diam., usually with a rancid odor during development; matures late summer to autumn.

ROUGHLEAF DOGWOOD

HABITAT/RANGE Native. Moist woods, thickets, bottomlands, or dry, rocky uplands, often where calcium is present, 25–600 m; distributed chiefly in the Midwest, Ohio to S.D., south to ne. Ga., c. Ala., La., and Tex.

SIMILAR SPECIES Toughleaf Dogwood can be distinguished by its blue fruit, shaggy-hairy twigs, and a predominately eastern distribution.

TOUGHLEAF DOGWOOD *Cornus asperifolia* Michx.
A.K.A. COASTAL ROUGHLEAF DOGWOOD

QUICK ID Recognized by the combination of light blue fruit and opposite leaves, the upper surface with the feel of fine sandpaper.

Deciduous, usually a shrub, sometimes a small, slender tree 1–5 m tall, to about 18 cm diam. Erect, single trunk or multiple; crown rounded or irregularly spreading. **BARK** Gray, scaly. **TWIG** Brown at first, becoming gray; hairy with shaggy or appressed hairs; pith white. **LEAF** Opposite, simple, elliptic or ovate, rarely lanceolate; tip abruptly tapered to an elongate point; margins entire. Upper surface dull, dark green, with the feel of fine sandpaper due to the presence of short, stiff hairs; lower surface paler, hairy, the hairs gray or rusty. Blade 2–8 cm long, 1–4 cm broad; petiole 2–5 mm long. **FLOWER** Petals creamy white, 3 mm long; produced in flat-topped or convex clusters 3–4 cm broad. Spring. **FRUIT** Sparsely hairy, light blue drupe, about 8 mm diam.; produced in branched clusters; matures late summer to autumn.

HABITAT/RANGE Native. Well-drained calcareous woodlands, usually in association with neutral or basic soils, rarely in bottomlands, 25–200 m; southeastern coastal plains, e. N.C. south to c. Fla., west to s. Ala.

SIMILAR SPECIES Roughleaf Dogwood can be distinguished by its white fruit, smooth twigs, and predominantly Midwestern distribution. Some taxonomists consider Toughleaf Dogwood and Roughleaf Dogwood to represent a single species, but the two occupy separate ranges and differ markedly in fruit color.

TOUGHLEAF DOGWOOD

STIFF DOGWOOD *Cornus foemina* Mill.
A.K.A. STIFF CORNEL DOGWOOD

QUICK ID Distinguished by the combination of opposite leaves with a smooth upper surface, clusters of blue to purple fruit, and typically wetland habitat.

Deciduous shrub or small, slender tree to about 8 m tall, to about 8 cm diam. Erect, single trunk or multiple, sometimes thicket-forming from the production of numerous root suckers; crown rounded, with ascending or irregularly spreading branches. **BARK** Brownish gray. **TWIG** Smooth, hairless, green at first, becoming reddish brown, maroon, or tan; pith of year-old twigs white. **LEAF** Opposite, simple, lanceolate, elliptic, or ovate; tip abruptly tapered to a point; margins entire. Upper surface usually dark green, varying to yellow-green or grayish green, sparsely hairy, smooth to the touch; lower surface paler, hairless or with short, appressed hairs. Blade 2–10 cm long, 1–4 cm broad; petiole about 1 cm long, hairy, with short grayish hairs. **FLOWER** Petals creamy white, 3–4 mm long; produced in convex clusters 3–7 cm broad. Spring. **FRUIT** Rounded or ellipsoid blue or purplish drupe, 4–6 mm diam.; matures late summer to autumn.

HABITAT/RANGE Native. Swamps, stream margins, bottomlands, often where water stands for extended periods; widespread, chiefly in the southeastern coastal plains, also in the Piedmont and central inlands, N.J. south to Fla., west to s. Ill. and Mo., e. Tex.

SIMILAR SPECIES Toughleaf Dogwood and Roughleaf Dogwood are similar but have rough upper leaf surfaces and are not typically found in wetland habitats. Silky Dogwood can be distinguished from Stiff Dogwood by combination of its mounding stature, shaggy young twigs, and brownish to tawny pith.

STIFF DOGWOOD

Toughleaf Dogwood

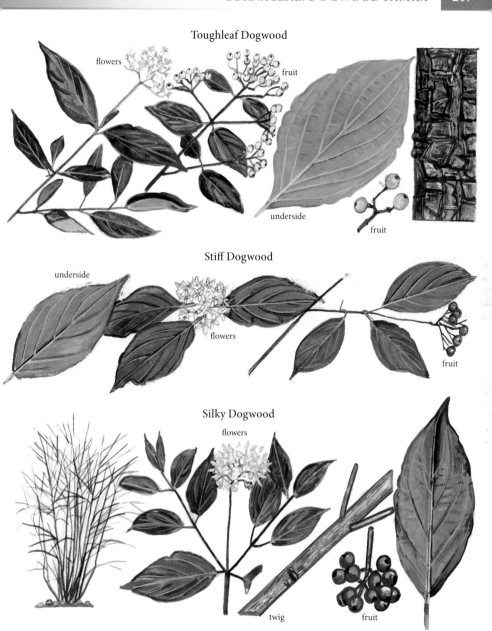

flowers

fruit

underside

fruit

Stiff Dogwood

underside

flowers

fruit

Silky Dogwood

flowers

twig

fruit

SILKY DOGWOOD *Cornus amomum* Mill.

Multistemmed wetland shrub to about 5 m tall. **TWIG** Young twigs are shaggy-hairy with silvery or rusty hairs. **LEAF** Mostly oval, 3–10 cm long and 2–8 cm broad, with a petiole to about 2 cm long. **HABITAT/RANGE** Native; occurs in similar wetland habitats to Stiff Dogwood, often in standing water of lake margins; e. Canada and U.S.

ROUNDLEAF DOGWOOD *Cornus rugosa* Lam.

QUICK ID A usually shrubby dogwood, recognized by the green twigs with purplish spots, bright red fruit stalks, and greenish, bluish-white, or light blue drupes.

Deciduous, usually a shrub, rarely arborescent, 1–4 m tall. Erect, often with a single main trunk, sometimes with several trunks; crown dense, rounded. **TWIG** Green or yellow-green, hairless, often mottled with red, usually with wartlike lenticels; pith white. **LEAF** Opposite, simple, ovate to circular; base rounded or broadly wedge-shaped; tip abruptly bluntly pointed or, less often, rounded; margins entire. Upper surface with the texture of fine sandpaper, veins conspicuously impressed; lower surface softly white-hairy. Blade 7–12 cm long, 3–10 cm broad; petiole 5–12 mm long, reddish. **FLOWER** White, individually tiny, produced in numerous flat-topped clusters. Late spring to early summer. **FRUIT** Bluish-white, greenish-white, or light blue drupe, more or less round, to about 6 mm diam., born on red stalks; stone uniform pale tan, unstriped; matures summer.

HABITAT/RANGE Native. Moist or dry rocky sites, usually where well drained, 0–850 m; N.B. west to Man., south to Va. and Ill.

SIMILAR SPECIES Red-osier Dogwood usually has red stems and white drupes that are slightly larger than those of Roundleaf Dogwood.

RED-OSIER DOGWOOD *Cornus sericea* L.

QUICK ID A widespread, shrubby, wetland species with red twigs contrasting with the white fruits.

Shrub, 1–3 m tall, often forming dense thickets in moist sites. Overlaps in range with Roundleaf Dogwood, differing from it by its bright red twigs and the typically white drupe, 7–9 mm diam., with a yellow-striped, dark brown stone.

HABITAT/RANGE Native; moist areas, often along streams, 450–2,700 m; Alaska to Lab., south in the East to ne. U.S.; also throughout the West.

CORNELIAN CHERRY *Cornus mas* L.

QUICK ID Distinguished from other dogwoods in the East by the copious yellow flowers that appear in early spring prior to leaf emergence.

Deciduous, large shrub or small, densely branched tree, 5.5–7.5 m tall, 15–30 cm diam. Erect at first, broadly spreading and arching at maturity, usually with numerous trunks from the base. **BARK** Medium or light brown, more or less smooth. **TWIG** Red, hairy, ridged; pith white. **LEAF** Opposite, simple, becoming leathery on some plants; ovate or broadly elliptic; base rounded or wedge-shaped; tip abruptly narrowed to a short point; margins entire or wavy. Upper surface lustrous dark green, finely hairy, veins deeply impressed and conspicuous; lower surface paler, finely hairy. Potentially turns purple or yellow in autumn. Blade 5–10 cm long, 2.5–7 cm broad; petiole about 1 cm long. **FLOWER** Yellow, 6–9 mm diam., produced in numerous rounded umbels about 2.5 cm wide. Early spring. **FRUIT** Bright red cherry-like drupe about 15 cm long, stones 2; matures summer.

HABITAT/RANGE Introduced, native to Europe and Asia; rarely naturalized in ne. U.S.

ROUNDLEAF DOGWOOD   RED-OSIER DOGWOOD

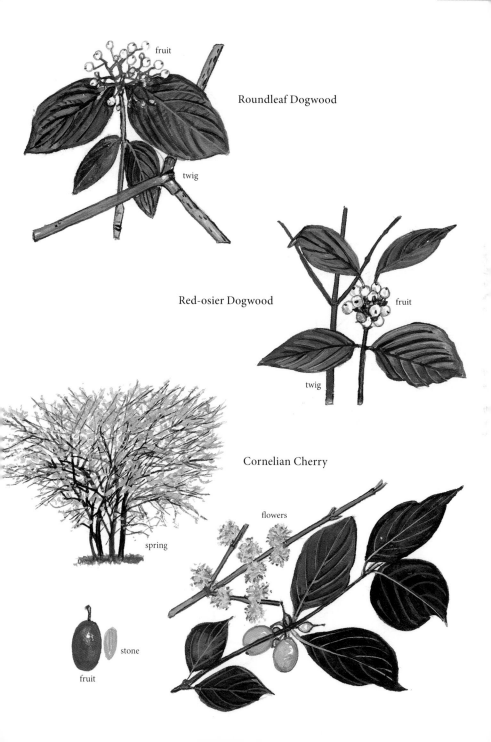

Roundleaf Dogwood

fruit

twig

Red-osier Dogwood

fruit

twig

Cornelian Cherry

spring

flowers

fruit

stone

ALTERNATELEAF DOGWOOD *Cornus alternifolia* L.f.

QUICKID A shrub or small tree with a distinctively layered, horizontal branching structure, and the only eastern dogwood with alternate rather than opposite leaves.

Deciduous shrub or small tree, 4–9 m tall; trunk usually 8–15 cm diam., potentially to 55 cm. Erect, usually a single trunk, sometimes multiple; crown spreading, the branches usually appearing horizontally layered and turned upward at the tip. **BARK** Reddish brown, smooth, faintly vertically striped, becoming slightly fissured at maturity. **TWIG** Reddish, reddish brown, or green when young, becoming smooth, lustrous, and dark green or dark reddish purple; the ultimate lateral twig usually longer than and extending beyond the terminal twig; pith white. **LEAF** Alternate, those at the tip of the shoot often closely clustered and appearing opposite or whorled, those lower on the stem evidently alternate; simple, ovate or oval, base rounded or wedge-shaped, tip abruptly tapered to a long point, margins entire. Upper surface dark green, hairless or virtually so, veins conspicuous; lower surface paler, hairy. Turns yellow, red, or purple in autumn. Blade 5–12 cm long, 2.5–8 cm broad; petiole slender, 1–6 cm long, grooved, hairy or hairless. **FLOWER** Individually tiny, petals creamy white, produced in a showy flat-topped or convex inflorescence 3–6 cm broad. Spring to early summer. **FRUIT** Rounded, sparsely hairy blue drupe, 4–7 mm diam.; produced on reddish stalks; matures early autumn.

HABITAT/RANGE Native. Moist rich woods, slopes and ravines, thickets, stream banks, swamp margins, floodplains, bottoms of steep slopes, 50–1,900 m; nearly throughout the East, Man. east to Nfld., south to nw. Fla., Ark., and Miss.

ALTERNATELEAF DOGWOOD

SIMILAR SPECIES Flowering Dogwood is similar but all leaves are clearly opposite, and its flower cluster is subtended by large, showy white bracts; Alternateleaf Dogwood is the only dogwood that has a layered form with branches upturned at their tips.

KOUSA DOGWOOD *Cornus kousa* Hance

QUICKID Recognized by the combination of opposite leaves, flower clusters subtended by 4 long-pointed creamy-white petal-like bracts, and rounded, knobby fruit.

Deciduous, small tree, 7.5–9 m tall, 15–20 cm diam. Erect, single short trunk at maturity, usually branching low to the ground; crown broad, rounded, about as broad as tall. **BARK** Smooth and uniformly gray when young, exfoliating and becoming mottled with shades of gray, copper, and olive with age. **TWIG** Light brown, tinged purple or green. **LEAF** Opposite, simple, ovate or elliptic, base narrowly wedge-shaped, tip long-tapered. Upper surface, dark green, veins conspicuous but not deeply impressed; lower surface paler, with hairs at least in the vein axils. Potentially turns brilliant red, orange, or purple in autumn. Blade 5–10 cm long, 2.5–5 cm broad; petiole about 5 mm long. **FLOWER** Individually tiny, greenish or yellowish, borne in compact clusters, 12–20 mm broad; inflorescence subtended by 4 large, long-pointed, usually white bracts to about 5 cm long that are sometimes tinged pinkish or reddish at the tip. Late spring. **FRUIT** Cluster of small drupes fused into a knobby red or reddish-orange, raspberry-like aggregate about 2.5 cm diam., produced on stalks to about 5 cm long; matures summer to autumn.

HABITAT/RANGE Introduced from Asia; widely cultivated in the East, sparingly naturalized in se. N.Y.

SIMILAR SPECIES Flowering Dogwood can be distinguished by its nontapering, notch-tipped bracts.

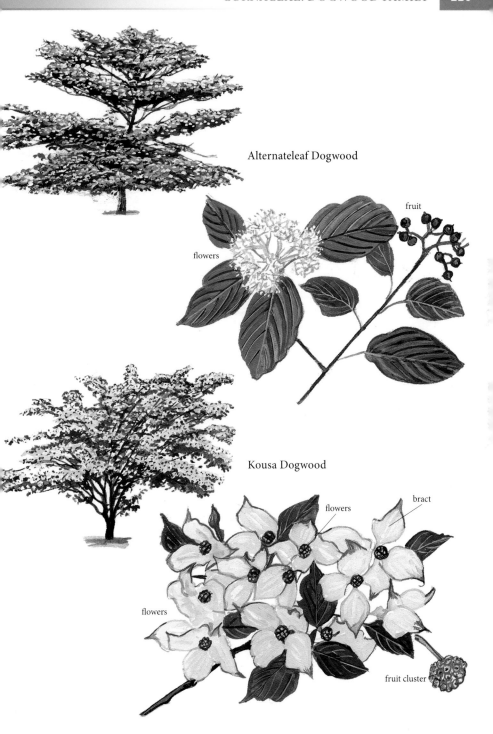

Alternateleaf Dogwood

flowers

fruit

Kousa Dogwood

flowers

bract

flowers

fruit cluster

CYRILLACEAE: TITI FAMILY

This is a small family of 2 genera and 2 species distributed from the se. U.S. to the West Indies and n. South America. Species in the family are trees or shrubs with alternate leaves, elongate, cylindric (racemose) inflorescences, and small white flowers. Species of Cyrillaceae are closely allied to plants of the heath family (Ericaceae), and at least one species of titi has been included within the heath family by some taxonomists. The sweetpepperbushes of the genus *Clethra* (Clethraceae) are also sometimes included within the Cyrillaceae. The family's common name is pronounced *tie-tie*.

BLACK TITI *Cliftonia monophylla* (Lam.) Britton ex Sarg.
A.K.A. BUCKWHEAT TREE

QUICK ID Recognized by its wetland habitat, mostly elliptic leaves with obscure venation, erect racemes, and small, fragrant white flowers borne in abundance.

Evergreen shrub or small, slender tree to about 18 m tall and 60 cm diam. Erect, single trunk or multiple, often somewhat contorted. Crown dense, irregular, especially on isolated plants in sunny locations; plants in swamps and along swampy margins often form dense stands with their crowns intermixed. **BARK** Smooth, dark gray or nearly black, becoming shallowly fissured on old trees. **TWIG** Grayish. **LEAF** Alternate, simple, leathery, elliptic or slightly wider above the middle; tip bluntly pointed; margins entire. Upper surface dark green, veins obscure; lower surface paler, sometimes with a bluish-white tinge. Blade 2.5–10 cm long, 1.2–1.8 cm broad; petiole to about 3 mm long. **FLOWER** Bisexual, fragrant, radially symmetric, petals 5, white, sometimes tinged pink, sepals 5, enclosing only the base of the corolla; inflorescence an erect raceme to about 7 cm long; borne in abundance, rendering dense stands of this species along wetland margins very attractive. Early spring. **FRUIT** Dry, capsule-like but indehiscent drupe with 2–5 wings, 5–7 mm long, more or less golden amber when fresh, becoming dark brown and persisting on the tree for most of the year; matures summer to autumn.

HABITAT/RANGE Native. Swamps, swamp margins, wet depressions within flatwoods, shrub-tree bogs, margins of pineland streams, often forming dense colonies that stretch for many meters, 0–100 m; southeastern coastal plains, S.C. south to c. Fla., west to La.

SIMILAR SPECIES Potentially confused with Titi, with which it often grows intermixed; Titi is distinguished by its later flowering period, evident leaf venation, and egg-shaped, capsular, wingless fruit.

TITI *Cyrilla racemiflora* L.
A.K.A. SWAMP TITI

QUICK ID The combination of spray-like clusters of racemes, late-spring or early-summer flowering time, leaves with entire margins, and wetland habitat is usually enough to distinguish this species.

Deciduous, semi-deciduous, or occasionally evergreen shrub or small tree to about 13 m tall and 40 cm diam. Erect or low-branching, single trunk or multiple from near the base, often suckering and producing multiple trunks and forming thickets, especially following fire; crown open, irregular, often more or less vertically elongate where it dominates swamps, dense and irregular in densely vegetated wetlands. **BARK** Reddish, stripping and flaking, sometimes becoming grayish with

BLACK TITI

TITI

flowers

flower

fruit

fruit

Black Titi

fruit

Littleleaf Titi

Titi

fruit

fruit

flowers

fruit

age, mostly near the base. **TWIG** Angled, ridged, reddish brown. **LEAF** Alternate, simple, stiff, leathery; narrowly obovate, oblanceolate, or narrowly elliptic; tip bluntly pointed; margins entire. Upper surface medium or dark green, venation conspicuous; lower surface paler. Blade 1–10 cm long, 0.5–2.5 cm broad, size varying considerably by habitat and from tree to tree; petiole 3–10 mm long. **FLOWER** Bisexual, radially symmetric; petals 5, white; sepals 5, enclosing only the base of the corolla; inflorescence an elongate raceme, 2–15 cm long, varying in length in proportion to the length of the leaf; produced in clusters near the terminus of the previous year's growth. Late spring to early summer. **FRUIT** Dry, hard egg-shaped drupe, 2–2.5 mm long, the sepals persistent at the base; matures summer to autumn.

HABITAT/RANGE Native. Swamps and swamp margins, banks of small streams, shrub-tree bogs, flatwoods, and flatwood depressions, often in association with acid soils, 0–100 m; southeastern coastal plains, Va. south to c. Fla, west to e. Tex.

SIMILAR SPECIES Coastal Sweetpepperbush (*Clethra alnifolia*, Clethraceae), a shrub that often grows in association with Titi, produces a similar inflorescence but has toothed leaves. Black Titi can also grow in association with Titi and is sometimes confused with it, but can be distinguished by its earlier flowering period, upright rather than spreading racemes, and leaves with mostly obscure venation. Titi is a polymorphic species that expresses extreme variation. Plants with small leaves (less than 4 cm long) and short racemes (less than 5 cm long) have been treated as **Littleleaf Titi** (*Cyrilla parvifolia* Raf.). Plants with intermediate features are regularly encountered in the field, suggesting that extreme forms may only be ecological adaptations to differences in habitat.

EBENACEAE: EBONY FAMILY

The ebony family includes 2–6 genera and 450–500 species of trees and shrubs distributed in tropical and warm temperate regions. One genus and 4 species occur in North America, two of which are native; 3 species occur in the East, 1 native. **LEAF** Alternate and commonly 2-ranked, simple, often leathery, usually with nectar glands on the lower surface. **FLOWER** Few, clustered or solitary, usually unisexual, with male and female flowers borne on separate plants; petals and sepals 3–7, fused, the corolla urn-shaped, the sepals usually persistent and enlarging at the base of the fruit; stamens 6–20 or more, replaced by sterile stamens (staminodes) in female flowers, the ovary usually superior, with 3–8 chambers. **FRUIT** A berry, astringent until ripe or overripe.

The family provides valuable hardwoods, some ornamentals, and several kinds of fruit trees, and is probably best known for Ebony and persimmons. Dark chemical compounds, naphthoquinones, occur in nearly all tissues.

■ *DIOSPYROS*: EBONIES AND PERSIMMONS

A genus of about 480 species, constituting about 90% of the ebony family. Distributed in tropical and warm temperate regions, nearly half occurring naturally on the Malay Archipelago. Two native species occur in North America, 1 in the East; 2 introduced species are sparingly naturalized in Fla.

Deciduous trees or shrubs, usually with hard, dense wood. **BARK** Often dark or blackish, usually blocky or scaly. **LEAF** Alternate, simple, more or less leathery, margins usually entire (in species covered); petiole often glandular. **FLOWER** Unisexual, urn-shaped; petals 3–7, often recurved at the apex; sepals 3–7; ovary superior. **FRUIT** Large, several-seeded berry.

Diospyros supplies many valuable hardwoods, including the famous black ebony of commerce, and numerous edible fruits. In the tropics, leaves of 1 species are used for cigarette papers, the sticky fruit of another is used to caulk boats, and the fruit of a third is a source of black dye for silk.

EBONY *Diospyros ebenum* J. Koenig

Tree, to 30 m tall and 90 cm diam. in its native India and Sri Lanka, but much smaller in the U.S. Best known for its hard black wood. **LEAF** Hairless and rounded at the tip, distinguishing it from Common Persimmon. **HABITAT/RANGE** Introduced; recorded from a few locations in 2 counties in s. Fla.

MALAYSIAN PERSIMMON *Diospyros maritima* Blume

A tree, smaller than Ebony, 3–12 m tall, with silvery-green buds and scaly, flaking bark. **LEAF** Hairless beneath (unlike those of Common Persimmon), with 1 or 2 pairs of glands at the base of the lower surface, near the leaf's point of attachment to the petiole (distinguishing it from Ebony). **HABITAT/RANGE** Introduced from Asia; cultivated, rarely naturalized in se. Fla.

COMMON PERSIMMON *Diospyros virginiana* L.

QUICK ID Recognized by the combination of the orange ripe fruit and alternate, simple leaves with margins entire and often with blackish blemishes on the upper surface.

Deciduous tree, usually 15–20 m tall, to about 1 m diam.; sometimes flowering and fruiting when of a shrubby stature; occasionally spreading by root suckers and forming thickets. Erect, single straight trunk; crown rounded, usually with crooked branches. **BARK** Gray-brown and shallowly fissured on young trees, becoming dark gray to nearly black and divided into small squarish blocks by a network of horizontal and vertical fissures. **TWIG** Slender, grayish brown, with prominent leaf scars. **LEAF** Alternate, simple, ovate or elliptic;

COMMON PERSIMMON

Ebony

fruit

fruit

Malaysian
Persimmon

flower

Common Persimmon

spring

flowers

fruit

base rounded or wedge-shaped; tip usually abruptly contracted to a short point; margins entire. Upper surface lustrous green, often with blackish spots, hairless; lower surface paler, grayish green, usually at least slightly hairy, the hairiness variable. Blade 7–15 cm long, 3–8 cm broad; petiole 7–10 mm long, often with glands along the upper surface. **FLOWER** Male and female on separate trees; 1–2 cm long, corolla creamy white or greenish yellow; petals and sepals 4, fused; stamens 16, styles 4; female flowers with 8 nonfunctional stamens. Spring. **FRUIT** Rounded or vertically depressed, several-seeded berry, 4–5 cm diam., turning from green to yellow to orange at maturity; pulp astringent and unpalatable during ripening, becoming sweet when fully ripe; matures late summer to autumn.

HABITAT/RANGE Native. Occurs in a wide range of habitats: Fields, upland woods, flatwoods, longleaf pinelands, bottomlands, river and stream margins, disturbed roadsides, 0–1,100 m; Mass. and N.Y. west to Iowa, south to Fla. and e. Tex.

SIMILAR SPECIES Potentially mistaken for Sweetleaf (*Symplocos tinctoria*, Symplocaceae), with which it sometimes occurs; the leaf margin of Sweetleaf is obscurely toothed.

Notes: The pulp of the fruit is used in rural regions as an ingredient in puddings, cakes, and beer.

ELAEAGNACEAE: OLEASTER FAMILY

A small family of 3 genera and 45–64 species of deciduous or evergreen, stiffly branched, often thorny shrubs and trees distributed primarily in the Northern Hemisphere, extending south into Australia. Three genera and 7 species occur in North America, 4 species native.

Foliage and twigs are covered by small silvery, golden, or brown scalelike hairs that often impart a grayish hue to the plant. **LEAF** Opposite or alternate, simple, with entire, sometimes wavy margins. **FLOWER** Radially symmetric, bisexual or unisexual; when unisexual, male and female usually borne on separate plants, or sometimes with unisexual and bisexual flowers intermixed on the same plant. Petals absent; sepals 2–8, fused, forming an elongate hypanthium bearing 4 or 8 stamens at the top; ovary superior, 1-celled. **FRUIT** Drupelike, commonly yellow, tan, or red, the hypanthium becoming fleshy or mealy, the inside layer usually hardened and completely enclosing a single achene.

Several species are grown as ornamental shrubs or trees, or windbreaks, or for mine reclamation. Fruits are used as food by humans and wildlife. The wood is a minor source of decorative lumber for novelty items.

SEA-BUCKTHORN *Hippophae rhamnoides* L.
A.K.A. SEABERRY

QUICK ID **A willowlike shrub or small tree, distinguished by its stiff, thorny branches, narrow silvery leaves, and crowded clusters of orange fruit.**

Deciduous thorny shrub or very small tree, 3–8 m tall; crown rounded, dense or spreading. **LEAF** Alternate, simple; narrowly linear; margins entire. Surfaces vested with silvery scales. Blade 2.5–8 cm long, stalkless. **FLOWER** Unisexual, male and female on separate plants, tiny, yellow, produced in spikes (male) or axillary clusters (female) prior to new leaf growth. Spring. **FRUIT** Drupelike, rounded or ellipsoid, 6–10 mm long, bright orange; seed dark brown to nearly black; matures late spring, persisting through winter.

HABITAT/RANGE Introduced; cultivated in North America for its grayish foliage and abundant orange fruit; naturalized in Que., Sask., and Alta.

Notes: Hippophae is a genus of 7 species native to Europe and Asia; this is the only one introduced in North America.

◼ *ELAEAGNUS*: OLEASTERS

A genus of about 67 species distributed in Asia, s. Europe, and North America. Five species occur in North America, 1 a native shrub of the North and West. At least 3 of the naturalized *Elaeagnus*, including the 2 treated here, are notorious invasive species in the East, readily invading natural areas and displacing native flora. They are very weedy and extremely difficult to eradicate once established.

RUSSIAN OLIVE *Elaeagnus angustifolia* L.
A.K.A. OLEASTER

QUICK ID **Recognized by the combination of silvery scales on twigs and leaves, and the colorful olive-like fruit.**

Deciduous thorny shrub or small tree, 3–14 m tall, to 65 cm diam. Erect, single trunk; crown rounded, branches often ascending. **BARK** Dark reddish brown, fissured. **TWIG** Slender, silvery-scaly, becoming lustrous green, reddish in winter; often thorny or thorn-tipped. **LEAF** Alternate, simple, narrowly oblong, lanceolate, or oblanceolate; margins entire (rarely toothed). Upper surface grayish green; lower surface densely silvery-scaly. Blade 4–10 cm long, 1–3 cm broad; petiole about 2 mm

Sea-buckthorn

fruit

Russian Olive

flowers

fruit

fruit

fruit

flowers

Autumn Olive

long, silvery. **FLOWER** Bisexual, or sometimes with unisexual male flowers intermixed; tubular, with 4 spreading silvery-white or yellowish sepals; fragrant. Spring to summer. **FRUIT** Drupelike, rounded, 1.2–2 cm long, green to yellowish brown, sometimes tinged reddish; surface scaly; matures summer to autumn.

HABITAT/RANGE Introduced, native to Europe and w. Asia; established throughout the East except Fla., Ala., Miss., La., and Ark.

AUTUMN OLIVE *Elaeagnus umbellata* Thunb.

Deciduous or semi-deciduous multistemmed shrub or small tree, 1–6 m tall. **LEAF** Alternate, elliptic to long-elliptic, margins entire, wavy; upper surface bright green, lower surface densely covered with silvery and brown scales. Blade 5–8 cm long, 2–3 cm broad, petiole short, silvery. **FRUIT** Drupelike, reddish, the skin marked with silvery scales. **HABITAT/RANGE** Introduced; naturalized throughout the East as far south as nw. Fla.

SILVER BUFFALOBERRY *Shepherdia argenta* (Pursh) Nutt.

QUICK ID Distinguished by the narrow, opposite leaves, silvery on both surfaces, and the spine-tipped branches.

Deciduous shrub or small tree, 1–6 m tall, 10–30 cm diam. Trunk short, branched near the ground, branches rigid, ascending or spreading, thorn-tipped. **LEAF** Usually opposite; simple, thin and leathery, narrowly oblong to oblanceolate, covered with tiny silvery scales that impart a silvery-gray color to the entire plant. Blade 2–6 cm long, 5–15 mm broad; petiole 3–12 mm long. **FLOWER** Unisexual, male and female on separate plants, tiny, yellowish, solitary or in small umbel-like clusters. Spring to summer. **FRUIT** Drupelike, rounded, 6–9 mm diam., red with whitish speckles; matures summer to early autumn.

HABITAT/RANGE Native. Stream margins, prairies, shrublands, woodlands, 300–2,000 m; widely distributed in the West, entering our range from N.D. south to Nebr., east to Minn., Iowa, and Wis.; naturalized but not persisting in N.Y.

SIMILAR SPECIES *Shepherdia* includes 3 species, all native, the other two shrubby. Russian Olive (*Elaeagnus angustifolia*) is similar but its leaves are alternate.

SILVER BUFFALOBERRY

ERICACEAE: HEATH FAMILY

The heath family is a large, diverse assemblage of about 125 genera and 4,100 species of herbs, shrubs, trees, and a few vines, of which 46 genera and 212 species occur in North America. Distributed in a variety of habitats nearly worldwide, the family is rare in lowland tropics and generally absent from deserts. Species of this family form several distinct groups formerly recognized as separate families. Most species are green and photosynthetic, but 1 herbaceous group has white, yellow, or red plants that lack chlorophyll and, through intermediary (mycorrhizal) fungi, absorb all nutrients from the soil.

LEAF Usually alternate, occasionally opposite or whorled; simple, margins entire or toothed. Leaves reduced to scales in some herbaceous parasitic species. **FLOWER** Usually bisexual, radially symmetric or slightly bilateral, often more or less pendulous, and white to brightly colored. Sepals and petals each number 4 or 5, nearly separate to almost completely joined from base to tip, the corolla often lantern-, cup-, urn-, bell-, or funnel-shaped, or cylindric. Stamens usually 8–10, the anthers often opening by terminal pores and often bearing 2 projecting awns. The ovary has 2–10 chambers and may be superior or inferior. **FRUIT** A capsule, a berry, or a drupe with 1 to several stones.

The heath family provides blueberries, huckleberries, and cranberries. Many species and hybrids are grown as showy ornamentals. Before it was produced synthetically, oil of wintergreen originally came from the family. Many of the brushy and scrubby vegetation types of the world (heath, chaparral, maquis or macchia, fynbos, flatwoods) contain numerous species of Ericaceae. Some species, especially rhododendrons and Mountain Laurel in the East, are poisonous to livestock and can cause staggering, convulsions, and death if consumed in quantity.

Silver Buffaloberry

fruit

flowers

flower

fruit

Georgiaplume

fruit

GEORGIAPLUME *Elliottia racemosa*
Muhl. ex Elliott

QUICK ID Recognized by the large plumelike inflorescence of white flowers that usually appears in late June.

Deciduous shrub or small tree, 2–12 m tall, 5–20 cm
diam. Erect or leaning, single trunk; crown narrow,
with ascending branches. **BARK** Gray, furrowed
when young, becoming blocky and similar to that
of Sourwood (*Oxydendrum arboreum*). **TWIG**
Greenish or orange-brown when young, becoming
grayish brown and roughened. **LEAF** Alternate, simple, ovate, oblong, or narrowly elliptic; base tapered
or wedge-shaped; tip acute or abruptly pointed,
with a short bristle at the apex; margins entire, flat.
Upper surface dark green, hairless; lower surface
paler, sparsely hairy. Blade 5–12 cm long, 2–4.5 cm
broad; petiole 6–14 mm long. **FLOWER** Bisexual,
about 2 cm long; petals 4, narrowly linear, white;
produced in showy terminal racemes or panicles,

15–30 cm long. Early summer to midsummer.
FRUIT Four-lobed brown to blackish capsule, about
1 cm diam.; matures autumn, persisting into winter.

HABITAT/RANGE Native. Rare and restricted to
a few locations in Ga.

Notes: *Elliottia* is a small genus of 4 species. Two
are endemic to Japan and 2 to North America; the
other is a western shrub.

GEORGIAPLUME

SOURWOOD *Oxydendrum arboreum* (L.) DC.

QUICK ID The combination of typically leaning habit, deeply corrugated bark, finely toothed oblong leaves, and spray-like clusters of arching or curving racemes distinguishes Sourwood.

Deciduous shrub or moderately large tree, 25–35 m tall, 70 cm diam. Erect, single trunk, often leaning and typically producing 1 to several strictly erect treelike branches along the upper side. **BARK** Usually reddish brown, sometimes gray-brown; deeply, distinctly, and coarsely horizontally and vertically furrowed. **TWIG** Slender, somewhat zigzag, yellowish green, hairless or finely hairy; sap has a sour taste. **LEAF** Alternate, simple, elliptic or oblong, occasionally ovate or obovate; base wedge-shaped; tip tapering to a moderately elongate point; margins finely toothed or entire. Upper surface dull or yellowish green, hairless, or hairy on the midvein and occasionally on the blade tissue; lower surface paler, usually hairy. Turns bright red in autumn. Blade 10–23.5 cm long, 2–8 cm broad; petiole 1.5–2 cm long, usually reddish green. **FLOWER** Bisexual, white or tinged pinkish, petals and sepals 5, produced in clusters of elongate, arching or curving racemes, each with 15–50 flowers. Early summer to midsummer. **FRUIT** Egg-shaped, slightly ribbed, 5-parted brown capsule, 3.5–8.5 mm long, 2–4 mm broad, splitting to release 25–100 seeds; matures late summer to autumn.

HABITAT/RANGE Native. Well-drained acidic woodlands, upland forests, lower to midlevel mountain slopes, bluffs, ravines, stream margins, occasionally in coarse, dry coastal sands, 0–1,700 m; widespread in the East, N.Y. to Ill. south to nw. Fla. and La.

Notes: Sourwood is the only species in its genus and is one of the few unquestionably arborescent members of the heath family in e. North America. It is well known for its splendid autumn color and as the source of sourwood honey. It is a popular ornamental in southern landscapes for its summer flowers and fall foliage. It is essentially pest-free and is tolerant of sun and shade.

FLORIDA HOBBLEBUSH *Agarista populifolia* (Lam.) Judd
A.K.A. AGARISTA, PIPESTEM

QUICK ID Recognized by the combination of toothed evergreen leaves, arching habit, and urn-shaped white flowers.

Evergreen shrub or small shrubby tree, 4–7 m tall, to 7 cm diam. Erect or more often vase-shaped, with 1 to several main trunks arising from near the base; crown ascending, spreading, the branches often arching. **BARK** Smooth, reddish brown, slightly peeling. **TWIG** Brown, usually hairless, sometimes finely hairy, the hairs sometimes gland-tipped; pith chambered. **LEAF** Alternate, simple, thick, lanceolate; base wedge-shaped or rounded; tip tapering to a point; margins toothed or entire. Upper surface lustrous, dark green, sometimes with glandular hairs; lower surface paler, often with gland-tipped hairs. Blade 4–10 cm long, 1–4 cm broad; petiole 5–8 mm long. **FLOWER** Cylindric with a slightly constricted neck, white; petals and sepals 5, fused; stamens 10, stigma 1. Spring. **FRUIT** Rounded or egg-shaped, 5-parted capsule with 125–250 dustlike seeds; matures late summer.

HABITAT/RANGE Native. Acid swamps, ravines, dryish slopes, often along streams or springs, 0–50 m; extreme s. N.C. south to ne. Fla.

Notes: *Agarista* is a genus of 31 species distributed in Mexico, Central and South America, Africa, and islands of the Indian Ocean; this is the only species in North America.

SOURWOOD

FLORIDA HOBBLEBUSH

Sourwood

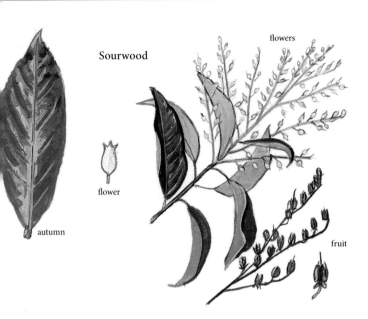

flowers

flower

autumn

fruit

Florida Hobblebush

flowers

fruit

SPARKLEBERRY   *Vaccinium arboreum*
Marshall
A.K.A. FARKLEBERRY

QUICK ID Recognized by the reddish bark, bell-shaped flowers, and lustrous green leaves with a tiny point at the tip.

Evergreen (late deciduous in colder climates) shrub or small tree, 8–14 m tall, to 35 cm diam. Erect, usually a single trunk; crown rounded, usually with contorted branches. **BARK** Reddish brown, mottled gray, often peeling in plates or sheets to reveal reddish inner bark. **TWIG** Red or greenish, hairy at first, hairless by 2nd year. **LEAF** Alternate, simple, firm, elliptic, oval, or nearly circular; base wedge-shaped; apex tipped with the extension of the midvein; margins more or less entire, often glandular. Upper surface lustrous, dark green, hairy along the midvein; lower surface paler, hairy along the midvein. Potentially turns red in autumn. Blade 2–7 cm long, 1–4 cm broad; petiole absent or to about 3 mm long. **FLOWER** White, corolla cup-shaped, about 4 mm long, produced in abundance in spray-like racemes. Spring. **FRUIT** Lustrous black berry, somewhat dry, 5–9 mm diam.; matures late summer to autumn.

HABITAT/RANGE Native. Dry sandy woodlands, thickets, and clearings, sometimes where limestone is present, 0–800 m; in the Southeast, Va. to s. Fla., west to e. Kans. and e. Tex.

SIMILAR SPECIES The flowers of Deerberry (*V. stamineum* L.), a large shrub or small tree widespread in the East from Ont. to Fla. and west to Kans. and Tex., are also open and bell-shaped but have conspicuously protruding stamens.

Notes: The blueberry genus (*Vaccinium*) includes about 500 deciduous shrubs, less often trees and creeping vines, distributed in Mexico, the West Indies, Central America, n. South America, Europe, and Asia. About 30 species occur in North America. Species have alternate, simple leaves, bisexual 4- or 5-parted flowers, and rounded, fleshy berries with 2–40 seeds. Many species of blueberry are similar to one another, often making identification difficult. Centuries of cultivation and use by Native Americans and European settlers has probably contributed to natural hybridization that has blurred morphological distinctions between species.

RUSTY STAGGERBUSH   *Lyonia ferruginea* (Walter) Nutt.

QUICK ID Distinguished by the scaly yellowish-green or dark green leaves, and flowers borne on twigs of the current season.

Evergreen shrub or small tree, 6–12 m tall, to about 23 cm diam. Erect or angled, single trunk; crown ascending and spreading. **BARK** Reddish to brown, scaly. **LEAF** Alternate, simple, leathery, elliptic, ovate, or obovate; base tapered; tip bluntly pointed; margins entire, often wavy. Upper surface dull to semi-lustrous, yellow-green or dark green, often scaly, the scales usually falling early; lower surface persistently densely scaly, hairy along the midvein. Blade 1–9 cm long, 0.5–3 cm broad; petiole 3–7 mm long. **FLOWER** Urn-shaped, 2–4 mm long, often widest at the base; petals 5, white; produced on the previous year's twigs, prior to new growth. Spring. **FRUIT** Egg-shaped, 5-angled, hairy capsule, 3–6 mm long; matures summer to autumn.

HABITAT/RANGE Native. Flatwoods, pine–oak forests, sand scrub, 0–100 m; se. S.C. and se. Ga., south to c. and nw. Fla.

SIMILAR SPECIES In this genus of 36 species (5 in North America), distributed in e. U.S., Mexico, the West Indies, and Asia, only Rusty Staggerbush forms a tree. The shrub Poor-grub (*L. fruticosa* [Michx.] G.S. Torr.), distributed from S.C. to the s. Fla. peninsula and Fla. panhandle, is similar but usually produces flowers and fruit on new growth, after the twigs are fully developed.

SPARKLEBERRY   RUSTY STAGGERBUSH

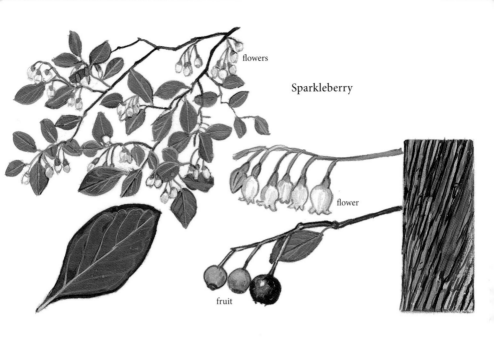

flowers

Sparkleberry

flower

fruit

Rusty Staggerbush

underside

flowers

fruit

■ *RHODODENDRON:* RHODODENDRONS

Evergreen or deciduous shrubs or small trees. A genus of about 1,000 species, 25 in North America; also distributed in Europe, Asia, and Australia. Many species are cultivated for their showy flowers and attractive form. Two main groups are recognized, 1 evergreen, the other deciduous. Native deciduous species are often referred to as native azaleas, and the evergreen species as rhododendrons.

CATAWBA ROSEBAY *Rhododendron catawbiense* Michx.

QUICK ID Distinguished by its large pink flowers and evergreen leaves with a rounded base.

Evergreen shrub or small tree, 3.5–7 m tall, to about 10 cm diam. Shrubby, single trunk, often branching close to the ground. **BARK** Smooth, becoming furrowed and shredding. **LEAF** Alternate, simple, narrowly or broadly elliptic; base rounded; tip bluntly pointed; margins entire, often rolled under, especially during extreme cold or drought. Upper surface dark, lustrous green; lower surface paler. Blade 6–15 cm long, 3.5–6 cm broad; petiole 1–3 cm long. **FLOWER** Corolla pink, broadly bell-shaped, about 6 cm diam.; petals and sepals usually 5; stamens 10. Early summer. **FRUIT** Linear or oblong capsule covered with reddish-brown hairs, 10–23 mm long, produced on erect stalks; matures summer to autumn.

HABITAT/RANGE Native. Mountain slopes, ridges, balds, 500–2,000 m, rarely lower; Va. and W. Va. south to n. Ga., west to Ky. and ne. Ala.

SIMILAR SPECIES Great Laurel can be distinguished by its white flowers and wedge-shaped leaf base.

CATAWBA ROSEBAY

GREAT LAUREL *Rhododendron maximum* L.
A.K.A. ROSEBAY RHODODENDRON

QUICK ID Recognized by its mostly white flowers and evergreen leaves with a wedge-shaped base.

Evergreen large shrub or small tree, to 10 m tall, 30 cm diam. Erect, single trunk, often densely branched from near the base. **BARK** Reddish brown, smooth, becoming shallowly furrowed, shredding. **LEAF** Alternate, simple, narrowly or broadly elliptic; base wedge-shaped; tip short-pointed; margins entire, usually flat. Upper surface lustrous green, usually hairless; lower surface paler green or brownish, finely hairy. Blade 9–30 cm long, 2–8 cm broad; petiole 1–3 cm long. **FLOWER** Corolla white, often tinged pink, with greenish-yellow spots on the upper side of the petals; petals united and cuplike below, spreading and overlapping above, about 4 cm diam.; petals and sepals usually 5; stamens 10. Spring to early summer. **FRUIT** Elongate capsule, 8–20 mm long, glandular-hairy; matures late summer to autumn.

HABITAT/RANGE Native. Low woods, stream banks, mesic forests, lower slopes, 0–1,900 m; N.S. and Maine south to n. Ga., west to e. Ohio, e. Ky., and e. Tenn.

SIMILAR SPECIES Catawba Rosebay can be distinguished by its pink flowers and more rounded leaf base.

GREAT LAUREL

Catawba Rosebay

flowers

Great Laurel

flowers

flower bud

MOUNTAIN LAUREL *Kalmia latifolia* L.

QUICKID Recognized by the combination of evergreen dark green leaves, cup-shaped flowers with 10 stamens, the anthers embedded in the corolla, and rounded fruit capsules.

Evergreen, typically a large spreading shrub, rarely a small tree to about 9 m tall, 30 cm diam. Upright, often with numerous crooked branches from near the base. **BARK** Reddish brown, slightly scaly. **TWIG** Round in cross section, slightly sticky with glandular hairs. **LEAF** Alternate, sometimes appearing whorled near branch tips; simple, leathery, lanceolate, elliptic, or oblanceolate; base wedge-shaped; tip acute; margins entire. Upper surface dark, lustrous green, usually hairless or finely hairy with stalked hairs, mainly on the midvein, veins obscure; lower surface paler green, often with stalked glands. Blade 2–12 cm long, 3–5 cm broad; petiole 1–4.5 cm long, sometimes with stalked glands. **FLOWER** Cup- or bowl-shaped, 1–2 cm diam., varying pink to reddish or white; petals 5, fused; stamens 10, recurved, the anthers lodged in darkened pockets within the corolla; produced in many-flowered terminal panicles. Spring to summer, depending on elevation. **FRUIT** Rounded, glandular-hairy capsule, 3–5 mm broad, 4–7 mm long; matures late summer to autumn.

HABITAT/RANGE Native. Mountain slopes, ravine bottoms, bluffs, along woodland streams, rocky or sandy hardwood forests, sometimes forming dense thickets, 0–1,900 m; Maine south to nw. Fla., west to Ind. and La.

MOUNTAIN LAUREL

Notes: Kalmia is a genus of 10 species, 8 in North America (also in the West Indies, Europe, and Asia); only Mountain Laurel forms a tree. Evergreen *Rhododendron* species are similar, but their flowers lack the lodged anthers in the corolla.

EUPHORBIACEAE: SPURGE FAMILY

The spurges constitute a large family of more than 200 genera and nearly 6,000 species, ranging from small herbs to massive trees. Recent phylogenetic work has separated the sections of this large family into 3 smaller families: Euphorbiaceae, Phyllanthaceae (including *Bischofia* and *Phyllanthus*), and Putranjivaceae (including *Drypetes*). Here we treat them in the traditional classification.

Many species have milky sap. **LEAF** Alternate, 2-ranked, or opposite; usually simple, but sometimes palmately compound or simple and deeply palmately lobed. **FLOWER** Unisexual, the sexes on the same or separate plants; when on the same plant they are often aggregated in a cyathium, a small cup resembling a tiny flower. A calyx may be present; petals are usually lacking. Stamens vary from 1 to many. The ovary is usually 3-chambered but may be 2- to many-chambered. **FRUIT** Usually a capsule that splits open along the partitions between chambers (schizocarp).

Most species native to the U.S. are herbaceous; a few native subtropical species are shrubs or trees. A number of non-native species have been introduced for horticultural purposes, several of which have become naturalized in the East. This is especially true in s. Florida, where several are recognized as invasive species. Many economically valuable products are obtained from the family, among them rubber, castor and tung oils, dyes, timber, and many ornamentals, including Poinsettia (*Euphorbia pulcherrima* Willd. ex Klotzsch).

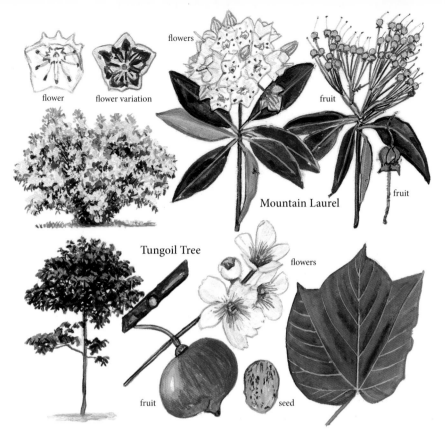

flowers

flower

flower variation

fruit

Mountain Laurel

fruit

Tungoil Tree

flowers

fruit

seed

■ *ALEURITES*: ALEURITES

Aleurites is a genus of about 5 species distributed in Asia and Hawaii, at least two of which occur in the Southeast.

TUNGOIL TREE *Aleurites fordii* Hemsl.

QUICK ID Easily recognized by the long-stalked, ovate, palmately veined leaves and distinctive petiole glands.

Deciduous tree to about 12 m tall, 40 cm diam. Erect, single trunk; crown rounded. **BARK** Gray, smooth or slightly roughened. **TWIG** Stout, hairless, developing oblong lenticels; exuding milky sap when broken. **LEAF** Alternate, simple, ovate, often 3-lobed; base heart-shaped or truncate; tip abruptly sharp-pointed; margins entire, sinuses of marginal lobes often with conspicuous glands. Upper surface dark green, hairless, with 5 primary veins arising from the base; lower surface paler, gray-green, usually hairy. Blade 5–30 cm long,

3–30 cm broad; petiole as long, or nearly as long, as the blade, hairy at first, with 2 conspicuous reddish glands on the upper side near the point of attachment with the blade, subtended at first by conspicuous stipules, these soon falling. **FLOWER** Radially symmetric, about 4 cm diam., male and female in the same inflorescence, usually with a single female flower at the center of a cyme; sepals 2; petals 5–8, spreading, white with reddish-yellow veins inside at the base. Spring. **FRUIT** Rounded green or red capsule, 4–8 cm diam., splitting to release 3–5 flattened or rounded seeds; matures late summer to autumn.

HABITAT/RANGE Introduced from China; cultivated for its oily seeds, established in s. Ga. and nw. Fla., west to e. La., mostly within 250 km of the coast.

SIMILAR SPECIES See Indian Walnut.

Notes: Some experts treat Tungoil Tree as *Vernicia fordii* (Hemsl.) Airy Shaw.

INDIAN WALNUT *Aleurites moluccana* (L.) Willd.

Evergreen tree, to about 20 m tall. **LEAF** Ovate to 5-lobed, very similar to leaf of Tungoil Tree but lacking glands in the sinuses of the marginal lobes. **FRUIT** Globose to ovoid, green to brown, 4–6 cm diam., indehiscent, usually with 1 or 2 seeds; sometimes called "candlenut." **HABITAT/RANGE** Introduced; native to Polynesia and Southeast Asia, naturalized in s. Fla.

■ *DRYPETES*: MILKBARKS

This is a pantropical genus of about 200 species, distributed mostly in the Old World. About 12 species occur in the American tropics, 2 native to North America. Members of this genus constitute the only species outside the order of mustard plants (Brassicales) that are known to contain mustard oils.

MILKBARK *Drypetes diversifolia* Krug & Urb.

QUICK ID Recognized by the combination of milky-white bark, stiff leaves, petalless flowers with 5 hairy sepals, and subtropical hammock habitat.

Evergreen shrub or small tree to about 12 m tall. Erect, single main trunk; crown rounded, compact. **BARK** Milky white, smooth or slightly roughened, often decorated with lichens. **LEAF** Alternate, simple, stiff, elliptic, oval, or oblong; base broadly wedge-shaped; tip blunt or rounded, sometimes notched; margins usually entire, those of young leaves sometimes sharply toothed. Upper surface dark green, lower surface paler. Blade variable in size and shape, 8–13 cm long, 2.5–5 cm broad; petiole 5–15 mm long. **FLOWER** Unisexual, tiny, male and female

borne in axillary clusters on separate plants, about 5 mm diam., greenish or greenish white, petals absent, sepals usually 5, hairy. Mostly spring to early summer. **FRUIT** Egg-shaped white drupe, 1–2.5 cm diam.; matures mostly summer to autumn.

HABITAT/RANGE Native. Hammocks; southernmost Fla. and Fla. Keys.

GUIANA PLUM *Drypetes lateriflora* (Sw.) Krug & Urb.

QUICK ID Recognized within subtropical hammocks by the lanceolate or oblong leaves, petalless flowers with 4 hairy sepals, and fuzzy red fruit.

Evergreen shrub or small tree, to about 10 m tall. Erect, single slender trunk; crown of drooping branches. **BARK** Smooth, light brown. **LEAF** Alternate, simple, leathery, lanceolate, elliptic, or oblong; base wedge-shaped or rounded, often oblique; tip often abruptly sharp-pointed; margins entire. Upper surface dark green; lower surface paler. Blade 8–12 cm long, to 6 cm broad; petiole 10–15 mm long. **FLOWER** Unisexual, tiny, male and female borne in axillary clusters on separate plants, 4–5 mm diam., greenish, petals absent; sepals usually 4, hairy. Spring. **FRUIT** Round, single-seeded, fuzzy, bright red drupe, 7–10 mm diam.; matures autumn.

HABITAT/RANGE Native. Hammocks; se. Fla. and Fla. Keys.

SIMILAR SPECIES Lancewood (*Ocotea coriacea*) and Redbay (*Persea borbonia*), both in Lauraceae, are similar small evergreen trees that occur with Guiana Plum, but they have small blue-black drupes (those of Lancewood held in a red or yellow cup) rather than hairy red fruit.

MILKBARK

GUIANA PLUM

Indian Walnut

flowers

fruit

seed

fruit section

Milkbark

Guiana Plum

fruit

young leaf
with small
teeth

fruit

OYSTERWOOD *Gymnanthes lucida* Sw.
A.K.A. CRABWOOD

QUICK ID No other tree of the Florida subtropical hammocks has leaves with an eared base.

Evergreen shrub or small tree, to about 10 m tall, about 20 cm diam. Erect, single trunk; crown narrow. **BARK** Smooth or finely fissured, grayish or brown. **TWIG** Green at first, usually with numerous raised lenticels; sap more or less watery. **LEAF** Alternate, simple, leathery, elliptic; base minutely but distinctly eared; tip rounded or blunt; margins entire or minutely toothed near the tip, the teeth of newer leaves often gland-tipped. Upper surface dark green; lower surface paler. Blade 3–12 cm long, 1–4 cm broad; petiole usually less than 1 cm long. **FLOWER** Unisexual, male and female on the same tree, petals and sepals absent or rudimentary, male flowers in elongate racemes, to about 5 cm long, shorter than the leaves, female flower solitary at the tip of a long stalk arising from the base of the male raceme. Summer to winter. **FRUIT** Rounded, 3-parted, dark brown capsule, to about 12 mm diam.

HABITAT/RANGE Native. Hammocks; s. Fla. and Fla. Keys.

Notes: Gymnanthes is a small genus of about 12 species distributed primarily in the American tropics; Oysterwood is the only species native to North America.

MANCHINEEL *Hippomane mancinella* L.
A.K.A. POISON GUAVA

QUICK ID Distinguished by the finely toothed yellow-green leaves with a yellowish central vein, the spikelike inflorescence, and the comparatively large yellowish fruit.

Deciduous shrub or small tree, to about 15 m tall, potentially to 60 cm diam., but usually much smaller than this in the U.S. Erect, single trunk; crown broad, spreading, with forking branches. **BARK** Gray or brown, finely fissured or warty. **TWIG** Green, becoming brown, exuding poisonous white sap that is extremely irritating to the skin. **LEAF** Alternate, simple, ovate or elliptic; base rounded or slightly flattened; tip rounded or short-pointed; margins minutely and finely toothed. Upper surface light yellow-green, midvein yellowish; lower surface paler. Blade 5–10 cm long, 3–8 cm broad; petiole slender, to 6 cm long, with a distinctive gland at the point of attachment to the blade. **FLOWER** Male and female on the same tree, greenish, several male flowers along the outer half of an erect spike to 10 cm long, female flowers 2 or 3 at the base of the male spike. Year-round. **FRUIT** Rounded yellowish-green apple-like drupe of 6–9 cells, 2–4 cm diam., extremely poisonous if ingested. Year-round.

HABITAT/RANGE Native. Hammocks, mostly along the coast; extreme s. Fla. and Fla. Keys.

Notes: Hippomane is a genus of 1 species of the American tropics, including se. North America. Manchineel is rare in the wild owing to intentional eradication. Ostensibly extremely poisonous; the fruit is reportedly deadly if consumed. Not easily confused with other trees of subtropical coastal hammocks.

JAVANESE BISHOPWOOD *Bischofia javanica* Blume

Evergreen tree to about 20 m tall, with finely fissured gray-brown bark. Erect, single trunk, crown dense, rounded. Distinguished in s. Fla. by its 3-parted leaves and milky sap. **LEAF** Alternate, compound, blade 25–36 cm long, petiole 8–20 cm long. Trifoliolate, leaflets ovate, elliptic, or obovate, 7–20 cm long, 4–8 cm broad, margins toothed. **FLOWER** Greenish yellow, in drooping panicles; male and female on separate trees. Late summer to autumn. **FRUIT** Rounded, fleshy capsule, 6–13 cm diam., splitting into 3 segments; matures autumn. **HABITAT/RANGE** Introduced from Asia; established in hammocks, pine flatwoods, and swamps in s. Fla. Invasive. *Notes:* 1 of 2 species in the genus.

OYSTERWOOD   MANCHINEEL

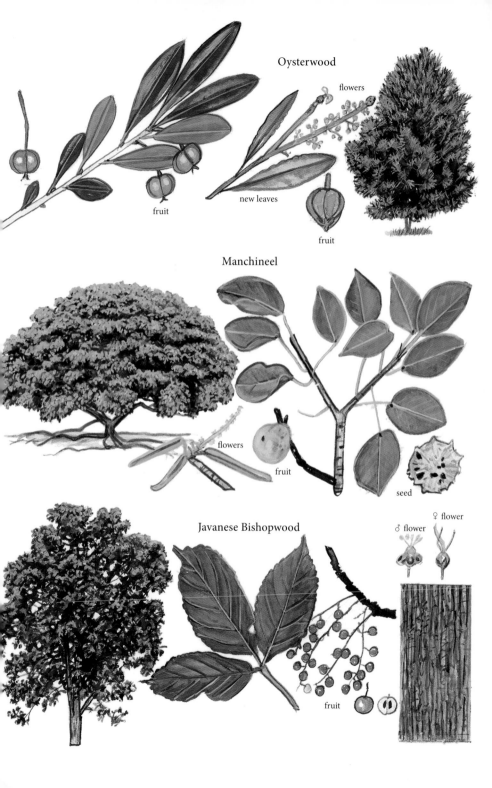

Oysterwood

fruit

flowers

new leaves

fruit

Manchineel

flowers

fruit

seed

Javanese Bishopwood

♂ flower

♀ flower

fruit

INDIAN TREE SPURGE *Euphorbia tirucalli* L.
A.K.A. PENCIL RUBBER HEDGE, PENCIL TREE

Succulent shrub or small tree, potentially to 9 m tall, 15 cm diam., with numerous jointed, ascending, pencil-diameter green branches. Easily recognized by the nearly leafless green stems and cactus-like appearance. **BARK** Dark green, smooth. **LEAF** Absent, or alternate, simple, spoon-shaped, more or less succulent; blade 1.5–2.5 cm long, less than 5 mm broad. **FLOWER** Tiny, yellowish, borne in dense ball-like heads, 1–2 cm diam. Year-round. **FRUIT** Rounded, 3-parted capsule on a stout stalk. **HABITAT/RANGE** Introduced from Africa; established in sw. Fla. and Fla. Keys. *Notes:* This large genus of nearly 2,000 species is represented in the U.S. mostly by herbaceous species. **Mottled Spurge** (*E. lactea* Haw.), another cactus-like species, has been reported in Fla. but is not currently known to be established there.

Mottled Spurge

SANDBOX TREE *Hura crepitans* L.

Evergreen tree to about 30 m tall. Erect, single trunk, often densely spiny. Sap clear, sticky. Recognized by the combination of heart-shaped leaves, spiny stem and branches, and many-chambered fruit. **LEAF** Alternate, simple, ovate; margins vary from entire to coarsely toothed. Blade 11–16 cm long, to about 5–12 cm broad. **FLOWER** Male and female on the same tree, male flowers in long-stalked terminal catkins, female flowers solitary in the leaf axils; petals absent; styles fused into a fleshy column; stigmas fused into an umbrella-like disk. **FRUIT** Large, vertically compressed woody capsule, to 8 cm diam., longitudinally grooved

and segmented into 12–15 chambers; green, becoming pinkish brown; splits forcibly and clearly audibly at maturity (spring to summer) to expel the seeds. **HABITAT/RANGE** Introduced from tropical America; established in s. Fla. and Fla. Keys. *Notes:* The genus contains about 3 species.

■ *JATROPHA*: NETTLESPURGES

A genus of about 200 species, many with showy, ornamental flowers. Mostly tropical and warm temperate in distribution; 4 species have been introduced to Fla. from Cuba or tropical America, and as many as 6 herbs, shrubs, and subshrubs are native to the Southwest.

BARBADOS NUT *Jatropha curcas* L.
A.K.A. NUTMEG PLANT, PHYSIC NUT

QUICK ID Recognized by the combination of large, palmately lobed leaves, green to yellowish-white flowers, and large ellipsoid, 2- or 3-valved fruit.

Deciduous large shrub or small tree, to about 6 m tall, 16 cm diam. Erect, single trunk, usually low-branching; crown thin, rounded, with few spreading branches. **BARK** Light brown, smooth or somewhat warty. **TWIG** Stout, light green, becoming gray, smooth, with whitish lenticels. **LEAF** Alternate, simple, heart-shaped, often palmate with 3–5 lobes; base rounded or cordate; tip abruptly sharp-pointed. Upper surface dull green, veins palmate, impressed, yellowish; lower surface paler, veins raised. Blade averaging about 15 cm long and broad; petiole 6–18 cm long. **FLOWER** Yellowish green, male and female on the same tree, borne from the leaf axils in branched clusters 3–8 cm long. Spring to autumn. **FRUIT** Rounded or ellipsoid yellow capsule, 2.5–3 cm diam., with 2 or 3 oblong black seeds, 1.5–2 cm long; present nearly year-round.

HABITAT/RANGE Introduced from tropical America; escaped and established mostly along the coast in s. Fla.

SIMILAR SPECIES Similar species of *Aleurites* can be distinguished by the glands on the petiole near the point of leaf attachment. See also Peregrina.

Indian Tree Spurge

flower cluster

Sandbox Tree

♀ flower

♂ catkin

fruit

fruit

Barbados Nut

PEREGRINA *Jatropha integerrima* Jacq.

Deciduous, typically a shrub with several trunks, rarely arborescent, 4–5 m tall. Closely related to Barbados Nut. **LEAF** Alternate, simple, often with sharp-pointed lobes at the base of the blade. **HABITAT/RANGE** Introduced to Fla. from Cuba and naturalized from ornamental plantings in s. Fla. and Fla. Keys.

CORALBUSH *Jatropha multifida* L.
A.K.A. CORALPLANT

Evergreen or deciduous shrub or small tree to about 5 m tall, 8 cm diam. **BARK** Brown, smooth, with raised lenticels. **LEAF** Alternate, simple, deeply palmately divided into several narrow, toothed or divided lobes. Blade 15–30 cm long and broad; petiole 10–20 cm long, subtended by a distinctive fringed stipule to about 1.5 cm long. **FLOWER** Red, male and female in the same long-stalked branched cluster arising from the top of the main stem, petals present, sepals not petal-like. **FRUIT** Three-parted capsule with mottled seeds. **HABITAT/RANGE** Introduced from the West Indies; naturalized in s. Fla.

GRAHAM'S MANIHOT *Manihot grahamii* Hook.

QUICK ID Easily distinguished by the alternate, simple, deeply divided leaves, yellowish flowers with a petal-like calyx, and a naturalized distribution mostly in c. and n. Fla.

Deciduous shrub or small tree, to about 7 m tall, 20 cm diam. Erect, single trunk; new growth herbaceous. **BARK** Light brown with circular lenticels. **TWIG** Green, hairless, often glaucous. **LEAF** Alternate, simple, deeply palmately divided into 5–11 leaflike segments, the segments 5–15 cm long and often flared or fiddle-shaped near the tip. Upper surface usually dark green; lower surface paler, often glaucous, with a bluish-green cast. Blade 8–15 cm long and broad; petiole to about 20 cm long. **FLOWER** Yellowish green, male and female borne in the same inflorescence; petals absent, sepals 5, petal-like, at least partially fused, the calyx about 1.5 cm long; inflorescence branched, the branches to about 10 cm long. Summer. **FRUIT** Rounded, several-sided capsule, about 1.5 cm diam.; matures autumn to winter.

HABITAT/RANGE Introduced from South America; naturalized in c. and n. Fla., sw. Ala., and La.

SIMILAR SPECIES The leaves of the buckeyes (*Aesculus*, Sapindaceae) are similar in form but are opposite and compound, with toothed leaflets. Leaves of Coralbush (*Jatropha multifida*) are also similar, but the flowers are red.

Notes: Manihot is a genus of about 125 species, 2 naturalized in North America; the other is a herb or subshrub sparingly naturalized in a few counties in s. Fla., Ala., and Tex. **Castor Bean** (*Ricinus communis* L.), a large, softly woody shrub (rarely treelike) with palmately lobed leaves, bristly capsules, and large, highly poisonous gray, black, and reddish-brown seeds, has escaped cultivation and is widely established in warmer parts of the East.

Castor Bean

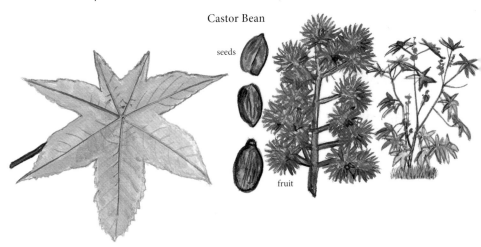

seeds

fruit

Peregrina

flowers

fruit

Coralbush

flowers

fruit

Graham's Manihot

flowers

fruit

TAHITIAN GOOSEBERRY TREE *Phyllanthus acidus* (L.) Skeels

QUICKID Recognized by its greenish or pinkish twigs lined with up to 50 drooping, ovate leaves.

Deciduous large shrub or small tree, 8–10 m tall, to about 15 cm diam. Erect, single trunk; crown spreading. **BARK** Greenish gray, scaly, slightly fissured. **TWIG** Stout, about 1 cm diam., brownish gray, green, or pinkish; deciduous and falling with the leaves. **LEAF** Alternate, simple, borne along a pinkish twig 15–50 cm long and often appearing compound. Ovate, base rounded, tip rounded or pointed, margins entire. Upper surface green, hairless; lower surface paler. Blade 4–7.5 cm long, to 4 cm broad; petiole about 3 mm long. **FLOWER** Green to whitish green or yellowish green, suffused with wine red, the female flowers 1.5–2 cm diam.; both sexes intermingled in many-flowered fascicles on leafless branchlets. Year-round. **FRUIT** Fleshy drupelike capsule, 1.5–2 cm diam., with several smooth brown seeds; matures spring to late summer.

HABITAT/RANGE Introduced from Brazil; cultivated and established in sw. Fla.

Notes: Phyllanthus is a genus of several hundred species, 8 native to North America, 6 introduced. This is the only one that forms a tree.

CHINESE TALLOW *Sapium sebiferum* (L.) Roxb.
A.K.A. POPCORN TREE

QUICKID The ovate leaves with an abruptly narrowed tip and a long petiole distinguish this species.

Deciduous shrub or tree, 6–17 m tall, 30–90 cm diam. Erect, single trunk, sometimes mildly contorted; crown slender, upright, the branches spreading or ascending. **BARK** Grayish brown,

smooth at first, becoming scaly, somewhat furrowed and roughed with age. **TWIG** Green and glaucous at first, becoming tan, usually with scattered circular orange lenticels. **LEAF** Alternate, simple, mostly ovate or nearly rhombic, occasionally widest at the middle and broader than long; base rounded or broadly wedge-shaped; abruptly narrowing to an elongate tip; margins entire. Upper surface green or yellow-green, central vein yellowish, turning reddish in autumn; lower surface paler. In autumn turns pinkish red, purplish red, orange-red or red. Blade 3–6 cm long, 2–5 cm broad; petiole 2–6 cm long, slender, hairless, the upper side with a pair of glands at the point of blade attachment, oozing milky sap when broken. **FLOWER** Yellowish, petals absent, male and female intermingled in a cylindric spikelike inflorescence to about 20 cm long. Spring. **FRUIT** Three-lobed capsule, splitting at maturity (summer to autumn) to reveal 3 dull white seeds.

HABITAT/RANGE Introduced from China and Japan; cultivated and now a pernicious weed invading stream banks, pond margins, wet ditches, and uplands; widely established across the Southeast from N.C. south to Fla., west to Ark., e. Tex., and La., especially near the coast.

SIMILAR SPECIES The leaflets of Indian Rosewood (*Dalbergia sissoo*, Fabaceae), a well-known invasive species in s. Fla., are similar in shape, but the leaves are compound. The related **Milktree** (*S. glandulosum* [L.] Morong) has been reported from one location in extreme nw. Fla., but is not known to occur there presently. It is native to the West Indies and differs from Chinese Tallow by its narrowly elliptic leaves with finely toothed margins.

Notes: Sapium is genus of 20–25 species, 2 introduced in North America. Chinese Tallow, which is also known as *Triadica sebifera* (L.) Small, was introduced to S.C. in the 1700s and has been cultivated for seed oil, ornamental use, and as a honey plant for beekeepers. Many observers place it among the most malicious invasive species of the southeastern coastal plains.

Tahitian Gooseberry Tree

flower

flowers

fruit

Chinese Tallow

flowers

fruit

autumn

Milktree

flowers

fruit

splitting fruit

seed

leaf margin

FABACEAE: BEAN OR PEA FAMILY

The bean family includes approximately 730 genera and more than 19,000 species, and constitutes the third largest plant family, exceeded in size only by the sunflower (Asteraceae) and orchid (Orchidaceae) families. More than 45 genera and 110 species of trees of Fabaceae occur north of Mexico, from the hot arid Southwest and humid Southeast northward. The family is also known as the Leguminosae, an old name derived from early European words for "vegetable" and "plant with a seed pod."

LEAF All members of the family have compound leaves, those of most species pinnately or bipinnately compound, although the leaves of some species treated here are unifoliolate and appear simple. The leaves are usually alternate. At night or during hot periods, leaflets may fold together, apparently a water-conservation mechanism. Species with glands on the leaves often attract ants, which may attack insects or animals that would otherwise feed upon the plant. **FLOWER** Usually bisexual and fundamentally arranged in multiples of 5, except for the single simple pistil. **FRUIT** A legume and the unifying feature of the family. The pea pod is a good example of this type of fruit. It is 1-chambered, derived from a superior, simple ovary, with 2 rows of seeds hanging from the upper suture; when mature it is dry and elastically dehisces (splits open) along the upper and lower sutures. From this prototype various types of legumes have evolved, some with few seeds, some indehiscent, some breaking into 1-seeded sections.

The family is commonly divided into 3 major groups, subfamilies Caesalpinioideae, Mimosoideae, and Papilionoideae. For the most part each subfamily is easily recognized by the structure of the corolla and stamens. The treatment here is organized by subfamily, and each section is introduced with a brief subfamily description. The family is worldwide in distribution, and species are found in all habitats. They form one of the world's most economically and ecologically important plant families, providing food for humans and livestock, as well as high-quality lumber, sources of dye, spectacular ornamental plants, and habitat and food for wildlife. Many members of the family are well known for their ability to fix atmospheric nitrogen and improve soil fertility. Root nodules provide habitat for the bacteria *Rhizobium*, which use atmospheric nitrogen in their metabolism, making it available to all living systems through soil enrichment.

SUBFAMILY CAESALPINIOIDEAE: SENNAS AND THEIR RELATIVES

The subfamily Caesalpinioideae includes the sennas, cassias, orchid trees, locusts, redbuds, and their relatives. It is primarily tropical and subtropical, consists mostly of shrubs and trees, and includes about 180 genera and 3,000 species. **LEAF** Alternate, occasionally clustered; usually pinnate, sometimes bipinnate, or sometimes unifoliolate and appearing simple; in some species, especially in the genus *Senna*, the petiole beard glands. **FLOWER** Usually bisexual, more or less bilateral, the upper petal positioned interior to the lateral petals (wings) and enclosed by them in bud; stamens 10 or fewer, separate or at least partially united, often opening by terminal pores.

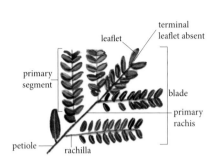

Bipinnately Compound Leaf

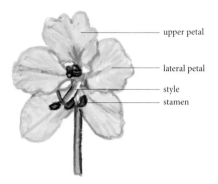

Caesalpinioid Legume Flower
(pp. 250–263)

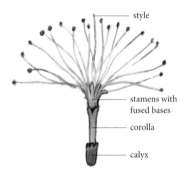

Mimosoid Legume Flower
(pp. 264–279)

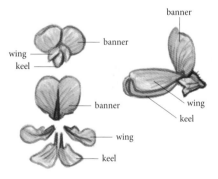

Papilionoid Legume Flower
(pp. 280–293)

■ *BAUHINIA*: ORCHID TREES

Bauhinia is a genus of about 250 species of trees, shrubs, and woody vines distributed in tropical regions of Mexico, the West Indies, Central and South America, Asia, Africa, and Australia; 5 species (4 trees) occur in North America, 1 native to the West. At least 10 species are used ornamentally.

ORCHID TREE *Bauhinia variegata* L.
A.K.A. MOUNTAIN EBONY

QUICK ID Orchid Tree is recognized by the combination of its apparently 2-lobed leaves and comparatively large, showy flowers.

Evergreen or deciduous tree to about 8 m tall. Erect, usually single trunk; crown more or less rounded or vertically flattened and spreading. **BARK** Grayish, smooth at first, becoming slightly roughened. **TWIG** Brownish or grayish brown, hairy at first, becoming nearly hairless. **LEAF** Alternate, unifoliolate (appearing simple), 2-ranked; usually deeply notched from the tip nearly to the heart-shaped base, the blade thus appearing to be divided into 2 symmetric lobes; margins entire. Upper surface soft yellow-green with 7–9 palmate veins; lower surface paler, the veins raised and conspicuous. Blade 3–10 cm long, 2.5–5 cm broad; petiole 5–30 mm long. **FLOWER** Bisexual, 7.5–10 cm diam.; petals 5, varying purple, reddish, pinkish, or white, 1 with a deep purple or yellow streak or blotch at base; functional stamens 5, nonfunctional stamens 5. Winter to spring, usually when the tree is leafless. **FRUIT** Flattened legume, 13–23 cm long, to about 2 cm broad, less than 2 mm thick, tapering to base; seeds 10–25, brown; matures summer to autumn.

HABITAT/RANGE Introduced from tropical Asia; escaped from cultivation and established in hardwood hammocks, pine flatwoods, and coastal swamps; s. Fla. (where it is treated as an invasive species), previously reported for La. and Tex. but probably not naturalized there.

NAPOLEON'S PLUME *Bauhinia monandra* Kurz

Cultivated in the s. U.S. and previously reported as naturalized in Fla. and Tex., **FLOWER** Often pink but with only 1 fertile stamen; appearing in summer. **HABITAT/RANGE** Introduced; cultivated in the U.S. and previously reported as naturalized in Fla. and Tex.

PURPLE ORCHID TREE *Bauhinia purpurea* L.
A.K.A. BUTTERFLY TREE

Distinguished by its mostly autumn flowering period and its flowers with 3 functional stamens. **HABITAT/RANGE** Introduced; naturalized in s. Fla.

WHITE ORCHID TREE *Bauhinia aculeata* L.

FLOWER White, with 10 fertile stamens, appearing mostly in summer. **LEAF** Leaves subtended by spines. **HABITAT/RANGE** Introduced; naturalized in s. Fla.

White Orchid Tree

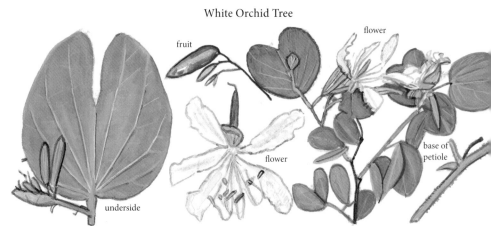

fruit

flower

flower

base of petiole

flower

underside

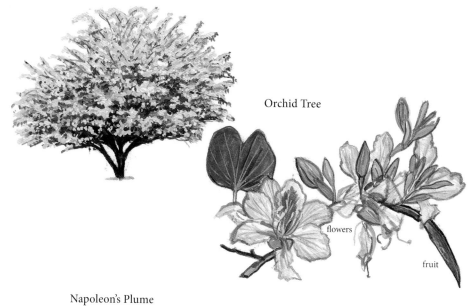

Orchid Tree

flowers

fruit

Napoleon's Plume

seed

Purple Orchid Tree

flowers

flowers

fruit

PRIDE-OF-BARBADOS *Caesalpinia pulcherrima* (L.) Sw.
A.K.A. DWARF POINCIANA, BIRD OF PARADISE

QUICK ID In s. Fla. the species is distinguished by its combination of pinnately compound leaves, showy red and yellow flowers, and mostly unarmed or mildly spiny branches.

Evergreen shrub or small tree, 3–5 m tall, 7–13 cm diam. Vase-shaped, low-branching; crown flat-topped, spreading, the branches mildly armed with scattered 5-mm-long spines. **BARK** Light gray, smooth, becoming slightly fissured. **LEAF** Alternate, bipinnate, blade 15–30 cm long, 16–28 cm broad, with 5–10 pairs of major lateral segments, terminal segment absent, each segment with 5–12 pairs of ultimate leaflets and no terminal leaflet; petiole stout, 5–10 cm long. Leaflets 1–2.5 cm long, 5–10 mm broad, oblong, base asymmetric; tip round, often notched and with a minute point; margins entire. **FLOWER** Bisexual, about 4 cm diam., petals 5, yellow or orange-yellow, often turning red with age, sometimes red with a yellow border; stamens 10, slender, red or yellow, 4–6 cm long. Year-round. **FRUIT** Flat legume, 6–10 cm long, 1.5–2 cm broad, seeds about 1 cm diam.; matures year-round.

HABITAT/RANGE Introduced from tropical America; widely planted, naturalized in s. Fla.

Notes: Caesalpinia is a genus of 70–165 species of tropical and subtropical shrubs, trees, and vines; about 10 occur in North America, 6 native, with an additional 4 species in s. Fla., all of which are spiny, scrambling shrubs or vines.

JERUSALEM THORN *Parkinsonia aculeata* L.

QUICK ID Easily recognized by the linear leaf segments and numerous short leaflets.

Deciduous or nearly evergreen scraggly, spiny shrub or small tree in the East (arborescent, to about 12 m tall in the West). Erect or drooping; crown often rounded, with pendulous branches. **BARK** Smooth, green or yellowish green, becoming brown or reddish brown. **TWIG** Hairless, green or yellowish green, with green, black, or brown spines to about 2.5 cm long. **LEAF** Alternate, bipinnate or rarely pinnate, often appearing pinnate due to lack of a distinct petiole; segment blade 20–40 cm long, 6–10 mm broad; petiole essentially absent. Major leaf segments 1–3, linear, arising from a central point near the base of the leaf, rachilla yellowish green, photosynthetic. Leaflets in 20–30 pairs, widely spaced, linear or oblanceolate, 5–8 mm long, quickly deciduous, leaving the long, drooping rachilla leafless. **FLOWER** Bisexual, about 2 cm diam.; petals 5, yellow, about 12 mm long; stamens 10; inflorescence a short, congested terminal cluster of short racemes, each with 2–15 flowers. Spring to autumn. **FRUIT** Narrow or oblong legume, 2–10 cm long, 5–6 mm diam., nearly round in cross section, often slightly constricted between the seeds; matures summer.

HABITAT/RANGE Introduced to the East from the Southwest or Mexico; broadly cultivated and naturalized, especially in Fla., where it is more often a shrub than a tree.

Notes: Parkinsonia is a genus of 10 species distributed in warm, dry areas of the world, from sea-level to moderate elevations. All species are cold-sensitive. The single species in the East is native to the West and is naturalized from cultivation.

JERUSALEM THORN

Pride-of-Barbados

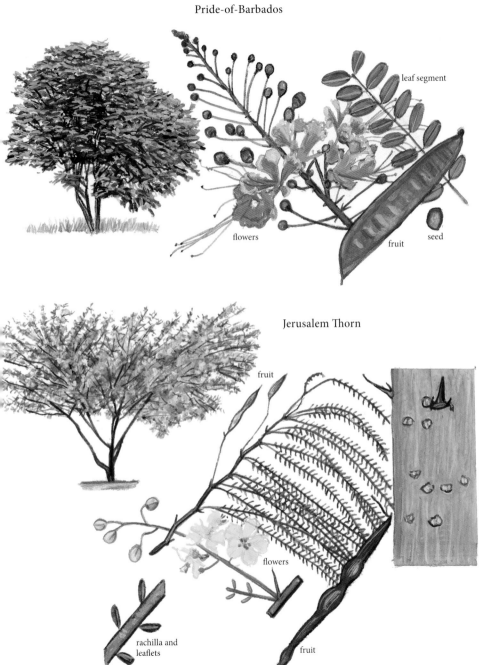

leaf segment

flowers

fruit

seed

Jerusalem Thorn

fruit

flowers

rachilla and
leaflets

fruit

■ *CASSIA*: CASSIAS

Cassia is a relatively large genus that once included numerous species now classified in the genera *Chamaecrista* and *Senna*.

GOLDEN SHOWER *Cassia fistula* L.

QUICK ID Identified by the combination of evenly compound leaves with large leaflets and showy yellow flowers.

Deciduous tree to about 20 m tall, 30 cm diam. Erect, single trunk, often branching from near the ground; crown ellipsoid, with ascending branches. **BARK** Gray, smooth, becoming roughened, brownish, and darkening with age. **TWIG** Finely hairy to nearly hairless. **LEAF** Alternate, pinnate, blade 20–40 cm long, 13–28 cm broad, divided into an even number of leaflets; petiole to about 8 cm long. Leaflets 6–16, in 3–8 pairs, terminal leaflet absent, elliptic or broadly lanceolate, base rounded, tip bluntly pointed, 6–20 cm long, 4–5 cm broad, those toward the tip of leaf longer. **FLOWER** Bisexual, 3–6 cm diam., stalk to 8 cm long; petals 5, pale or bright yellow; stamens 10, 7 fertile, 3 elongate, arching, 2.5–4 cm long and exerted beyond the corolla; inflorescence a drooping raceme 20–40 cm long. Spring to summer. **FRUIT** Narrow, cylindric, lustrous, dark brown legume, 30–60 cm long, 1.5–2 cm diam.; not constricted between the seed compartments, sometimes with ringed depressions near the apex; matures summer to autumn.

HABITAT/RANGE Introduced from Southeast Asia; cultivated in warmer climates, sparingly naturalized in Fla.

SIMILAR SPECIES At least 3 other non-native *Cassia* species have previously been reported as occurring in Fla., none of which is currently known to be naturalized there; they are illustrated below.

PINK SHOWER *Cassia javanica* L. var. *indochinensis* Gagnep.
A.K.A. APPLE BLOSSOM

FLOWER Pinkish or reddish, with 5 dark red sepals. **LEAF** Leaflets comparatively small. **HABITAT/RANGE** Introduced from tropical Asia; cultivated in s. Fla.

PINK SHOWER *Cassia grandis* L.f.

Like *C. javanica*, this tree is also called Pink Shower and bears pink flowers; it can be distinguished by its conspicuously hairy young growth. **HABITAT/RANGE** Introduced; native from the Caribbean to n. South America; cultivated in s. Fla.

AFRICAN PIPE CASSIA *Cassia afrofistula* Brenan

FLOWER Yellow, with shorter stamens than those of Golden Shower, not exerted beyond the corolla. **HABITAT/RANGE** Introduced from Africa; cultivated in s. Fla.

Golden Shower

fruit

flowers

Pink Shower
(*Cassia javanica*)

fruit

seeds

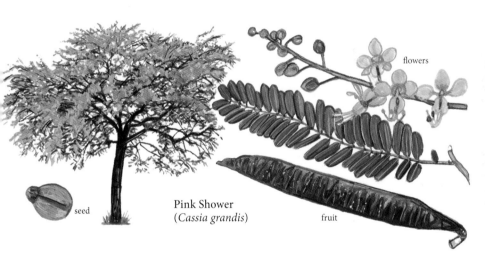

seed

Pink Shower
(*Cassia grandis*)

flowers

fruit

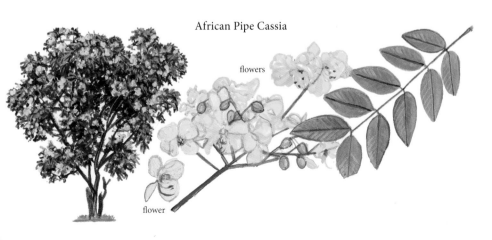

African Pipe Cassia

flowers

flower

EASTERN REDBUD *Cercis canadensis* L.

QUICK ID Recognized by the combination of magenta flowers, heart-shaped leaves, and flattened legumes.

Deciduous tree, 8–14 m tall, 20–80 cm diam. Erect, single short trunk with low branches; crown spreading, vertically flattened, or rounded. **BARK** Grayish brown, more or less smooth, becoming finely fissured with scaly ridges. **TWIG** Light brown, slender, slightly zigzag, smooth, with scattered lenticels. **LEAF** Alternate, appearing simple (unifoliolate), broadly ovate, about as broad at the base as long; base heart-shaped or flattened; apex abruptly pointed; margins entire. Upper surface dull medium or dark green, hairless, palmately veined, with 5–7 prominent, arching veins; lower surface paler, hairless or hairy throughout. Blade 7.5–12.5 cm long, 7.5–12.5 cm broad; petiole 4–10 cm long, swollen at both ends. **FLOWER** Bisexual, 10–12 mm long, sepals 5, dark magenta; petals 5, light to dark pink or magenta, corolla strongly bilateral; stamens 10, free; inflorescence a fascicled cluster of 4–8 flowers from the leaf axils. Spring, prior to the new leaves. **FRUIT** Flattened, oblong legume, 6–10 cm long, to about 1 cm broad, bottom margin often slightly curved; seeds flat, 6–8 mm long; matures late summer to autumn.

HABITAT/RANGE Native. Moist or dry woods and slopes, roadsides, 0–670 m; nearly throughout the East: Ont., N.Y., and Mass., south to c. Fla., west to Tex.

SIMILAR SPECIES Several non-native redbuds, including **Judas Tree** (*C. siliquastrum* L.) and **Chinese Redbud** (*C. chinensis* Bunge.), are sometimes cultivated in gardens and arboreta, but are not naturalized. In early spring Eastern Redbud is often confused at a distance with the cultivated Taiwan Cherry (*Cerasus campanulata* [Maxim.] A.N. Vassiljeva, Rosaceae), which blooms slightly earlier and has larger and darker flowers. The 2 are easily distinguished by leaves and fruit. Few other trees resemble Eastern Redbud.

Notes: Cercis is a genus of about 8 species, 2 native (1 eastern) to North America, of often low-branching deciduous trees and shrubs. Eastern Redbud is a widely used ornamental, especially in the Southeast, and is commonly

planted along with Flowering Dogwood (*Cornus florida*, Cornaceae) to beautify urban and suburban streets.

ROYAL POINCIANA *Delonix regia* (Bojer ex Hook.) Raf.

a.k.a. FLAME TREE, FLAMBOYANT TREE

QUICK ID Recognized by its combination of showy scarlet flowers, large bipinnate leaves, and large, dark legume.

Briefly deciduous tree, 5–32 m tall, 50–105 cm diam. Erect, single trunk, somewhat low-branching and buttressed; crown broad, spreading, usually broader than tall, umbrella-like. **BARK** Brownish, smooth, often with a silvery cast. **TWIG** Stout, dark green, becoming light brown or grayish brown. **LEAF** Alternate, bipinnate, 20–50 cm long, to about 20 cm broad, with 10–20 pairs of primary leaf segments; petiole averaging about 9 cm long. Leaflets 10–26 pairs per segment, oblong or narrowly elliptic, 5–15 mm long, about 4 mm broad; base and tip usually rounded. Upper surface yellow-green or soft green; lower surface paler. Leaves often turn yellow before falling. **FLOWER** Bisexual, 8–25 cm diam.; petals 5, 4–7 cm long, flaring near the apex, abruptly narrowed below, the lower 4 scarlet or yellow, the upper 1 (standard) varicolored red, yellow, and white, often with red nectar guides; corolla bilateral; stamens 10, the filaments scarlet. Spring to early summer. **FRUIT** Long, hard, flat blackish or dark brown legume, 35–50 cm long, 4–6 cm broad, 5–10 mm thick; persisting for several months.

HABITAT/RANGE Introduced from Madagascar; widely cultivated and established in s. Fla., potentially invasive.

SIMILAR SPECIES Several non-native trees of various genera in s. Fla. have large bipinnate leaves, but no other species has such ornate scarlet flowers or large black fruit.

Notes: Delonix is a genus of 11 deciduous, mostly white-flowered, nocturnally blooming trees, 9 endemic to Madagascar, 2 native to Africa, none native to North America. Other than *D. regia*, few are cultivated outside of their native range.

EASTERN REDBUD

flowers

Eastern Redbud

fruit

seeds

Royal Poinciana

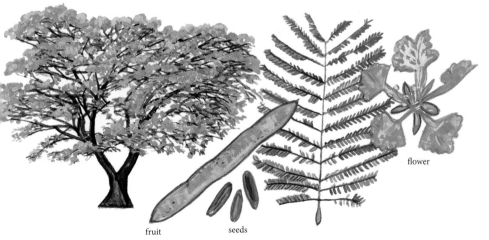

flower

fruit

seeds

■ *GLEDITSIA*: LOCUSTS

A genus of about 13 species distributed in East Asia, e. North America, and n. India; 2 are native to North America.

Deciduous trees, recognized by pinnate or bipinnate leaves and usually conspicuous thorns. **BARK** Gray, often beset with sharp-pointed simple or branched thorns. **LEAF** Alternate, evenly pinnate or evenly bipinnate (no terminal leaflet), leaflets opposite or sub-opposite. **FLOWER** Small, radially symmetric, functionally unisexual, male and female borne on separate trees; inflorescence a spike or raceme, 2–10 cm long, arising well after the new leaves have developed. **FRUIT** Stalked, flattened legume with 1 to many seeds.

WATER LOCUST *Gleditsia aquatica* Marshall

QUICKID Distinguished by the pinnate to bipinnate leaves, watery habitat, and distinctive ovate fruit.

Deciduous tree, 25–30 m tall, to about 70 cm diam. Erect, single trunk, often armed with long, sharp, simple or branched thorns 7–15 cm long; crown cylindric or narrowly spreading, large branches also thorny. **BARK** Grayish brown to blackish; smooth, narrowly furrowed, or warty. **LEAF** Alternate, pinnate and bipinnate; blade to about 16 cm long, pinnate blade to about 7 cm broad, bipinnate blade 15–21 cm broad; petiole 3–5 cm long. Pinnate leaves with 7–12 pairs of leaflets; bipinnate leaves with 4 or 5 pairs of major leaf segments, each with 7–9 pairs of leaflets. Leaflets elliptic, 1–4 cm long, margins often minutely bluntly toothed; surfaces hairless or finely hairy, especially along the midvein. **FLOWER** Small, radially symmetric, greenish yellow. Spring. **FRUIT** Flattened, ovate or slightly elongate legume, 3–8 cm long, with 1–3 seeds; matures autumn.

HABITAT/RANGE Native. Swamps, sloughs, floodplains, to about 75 m; S.C. and w. Tenn. south to c. Fla., west to Mo. and e. Tex.; cultivated outside of this range.

SIMILAR SPECIES The similar Honey Locust can be distinguished by the elongate legume, usually more than 20 cm long.

Notes: Water Locust and Honey Locust hybridize in scattered locations along the Gulf Coast, producing Texas Honey Locust (*G.* × *texana* Sarg.), characterized by fruit pods intermediate in size between those of the parent species.

HONEY LOCUST *Gleditsia triacanthos* L.

QUICKID Recognized by the combination of pinnate and bipinnate leaves, large, conspicuous thorns, and elongate legume.

Deciduous tree, potentially 30–45 m tall, 60–160 cm diam., often smaller. Erect, single trunk, often armed with stout, strong, frequently branched thorns that are sharp and piercing to the touch; crown broad, open, large branches also thorny. **BARK** Reddish, becoming brown, deeply furrowed, with narrow ridges. **TWIG** Slender, greenish red, becoming brown. **LEAF** Alternate, pinnate and bipinnate; blade to about 16 cm long, pinnate blade to about 7 cm broad, bipinnate blade 15–21 cm broad; petiole 2–5 cm long. Pinnate leaves with 10–14 pairs of leaflets; bipinnate leaves with 2–8 pairs of major leaf segments, each with 5–10 pairs of leaflets. Leaflets elliptic, 1.2–3.5 cm long, margins entire or minutely bluntly toothed. Upper surface hairless or finely hairy, especially along the midvein; lower surface usually hairy along the midvein and sometimes other veins. **FLOWER** Small, radially symmetric, greenish yellow. Spring. **FRUIT** Long, flattened, often curved, twisted, or contorted reddish-brown or blackish legume, 20–45 cm long, 2–4 cm broad, with a stout stalk; seeds numerous, flat; matures autumn.

HABITAT/RANGE Native. Uplands, open woods, dry coastal hammocks, bottomlands, 0–600 m; throughout the East, south to nw. Fla.

WATER LOCUST   HONEY LOCUST

Water Locust

fruit

Honey Locust

twig

flowers

fruit

thorn

seeds

KENTUCKY COFFEETREE
Gymnocladus dioicus (L.) K. Koch

QUICK ID Distinguished by its combination of large leaflets, large flowers, scaly bark, and inflated fruit.

Deciduous tree, 18–30 m tall, 50–150 cm diam. Erect, single relatively low-branching trunk; crown narrow or broad, pyramidal or rounded. **BARK** Reddish brown, becoming gray, irregularly fissured, conspicuously curly-scaly. **TWIG** Stout, reddish brown, densely hairy when young, with orange lenticels. **LEAF** Alternate, bipinnate, 30–90 cm long, 45–60 cm broad, with 3–5 pairs of major segments; petiole about 8 cm long, swollen at base. Leaflets 3–7 pairs per segment, 2–6 cm long, 2–3 cm broad; ovate, tip pointed; margins entire. Upper surface light green, hairy, becoming hairless; lower surface yellowish green. Turns yellow in autumn and falls early. **FLOWER** Unisexual, male and female on separate trees; male flowers in narrow clusters 7–10 cm long, sepals and petals 5, white, stamens 10; female flowers in racemes 25–30 cm long. Late spring to early summer. **FRUIT** Tough, hard, inflated, dark reddish-brown woody legume, 15–25 cm long, 4–5 cm broad; seeds 4–7, hard-coated, to about 2 cm long, nearly round, blackish brown; matures autumn.

HABITAT/RANGE Native. Floodplains and terraces of large alluvial rivers, damp rich soils, bottoms of ravine slopes, 100–600 m; N.Y. and Mass., west to e. N.D., south to n. Ga., n. Ala., and e. Tex.

SIMILAR SPECIES Honey Locust (*Gleditsia triacanthos*) differs in having smaller leaflets, smaller flowers, less scaly bark, flattened, twisted fruit, and copious thorns.

Notes: Gymnocladus is a genus of 2 species, the other native to China. Early settlers roasted the fruit of this species for use as a coffee substitute.

KENTUCKY COFFEETREE

■ *PELTOPHORUM*: YELLOW POINCIANAS

Peltophorum is a pantropical genus of about 8 species, two of which are introduced, cultivated, and naturalized in North America. **LEAF** Alternate, bipinnate, with an even number of primary leaf segments. **FLOWER** Bisexual, yellow; petals 5, often with frilly margins. **FRUIT** Flat, winged legume, tapering to a pointed base and tip.

HORSEBUSH *Peltophorum dubium*
(Spreng.) Taub.

QUICK ID Recognized by the combination of yellow flowers, bipinnate leaves, and a flattened legume that is pointed at both ends.

Deciduous or semideciduous tree, to about 13 m tall. Erect, single trunk, high branching; crown broad, spreading, lowermost branches often slightly drooping. **BARK** Gray or light gray, somewhat smooth. **LEAF** Alternate, bipinnate, blade 20–45 cm long, about 20 cm broad, with 15–25 pairs of primary segments, the middle segments longer than those near the apex and base; petiole to about 4 cm long. Leaflets 10–25 pairs per segment, oblong, asymmetric at base, 5–10 cm long, to about 5 mm broad; upper surface dark green, lower surface paler. **FLOWER** Bisexual, 2–3.5 cm diam., bilateral, yellow, produced abundantly; buds yellowish. Summer. **FRUIT** Flattened, winged legume, 6–10 cm long, 2–2.5 cm broad; seeds 1–3; matures late summer to early autumn.

HABITAT/RANGE Introduced from South America; cultivated and escaped in c. and s. Fla.

SIMILAR SPECIES Yellow Poinciana is distinguished by its larger flowers and leaflets.

YELLOW POINCIANA *Peltophorum pterocarpum* (DC.) Backer ex K. Heyne
A.K.A. PELTOPHORUM

Deciduous or semideciduous tree, very similar in most respects to Horsebush. **LEAF** Leaflets larger, 1–2 cm long, with evident secondary veins. **FLOWER** 3–4 cm diam., buds rust-colored. **HABITAT/RANGE** Introduced from Sri Lanka, Malay Archipelago, Indonesia, and n. Australia; cultivated and established in s. Fla.

Kentucky Coffeetree

seed

fruit

autumn

Horsebush

flowers

fruit

seed

Yellow Poinciana

flowers

fruit

seed

leaflet

■ *SENNA*: SENNAS

A genus of about 350 species distributed mostly in the American tropics and slightly northward, especially in xeric regions. At least 28 species occur in North America, about 18 native. Well known as a source of ornamental plants, the genus has been included taxonomically within the genus *Cassia*. Mostly evergreen trees, shrubs, and herbs, sennas are recognized by their pinnate leaves, relatively large leaflets, bright yellow flowers, and indehiscent legumes. **LEAF** Alternate, pinnate, with an even number of leaflets. **FLOWER** Bisexual, slightly bilateral, yellow or yellow-orange, petals 5; stamens 10, 5–10 functional. **FRUIT** A legume, usually oblong, laterally compressed or cylindric, sometimes winged, indehiscent; seeds usually numerous.

ARGENTINE SENNA *Senna corymbosa*
(Lam.) H.S. Irwin & Barneby
A.K.A. Argentine Wild Sensitive Plant

Evergreen shrub or small tree, 1–3.5 m tall; erect or vase-shaped, single trunk or several. **LEAF** Alternate, pinnate, usually with 2 or 3 pairs of opposite leaflets, the lower pair separated by an erect gland; leaflets oblanceolate, lanceolate, or narrowly elliptic, base rounded, tip bluntly or abruptly short-pointed, 2–5 cm long, 4–5 mm broad, terminal pair the largest. **FLOWER** Bisexual, 2–2.5 cm diam., bright yellow; produced in axillary clusters of 4–12 flowers; stamens 10, 7 fertile, 3 much reduced. Late summer to autumn. **FRUIT** Oblong, cylindric legume, 4–10 cm long, 7–10 mm diam., light green, maturing brown. **HABITAT/RANGE** Introduced; cultivated in the Southeast, established in Fla., Ga., Miss., Tex., perhaps elsewhere.

GLOSSY SHOWER *Senna surattensis*
(Burm. f.) H.S. Irwin & Barneby

Evergreen shrub or small tree, to about 5 m tall, 10–15 cm diam. Erect, single trunk; crown rounded. Distinguished by having glands between nearly all the leaflet pairs. **LEAF** Alternate, pinnate, with 6–10 pairs of opposite leaflets, rachis bearing glands between the leaflet pairs. Leaflets oval or elliptic, rounded at tip, 2–3.5 cm long, to about 1.5 cm broad; petiole 6–20 cm long. **FLOWER** Bisexual, 2.5–5 cm diam., yellow, petals 5, stamens 10. Year-round. **FRUIT** Flattened brown legume, 7–10 cm long, to about 1.4 cm broad, slightly constricted between the seed cavities, with a tooth-like extension at tip.

HABITAT/RANGE Introduced from the Old World tropics; cultivated and escaped in s. Fla.

SIMILAR SPECIES Cassia Amarilla (*Senna spectabilis* [DC.] H.S. Irwin & Barneby), introduced from tropical America and cultivated in s. Fla., has leaves 20–30 cm long, with 8–13 pairs of ovate or lanceolate leaflets, each 4–6 cm long; yellow flowers with 7 fertile stamens; and a legume with irregular horizontal ridges, 15–25 cm long, about 1 cm diam.

TAMARIND *Tamarindus indica* L.

QUICK ID Recognized by the combination of pinnate leaves, blackish trunk, often zigzag twigs, and variable fruit.

Evergreen or briefly deciduous, potentially massive tree, 20–30 m tall, diam. to about 1.5 m in the U.S., reportedly to 7.5 m in its native range. Erect, single trunk, often somewhat buttressed at base; crown of strong, spreading branches that usually droop gracefully at the tips; twigs and small branches often zigzag. **BARK** Smooth and dark gray at first, becoming blackish, horizontally cracked, and vertically fissured. **TWIG** Somewhat zigzag. **LEAF** Alternate, pinnate, the blade 7.5–15 cm long, 2–6 cm broad, folding at night; petiole about 5 mm long. Leaflets in 10–20 pairs, even in number, oblong, oblique at the base, more or less squared at the apex, 1–2.5 cm long, 5–6 mm broad; upper surface dark green or yellowish green, lower surface paler. **FLOWER** Bisexual, about 2.5 cm diam., bilateral; sepals 4; petals 3, yellowish, with pinkish streaks and crinkled margins; functional stamens 7. Spring to summer. **FRUIT** Often bulging, light brown legume, varying from straight to curved and from laterally flattened to more or less round in cross section, 4–15 cm long, 2–2.5 cm broad; matures summer to autumn.

HABITAT/RANGE Introduced from tropical Africa and India; escaped from cultivation and established in s. Fla.

SIMILAR SPECIES Wild Tamarind (*Lysiloma latisiliquum*) also has zigzag twigs, but its trunk is pale (whitish to gray) rather than blackish, and its flat, twisted pod is not widely variable in shape and size.

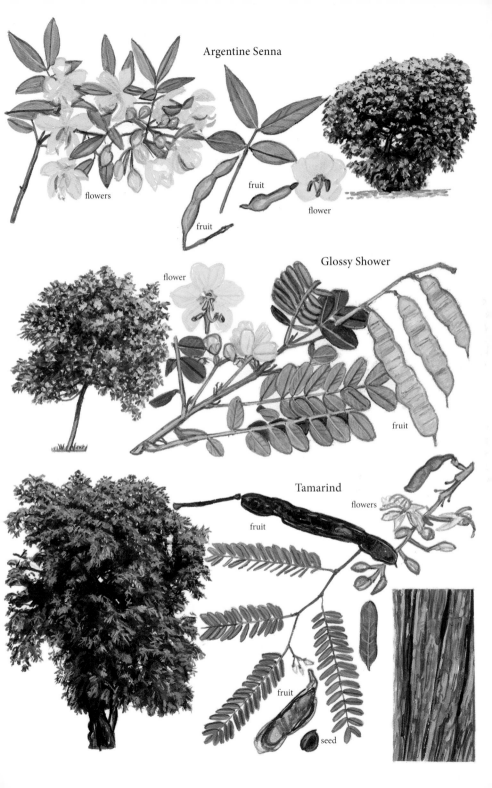

Argentine Senna

flowers

fruit

fruit

flower

Glossy Shower

flower

fruit

Tamarind

fruit

flowers

fruit

seed

SUBFAMILY MIMOSOIDEAE: MIMOSAS AND THEIR RELATIVES

The subfamily Mimosoideae consists largely of tropical and subtropical trees and shrubs, and has about 56 genera and up to 3,000 species, including the acacias, wattles, mimosas, wild tamarinds, blackbeads, and relatives. Members of this subfamily are most easily recognized by their typically rounded or spikelike inflorescences composed of small symmetric flowers. **LEAF** Alternate, often bipinnate; many bear glands on the stalk. **FLOWER** Usually bisexual, radial, small, aggregated into heads or spikes; petals do not overlap in bud; stamens 10 to many, usually conspicuous and showy.

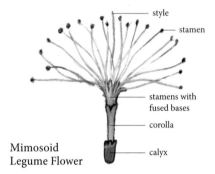

style
stamen
stamens with fused bases
corolla
calyx

Mimosoid Legume Flower

■ *ACACIA*: ACACIAS

A genus of about 960 species worldwide, mostly in tropical and subtropical regions of the Southern Hemisphere; 2 species are established in Fla., neither native. The genus *Acacia* achieves its greatest diversity in Australia, where there are hundreds of species. *Acacia* previously included about 1,350 species, but recent consensus and ongoing work among specialists has placed many of these into segregate genera, including *Vachellia*, which follows *Acacia*.

Usually evergreen trees and shrubs. **BARK** Usually hard and persistent, often furrowed, and in some species with a commercially significant tannin content. **LEAF** Alternate, bipinnately compound, or more often a phyllode, an apparent leaf consisting of a flattened, expanded petiole that resembles a narrow, often curved blade. **FLOWER** Bisexual, small, with 5 inconspicuous sepals and petals and numerous separate stamens; produced in globose heads or spikes, themselves usually aggregated into racemes or branched inflorescences. Plants usually floriferous and showy; the copious pollen is allergenic to many. **FRUIT** A legume; straight, curved, or contorted, usually flat or somewhat swollen, often constricted between the seeds, the sides leathery or papery, dehiscing (splitting) along 1 or both sutures; seeds usually have a nutrient-rich aril that caps the seed and fosters seed dispersal by animals.

EARLEAF ACACIA *Acacia auriculiformis* A. Cunn. ex Benth.

QUICK ID Recognized in s. Fla. by the combination of sickle-shaped phyllodes with parallel veins, and a flattened and twisted legume with the seeds dangling from yellow threads.

Evergreen shrub or tree, 15–20 m tall, 50–60 cm diam., potentially larger in its native range. Erect, usually single trunk, sometimes multiple; crown compact, somewhat spreading. **BARK** Pale gray to creamy white at first, becoming light gray with shallow vertical furrows. **TWIG** Smooth, hairless, green or greenish yellow, becoming grayish or grayish brown. **LEAF** Alternate, phyllode, reduced to a flattened, expanded petiole that resembles a leaf in form but lacks blade tissue; somewhat linear to narrowly elliptic, curved and sickle-shaped; base rounded or narrowly wedge-shaped; tip pointed. Upper and lower surfaces dark yellow-green, lustrous, with 3–7 longitudinal veins arising from the base. Phyllode 10–20 cm long, 1.2–5 cm broad; petiole 7–12 mm long. **FLOWER** Bisexual, 1.6–2.4 mm diam., yellow; inflorescence a cluster of axillary spikes 5–8 cm long. Summer to autumn. **FRUIT** Flattened, oblong reddish-brown legume, averaging 5–8 cm long, twisted, not constricted between seed cavities; seed black, flattened, often dangling from the split edge of the pod on a yellowish or orange threadlike extension; matures late spring and summer.

HABITAT/RANGE Introduced from Australia; widely and abundantly naturalized in scrub, sandhills, dunes, hammocks, margins of tidal marshes, disturbed woodlands and roadsides, in southernmost Fla., where it is considered invasive and difficult to control.

SIMILAR SPECIES The phyllodes of Water Wattle are straight, narrower, and long-tapering from base to tip.

fruit

seed

fruit

flowers

Earleaf Acacia

Water Wattle

fruit

flowers

WATER WATTLE *Acacia retinodes*
Schltdl.

QUICK ID Recognized by the combination of narrow, straight-sided phyllodes, a flattened legume, and flowers borne in rounded yellow heads along an elongate axis.

Evergreen shrub or small tree, 6–10 m tall, 24–30 cm diam. Erect, single trunk, more often dividing at ground level into 2 or more trunks; combined crown of main trunks flat-topped or rounded. **BARK** Smooth, reddish brown. **TWIG** Hairless, reddish brown. **LEAF** Alternate, reduced to a flattened phyllode; straight to slightly sickle-shaped, linear-lanceolate to narrowly oblanceolate; narrowly tapering, with an obscure gland at the base; tip rounded. Upper and lower surfaces dark, lustrous green, pinnately veined, central vein conspicuous, lateral veins inconspicuous. Phyllode 3–20 cm long, 3–14 mm broad; petiole absent or to about 5 mm long. **FLOWER** Bisexual, yellow or cream, produced in densely flowered, rounded heads 5–7 mm diam.; 5–9 heads along a central axis in an axillary inflorescence. Year-round. **FRUIT** Flat, narrow, oblong, more or less straight-sided brown legume, 3–16 cm long, 6–18 mm broad; lacking constrictions between the seed cavities; matures summer.

HABITAT/RANGE Introduced from Australia; naturalized from cultivation in s. Fla. and Calif., largely restricted to disturbed sites.

SIMILAR SPECIES Earleaf Acacia can be distinguished by having sickle-shaped phyllodes 12–50 mm broad and flower heads mostly in short spikes.

■ *VACHELLIA*: VACHELLIAS

The genus *Vachellia* includes about 163 species of shrubs or small trees, most of which were formerly included within the genus *Acacia*. About 9 arborescent species occur in North America; 6 in the East, 4 of which are native.

CINNECORD *Vachellia choriophylla*
(Benth.) Seigler & Ebinger

QUICK ID Recognized in s. Fla. by the combination of a circular gland on the petiole, short-lasting stipular spines, leaflets 1–2 cm long, and fewer than 4 pairs of primary leaf segments.

Evergreen, small, spineless, bushy shrub, rarely a small tree to about 9 m tall. Erect, usually bushy, single short trunk, often branching close to ground level. **LEAF** Alternate, bipinnate, rachis averaging about 4 cm long; petiole 1–5 cm long, bearing a circular gland; 1–3 pairs of primary segments, with a stalked gland between each pair. Leaflets 3–5 opposite pairs per segment, 1–3 cm long, to about 7 mm broad; elliptic, tip rounded or notched; margins entire, often slightly curled under; upper surface lustrous dark green, lower surface paler. **FLOWER** Bisexual, tiny, tubular, produced in a dense, globular, bright yellow cluster to about 8 mm diam. Spring to early summer. **FRUIT** More or less flattened legume, 5–8 cm long, 1.5–2.5 cm broad; splits along 2 sutures to reveal whitish pulp and several brown seeds to about 8 mm long; matures summer.

HABITAT/RANGE Native. Ecotones separating hammocks and mangroves; s. Fla. and Fla. Keys.

SIMILAR SPECIES Sweet Acacia and Pineland Acacia also have circular petiole glands, but retain their stipular spines, and the leaflets do not exceed 1 cm long. The petiole of Poponax has an elliptic gland and stipular spines that are fused at the base.

BULLHORN WATTLE *Vachellia cornigera* (L.) Siegler & Ebinger

A large shrub or small tree armed with pairs of large, curved, swollen stipular spines that are fused at the base and resemble a pair of small bullhorns. The only *Vachellia* in Fla. with a spikelike inflorescence. **LEAF** Alternate, bipinnate, with 2–8 pairs of primary leaf segments bearing 15–20 pairs of leaflets, each 7–8 mm long; petiole has a large gland near the base of the blade. **FLOWER** Tiny, cream or yellow, borne in a spike 2–3 cm long that is covered at the base with 2 large bracts. **FRUIT** Legume, round in cross section, 2–5 cm long, to about 1.5 cm diam. **HABITAT/RANGE** Introduced from Central America; established in c. Fla. peninsula.

SWEET ACACIA *Vachellia farnesiana* (L.) Wight & Arn. **var.** *farnesiana*

QUICK ID Recognized by the combination of its alternate, bipinnate leaves, small leaflets, globular yellow flower clusters, hairy petiole and leaf axis, and leaflets with evident lateral secondary venation.

Deciduous shrub or small, many-branched tree to about 5 m tall. Erect or shrubby, branches usually zigzag. **LEAF** Alternate, often crowded on spur twigs, bipinnate, blade 2–10 cm long, with 2–6 pairs of primary segments, rachis hairy; petiole 6–10 mm long, hairy, usually subtended by a pair of conspicuous stipular spines to about 4 cm long. Leaflets 10–25 pairs per segment, 3–6 mm long, secondary venation between the major lateral veins usually evident on lower surface, though less so from about Miss. westward. **FLOWER** Tiny, tubular, bright yellow, produced in rounded, headlike globular clusters 1–1.3 cm diam., the clusters on stalks 1.5–3 cm long. Spring. **FRUIT** Flattened, somewhat curved purplish-red legume, 5–8 cm long; matures summer.

HABITAT/RANGE Native. Mostly distributed in coastal shell middens, hammocks, and pinelands, to about 50 m; se. Ga. south to s. Fla., west to s. Calif.

CINNECORD

SWEET ACACIA

flower heads

Cinnecord

fruit

seeds

Bullhorn Wattle

flower spikes

stipular spines

flowers

fruit

Sweet Acacia

seeds

flower head

PINELAND ACACIA *Vachellia farnesiana* (L.) Wight & Arn. var. *pinetorum* (F.J. Herm.) Siegler & Ebinger

QUICK ID An acacia, distinguished by bipinnate leaves with 1–8 primary segments, the mature leaflets lacking evident secondary venation, and flowers in a rounded yellow head.

Deciduous shrub, distinguished from Sweet Acacia by its hairless petiole and leaf axis, and by the obscure secondary venation on the leaflets.

HABITAT/RANGE Native; restricted to s. Fla.

PORKNUT *Vachellia macracantha* (Humb. & Bonpl. ex Willd.) Siegler & Ebinger
A.K.A. LONG-SPINE ACACIA, STEEL ACACIA

QUICK ID Recognized by the combination of numerous primary leaf segments, small leaflets, headlike cluster of yellow flowers, and paired stipular spines.

Deciduous or evergreen, typically a small tree to about 7 m tall, 30 cm diam. Erect, single trunk; crown spreading, the plant often broader than tall. **BARK** Gray, grooved or furrowed. **TWIG** Slightly zigzag, grayish green, hairy, becoming light brown, with evident lenticels. **LEAF** Alternate, bipinnate, blade to about 21 cm long, 12 cm broad, with 10–25 pairs of primary segments, the axis hairy; petiole about 4 cm long, hairy, often subtended by paired stipular spines. Leaflets oblong, about 3 mm long, 20–30 pairs per segment. **FLOWER** Tiny, yellow, produced in rounded heads about 1 cm diam. Spring to summer. **FRUIT** Flattened brown legume, 5–13 cm long, 6–10 mm broad; matures summer to autumn.

HABITAT/RANGE Native. Coastal hammocks, margins of mangrove wetlands; s. Fla.

SIMILAR SPECIES All other *Vachellia* species with rounded flower heads have 8 or fewer primary leaf segments.

POPONAX *Vachellia tortuosa* (L.) Siegler & Ebinger
A.K.A. TWISTED ACACIA

QUICK ID Distinguished by the combination of elongate, elliptic glands on the petiole, fused stipular spines, 8 or fewer pairs of primary leaf segments, netlike leaflet venation, and zigzag twigs.

Deciduous or evergreen shrub or small tree, 3–6 m tall, to about 15 cm diam. Erect, single trunk; crown flat-topped. **BARK** Light gray, finely fissured. **TWIG** Green, becoming reddish brown, with whitish lenticels, hairy at first, conspicuously zigzag. **LEAF** Alternate, bipinnate, blade 3–5 cm long, to about 4 cm broad, with 4–8 pairs of primary segments; petiole to 1 cm long, with an elliptic gland and subtended by paired stipular spines that are fused at the base. Leaflets 10–20 pairs per segment, 4–7 mm long, linear or oblong, tip blunt; upper surface dull green, lateral secondary veins evident and reticulate, lower surface paler. **FLOWER** Tiny, yellow, produced in a rounded head 7–12 mm diam. Spring to summer. **FRUIT** Straight or curved oblong, often blackish legume, 4–7 cm long, 5–7 mm diam.; matures summer to autumn.

HABITAT/RANGE Native. Shell middens; s. Fla.

SIMILAR SPECIES Bee Wattle (*V. sphaerocephala* [Cham. & Schltdl.] Siegler & Ebinger), an introduced species naturalized in s. Fla., also has 8 or fewer pairs of primary leaf segments, elliptic petiole glands, and stipular spines fused at the base. It is distinguished from Poponax by the leaflets lacking evident lateral secondary veins.

PINELAND ACACIA

PORKNUT

POPONAX

Pineland Acacia

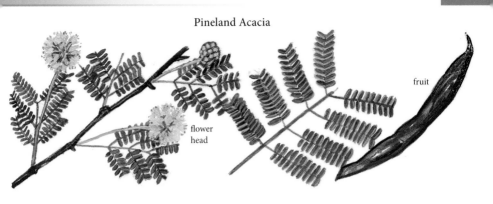

fruit

flower head

Porknut

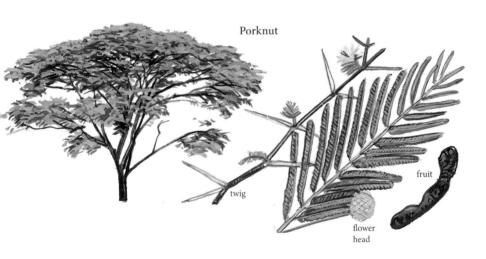

twig

fruit

flower head

Poponax

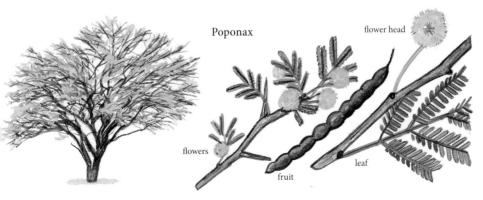

flower head

flowers

fruit

leaf

◼ *ALBIZIA*: ALBIZIAS

A genus of 120–140 species, distributed mostly in tropical or warm regions; 4 species occur in North America, none native.

Trees or shrubs, usually unarmed. **LEAF** Alternate, bipinnate; petiole and rachis glandular. **FLOWER** Bisexual, or bisexual and unisexual male; calyx usually bell- or funnel-shaped; corolla funnel-shaped, with 5 lobes; stamens numerous, joined at base, the free part extending well beyond the tip of the corolla; inflorescence usually a densely flowered head. **FRUIT** A legume, linear or oblong, with rounded or ovoid seeds.

SILKTREE *Albizia julibrissin* Durazz.
A.K.A. Mimosa

QUICK ID Recognized by the combination of bipinnate leaves and the pinkish inflorescence.

Deciduous tree to about 15 m tall. Erect, single short trunk, often leaning and divided into several low, large ascending branches; crown spreading, umbrella-like. **BARK** Light gray, more or less smooth to slightly roughened. **TWIG** Slightly zigzag, grayish. **LEAF** Alternate, bipinnate, blade 10–30 cm long, about 15 cm broad, with 5–15 pairs of (usually) evenly paired primary segments; petiole 3–5 cm long. Leaflets 13–35 pairs per segment, 5–15 mm long, 2–4 mm broad, those at the base of the segment somewhat smaller than those above, oblong, the upper margin more or less straight, the lower margin curved; margins entire, often hairy. Upper surface yellow-green, the main vein of the leaflet closely adjacent to the upper margin; lower surface paler, finely hairy. **FLOWER** Bisexual and male, individually small, tubular, radially symmetric, produced in a showy head, 4–6 cm diam., with a single bisexual flower in the center surrounded by numerous male flowers; filaments long, pink and white, forming the showy part of the inflorescence. Spring. **FRUIT** Flattened, more or less straight-sided legume, yellowish, turning light brown, to about 15 cm long, 2–3 cm broad, the seed cavities evident; seed flat, brown, 8–10 mm long; matures late summer to autumn.

HABITAT/RANGE Introduced from Asia; established across much of the East from N.Y. south to n. Fla., west to Mo. and Calif.; treated as invasive in many locations.

SIMILAR SPECIES Woman's Tongue is similar but has creamy-white flowers. The Asian species *A. kalkora* (Roxb.) Prain also has a pink inflorescence; it is cultivated in the U.S.

Notes: Silktree has been cultivated in the U.S. for more than 100 years. A fungal disease that enters the root and destroys the wood often kills older trees.

WOMAN'S TONGUE *Albizia lebbeck* (L.) Benth.

QUICK ID Recognized by the combination of bipinnate leaves and the large creamy-white inflorescence.

Deciduous tree or shrub, 12–15 m tall, potentially much larger in its native range. Erect, single trunk or sometimes multiple, with relatively low branches; sometimes spreading from root suckers; crown spreading and flat-topped when open-grown, more compact in closed woodlands. **BARK** Rough, gray, somewhat flaking and scaly. **TWIG** Brittle, green at first, becoming gray-brown. **LEAF** Alternate or sub-opposite, bipinnate, blade 15–20 cm long, to about 40 cm broad; petiole 5–10 cm long, with a gland near the base, stipules absent on young growth. Usually 2–4 pairs of opposite or sub-opposite primary segments, 5–20 cm long. Leaflets 3–10 pairs per segment, 1.5–6 cm long, 0.5–3.5 cm broad, oblong or narrowly elliptic, the central vein offset from the center; upper surface green or yellow-green, lower surface paler. **FLOWER** Bisexual, individually small, produced in loose, globular creamy-white or yellowish clusters, 4–9 cm diam., each cluster with 15–40 flowers; corolla to about 1 cm long, with 5 triangular lobes; stamens numerous, 1.5–3 cm long, white or creamy white, becoming yellow with age. Spring to autumn. **FRUIT** Flat legume, 12–35 cm long, 3–6 cm broad, yellowish brown; 3–12 flattened or ellipsoid brown seeds, 7–11 mm long. Present year-round.

HABITAT/RANGE Introduced from Asia; abundant and considered invasive in c. and s. Fla.

SIMILAR SPECIES Silktree has leaves with more than 4 pairs of primary segments and smaller leaflets, and a pinkish inflorescence. Both Indian Albizia and Tall Albizia have inflorescences less than 1.5 cm diam. See also Horseflesh Mahogany (*Lysiloma sabicu*) and Wild Tamarind (*Lysiloma latisiliquum*), which have similar leaves but lack the gland at the base of the petiole.

flower head

Silktree

flower
head

Woman's Tongue

fruit

leaflet underside

flower
heads

INDIAN ALBIZIA *Albizia lebbekoides* (DC.) Benth.

QUICK ID Recognized by the combination of greenish-yellow flower heads not exceeding about 1.5 cm diam. and bipinnately compound leaves with oblong leaflets 1–2.5 cm long.

Deciduous tree or shrub to about 15 m tall. Erect, single trunk; vase-shaped crown of long, ascending branches. **BARK** Grayish or reddish gray, roughened, somewhat scaly. **LEAF** Alternate, bipinnate, blade 5–13 cm long, to about 15 cm broad, with 3–8 pairs of opposite or sub-opposite segments; petiole about 2.5–6 cm long. Leaflets 15–25 pairs per segment, opposite, 1–2.5 cm long, 2–4 mm broad, oblong or narrowly oblong, the midvein offset from the center, base asymmetric; surfaces dull medium green. **FLOWER** Bisexual, produced in greenish-white heads about 1 cm diam. Summer. **FRUIT** Flattened, oblong yellowish-brown legume, 7–15 cm long, 1.5–2.5 cm broad, the seed cavities evident; matures autumn.

HABITAT/RANGE Introduced from tropical Asia; cultivated and established in s. Fla.

SIMILAR SPECIES Tall Albizia has elliptic leaflets, many of which are longer than 2.5 cm.

TALL ALBIZIA *Albizia procera* (Roxb.) Benth.

QUICK ID Recognized by the combination of bipinnate leaves, elliptic leaflets, and greenish-yellow flower heads.

Deciduous tree to about 30 m tall and 35 cm diam., usually not exceeding about 15 m tall in the U.S. Erect, single trunk, often branching low to the ground; crown upright, irregular, the branches sometimes contorted. **BARK** Grayish brown to whitish, smooth to slightly roughened. **LEAF** Alternate, bipinnate, blade 14–20 cm long, with 3–7 pairs of opposite segments, each 10–25 cm long; petiole to about 16 cm long. Leaflets 4–16 pairs per segment, 2–4 cm long, to about 1.3 cm broad, elliptic, midvein offset from center, lower surface hairy. **FLOWER** Bisexual, individually small,

produced in yellowish or greenish axillary heads 1–1.5 cm diam. Spring. **FRUIT** Flattened, light brown legume, 6–15 cm long, the seed compartments dark brown, squarish, conspicuous; matures autumn.

HABITAT/RANGE Introduced from tropical Asia; cultivated, established in s. Fla.

SIMILAR SPECIES Indian Albizia has oblong leaflets, the margins nearly parallel, that are 1–2.5 cm long.

PACARA EARPOD TREE *Enterolobium contortisiliquum* (Vell.) Morong

QUICK ID Recognized by the dark earlike or kidney-shaped legumes.

Deciduous or evergreen fast-growing tree to about 30 m tall in its native range, slightly smaller in the U.S. Erect, single trunk, with low branches; crown spreading, more or less flat-topped. **BARK** Grayish, slightly roughened, scaly. **TWIG** Reddish brown and finely striped. **LEAF** Alternate, bipinnate, blade 5–14 cm long, to about 14 cm broad, with 4–10 pairs of primary segments; petiole mostly 4–6 cm long. Leaflets 12–16 pairs per segment, 8–14 mm long, midvein off-center, 1 margin straight, the other curving and reminiscent of the bow of a boat, the tip pointed; upper surface lustrous medium green, lower surface paler. **FLOWER** Bisexual, tubular, produced in a creamy-white headlike fascicle of racemes 1–2 cm diam. Spring. **FRUIT** Dark, coiled, kidney-shaped legume, forming an irregular circle to about 6 cm diam.; present at nearly any time of year.

HABITAT/RANGE Introduced from tropical America; cultivated and escaped in c. and s. Fla., potentially invasive.

SIMILAR SPECIES Elephant's Ear (*E. cyclocarpum* [Jacq.] Griseb.) is similar and sometimes reported for Fla. It has larger fruit and more numerous leaflets.

Notes: Enterolobium is a genus of about 5 species distributed in the American tropics; none native to North America.

Indian Albizia

fruit

Tall Albizia

flower
head

fruit

Pacara Earpod Tree

fruit section

fruit

seed

■ *LYSILOMA*: WILD TAMARINDS

A genus of about 35 species, mostly of the American tropics; 3 species occur in North America, 2 native, with 1 native and 1 introduced species in the East.

Trees or shrubs, unarmed. **LEAF** Alternate, evenly bipinnate, leaflets usually numerous, the petiole with a conspicuous gland. **FLOWER** Bisexual, calyx bell-shaped, corolla more or less funnel-shaped, stamens numerous, usually extending well beyond the tip of the corolla; produced in conspicuous rounded heads. **FRUIT** A legume, linear or oblong, usually flattened or compressed; seeds ovate, flattened.

WILD TAMARIND *Lysiloma latisiliquum* (L.) Benth.
A.K.A. BAHAMA LYSILOMA

QUICKID Recognized by the combination of zigzag twigs and branches, whitish bark, very flat pods, and whitish inflorescences.

Evergreen or semideciduous tree, 10–20 m tall, to about 1 m diam. Erect, single trunk, relatively low-branching; crown of open-grown trees broad, spreading, usually of large, ascending branches, that of hammock-grown plants narrower. **BARK** Gray or whitish, smooth at first, eventually separating into large plate-like scales. **TWIG** Zigzag. **LEAF** Alternate, bipinnate, blade to about 5 cm long, 13 cm broad, with 2–4 pairs of primary segments, each to about 10 cm long; petiole 2–4 cm long, subtended at first by a conspicuous stipule. Leaflets 8–30 pairs per segment, opposite, even in number, 8–15 mm long, 3–5 mm broad, elliptic, oblong, or lanceolate; upper surface yellowish green, lateral venation evident, lower surface paler. **FLOWER** Tiny, tubular; sepals and petals 5, fused

at base; stamens 15–20, long, conspicuous, forming the showy part of the inflorescence, a pincushion-like head 1.5–2 cm diam. Spring to summer. **FRUIT** Flat, often twisted legume lacking conspicuous seed compartments; black at maturity but often eroding to expose the white interior, thus usually mottled; 6–10 cm long, 2–4 cm broad; matures autumn, but usually persists for much of the year.

HABITAT/RANGE Native. Hammocks, disturbed woodlands, often encroaching onto pinelands, usually coastal; s. Fla.

SIMILAR SPECIES Horseflesh Mahogany has fewer and larger leaflets.

Notes: This is a relatively large tree in s. Fla. Though native, it has weedy tendencies and may invade burned pinelands adjacent to hammocks. It is common in the upper Fla. Keys and the southern tip of the peninsula.

HORSEFLESH MAHOGANY *Lysiloma sabicu* Benth.

QUICKID Recognized by the creamy-white flowers in combination with 7 or fewer pairs of oval leaflets per segment, the leaflets more than 1.5 cm long.

Evergreen small tree to about 8 m tall, averaging 10–30 cm diam. Erect, single trunk; crown vase-shaped, with ascending branches, becoming spreading and more or less flat-topped. **BARK** Grayish brown, scaly, with loose plates. **LEAF** Alternate, bipinnate, blade 3–10 cm long, to about 12 cm broad, with 2–4 pairs of primary segments, each 2–4 cm long; petiole 1–2 cm long. Leaflets 3–7 pairs per segment, 1–2.5 cm long, about 1 cm broad, oval or obovate, base slightly wedge-shaped, tip rounded; upper surface dark green, lower surface paler. **FLOWER** White or creamy white, corolla tubular; stamens 15–20, elongate, showy; produced in heads averaging about 1.5 diam. Spring to autumn. **FRUIT** Flattened, oval, oblong, or narrowly linear legume 7–15 cm long, 2–4 cm broad, often larger than the leaves. Year-round.

HABITAT/RANGE Introduced from the West Indies; cultivated and established in s. Fla.

SIMILAR SPECIES The primary leaf segments of the native Wild Tamarind have more leaflets.

WILD TAMARIND

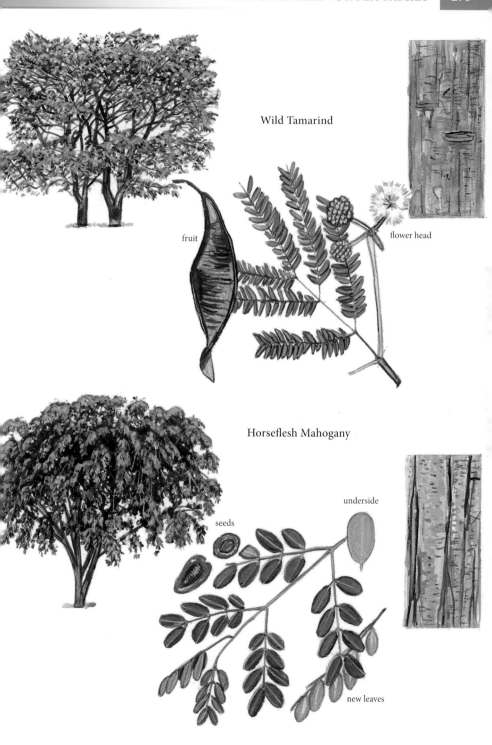

Wild Tamarind

fruit

flower head

Horseflesh Mahogany

seeds

underside

new leaves

WHITE LEADTREE *Leucaena leucocephala* (Lam.) de Wit

QUICK ID Recognized by the combination of bipinnate leaves, compact heads of creamy-white flowers, and flattened reddish-brown legumes.

Deciduous or evergreen shrub or small tree, to about 5 m tall, 5–10 cm diam. Erect, single trunk; crown spreading. **BARK** Smooth and grayish brown on young trees, becoming darker and roughened with age, with conspicuous lenticels and shallow vertical fissures. **TWIG** Gray-green, finely hairy. **LEAF** Alternate, bipinnate, blade 8–10 cm long, about 13 cm broad, with 4–9 pairs of primary segments; petiole 2.5–4 cm long. Leaflets 10–20 opposite pairs per segment, 8–14 mm long, oblong, tip pointed; upper surface gray-green, lower surface slightly paler. Leaflets fold together at night. **FLOWER** Bisexual, produced in rounded creamy-white heads 1–2 cm diam., on stalks 2–3 cm long. Year-round. **FRUIT** Flat reddish-brown legume, 8–15 cm long, 2–4 cm broad, borne in crowded, dangling clusters. Year-round.

HABITAT/RANGE Introduced from the West Indies; cultivated and escaped in s. Fla. and s. and e. Tex.; treated as an invasive species in the U.S.

SIMILAR SPECIES The wild tamarinds (*Lysiloma*) also have white flowers, but they are not borne in compact heads. The compact flower heads of *Acacia* and *Vachellia* are mostly yellow.

Notes: Leucaena is a genus of about 22 species distributed mostly in the American tropics; 2 are native to North America, none to the East.

RED BEADTREE *Adenanthera pavonina* L.
A.K.A. RED SANDALWOOD

QUICK ID Recognized by the alternate leaflets, curled and twisted pods, and scarlet seeds.

Deciduous tree to about 20 m tall in its native range, usually not exceeding about 12 m in the U.S. Erect, single trunk; crown spreading or rounded, dense. **BARK** Light brown or grayish brown with pinkish highlights, smooth at first, becoming finely furrowed. **LEAF** Alternate, bipinnate, blade 6–13 cm long, to about 20 cm broad, with 3–6 pairs of opposite or sub-opposite segments; petiole about 3 cm long, without a gland. Leaflets 8–18

per segment, alternate, 1.5–2.5 cm long, 1–1.5 cm broad, elliptic or oval; upper surface dark green, lower surface paler to grayish. **FLOWER** Bisexual, yellow or orange; petals 5, 2–3 mm long; inflorescence a slender, crowded axillary raceme to about 30 cm long. Spring. **FRUIT** Flattened, twisted legume, often forming a spiral, 10–30 cm long, about 1 cm broad, with 8–12 flat, lustrous scarlet seeds 5–10 mm long; matures late summer to autumn.

HABITAT/RANGE Introduced from tropical Asia; escaped and considered invasive in s. Fla.

Notes: The genus *Adenanthera* includes about 12 species of tropical Asia and Pacific islands.

HONEY MESQUITE *Prosopis glandulosa* Torr.

QUICK ID Recognized by the combination of stout spines, creamy flowers in dense spikes, bipinnate leaves with usually 2 segments and well-spaced oblong, hairless leaflets.

Deciduous tree or shrub, 1–10 m tall, usually much wider than tall. **TWIG** Often armed at nodes with 1 or 2 stout, sharp, pale spines to 5 cm long. **LEAF** Alternate or clustered on heavy spur twigs, bipinnate, flexible, with 1 or 2 pairs of primary segments, each 6–17 cm long; petiole 2–15 cm long. Leaflets 6–18 pairs per segment, usually 1–5 cm long, spaced 7–18 mm apart. **FRUIT** Cylindric legume, 8–20 cm long, constricted between seed cavities.

HABITAT/RANGE Native. Dry uplands, pastures, watercourses, 0–1,200 m; entering the East in La., Tex., and Okla.

Notes: Prosopis is a genus of about 45 long-lived shrubs or short-trunked trees; 4 species occur in North America north of Mexico.

HONEY MESQUITE

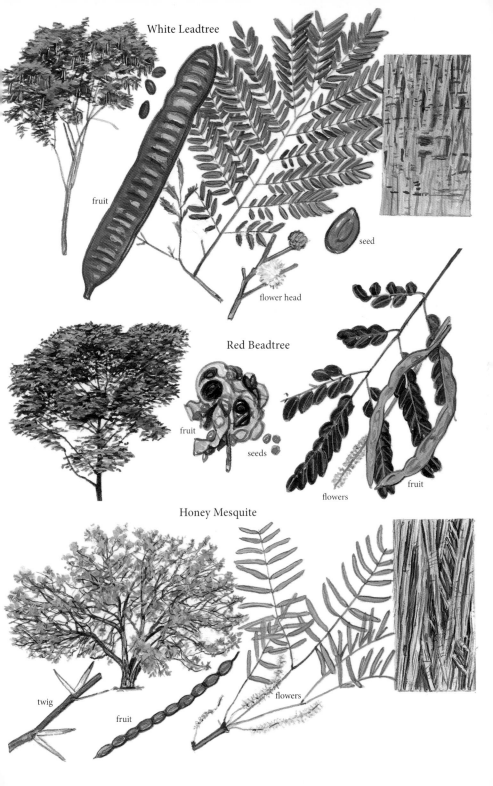

White Leadtree

fruit

seed

flower head

Red Beadtree

fruit

seeds

flowers

fruit

Honey Mesquite

twig

fruit

flowers

■ *PITHECELLOBIUM*: BLACKBEADS

The genus *Pithecellobium* includes about 18 species distributed mostly in the tropical and subtropical Americas.

MONKEYPOD   *Pithecellobium dulce* (Roxb.) Benth.

QUICKID Recognized by its bipinnate leaves with only 4 leaflets per blade.

Evergreen armed (rarely unarmed), fast-growing shrub or small tree to about 10 m tall in Fla., potentially to 22 m tall and 30–75 cm diam. Erect, single often crooked trunk, relatively low-branching; spreading crown of large ascending branches. **BARK** Smooth, light gray. **TWIG** Slender, somewhat drooping, zigzag, often spiny. **LEAF** Alternate, bipinnate, blade 2–5 cm long, to about 12 cm broad, with a single pair of primary segments, each with 1 pair of opposite leaflets; petiole 1–4 cm long, usually subtended by a pair of spines. Leaflets 2–6 cm long, to about 2 cm broad, oblong, elliptic, or nearly circular, tip rounded; margins entire; upper surface dull pale green, lower surface light green; new growth pinkish. **FLOWER** Bisexual, tiny, tubular, petals 5, corolla 2–3 mm long, hairy; stamens numerous, about twice as long as the corolla; produced in 1-cm-diam. ball-like, finely hairy greenish or whitish heads of 20–30 flowers. Spring. **FRUIT** Curved or coiled legume, 8–10 cm long, 8–12 mm broad, seed cavities evident; seeds lustrous black, partially enclosed in a whitish aril; matures summer to autumn.

HABITAT/RANGE Introduced from tropical America; cultivated, escaped, and established in s. Fla.

SIMILAR SPECIES Three native species of *Pithecellobium* also occur in s. Fla., all shrubs with bipinnate leaves that have only 4 leaflets. Bahama Blackbead (*P. bahamense* Northr.) is similar, but its leaflets reach only 2–2.5 cm long. See also Catclaw Blackbead and Florida Keys Blackbead.

CATCLAW BLACKBEAD   *Pithecellobium unguis-cati* (L.) Benth.

QUICKID A blackbead recognized by the combination of stipular spines, a shrubby stature, hairless flowers, leaflets 3–5 cm long and dull above, and greenish-yellow to pinkish flowers.

This is the native blackbead most likely to reach arborescent proportions. It differs from Monkeypod in having a hairless (or nearly so) inflorescence.

HABITAT/RANGE Native; found frequently on shell middens and in coastal hammocks, s. Fla.

CATCLAW BLACKBEAD

FLORIDA KEYS BLACKBEAD
Pithecellobium keyense Britton ex Britton & Rose

QUICKID The only blackbead in s. Fla. that lacks stipular spines.

Shrub; similar to other Fla. blackbeads but lacks spines.

HABITAT/RANGE Native; s. Fla. and Fla. Keys.

FLORIDA KEYS BLACKBEAD

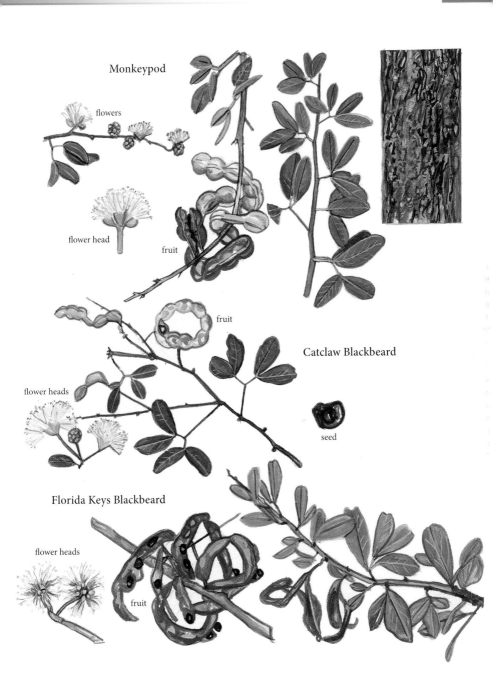

Monkeypod

flowers

flower head

fruit

fruit

Catclaw Blackbeard

flower heads

seed

Florida Keys Blackbeard

flower heads

fruit

SUBFAMILY PAPILIONOIDEAE: PEAS, BEANS, AND THEIR RELATIVES

Members of the subfamily Papilionoideae are usually easily recognized by their typical "pea-like" flowers. The subfamily ranges from the hot tropics to cold areas, from wet habitats to dry deserts, and consists of many herbaceous species in addition to shrubs and trees. There are up to 500 genera and 10,000 species worldwide.

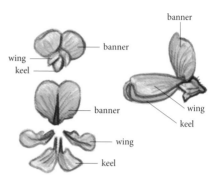

Papilionoid Legume Flower

LEAF Alternate, usually pinnate, but sometimes unifoliolate and appearing simple by reduction. **FLOWER** Bisexual, 5-petaled and strongly bilateral, with 1 large upper petal (the banner or standard) inserted outside of the other petals, which include 2 usually spreading lateral petals (wings), and 2 lower petals that are usually fused along their lower edge and collectively referred to as the keel. Such flowers are said to be papilionaceous. Sepals united, calyx bell-shaped or tubular, sometimes 2-lipped, often 5-lobed, sometimes appearing 4-lobed. There are usually 10 stamens, sometimes all free, sometimes all fused, and sometimes with 9 fused into a single group and the 10th uppermost and free. Inflorescence variable, usually a raceme, sometimes a spike, rarely a panicle or a dense head.

KENTUCKY YELLOWWOOD
Cladrastis kentukea (Dum. Cours.) Rudd

QUICK ID Easily recognized by the pinnately compound leaves with relatively broad, alternate leaflets.

Deciduous, relatively rare, slow-growing tree to about 18 m tall, 60 cm diam. Erect, single straight trunk, often branching rather low; crown broad, rounded or oval, the lowermost branches often drooping at the tips. **BARK** Smooth, splotched light and dark gray. **TWIG** Slender, zigzag, brittle. **LEAF** Alternate, pinnate, blade 20–30 cm long, to about 25 cm broad; petiole 10–15 cm long. Leaflets 5–11, usually alternate, averaging 4–15 cm long, 2–7 cm broad; ovate, elliptic, or obovate, base broadly

wedge-shaped, tip pointed; margins entire; upper surface soft green, lower surface paler. Turns orange-yellow in autumn. **FLOWER** Bisexual, white (sometimes pinkish), 1.8–2.5 cm long; sepals 5; petals 5, the standard nearly circular, the wings narrow; produced in hanging panicles 30–35 cm long. Spring. **FRUIT** Persistent, dangling legume; thin, flat, 3–8 cm long, 8–11 mm broad; matures summer to autumn.

HABITAT/RANGE Native. Ravines, slopes, bluffs, ridges, river valleys, usually in rich, well-drained soils, to about 1,080 m; N.Y. and Va. to S.C., west to s. Ind., s. Ill., Mo., and Okla.; widely cultivated and likely established beyond its natural range.

Notes: *Cladrastis* is a genus of about 7 species, most of which are confined to Asia; a single species occurs in North America.

DOTTED LANCEPOD *Lonchocarpus punctatus* Kunth

QUICK ID Recognized by the combination of pinnate leaves, purplish to white flowers, and flattened, pointed legumes.

Deciduous or evergreen shrub or tree to about 20 m tall. Erect, single trunk; crown dense, rounded or

KENTUCKY YELLOWWOOD

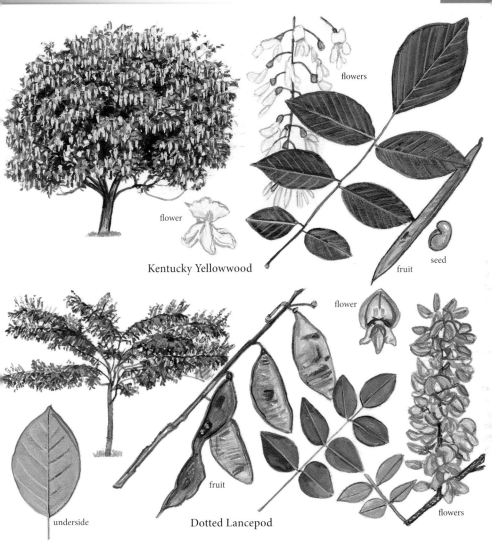

flowers

flower

Kentucky Yellowwood

fruit

seed

flower

fruit

underside

Dotted Lancepod

flowers

slightly flat-topped. **TWIG** Zigzag. **LEAF** Alternate, pinnate, blade to about 16 cm long, to 12 cm broad; petiole 4–9 cm long. Leaflets 2–8 pairs, opposite, to about 6 cm long, 2 cm broad, oval or oblong; upper surface medium or dark green, lower surface paler. **FLOWER** Bisexual, pinkish purple to white, 10–15 mm long, standard petal upright, finely hairy; produced in conspicuous axillary racemes to 9 cm long with stalks 2–3 cm long. Year-round. **FRUIT** Flattened brown legume to about 15 cm long, tapered to a point at both ends; seeds usually 1, sometimes several, more or less flat. Year-round.

HABITAT/RANGE Introduced from South America; escaped from cultivation and established in s. Fla.

Notes: Lonchocarpus is a genus of about 150 species distributed in tropical and subtropical regions of America, Africa, and Australia; this is the only species introduced to North America.

INDIAN ROSEWOOD *Dalbergia sissoo*
Roxb. ex DC.

QUICK ID No other s. Fla. tree has compound leaves with alternate leaflets on a zigzagging rachis.

Evergreen or partly deciduous tree, to about 18 m tall, 35 cm diam.; larger in its native range. Erect, single often crooked trunk, relatively low-branching; crown rounded, the lower branches often drooping or angling downward. **BARK** Gray, becoming scaly, furrowed, and flaking at maturity. **LEAF** Alternate, pinnate, central rachis zigzagging; blade to about 3 cm long, 9 cm broad; petiole to about 2.5 cm long. Leaflets 3–7, alternate and well spaced, each often giving the impression of a simple leaf; broadly oval to nearly circular, to about 8 cm long and broad; base broadly wedge-shaped, tip abruptly short-pointed; upper surface light green, lower surface slightly paler. **FLOWER** Bisexual, yellowish or white, fragrant, about 1 cm long; sepals and petals 5; inflorescence an axillary panicle. Spring to summer. **FRUIT** Flattened brown legume to about 8 cm long, 1 cm broad; matures autumn.

HABITAT/RANGE Introduced from India, Nepal, and Pakistan; established from cultivation and invasive in s. Fla.

SIMILAR SPECIES The simple leaves of Chinese Tallow (*Sapium sebiferum*, Euphorbiaceae) are similar to the leaflets of Indian Rosewood's pinnately compound leaf.

Notes: Dalbergia is a mostly tropical genus of about 100 species. Two scrambling shrubs also occur in s. Fla.

■ *ERYTHRINA*: CORAL TREES

The genus *Erythrina* includes about 100 species from tropical and warm temperate regions; 2 species are naturalized in the East.

CORALTREE *Erythrina crista-galli* L.

Deciduous small tree. Its leaves are also trifoliolate, like those of Coralbean, but the leaflets are not lobed. **HABITAT/RANGE** Introduced from South America; cultivated in the South and reported naturalized from n. Fla. and Ga. west to Tex.

CORALBEAN *Erythrina herbacea* L.
A.K.A. REDCARDINAL, CARDINAL SPEAR, CHEROKEE BEAN

QUICK ID Easily recognized by the bright red flowers, leaves with 3 leaflets, and distinctive fruit.

Deciduous, usually a soft-wooded or herbaceous shrub except in s. Fla., where it becomes a small tree to about 5 m tall. Erect, usually with multiple trunks, sometimes a single trunk; crown spreading, irregular. **BARK** Tree-size plants have smooth yellowish bark. **LEAF** Alternate, trifoliolate, blade to about 3 cm long, to about 12 cm broad; petiole 6–8 cm long, often subtended by a pair of short, sharp spines. Leaflets 2.5–8 cm long, to about 6 cm broad, 3-lobed, ovate, widest and often somewhat flattened at the base, tip abruptly short- or long-pointed; upper surface dark to medium green. **FLOWER** Bisexual, bright red or scarlet, 3–8 cm long, papilionaceous but appearing tubular, the standard and wings elongate and closely overlapping. Inflorescence an erect raceme, the flowers spreading. Spring to early summer. **FRUIT** Cylindric, oblong legume, 6–20 cm long, 1–1.5 cm diam., constricted between the seed compartments; turns black and splits to reveal white seeds completely covered with a bright red aril; matures late summer to autumn.

HABITAT/RANGE Native. Hammocks and pinelands, usually where dry, to about 100 m; southeastern coastal plains, from se. N.C. south to s. Fla. and west to e. Tex, becoming a tree only in s. Fla.

SIMILAR SPECIES Indian Rosewood has similar leaflets, but they number up to 7 per leaf. See also Coraltree.

CORALBEAN

Indian Rosewood

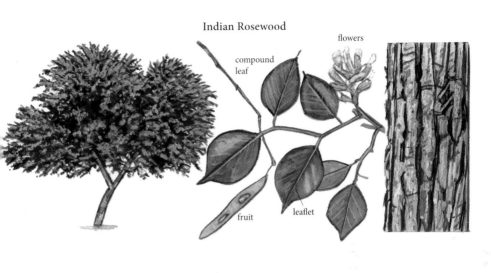

compound leaf

flowers

fruit

leaflet

Coraltree

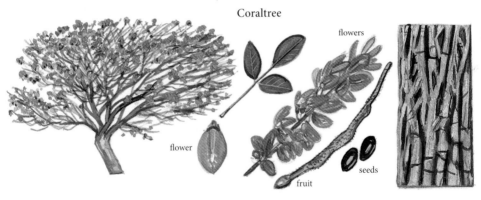

flowers

flower

fruit

seeds

Coralbean

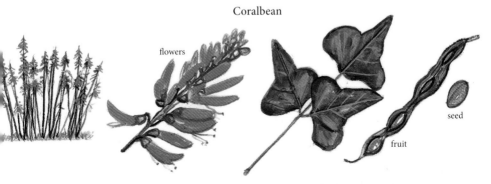

flowers

fruit

seed

FLORIDA FISHPOISON TREE *Piscidia piscipula* (L.) Sarg.
A.K.A. JAMAICA DOGWOOD, FISHFUDDLE TREE

QUICK ID Recognized by the combination of pinnate leaves, leaflets with conspicuous venation and rolled margins, and 4-winged papery fruit.

Deciduous or nearly evergreen, large shrub or tree, to about 15 m tall, about 15 cm diam. Erect, single trunk or sometimes several closely clustered; crown ascending or spreading, dense on shrubby plants. **BARK** Grayish brown, often mottled, smooth at first, becoming finely fissured, sometimes with faint horizontal lines. **LEAF** Alternate, pinnate, blade 5–7 cm long, 13–16 cm broad; petiole 2.5–4 cm long. Leaflets 5–11, 4–10 cm long, 2.5–6 cm broad; oval or broadly elliptic, base broadly wedge-shaped or rounded, tip abruptly short-pointed; margins wavy, often revolute. Upper surface grayish green, dull, essentially hairless, veins impressed and conspicuous; lower surface paler, hairy with appressed hairs at first, becoming mostly hairless. **FLOWER** Bisexual, white, lavender, pinkish, or purple, 1.6–2 cm long; stalks hairy, 2–7 mm long; inflorescence an elongate, many-flowered panicle 5–10 cm long. Spring, before the new leaves. **FRUIT** Light brown legume, 2–10 cm long, 2–4 cm broad, with 4 broad, thin, ruffled or lacerated papery wings, 1–6 seeds; matures summer to autumn.

HABITAT/RANGE Native. Margins of coastal hammocks and woodlands, pinelands, roadsides; s. Fla.

SIMILAR SPECIES The leaflets of Karum Tree (*Pongamia pinnata*) are lustrous above, and the fruit is a flat 1-seeded legume.

Notes: Piscidia is a genus of about 10 species, distributed mostly in the American tropics, including the West Indies and Mexico. The decay-resistant trunk of this and related species has reportedly been used in boat building as the central axis, or dog, of a vessel, hence the common name Jamaican Dogwood. The monikers "fishpoison" and "fishfuddle" refer to the practice of immersing the tree's bark in water to poison or intoxicate fish temporarily, causing them to float to the surface for easy capture.

YELLOW NECKLACEPOD *Sophora tomentosa* L. subsp. *bahamensis* Yakovlev

QUICK ID No other species in s. Fla. has the combination of pinnately compound leaves with opposite and alternate leaflets, yellow flowers, and distinctive necklace-like fruit.

Evergreen or deciduous, usually a thicket-forming shrub, rarely forming a small tree to about 6 m tall. Erect, ascending, or leaning, single trunk or multiple; crown open, irregular, sometimes more or less columnar. **BARK** Yellowish brown. **LEAF** Alternate, pinnate, blade 15–25 cm long, to about 10 cm broad; petiole averaging about 4 cm long. Leaflets 11–21, thick and leathery, alternate and opposite, 2–5 cm long, 1–2 cm broad; obovate, elliptic, or oval, base and tip rounded; margins entire; upper surface dull green at first owing to silky hairs, becoming less hairy and lustrous green at maturity; lower surface hairy. **FLOWER** Bisexual, bright yellow, 2–2.5 cm long; produced in elongate terminal racemes, 10–33 cm long. Year-round. **FRUIT** Legume, 5–20 cm long, 5–10 mm diam., conspicuously constricted between the seed cavities, reminiscent of a beaded necklace. Year-round.

HABITAT/RANGE Native. Margins of coastal hammocks and woodlands, coastal scrub, 0–10 m; coastal peninsular Fla.

FLORIDA FISHPOISON TREE

YELLOW NECKLACEPOD

Florida Fishpoison Tree

flowers

fruit

seed

flowers

developing fruit

Yellow Necklacepod

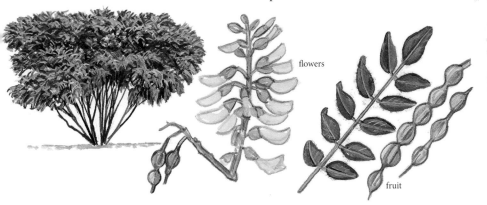

flowers

fruit

SIMILAR SPECIES The similar *S. tomentosa* subsp. *occidentalis* (L.) Brummitt, a mostly shrubby subspecies of Tex., is now naturalized in Fla.; its leaves are hairier and more grayish green at maturity than the sparsely hairy green mature leaves of the Florida subspecies. The leaves of Mexican Alvaradoa (*Alvaradoa amorphoides*, Picramniaceae) and, to a lesser degree, Paradisetree (*Simarouba glauca*, Simaroubaceae) are reminiscent, but neither of these latter species produces yellow flowers.

Notes: Both subspecies are popular garden plants; subsp. *occidentalis* is now well established in s. Fla. and is often mistaken for the native subspecies. The genus contains about 50 species of herbs, shrubs, and trees, 4 native to North America, all with alternate, pinnately compound leaves, blue to yellow 5-petaled flowers, and an essentially stalkless, dangling legume, usually constricted between the seeds and often resembling a string of beads. The seeds are usually toxic.

■ *STYPHNOLOBIUM*: NECKLACEPODS

A small genus of 3–7 species of shrubs and trees. **LEAF** Alternate, pinnately compound. **FLOWER** Bisexual. **FRUIT** A distinctive beadlike legume, the seeds toxic. Species in this genus have long been included within a broader interpretation of the genus *Sophora*, but unlike *Sophora* species, they lack the ability to fix atmospheric nitrogen.

EVE'S NECKLACEPOD *Styphnolobium affine* (Torr. & Gray) Walp.

QUICK ID Recognized by the combination of pinnate leaves, pink or white flowers, and black leathery legumes with conspicuous seed compartments.

Deciduous, usually a shrub 2–5 m tall, rarely a small tree to about 10 m tall. Erect, single slender trunk or multiple; crown ascending, spreading, sparse. **BARK** Reddish brown, irregularly ridged and furrowed, becoming scaly and roughened. **TWIG** Smooth, green. **LEAF** Alternate, pinnate, blade 10–20 cm long, to about 8 cm broad. Leaflets 13–17, often alternate, 2–4 cm long, 1–2 cm broad, oval, base rounded or broadly wedge-shaped, tip bluntly rounded, notched at the tip; margins entire; upper surface medium green, lustrous, veins conspicuous. **FLOWER** Bisexual, fragrant; calyx 3–5 mm long; corolla pink or white, 1–1.5 cm long; produced in drooping, terminal racemes of 6–15 flowers, 7–13 cm long. Late spring to early summer. **FRUIT** Oblong blackened leathery legume, 2–8 cm long, 7–8 mm diam., the seed compartments conspicuous, beadlike; seeds 2–6, brown, about 5 mm long; matures late summer, persisting into autumn.

HABITAT/RANGE Native. Upland woods, ravine bottoms, floodplains, stream margins, limestone slopes, roadsides, often where limestone is abundant, to about 100 m; nw. La., sw. Ark., s. Okla., c. and e. Tex.

SIMILAR SPECIES Species of the similar genus *Sophora* have yellow flowers.

JAPANESE PAGODA TREE
Styphnolobium japonicum (L.) Schott

QUICK ID Recognized by the combination of pinnate leaves, white or yellowish-white flowers, and yellowish-brown, necklace-like legume.

Deciduous tree to about 21 m tall. Erect, single trunk; crown broad, rounded. **BARK** Gray-brown, ridged, with elongate vertical furrows. **TWIG** Lustrous green, with lighter lenticels. **LEAF** Alternate, pinnate; blade 15–25 cm long, to about 11 cm broad. Leaflets 7–17, alternate and opposite, each 2.5–5 cm long; ovate, base rounded, tip pointed; margins entire; upper surface lustrous medium green, lower surface paler, hairy. **FLOWER** Bisexual; corolla white or yellowish white, about 1 cm long, produced in hanging panicles to about 35 cm long. Summer. **FRUIT** Hairless yellow-green to light brown legume, 8–20 cm long, seed compartments conspicuous, beadlike; matures autumn, persisting into winter.

HABITAT/RANGE Introduced from Asia; cultivated and naturalized from Pa. and Ohio south to N.C.

SIMILAR SPECIES Eve's Necklacepod can be distinguished by the blackish leathery legume.

TEXAS KIDNEYWOOD *Eysenhardtia texana* Scheele
A.K.A. BEE-BRUSH

QUICK ID Recognized by its pinnate leaves with small leaflets and its dense spikes of small white flowers with petals rather equal in size to one another.

Tardily deciduous, usually open shrub, rarely a small tree to about 5 m tall. **LEAF** Alternate, pinnately compound, with 7–23 pairs of obovate

EVE'S NECKLACEPOD

TEXAS KIDNEYWOOD

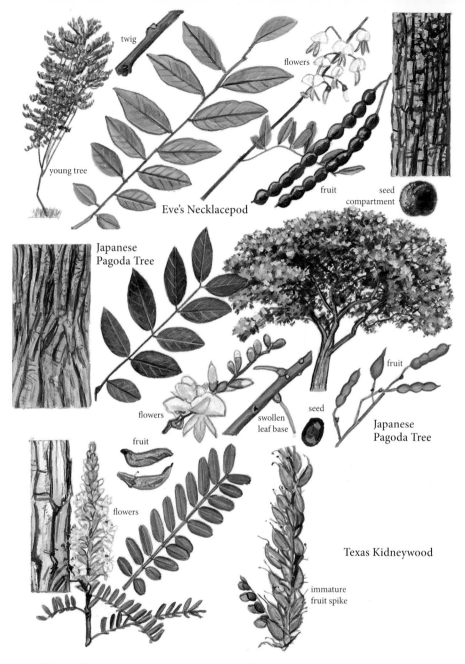

twig

flowers

young tree

fruit

seed compartment

Eve's Necklacepod

Japanese Pagoda Tree

flowers

swollen leaf base

seed

fruit

Japanese Pagoda Tree

fruit

flowers

flowers

Texas Kidneywood

immature fruit spike

or elliptic leaflets, each 4–12 mm long. **FLOWER** White, produced in dense spikes, 3–10 mm long. **FRUIT** Oblong legume, 5–8 mm long.

HABITAT/RANGE Native, a mostly western species, barely entering our area in c. Tex.

Notes: Eysenhardtia is a genus of about 15 species of unarmed, mostly deciduous shrubs and small trees distributed primarily in Mexico. The foliage of most species is gland-dotted, with a resinous, often citrus-like odor.

■ *ROBINIA*: LOCUSTS

A genus of 4 species and several natural hybrids, confined mostly to temperate regions of the U.S. and Mexico; 4 are native to North America, 3 to the East. At least 2 species are widely cultivated, obscuring their original range limits.

Deciduous trees and shrubs. **LEAF** Alternate, pinnately compound, with numerous elliptic to lanceolate leaflets; in some species the leaf is armed with spines at the base of the petiole. **FLOWER** Bisexual, white, pink, purple, or rose-purple. **FRUIT** Oblong, flattened papery legume.

BLACK LOCUST *Robinia pseudoacacia* L.

QUICK ID Recognized by the combination of hanging clusters of creamy-white flowers, pinnate leaves subtended by a pair of sharp-pointed spines, and coarse, ridged and furrowed blackish bark.

Deciduous tree, to about 25 m tall, 1–1.5 m diam. Erect, single straight or crooked trunk; crown open, irregular, with ascending branches, sometimes spreading when open-grown. **BARK** Gray or dark gray-brown, coarse, becoming deeply furrowed, often developing large forking ridges and large plates. **TWIG** Slender, brittle, reddish brown. **LEAF** Alternate, pinnate; blade 20–36 cm long, 4–12 cm broad; petiole averaging about 3 cm long, subtended by a pair of sharp-pointed spines. Leaflets 7–25, 2–6 cm long, 1–2.5 cm broad; thin, elliptic, oblong, or ovate, base rounded or bluntly wedge-shaped, apex rounded, usually tipped with a small tooth; margins entire; upper surface medium green or yellowish green, hairless, lower surface gray-green. **FLOWER** Bisexual, fragrant, white or creamy white, the standard with a dull yellow patch; calyx 6–9 mm long, corolla 1.5–2.5 cm long; produced from the leaf axils in an elongate, drooping raceme. Spring to early summer. **FRUIT** Oblong, flat legume, 5–10 cm long, about 1 cm broad; matures late summer to autumn, persisting throughout the winter.

HABITAT/RANGE Native. Moist woods, stream margins, river bottoms, to about 1,000 m; original native range probably confined to the s. Appalachians and the Ozark Mountains. Widely cultivated and established nearly throughout North America and parts of Europe; common in pastures, fencerows, and disturbed roadsides.

SIMILAR SPECIES The flowers of Clammy Locust and Bristly Locust are usually pinkish or rose-purple.

CLAMMY LOCUST *Robinia viscosa* Vent.

QUICK ID Recognized by the combination of pinnate leaves, pinkish-purple flowers, and sticky twigs, flower stalks, and fruit.

Deciduous shrub or small tree, usually not exceeding about 4 m tall, potentially to 10 m tall and 25 cm diam. Erect, single trunk, sometimes branching close to the ground; crown ascending. **BARK** Reddish brown. **TWIG** Sparsely or densely covered with sticky, glandular hairs. **LEAF** Alternate, pinnate; blade 8–15 cm long, averaging about 5 cm broad; petiole 1–2 cm long, sometimes subtended by slender stipular spines. Leaflets 13–21, each 2.5–4.5 cm long, 10–17 mm broad, elliptic or oval, base rounded, tip rounded or blunt; margins entire; upper surface dull green, mostly hairless, lower surface paler, densely and persistently hairy. **FLOWER** Bisexual, pink or pinkish purple, rarely white; calyx 7–9 mm long; corolla 2–2.5 cm long; produced in pendent racemes; flower stalks sticky with glandular hairs. **FRUIT** Flattened, oblong legume, 5–13 cm long, 8–12 mm broad, usually

BLACK LOCUST

CLAMMY LOCUST

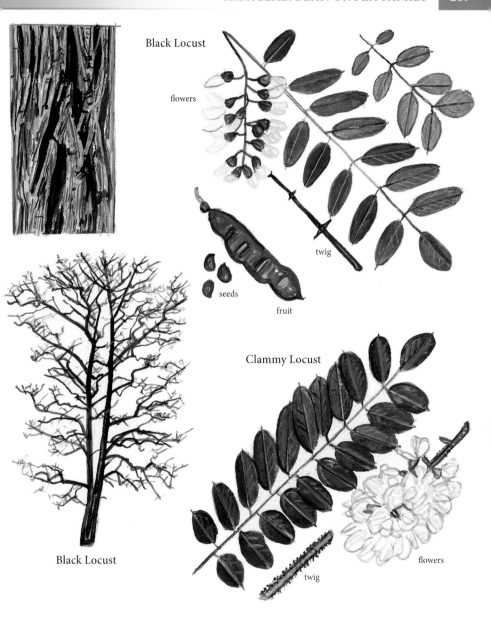

Black Locust

flowers

seeds

fruit

twig

Black Locust

Clammy Locust

twig

flowers

covered with glandular hairs 1–2 mm long; matures summer to early autumn.

HABITAT/RANGE Native. Occurs naturally on rock outcrops, along forest edges, and in thin woodlands at higher elevations in the s. Appalachians, 500–4,000 m; rare endemic to the Southeast, but widely cultivated, established well beyond the native range depicted on the accompanying map.

SIMILAR SPECIES The Black Locust has creamy-white flowers and lacks the sticky hairs on twigs, flower stalks, and fruit.

BRISTLY LOCUST *Robinia hispida* L.

QUICKID Distinguished by the alternate pinnate leaves and conspicuously and densely hairy twigs that lack sticky glands.

Deciduous shrub, similar to, and sometimes confused with, Clammy Locust. Twigs, leaf petioles, and inflorescences densely hairy, the hairs 1–5 mm long and lacking sticky glands. **LEAF** Pinnate, with 9–13 leaflets, the lower surfaces usually nearly hairless at maturity.

HABITAT/RANGE Native; endemic to the Southeast, but widely planted and now established well beyond its original range.

SIBERIAN PEA TREE *Caragana arborescens* Lam.
A.K.A. SIBERIAN PEA SHRUB

QUICKID Recognized by its evenly pinnate leaves and yellow flowers, and the dense, shrubby form.

Deciduous shrub or small tree, to about 7 m tall. Vase-shaped or rounded, single trunk or more often with multiple trunks and branching close to the ground; crown usually dense, rounded. **BARK** Grayish brown. **TWIG** Hairy. **LEAF** Alternate, pinnate, blade 3–9 cm long, to about 3 cm broad; petiole 1–10 cm long, subtended by spine- or soft-tipped stipules. Leaflets 3–6 pairs, even in number, 1–4 cm long, 5–15 mm broad; elliptic, ovate, or oblong, base wedge-shaped, apex rounded or flattened, with a tiny tooth at the tip; upper and lower surfaces hairy at first, becoming nearly hairless. **FLOWER** Bisexual; corolla 1.5–2.3 cm long, yellow; calyx 4.5–8 mm long. Inflorescence technically a raceme but reduced to a single flower. Late spring to early summer. **FRUIT** Reddish-brown legume, linear or oblong, 2.5–6 cm long, 4–7 mm diam.; seeds 3–8, varying from greenish yellow to dark reddish brown, 4–6 mm long; matures summer.

HABITAT/RANGE Introduced from Asia. Established in pastures, fields, woodlands, and along fencerows and roadsides, 100–2,500 m; N.B. west to Alaska, south to Mass., Ill., and Nebr. in the East, more widespread in the West.

Notes: Caragana is a genus of about 80 species; 2 other species are established in North America, both shrubs with only 2–4 leaflets per leaf. Many species have been introduced to horticulture and are likely to be encountered in arboreta and gardens.

QUICKSTICK *Gliricidia sepium* (Jacq.) Kunth
A.K.A. KAKAWATI

QUICKID Recognized by its combination of pinkish flowers, large blackish fruit, and odd-pinnate leaves.

Deciduous shrub or small tree, to about 10 m tall, 20 cm diam. Erect, single trunk; crown irregular, spreading. **BARK** Smooth, grayish. **LEAF** Alternate, pinnate; blade 7–15 cm long, 10–12 cm broad; petiole averaging 6 cm long. Leaflets 7–15, each 3–8 cm long, 1–3.5 cm broad; ovate, lanceolate, or elliptic, margins entire; upper surface dull green, lower surface paler, hairy. **FLOWER** Bisexual, corolla white or pink, 1.5–2.2 cm long; calyx 4–5 mm long; inflorescence a raceme at the branch tips, 5–12 cm long. Spring. **FRUIT** Flattened blackish legume, 10–15 cm long, 5–10 mm broad; matures summer.

HABITAT/RANGE Introduced from Mexico and Central and South America; cultivated and established in s. Fla., especially Key West.

SIMILAR SPECIES Black Locust (*Robinia pseudoacacia*) is similar but has white flowers and smaller fruits and does not overlap in range with Quickstick.

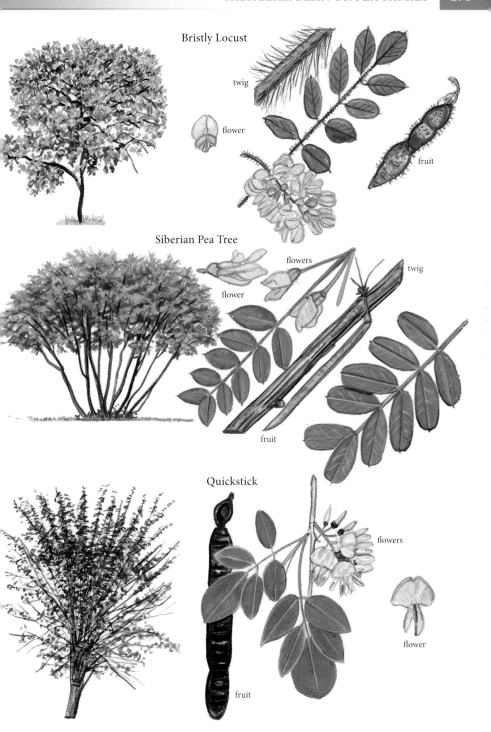

Bristly Locust

twig

flower

fruit

Siberian Pea Tree

flowers

flower

twig

fruit

Quickstick

flowers

flower

fruit

KARUM TREE *Pongamia pinnata* (L.) Merr.
A.K.A. Pongame Oiltree, Poonga-oil Tree

QUICK ID Distinguished in s. Fla. by the combination of pinkish or lavender flowers, pinnately compound leaves with ovate leaflets, and semicircular fruit.

Deciduous or late-deciduous tree, to about 10 m tall, 15–60 cm diam., potentially larger. Erect or ascending, single trunk, often very low branching, with several main branches arising from near the base. **BARK** Light brown, smooth or slightly roughened. **LEAF** Alternate, pinnate; blade 10–20 cm long, to about 16 cm broad; petiole 5–15 cm long. Leaflets 5–7, each 4–8 cm long, 2–4 cm broad; ovate, base rounded, tip pointed; margins entire; upper surface hairless, reddish at first, becoming lustrous bright green, then turning yellow, veins conspicuous; lower surface paler. **FLOWER** Bisexual, whitish, pinkish, or lavender, about 1.3 cm long; produced from the leaf axils in pendent panicles or raceme-like clusters. Spring to summer. **FRUIT** Flat, semicircular, dangling, 1-seeded yellowish to brownish (green at first) legume, 3–4 cm long, about 2 cm broad; matures summer to autumn.

HABITAT/RANGE Introduced from Southeast Asia; cultivated and established in s. Fla.

Notes: The fruits of Karum Tree are rich in oil; the tree is often used as a sustainable source of biodiesel fuel. As treated here, the genus *Pongamia* includes only a single species. It is sometimes included in the genus *Millettia*.

VEGETABLE HUMMINGBIRD *Sesbania grandiflora* (L.) Pers.
A.K.A. Scarlet Wisteria, Christmas Bells

QUICK ID Recognized by the combination of the pinnately compound leaves and large pink, white, or yellow flowers that are present nearly year-round.

Deciduous or evergreen small tree, 5–10 m tall, 15–30 cm diam. Erect, single trunk; crown sparsely branched, open. **BARK** Gray, thick, rough, furrowed, with thick plates. **TWIG** Finely hairy. **LEAF** Alternate, pinnate; blade 15–35 cm long, to about 10 cm broad; petiole about 4 cm long. Leaflets 10–25 pairs, opposite or nearly so, 2–7 cm long, 7–15 mm broad; oblong, the margins mostly parallel, base asymmetric, tip flattened or rounded, usually minutely notched; upper and lower surfaces pale green, hairless at maturity. **FLOWER** Bisexual, large, white, pink, or yellow, corolla 5–10 cm long, standard to about 8 cm broad; produced in axillary racemes of 2–5 flowers. Year-round. **FRUIT** Slender brown legume 20–45 cm long, 6–9 mm diam., with up to 50 kidney-shaped, dark brown seeds. Year-round.

HABITAT/RANGE Introduced from tropical Asia; cultivated and established in s. Fla.

Notes: The genus *Sesbania* includes about 50 species, mostly of temperate and warm tropical regions. Nearly all others in the East are herbaceous, and none has equally large flowers.

GOLDEN CHAIN TREE *Laburnum anagyroides* Medik.
A.K.A. Golden Rain Tree, Common Laburnum

Deciduous, tree to about 10 m tall. Erect, trunk slender, crown irregular with slightly drooping twigs. **LEAF** Alternate, palmately compound, with 3 ovate or broadly lanceolate leaflets, each 3–7 cm long, grayish green with appressed hairs. **FLOWER** Bright yellow, 1.5–2 cm long, produced in a loose, narrow, elongate, pendent, many-flowered cluster 10–40 cm long. **FRUIT** Plump, lightly hairy brown legume; constricted between the seed compartments. **HABITAT/RANGE** Introduced from Europe; cultivated and marginally escaped, mostly in Mass., more widespread in the West.

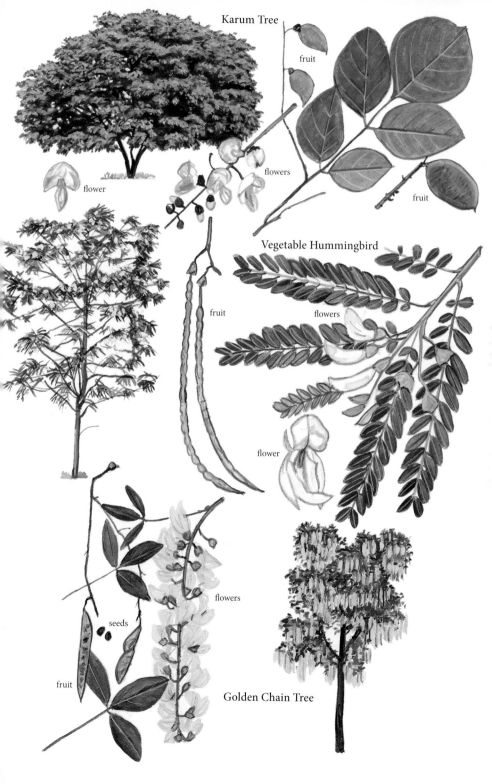

Karum Tree

fruit

flowers

flower

fruit

Vegetable Hummingbird

flowers

fruit

flower

flowers

seeds

fruit

Golden Chain Tree

FAGACEAE: BEECH OR OAK FAMILY

Fagaceae comprises a collection of 9 genera and 600–800 species of trees and shrubs, naturally occurring mostly in the Northern Hemisphere. Five genera and nearly 100 species occur in North America north of Mexico, and are absent or rare only in the northern Great Plains, the northern Rocky Mountains, and the deserts of the Southwest. The oaks (*Quercus*) constitute the family's largest genus; the approximately 44 oak species native to eastern North America are joined by 3 species of chestnuts (*Castanea*) and a single species of beech (*Fagus*).

Evergreen or deciduous trees and shrubs. **LEAF** Alternate, simple, and variously lobed, toothed, or entire. **FLOWER** Members of the family are monoecious and characterized by tiny unisexual, wind-pollinated flowers borne in separate inflorescences on the same plant. Individual flowers are radially symmetric, lack petals, and are produced in rigid or flexible catkins, the female flowers few or only 1 per catkin, the male flowers usually more numerous. **FRUIT** The family's most distinctive character is the fruit, 1 or more nuts partially or completely enclosed within a scaly or spiny cupule (variously called a cup, cap, or involucre).

Many species of this family are economically important as sources of lumber, fuel, and food, and are also widely used in habitat restoration and as ornamentals. Perhaps no family of woody plants provides more ecological services to a wider array of wildlife. Trees of some species, especially the oaks, may live several hundred years and grow to very large proportions. When growing within the confines of cities and towns, such ancient matriarchs are often revered, named, and even protected by ordinance.

■ *CASTANEA*: CHESTNUTS

Castanea includes as many as 10 species in North America, Europe, and Asia. Seven species occur in North America, of which 4 are native; none occurs in the West. Most species in the genus are similar in leaf and fruit and are difficult to distinguish from one another; chestnuts can be distinguished from other trees by the combination of alternate leaves with bristle-tipped marginal teeth, conspicuous parallel lateral leaf veins, and the spiny cupule enclosing 1–3 nuts.

Deciduous shrubs and trees ranging from small shrubs 1 m tall to huge single-trunked trees 30 m tall, with a trunk to 3 m diam. **BARK** On young trees smooth, brown, and vertically streaked with narrow, light brown ridges, on some species with horizontal streaks; older trees developing broad, flat, sometimes scaly ridges separated by shallow fissures. **TWIG** Reddish brown, hairless or hairy, sometimes marked with lenticels. Pith 5-angled in cross section. Buds egg-shaped, greenish, to about 8 mm long. **LEAF** Alternate, simple, to about 28 cm long. Veins prominent, parallel, up to about 20 per side. Margins with large or small blunt or sharp teeth, each typically terminated by a single lateral vein often forming a bristle-like tip. **FLOWER** Unisexual (plants monoecious), individually tiny, produced in densely flowered unisexual or bisexual inflorescences (catkins or aments), or as solitary flowers. Male catkins more or less erect or ascending, conspicuous, to about 20 cm long, produced on short stalks in the axils of developing leaves. Female flowers usually inconspicuous, either solitary or in clusters of 2 or 3 in the axils of fully expanded leaves, often at the base of the male inflorescence. **FRUIT** Distinctive spiny cupule with 2–4 valves that splits at maturity to expose 1–3 shiny nuts, rounded on both sides or rounded on 1 side and flattened on the other side; usually matures late summer to autumn.

Members of the genus occur in pinelands, mixed forests of oaks and other hardwoods, and on disturbed sites as escapees from nearby plantings, 0–1,000 m. Species of *Castanea* are wind-pollinated, interfertile, and hybridize readily. Natural crosses between native and non-native species are common and often make precise identification difficult. Several species are valued for their sweet, edible nuts as

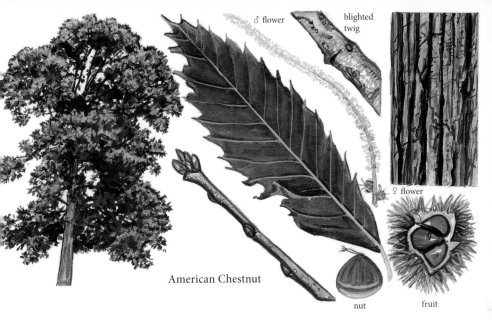

♂ flower   blighted twig

♀ flower

American Chestnut

nut   fruit

well as for their decay-resistant wood. The American Chestnut was formerly among the dominant trees of e. North America's deciduous forests but has been nearly eliminated by chestnut blight, a fungal disease caused by *Cryphonectria parasitica* that was introduced to the U.S. from Europe in the early 1900s. Most plants that remain today are sprouts from diseased stumps. Despite continuing efforts to produce blight-resistant trees, nearly all populations within the American Chestnut's natural range remain infected, and the outlook for this and perhaps other native species of *Castanea* appears dire.

AMERICAN CHESTNUT *Castanea dentata* (Marsh.) Borkh.

QUICK ID Recognized by the combination of large, coarsely toothed, mostly hairless yellow-green leaves with bristle-tipped marginal teeth, and the fruit a spiny bur containing flattened nuts.

Deciduous, formerly a medium to large tree to about 30 m tall, 3 m diam.; now occurring mostly as stump sprouts and seldom exceeding about 7 m tall. Mature trees erect with 1 straight trunk. **BARK** On young trees smooth, brown, vertically and irregularly streaked with tan; at maturity darker brown and developing broad, flat, scaly plates divided by shallow fissures. **TWIG** Hairless, brown, spotted with creamy-brown lenticels. Buds slightly offset but appearing terminal, hairless, greenish brown,

egg-shaped, 5–8 mm long. **LEAF** Alternate, simple, thin, papery, obovate or oblanceolate, sometimes widest toward the middle; margins coarsely toothed with large triangular, bristle-tipped teeth, the bristles often exceeding 2 mm long. Upper surface lustrous, yellow-green, hairless; lower surface paler, hairy when young, becoming hairless or usually with minute hairs at least along the veins. Turns yellow in autumn. Blade 9–30 cm long, 3–10 cm broad; petiole 1–3 cm long. **FLOWER** Male flowers creamy white, aromatic, borne in dense, irregularly spaced clusters in a narrow, spicate inflorescence 12–20 cm long. Female flowers inconspicuous, tiny, borne at the base of some male inflorescences. **FRUIT** Densely spiny, 4-valved bur to about 7.5 cm diam., enclosing 1–3 nuts. Nuts lustrous brown, usually flattened on at least 1 side, 1.8–2.5 cm broad, apex terminated by a narrow beak about 8 mm long.

HABITAT/RANGE Native. Well-drained rocky upland soils on hills and mountain slopes,

AMERICAN CHESTNUT

AMERICAN CHESTNUT *continued*

0–1,200 m; Maine, N.Y., and Ont. south to nw. Fla., west to Mo. and La., cultivated from Mich. and Wis. south to Ind. and Ill.; formerly achieved its largest size in the s. Appalachians.

SIMILAR SPECIES The native chinquapins have rounded instead of flattened nuts held in 2-valved cupules, and the lower surface of the leaves usually bears star-shaped hairs at maturity. Spanish Chestnut, Japanese Chestnut, and Chinese Chestnut have variously hairy lower leaf surfaces. The leaves of Sawtooth Oak (*Quercus acutissima*) are reminiscent but much smaller.

Notes: In its former grandeur the American Chestnut was a dominant, valuable, and well-used tree of e. North America. The nuts are sweet and edible and were used as food by humans and a variety of wildlife, including deer, squirrels, and chipmunks. The decay-resistant wood was used for furniture, railroad ties, and fencing, and tannins in the bark and wood were used in tanning leather. The fungal blight introduced to the U.S. from Europe in 1904 has eliminated virtually all large specimens of this species and has relegated it to a minor place in the eastern deciduous forest. Recent efforts at saving the species have focused on propagating and distributing offspring of a few recently discovered and apparently blight-resistant trees. Breeding programs that cross American Chestnut with blight-resistant Chinese Chestnut and Japanese Chestnut have also met with some success, but result in offspring that are not genetically pure.

CHINQUAPIN *Castanea pumila* Mill.
A.K.A. Chinkapin, Dwarf Chestnut

QUICK ID **Distinguished by the combination of alternate, coarsely toothed leaves, a petiole less than 8 mm long, a dense inflorescence with flowers nearly concealing the axis, and the spiny bur with spines less than 1 cm long enclosing a nut that is rounded on both sides.**

Deciduous shrub or tree, to 15 m tall, 60 cm diam. Often with multiple leaning trunks arising from a clustered base; crown irregularly rounded. **BARK** Gray, splotchy, smooth when young, becoming scaly and narrowly fissured with maturity. **TWIG** Grayish or reddish brown, minutely hairy when young, sometimes becoming mostly hairless at maturity. **LEAF** Alternate, simple, somewhat stiff and leathery, narrowly elliptic to oblanceolate, often widest near the middle and tapering to a wedge-shaped base; margins coarsely and sharply toothed, the teeth bristle-tipped and curved toward the leaf tip. Upper surface lustrous bright green, varying to dull green; lower surface on some plants silvery gray with a conspicuous covering of stellate whitish hairs, on other plants nearly hairless. The silvery-gray color of the lower surface of the leaves of some trees is distinctive among the chestnuts and chinquapins. Leaf turns yellowish brown in autumn. Blade 4–21 cm long, 2–8 cm broad; petiole 3–7 mm long. **FLOWER** Male flowers creamy white, borne in a densely flowered catkin, 10–18 cm long, flowers so densely packed as to obscure the axis of the inflorescence. Female flowers small, inconspicuous, borne singly or in few-flowered clusters near the bases of some male inflorescences. **FRUIT** Spiny 2-valved bur, 3–4 cm diam., usually enclosing 1, rarely 2, nuts. Nuts lustrous, dark brown to almost black, round in cross section, 7–20 mm diam.

HABITAT/RANGE Native. Open woods, sandy pinelands, usually where relatively dry, 0–1,000 m; Mass. south to c. Fla., west to Ky., e. Okla., and Tex.

SIMILAR SPECIES Ozark Chinquapin can be distinguished by its hairless twigs, a petiole 8–10 mm long, and the spines on the cupule often exceeding 1 cm long. The fruits of American Chestnut are 4-valved, and the lower surface of the leaves appears hairless.

Notes: Chinquapin has been divided into several distinct species by various authors. Some experts treat the shrubby, rhizomatous form of n. Fla. and s. Ga. as *C. alnifolia* Nutt. Other experts distinguish

CHINQUAPIN

OZARK CHINQUAPIN

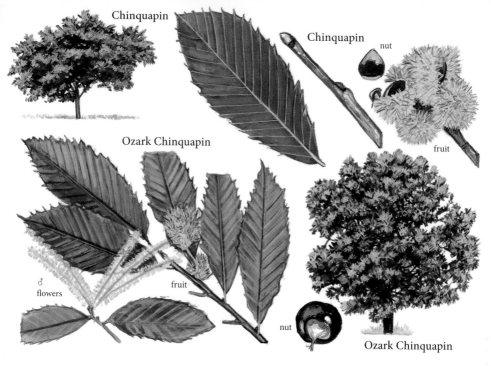

Chinquapin

Chinquapin

nut

Ozark Chinquapin

fruit

♂ flowers

fruit

nut

Ozark Chinquapin

C. floridana (Sarg.) Ashe, a shrub or small tree of the southeastern coastal plains, by the lower surfaces of the leaves being sparsely, if at all, hairy. Many modern taxonomists consider all of these forms to represent a single species, attributing perceived morphological differences to clinal, ecological, and geographical variation. Trees affected by chestnut blight are encountered, though the impact has not been as great as it has on American Chestnut.

OZARK CHINQUAPIN *Castanea ozarkensis* Ashe

QUICK ID A chestnut, distinguished by the combination of hairless twig, rounded nut, and its occurrence chiefly in Ark. and adjacent states.

Deciduous tree, sometimes a multitrunked shrub, formerly to 20 m tall, 1 m diam., now usually sprouting from diseased stumps and not exceeding about 10 m tall. **BARK** Brown, becoming moderately or deeply fissured with age. **TWIG** Stout, hairless, ashy gray. **LEAF** Alternate, simple, oblanceolate to narrowly obovate; margins coarsely toothed, the teeth bristle-tipped and curving toward the leaf tip. Upper surface lustrous, yellow-green, hairless; lower surface usually with a dense or sparse covering of stellate whitish hairs, sometimes nearly

hairless. Blade 12–22 cm long, 3–10 cm broad; petiole usually 8–10 mm long. **FLOWER** Male flowers borne in a narrow, elongate catkin, 15–20 cm long. Female flowers solitary at the base of some male inflorescences. **FRUIT** Two-valved spiny bur concealing a single rounded or oval nut, 9–19 mm long, 8–14 mm broad.

HABITAT/RANGE Native. Deciduous forests, 150–600 m; restricted mostly to the Ozark and Ouachita mountains of Ark., also reported in e. Okla., ne. Tex., n. La., s. Mo.; previously reported from n. Ala. but apparently no longer extant there owing to chestnut blight.

SIMILAR SPECIES American Chestnut differs in having nuts usually flattened on at least 1 side and mature leaves hairless or minutely hairy along veins beneath. Chinquapin can be distinguished by its combination of cupule spines less than 1 cm long, twigs minutely and finely hairy, and petiole usually less than 8 mm long.

Notes: Ozark Chinquapin shows affinities to both American Chestnut and Chinquapin; some experts suggest that *C. ozarkensis* is merely a subspecies of the more wide-ranging *C. pumila.* The chestnut blight that attacks American Chestnut has also substantially reduced Ozark Chinquapin numbers.

CHINESE CHESTNUT *Castanea mollissima* Blume

QUICK ID Distinguished among chestnuts by the lower surface of the leaf usually densely covered with hairs, at least along the major veins, but lacking scalelike glands.

Deciduous tree, sometimes shrubby, 15–30 m tall, to about 1.5 m diam. Single trunk or several. Crown spreading, often with low branches. **BARK** Gray-brown, rough, scaly, divided into irregular furrows. **TWIG** Pubescent with long hairs when young, hairs shorter with age. **LEAF** Alternate, simple, varying elliptic, oblong, or lanceolate, with bluntly toothed margins and conspicuous parallel veins, the tip of each vein extending beyond the tip of a marginal tooth as a curved bristle. Upper surface lustrous yellow-green; lower surface densely hairy, at least along the veins, lacking scalelike glands. Blade 10–17 cm long, 3–7 cm broad; petiole 1–2 cm long. **FLOWER** Male flowers white, tiny, borne in a slender, densely flowered catkin 9–13 cm long. Female flowers borne in short catkins less than 2 cm long at the base of some male catkins. **FRUIT** Spiny bur, 5–8 cm diam., enclosing 2 or 3 lustrous reddish-brown nuts that are typically flattened on 1 or 2 sides.

HABITAT/RANGE Introduced from China. Occasionally cultivated and naturalized in the e. U. S. from about Mass. and Ill. south to Fla.

SIMILAR SPECIES Similar to, and often difficult to distinguish from, Japanese Chestnut and American Chestnut. American Chestnut has more sharply toothed leaves; Japanese Chestnut has bluntly toothed leaves, the margin on some leaves appearing almost entire except for the marginal bristles, and glandular scales on the lower leaf surface.

Notes: This is the most common non-native chestnut in cultivation. Numerous cultivars and hybrids are recognized, which contributes to the difficulty of distinguishing between cultivated and native species.

JAPANESE CHESTNUT *Castanea crenata* Siebold & Zucc.

QUICK ID Distinguished among chestnuts by the lower leaf surface often densely hairy and dotted with glandular scales, and the leaf margins bluntly toothed or sometimes appearing entire except for bristles.

Deciduous tree or large shrub, to about 15 m tall. One or a few short trunks. Crown broad, spreading. **BARK** Grayish, often splitting at maturity. **TWIG** Finely pubescent when young, becoming hairless with age. **LEAF** Alternate, simple, elliptic or oblong, rounded to somewhat heart-shaped at base; margins bluntly toothed, the teeth sometimes essentially reduced to bristles. Upper surface lustrous, dark green, veins conspicuous, parallel, usually extending beyond the leaf margin as a bristle; lower surface with a combination of dense tangled hairs and minute glandular scales. Blade 8–16 cm long, 2–4 cm broad; petiole 0.5–2.5 cm long. **FLOWER** Male flowers borne when closely spaced clusters in an ascending or erect catkin. Female flowers inconspicuous, borne near the base of some male catkins. **FRUIT** Spiny bur, 5–6 cm diam., usually containing 2 or 3 nuts, occasionally up to 5. Nuts lustrous, reddish brown, 2–3 cm broad.

HABITAT/RANGE Introduced from Japan. Occasionally cultivated and marginally naturalized in disturbed pinelands in c. Fla.

SIMILAR SPECIES Chinquapin is similar, distinguished by the lower leaf surface being either nearly hairless or silvery gray with a conspicuous covering of stellate whitish hairs (but without tangled hairs or minute glandular scales).

Notes: This species is resistant to chestnut blight and has been interbred with American Chestnut to produce blight-resistant strains of that species.

SPANISH CHESTNUT *Castanea sativa* Mill.
A.K.A. SWEET CHESTNUT, EUROPEAN CHESTNUT

QUICK ID The combination of large leaves with spreading teeth and a relatively long petiole, yellowish male catkins, large female flowers, and a flattened nut are diagnostic within the genus.

Deciduous heavy-branched tree, to 30 m tall, usually to about 1.5 m diam. Typically with a single erect trunk. Crown vertically elongate, irregularly branched. **BARK** Young bark somewhat silvery and horizontally banded, at maturity becoming reddish brown to grayish, with rounded ridges and moderately deep furrows that sometimes spiral the trunk. **TWIG** Brown, with conspicuous lenticels; bud offset at tip, often appearing terminal. **LEAF** Alternate, simple, stiff, oblong to elliptic; margins

fruit

Chinese Chestnut

nut

autumn

Spanish Chestnut

fruit

nut

Japanese Chestnut

nut

fruit

coarsely toothed, the teeth about 1 cm long, each tipped with the bristlelike extension of a conspicuous lateral vein; margins raggedly fringed in some cultivated plants. Blade 12–22 cm long, to about 5 cm broad; petiole 30 mm long or more. **FLOWER** Male flowers creamy yellow, borne in irregularly spaced clusters along the axis of an erect catkin, 15–20 cm long, the greenish axis clearly visible. Female flowers in conspicuous clusters near the bases of some male catkins. **FRUIT** Four-valved capsule, splitting at maturity to reveal 4 nuts. Nut lustrous brown, rounded on 1 side, flattened on the other, 2–3 cm broad.

HABITAT/RANGE Introduced; probably native to coastal areas of the Mediterranean and w. Asia.

Escaped from cultivation and scarcely naturalized in a few e. states, including N.Y., Mass., Pa., and Ala.

SIMILAR SPECIES American Chestnut has creamy-white male catkins, and smaller, less conspicuous female flowers.

Notes: Spanish Chestnut has been cultivated for at least 2,000 years and is the chief source of commercial chestnuts. The wood has been used as a substitute for oak and has proven particularly durable in applications where it comes into contact with the soil. Spanish Chestnut is susceptible to chestnut blight in North America, though apparently less so in Europe.

■ *FAGUS*: BEECHES

The genus *Fagus* is comprised of 8–10 species; 1 native and 1 non-native species occur in North America, mostly in the East, from Que. to e. Tex. and n. Fla. Deciduous, moderate to large trees, to at least 30 m tall, 1.5 m diam. Erect, single trunk, crowns of open-grown and canopy trees broad, spreading; crowns of understory trees usually narrower. **BARK** Smooth, blue-gray or silvery gray, some species developing shallow furrows and ridges. **TWIG** Green at first, becoming splotchy gray at maturity. Lateral buds reddish brown, elongate, cigarlike or torpedo-shaped, tapering to an acute tip. Terminal buds long, narrow, more or less torpedo-shaped. **LEAF** Alternate, simple, 2-ranked, elliptic or ovate, margins bluntly or sharply toothed, lateral veins parallel, each vein terminating at the tip of a marginal tooth. Upper surface lustrous, dark green, varying to coppery brown; lower surface paler, with tufts of hairs in the major vein axils or single hairs along major veins and sometimes between the veins. Leaves turning brown in autumn, usually remaining on the tree most of the winter (macrescent), sometimes into early spring in southern populations. **FLOWER** Male flowers produced in dangling, globular heads. Female flowers in short clusters of 2–4 flowers in the axils of the upper leaves. **FRUIT** Four-valved prickly cupule concealing 2 nuts. Fruit is produced in intervals of 2–8 years, typically maturing in autumn following frost, the cupule remaining on the tree into the following summer.

Beeches are potentially large, majestic trees with a handsome shape. Some references suggest that they are short-lived trees, but specimens of American Beech 300–400 years old have been recorded. Beeches may be confused with several of the elms (Ulmaceae); the leaves of elms are asymmetric at the base and the fruits are flat, disk-like samaras.

AMERICAN BEECH   *Fagus grandifolia*
Ehrh.

QUICK ID   Readily identified by the combination of the smooth blue-gray bark, coarsely toothed leaves with 9–14 pairs of parallel lateral veins, and elongate, torpedo-shaped buds.

Deciduous tree, 5–30 m tall, to 1.5 m diam. Erect, single trunk. Crown broad, open, with numerous stout, spreading branches. **BARK** Smooth, thin, bluish to ashy gray, somewhat mottled; often developing cankers, splitting, and becoming darker with age. **TWIG** Green at first, becoming mottled gray to brownish at maturity, with or without hairs, usually zigzag. Terminal and lateral buds chestnut brown, elongate, slender, 1–2 cm long, widest toward the base and tapering to an acute tip, torpedo-shaped. **LEAF** Alternate, simple, ovate, elliptic, or oval, margins coarsely toothed, lateral veins parallel, 9–14 per side, each terminating at the tip of a marginal tooth. Upper surface lustrous dark green, usually hairy along the midvein; lower surface paler, hairy along the major veins and often between the veins, sometimes the blade tissue of the lower surface hairless. Turns yellow, lustrous brown, then pale brown in autumn, remaining on the tree well into winter. Blade usually 4–12 cm long, 2–7 cm broad; petiole 2–10 mm long. **FLOWER** Male flowers tiny, numerous, borne in dangling globular heads at the end of a slender, silky-hairy stalk; female flowers tiny, inconspicuous, borne singly or in pairs on a stout, silky-hairy stalk. **FRUIT** Bristly 4-valved cupule containing 1–3 (usually 2) 3-angled or 3-ridged nuts.

HABITAT/RANGE Native. Rich woods, moist slopes, eastern deciduous forests, and mixed hardwood and pine forests, 0–1,250 m; throughout much of the East from N.B. and Ont. south to n. Fla. and Tex.

SIMILAR SPECIES European Beech can be distinguished by the combination of coppery to dark purple leaves with lateral veins mostly numbering 9 or fewer per side. American Elm (*Ulmus americana*, Ulmaceae) is easily distinguished by its ridged and flaking bark, short, egg-shaped leaf buds, and leaves asymmetric at the base. American Beech is noted for retaining brown leaves well into winter, a condition that may be confused at a distance with Hophornbeam (*Ostrya virginiana*, Betulaceae), which also retains brownish leaves.

Notes: The nut of American Beech is a favorite food of small mammals and birds, especially

AMERICAN BEECH

♀ flowers

♂ flowers

fruit

fruit

nut

autumn

American Beech

grosbeaks. However, mature trees usually produce abundant fruit only once every few years, particularly in the South, making it unreliable as an annual crop. At elevations above 1,000 m, especially on exposed bluffs, beech trees often appear diseased, stressed, and stunted. American Beech reaches its most majestic proportions in the Ohio and Mississippi river valleys. In northern forests, beech occurs in mixed woodlands with Sugar Maple, birch, and hemlock. At its southern extreme, it inhabits sites with Southern Magnolia and Spruce Pine and is a dominant component of what has been called beech-magnolia hammock. During pre-glacial times, American Beech probably ranged throughout North America as far west as Calif.

EUROPEAN BEECH *Fagus sylvatica* L.
A.K.A. COMMON BEECH

QUICK ID The combination of its large size, bluntly toothed leaves with 5–9 pairs of lateral veins, smooth silvery-gray bark, and spiny fruit is diagnostic.

Deciduous, potentially massive tree, to about 30 m tall, 2.3 m diam. in North America, potentially larger in Europe. Erect, single trunk. Crown broad, spreading, with large, stout branches. **BARK** Silvery gray, smooth, developing shallow horizontal or crisscrossed ridges with maturity. **TWIG** Reddish brown at maturity; terminal and lateral buds elongate, torpedo-shaped. **LEAF** Alternate, simple, elliptic, oval, or ovate; lateral veins mostly 5–9 per side; lateral veins parallel, margins bluntly toothed to nearly entire, sometimes appearing scalloped. Upper surface

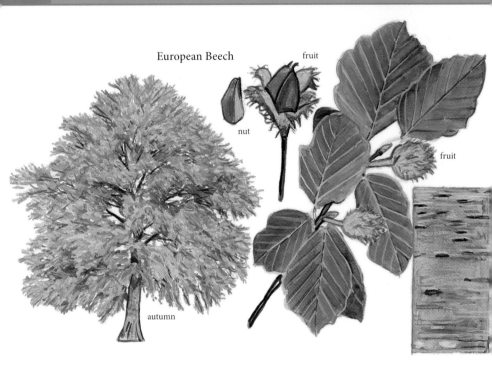

European Beech

fruit

nut

fruit

autumn

EUROPEAN BEECH *continued*

lustrous green, varying to more or less coppery brown, purplish, or blackish purple; lower surface paler. Blade 5–10 cm long, to 5 cm broad; petiole to about 1 cm long. **FLOWER** Male flowers borne in a globular catkin dangling on an elongate stalk. Female flowers individually inconspicuous, borne in a short-stalked catkin. **FRUIT** Short-stalked, spiny cupule, splitting at maturity to reveal a pair of 3-ridged nuts.

HABITAT/RANGE Introduced from Europe. Cultivated in the Northeast; sparingly naturalized from Maine to Ont., south to Md. and Del.

SIMILAR SPECIES American Beech can be distinguished by its green leaves with lateral veins usually numbering more than 9 per side.

Notes: This is a popular landscape tree throughout Europe and increasingly in the U.S. Numerous cultivars are recognized, including Copper Beech (*F. sylvatica* 'Atropunicea'), with purplish leaves, and Weeping Beech (*F. sylvatica* 'Pendula'), with strongly drooping branches; both are planted in the U.S.

■ *QUERCUS*: OAKS

Quercus comprises approximately 450 species of evergreen and deciduous trees and shrubs. Nearly 100 species occur in North America north of Mexico, approximately 44 in the e. U.S., at elevations of 0–2,000 m. Oaks can be identified to the genus by the combination of the clustered buds at the tips of the twigs, the 5-ranked alternate leaves, and the acorn fruit.

Evergreen or deciduous shrubs or trees, ranging from shrubs 1 m tall to massive, single-trunked trees to 40 m tall, 3 m diam. **BARK** Varying from scaly to furrowed or blocky; can be helpful in identification. **TWIG** Lateral and terminal buds clustered at tip of twig, usually egg-shaped, and protected by several overlapping scales. **LEAF** Alternate, simple, borne in 5 rows, those near the end of the branch often closely crowded and appearing whorled. Margins pinnately lobed, entire, or coarsely toothed; shape, size, and marginal features extremely variable, depending upon age, position on the tree, sunlight, and effects of hybridization. **FLOWER** Unisexual (plants monoecious, having both male and female flowers), tiny, individually inconspicuous, produced in unisexual inflorescences called catkins or aments. Male inflorescences are up to about 15 cm long and borne in pendent clusters, typically at the base of emerging shoots. Female inflorescences arise in short, inconspicuous single- or several-flowered spikes in the axils of developing leaves. Differences in flowers and inflorescences are minute and unreliable for field identification. **FRUIT** An acorn, a specialized structure in which a thin-shelled nut rests in a cup (variously referred to as an involucre, cap, or cupule) composed of flat or knobby, usually appressed scales. Acorns typically mature in autumn, but are sometimes retained on the tree into spring.

Oaks are wind-pollinated and produce copious pollen, which probably contributes to significant hybridization among oak species. Pollen is produced in spring and is a well-known allergen. The genus is important for lumber, cork, and the acorns, which are a source of human, wildlife, and livestock food and of tannin and dyes. Sudden oak death, a fungal infection cause by the pathogen *Phytophora ramorum*, is potentially a serious threat to western forests. The pathogen has been reported in the East primarily from shipments of western plants and could also become problematic for eastern forests.

Oak Taxonomic Sections

North American oaks are divided into 3 groups, commonly referred to as white oaks, red (or black) oaks, and intermediate (or golden) oaks. Only white and red oaks are represented in e. North America by native species. The groups differ primarily in wood anatomy, leaf form, characteristics of the acorn cup, and the time required for fruit maturation. With 1 exception, the species presented here are grouped by section and similarity, beginning with the white oaks.

WHITE OAKS: SECTION *QUERCUS*

White oaks lack true bristles on the leaves (but may produce bristlelike extensions of the midvein or lateral veins), have knobby cup scales and fruits that mature in autumn of the 1st year, and the inside of the nut's shell is nearly hairless. Since white oaks produce a crop of acorns each year, all acorns on a given tree are typically of a single age class.

WHITE OAK   *Quercus alba* L.

A.K.A. EASTERN WHITE OAK, STAVE OAK

QUICK ID The combination of scaly grayish-white bark and leaves with 7–10 deeply cut lobes is distinctive.

Deciduous tree, to about 30 m tall, 2.8 m diam. Erect, with a single straight trunk. Crown broad, spreading, branching at nearly right angles from the trunk; lateral branches on old open-grown trees to 15 m long or more; crown of forest-grown trees shorter, narrower. **BARK** Grayish white, loose, scaly, flaking in vertical strips, shallowly to moderately ridged and furrowed. **TWIG** Reddish green at first, becoming gray, essentially glabrous at maturity. Terminal and lateral buds small, often not exceeding about 3 mm long, scales hairless. **LEAF** Alternate, simple, elliptic, oblong, or obovate; margins of mature blades deeply cut into 7–10 narrow (usually 3 or 4 per side), finger-like lobes with rounded tips. Upper surface green, lower surface grayish or whitish, both surfaces essentially hairless at maturity. New leaves reddish and hairy, turning pink, then silvery, then green; autumn color red, yellow, or reddish brown, often slow to develop and splotchy. Blade 5–20 cm long, 3–10 cm broad; petiole 1–2.5 cm long. **FRUIT** Acorn, cup shallow, 10–12 mm deep, enclosing about ¼–½ of the nut; nut light brown, 1–2.5 cm long; at least some fruit stalks 2.5 cm or longer.

HABITAT/RANGE Native. Hardwood forests of varying soil moisture, dry slopes to well-drained lowland woods; 0–1,370 m; throughout the e. U.S.; Maine and Minn., south to n. Fla. and e. Tex.

SIMILAR SPECIES The similar Bluff Oak (*Q. austrina*) is distinguished by its smaller acorns and leaves with fewer, shallower lobes; Durand Oak (*Q. durandii*) has a dense covering of tightly appressed stellate pubescence on the lower surface of

WHITE OAK

White Oak

autumn

fruit

WHITE OAK *continued*

mature leaves; Swamp White Oak (*Q. bicolor*) has a whitish and felty pubescence on the lower surface; Bur Oak (*Q. macrocarpa*) has often fiddle-shaped leaves and its very large acorns have a fringed cup; the non-native English Oak (*Q. robur*) has an eared leaf base.

Notes: White Oak is one of the largest and most important lumber trees of the white oak group. The common name Stave Oak results from its use in the manufacture of barrel staves. White Oak acorns taste sweet and are an important wildlife food but are produced in abundance only at intervals, typically every 4–10 years. Open-grown trees may produce acorns when only 20 years old but will continue to produce until they are 200 years old. Seedlings are generally produced only in years of heavy acorn production; during years of light production, nearly all acorns are eaten or damaged, chiefly by rodents. Nearly 200 species of wildlife use the acorns as food, including squirrels, deer, chipmunks, Raccoons (*Procyon lotor*), and a wide variety of birds. Deer also browse the foliage of young trees.

BLUFF OAK *Quercus austrina* Small
A.K.A. BASTARD WHITE OAK

QUICKID The combination of scaly grayish bark and leaves with 5–7 shallow and irregular lobes is characteristic.

Deciduous tree, typically to about 25 m tall and to 80 cm diam. Erect, with a single straight trunk. Crown narrow or narrowly spreading in a forest setting, somewhat spreading when open-grown. **BARK** Light gray, scaly, becoming slightly furrowed with age, similar to that of White Oak but often somewhat less scaly on the lower trunk. **TWIG** Reddish brown, often green on 1 side, reddish on the other, usually with creamy-white corky lenticels. Buds reddish brown, 3–5 mm long, egg-shaped, finely hairy. **LEAF** Alternate, simple, obovate or oblong, margins with 5–7 shallow, irregular lobes, these varying in size. Upper surface green, lower surface paler, both surfaces essentially hairless at maturity, or lower surface finely and minutely hairy, at least in the vein axils. Blade 3–15 cm long, 2–8 cm broad; petiole 3–5 mm long. **FRUIT** Acorn, cup shallow, 6–10 mm deep, with grayish scales, enclosing about ⅓ of the nut; nut shiny brown,

Bluff Oak

underside

fruit

buds

egg-shaped or ellipsoid, to about 17 mm long; fruit stalks to about 1.5 cm long.

HABITAT/RANGE Native. Moist to somewhat dry soils of deciduous forests, bluffs, ravine slopes, and calcareous woods, often where soil pH is near-ly neutral, 0–200 m; spottily distributed in, and likely restricted to, the southeastern coastal plains from N.C. to Miss., including n. Fla.

SIMILAR SPECIES Often confused with, and misidentified as, Durand Oak (*Q. durandii*) and, to a lesser degree, White Oak (*Q. alba*). Durand Oak has a densely hairy lower leaf surface (especially on crown leaves) and a shallower acorn cup, enclosing just ¼ of the nut. The leaves of White Oak typically have more than 7 lobes.

Notes: Bluff Oak is among the most confusing of eastern white oaks. Some observers have included

it within Durand Oak, for which it is often misidentified. The confusion in identity between Durand Oak and Bluff Oak has resulted in range maps that sometimes show far more extensive geographic coverage for Bluff Oak than the species actually enjoys. The acorns provide a food source for wildlife.

BLUFF OAK

DURAND OAK *Quercus durandii* Buckley
A.K.A. BIGELOW OAK, DURAND WHITE OAK

QUICK ID The leaves with shallow lobes mostly near the tip, the lower surface silvery and often with tightly appressed stellate pubescence, and the shallow acorn cup enclosing ¼ or less of the nut are diagnostic.

Deciduous tree, 15–20 m tall. Erect, with 1 or multiple trunks. Crown more or less rounded, with spreading branches. **BARK** Grayish brown, becoming papery, flaking, and furrowed. **TWIG** Gray or brown, slender, hairy at first, becoming hairless or very finely hairy with age. Buds reddish brown, egg-shaped, to 3 mm long, hairless, or scales with hairy margins. **LEAF** Alternate, simple, widest toward the tip and narrowing to the base; margins entire or shallowly lobed, often 3-lobed mostly near the tip, or sometimes undulate throughout. Upper surface dark green; lower surface often silvery or whitish green, sometimes pale green, on leaves of the crown usually with a dense covering of tightly appressed stellate pubescence beneath, leaves lower on the tree usually nearly hairless beneath. Blade 3–12 cm long, 2.5–6 cm broad; petiole 2–6 mm long. **FRUIT** Acorn, cup exceedingly shallow, less than about 8 mm deep, typically covering about ¼ of the nut or less; nut light brown, 7–19 mm long.

HABITAT/RANGE Native. Low, wet sites, often in association with alluvial and limestone soils; 0–400 m; se. N.C., south to sc. Tex.

SIMILAR SPECIES See "Similar Species" section of White Oak (*Q. alba*). Most often confused with Bluff Oak (*Q. austrina*) and Boynton Oak (*Q. boyntonii*), less often with Water Oak (*Q. nigra*). Boynton Oak has dense yellowish or rusty-brown hair on the leaves and twigs, and a deeper acorn cup, enclosing ⅓–½ of the nut. Water Oak has conspicuous grayish tufts in the vein axils of the lower leaf surface. The closely related and similar **Q. durandii** var. **breviloba** (Torr.) Palmer is typically a thicket-forming shrub less than 5 m tall with multiple trunks and more continuously lobed leaf margins. It is confined in our area mostly to a few counties in sc. Okla., and the Edwards Plateau and northern plains of ec. Tex.

Notes: This species is treated as *Q. sinuata* Walter by some authors.

BOYNTON OAK *Quercus boyntonii* Beadle

QUICK ID The small plant size, hairy young twigs, and typically 3-lobed leaves with a hairy lower surface are important for identification.

Deciduous or semi-evergreen, typically a thicket-forming shrub to about 2 m tall, rarely arborescent to about 6 m tall. **BARK** Brown or dark gray, scaly, furrowed. **TWIG** Light brown, hairy with yellowish hairs at first, becoming less hairy or glabrous at maturity. Buds reddish brown, egg-shaped, sparsely hairy. **LEAF** Alternate, simple, widest toward the tip, margins with 3–5 irregular lobes, especially on the distal half, this often with 3 rounded lobes. Upper surface dark, lustrous green and nearly hairless at maturity; lower surface densely covered with stellate rusty or yellowish-brown hairs. Blade 5–12 cm long, 2–7 cm broad; petiole 5–10 mm long, hairy. **FRUIT** Acorn, cup more or less shallow, 5–10 mm deep, enclosing ⅓–½ of the nut; nut light brown, egg-shaped, hairless, 10–17 mm long, 1 or 2 together on a stalk to 1 cm long.

HABITAT/RANGE Native. Sandy pine forests, stream margins, 0–200 m; rare, known only from e. Tex and n. Ala. Most common at Lookout Mountain, Ala.

DURAND OAK   DURAND OAK, var. *breviloba*   BOYNTON OAK

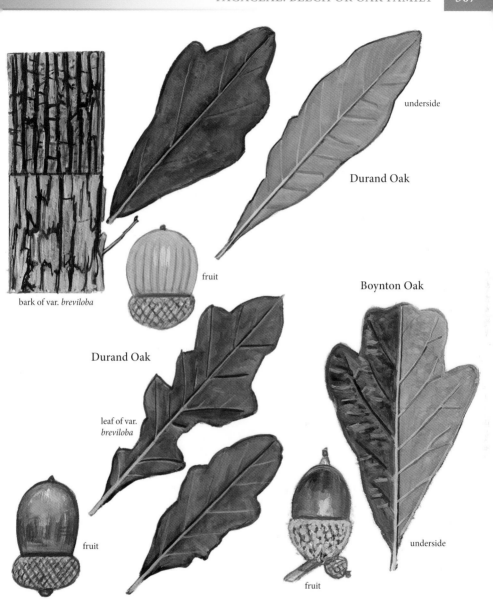

bark of var. *breviloba*

fruit

Durand Oak

underside

Durand Oak

leaf of var. *breviloba*

fruit

Boynton Oak

fruit

underside

SIMILAR SPECIES The leaves and acorns are very similar to those of Sand Post Oak (*Q. margarettae*) and, to a lesser degree, Post Oak (*Q. stellata*). The leaf blades of Post Oak are usually 10–18 cm long, and those of Sand Post Oak usually have 4 or 5 lobes. The leaves are similar to those of Durand Oak (*Q. durandii*), but that has hairless twigs and a whitish or silvery pubescence on the leaf lower surface. Swamp Post Oak (*Q. similis*) also has similar leaves, but with 2 or 3 pairs of lobes, and is a large tree.

Notes: Boynton Oak was originally considered to be a variety of Post Oak and may be more widespread than its currently known range suggests.

SWAMP WHITE OAK   *Quercus bicolor* Willd.
A.K.A. WHITE OAK, BLUE OAK

QUICK ID Easily distinguished by the combination of toothed leaves that are whitish and felty beneath, a long fruit stalk, and typically wetland to moist habitat.

Deciduous tree, to about 30 m tall, 2 m diam. Crown irregular, rugged, often somewhat open, with both ascending and drooping branches. **BARK** Dark gray, with scaly, flattened ridges and deep furrows. **TWIG** Light brown, slender, hairless. Buds light or dark brown, 2–3 mm long, more or less egg-shaped, hairless except sometimes near the apex. **LEAF** Alternate, simple, widest just above the middle and tapering to the base; margins coarsely and bluntly toothed or shallowly and regularly lobed throughout, sometimes entire near the base and toothed toward the tip, 5–7 teeth per side, each tooth with an arching lateral vein terminating at its apex. Upper surface dark, lustrous green; lower surface often whitish with a dense velvety covering of appressed, stellate hairs. Blade 8–18 cm long, 4–11 cm broad; petiole 1–2.5 cm long. **FRUIT** Acorn, cup 10–15 mm deep, enclosing ½–¾ of the nut, finely grayish-hairy, sometimes appearing fringed at the rim; nut light brown, 1.5–3 cm long, 1 or 2 at the end of a stalk 4–10 cm long.

HABITAT/RANGE Native. Moist, poorly drained, organic mucky or peaty soils, swamps, moist slopes, usually where the water table is high, but does not tolerate permanent inundation; 0–1,000 m; widespread across s. Canada and the n. U.S., from about Ont., Que., se. Minn., and sw. Maine to Tenn., N.C., and n. Ala.

SIMILAR SPECIES Bur Oak (*Q. macrocarpa*) has a much larger acorn, more deeply lobed leaves, and finely hairy twigs; Overcup Oak (*Q. lyrata*) has deeply lobed leaves and acorns that are ⅔ to completely covered by the cup; the leaves of Swamp Chestnut Oak (*Q. michauxii*) are rusty- or yellowish-felty beneath; leaves of Chinquapin Oak (*Q. muehlenbergii*) are sometimes whitish beneath but only finely hairy and not feltlike to the touch.

Notes: The epithet *bicolor* references the difference in color between the upper and lower surfaces of the leaf. Swamp White Oak hybridizes with several oak species to produce an array of intermediate leaf shapes. This oak achieves its largest size in n. Ohio and w. N.Y., where average annual temperatures are usually less than 16° C. Swamp White Oak occurs in several forest types and often grows in combination with American Elm, Red Maple, Silver Maple, American Sycamore, Pin Oak, and Black Ash. Trees of this species can live 350 years. The wood is hard and strong, and is often harvested and sold simply as "white oak." The acorns are a valuable food source for an array of wildlife, especially waterfowl.

ENGLISH OAK   *Quercus robur* L.

QUICK ID A large oak distinguished by the combination of the leaf with an eared base and very short petiole and the long fruit stalk.

Deciduous tree, to 30 m tall, 1.5 m diam. Erect, single trunk. Crown broad, spreading, often with low, twisted branches. **BARK** Gray, scaly, finely vertically fissured into narrow plates. **TWIG** Reddish brown, slender, hairless. Buds angled, egg-shaped, 2–3 mm long, hairless. **LEAF** Alternate, simple, narrowly elliptic, sometimes widest toward the tip, distinctly eared or heart-shaped at base; margins with 5–7 rounded lobes. Upper surface dark green; lower surface more or less bluish white. Blade 7–15 cm long, 3–9 cm broad; petiole 3–6 mm long. **FRUIT** Acorn, cup goblet-shaped, grayish, hairy, enclosing ¼–½ of the nut; nut brown, hairless, egg-shaped, oblong, or nearly cylindric, 1.5–3 cm long, 3–5 borne at the end of a stalk 3–8 cm long.

HABITAT/RANGE Introduced from Europe. Extremely cold-tolerant, planted for ornament in ne. and nw. U.S. and s. Canada; occasionally escaped from cultivation and persisting, rarely naturalized.

SIMILAR SPECIES The similar leaves of White Oak (*Q. alba*) lack the strongly eared base and have

SWAMP WHITE OAK

Swamp White Oak

underside

fruit

English Oak

fruit

a longer petiole and a shorter fruit stalk, averaging less than 3.5 cm.

Notes: Relatively fast-growing and introduced to North America in colonial times, English Oak is valued for its high-quality wood, which has been used in furniture making, shipbuilding, and in the construction of English castles and churches. More than 40 cultivars are recognized, varying mostly in leaf color and shape.

TURKISH OAK *Quercus cerris* L.
A.K.A. TURKEY OAK

QUICK ID Easily identified by leaves with 6–12 pairs of rounded lobes in combination with elongate, recurved scales adorning the acorn cup.

Deciduous tree, potentially to 40 m tall, usually not exceeding about 15 m, to about 2 m diam. Erect, with a single trunk. Crown rounded, symmetric, more or less consistent in form from tree to tree. **BARK** Dark gray, ridged, deeply furrowed. **TWIG** Usually densely hairy. Buds egg-shaped, hairy, usually subtended by persistent stipules. **LEAF** Alternate, simple, narrowly oblong or somewhat wider toward the tip, varying rounded, acute, or nearly heart-shaped at base; margins with 6–12 pairs of more or less bristle-tipped, irregularly shaped lobes. Upper surface dark green, slightly roughened to the touch; lower surface paler, densely hairy at first, becoming less hairy and with hairs mostly on the veins at maturity. Blade 7–14 cm long, 3–5 cm broad; petiole 1–2 cm long. **FRUIT** Acorn, cup to about 2 cm deep, enclosing about ½ the nut, covered with conspicuous, elongate, recurved, bristlelike scales 4–8 mm long, appearing mossy; nut 2.5–4 cm long, 1–4 in stalkless clusters.

HABITAT/RANGE Introduced; native to Europe and Asia Minor. Planted in the U.S., rarely or occasionally naturalized.

Notes: Turkish Oak has traditionally been treated as a member of the Old World section *Cerris*, but is considered by some experts to be included within the white oaks. The common name references the country of Turkey. This species should not be confused with the native Turkey Oak (*Q. laevis*) of the southeastern coastal plains.

BUR OAK *Quercus macrocarpa* Michx.
A.K.A. MOSSYCUP OAK

QUICK ID Distinguished by the combination of fiddle-shaped leaf, winged twigs, and large acorn with fringed cup.

Deciduous tree, 30–50 m tall at maturity, to about 2 m diam. Erect, with a single trunk. Crown spreading, rounded in profile, with relatively large, rugged branches. **BARK** Dark gray, with relatively wide, flattened, scaly ridges between deep vertical furrows. **TWIG** Reddish, grayish, or yellowish, densely hairy at first, eventually becoming hairless and developing wide, flat, conspicuous corky wings to 3 cm wide. Terminal buds reddish brown, 2–6 mm long, hairless or slightly hairy; lateral buds slightly smaller. **LEAF** Alternate, simple, elliptic to obovate, often fiddle-shaped, typically widest toward the rounded apex; margins deeply lobed, the 6–8 lobes (3 or 4 per side) increasing in size toward the tip of the blade, terminal lobes often fused into a semicircular apex and conspicuously separated from the next lower pair of lobes by deep, narrow sinuses. Upper surface lustrous, dark green or grayish, essentially hairless; lower surface pale green or slightly whitish, with a thin covering of minute branched hairs. Blade 7–25 cm long, 5–15 cm broad; petiole 15–25 mm long. **FRUIT** Acorn, cup 1.5–5 cm deep, enclosing ½ to nearly all of the nut and usually fringed with numerous hairy scales, those at the rim often with conspicuous soft awns 5–10 mm long; nut light brown, ellipsoid, finely hairy, 2.5–5 cm long, 1–3 on a stout stalk 6–20 mm long.

HABITAT/RANGE Native. Bottomlands, poorly drained woods, sandy plains, dry uplands, prairies, often in association with limestone or clay soils, 0–1,000 m; Man., Ont., and N.B. southward to Tenn., Okla., Va., and in ec. Tex. nearly to the Gulf Coast.

SIMILAR SPECIES The leaf of White Oak (*Q. alba*) is more regularly divided, with rounded lobes, and the lower leaf surface is essentially hairless; Post Oak (*Q. stellata*) lacks the rounded apex of some Bur Oak leaves, and the twigs do not form corky wings.

Notes: Bur Oak has the largest acorns of any oak species north of Mexico. It is also the most northerly ranging and cold-tolerant of native American

BUR OAK

autumn

Turkish Oak

fruit

Bur Oak

fruit

under-side

winged twig

oaks, tolerating harsh environmental conditions well into Canada but often becoming shrubbier with greater exposure, especially nearest its north-western extent. Acorn size is smaller and the cup scales less conspicuous in northern plants, with the largest dimensions expressed at the southern extent of the range. The acorns are an important wildlife food. The wood is valued for its high-quality lumber, which is sold as "white oak." Bur Oak is easy to grow and is used as a street and yard tree within and outside of its native range. Many Bur Oaks have secured a place in history as treaty and council oaks and were important trees during westward expansion.

OVERCUP OAK *Quercus lyrata* Walter
A.K.A. SWAMP POST OAK

QUICK ID The nearly completely enclosed nuts, from which this species takes its common name, can be found on the ground at almost any time of year and are diagnostic.

Deciduous tree, to about 20 m tall, 2–3 m diam. Erect, with a single trunk. Trunk usually short; crown of forest-grown trees narrowly rounded, symmetric, with slender, often drooping branches; crown of open-grown trees often with lateral branches spreading nearly perpendicular to the trunk. **BARK** Grayish or dark gray, scaly, finely fissured into narrow, irregular ridges, sometimes appearing twisted or swirling on the trunk. **TWIG** Gray or reddish gray, slender, lacking hairs at maturity. Buds essentially egg-shaped, to about 3 mm long, scales chestnut brown, finely hairy. **LEAF** Alternate, simple, variable, typically widest nearer the tip, tapering toward the base, suggesting the shape of a lyre; margins with up to 10 rounded lobes, 3–5 lobes per side, the proximal pair smaller, often separated from those above by a wide sinus. Upper surface lustrous, medium or dark green, mostly hairless; lower surface paler, sometimes whitish, on young trees sometimes lacking hairs, on older trees usually covered with branched hairs, sometimes becoming sparsely hairy or nearly hairless late in the season. Blade 10–20 cm long, 5–10 cm broad; petiole 0.8–2 cm long. **FRUIT** Acorn, cup to about 4 cm deep, usually covering all or nearly all of the nut; nut light brown, more or less ellipsoid, finely hairy, 2.5–5 cm long, 1 or 2 at the end of a stalk to 4 cm long.

HABITAT/RANGE Native. River bottoms and floodplain forests of large alluvial rivers, typically on low-lying clay or silty-clay flats, 0–200 m; essentially restricted to the southeastern coastal plains from about Del. and s. Ill. south to n. Fla. and e. Tex.

SIMILAR SPECIES The leaves of Swamp White Oak (*Q. bicolor*) are more nearly toothed than lobed. White Oak (*Q. alba*) is an upland species with scaly whitish bark and leaves more deeply and regularly divided. Bluff Oak (*Q. austrina*) is superficially similar but does not overlap in habitat. Texas Red Oak (*Q. texana*) occurs in river floodplains, but its leaves have distinct bristles at the tips of the lobes. Some Overcup Oak leaves reminiscent of those of Post Oak (*Q. stellata*), but forest-grown trees of these species are easily separated by habitat—wet lowlands for the former, dry uplands for the latter.

Notes: Overcup Oak often occurs on the lowest parts of river bottoms and can withstand considerable periods of inundation. Trees on favorable sites can be 300–400 years old. Associates in this habitat include Bald Cypress, Diamondleaf Oak, Swamp Chestnut Oak, Water Hickory, and Water Tupelo. Although found in nature mainly in floodplains and riverine wetlands, Overcup Oak adapts well to drier upland sites and is sometimes used for ornamental plantings. The wood is usually sold as "white oak" but is inferior to the wood of most other white oaks. Most trees of this species require 25–30 years to produce acorns. The acorns are less often used by wildlife than those of other white oaks and are more frequently distributed by water than by squirrels.

POST OAK *Quercus stellata* Wangenh.

QUICK ID Most easily identified in the southern and eastern parts of its range by the cross-shaped leaves with rectangular lobes.

Deciduous tree, 10–20 m tall, 30–60 cm diam. Erect, single trunk. Crown rounded, spreading and ascending, more or less openly branched with somewhat gnarled, crooked branches that are often produced fairly low on the trunk. **BARK** Grayish, dull, moderately scaly, irregularly ridged and furrowed. **TWIG** Yellowish becoming grayish, densely clothed with branched hairs. Buds reddish brown, more or less egg-shaped or rounded, to about 4 mm long. **LEAF** Alternate, simple, widest toward the tip, varying significantly in shape and size, U-shaped or tapered at base; margins with 4–8 lobes, the distal pair often appreciably larger, rectangular in outline, and divergent at nearly

OVERCUP OAK

POST OAK

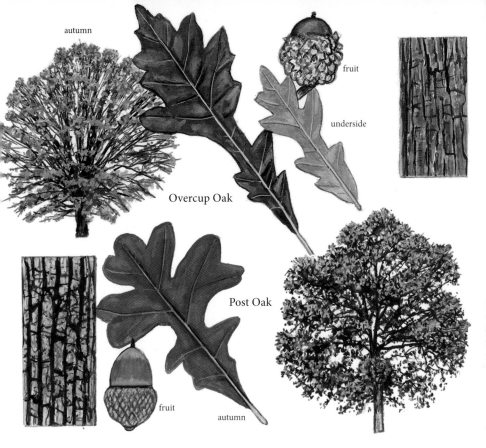

autumn

Overcup Oak

fruit

underside

Post Oak

fruit

autumn

right angles to the axis, the blade of many leaves thus forming the shape of a cross. Upper surface lustrous, dark green, usually with the feel of fine sandpaper; lower surface often yellowish, densely covered with a mat of stellate hairs. Blade 10–18 cm long, 5–15 cm broad; petiole to about 3 cm long. **FRUIT** Acorn, cup 7–18 mm deep, enclosing ⅓–⅔ of the nut, scales gray and hairy; nut light brown, more or less egg-shaped or rounded, 1–2 cm long.

HABITAT/RANGE Native. Typically occurring in dry, upland, sandy or gravelly woods, often in association with Longleaf Pine, or in dry, mixed deciduous forests, 0–1,500 m, usually not exceeding about 1,000 m; occupying a broad range across the e. U.S. from Mass. and Iowa south to Fla. and ec. Tex.

SIMILAR SPECIES Few to numerous leaves on any tree may lack the distinctive cross shape. The very similar Sand Post Oak (*Q. margarettae*) has twigs that mostly lack hairs at maturity, and overall smaller leaves with the lower surface velvety and upper surface smooth. The often associated Blackjack Oak

(*Q. marilandica*) has leaves with a lustrous, hairless upper surface and a rusty-haired lower surface. The similar Bur Oak (*Q. macrocarpa*) has fringed acorn cups, corky wings on older twigs, and a rounded leaf apex. Leaves of Southern Red Oak (*Q. falcata*) also have a U-shaped base, but have bristles at the tips of the lobes and are not cross-shaped in outline.

Notes: Post Oak is important to wildlife. The acorns provide high-energy winter food for Wild Turkey (*Meleagris gallopavo*), Whitetail Deer (*Odocoileus virginianus*), squirrels, and other rodents, and cavities in the trunk and branches provide nest sites for birds and small mammals. The leaves, buds, and acorns are toxic to cattle, sheep, and goats, which is especially problematic in rangelands of the Southwest. The wood is sold as "white oak" and is used in a wide assortment of applications where decay resistance is important, including railroad ties, mine timbers, fence posts, construction lumber, siding, and flooring. In northern forests Post Oak grows with White Pine and Chestnut Oak; in the South it is often associated with Longleaf Pine.

SAND POST OAK *Quercus margarettae*
(Ashe) Small
a.k.a. Dwarf Post Oak, Runner Oak, Scrubby Post Oak

QUICK ID **Distinguished by the combination of comparatively small leaves, the lower surface velvety, and hairless grayish mature twigs.**

Deciduous small tree or shrub, averaging about 12 m tall, potentially to about 25 m, 1 m diam. Crown dense, rounded. **BARK** Gray, scaly, finely ridged and furrowed. **TWIG** Green or reddish and hairy with branched hairs at first, becoming gray and nearly hairless at maturity. Buds reddish brown, egg-shaped, usually 2–3 mm long. **LEAF** Alternate, simple, widest toward the tip, tapering at the base; margins with 2 or 4 pairs of more or less rounded lateral lobes, the terminal lobe often with 3 smaller lobes, the main pair of lateral lobes usually diverging at slightly less than right angles from the axis, the leaf outline somewhat cross-shaped. Upper surface lustrous, dark green, hairless or with a few branched hairs, not rough to the touch; lower surface velvety with a dense covering of branched hairs. Blade 2–15 cm long, 2–8 cm broad; petiole 3–15 mm long. **FRUIT** Acorn, cup enclosing ⅓–⅔ of the nut; nut light brown, 15–25 mm long.

HABITAT/RANGE Native. Sandy woods and pinelands, 0–600 m; southeastern coastal plains, Va. south to Fla., west to Mo., Okla., and Tex.

SIMILAR SPECIES Most easily confused with Post Oak (*Q. stellata*) and Durand Oak (*Q. durandii*). Post Oak is distinguished by its much hairier yellowish twigs in combination with the upper surface of the leaf being finely sandpapery, and the lower having a covering of branched hairs. Durand Oak is distinguished by some leaves being unlobed and the lower surface of the crown leaves having a silvery or whitish sheen.

Notes: Trees displaying characteristics intermediate between Post Oak and Sand Post Oak occur in the Cross Timbers region of Tex. and may represent a hybrid.

SWAMP POST OAK *Quercus similis* Ashe
a.k.a. Delta Post Oak, Bottomland Post Oak, Yellow Oak

QUICK ID The combination of irregularly lobed leaves, hairy twigs, and wetland habitat is distinctive.

Deciduous tree, potentially to about 30 m tall, 1.4 m diam. Erect, single trunk. **BARK** Gray or grayish brown, slightly scaly, finely ridged and furrowed. **TWIG** Gray, slender, persistently and conspicuously hairy at maturity. **LEAF** Alternate, simple, widest toward the tip, base tapering or rounded, margins with 2 or 3 pairs of shallow, irregular lobes, but blade not distinctly cross-shaped. Upper surface dark green, lustrous, sparsely hairy; lower surface paler, grayish, sparsely hairy. Blade 7–12 cm long, 5–8 cm broad; petiole to about 1 cm long. **FRUIT** Acorn, cup 10–12 mm deep, grayish, hairy, enclosing ⅓–½ of the nut; nut light brown, about 15 mm long.

HABITAT/RANGE Native. River valleys, wet bottomlands, 0–300 m; S.C. to e. Tex.

SIMILAR SPECIES Post Oak (*Q. stellata*) and Sand Post Oak (*Q. margarettae*) occur in drier habitat, not in wetlands. In Bluff Oak (*Q. austrina*) the lower leaf surface is hairless at maturity or finely and minutely hairly, mostly in vein axils. Some leaves on any Swamp Post Oak tree may have the general shape and appearance of those of Overcup Oak (*Q. lyrata*), but Overcup's mature twigs are hairless, and its nuts are nearly enclosed by the cup.

SAND POST OAK

SWAMP POST OAK

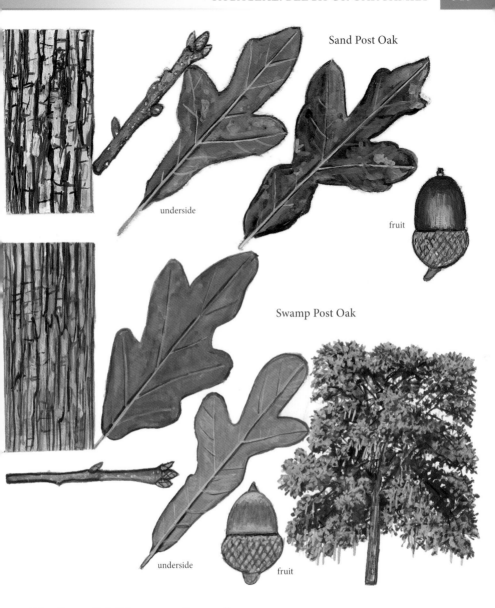

Sand Post Oak

underside

fruit

Swamp Post Oak

underside

fruit

Notes: Swamp Post Oak grows mostly on well-drained ridges and terraces in low bottoms of alluvial rivers, in association with Blackgum, Cherrybark Oak, Green Ash, Shumard Oak, and Swamp Chestnut Oak. This species is often included as a variety of Post Oak and has also been referred to as *Q. stellata* var. *paludosa* Sarg. and *Q. mississipiensis* Ashe.

SOUTHERN LIVE OAK *Quercus virginiana* Mill.

QUICK ID Recognized by the combination of mature leaves with the upper surface lustrous, dark green and the lower with densely matted grayish hairs, a broadly spreading crown, and blocky grayish bark.

Evergreen tree, potentially to about 20 m tall, 3 m diam. Erect, with a single, often massive, trunk; trunk of open-grown trees usually short, branching within 3 m of the ground; trunk of forest-grown trees typically slightly leaning and branching at 10 m or more above the ground. Crown broad, spreading, with large ascending, arching, or laterally spreading branches. **BARK** Rough, gray, conspicuously and deeply divided into irregular, blocky plates. **TWIG** Grayish, minutely hairy at first, becoming more or less hairless with age. Buds reddish brown, more or less egg-shaped, 1–2 mm long. **LEAF** Alternate, simple, stiff, usually elliptic or slightly wider toward the tip; margins mostly flat, entire at maturity, variously toothed when young. Upper surface lustrous, dark green; lower surface obscured by a dense mat of grayish hairs, often appearing hairless to the naked eye. Blade 2–10 cm long, 2–5 cm broad; petiole usually not exceeding about 1 cm long. **FRUIT** Acorn, cup 8–15 mm deep, enclosing ⅓–½ of the nut; nut shiny brown to nearly black, more or less egg-shaped with a rounded or blunt tip, hairless, 1–2.5 cm long, 1–3 on a stalk 1–2 cm long.

HABITAT/RANGE Native. Occurs naturally in dry or moist woodlands and hammocks, 0–100 m; southeastern coastal plains, N.C. to e. Tex., especially near the coast (throughout Fla.), commonly planted or allowed to survive in pastures, also along streets, and in parks and residential landscapes.

SIMILAR SPECIES Texas Live Oak (*Q. fusiformis*) is similar and intergrades with Southern Live Oak along the s. Tex. Gulf Coast and between the Brazos River and Edwards Plateau, making precise identification difficult. Typical Texas Live Oaks have longer (2–3 cm) and more pointed acorns, and at least a few mature leaves with 1–3 marginal teeth. Sand Live Oak (*Q. geminata*) has conspicuously revolute leaves with deeply impressed veins on the upper surface.

Notes: Hybrids between Live Oak and Sand Live Oak are reported. Collections of apparent Sand Live Oak nuts from sites where the 2 species occur together, especially in inland sandhills, usually produce trees of both types, even when the nuts are collected from the same tree.

OGLETHORPE OAK *Quercus oglethorpensis* Duncan

QUICK ID Recognized within its habitat by its narrow, entire-margined leaves, which are yellowish and felty-hairy beneath.

Deciduous tree, to about 20 m tall and nearly 1 m diam.; trunk sometimes with late-developing lateral branches arising from dormant (epicormic) buds (often referred to as adventitious or epicormic branches). **BARK** Light gray or whitish, scaly, similar to White Oak (*Q. alba*). **LEAF** Alternate, simple, narrowly elliptic, often widest near the tip; margins entire, sometimes slightly wavy or lobed near the tip. Upper surface lustrous, dark green, often with the texture of fine sandpaper; lower surface yellowish, felty-hairy, especially along the midvein. Blade 5–15 cm long, 2–4.5 cm broad; petiole 2–7 mm long.

HABITAT/RANGE Native. Bottomlands of alluvial rivers, 0–200 m; rare, mostly ne. Ga. and adjoining S.C.; small colonies are also reported in La. and Miss.

SOUTHERN LIVE OAK

OGLETHORPE OAK

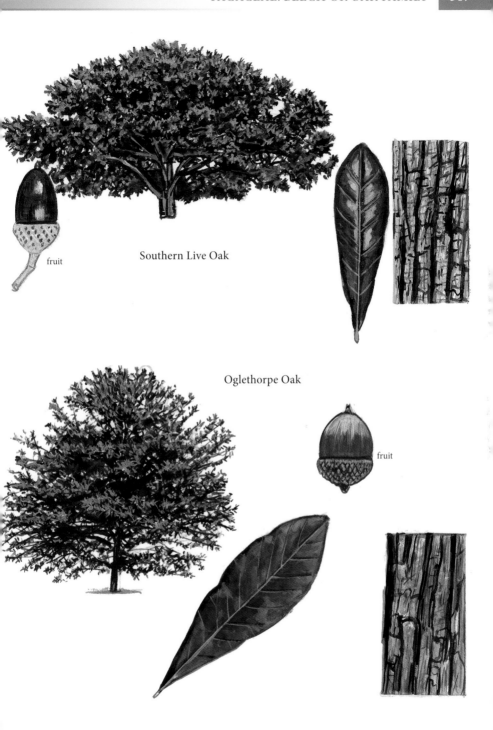

fruit

Southern Live Oak

Oglethorpe Oak

fruit

SAND LIVE OAK *Quercus geminata* Small

QUICK ID Most easily distinguished by its conspicuously revolute leaves, with deeply impressed veins and matted grayish pubescence on the lower surface.

Evergreen tree (rarely shrubby), to about 10 m tall, 50 cm diam. Erect, single trunk. Crown spreading, rounded in outline, with several large branches. **BARK** Medium or dark gray, vertically ridged and furrowed, the ridges separated into small vertical plates. **TWIG** Slender, yellowish at first, becoming gray, finely hairy. Buds reddish brown, less than 3 mm long. **LEAF** Alternate, simple, stiff, narrowly elliptic, margins entire, usually conspicuously and strongly rolled under (revolute), the blade reminiscent of an inverted boat. Upper surface lustrous, dark green, usually with deeply impressed veins; lower surface grayish with a covering of densely matted hairs. Blade 2–12 cm long, 0.5–4 cm broad; petiole usually 3–10 mm long. **FRUIT** Acorn, cup 8–15 mm deep, grayish, enclosing about ⅓ of the nut; nut dark brown, egg-shaped, without hairs, 1.6–2.5 cm long, 1–3 on a stout stalk 1–10 cm long.

HABITAT/RANGE Native. Scrub, dry pinelands, hammock margins, coastal woodlands, usually in sandy soils, 0–200 m; southeastern coastal plains, N.C. to La.

SIMILAR SPECIES The leaves of Southern Live Oak (*Q. virginiana*) are flatter, lacking revolute margins.

Notes: The leaves of Sand Live Oak vary significantly in correlation with habitat, exposure, drainage, and soil moisture. On xeric sites in full sun the leaves are often extremely narrow and severely revolute. The crowns of trees growing along the Atlantic Coast are subject to strong onshore winds and often appear pruned and wedge-shaped.

TEXAS LIVE OAK *Quercus fusiformis* Small
A.K.A. SCRUB LIVE OAK

QUICK ID Recognized by the combination of mature leaves with at least a few marginal teeth, the lower surface with matted grayish or whitish hairs, and pointed, long-tapering acorns.

Semievergreen tree (leaves persisting through winter, falling en masse and immediately replaced in spring), usually to about 12 m tall, often shrubby and thicket-forming and less than 3 m tall. Crown broad and spreading on larger trees, with several stout, ascending branches. **BARK** Dark brown to nearly black, furrowed, blocky, with scaly ridges. **TWIG** Gray, sparsely or moderately covered with matted hairs. Buds shiny, dark red, more or less egg-shaped, 1–3 mm long. **LEAF** Alternate, simple, lanceolate or oblong-elliptic, stiff, mostly flat, often entire, commonly with 1–3 marginal teeth per side. Upper surface green or dark green, lustrous, smooth, hairless or with a few scattered hairs; lower surface whitish or grayish, covered with overlapping branched hairs, the veins inconspicuous. Blade 2–9 cm long, 1–3 cm broad; petiole 2–8 mm long. **FRUIT** Acorn, cup 8–15 mm deep, enclosing ¼–½ of the nut; nut shiny brown, tapering to a pointed tip, 2–3 cm long, 1–3 on a stalk 3–30 mm long.

HABITAT/RANGE Native. Rocky limestone sites, granitic rubble, clay-based grasslands, scrub, open woods, often in association with calcareous loamy soils, 0–500 m; sc. Tex. and sw. Okla.

SIMILAR SPECIES Southern Live Oak (*Q. virginiana*) intergrades with Texas Live Oak along the s. Tex. Gulf Coast and between the Brazos River and Edwards Plateau, making precise identification difficult. Typical Southern Live Oaks have shorter, blunt-tipped acorns, and the mature leaves typically lack marginal teeth.

SAND LIVE OAK

TEXAS LIVE OAK

Sand Live Oak

underside

fruit

Texas Live Oak

fruit

underside

CHESTNUT OAK *Quercus montana* Willd.
A.K.A. Mountain Chestnut Oak

QUICK ID Recognized by the combination of furrowed bark, leaves with toothed margins and the lower surface bearing long hairs along the midvein and closely appressed hairs on the tissue, and the mountain habitat.

Deciduous tree, to 30 m tall, 1.8 m diam. Erect, single trunk. Crown broad, open, spreading on open-grown trees, narrower on forest-grown trees. **BARK** Reddish brown to dark gray or nearly black, deeply furrowed between broad, coarse ridges, furrows often V-shaped. **TWIG** Light brown, hairless. Buds 4–8 mm long, light brown, more or less egg-shaped, scales glabrous. **LEAF** Alternate, simple, widest toward the tip and rounded at the base, the amount of tissue on either side of the midvein often unequal at the base, lateral veins in 10 or more pairs, more or less parallel, arching or ascending, each terminating at the tip of a marginal tooth; margins coarsely and regularly toothed with low, wide, blunt, rounded teeth, sometimes appearing scalloped. Upper surface dark green; lower surface paler, with tufts of longish hairs along the midvein and shorter hairs on the blade tissue. Turns yellow in autumn. Blade 10–20 cm long, 6–10 cm broad; petiole 1–3 cm long. **FRUIT** Acorn, cup 9–15 mm deep, enclosing ⅓–½ of the nut, scales gray, tipped with red; nut light chestnut brown, 2–4 cm long, 1–3 on stalks to 2 cm long, or sometimes stalkless.

HABITAT/RANGE Native. Thin, fast-draining soils of steep mountain slopes and ridges, 500–1,500 m; mostly distributed in the Piedmont and mountains from Maine to Ala. and Miss.

SIMILAR SPECIES Distinguished from similarly leaved white oaks, including Swamp White Oak (*Q. bicolor*), Swamp Chestnut Oak (*Q. michauxii*),

Chinquapin Oak (*Q. muehlenbergii*), and the more or less shrubby Dwarf Chinquapin Oak (*Q. prinoides*), by the dark, non-scaly, deeply furrowed bark. Many of these species are often misidentified.

Notes: Chestnut Oak is often seen referenced as *Q. prinus*, an ambiguous name that has been applied to more than 1 species. Squirrels, Whitetail Deer (*Odocoileus virginianus*), chipmunks, mice, and Wild Turkey (*Meleagris gallopavo*) use the acorns for food, but good acorn crops are intermittent, occurring once every 4 or 5 years. Chestnut Oak grows in association with Black Cherry, Blackgum, Red Maple, Northern Red Oak, Scarlet Oak, Sugar Maple, Sweet Birch, Tuliptree, and White Oak. Chestnut Oak leaves are a preferred food for the Gypsy Moth (*Lymantria dispar*) caterpillar, which defoliates the host tree.

SWAMP CHESTNUT OAK *Quercus michauxii* Nutt.
A.K.A. Basket Oak, Cow Oak

QUICK ID Recognized by the combination of leaves with coarsely toothed margins and a felty-hairy lower surface, scaly grayish-white bark, and large acorns.

Deciduous, fast-growing tree, to 40 m tall, 2 m diam. Erect, single trunk, usually clear of branches for at least 12 m. Crown spreading, becoming rounded, with large lateral and ascending branches. **BARK** Whitish gray, scaly, flaking, peeling. **TWIG** Reddish brown, slender, sparsely hairy. Bud reddish brown, egg-shaped, finely hairy or hairless. **LEAF** Alternate, simple, much wider toward the tip, tapering to a narrowed or rounded base; margins coarsely and conspicuously toothed with large, bluntly pointed teeth, each terminated by a single arching or ascending lateral vein; veins conspicuously parallel, on mature leaves usually numbering 15–20 per

CHESTNUT OAK

SWAMP CHESTNUT OAK

Chestnut Oak

fruit

fruit

Swamp Chestnut Oak

side. Upper surface dull green or yellowish green; lower surface felty-hairy, yellowish. Turning dull yellow or splotched red and green in autumn. Blade 10–22 cm long, 7–15 cm broad; petiole to about 2 cm long. **FRUIT** Acorn, cup 15–25 mm deep, enclosing ½ of the nut or more, with loose, knobby grayish or light brown scales; nut large, light brown, rounded or egg-shaped, hairless, 2.5–3.5 cm long, 1–3 on stalks 2–3 cm long, or stalkless.

HABITAT/RANGE Native. Bottomlands, swamp margins, and rich, moist, often sloping woods, 0–600 m; Pa. and Del., south to n. Fla., west to e. Tex, Ark., sw. Mo., s. Ill.

SIMILAR SPECIES The several similar white oaks have smaller acorns and lack rusty-felty hairs on the lower leaf surface. The bark of Swamp Chestnut Oak is most similar to that of White Oak (*Q. alba*) and Bluff Oak (*Q. austrina*), with which it sometimes associates; they can be distinguished by the leaf margins with rounded lobes rather than coarse teeth.

Notes: Swamp Chestnut Oak is sometimes referred to as *Q. prinus*, an ambiguous name that has been applied to more than 1 species. The name Basket Oak is a reference to the use of the wood in fabricating baskets, and the name Cow Oak to the acorns being eaten by cows.

CHINQUAPIN OAK *Quercus muehlenbergii* Engelm.

A.K.A. CHINKAPIN OAK, YELLOW CHESTNUT OAK

QUICK ID Best identified by the combination of scaly bark, calcareous habitat, and leaves mostly with 10–14 pairs of parallel veins, each vein terminating in a marginal tooth.

Deciduous tree, 20–33 m tall, 60–90 cm diam. Erect, single trunk; crown of forest-grown trees narrow, rounded, dense, with relatively small branches; crown broader and spreading on open-grown trees. **BARK** Ashy gray, thin, scaly, and flaking. **TWIG** Reddish brown, finely hairy at first, becoming gray and nearly hairless in the 2nd year. Terminal and lateral buds similar, reddish brown, 2–4 mm long, scales with pale margins. **LEAF** Alternate, simple, widest toward the tip, lateral veins parallel, averaging 10–14 per side, terminating at the tips of the marginal teeth; margins coarsely toothed with large curved dentations usually pointing toward the tip of the leaf. Upper surface lustrous, dark green; lower surface paler, sometimes whitish and minutely hairy. Blade 5–15 cm long, 4–8 cm broad; petiole 1–3 cm long. **FRUIT** Acorn, cup shallow, to about 10 mm deep, with appressed grayish-hairy scales, covering ⅓–½ of the nut; nut light brown, oblong or egg-shaped, 1–2 cm long.

HABITAT/RANGE Native. Mixed forests and woodlands, occurring mostly on neutral or alkaline calcareous soils in association with limestone, 0–2,300 m elevation; distributed throughout much of the East from Vt. and Wis. south to n. Fla. and west to N.M.

SIMILAR SPECIES Chestnut Oak (*Q. montana*), Swamp Chestnut Oak (*Q. michauxii*), and Dwarf Chinquapin Oak (*Q. prinoides*) have similar chestnut-like leaves but lack Chinquapin

Oak's combination of small acorns, scaly grayish bark, and leaves averaging 10–14 veins per side. The leaves of Swamp Chestnut Oak are felty-hairy beneath.

Notes: Chinquapin Oak does not usually grow in sufficient numbers or reach sufficient size to make it commercially marketable. Mammals and birds eat its acorns, but its somewhat scattered distribution renders it less important as a wildlife food than some other oaks. This species is largely intolerant of shade, except when very young, and achieves its best stature in open woodlands.

DWARF CHINQUAPIN OAK *Quercus prinoides* Willd.

QUICK ID Distinguished by the combination of habitat, shrubby size, multistemmed habit, and coarsely toothed leaves with 10 or fewer pairs of lateral veins per leaf.

Deciduous, typically a large, multitrunked shrub, occasionally reaching about 5 m tall. **BARK** Thin, gray, with scaly ridges. **LEAF** Alternate, simple, mostly widest toward the tip, similar to that of Chinquapin Oak, usually with fewer than 10 pairs of widely spaced veins per blade, margins coarsely toothed. Blade 4–14 cm long, 2–6 cm broad; petiole 8–20 cm long.

HABITAT/RANGE Native. Overlapping in range with Chinquapin Oak but occurring mostly on shale or neutral, often acidic sand, 0–500 m; N.Y. and N.H. south to n. Ga. and n. Ala., west to Okla.

Notes: Sometimes treated as a variety of Chinquapin Oak (*Q. muehlenbergii*), which is distinguished by its arborescent habit, adaptation to alkaline soils, and leaf veins usually 10–14 per side.

CHINQUAPIN OAK

DWARF CHINQUAPIN OAK

Chinquapin Oak

autumn

fruit

Dwarf Chinquapin Oak

underside

fruit

Turkey Oaks: Section *Cerris*

Sawtooth Oak and Cork Oak are closely related non-native species of the taxonomic section *Cerris*, sometimes treated as a section of the white oaks. They are planted and occasionally naturalized in the Southeast, especially near La. The form and shape of their leaves are similar to the chinquapin oaks and chestnut oaks, but are distinguished by the bristle-tipped teeth at the tip of the lobes.

SAWTOOTH OAK   *Quercus acutissima*
Carruth.

A.K.A. JAPANESE CHESTNUT OAK

QUICKID The fringed acorn cup and narrow leaf with bristle-tipped teeth are diagnostic.

Deciduous tree, 10–21 m tall, to about 1.5 m diam. Erect, single trunk; crown dense, rounded or pyramidal. **BARK** Dark gray with lighter gray scales, deeply furrowed at maturity. **LEAF** Alternate, simple, oblong or obovate, margins with 12–16 pairs of sharp, bristle-tipped teeth; veins parallel, conspicuous. Upper surface lustrous green, hairless; lower surface paler, hairless at maturity except for conspicuous tufts in the main vein axils. Blade 10–20 cm long, 2–6 cm broad; petiole 1.5–2.5 cm long. **FRUIT** Acorn, cup enclosing ⅓–⅔ of the nut, rim adorned with comparatively long, spreading, recurved, hairlike scales forming a distinctive fringe; nut 1–2.5 cm long.

SIMILAR SPECIES Chinquapin (*Castanea pumila*) has similar leaves but is distinguished by its spiny, burlike fruit.

HABITAT/RANGE Introduced from Asia. Reported naturalized in scattered sites, from Penn. to N.C. and Ga. to La.

Notes: Planted primarily for wildlife food and cover due to its fast growth and abundant fruit. Tolerant of drought, soil compaction, and air pollution; sometimes used for urban and highway beautification.

CORK OAK   *Quercus suber* L.

QUICKID The oval, lustrous, dark green leaves with marginal teeth distinguish Cork Oak.

Evergreen tree to about 20 m tall, diam. 2–3 m. Erect, with a single often contorted trunk and low, twisted branches. Crown spreading, cylindric or dome-shaped. **BARK** Gray or reddish brown, producing deep, irregular furrows and thick corky ridges. **TWIG** Gray-brown, with abundant woolly hairs. **LEAF** Alternate, simple, thick, leathery, ovate, oblong, or oval; margins entire or more often with 4 or 5 pairs of sharp-pointed teeth. Upper surface lustrous, dark green; lower surface grayish, hairy. Blade 2.5–8 cm long, 1.5–4 cm broad. **FRUIT** Acorn, cup enclosing about ½ of the nut, upper scales upright, sometimes spreading; nut egg-shaped, 1.5–3 cm long.

HABITAT/RANGE Introduced from the Mediterranean. Planted as an ornamental in the U.S.

Notes: Cultivated in Europe for centuries, especially in wine-producing regions, where the bark was periodically stripped for use in bottle corks.

Red Oaks: Section *Lobatae*

Red oaks are strictly North American in distribution, usually bear bristles at the tips of the leaves and marginal lobes, and have smooth cup scales and fruits that mature in the 2nd year; the inside of the nutshell is hairy. Red oaks sometimes have 2 age classes of acorns (1st year and 2nd year) on a single tree.

SIMILAR RED OAKS

Northern Red Oak has shallowly lobed, essentially hairless leaves, a comparatively long petiole, and an often shallow acorn cup. Several red oaks have similar leaves and can be difficult to distinguish. Following is a round-up of characters helpful, but not always definitive, for distinguishing the species. The leaves of Southern Red Oak (*Q. falcata*) are U-shaped at the base and densely hairy beneath. Cherrybark Oak (*Q. pagoda*) is the only oak in this group with bark reminiscent of Black Cherry (*Prunus serotina*, Rosaceae). Turkey Oak (*Q. laevis*) has a twisted petiole that orients the leaf more or less perpendicular to the ground. The lower branches of Pin Oak (*Q. palustris*) are wide-spreading and demonstrably drooping, the leaves usually with 2 or 3 lobes per side, the terminal lobe about ⅓ the length of the middle lobes. The leaves of Northern Pin Oak (*Q. ellipsoidalis*) typically have 2 lobes per side, C-shaped sinuses, and the length of the terminal lobe equal to that of the lateral lobes. Shumard Oak (*Q. shumardii*) leaves are hairless except for small tufts in the vein axils on the lower surface, and the petiole doesn't exceed about ⅓ the length of the blade. The petiole of Black Oak (*Q. velutina*) is ⅓–½ the length of the leaf blade, which has hairy veins and tufts of hairs in the vein axils beneath.

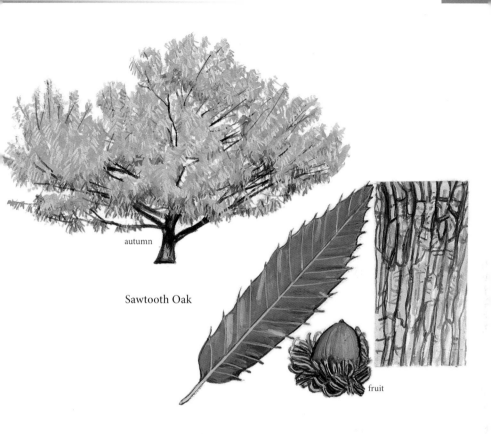

autumn

Sawtooth Oak

fruit

Cork Oak

underside

fruit

NORTHERN RED OAK *Quercus rubra* L.
A.K.A. RED OAK, EASTERN RED OAK, MOUNTAIN OAK

QUICK ID The shallowly lobed, essentially hairless leaves, comparatively long petiole, and often shallow acorn cup help distinguish Northern Red Oak.

Deciduous tree, to about 30 m tall, 2 m diam. Erect, single trunk, forest-grown trees straight and free of limbs for 10–15 m, open-grown trees often low-branching, producing a dense, spreading, more or less rounded or conical crown. **BARK** Light or medium gray, somewhat smooth on young trees, becoming darker gray and developing deep furrows between narrow ridges with maturity, the ridges often broken into irregular vertical plates. **TWIG** Reddish brown, hairless. Buds reddish brown, 4–7 mm long, hairless or the apical half conspicuously hairy. **LEAF** Alternate, simple, ovate, elliptic, or obovate, base often nearly truncate, margins usually with 4 or 5 primary lobes per side, the main lobes with smaller secondary lobes, all of which are conspicuously bristle-tipped; the sinuses dividing the primary lobes shallow, usually about ½ the length of the lobe. Upper surface medium green, hairless; lower surface paler, often whitish, hairless except for tufts in the vein axils. Turns red in autumn. Blade 12–20 cm long, 6–12 cm broad; petiole 2.5–5 cm long. **FRUIT** Acorn, cup 5–12 mm deep, of 2 forms, some shallow and enclosing about ¼ of the nut, others deeper and covering ½ of the nut; nut lustrous chestnut brown, 1.5–3 cm long.

HABITAT/RANGE Native. Moist slopes and well-drained uplands, occasionally drier sites, usually on well-drained loam or silty clay loam, occasionally forming nearly pure stands, 0–1,800 m; widespread across the e. U.S. from Ont., Que., and N.S. south to Okla., La., Ala., Ga., N.C., S.C.

SIMILAR SPECIES See "Similar Red Oaks," p. 324.

Notes: Northern Red Oaks with shallow acorn cups are sometimes referred to as var. *rubra*; those with deeper cups, as var. *borealis* (F. Michx.) Farw. This is one of the most important red oaks for lumber; it is also planted for shade and ornament. The acorns are valuable to an array of insects and other wildlife, which can damage or consume 80–100% of the annual crop.

BLACK OAK *Quercus velutina* Lam.
A.K.A. YELLOW OAK, QUERCITRON OAK, YELLOW-BARK OAK, SMOOTH-BARK OAK

QUICK ID Recognized by the combination of uniformly hairy and comparatively large buds, leaf tissue essentially hairless on the lower surface, and thick, rugged, nearly black bark.

Deciduous tree to about 25 m tall, 1.5 m diam. Erect, single trunk. Crown somewhat open, ascending, narrow, with relatively large branches. **BARK** Thick, dark gray or brown at first, becoming nearly black, even on relatively young trees, deeply and roughly ridged and furrowed, the vertical ridges broken by numerous irregular horizontal fissures; inner bark bright yellow or orange-yellow. **TWIG** Somewhat stout, reddish brown, finely hairy or hairless. Terminal buds egg-shaped, comparatively large, 6–13 mm long, densely hairy, angled, sharp-pointed. **LEAF** Alternate, simple, obovate or ovate, base wide-angled or nearly truncate; margins with 4 or 5 primary lobes per side, these with secondary lobes, each lobe bristle-tipped, some leaves on any tree with the sinuses between the lobes relatively shallow, often with abundant tissue on either side of the leaf axis, especially toward the tip. Upper surface lustrous, dark green, hairless, with raised veins; lower surface paler, also with raised veins, generally hairless at maturity, except along the veins, with scurfy (scaly or flaking) tufts in the vein axils. Turning yellowish or reddish brown in autumn. Blade 10–30 cm long, 8–15 cm broad; petiole 2.5–7 cm long. **FRUIT** Acorn, cup 7–14 mm deep, finely hairy outside, densely hairy inside, enclosing about ½ of the nut, scales loose and forming a slight fringe at the rim; nut reddish brown, 1–2 cm long, rounded or somewhat egg-shaped, essentially hairless.

NORTHERN RED OAK

BLACK OAK

Northern Red Oak

fruit

developing
fruit

autumn

Black Oak

fruit

HABITAT/RANGE Native. Grows best in upland woods and lower slopes on rich, well-drained soils, often where clay is present, sometimes also growing on dry, sandy soils and on glacial hillsides, 0–1,500 m; widespread in e. North America from Minn. and Ont. south to n. Fla. and e. Tex.

SIMILAR SPECIES Most often confused with Northern Red Oak (*Q. rubra*) and Scarlet Oak (*Q. coccinea*), both of which have hairs on the lower leaf surface restricted largely to the vein axils, and leaves also somewhat similar to Pin Oak (*Q. palustris*), Northern Pin Oak (*Q. ellipsoidalis*), and Shumard Oak (*Q. shumardii*); however, all of these oaks have buds not exceeding about 8 mm long.

Notes: Black Oak bark is rich in tannins suitable for tanning leather. Its lumber is sold as "red oak" and is used for furniture and flooring. The acorns provide a source of food for squirrels, Whitetail Deer (*Odocoileus virginianus*), mice, voles, and Wild Turkey (*Meleagris gallopavo*) and other birds.

SCARLET OAK *Quercus coccinea* Münchh.

QUICK ID The deeply cut leaves in combination with 1 or more pitted rings at the acorn apex are diagnostic.

Deciduous, fast-growing tree, to about 30 m tall, to 1.5 m diam. Erect, single trunk, often swollen at the base, usually lacking stubs of dead branches. Crown rounded, open, with spreading branches. **BARK** Thin, brown to dark gray, nearly black on some trees, becoming finely ridged and furrowed and sometimes scaly. **TWIG** Slender, reddish, orange-brown, or purplish, becoming hairless. Buds reddish brown, to about 7 mm long, distinctly angled in cross section, typically hairy only at the apex. **LEAF** Alternate, simple, oblong or elliptic; margins typically with 5–7 narrow lobes, each becoming widest at the apex and furnished with several bristle-tipped secondary lobes, primary lobes divided by deep sinuses, often leaving a comparatively narrow band of tissue along the midvein. Upper surface lustrous, bright green, hairless; lower surface paler, moderately lustrous, hairless or with tufts of hairs in few to many of the major vein axils. Turns brilliant scarlet-red in autumn. Blade 7–16 cm long, 6–15 cm broad; petiole 2.5–6 cm long. **FRUIT** Acorn, cup 7–15 mm deep, enclosing ⅓–½ of the nut, scales finely hairy; nut 1.5–2 cm long, finely hairy, adorned at the apex with concentric, finely pitted rings.

HABITAT/RANGE Native. Well-drained slopes, dry uplands, ridges, usually in relatively poor soils, generally on middle to upper south-facing slopes in the s. Appalachians and middle to lower slopes farther north, perhaps achieving its best development in the Ohio River valley, 0–1,500 m; widespread across the e. U.S. from s. Wis. and s. Maine south to Ark. and sw. Ga.

SIMILAR SPECIES The closely related Northern Pin Oak (*Q. ellipsoidalis*) is distinguished by the combination of trunk with stubs of dead branches, slightly smaller buds, and acorns usually lacking rings at the apex; Shumard Oak (*Q. shumardii*) by the hairless buds; Northern Red Oak (*Q. rubra*) by the less deeply cut leaves; and Pin Oak (*Q. palustris*) by the smaller acorn.

Notes: Fast growth, attractive form, and brilliant fall color have made Scarlet Oak a popular street and landscape tree across its range; it is also commonly cultivated in Europe. The thin bark makes this oak susceptible to damage from fire. It is a major component of more than a dozen eastern forest types and often grows in association with White Pine, Sourwood, hickories, Flowering Dogwood, Red Maple, Sour Gum, and White Oak, Black Oak, and Post Oak.

NORTHERN PIN OAK *Quercus ellipsoidalis* E.J. Hill
A.K.A. JACK OAK, HILL'S OAK, BLACK OAK

QUICK ID The retention of dead branch stubs on the lower trunk, the deeply cut leaves, and the comparatively small acorns help distinguish Northern Pin Oak.

Deciduous tree, sometimes shrubby at the northern extent of its range, to about 20 m tall, 1 m or more diam. Erect, single trunk, stubs of dead branches often present on lower trunk. Crown narrow, oblong or cylindric, with numerous forked branches. **BARK** Dark grayish brown, smooth on young trees, becoming vertically divided into shallow furrows and thin ridges. **TWIG** Slender, bright red or dark reddish brown, hairless at maturity. Terminal buds 3–6 mm long, egg-shaped, angled in cross section, typically silvery- or tawny-hairy at the apex. **LEAF** Alternate, simple, elliptic, flattened or broadly angled at the base; margins with 5–7 narrow, deeply divided lobes, the primary lobes widest toward the apex and furnished with several bristle-tipped secondary lobes; sinuses between the primary lobes greater than ½ the lobe length, often leaving a comparatively narrow band of tissue along the midvein. Upper surface bright green, lustrous, hairless; lower surface paler, moderately lustrous, hairless or with small tufts of hairs in the axils of main veins. Turns bright orange-red in

SCARLET OAK   NORTHERN PIN OAK

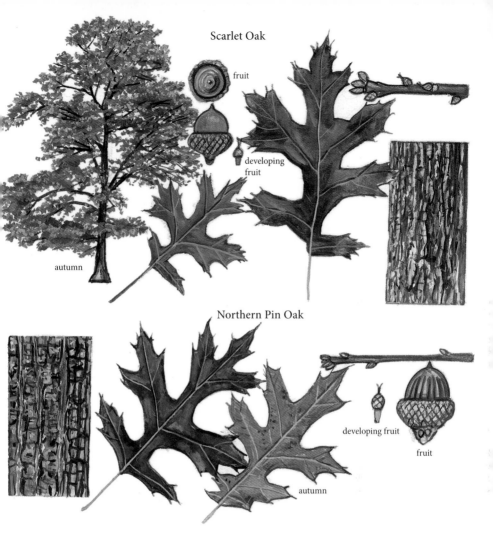

Scarlet Oak

fruit

developing fruit

autumn

Northern Pin Oak

developing fruit

fruit

autumn

autumn. Blade 7–13 cm long, 5–10 cm broad; petiole 2–5 cm long. **FRUIT** Acorn, cup 6–11 mm deep, enclosing ⅓–½ of the nut; nut dark brown, 1–2 cm long, sometimes with vertical stripes, usually lacking concentric rings at the apex.

HABITAT/RANGE Native. Dry, sandy, fire-prone uplands, rarely on slightly moist sites, sometimes in moist woods along ponds and streams, 150–500 m; Ont. south to Iowa, east to n. Ill., n. Ohio, and Mich.

SIMILAR SPECIES The closely related Scarlet Oak (*Q. coccinea*) is distinguished by the trunk lacking stubs of dead branches, slightly larger buds, and acorns with 1 or more concentric rings at the apex; Shumard Oak (*Q. shumardii*) by the hairless

buds; Northern Red Oak (*Q. rubra*) by the less deeply cut leaves; and Pin Oak (*Q. palustris*) by the acorns predominantly not exceeding 16 mm long.

Notes: Northern Pin Oak is closely related to, and sometimes considered to be a northern expression of, Scarlet Oak. It is the most drought-tolerant of e. North American oaks. It often grows in association with American Elm, Black Cherry, Shagbark Hickory, Jack Pine, Red Pine, and White Pine, and Black Oak, Bur Oak, Northern Red Oak, Scarlet Oak, and White Oak. Acorns are produced in abundance once every 2 or 3 years and are a food source for Whitetail Deer (*Odocoileus virginianus*), Black Bear (*Ursus americanus*), squirrels, Wild Turkey (*Meleagris gallopavo*), grouse, and other birds.

PIN OAK *Quercus palustris* Münchh.
A.K.A. SWAMP OAK

QUICK ID Recognized by the combination of small acorns, drooping lower branches, and deeply cut leaves with the 1st and 2nd pair of lobes diverging at nearly right angles to the axis.

Deciduous tree to about 25 m tall, 1.5 m diam. Erect, single trunk, often with low branches. Crown large, tall, symmetric, conical or cylindric, upper branches ascending, middle branches horizontal, lower branches often conspicuously drooping (old trees may lose the lower branches and have all branches either ascending or horizontally spreading). **BARK** Gray, smooth on young trees, becoming finely furrowed and shallowly ridged with age. **TWIG** Slender, lustrous reddish brown, hairless at maturity. Terminal buds reddish or chestnut brown, 2–5 mm long, egg-shaped with a pointed tip, essentially hairless except at the apex. **LEAF** Alternate, simple, elliptic or obovate, margins with 5–7 primary lobes, these furnished near the apex with several bristle-tipped secondary lobes, primary lobes separated by deep sinuses, the 1st and (sometimes) 2nd pairs of lobes diverging at nearly right angles from the leaf axis, the central lobe at least 3 times as long as the narrowest width of the blade. Upper surface yellow-green, lustrous, veins visibly raised; lower surface essentially hairless except for tufts in the vein axils. Turns scarlet-red in autumn. Blade 5–16 cm long, 5–12 cm broad; petiole 2–6 cm long. **FRUIT** Acorn, cup shallow, 3–6 mm deep, enclosing about ¼ of the nut; nut egg-shaped or rounded, comparatively small, less than 16 mm long, usually conspicuously vertically striped.

HABITAT/RANGE Native. Lowland woods, river bottomlands, swamp margins, poorly drained uplands where clay is present, 500–1,000 m, widely planted as a street and yard tree above 1,000 m; Mass. and N.Y. south and west to Kans. and Okla.

SIMILAR SPECIES See Northern Red Oak for comparisons of red oaks with lobed leaves. The leaves of Black Oak (*Q. velutina*) are hairy along the veins beneath. Northern Pin Oak (*Q. ellipsoidalis*), Scarlet Oak (*Q. coccinnea*), Shumard Oak (*Q. shumardii*), and Northern Red Oak (*Q. rubra*) lack Pin Oak's demonstrably drooping lower branches. Scarlet Oak's nuts have concentric circles at the apex, and many of its acorns are greater than 16 mm long.

Notes: This is a relatively fast-growing tree with hard, heavy wood suitable for construction and firewood. It is tough and resistant to disturbance, which has led to it becoming a very popular landscape and street tree, even along sidewalks of heavily populated metropolitan areas. It is the dominant species in pin oak–sweetgum forests, where it grows in association with Sour Gum, Green Ash, Red Maple, Shagbark Hickory, Shellbark Hickory, and several oaks, including Bur Oak, Overcup Oak, White Oak, and Willow Oak. The acorns are an important food source for migrating waterfowl, as well as for a variety of small mammals and other birds. Although sometimes called Swamp Oak, it is tolerant of flooding and inundation only during the dormant season; repeated growing-season floods over several consecutive years can kill the tree.

SHUMARD OAK *Quercus shumardii* Buckley

QUICK ID Most easily distinguished by the combination of deeply cut leaves, hairless terminal buds, and a shallow acorn cup enclosing less than ⅓ of the nut.

Deciduous tree, potentially to about 40 m tall, typically 30 m, 2 m diam. Erect, single trunk, lower trunk often somewhat buttressed or fluted, usually high-branching and clear of branches below. Crown open, spreading, with ascending and spreading branches. **BARK** Pale gray, smooth on young trees, becoming finely ridged and furrowed (more deeply furrowed on very old trees), with pale gray ridges and darker furrows. **TWIG** Gray or light brown, slender, hairless. Terminal buds more or less egg-shaped, 4–8 mm long, angled in cross section, hairless. **LEAF** Alternate, simple, elliptic or obovate,

PIN OAK   SHUMARD OAK

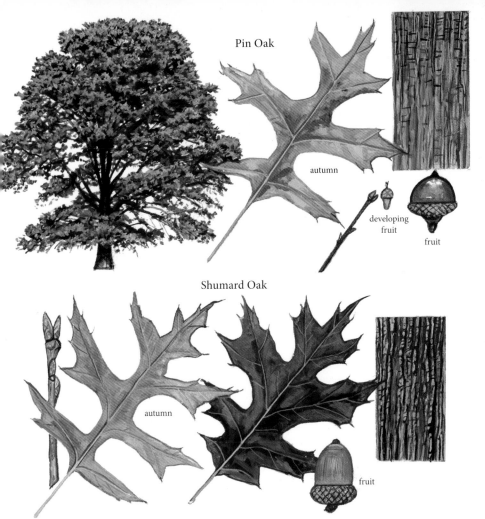

Pin Oak

autumn

developing fruit

fruit

Shumard Oak

autumn

fruit

base flattened or wide angled; margins with 5–9 primary lobes, each lobe widest at the apex and furnished with several bristle-tipped secondary lobes. Upper surface pale yellow-green, lustrous, hairless; lower surface lustrous, about the same color as the upper, with conspicuous tufts of hairs in the axils of primary veins. Turning more or less brownish with small purple spots in autumn. Blade 7–20 cm long, 6–15 cm broad; petiole 2–6 mm long. **FRUIT** Acorn, cup 7–12 mm deep, enclosing ⅓ or less of the nut; nut light brown, lustrous, 2–3 cm long.

HABITAT/RANGE Native. Mixed forests, moist slopes and woodlands, riverbanks, bottomlands, often where limestone is present, 0–500 m; s. Mich. southwest to e. Kans. and c. Tex, east to s. Penn., the Carolinas, and n. Fla.

SIMILAR SPECIES Pin Oak (*Q. palustris*) can be distinguished by its much smaller acorn; the acorn cups of Northern Red Oak (*Q. rubra*) and Texas Red Oak (*Q. texana*) cover more than ⅓ of the nut.

Notes: This is among the largest red oaks in the se. U.S. Under cultivation it is fast-growing and tolerant of harsh and dry conditions and varying soils. It is a popular landscape tree in the South and is increasingly used to decorate parking lots, medians, roadsides, and large suburban lawns. In nature it usually occurs as individual trees within the forest canopy and generally does not form pure stands. Associates in its natural habitat include American Elm, Winged Elm, Green Ash, White Ash, several hickories, Tuliptree, Sour Gum, Cherrybark Oak, Southern Red Oak, Water Oak, and White Oak.

MAPLE-LEAF OAK *Quercus acerifolia*
(Palmer) Stoynoff & Hess

QUICK ID Distinguished by maplelike leaves that are broader than long.

Deciduous small tree, to about 15 m tall. **LEAF** Broadly elliptic to nearly round, maplelike in form. Blade 7–14 cm long, 10–15 cm broad; petiole 2–4.5 cm long. **FRUIT** Acorn, cup 4–7 mm deep, enclosing less than ⅓ of the nut; nut egg-shaped, to about 2 cm long.

HABITAT/RANGE Native. Dry slopes and ridges, 500–800 m; rare and restricted to only a few counties in ec. Ark.

Notes: Closely related to Shumard Oak (*Q. shumardii*) and sometimes considered a variant of that species, when it is treated as *Q. shumardii* var. *acerifolia* Palmer.

CHERRYBARK OAK *Quercus pagoda* Raf.
A.K.A. PAGODA OAK

QUICK ID The combination of the leaf with 5–11 marginal lobes and a hairy lower surface, comparatively large buds, bark somewhat similar to that of Black Cherry (*Prunus serotina*, Rosaceae), and bottomland habitat helps distinguish Cherrybark Oak.

Deciduous, potentially very large tree, 30–40 m tall, to 2.5 m diam. or more. Erect, single trunk, usually clear of branches below, especially in forest-grown trees. Crown of open-grown trees spreading, that of forest-grown trees narrower. **BARK** Smooth at first, becoming scaly and resembling the bark of Black Cherry, especially on fast-growing trees, darker at maturity, with shallow furrows and scaly ridges; ridges often with a reddish tinge. **TWIG** Yellowish

brown or reddish purple, slender, grayish-hairy at first, sometimes becoming glabrous by autumn. Terminal buds brown, narrowly egg-shaped, comparatively large, 4–9 mm long, 5-angled in cross section, finely hairy. **LEAF** Alternate, simple, ovate or elliptic to nearly obovate, base flattened or wide-angled; margins with 5–11 lobes, often diverging at nearly right angles from the midrib, each lobe often with 2 or more smaller secondary lobes, all lobes bristle-tipped. Upper surface lustrous, dark green, hairy at first, essentially hairless at maturity; lower surface paler, densely grayish-hairy, soft to the touch. Turns bright, clear yellow in autumn. Blade 9–20 cm long, 6–16 cm broad; petiole 2–6 cm long. **FRUIT** Acorn, cup 3–7 mm deep, enclosing ⅓–½ of the nut; nut 1–1.5 cm long, brown, striped, rounded, finely hairy.

HABITAT/RANGE Native. Chiefly grows in floodplain forests, bottomlands, lower slopes along large rivers, usually in areas only periodically and briefly flooded, often in association with neutral soils, sometimes in drier sites, 0–300 m; se. U.S., Mississippi River valley, Va. south to n. Fla., west to e. Tex., s. Ill.

SIMILAR SPECIES Similar to, and sometimes considered a variant of, Southern Red Oak (*Q. falcata*), which has leaves typically with a U-shaped leaf base. Distinguished from most oaks with similar leaves by its wetland habitat. Overcup Oak (*Q. lyrata*), a white oak that also occurs in wetlands, has a nut 2.5–5 cm long and nearly completely enclosed by the cup.

Notes: This is one of the largest and fastest growing of southern oaks. Under optimum conditions it becomes an important component of floodplain forests, often sharing canopy dominance with Swamp Chestnut Oak, Water Oak, Willow Oak, and Diamondleaf Oak. Other trees sharing similar habitat include Green Ash, White Ash, Shellbark Hickory,

MAPLE-LEAF OAK

CHERRYBARK OAK

Maple-leaf Oak

autumn

Cherrybark Oak

fruit

Shagbark Hickory, Water Locust, and Honey Locust. Cherrybark Oak typically begins producing fruit at about 25 years old and yields abundant acorn crops every 1 or 2 years for at least 100 years thereafter. Fast growth makes Cherrybark Oak a valuable timber tree; it is considered by some to be one of the best timber trees of the red oak group. The branch-free trunks of forest-grown trees produce high-quality lumber that is used in the fabrication of furniture and interior trim.

SOUTHERN RED OAK *Quercus falcata* Michx.
A.K.A. SPANISH OAK

QUICK ID The leaf, with its U-shaped base in combination with the extended, often curving (sickle-shaped), straplike terminal lobe, is diagnostic.

Deciduous tree, typically to about 30 m tall, 2 m diam., potentially much larger. Erect, single trunk. Crown somewhat narrow at first, becoming more or less rounded with low, spreading branches, often appearing lustrous and drooping due to the shiny, pendent leaves. **BARK** Dark gray, mixed with black on older trunks, deeply furrowed and ridged, roughened with scaly, irregular, blocky plates. **TWIG** Reddish brown, slender, hairy. Terminal buds hairy, egg-shaped, usually 2–4 mm long. **LEAF** Alternate, simple, usually ovate, varying to elliptic, base rounded, typically U-shaped, especially on crown leaves; margins with 3–7 bristle-tipped lobes, the terminal lobe often the longest, usually narrow, straplike, and curving. Upper surface lustrous, dark green; lower surface grayish or rusty hairy with a decidedly rusty cast. Turns brownish yellow in autumn. Blade 10–30 cm long, 6–16 cm broad; petiole 2–6 cm long. **FRUIT** Acorn, cup shallow, 3–7 mm deep, enclosing ⅓ of the acorn or less; nut orange-brown, 1–1.5 cm long.

HABITAT/RANGE Native. Dry, sandy upland woods, pinelands, usually associated with sandy or clay-loam soils, 0–800 m; Del. to s. Mo., south to e. Okla., e. Tex., and n. Fla.

SIMILAR SPECIES Similar to Cherrybark Oak (*Q. pagoda*) and Turkey Oak (*Q. laevis*), neither of which have Southern Red Oak's U-shaped leaf base. The leaves of Post Oak (*Q. stellata*) also often have a U-shaped base, but the twigs and lower surface of the leaves are covered with stellate grayish pubescence.

Notes: Southern Red Oak is one of the more common southern oaks, often seen growing naturally in pastures, thick woods, and roadside woodlands. Although typically found in nature in dry, well-drained woods, it is among the first of the oaks to suffer during long periods of low rainfall. Leaves of drought-stressed trees often turn brown in large patches, and entire trees can succumb during severe water shortages. It is moderately tolerant of shade and grows best along the edges of, or within, relatively open woodlands. Associates include Loblolly Pine, Longleaf Pine, Virginia Pine, and Shortleaf Pine; Black Oak, Blackjack Oak, and Post Oak; and other upland trees including Sweetgum, Sour Gum, and hickories. Southern Red Oak is a dominant component of the relatively recently recognized black oak–red oak–shortleaf pine forest association.

TURKEY OAK *Quercus laevis* Walter

QUICK ID Identified by its small stature in combination with its twisted petioles, at least some leaves 3-lobed and resembling a turkey footprint, and dry, often sandy habitat.

Deciduous small tree or shrub, potentially to 20 m, usually not exceeding about 13 m tall or about 50 cm diam. Typically erect, single trunk, more or less straight to sometimes slightly contorted, plants often appearing scrubby. Crown narrow to somewhat spreading, open, irregular, with contorted branches. **BARK** Dark gray to nearly black, with vertical furrows and roughened ridges, ridges often horizontally divided into smaller plates, appearing blocky. **TWIG** Stout, brown at first, becoming gray with maturity, varying sparsely hairy to hairless. Terminal and surrounding buds reddish brown, narrowly egg-shaped or ellipsoid, comparatively large, 6–13 mm long, hairy. **LEAF** Alternate, simple, broadly elliptic or broadly ovate; margins typically with 3–7 bristle-tipped lobes, lobes widest near the midvein, becoming narrower, long-tapering, and pointed at the apex; base usually more or less V-shaped. Upper surface lustrous yellow-green, hairless; lower surface varying rusty to pale green, usually with conspicuous tufts of hairs in the axils of major veins. Often turns scarlet-red in autumn, sometimes merely brown.

SOUTHERN RED OAK   TURKEY OAK

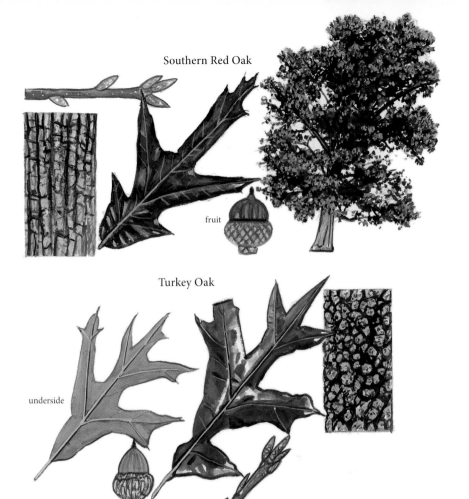

Southern Red Oak

fruit

Turkey Oak

underside

fruit

Blade 7–30 cm long, 8–15 cm broad; petiole averaging about 1 cm long, twisted so that the planes
of many leaves on any plant are oriented perpendicular to the ground. **FRUIT** Acorn, cup 9–14 mm
deep, enclosing about ⅓ of the nut, scales hairy,
with reddish margins; nut medium or dark brown,
2–3 cm long.

HABITAT/RANGE Native. Deep, well-drained
sandy ridges, sunny hammocks, often associated with Longleaf Pine and Slash Pine uplands, to
about 150 m; outer coastal plain, se. Va. south and
west to extreme e. La.

SIMILAR SPECIES Southern Red Oak (*Q. falcata*) is a larger tree, with leaves hairy throughout
on the lower surface, and at least some U-shaped
at the base; Cherrybark Oak (*Q. pagoda*) is also
larger and occurs mostly in wetter habitats; the
petioles of these species are not twisted as in
Turkey Oak.

Notes: Do not confuse the common name of this
species with that of *Q. cerris*, which is named for the
country of Turkey. At least some leaves on any plant
of *Q. laevis* are 3-lobed, distinctly resembling in
outline the footprint of the American Wild Turkey
(*Meleagris gallopavo*). Turkey Oak is slow-growing,
relatively short-lived, and intolerant of shade. It
was formerly a dominant understorey species in
the longleaf pinelands that once covered 35 million
hectares across the southeastern coastal plains.

BUCKLEY OAK *Quercus buckleyi* Nixon & Dorr

QUICK ID Identified by the combination of its Tex.–Okla. range, habitat, and sharply lobed leaves with a hairless lower surface except for inconspicuous tufts in the vein axils.

Deciduous tree to about 15 m tall, 20–50 cm diam. Erect, often with several trunks, occasionally with a single trunk. **BARK** Smooth and gray or furrowed and black. **TWIG** Slender, reddish brown, lustrous, slightly hairy in the 1st year, becoming gray, hairless, and nonlustrous. Terminal buds 3–5 mm long, reddish brown, broadly or narrowly egg-shaped, rounded or 5-angled, often with an acute point, finely hairy, especially near the apex. **LEAF** Alternate, simple, broadly elliptic, ovate, obovate, or nearly circular, wide-angled or nearly truncate at the base, tissue asymmetric on either side of the midrib at the base; margins usually with 2 or 3 primary lobes per side, each with 2 or more secondary lobes, most tipped with bristles 2–8 mm long, usually resulting in a total number of 12–35 per leaf; lobes deeply separated, the depth of the sinuses between them usually exceeding ½ the length of the adjacent lobes, typically leaving a narrow strip of tissue paralleling the midrib; the basal lobes often narrowly wedge-shaped and sometimes lacking secondary lobes. Upper surface lustrous, dark green or yellowish green, quickly becoming hairless; lower surface paler, coppery green, hairless or with inconspicuous triangular tufts in the main vein axils. Blade 7–10 cm long, 5–8 cm broad, petiole 2–4.5 cm long. **FRUIT** Acorn, cup 5–11 mm deep, enclosing ⅓–½ of the nut; nut brown, narrowly ovoid, ellipsoid, or cylindric, finely hairy or hairless, sometimes faintly ringed with minute pits at the apex, 14–20 mm long.

HABITAT/RANGE Native. Limestone ridges, calcareous slopes, creek bottoms, 150–500 m; c. Okla. and the Edwards Plateau region of Tex.

SIMILAR SPECIES Similar to, and abutting the ranges of, Shumard Oak (*Q. shumardii*) and Texas Red Oak (*Q. texana*), both of which have conspicuous tufts of hairs in the vein axils on the lower surface of the leaf.

Notes: Buckley Oak was first recognized as a distinct species in 1985. For many years it was erroneously confused with Texas Red Oak, or thought to be a variety of either Shumard Oak or Northern Red Oak. It is of conservation concern due to its limited numbers and narrow range.

TEXAS RED OAK *Quercus texana* Buckley
A.K.A. NUTTALL'S OAK

QUICK ID The wetland habitat, relatively deep acorn cup, and deeply lobed leaf with conspicuous tufts of hair in the vein axils on the lower surface help identify Texas Red Oak.

Deciduous tree, to 28 m tall, 1.3 m diam. Erect, single trunk. Crown of open-grown trees spreading and elongate, crown of forest-grown trees narrower and shorter. **BARK** Smooth, dark brown, especially on young trees, becoming shallowly divided into broad, flat ridges on large trees. **TWIG** Grayish or reddish brown, slender, hairless. Terminal buds egg-shaped, 3–7 mm long, graybrown, hairless except along the scale margins and apex. **LEAF** Alternate, simple, ovate, elliptic, or obovate, base wide-angled or flattened, asymmetric on either side of the midvein; margins with 6–11 lobes, each often with 2 or more secondary lobes, all lobes sharp-pointed and bristle-tipped. Upper surface medium or dark green, hairless; lower surface hairless except for conspicuous tufts in the vein axils. Blade 7–20 cm long, 5–13 cm broad; petiole 2–5 cm long. **FRUIT** Acorn, cup 10–16 mm deep, outer surface hairless or finely hairy, inner surface sparsely to conspicuously hairy, enclosing ⅓–½ of the nut; nut broadly egg-shaped or ellipsoid.

HABITAT/RANGE Native. Floodplains and bottomland woods, typically in wet clay soils, 0–200 m; restricted largely to the Mississippi River drainage basin, Ala. west to e. Tex., north to se. Mo. and s. Ill.

BUCKLEY OAK

TEXAS RED OAK

Buckley Oak

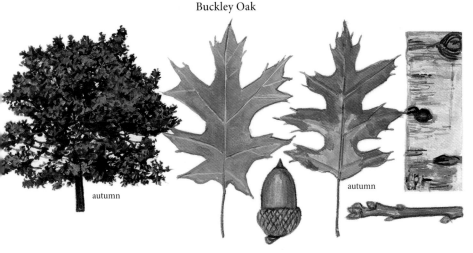

autumn

autumn

Texas Red Oak

autumn

developing fruit

fruit

SIMILAR SPECIES Shumard Oak (*Q. shumardii*) is similar but has gray bark, and its acorn cup is shallow, encloses less than ⅓ of the nut, and is essentially hairless inside. The leaves of Buckley Oak (*Q. buckleyi*) are hairless below, or with small, inconspicuous tufts of hairs in the vein axils. The leaves of Cherrybark Oak (*Q. pagoda*) are uniformly hairy below.

Notes: Texas Red Oak is fast-growing, bearing acorns in 20 years or less and reaching harvestable size in about 70 years. It is valued most as a wildlife food and is regularly used in the development of green-tree reservoirs, specially designed feeding grounds for wintering and migrating waterfowl. The acorns are also a valued food source for hogs, rodents, Whitetail Deer (*Odocoileus virginianus*), Wild Turkey (*Meleagris gallopavo*), and other wildlife. Good seed crops are produced every 3 or 4 years and are disseminated by water, mammals, and birds. Its acorn crops rarely fail, making it one of the best mast-producing species in bottomland woods. Germination is dependent upon the availability of openings in the forest canopy. However, in the absence of killing floods, seedlings can grow in shade for up to 10 years once established. Texas Red Oak has been confused in the literature with Buckley Oak; the two are morphologically distinct and well separated geographically. It is also often seen listed by the synonym *Q. nuttallii*, a name that lacks precedence under the rules of botanical nomenclature.

BEAR OAK *Quercus ilicifolia* Wangenh.

QUICK ID The small plant size, rocky habitat, and hairy lower surface of the leaves distinguish the species.

Deciduous small tree or gangly shrub, usually not exceeding about 5 m tall, sometimes to 12 m tall, 5–15 cm diam., with 1 or more short, contorted trunks. Crown dense and rounded. **BARK** Gray, becoming shallowly furrowed and scaly. **TWIG** Yellowish brown, slender, hairy. Terminal buds chestnut brown, egg-shaped, to about 3 mm long, finely hairy at the apex. **LEAF** Alternate, simple, ovate, elliptic, or obovate, base wedge-shaped; margins with 3–7 shallow, pointed or somewhat squarish, bristle-tipped lobes. Upper surface lustrous, dark green; lower surface paler, conspicuously hairy. Turns yellow in autumn. Blade 5–12 cm long, 3–9 cm broad; petiole 10–25 mm long. **FRUIT** Acorn, cup 10–17 mm deep, enclosing about ¼–½ of the nut; nut egg-shaped, faintly vertically striped, 9–16 mm long.

HABITAT/RANGE Native. Dry soils and exposed rocky outcrops, often in mountainous terrain, 0–1,500 m; Ont. and s. Maine to Va.

Notes: Individual aboveground stems of Bear Oak are short-lived, usually not persisting for more than about 20 years, but arise from a large, long-lived taproot that may be as much as 20 cm thick and extend to 90 cm deep. The acorns are produced in abundance, probably due to the harsh environment in which Bear Oak grows.

BEAR OAK

GEORGIA OAK *Quercus georgiana* M.A. Curtis

QUICK ID The combination of comparatively small leaves with conspicuously bristle-tipped lobes and the granite-outcrop habitat is distinctive.

Deciduous tree, or sometimes a shrub, to about 15 m tall, 10–30 cm diam. Usually erect with a single trunk. Crown compact, dense. **BARK** Grayish or light grayish brown, often with darker horizontal markings, smooth when young, becoming shallowly fissured between broad, flat plates. **TWIG** Reddish, slender, hairless, with prominent light brown lenticels. Terminal buds reddish brown, egg-shaped, 3–5 mm long. **LEAF** Alternate, simple, ovate, elliptic, or obovate, base narrowly wedge-shaped; margins with 3–7 shallow or moderately deep lobes, lobes often wedge-shaped, each terminated by a conspicuous, elongate bristle. Upper surface lustrous, yellow-green, hairless; lower surface hairless except for tufts in the vein axils. Blade 4–13 cm long, 2–9 cm broad; petiole 6–23 mm long. **FRUIT** Acorn, cup shallow, 4–6 mm deep, enclosing about ⅓ of the nut; nut rounded or egg-shaped, outer surface hairless.

HABITAT/RANGE Native. Granite outcrops and dry slopes of the Piedmont, 50–1,500 m; rare, sparsely distributed in portions of Ala., Ga., and S.C.

SIMILAR SPECIES Bear Oak (*Q. ilicifolia*) is distinguished by its more mountainous or dry, barren, usually sand and rocky habitat, shrubby growth form, and the hairy lower surface of the leaf.

Notes: Georgia Oak was originally described from collections at Stone Mountain, Ga., where it is best known and easily seen.

GEORGIA OAK

Bear Oak

underside

fruit

Georgia Oak

developing fruit

fruit

DARLINGTON OAK *Quercus hemisphaerica* W. Bartram ex Willd.
A.K.A. LAUREL OAK

QUICK ID The only eastern oak with wholly hairless lanceolate leaves.

Semi-deciduous tree, to 35 m tall, to about 2 m diam.; leaves fall mostly at once in spring, then are immediately replaced by new growth. Crown elongate, cylindric, densely foliaged. **BARK** Smooth, gray on young trunks, becoming darker, sometimes nearly black, shallowly ridged, furrowed on very old trees. **TWIG** Light brown, reddish brown, or gray, slender, hairless. Terminal buds dark brown, egg-shaped, hairless except along the margins of the scales. **LEAF** Alternate, simple, leathery, lanceolate, narrowly elliptic, or widest toward the tip, base tapering and narrowly wedge-shaped, margins entire. Upper surface lustrous, dark green, hairless; lower surface paler, bright green, hairless. Blade 3–10 cm long, 1–3 cm broad; petiole 1–6 mm long. **FRUIT** Acorn, cup 3–10 mm deep, enclosing ¼–⅓ of the nut; nut egg-shaped or rounded, dark brown, flattened at base, 9–20 mm long.

HABITAT/RANGE Native. Sandhills, dry slopes, disturbed uplands, 0–150 m; southeastern coastal plains, Va. south to Fla., west to se. Tex. and s. Ark.

SIMILAR SPECIES Diamondleaf Oak (*Q. laurifolia*) differs in the lower surface of the leaves occasionally with tufts of hairs in the vein axils and in its floodplain habitat; Bluejack Oak (*Q. incana*) differs in the leaves having a bluish or grayish tint.

Notes: Before European settlement, Darlington Oak occupied a narrow zone between upland sandhill and mesic forests. With fire suppression it expanded into disturbed uplands and is now common on lawns and in other open places.

DIAMONDLEAF OAK *Quercus laurifolia* Michx.
A.K.A. LAUREL OAK, SWAMP LAUREL OAK

QUICK ID The combination of wetland habitat and rhombus-shaped leaves distinguish this species in nature; no other cultivated oak has rhombic leaves.

Deciduous tree, but with leaves falling slowly over winter, to 40 m tall, 1–2 m diam. Erect, single trunk, often with narrow, flange-like buttresses at the base that can extend 1 m or more from the trunk and be up to 2 m tall. Crown of forest-grown trees open, with several ascending branches, that of open-grown trees dense, somewhat taller than wide. **BARK** Grayish, dark gray, or almost black, vertically ridged and furrowed. **TWIG** Reddish brown or dark brown, slender or stout, hairless. Buds egg-shaped, red-brown, 2–6 mm long, hairless except for tufts at the apex. **LEAF** Alternate, simple, stiff, elliptic or broadly elliptic, few to many on any tree conspicuously rhombic or diamond-shaped, tapering to the base; margins entire, with a bristle only at the leaf tip. Upper surface dark, lustrous green, hairless; lower surface paler, hairless or occasionally with tufts of hairs in the axils of major veins. Blade 3–12 cm long, 2–4 cm broad; petiole to about 5 mm long. **FRUIT** Acorn, cup shallow, 4–9 mm deep, outer surface finely hairy, enclosing ¼–½ of the nut; nut dark brown, rounded or egg-shaped, 6–12 mm long.

HABITAT/RANGE Native. Floodplain forests and bottomlands, 0–150 m, often planted for roadside beautification; generally restricted in distribution to the southeastern coastal plains, Va. south to Fla., west to e. Tex., s. Ark.

SIMILAR SPECIES Most similar to, and sometimes considered to be the same species as, Darlington Oak (*Q. hemisphaerica*), which occurs naturally in drier habitats and has lanceolate rather

DARLINGTON OAK

DIAMONDLEAF OAK

Darlington Oak

autumn

underside

fruit

Diamondleaf Oak

fruit

than a mixture of lanceolate and rhombic leaves. The wetland Willow Oak (*Q. phellos*), often also planted as a street tree, has much narrower leaves; Shingle Oak (*Q. imbricaria*) has a uniformly hairy lower leaf surface.

Notes: Although the scientific name for this species is *laurifolia*, the name Laurel Oak is more often applied to the similar *Q. hemisphaerica*, a situation that can be attributed to the long-held opinion that these 2 plants represent a single species. Here we have emphasized names intended to reduce this confusion. This species is regularly used as a street tree these days, way out of its natural habitat.

WILLOW OAK *Quercus phellos* L.

QUICK ID No other eastern oak has such narrow leaves with tufts of hairs in the vein axils on the lower surface.

Deciduous tree, to 30 m tall, 1 m diam. Erect, single straight, tall, slender trunk; lower trunk of forest-grown trees often with stubs of self-pruned branches. Crown of open-grown trees pyramidal or oval, dense, low-branching, the lower branches often drooping or angling slightly downward at the tip; crown of forest-grown trees full, symmetric, cylindric, with a rounded top. Branches often produce numerous short, spurlike branchlets, similar to those of Pin Oak (*Q. palustris*). **BARK** Smooth and light gray when young, becoming darker gray and shallowly and narrowly fissured with age. **TWIG** Brown, slender, hairless. **LEAF** Alternate, simple, usually linear, lanceolate, narrowly elliptic, or narrowly oblong, sometimes slightly wider near the tip; margins entire. Upper surface dark green, hairless; lower surface paler green, with conspicuous tufts of hairs in the axils of the major veins. Blade 5–12 cm long, 1–2 cm broad; petiole 2–6 mm long. **FRUIT** Acorn, cup shallow, 3–7 mm deep, enclosing ¼–⅓ of the nut; nut brown, egg-shaped to nearly rounded, often vertically striped.

HABITAT/RANGE Native. Bottomland and lowland woods, floodplains, stream banks, river terraces, usually in association with alluvial soils, occasionally on uplands; reaching its greatest abundance and largest size in floodplain forests of the Mississippi River, 0–400 m; cultivated for ornament in residential and commercial landscapes and for median and roadside beautification; N.J. and Del. south to n. Fla., west to Ky., e. Okla., and e. Tex.

SIMILAR SPECIES Darlington Oak (*Q. hemisphaerica*) lacks tufts of hairs in the vein axils on the lower surface of the leaf. The leaves of Diamondleaf Oak (*Q. laurifolia*) and Shingle Oak (*Q. imbricaria*) are predominantly broader than 2 cm.

Notes: Willow Oak is a fast-growing, long-lived oak that bears acorns in as few as 20 years. It produces an abundant crop annually, making it an excellent mast producer for wintering and migrating waterfowl. The acorns also provide food for squirrels, Whitetail Deer (*Odocoileus virginianus*), and Wild Turkey (*Meleagris gallopavo*), as well as jays, woodpeckers, and grackles. Willow Oak is a component of several bottomland hardwood forest types and grows in association with Cherrybark Oak, Swamp Post Oak, Diamondleaf Oak, Overcup Oak, Shumard Oak, Swamp Chestnut Oak, Texas Live Oak, and White Oak, as well as Eastern Cottonwood, Green Ash, Red Maple, Sugarberry, and Water Hickory. Its use as a timber tree is mostly for pulp, but its fast growth, moderate size, and dense crown have contributed to its popularity as a residential shade tree. It is intolerant of fire, which can kill trees of this species outright if hot enough.

BLUEJACK OAK *Quercus incana* W. Bartram

QUICK ID Bluish-gray leaves with entire margins and a dense covering of grayish hairs on the lower surface, combined with a xeric habitat, distinguish this oak.

Deciduous tree (sometimes retaining leaves until spring in mild winters), potentially to 15 m tall, 1 m diam., usually not exceeding about 6 m tall, 30 cm diam. Erect, single trunk, crown thin, irregularly branched, with an ashy-gray hue at a distance. **BARK** Gray, becoming blackish with age, deeply and roughly furrowed, transversely divided into blocky plates. **TWIG** Grayish or brown, densely

WILLOW OAK

BLUEJACK OAK

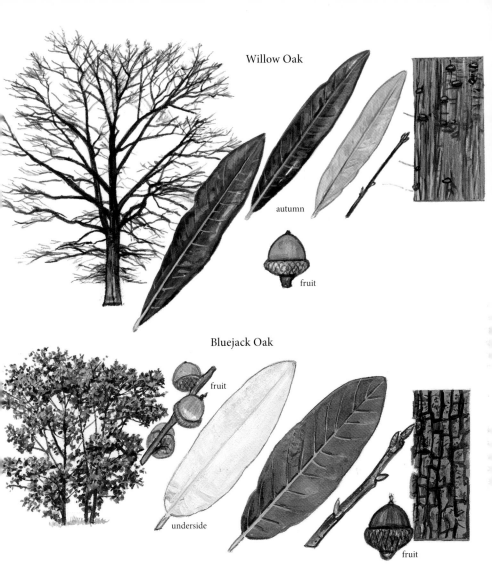

Willow Oak

autumn

fruit

Bluejack Oak

fruit

underside

fruit

to moderately hairy, especially when young. Terminal buds dark reddish brown, egg-shaped, hairy. **LEAF** Alternate, simple, stiff, narrowly ovate, elliptic, or slightly obovate; margins entire. Upper surface essentially hairless, lower surface densely and compactly covered with short grayish hairs, the blade with a decidedly bluish or grayish cast. Blade 3–10 cm long, 1–3 cm broad; petiole 2–8 mm long. **FRUIT** Acorn, cup 4–8 mm deep, enclosing about ¼–½ of the nut; nut egg-shaped, ellipsoid, or rounded, 10–17 mm long.

HABITAT/RANGE Native. Well-drained sandy ridges, dunes, longleaf pine sandhills, 0–250 m; southeastern coastal plains, N.C. south to Fla., west to e. Tex.

SIMILAR SPECIES The leaves of Darlington Oak (*Q. hemisphaerica*) are similar in shape but hairless.

Notes: This is one of several "scrub" oaks, growing in a variable association including Blackjack Oak, Chapman Oak, Myrtle Oak, Sand Live Oak, Sand Post Oak, and Turkey Oak.

SHINGLE OAK *Quercus imbricaria*
Michx.

QUICK ID Distinguished by the oblong, dark green leaves with the lower surface hairy, in combination with the comparatively long petiole.

Deciduous tree, 20–30 m tall, to 1.7 m diam. Erect, single trunk. Forest-grown trees often clear of branches for ½ their height, their crown narrow, round-topped; crown of open-grown trees pyramidal, low-branching, mostly wider than tall, with several large, spreading branches. Lower branches sometimes drooping, similar to those of Pin Oak. **BARK** Grayish brown, shallowly and narrowly ridged and furrowed. **TWIG** Greenish brown or brown, lustrous, slender, hairless or sparsely hairy. Buds brown, egg-shaped, 3–6 mm long, finely hairy along the scale margins. **LEAF** Alternate, simple, stiff, leathery, narrowly elliptic or oblong, sometimes widest toward the apex; tip sharply or bluntly pointed, bristle-tipped, the bristle sometimes falling with age; margins entire. Upper surface lustrous, dark green, hairless; lower surface more or less persistently and uniformly hairy. Blade 8–20 cm long, 2–7 cm broad; petiole 1–2 cm long. **FRUIT** Acorn, cup moderately shallow, 5–9 mm deep, outer surface finely hairy, enclosing ⅓–½ of the nut; nut dark chestnut brown, egg-shaped or nearly rounded, 9–18 mm long.

HABITAT/RANGE Native. Dry to moist slopes, bottomlands and lower slopes along rivers and streams, 100–700 m, but planted at higher elevations, especially as an ornamental or shade tree; Pa. west to s. Wis. and e. Kans., south to n. Ark., Tenn., and w. N.C., disjunct to extreme ne. Tex. and nw. La.

SIMILAR SPECIES Similar to, but not appreciably overlapping in range with, Diamondleaf Oak (*Q. laurifolia*), which is distinguished by the lower surface of the leaves hairless or occasionally with tufts of hairs in axils of major veins.

Notes: The wood of this species was formerly used in the fabrication of shingles, hence the common name. The epithet *imbricaria* means overlapping, as with shingles. The wood has also been used in the construction trades.

WATER OAK *Quercus nigra* L.

QUICK ID The highly variable but typically spatulate leaves with tufts of grayish hairs in the vein axils of the lower surface are usually diagnostic.

Semi-deciduous or deciduous tree, typically losing leaves gradually over the winter, or leaves retained until spring and falling all at once, especially in the southernmost parts of the range, to 30 m tall, to about 2 m diam. Erect, single trunk. Crown dense, rounded, symmetric. **BARK** Grayish, smooth on young trees, becoming shallowly and narrowly fissured with maturity, root collar at base of trunk on older trees usually producing conspicuous, rounded, humplike protuberances. **TWIG** Reddish brown, slender, glabrous at maturity. Buds reddish brown, egg-shaped, 3–7 mm long. **LEAF** Alternate, simple, extremely variable in shape, elliptic, lanceolate, usually widest toward the tip, at least a few leaves on any tree decidedly spatulate; margins entire, sometimes with 3 lobes at the apex. Upper surface lustrous, hairless, veins more or less impressed; lower surface paler, hairless except for conspicuous grayish tufts in the vein axils. Blade 3–15 cm long, 1.5–7 cm broad, petiole 2–9 mm long. **FRUIT** Acorn, cup saucer-shaped, 2–5 mm deep, enclosing ¼ of the nut or less; nut dark, nearly black, egg-shaped, 9–14 mm long.

HABITAT/RANGE Native. Grows naturally in lowlands, bottoms along alluvial rivers, moist hammocks, now well established on a variety of upland sites and widely planted as a shade tree in residential and commercial landscapes, 0–450 m; widespread in the Southeast, Del., Ark. and e. Okla. south to Fla. and Tex.

SIMILAR SPECIES Most often confused with Durand Oak (*Q. durandii*), which can be distinguished by at least some leaves being silvery beneath with a dense covering of inconspicuous stellate hairs. Both Blackjack Oak

SHINGLE OAK

WATER OAK

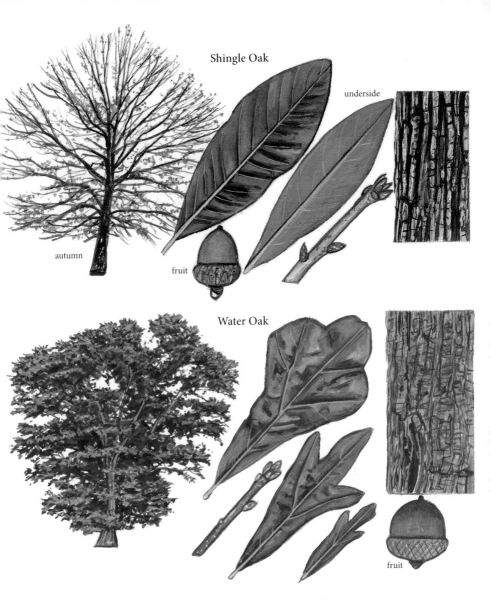

Shingle Oak

underside

autumn

fruit

Water Oak

fruit

(*Q. marilandica*) and Arkansas Oak (*Q. arkansana*) have hairy twigs.

Notes: This is a fast-growing, opportunistic, and often-planted tree that soon colonizes cleared land. Prior to European settlement, Water Oak was probably confined to riverine and bottomland wetlands, and was prevented from invading the uplands by naturally occurring fire. Fire suppression, forestry practices, land clearing, and development over the past 200 years have allowed Water Oak to colonize forested lands, clearings, and other disturbed sites, making it a dominant tree in suburban uplands. Water Oaks bear fruit in about 20 years, earlier than some other oaks, and usually produce good acorn crops at least every 2 years. Under ideal conditions, Water Oak may grow 60 cm per year. The tree is intolerant of fire and can be eliminated through regular burning. Common associates in southern forests include Blackjack Oak, Southern Red Oak, Sassafras, Common Persimmon, Sweetgum, and Flowering Dogwood.

BLACKJACK OAK *Quercus marilandica*
Münchh.

<u>QUICK ID</u> Distinguished by the combination of leaves with the upper surface dark green and the lower orange-brown, and the tawny-hairy buds.

Deciduous tree, rarely shrublike, typically not exceeding 20 m tall and 45 cm diam., potentially larger. Erect, usually single trunk. Crown irregularly shaped, more or less compact, with short, stout, contorted branches. **BARK** Dark gray to nearly black, roughened with scaly ridges, somewhat resembling that of Black Oak (*Q. velutina*). **TWIG** Grayish brown, slender, finely to densely hairy. Terminal buds conical or ellipsoid, usually angled in cross section, 5–10 mm long, covered with conspicuous yellowish-brown hairs. **LEAF** Alternate, simple, thick, stiff, equally broad as long, obovate or nearly triangular, typically much the widest toward the tip; base rounded or modestly heart-shaped; margins usually with 3–5 shallow, bristle-tipped lobes, sometimes more or less unlobed and the leaf broadly spatulate. Upper surface lustrous, dark green, hairless; lower surface orange-brown, sometimes feltlike, with a dense or moderate covering of rusty hairs; veins on both surfaces conspicuously raised. Blade 7–20 cm long, 7–20 cm broad, petiole 5–20 mm long. **FRUIT** Acorn, cup 6–10 mm deep, covering ⅓–½ of the nut; nut egg-shaped or ellipsoid, minutely hairy or hairless, 1.2–2 cm long.

HABITAT/RANGE Native. Dry hills and ridges, flatwoods, upland mixed woodlands, typically where clay is present in the soil column, 0–900 m; widespread but spotty in the e. U.S. from about R.I. to Iowa, south to Fla. and ec. Tex.

SIMILAR SPECIES Most easily confused with Arkansas Oak (*Q. arkansana*), which may be distinguished by its much smaller and mostly hairless terminal bud; marginally similar to Water Oak (*Q. nigra*), which has twigs hairless at maturity.

Notes: This is a slow-growing, relatively short-lived tree that reaches its best form on clay-based uplands. It is intolerant of heavy shade and is usually found along edges or in sunny openings, often in pine-dominated woodlands. On better sites, where it reaches its maximum size, it grows with Pignut Hickory, Mockernut Hickory, Black Oak, Post Oak, Bluejack Oak, Southern Red Oak, and Turkey Oak. On harsh sites it sometimes grows as a shrub, often forming thickets with Pitch Pine and Bear Oak. Trees growing at the extreme western extent of the range often exhibit tufts of grayish hairs in the vein axils on the lower surface of the leaves; plants meeting this description are sometimes referred to as var. *ashei* Sudw.

Confusing Scrub Oaks

Three species of scrub oaks of sandy habitats in the outer coastal plain often occur together and can easily be confused when first encountered. Arkansas Oak and Myrtle Oak are red oaks. Chapman Oak is a white oak. They are included together here for easy comparison.

CHAPMAN OAK *Quercus chapmanii*
Sarg.

<u>QUICK ID</u> Most easily identified by the combination of a xeric habitat, knobby acorn cup, and leaves that are oblong, dark green and lustrous on the upper surface, with wavy margins.

Deciduous or semievergreen shrub or small tree, potentially to about 13 m tall and 65 cm diam., usually not exceeding about 3 m tall and 10 cm diam. Crown of mature understory specimens spreading, vertically flattened, with several, often contorted

BLACKJACK OAK

CHAPMAN OAK

Blackjack Oak

fruit

underside

Chapman Oak

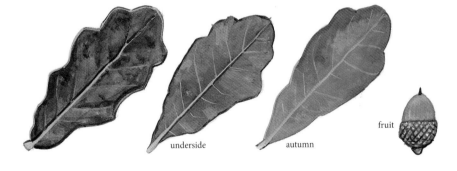

underside

autumn

fruit

branches. **BARK** Brown, scaly and flaking, typical of many white oaks. **TWIG** Yellowish, very slender, densely finely hairy. **LEAF** Alternate, simple, oblong, obovate, or oblanceolate, thick and leathery; margins entire, often wavy, slightly if at all rolled under. Upper surface dark green, conspicuously lustrous, hairless or with very fine hairs; lower surface grayish or yellowish, hairy, often least hairy on the veins. Blade 3–7 cm long, 1.5–3 cm broad; petiole 1–3 mm long. **FRUIT** Acorn, cup shallow, 5–11 mm deep, enclosing ⅓–½ of the nut, scales knobby, gray, finely hairy; nut egg-shaped or ellipsoid, 1.2–2 cm long.

HABITAT/RANGE Native. Sandy back dunes and pinelands, oak scrub, usually in xeric habitats, 0–100 m; coastal zone, S.C., Ga., Fla.

SIMILAR SPECIES Sometimes confused with Arkansas Oak (*Q. arkansana*), which is distinguished by an often shallower acorn cup and at least some leaves with long petioles. The leaves of Myrtle Oak (*Q. myrtifolia*) are yellowish green above and the margins are conspicuously rolled under.

ARKANSAS OAK *Quercus arkansana*
Sarg.

A.K.A. ARKANSAS WATER OAK

QUICK ID Distinguished by the stiff, rounded to broadly elliptic or obovate leaf that is grayish or yellowish green above and grayish green beneath.

Deciduous tree, to about 19 m tall, 1 m diam. Erect, single trunk, often crooked or contorted, especially on young understory trees in very dry habitat. Crown narrow and rounded, densely or sparsely branched. **BARK** Smooth, grayish, and with creamy splotches when young, becoming nearly black and deeply furrowed and ridged with age. **TWIG** Slender, grayish-hairy to nearly hairless; terminal buds egg-shaped, the upper scales usually fringed with minute hairs. **LEAF** Alternate, simple, stiff, often about as broad as long, varying from broadly obovate to more or less oval, circular, or broadly elliptic, at least some leaves with 3 bristle-tipped lobes at the apex. Upper surface grayish green or yellowish green; lower surface green or grayish green, hairy on the veins, some leaves also hairy on the tissue, some not, others nearly hairless throughout. Blade 6–15 cm long, 3–10 cm broad; petiole 1–2 cm long. **FRUIT** Acorn, cup shallow, 5–9 mm deep, outer surface finely hairy, enclosing ¼–½ of the nut; nut dark brown or blackish, 6–16 mm long; borne on a stalk to about 3 cm long.

HABITAT/RANGE Native. Sandy, well-drained pine–oak–hickory woods, 0–150 m; spottily distributed from extreme e. Tex. and sw. La. to w. Ga. and nw. Fla., apparently absent from Miss.

SIMILAR SPECIES Distinguished from most other oaks by the combination of leaf shape and habitat; the similar and associated Myrtle Oak (*Q. myrtifolia*) and Chapman Oak (*Q. chapmanii*) have generally smaller leaves with much shorter petioles, and Chapman has a knobby acorn cup. Also potentially confused with Blackjack Oak (*Q. marilandica*), which has a stiffer leaf whose lower surface is covered with orange hairs.

Notes: Arkansas Oak is usually abundant and common where it occurs, but populations of the species tend to be localized and occupy relatively small geographic areas.

MYRTLE OAK *Quercus myrtifolia* Willd.

QUICK ID Recognized by the combination of sandy-scrubby, often coastal habitat and yellow-green leaves with the upper surface hairless and the margins slightly but conspicuously rolled under.

Evergreen shrub or small tree, potentially to 12 m tall, to 50 cm diam., often much smaller. Usually a single trunk, sometimes several, often crooked or contorted. Crown dense, compact. **BARK** Gray, smooth when young, becoming darker and shallowly ridged and furrowed with age. **TWIG** Reddish brown, very slender, usually hairy, rarely hairless; terminal bud ovoid, brown, upper scales usually hairy along the margins. **LEAF** Alternate, simple, stiff, leathery, elliptic or obovate, base and tip rounded; margins entire, often conspicuously rolled under, sometimes with a few marginal bristles. Upper surface yellow-green, hairless; lower surface hairless except for conspicuous tufts mostly in the major vein axils. Blade 1.5–5 cm long, 1–2.5 cm broad; petiole 1–5 mm long. **FRUIT** Acorn, cup shallow, 5–9 mm deep, enclosing ¼–⅓ of the nut; nut egg-shaped or rounded, green at first, dark brown at maturity, 9.5–14 mm long.

HABITAT/RANGE Native. Dunes, coastal sandhills, oak-dominated scrub, usually in deep sand

ARKANSAS OAK

MYRTLE OAK

Arkansas Oak

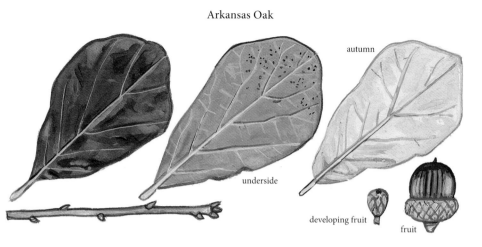

autumn

underside

developing fruit

fruit

Myrtle Oak

underside

fruit

fruit

developing fruit

and xeric habitats, 0–100 m; largely coastal from S.C. south throughout Fla., west to Miss.

SIMILAR SPECIES Due primarily to their overlapping habitats, Myrtle Oak is most often confused with Chapman Oak (*Q. chapmanii*), which can be distinguished by the leaves being oblong and dark green above. Arkansas Oak (*Q.*

arkansana) has larger leaves, many with much longer petioles. Also very similar to the shrubby Florida Oak (*Q. inopina* Ashe), a Florida endemic restricted to sand scrub of the central peninsula. Leaves of Florida Oak are conspicuously rolled under, the lower surface is often beset with tiny golden scales, and the leaf blade is usually at least twice as long as wide.

HAMAMELIDACEAE: WITCH-HAZEL FAMILY

The witch-hazel family is a relatively small group of temperate and tropical trees and shrubs distributed in North America, Mexico, Central America, East Asia, Africa, Australia, and the Pacific islands. The family includes about 25 genera and 80 species, with 2 genera and 5 species in North America, all native. In addition to *Hamamelis*, covered here, the family includes *Fothergilla*, an e. North American genus of 2 shrubs, both with leaves similar to those of witch-hazels. The popular landscape shrub Loropetalum (*Loropetalum chinensis* [R. Br.] Oliv.) is also in this family.

The family is well known for its tendency toward autumn and winter flowering, its capsule fruit that sometimes splits forcibly to expel the seeds, and the broad, bluntly toothed leaves. Forked branches of witch-hazel have been used as divining rods, and the leaves, bark, and twigs have been used medicinally.

■ *HAMAMELIS*: WITCH-HAZELS

A genus of 4 or 5 species, 3 native to North America, all confined to the eastern half of the U.S.

Deciduous shrubs or trees, often suckering from the base, recognized by scalloped leaves and straplike flower petals. Erect, single trunk or multiple. **BARK** Gray, often mottled with darker gray or brown splotches. **TWIG** Finely covered with star-shaped hairs. **LEAF** Alternate, simple, usually broadly elliptic, margins scalloped. **FLOWER** Bisexual; petals 4, usually ribbon- or straplike; corolla yellow, red, or orange-red; functional stamens 4, nonfunctional stamens 4; styles 2. **FRUIT** Two-valved woody or leathery capsule; seeds 2 per capsule, lustrous black, forcibly expelled from the capsule at maturity.

AMERICAN WITCH-HAZEL
Hamamelis virginiana L.

QUICK ID Quickly distinguished by the ovate, scalloped leaves with an asymmetric base, the surfaces sparsely to moderately covered with star-shaped hairs

Deciduous shrub or small tree to about 8 m tall, 30 cm diam. Erect or leaning, single trunk or multiple, often low-branching; crown broad, rounded. **BARK** Smooth, grayish, splotched darker gray and brown. **TWIG** Zigzag, tipped in winter with a conspicuous naked bud. **LEAF** Alternate, simple, 2-ranked, oval or obovate; base asymmetric; tip bluntly pointed; margins scalloped or wavy. Upper surface dark green, often beset with distinctive cone-shaped galls. Blade 4–15 cm long, 2–10 cm broad; petiole 7–20 mm long, hairy at first, subtended by a stipule that soon falls following leaf expansion. Turns pale yellow in autumn. **FLOWER** Yellow, with 4 ribbonlike petals, 1–2.5 cm long; produced in 3-flowered clusters along the twigs and branches. Autumn to winter. **FRUIT** Hairy, 4-pointed, 2-valved greenish or grayish capsule 1–1.6 cm long; seeds 5–9 mm long; matures summer to autumn.

HABITAT/RANGE Native. Moist slopes and woods, ravines, 0–1,500 m; widespread in the East, N.S. and Maine south to Fla., west to Minn. and Tex.

SIMILAR SPECIES One of only a few native trees or woody shrubs that flower in late autumn and winter. Other native species (see Ozark Witch-hazel) are nearly always shrubby in form. A Chinese species (*H. mollis* Oliv.) is cultivated in the U.S. and is rarely established; its leaves are densely hairy below, and it blooms in spring.

AMERICAN WITCH-HAZEL

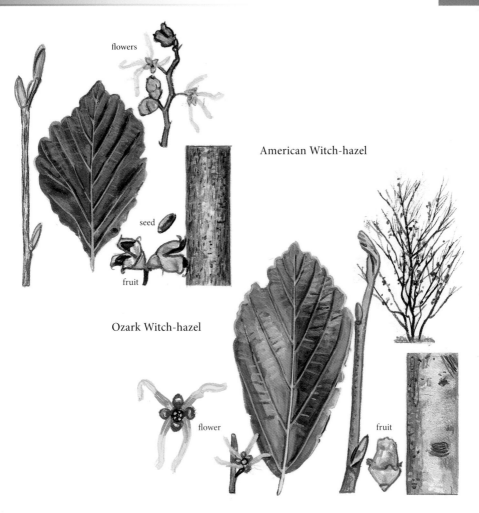

flowers

American Witch-hazel

seed

fruit

Ozark Witch-hazel

flower

fruit

OZARK WITCH-HAZEL *Hamamelis vernalis* Sarg.

QUICK ID Distinguished by the combination of its alternate, scalloped leaves, mostly reddish flowers, and typically late-winter and early-spring flowering time.

A shrub, rarely exceeding 2–3 m tall. It blooms later in the winter than American Witch-hazel, and has mostly red flowers.

HABITAT/RANGE Native; distribution centered in the Ozark Mountains of Ark., Mo., and Okla.

SIMILAR SPECIES Camp Shelby Witch-hazel (*H. ovalis* S.W. Leonard) is very similar to Ozark Witch-hazel; it occurs chiefly in Miss. and Ala.

OZARK WITCH-HAZEL

ILLICIACEAE: STAR ANISE FAMILY

This small family, distributed mostly in Southeast Asia, se. North America, and the American tropics, includes a single genus, *Illicium*, with about 40 species. All species contain ethereal aromatic oils that impart a distinctive pungent aroma when the leaves are crushed or bruised. **FLOWER** The primitive flowers are subtended by several sepal-like bracts and often produce numerous tepals, stamens, and pistils. **FRUIT** A unique, star-shaped collection of individual follicles.

FLORIDA ANISETREE *Illicium floridanum* J. Ellis

QUICK ID The hairless, elliptic, dark green leaves with a strong aroma of anise when crushed are distinctive.

Evergreen shrub, rarely a small understory tree, to about 8 m tall. Erect or ascending, single trunk or multiple. **TWIG** Tip of twig red at first, becoming gray, hairless. **LEAF** Alternate, those at the tip of the branch often closely set and appearing whorled; somewhat leathery, simple, narrowly elliptic, bluntly pointed at tip; margins entire. Upper surface dark green, veins obscure, hairless; lower surface minutely gland-dotted. Blade 6–20 cm long, 2–6 cm broad; petiole 1–2 cm long, often reddish. **FLOWER** 2.5–6 cm diam., red; sepal-like bracts 3–6, tepals 21–33, pistils 11–15, stamens 30–40. Spring. **FRUIT** Circular, star-shaped collection of single-seeded follicles, green at first, turning dark brown with age; matures late summer.

HABITAT/RANGE Native. Lower slopes of ravines, stream margins, often near water's edge, 0–500 m; nw. Fla. west to e. La., north to c. Ala.

SIMILAR SPECIES The mostly shrubby **Ocala Anise** (*Illicium parviflorum* Michx. ex Vent.) is closely related, but has smaller yellow flowers with 11–16 tepals; endemic to swamp margins in c. Fla.

FLORIDA ANISETREE

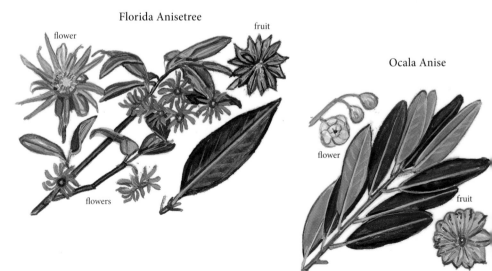

Florida Anisetree

flower

fruit

flowers

Ocala Anise

flower

fruit

JUGLANDACEAE: WALNUT FAMILY

The hickories and walnuts, and their relatives comprise a small to medium-size family of mostly trees distributed in Eurasia and the Western Hemisphere. There are 9 genera and more than 60 species; 23 species (18 native) occur in North America; 16 species occur in the East, 13 native.

LEAF Aromatic, alternate, pinnately compound, usually with a terminal leaflet (odd-pinnate). **FLOWER** Tiny, unisexual, both sexes on the same plant, borne on the previous year's twigs or at the base of the current year's growth. Flowers have a 4-lobed calyx, or the calyx is absent. Male flowers have 3–50 stamens; pistillate flowers have a single inferior ovary with 2 usually feathery stigmas. Plants are wind-pollinated. **FRUIT** Typically called a nut but in some species (especially the walnuts) more closely resembles a drupe, because the husk develops from the pericarp (the fruit wall). The large seed, or kernel, is oily and often edible.

The family Juglandaceae provides valuable hickory, pecan, and walnut lumber. Commercial varieties of pecans and walnuts are grown in extensive orchards in temperate regions of the world for the edible seeds from which oil can be pressed. A number of species are grown as ornamentals, enjoyed for their stately form, dense shade, and autumn foliage.

■ *JUGLANS*: WALNUTS

A genus of 21 species worldwide growing from low to moderate elevations, 6 native to North America, at least 3 introduced, rarely naturalized; 4 species in the East, 2 native.

Deciduous large shrubs or trees. **BARK** Smooth and gray when young, often fissured and scaly when older. **TWIG** Usually covered with glandular hairs; pith chambered, brown; leaf scars triangular or 3-lobed; terminal buds bluntly pointed, usually flattened, hairy. **LEAF** Alternate, pinnately compound, usually with a terminal leaflet (odd-pinnate), often with a spicy scent; foliage yellowish in autumn. **FLOWER** Unisexual, male and female borne on the same tree. Spring. **FRUIT** Globose or broadly ovoid nut enclosed in a green husk or rind that dries, blackens, and does not split (referred to by some experts as a drupe); nutshell tan to brown or blackish, smooth, grooved, or wrinkled, splitting in half upon germination. Seed (kernel) edible, large, oily, wrinkled and lobed.

Walnuts provide economically important nuts, dyes, and valuable dark-hued lumber used in the fabrication of cabinetry, gunstocks, and decorative items. The nuts are an important food source for small mammals.

Walnut

husk does not split open

Hickory

fruit splits along seams in the husk

BLACK WALNUT *Juglans nigra* L.

QUICK ID Recognized by the relatively long, pinnate leaves, many with the terminal leaflet absent or much reduced in size.

Deciduous large tree, 30–50 m tall, to about 2 m diam. Erect, single straight trunk; crown somewhat rounded and open on open-grown trees, more narrow when forest-grown. **BARK** Light grayish brown or reddish and scaly at first, becoming rough, deeply and irregularly fissured, the fissures often interlacing; nearly black at maturity. **TWIG** Dark brown, pale-hairy, with raised lenticels; pith chambered; bud copiously covered with blond hairs. **LEAF** Alternate, pinnately compound, odd-pinnate, often appearing even-pinnate owing to loss of the terminal leaflet; blade to about 40 cm long, 18 cm broad; petiole 4–8 cm long. Leaflets 8–23, opposite, each 4–9 cm long, 2–4 cm broad, narrowly ovate or lanceolate, base rounded or wedge-shaped, tip narrowing to a sharp point, margins toothed. Upper surface dark green, venation conspicuous; lower surface paler, shaggy-hairy at least along the veins. Turns yellowish or yellowish brown in autumn. **FLOWER** Male flowers in pendent catkins 7–15 cm long, stamens 8–40; female flowers solitary or in a few-flowered, densely woolly spike at the branch tips, styles 2. Spring. **FRUIT** Rounded nut or drupe, 5–8 cm diam., husk green, thick, tacky, staining, somewhat spongy, not splitting; nutshell dark brown, 2-valved, ridged and grooved; kernel oily; matures summer to autumn.

HABITAT/RANGE Native. Rich woods, slopes, floodplains, calcareous uplands, 0–1,000 m; nearly throughout the East, from Vt., Minn., and S.D., south to nw. Fla. and e. Tex.

SIMILAR SPECIES Butternut is similar, but has a sticky ellipsoid, mostly 4-angled fruit husk holding a nut with 4–6 conspicuous wings.

Notes: Black Walnut is a frequently cultivated ornamental, especially along roadsides and in parking lots. It is a slow-growing tree, prized for its beautifully grained wood. Most large, old-growth Black Walnut has been cut for use in furniture fabrication.

BUTTERNUT *Juglans cinerea* L.
A.K.A. WHITE WALNUT

QUICK ID Recognized by the combination of long, pinnate leaves with numerous leaflets and a sticky, mostly 4-angled fruit husk.

Deciduous tree, 20–30 m tall, to about 1 m diam. Erect, single straight trunk; crown open, often rounded and somewhat flat-topped when open-grown, narrower when forest-grown. **BARK** Light gray or brownish, thick, deeply furrowed. **TWIG** Lustrous, reddish-brown or gray, hairy or hairless; bud 12–18 mm long, whitish, hairy. **LEAF** Alternate, pinnately compound; blade to about 50 cm long, 20 cm broad; petiole 2–4 cm long. Leaflets 11–17, opposite, with a terminal leaflet, each 5–11 cm long, to about 6 cm broad, narrowly ovate or lanceolate, base unevenly rounded, tip tapering to a point, margins toothed. Upper surface yellowish green; lower surface paler, hairy, glandular and often sticky to the touch, especially when young. Turns yellowish or yellowish brown in autumn. **FLOWER** Male flowers in cylindric, hairy greenish-yellow catkins 6–14 cm long; female flowers in spikes of 4–7 flowers at the branch tips. Spring. **FRUIT** Ellipsoid or ovoid nut or drupe, 5–8 cm long, abruptly pointed or tapering at the apex; husk thick, sticky to touch, hairy, 4-ridged, brown, not splitting; nutshell with 4–6 winglike ridges; kernel oily; matures summer to autumn.

HABITAT/RANGE Native. Rich woods, floodplains of small streams, river terraces, rocky slopes, 0–1,000 m; irregularly distributed, N.B. west to

BLACK WALNUT

BUTTERNUT

Black Walnut

twig

fruit

nut

Butternut

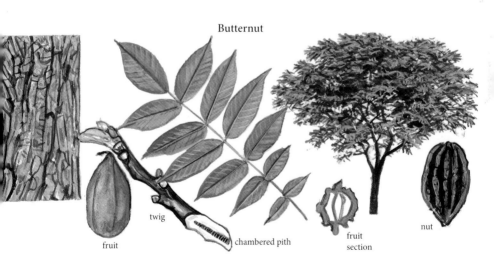

twig

chambered pith

fruit

fruit
section

nut

Minn., south to S.C., n. Ga., n. Ala., n. Miss., and e. Ark.

SIMILAR SPECIES The fruit husk of Black Walnut is round and lacks ridges and angles.

Notes: This species is of conservation concern owing primarily to butternut canker, a fungal disease caused by *Sirococcus clavigignenti-juglandacearum* that kills the tree. As a result, the range and numbers of this species are being reduced across the East.

ENGLISH WALNUT *Juglans regia* L.

QUICKID Recognized by the combination of large rounded or ellipsoid fruit and pinnately compound leaves with 5–9 leaflets.

Deciduous fast-growing tree to about 25 m tall, 13–130 cm diam. Erect, single straight, slender trunk; crown of large ascending branches, spreading on open-grown trees, considerably narrower in dense stands. **BARK** Smooth and brownish, becoming silvery gray and deeply and irregularly furrowed, the furrows separated by broad, flat ridges. **TWIG** Brownish, the pith chambered. **LEAF** Alternate, pinnately compound; blade 25–40 cm long. Leaflets 5–9, opposite, with a terminal leaflet; each 6–18 cm long, 3–8 cm broad, ovate or elliptic, base broadly wedge-shaped, tip pointed, margins usually entire. Upper surface lustrous green; lower surface paler, hairless except for the vein axils. **FLOWER** Male flowers in spikes 5–15 cm long, stamens 6–40. Spring. **FRUIT** Ellipsoid or nearly rounded nut or drupe, 4–6 cm diam.; husk green; matures summer to autumn.

HABITAT/RANGE Introduced from Asia; cultivated in cooler portions of the East, probably not naturalized.

SIMILAR SPECIES Black Walnut and Butternut have pinnately compound leaves with more leaflets.

JAPANESE WALNUT *Juglans ailantifolia*
Carrière
A.K.A. HEARTNUT

QUICKID Recognized by the combination of long, pinnately compound leaves and large greenish fruits in clusters of 4–10.

Deciduous tree to about 20 m tall, 15–20 cm diam. Erect, single trunk, crown broad, rounded. **BARK** Gray, deeply and roughly ridged and furrowed. **TWIG** Pith chambered. **LEAF** Alternate, pinnately compound; blade 50–90 cm long, with a long-stalked terminal leaflet. Leaflets 11–17, opposite, each 7–16 cm long, 3–5 cm broad; narrowly ovate, ovate-oblong, or elliptic, base rounded, tip pointed, margins toothed. Upper surface lustrous yellow-green, lower surface paler, both surfaces downy-hairy. **FLOWER** Male flowers individually small, produced in yellowish-green catkins 15–30 cm long. Spring. **FRUIT** Ellipsoid nut or drupe, 3–5 cm diam., husk green, hairy; usually 4–10 per cluster; matures autumn.

HABITAT/RANGE Introduced from Japan; reportedly naturalized in New England.

SIMILAR SPECIES The fruits of other walnuts usually do not exceed 3 per cluster.

CHINESE WINGNUT *Pterocarya stenoptera* C. DC.

QUICKID Recognized by the leaves with 11–21 leaflets and a partially winged rachis, in combination with winged nutlets borne along an elongated spike.

Deciduous tree to about 30 m tall. **LEAF** Alternate, pinnately compound; usually evenly pinnate, rarely odd-pinnate, rachis usually at least partially winged. Leaflets mostly 11–21; each 8–12 cm long, 2–3 cm broad; long-elliptic or lanceolate, margins toothed. **FLOWER** Unisexual, green, male and female flowers in separate inflorescences on the same tree. **FRUIT** Two-winged nutlet, produced at regular intervals along a spike 20–45 cm long; nutlets ellipsoid, 6–9 mm long; wings 13–24 mm long, 3–6 mm broad, often linear.

HABITAT/RANGE Introduced from China; reportedly established in 2 parishes of e. La.

Notes: Pterocarya is a genus of 6 species distributed in e. and sw. Asia.

English Walnut

kernel

nut

Japanese Walnut

fruit

nut

twig

Chinese Wingnut

fruit

fruit

■ *CARYA*: HICKORIES

A genus of 18 species distributed in e. North America, Mexico, and Asia; 11 species occur in North America, all native in the East.

Deciduous trees to about 50 m tall. **BARK** Gray, more or less smooth at first, becoming finely or moderately furrowed, the furrows often forming a diamond pattern. **TWIG** Varying greenish to reddish brown; pith solid; bud scales valvate (clam-like) or imbricate (overlapping). **LEAF** Alternate, pinnately compound, terminal leaflet conspicuous. Leaflets 3–21, opposite, usually hairy, hairs sometimes confined to the vein axils of the lower surface. **FLOWER** Unisexual, male and female borne on the same tree, the male flowers in catkins usually on 1st-year twigs, the female flowers in terminal spikes. Spring. **FRUIT** A nut, enclosed in a thick or thin husk, usually splitting at maturity along several sutures; nutshell brown, reddish brown, or tan. Matures late summer to autumn.

The hickories are widely used and commercially valuable for their nuts and wood, especially in applications that require strength and shock resistance. Several North American species are cultivated for timber in Europe. The nuts are a favored and important wildlife food. Taxonomically, the hickories are divided into 2 groups, those with valvate bud scales and those with imbricate bud scales.

WATER HICKORY *Carya aquatica* (F. Michx.) Elliott
A.K.A. WATER PECAN

QUICK ID Recognized by the combination of typically wetland habitat, scaly bark, pinnate leaves with slightly recurved leaflets, and flattened fruit.

Deciduous tree to about 35 m tall and about 1 m diam. Erect, single straight trunk, the base often fluted with narrow buttresses; crown narrowly rounded when forest grown, spreading when open-grown. **BARK** Grayish, loosely exfoliating or splitting into narrow, elongated strips or plate-like, shaggy scales. **TWIG** Slender, dark brown with scattered pale lenticels; bud scales valvate. **LEAF** Alternate, pinnately compound, with a conspicuous terminal leaflet; blade 17–27 cm long, 15–20 cm broad; petiole 3–6 cm long. Leaflets 7–17, usually 9 or 11, each 7–10 cm long, 1–3 cm broad, nearly stalkless, narrowly lanceolate, often slightly recurved, base rounded or tapered, tip long-tapered to an acute point; margins toothed or nearly entire. Upper surface light green or yellowish green, hairless at maturity, lower surface paler, usually hairy, especially along the veins. **FLOWER** Male flowers in catkins 6–7.5 cm long, 4–5 mm broad. Spring. **FRUIT** Husk-covered nut, the husk with 4 ridged sutures, somewhat laterally flattened, oval in outline, abruptly narrowed and bluntly pointed at both ends, 2.5–4 cm long, thin, splitting to base; nutshell angled, kernel bitter; matures autumn.

HABITAT/RANGE Native. Floodplains, levees, river- and stream banks, margins of freshwater bayous, 0–200 m; southeastern coastal plains, Va. and s. Ill., south to c. Fla., west to Ark. and e. Tex.

SIMILAR SPECIES The nuts of Pecan are round in cross section and the kernel of the nut is sweet.

Notes: This is one of 4 species with valvate bud scales.

PECAN *Carya illinoinensis* (Wangenh.) K. Koch

QUICK ID Recognized by the combination of pinnately compound leaves with numerous leaflets, grayish-scaly bark, and a distinctive nut.

Deciduous, potentially large tree, 40–60 m tall, to 2.5 m diam. in natural habitat; cultivated plants usually smaller. Erect, single straight trunk, open-grown plants often branching within 1–2 m of the ground; crown of cultivated trees usually vase-shaped, with several large ascending branches; crown of forest-grown trees in natural habitat narrowly rounded. **BARK** Grayish or light brown,

WATER HICKORY   PECAN

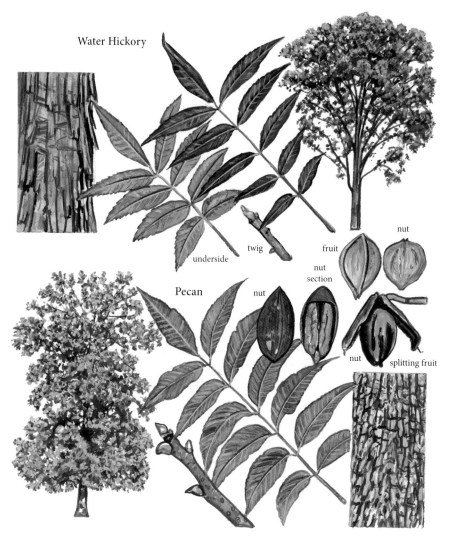

Water Hickory

underside

twig

fruit

nut

nut
section

Pecan

nut

nut

nut

splitting fruit

often tinged reddish, eventually dividing into narrow, scaly ridges. **TWIG** Purplish brown, more or less hairy, with elongated buff-colored lenticels; buds valvate. **LEAF** Alternate, pinnately compound, terminal leaflet conspicuous; blade 15–60 cm long, 15–30 cm broad; petiole 5–9 cm long. Leaflets 5–17, commonly 9 or more, each 8–20 cm long, 2.5–7.5 cm broad, recurved, drooping, lanceolate, base wedge-shaped, often asymmetric, tip tapered to a long point, margins toothed. Upper surface dark green, usually hairless; lower surface paler, hairless or with scattered hairs along the veins. **FLOWER** Male flowers in slender catkins 12–18 cm long, 5–6 mm diam. Spring. **FRUIT** Husk-covered nut, 3–5 cm long, sutures narrowly ridged; husk

thin, 3–4 mm thick, splitting to base; nutshell ellipsoid, rich dark brown; kernel edible; matures autumn.

HABITAT/RANGE Native. Along streams and in floodplains of the Mississippi River drainage basin; widely planted and naturalized well east of the range depicted on the accompanying map, 0–600 m.

SIMILAR SPECIES The nut of Water Hickory is flattened, and the kernel is bitter.

Notes: Pecan has given rise to many cultivars that are widely grown for the sweet kernel of the nut.

BITTERNUT HICKORY *Carya cordiformis* (Wangenh.) K. Koch

QUICK ID Distinguished by the comparatively small nuts, leaves with 7 or 9 leaflets, and valvate sulfur-yellow buds.

Deciduous tree to about 35 m tall and about 1.2 m diam. Erect, single trunk; crown open, rounded, especially when open-grown. **BARK** Light gray or grayish brown, often with a yellowish cast, smooth or finely furrowed, the ridges often interlacing. **TWIG** Greenish brown or dark brown with buff-colored lenticels; bud scales valvate, yellow, with resinous yellowish or copperish scales and a few hairs. **LEAF** Alternate, pinnately compound, terminal leaflet conspicuous; blade 14–30 cm long, to about 18 cm broad; petiole 4.5–6 cm long. Leaflets 7–11, usually 7–9, each 10–15 cm long, 2–3 cm broad; mostly lanceolate, base symmetric or slightly asymmetric, more or less rounded; tip pointed; margins toothed. Upper surface dark green, hairless or hairy; lower surface paler, the tissue sparsely or densely covered with grayish or rusty-brown resinous scales. **FLOWER** Male catkins clustered, slender, 6–10 cm long, about 4 mm diam. Spring. **FRUIT** Rounded, husk-covered nut, 1.5–3 cm diam., husk scaly, thin, 2–3 mm thick, slightly ridged; nutshell 4-angled; matures autumn.

HABITAT/RANGE Native. Low woods, moist hammocks, riverbanks, floodplains, slopes, upland woodlands, 0–900 m; widespread in the East, Maine to Minn. and e. Nebr., south to nw. Fla. and e. Tex.

SIMILAR SPECIES Pecan and Water Hickory also have valvate buds, but have leaves with many more leaflets and ellipsoid or flattened nuts. Nutmeg Hickory also has valvate buds and similar leaves, but is distinguished by its exfoliating bark.

NUTMEG HICKORY *Carya myristiciformis* (F. Michx.) Elliott

QUICK ID Mature tree recognized by the combination of alternate, pinnately compound leaves predominantly with 7 or 9 leaflets and scaly, exfoliating bark.

Deciduous tree to 35 m tall, 70 cm diam. Erect, single straight, slender trunk; crown open, rounded. **BARK** Gray or dark reddish brown, smooth or somewhat shaggy; shallowly and irregularly furrowed, separating into long strips or scales. **TWIG** Slender, brown or bronze, hairless, scaly; bud bronze, hairless, densely scaly, egg-shaped, 4–6 mm long, scales valvate. **LEAF** Alternate, pinnately compound; blade 30–60 cm long, to about 16 cm broad; petiole 3–10 cm long. Leaflet 5–9, usually 7 or 9, each 3–17 cm long, 1–8 cm broad; ovate, obovate, or elliptic, tip abruptly short-pointed, margins finely or coarsely toothed. Upper surface dark green, new leaves hairy along the midvein; lower surface of new leaves with single and branched hairs, especially along the midvein, blade tissue scaly, with a bronze cast. **FLOWER** Male catkins stalked, comparatively short, to about 6 cm long. Spring. **FRUIT** Husk-covered tan or bronze nut, obovoid or ellipsoid, 2–3 cm long, 1.5–2 cm diam.; husk thin, to about 2 mm thick, splitting to base at maturity; nutshell mottled reddish brown and tan, moderately thick; kernel sweet; matures autumn.

HABITAT/RANGE Native. River bottoms, stream margins, bluffs, hillsides, 0–500 m; uncommon or rare, N.C., disjunct west to Ala., Okla., and e. and sc. Tex.

SIMILAR SPECIES Other hickories with valvate buds lack Nutmeg Hickory's shaggy, exfoliating bark.

BITTERNUT HICKORY

NUTMEG HICKORY

Bitternut Hickory

autumn

fruit

fruit with
husk cut away

nut

Nutmeg Hickory

fruit

nut

PIGNUT HICKORY *Carya glabra* (Mill.)
Sweet

QUICK ID Recognized by the combination of leaves with mostly 5 or 7 essentially hairless leaflets and the snoutlike extension at the base of the fruit.

Deciduous tree, 25–40 m tall, to about 1.3 m diam. Erect, single straight trunk; crown broad, ascending and spreading, especially when open-grown, narrower when forest-grown. **BARK** Grayish, tight, finely to moderately furrowed, the intervening ridges crisscrossing and diamond patterned. **TWIG** Purplish brown with elongated buff-colored lenticels, often with a few persistent hairs; bud with overlapping scales. **LEAF** Alternate, pinnately compound, terminal leaflet evident, often larger than the lateral ones; blade 11–25 cm long, to about 20 cm broad; petiole 6–7 cm long. Leaflets usually 5 or 7, rarely 3; each 8–16 cm long, 3–5 cm broad; elliptic, lanceolate, or ovate, base wedge-shaped, tip narrowing to a point, margins sharply and coarsely toothed. Upper surface dark green, hairless; lower surface paler, usually hairless on the tissue, often with small tufts of hairs in the major vein axils. Turns rusty yellow in autumn. **FLOWER** Male catkins slender, usually 5–7 cm long, about 5 mm diam. Spring. **FRUIT** Ellipsoid, rounded, or obovoid husk-covered nut, 2.5–6 cm long; husk moderately thin, 2–5 mm thick, valves 2–5, usually splitting irregularly and only partially to base, often with a snoutlike protrusion at the base; nutshell tan, thick, not angled; kernel sweet; matures autumn.

HABITAT/RANGE Native. Well-drained moist uplands, margins of floodplains, slopes, dry rocky soils, 0–800 m; widespread in the East, s. N.H. west to Ill., e. Kans., e. Okla., south to c. Fla. and e. Tex.

SIMILAR SPECIES Sand Hickory is distinguished by the hairy petiole and rachis of the leaf.

Notes: Pignut Hickory is a variable species and includes forms with hairy leaves. Though not treated as distinct here, the form sometimes treated as *C. ovalis* (Wangenh.) Sarg. is similar in many respects, but has conspicuously exfoliating or scaly bark and fruits that consistently split completely to the base.

SAND HICKORY *Carya pallida* (Ashe)
Engl. & Graebn.

QUICK ID Recognized by buds 4–11 mm long with overlapping scales, leaves (including petiole) usually not exceeding about 25 cm long, leaf rachis with branched hairs, and lower surface of leaflets decorated with whitish or reddish scales.

Deciduous, usually a small tree, 10–15 m tall, rarely to about 35 m, to about 1 m diam. Erect, single trunk; crown spreading. **BARK** Pale or dark gray, tight, roughened with interlacing fissures and ridges in a somewhat diamond-like pattern. **TWIG** Reddish or purplish, becoming gray or nearly black, hairy at first, becoming hairless; buds with overlapping scales, 4–11 mm long. **LEAF** Alternate, pinnately compound, the rachis hairy with branched hairs, terminal leaflet conspicuous; blade 10–25 cm long, 18–24 cm broad; petiole 3–8 cm long. Leaflets 3–9, usually 7, each 7–15 cm long, 2–5 cm broad; lanceolate, ovate, elliptic, or obovate, base rounded or wedge-shaped, tip tapering to a long point, margins finely toothed. Upper surface green, hairless; lower surface drab green or brownish, the tissue decorated with disk-like, pale reddish or whitish scales, these requiring magnification to see clearly. Turns yellowish in autumn. **FLOWER** Male catkins 5–13 cm long, about 4 mm diam. Spring. **FRUIT** Mostly obovoid husk-covered

PIGNUT HICKORY

SAND HICKORY

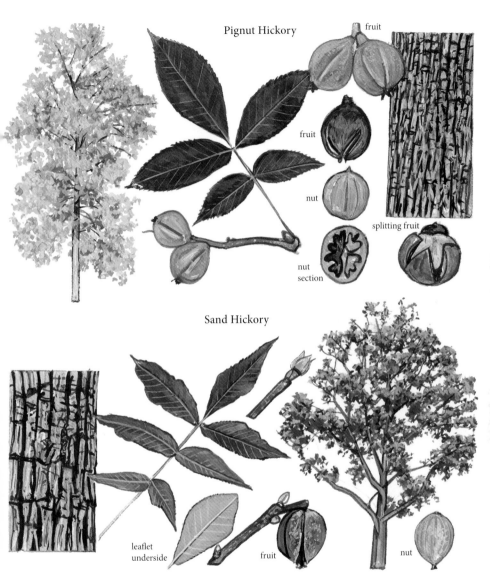

Pignut Hickory

fruit

fruit

nut

splitting fruit

nut
section

Sand Hickory

leaflet
underside

fruit

nut

nut, 1.5–4 cm long; husk relatively thin, 2–4 mm thick, 4-valved, 1 valve usually broader than the others, splitting completely to base; nutshell tan; kernel sweet; matures late autumn.

HABITAT/RANGE Native. Well-drained sandy uplands, often in association with Longleaf Pine, rocky bluffs, ridges, dry woods, 0–500 m; distributed mostly in the southeastern coastal plains and Piedmont, Del. and Va., south to nw. Fla., west to e. Mo. and e. La.

SIMILAR SPECIES The leaves of Mockernut Hickory are longer and copiously hairy with branched hairs; the petiole of Black Hickory is hairless or nearly so.

BLACK HICKORY *Carya texana* Buckley

QUICK ID Recognized by the combination of leaves mostly with 7 leaflets and hairs on the lower surface of leaflets usually concentrated near the base of the midvein.

Deciduous tree to about 41 m tall, 60–70 cm diam. Erect, single trunk; crown narrowly spreading when forest-grown, pyramidal when open-grown. **BARK** Dark gray or nearly black, sometimes with reddish highlights; deeply and irregularly ridged and furrowed, the ridges transversely divided, blocky, and scaly. **TWIG** Slender, rusty brown, densely scaly, becoming gray or brown and smooth; bud with overlapping scales. **LEAF** Alternate, pinnately compound, terminal leaflet conspicuous; blade 15–40 cm long, to about 30 cm broad; petiole 3–8 cm long. Leaflets 5–9, usually 7, each 3–15 cm long, 1–8 cm broad; ovate, obovate, or narrowly or broadly elliptic, base tapered or rounded, tip abruptly short-pointed, margins finely or coarsely toothed. Upper surface dark green, hairless, scaly at first, becoming glabrous; lower surface densely hairy (at least at the base of the midrib) to nearly hairless, with a dense covering of scales in spring that thins over time. **FLOWER** Male catkins slender, to about 16 cm long, stalk densely rusty-scaly. Spring. **FRUIT** Obovoid husk-covered brown or reddish-brown nut, 3–5 cm long, 2.5–3.5 cm diam.; husk relatively thin, 2–4 mm thick, splitting to base; nutshell tan, typically not angled; kernel sweet; matures autumn.

HABITAT/RANGE Native. Well-drained sandy soils, hills and hillsides, low flats, 0–500 m; s. Ill., w. Miss., and La. west to se. Kans. and e. Tex.

SIMILAR SPECIES Sand Hickory occurs mostly east of the Mississippi River, and its petiole and leaf rachis are finely hairy.

MOCKERNUT HICKORY *Carya tomentosa* (Poir.) Nutt.
A.K.A. WHITE HICKORY

QUICK ID Recognized by the combination of densely hairy pinnate leaves, thick twigs, tight bark, large buds, and the husk of the fruit to about 10 mm thick.

Deciduous tree to 36 m tall, about 1.5 m diam. Erect, single trunk, the branches large and relatively thick toward the extremities; crown broad, open. **BARK** Dark gray, with interlacing, diamond-like ridges and furrows; often irregularly pocked with fist-size depressions. **TWIG** Conspicuously stout, dark gray or dark brown; bud large, about 1.5 cm long, 1 cm broad, scales overlapping. **LEAF** Alternate, pinnately compound, terminal leaflet conspicuous; blade 30–50 cm long, to about 40 cm broad; petiole 3–12 cm long. Leaflets 5–9, often 7, the lowermost pair usually smaller than the others; each 4–19 cm long, 2–8 cm broad; ovate, broadly lanceolate or lanceolate-oblong to broadly elliptic, base rounded or wedge-shaped, tip abruptly short-pointed, margins coarsely toothed. Upper surface dark green or yellow-green, sparsely hairy with tufted hairs; lower surface dense with star-shaped hairs. Turns rusty orange-yellow in autumn. **FLOWER** Male catkins 15–20 cm long, 6–8 cm diam. Spring. **FRUIT** Rounded or obovoid husk-covered nut, 3–6 cm long; husk 4–10 mm thick, 4-valved, splitting partially or completely to the base; matures autumn.

HABITAT/RANGE Native. Well-drained soils of sandy uplands, slopes, ridges, and rocky hillsides, 0–900 m; N.Y., Mass., and Conn., south to c. Fla., west to se. Iowa, e. Okla., and e. Tex.

SIMILAR SPECIES No other hickory has the combination of non-shaggy bark and fruit husks exceeding 6 mm thick.

BLACK HICKORY

MOCKERNUT HICKORY

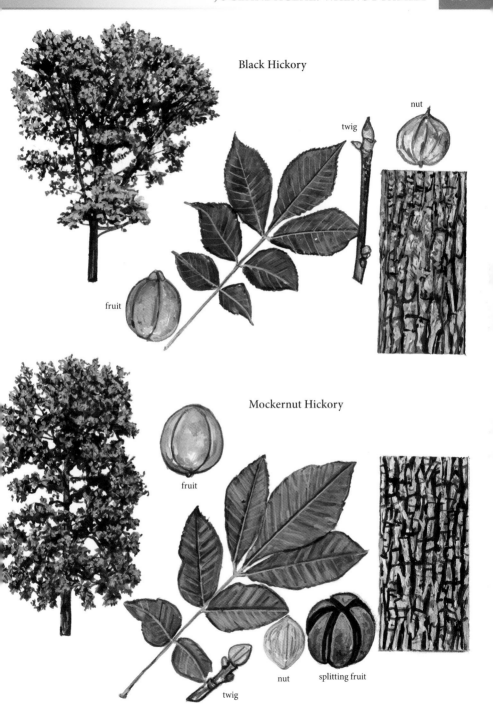

Black Hickory

nut

twig

fruit

Mockernut Hickory

fruit

nut

splitting fruit

twig

SHAGBARK HICKORY *Carya ovata*
(Mill.) K. Koch
A.K.A. SHELLBARK HICKORY

QUICK ID Recognized by the combination of often conspicuously exfoliating bark, leaves usually with 5 leaflets, and comparatively large, round nuts with thick husks.

Deciduous large tree to about 46 m tall, about 1.5 m diam. Erect, single straight trunk; crown broad, open, rounded at top. **BARK** Light gray, fissured, often conspicuously shaggy and exfoliating into long, loose, flattened plates, the ends often well separated and lifted from the trunk. **TWIG** Greenish, reddish, or orange-brown, hairy or hairless; bud large, 1–2 cm long, scales overlapping, usually dark brown and hairy. **LEAF** Alternate, pinnately compound, terminal leaflet conspicuous; blade 30–45 cm long, to about 50 cm broad; petiole 4–13 cm long. Leaflets 3–7, usually 5; each 4–26 cm long, 1–14 cm broad; ovate, obovate, or elliptic, tip acute or abruptly short-pointed, margins finely or coarsely toothed, lined with hairs. Upper surface dark yellow-green, usually hairless; lower surface paler, sometimes finely hairy, especially in the vein axils. Turns yellow in autumn. **FLOWER** Male catkins slender, 10–13 cm long. Spring. **FRUIT** Rounded husk-covered nut, often depressed at the tip, brown or reddish brown, 2.5–4 cm diam.; husk 4–15 mm thick, splitting to base; nutshell tan, thick; kernel sweet; matures late summer to autumn.

HABITAT/RANGE Native. Dry slopes at higher elevations, well-drained lowland woods, wet bottomlands, rocky hillsides, limestone outcrops, 0–1,400 m; widespread in the East, Ont. and Que. south to S.C. and n. Ga., west to se. Nebr., Okla., and e. Tex.

SIMILAR SPECIES The leaves of Shellbark Hickory usually have 7 or 9 leaflets.

Notes: The species is represented in the East by 2 varieties: Var. *australis* (Ashe) Little occurs within the range of var. *ovata* and is restricted to the c. South, including Ala., Ga., Miss., N.C., S.C., and Tenn. The twigs of var. *australis* often turn black by autumn and are slender and hairless, the buds are hairless, and the lower surface of the leaf is sparsely hairy. The twigs of var. *ovata* retain their reddish, greenish, or brownish color into autumn, and the buds and lower surface of the leaves are densely hairy.

SHELLBARK HICKORY *Carya laciniosa*
(F. Michx.) G. Don ex Loudon

QUICK ID Distinguished by the combination of leaves usually with 7 or 9 leaflets and shaggy bark.

Deciduous tree to about 41 m tall, 36–100 cm diam. Erect, single straight, slender trunk; crown narrow, oblong or cylindric, the lower branches often spreading or drooping. **BARK** Gray, thin and smooth on young trees, becoming fissured and separating into long, thick, persistent plates 1–1.2 m long, the ends curling away from the trunk. **TWIG** Orange-brown or buff; stout, angular, and hairy when young, becoming mostly hairless and round in cross section; terminal buds 2–3 cm long, scales overlapping. **LEAF** Alternate, pinnately compound; blade 50–80 cm long, to about 40 cm broad; petiole 6–13 cm long. Leaflets 5–11, usually 7; each 9–22 cm long, 3–12 cm broad; ovate, obovate, or elliptic, base narrowly tapered, rounded, or wedge-shaped, tip abruptly narrowed to a short or long point, margins toothed. Upper surface dark yellowish green, hairy along the midvein; lower surface hairy, with branched hairs. **FLOWER** Male catkins slender, stalked, to about 20 cm long. Late spring to early summer. **FRUIT** Rounded or ellipsoid husk-covered nut, tan or brown, 4.5–5 cm long, 4–5 cm diam.; husk finely hairy, 7–13 mm thick, splitting to base; nutshell tan, 4-angled; kernel sweet; matures autumn.

HABITAT/RANGE Native. Rich bottomlands, river terraces, floodplains, creek banks, cedar glades, 20–300 m; N.Y. and se. Iowa, south to Ga., Kans., Okla., Ark., and Tex.

SIMILAR SPECIES The leaves of Shagbark Hickory usually have 5 leaflets.

SHAGBARK HICKORY

SHELLBARK HICKORY

Shagbark Hickory

nut

fruit section

twig

fruit

Shellbark Hickory

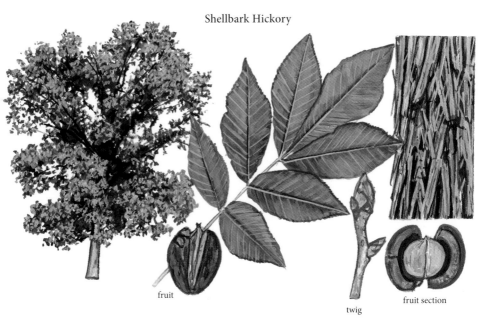

fruit

twig

fruit section

SCRUB HICKORY *Carya floridana* Sarg.

QUICK ID The only hickory in c. Fla. sand scrub with a scaly lower leaf surface.

Deciduous small or medium tree to about 25 m tall, 80 cm diam. Erect, single trunk; crown broad, rounded. **BARK** Pale gray or grayish brown, smooth at first, becoming finely furrowed with flat, interlacing ridges. **TWIG** Reddish brown flecked with gray, rusty-scaly at first; bud 5–10 mm long, scales overlapping and covered with rusty hairs and resinous yellowish scales. **LEAF** Alternate, pinnately compound; blade 5–12 cm long, to about 18 cm broad; petiole 3–6 cm long. Leaflets 3–7, usually 5; each 5–10 cm long, 2.5–5 cm broad; lanceolate, ovate, or elliptic, margins toothed. Lower surface rusty-scaly, with a bronze cast. **FLOWER** Male catkins 2–4 cm long, to about 2.5 mm diam. Spring. **FRUIT** Husk-covered nut, 2.5–4 cm long, husk thin, 2–3 mm thick, scaly, splitting to base at maturity; nutshell tan, thick; kernel sweet; matures late autumn.

HABITAT/RANGE Native. Endemic to sand scrub of c. Fla. peninsula, 0–50 m.

SCRUB HICKORY

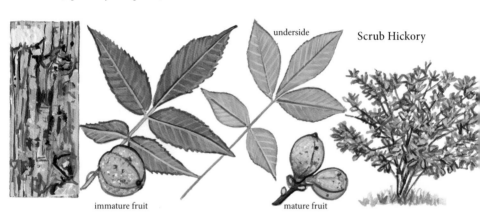

underside

Scrub Hickory

immature fruit

mature fruit

LAURACEAE: LAUREL FAMILY

The laurel family includes about 50 genera and 2,500 species of trees and shrubs (1 genus of climbing or scrambling vines), mostly from tropical and subtropical regions. Nine genera and about 13 species are native or naturalized in North America north of Mexico; 10 species of trees and shrubs occur in the East.

LEAF Plants of this family typically have alternate or opposite, simple leaves, though a few are leafless parasitic climbers. In many species leaves and other plant parts have cavities that contain highly aromatic oils that render crushed foliage spicily pungent. **FLOWER** Small, radial, bisexual or unisexual; when unisexual, usually borne on separate plants; yellow, yellow-green, or whitish, and borne in branched inflorescences. The petals and sepals are not well differentiated and are referred to here as tepals (some references may refer to the tepals as sepals, assuming the petals to be absent). Stamens vary from 3 to 12; commonly 9 are functional. **FRUIT** The ovary is usually superior and develops into a 1-seeded berry or drupe that is often fused to the cuplike base of the tepals.

The family provides the spices cinnamon and bay (the latter from Bay Laurel *Laurus nobilis* L.), camphor and sassafras oils, valuable timber, and the avocado, the latter a multi-million-dollar fruit crop in s. Fla. and s. Calif.

CAMPHORTREE *Cinnamomum camphora* (L.) J. Presl

QUICK ID All parts of this tree exude the odor of camphor when crushed.

Evergreen small to potentially large tree, to about 20 m tall, 2 m diam. Erect, with a single short trunk, sometimes producing several secondary trunks from the base; crown dense, oval, lustrous, often with low, spreading branches that become more or less ascending in the mid- and upper crown. **BARK** Dark cinnamon brown to dark steel gray, on young trees smooth or finely fissured, becoming more deeply furrowed at maturity; crushed bark with a camphorlike aroma. **TWIG** Green, often suffused with red, hairless. **LEAF** Alternate, simple, usually somewhat leathery at maturity, giving off a strong odor of camphor when crushed; ovate, elliptic, or lanceolate, base rounded or wedge-shaped, tip long-tapering to a narrow point, often with 2 main lateral veins from near the base; margins entire, somewhat thickened, often paler than the blade surface. Upper surface lustrous, dark green, hairless; lower surface paler, grayish green, hairless except sometimes in the vein axils. Blade 4–12 cm long, 2–5 cm broad; petiole to about 3 cm long. **FLOWER** Bisexual, tiny, 1–2 mm diam., with 6 greenish-white or creamy tepals. Spring. **FRUIT** Lustrous black drupe, 8–9 mm diam., borne in a cuplike receptacle; matures autumn to winter.

HABITAT/RANGE Introduced, native to Asia. Naturalized in disturbed sites, vacant lots, roadsides, upland woodlands, fencelines; established in the Southeast, N.C. south to Ga. and Fla., west to e. Tex.

SIMILAR SPECIES Lancewood (*Ocotea coriacea*), Redbay (*Persea borbonia*), and Swamp Bay (*Persea palustris*) also have evergreen leaves, but the leaf venation is pinnate and lacks Camphortree's 2 main lateral veins.

Notes: There are more than 200 species of *Cinnamomum*, most from India, China, and Japan. Camphortree was imported into the Southeast in an ill-fated attempt to establish a camphor industry. Extractions from this tree yield commercial camphor.

Camphortree

fruit

new leaf

■ *LINDERA*: SPICEBUSHES

Deciduous shrubs or small trees; 3 in e. North America, only 2 of which are sometimes trees. **BARK** Grayish, becoming darker with age. **LEAF** Alternate, simple, lanceolate, spicily aromatic; margins entire. **FLOWER** Unisexual and borne on separate plants, yellow, tepals deciduous, stamens 9; inflorescence a several-flowered cluster. **FRUIT** Ellipsoid to nearly rounded, bright red drupe.

NORTHERN SPICEBUSH *Lindera benzoin* (L.) Blume

QUICK ID The spicy, aromatic leaves that increase in size from the base to the tip of the twig are diagnostic.

Deciduous shrub or small tree, to about 5 m tall. Erect, single trunk; crown open, branches few, often spreading and spraylike. **TWIG** Spicily aromatic when bruised, hairy at first, becoming hairless, grayish brown, with pale raised lenticels. **LEAF** Alternate, simple, thin, spicily aromatic when crushed; obovate, oval, or elliptic, base and tip tapered, often abruptly pinched to a point; margins entire. Upper surface hairless, dark green; lower surface paler, grayish green, hairy at least along the midvein. Blade 6–15 cm long, 2–6 cm broad, the smallest leaves lowest on the twig, conspicuously increasing in size toward the twig tip; petiole about 1 cm long, usually hairy. **FLOWER** Yellow, tiny, borne in several-flowered clusters, male and female flowers on separate plants. Early spring, prior to leaf expansion. **FRUIT** Ellipsoid, bright red drupe, 8–10 mm long; matures autumn.

HABITAT/RANGE Native. Stream banks, moist woodlands, wetland margins, calcareous uplands, 0–1,200 m; throughout much of the East from Ont. and Maine south to n. Fla. and c. Tex.

NORTHERN SPICEBUSH

BOG SPICEBUSH *Lindera subcoriacea* Wofford

QUICK ID Distinguished by the faintly aromatic, small leathery leaves and typically swampy or boggy habitat.

Deciduous, usually a shrub not exceeding about 2 m tall, sometimes to about 4 m tall and treelike in shady swamps and stream bottoms. Crown open, spreading. **TWIG** Hairy at first, becoming nearly hairless with age. **LEAF** Alternate, simple, moderately leathery, faintly lemony aromatic when crushed, the strength of the aroma fading with age; elliptic or oblanceolate; margins entire, finely hairy on young leaves. Upper surface hairy at first, becoming hairless; lower surface hairy. Blade 4–8 cm long, 2–4 cm broad; petiole 3–10 mm long. **FLOWER** Individually tiny, about 2 mm diam., with 6 tepals. Spring, prior to leaf expansion. **FRUIT** Ellipsoid, bright red drupe about 10 mm long; matures autumn.

HABITAT/RANGE Native. Acidic evergreen-shrub bogs, swamps, and flooded margins of small streams, 0–200 m; rare, restricted largely to se. La. and s. Miss., reported elsewhere, esp. Fla. panhandle.

BOG SPICEBUSH

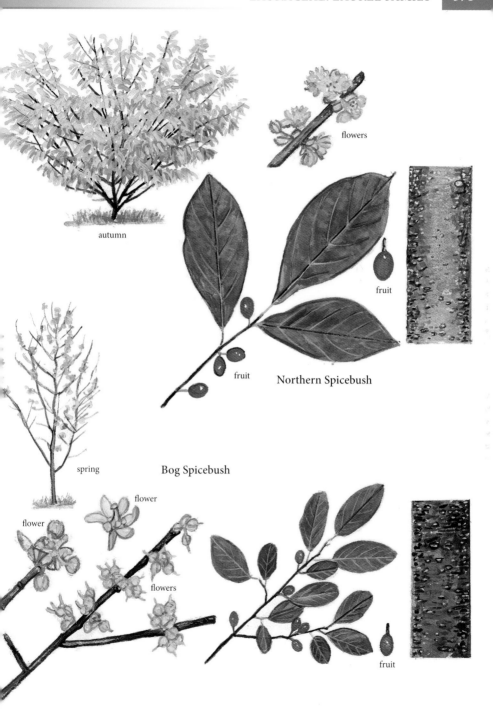

autumn

flowers

fruit

fruit

Northern Spicebush

spring

Bog Spicebush

flower

flower

flowers

flowers

fruit

■ *PERSEA*: BAYS

A genus of about 150 species worldwide, 3 native to North America, 1 introduced and naturalized; confined largely to the Southeast, from Md. to e. Tex.

Evergreen shrubs or medium-size trees; crowns dense or open, narrow or rounded. Identified by the combination of mildly aromatic evergreen lanceolate, entire-margined leaves, and fruit not subtended by a cup. The leaves on many trees are often distorted owing to the presence of insect galls. **BARK** Usually reddish brown to dark gray, becoming furrowed with age. **LEAF** Alternate, simple, lanceolate; margins entire. **FLOWER** Bisexual, tepals 6, usually white or yellowish, often hairy, the inner tepals usually longer than the outer ones, stamens 9; inflorescence an axillary cluster. **FRUIT** Nearly round, dark blue to nearly black drupe, not subtended by a cup.

A fungus, *Raffaelea lauricola*, first noted near Savannah, Ga., in 2002 and spread by the non-native ambrosia beetle *Xyleborus glabratus*, poses a significant threat to species in this genus. Many of the Redbay populations along the eastern seaboard have succumbed. No cure or remedy is known. Although usually referred to as laurel wilt or Redbay wilt, this disease affects other species within the laurel family, including Avocado.

REDBAY *Persea borbonia* (L.) Spreng.

QUICKID Distinguished by the combination of mildly aromatic lanceolate, lustrous, dark green leaves that are whitish beneath, and dark blue or blackish fruit.

Evergreen, occasionally a shrub, usually a small or medium-size tree to about 25 m tall, 1 m diam. Erect, single trunk; crown large, dense, more or less rounded. **BARK** Grayish and shallowly vertically fissured on young trees, becoming darker brownish gray and roughened with narrow, vertically interlacing furrows at maturity. **TWIG** Sparsely hairy with golden hairs when young, often appearing hairless without magnification. **LEAF** Alternate, simple, somewhat thick, leathery, mildly aromatic when crushed; lanceolate, margins entire. Upper surface lustrous, dark green; lower surface paler, often whitish, hairy with whitish or light brown hairs. Blade 2–16 cm long, 1.5–6 cm broad; petiole 1–2 cm long. **FLOWER** Tiny, tepals 6, greenish or greenish white. Spring. **FRUIT** Rounded or oblong, dark blue drupe to about 10 mm long, 8 mm diam.; peduncle about equal in length to the leaf petiole; matures autumn.

HABITAT/RANGE Native. Hammocks, moist hardwood forests, stable dunes, maritime forests, 0–100 m; southeastern coastal plains, N.C. south throughout Fla., west to se. Tex.

SIMILAR SPECIES The leaves of Swamp Bay display longer, rusty-brown hairs along the midrib beneath, and its fruit stalk is demonstrably longer than the petiole.

SILK BAY *Persea humilis* Nash

QUICKID Distinguished in its restricted sand-scrub habitat by having at least a few blackish twigs and by its evergreen lanceolate leaves being silky-hairy beneath.

Evergreen shrub or small tree to about 10 m tall, about 45 cm diam. Usually erect, single trunk, sometimes with multiple trunks. **BARK** Smooth, reddish brown, often marked with lenticels. **TWIG** Young twigs hairy with chestnut-brown hairs, older twigs often blackish. **LEAF** Alternate, simple, stiff; lanceolate, margins entire. Upper

REDBAY

SILK BAY

Redbay

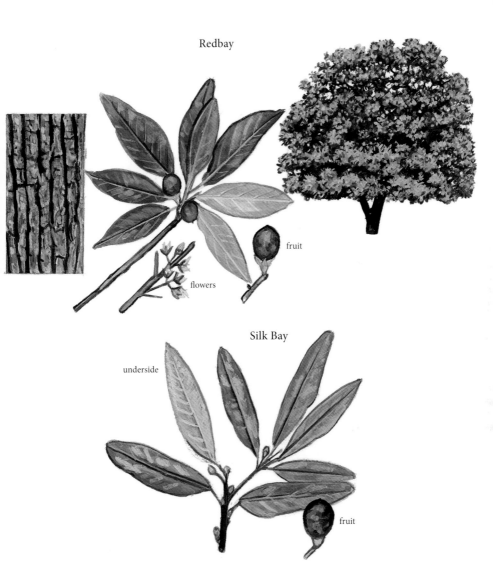

fruit

flowers

Silk Bay

underside

fruit

surface lustrous green, hairless or sparsely hairy; lower surface copiously covered with matted brownish hairs and distinctly silky to the touch. Blade 3–10 cm long, 1–3 cm broad; petiole 0.75–1.25 cm long. **FLOWER** Tiny, tepals 6, greenish. Spring to early summer. **FRUIT** More or less rounded, dark blue or blackish drupe, 1–1.5 cm diam.; matures autumn.

HABITAT/RANGE Native. Endemic to deep sands of the c. Fla. scrub, often in association with Sand Pine, 0–100 m.

SIMILAR SPECIES Swamp Bay and Redbay lack blackish twigs, and while they have hairs on the lower leaf surface, neither bears a copious covering of silky hairs like Silk Bay.

SWAMP BAY *Persea palustris* (Raf.) Sarg.

QUICK ID Distinguished by the combination of mildly aromatic lanceolate leaves that are hairy on the midvein beneath, and a blue-black drupe with a comparatively long stalk.

Evergreen shrub or small tree, to about 12 m tall, to about 1 m diam. Erect, single or multiple trunks. **TWIG** Conspicuously shaggy-hairy when young, becoming hairless and brown. **LEAF** Alternate, simple, lanceolate, margins entire. Upper surface dull or lustrous, yellowish green or dark green, hairless or hairy along the midrib; lower surface paler, hairy at least along the midrib and major veins, with comparatively long, shaggy brownish hairs, usually also hairy on the tissue throughout. Blade 5–20 cm long, 2–5 cm broad; petiole 1–2 cm long, shaggy-hairy. **FLOWER** Tiny, tepals 6, greenish. Spring to early summer. **FRUIT** Rounded or oblong, dark blue drupe to about 10 mm long, 8 mm diam.; peduncle longer than the petiole; matures autumn.

HABITAT/RANGE Native. Swamps, shrub bogs, Carolina bays, wet pinelands, maritime forests, marshes, 0–185 m; southeastern coastal plains, Md. south throughout Fla., west to e. Tex.

SIMILAR SPECIES The similar Redbay has short whitish hairs on the lower leaf surfaces and the fruit has a shorter stalk.

AVOCADO *Persea americana* Mill.

QUICK ID Distinguished by the combination of large yellowish-green fruit and lustrous, long-stalked leaves.

Evergreen fast-growing, often leaning small tree, 5–10 m tall, to 70 cm diam. Erect, single trunk; crown narrow to more or less rounded, symmetric or somewhat irregular. **BARK** Brown or gray, slightly furrowed; inner bark orange. **TWIG** Green and finely hairy when young, becoming brown; angular in cross section. **LEAF** Alternate, simple, leathery; elliptic or oblong, margins entire. Upper surface lustrous, dark green, essentially hairless; lower surface grayish green, hairy on veins. Blade 10–30 cm long, 5–12 cm broad; petiole 2–5 cm long, yellowish green, slightly hairy. **FLOWER** About 1 cm diam., tepals 6, greenish yellow, hairy. Late winter to early spring. **FRUIT** Large, more or less pear-shaped, yellowish green or reddish brown at maturity, skin tough and corky; fleshy contents edible, the avocado of commerce; matures autumn.

HABITAT/RANGE Introduced. Naturalized from cultivation in Fla.; 0–50 m.

PEPPERLEAF SWEETWOOD *Licaria triandra* (Sw.) Kosterm.

QUICK ID No other tree of s. Florida has the combination of spicy, aromatic leaves and a double-rimmed red cup subtending the fruit.

Evergreen small tree, 10–12 m tall, to 20 cm diam. Erect, single trunk; crown broad, rounded. **BARK** Dark brown, scaly and flaking at maturity. **TWIG** Slender, reddish when young, finely hairy, with raised lenticels. **LEAF** Alternate, simple, slightly leathery, spicily aromatic when crushed; narrowly elliptic, base wedge-shaped, tip abruptly narrowed to an elongated point; margins entire. Upper surface lustrous, dark green; lower surface paler. Blade 5–15 cm long, 2–7 cm broad; petiole 7–13 mm long. **FLOWER** Bisexual, 2–3 mm long, tepals 6, whitish, inflorescence a terminal or lateral panicle to 10 cm long; midwinter to late spring. **FRUIT** Ellipsoid blue drupe, 2–3 cm long, resting in a thickened, double-rimmed red cup; matures late spring to early summer.

HABITAT/RANGE Native. Hammocks, 0–10 m, s. Fla. Extremely rare and close to extirpation in the U.S.

SWAMP BAY   PEPPERLEAF SWEETWOOD

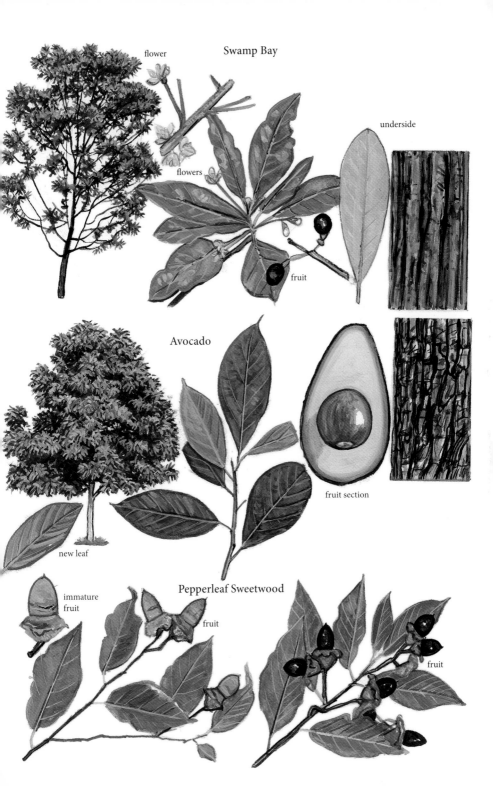

Swamp Bay

flower

flowers

underside

fruit

Avocado

new leaf

fruit section

Pepperleaf Sweetwood

immature fruit

fruit

fruit

LANCEWOOD *Ocotea coriacea* (Sw.) Britton

QUICK ID The combination of narrowly lanceolate, lustrous, dark green leaves, spreading white flowers, and a distinctive cup subtending the fruit distinguishes the species.

Evergreen small tree, to about 10 m tall, 15–30 cm diam. Erect, single trunk; crown narrow, densely branched. **BARK** Smooth, gray; inner bark brownish. **TWIG** Slender, green and somewhat hairy when young, becoming grayish and hairless. **LEAF** Alternate, simple, thick, leathery, aromatic when crushed; lanceolate, often folded slightly upward from the midrib, base wedge-shaped, tip gradually tapering to an elongated point; margins entire. Upper surface lustrous, dark green; lower surface paler. Blade 7–15 cm long, 2.5–5 cm broad; petiole 7–13 mm long. **FLOWER** Bisexual, about 8 mm diam., tepals white, spreading; inflorescence an axillary panicle 2.5–10 cm long. Mostly spring, potentially year-round. **FRUIT** Oval or ellipsoid, dark blue to nearly black drupe, 1–1.8 cm long, subtended by a persistent red or yellowish cup; matures summer to autumn, potentially year-round.

HABITAT/RANGE Native. Hammocks, 0–10 m; s. Fla.

SIMILAR SPECIES Species of the genus *Persea* have similar leaves but lack a distinctive cup subtending the fruit.

LANCEWOOD

SASSAFRAS *Sassafras albidum* (Nutt.) Nees

QUICK ID Easily distinguished by the presence of at least a few mitten-like leaves on any tree.

Deciduous, attractive tree, 9–18 m tall, to 66 cm diam. Erect, single trunk; crown columnar, open, more or less flat-topped, lateral branches spreading, more or less perpendicular to the trunk, often curving upward near the tip. **BARK** Aromatic; gray and somewhat smooth when young, becoming reddish or cinnamon brown and deeply furrowed between broad, flat ridges at maturity; distinctive and easily identified. **TWIG** Stout, hairy or not, grayish or yellowish green when young, becoming brown with age; spicily aromatic when crushed. **LEAF** Alternate, simple, thin; elliptic, ovate, or oblong, at least some leaves on any tree with the form of 2- or 3-lobed "mittens"; margins entire, often lobed. Upper surface dark or medium green, hairless; lower surface paler, usually hairy. Turns red, yellow, pink, salmon, or orange in autumn. Blade 8–15 cm long, 5–10 cm broad; petiole 2–3 cm long. **FLOWER** Individually tiny, unisexual, male and female on separate plants, yellow or yellowish green, borne in conspicuous ball-like racemes to about 5 cm diam., before leaf emergence; fragrant. Spring. **FRUIT** Ellipsoid, lustrous, dark blue drupe to about 1 cm long, resting in a conspicuous cup with a reddish stalk; matures autumn.

HABITAT/RANGE Native. Upland woods, dry woodlands, fencerows, suburban yards, old fields, often forming colonies, 0–1,500 m; throughout much of the East, Maine, Mich., and Iowa, south to n. Fla., west to e. Tex.

Notes: Sassafras has a long history of cultural uses. Native Americans and early colonists used the roots and bark to brew sassafras tea and as a flavoring for food. Current knowledge suggests this tree contains toxic compounds and should not be consumed.

SASSAFRAS

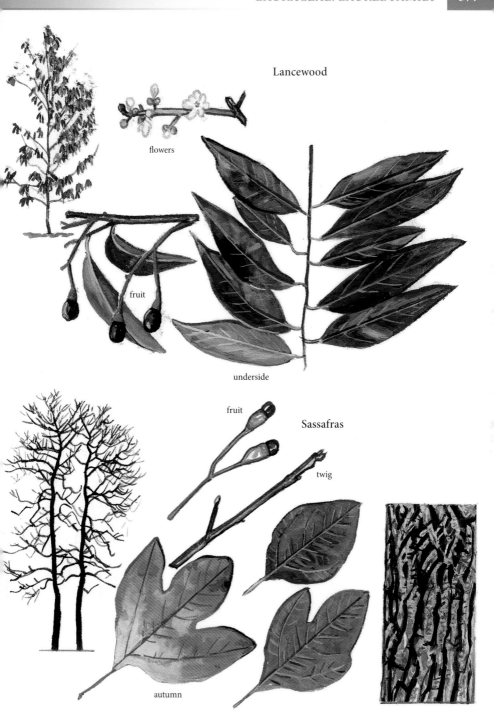

Lancewood

flowers

fruit

underside

fruit

Sassafras

twig

autumn

LEITNERIACEAE: CORKWOOD FAMILY

The corkwood family includes a single species distributed sporadically in the East. Some experts now include the genus *Leitneria* within the quassia family (Simaroubaceae), based on the hypothesis that the wind-pollinated flowers of corkwood evolved from flowers similar to the insect-pollinated flowers of the quassia family. Here we have chosen to retain corkwood in the family Leitneriaceae owing to a suite of unique and easily identifiable characters. This species should not be confused with *Stillingia aquatica* Chapm. (Euphorbiaceae), a shrub also known as corkwood.

CORKWOOD *Leitneria floridana* Chapm.

QUICK ID Recognized in its preferred habitat by the strictly upright form, narrowly elliptic leaves, unique catkins, and buff-colored lenticels in the reddish-brown bark.

Deciduous shrub or small tree, to about 5 m tall, 6 cm diam. Erect, single straight trunk; crown narrow, typically unbranched or nearly so. **BARK** Reddish brown, usually with conspicuous buff-colored corky lenticels. **LEAF** Alternate, simple, narrowly elliptic; margins entire. Upper surface lustrous, medium green, hairy at first, soon becoming hairless; lower surface paler, hairy at maturity. Blade 5–17 cm long, 2–5 cm broad; petiole 2–4 cm long. **FLOWER** Unisexual, male and female flowers borne on separate plants; male flowers in upright grayish-brown catkins 2–5 cm long along the upper part of the main stem; female flowers in reddish catkins 1–2 cm long, also arising directly from the upper stem. Late winter to early spring. **FRUIT** Single-seeded ellipsoid yellowish or brownish-yellow drupe, 1–2.5 cm long; seed pale brown, lightweight (like balsa wood); matures summer.

HABITAT/RANGE Native. Swamp margins, depression ponds or sinks, roadside ditches, margins of tidal marshes, 0–100 m; sporadically distributed in n. Fla., se. Tex., e. Ark., extreme se. Mo.

SIMILAR SPECIES The leaves of several bays of the genus *Persea* (Lauraceae) are similar, but lack the reddish-brown trunk with buff-colored lenticels.

Notes: Corkwood has the lightest-weight wood of any eastern tree; sections of the stem were once used as fishing floats.

CORKWOOD

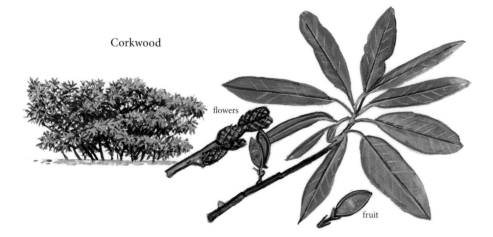

Corkwood

flowers

fruit

LYTHRACEAE: LOOSESTRIFE FAMILY

The loosestrife family includes about 31 genera and 625–650 species of herbs, trees, and shrubs, distributed mostly in tropical regions. The non-native Crapemyrtle is the only tree-sized member of the family that occurs in North America. Woody members of the family are recognized by the combination of opposite or nearly opposite leaves, flaky bark, flowers with crinkly petals and 10 or more stamens of unequal length, and capsular fruit.

CRAPEMYRTLE *Lagerstroemia indica* L.

QUICK ID The combination of rounded to elliptic sub-opposite to alternate leaves, showy flowers, and flaking bark is diagnostic.

Deciduous shrub or small tree to 7 m tall, 15 cm diam. Erect, single trunk or multiple; crown ascending and vase-shaped, rounded, or spreading. **BARK** Orange-brown, flaking and curling to reveal smooth inner bark. **LEAF** Alternate and sub-opposite on the same branch, simple, elliptic, obovate, ovate, or nearly rounded; margins entire. Upper surface lustrous green, usually hairless; lower surface paler, hairless or with minute hairs along the veins. Blade 2–6 cm long, 1–4 cm broad; petiole lacking or to about 2 mm long. **FLOWER** Averages about 3 cm diam., bisexual; petals usually 6, with crinkly margins, varying white, pink, purple, reddish, or lavender; borne in an elongated panicle, 20–30 cm long and broad. Summer. **FRUIT** Rounded or ellipsoid brown capsule, 10–12 mm long; matures late summer to autumn.

HABITAT/RANGE Introduced. Naturalized from plantings throughout the Southeast, rarely invading natural areas; Md. and Ind. south to Fla., west to e. Tex.

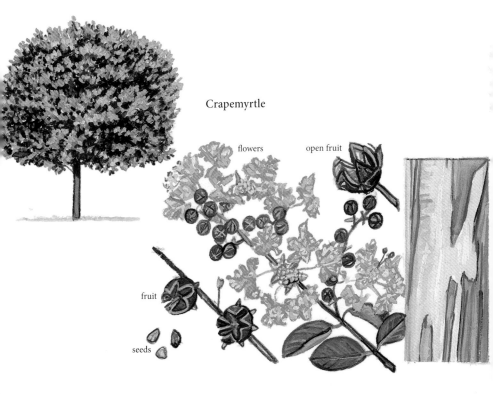

Crapemyrtle

flowers

open fruit

fruit

seeds

MAGNOLIACEAE: MAGNOLIA FAMILY

The magnolia family comprises 2 genera and about 225 species of trees and large shrubs, distributed mostly in the temperate regions of the Northern and Southern hemispheres; 1 species of *Liriodendron* and 8 species of *Magnolia* are native to e. North America. At least 3 non-native magnolias that are often used in gardening are naturalized rarely in North America.

Two of the species treated here are evergreen; the other 10 are deciduous. Members of this family are recognized by their distinctive leaves and flowers. **LEAF** Alternate, simple, with entire or lobed leaf margins (sometimes with an eared base); large, conspicuous stipules completely encircle the twig but are open on the side opposite the leaf stalk. **FLOWER** In most species large, solitary, bisexual, with fleshy, usually undifferentiated petals and sepals (collectively referred to here as tepals), an elongated central axis (receptacle), and numerous stamens and pistils. The flowers are usually diurnal, opening the 1st day, closing during the evening, and opening again the 2nd day, and are typically pollinated by beetles. They are also protogynous, meaning that the stigmas are receptive to pollen only prior to maturation of the anthers, which promotes out-crossing by reducing the opportunity for self-fertilization.

This is an ancient family dating at least to the late Cretaceous, 135–100 million years ago. The genus *Michelia*, a small group of evergreen trees and shrubs native to tropical Asia and formerly considered to represent a distinct genus, is now included within *Magnolia*.

TULIPTREE *Liriodendron tulipifera* L.
A.K.A. TULIP POPLAR, YELLOW POPLAR

QUICK ID The squarish, mostly 4-lobed leaves and clusters of upright samaras are diagnostic.

Deciduous large, sometimes massive tree, to 45 m tall, 3 m diam., commonly about half this size. Erect, single straight trunk; crown pyramidal and low-branching on open-grown trees, branching much higher on old trees. **BARK** Smooth or finely furrowed and whitish gray when young, becoming deeply and coarsely furrowed and darker gray at maturity. **TWIG** Stout, hairless at maturity, reddish brown or purplish, aromatic when crushed; pith whitish, chambered, solid between green partitions; terminal bud laterally flattened, rounded at the apex. **LEAF** Alternate, simple, somewhat thickened and firm, deeply and broadly notched at the tip into 2 lateral lobes, rounded or lobed at the base, sometimes more or less squarish in outline; margins entire. Upper surface lustrous, dark green or yellowish green; lower surface paler, often with a whitish bloom. Turns clear yellow in autumn. Blade 7–23 cm long, 12–20 cm broad; petiole 5–12 cm long, subtended by 2 conspicuous stipules that soon fall following leaf expansion. **FLOWER** About 5–7 cm diam., cup-shaped, tuliplike; tepals 6, inner 3 yellow, blotched with orange, outer 3 greenish. Spring. **FRUIT** Conelike aggregate, 4.5–8.5 cm long, of 2-seeded samaras, the samaras overlapping along a central axis, falling individually in autumn to leave the spindle-like axis visible at the tips of branches well into winter.

TULIPTREE

HABITAT/RANGE Native. Rich moist woods, slopes, mountain coves, 0–1,500 m; nearly throughout the East, Vt. to s. Mich., south to c. Fla., west to La.

SIMILAR SPECIES The only other tree with similar, distinctive leaves is Chinese Tuliptree (*L. chinense* [Hemsl.] Sarg.), which is occasionally cultivated but not known to naturalize in North America.

Notes: Tuliptree is a fast-growing species that can potentially reach 300 years old. It has wide commercial value in construction and furniture making and is used as a softwood replacement. Large, old-growth examples, like those at the Joyce Kilmer Memorial Forest in N.C., are particularly impressive.

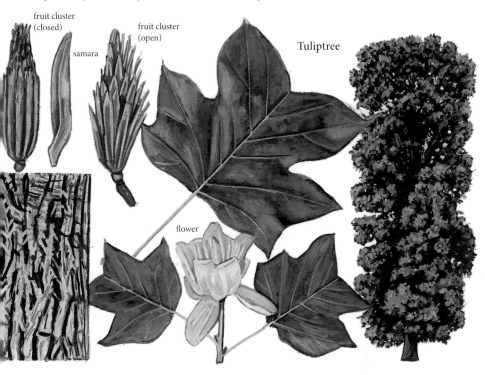

fruit cluster (closed)

samara

fruit cluster (open)

Tuliptree

flower

■ *MAGNOLIA*: MAGNOLIAS

Eight magnolias are native to North America north of Mexico, from Ont. and Maine south to s. Fla. and west to e. Tex.; 3 Asian species are naturalized.

Deciduous or evergreen trees or shrubs to at least 30 m tall. Erect or leaning, single trunk or multiple. **BARK** Usually smooth, grayish, becoming ridged, furrowed, and brownish in some species. **TWIG** Usually stout, buds terminal, subtended by an enlarged deciduous stipule, the base of which completely encircles the stem and remains evident even after the stipule has fallen. **LEAF** Alternate (on large-leaved species sometimes clustered below the flower and appearing whorled from a distance), simple, base tapering, rounded, or eared; margins entire, undulate in some species. Upper surface dark green or paler, lustrous or dull; lower surface greenish, yellow-green, brownish orange, grayish white, or chalky white. Blade to 100 cm long, to 30 cm broad; petiole 2–8 cm long. **FLOWER** Usually large and showy, solitary, bisexual, petals and sepals undifferentiated (tepals), 6–18 in 3 or more whorls, sometimes the outermost sufficiently distinct to appear as sepals; stamens and pistils numerous, spirally arranged along an erect axis (receptacle), stamens below, pistils above; stigmas maturing prior to the anthers (protogynous). **FRUIT** Numerous follicles borne embedded and congested in a conelike structure (follicetum); follicetum rounded or cylindric; individual follicles splitting along 1 side at maturity to reveal red-, pink-, or orange-coated seeds that sometimes dangle on a threadlike attachment.

Magnolias are usually distinguished by their fleshy flowers and distinctive leaves. The leaves of a few species may be confused with species of the closely related families Lauraceae and Annonaceae.

CUCUMBER-TREE *Magnolia acuminata* (L.) L.

QUICKID The combination of furrowed, scaly brown bark, obovate or elliptical leaves, comparatively large creamy or pale yellow flowers, and distinctive fruit is diagnostic.

Deciduous tree to 30 m tall, 1 m diam. Erect, single trunk; crown broad, vertically elongated, pyramidal, and low-branching on young or open-grown trees, usually shorter and high-branching on older or forest-grown trees. **BARK** Brownish, furrowed, somewhat scaly, becoming darker brown with age. **TWIG** Stout, reddish brown, hairless or silvery hairy; terminal bud narrowly ellipsoid, silvery hairy, 1–2 cm long. **LEAF** Alternate, simple, obovate, broadly elliptical, or ovate; base rounded or wedge-shaped, tip long- or short-pointed; margins entire, often undulate. Upper surface yellow-green or dark green, hairless; lower surface paler, hairless or distinctly hairy. Turns dingy yellow in autumn. Blade 10–30 cm long, 4–15 cm broad; petiole 2–4 cm long, subtended by conspicuous stipules 3–4 cm long. **FLOWER** 6–9 cm diam.; tepals usually 9, innermost erect, creamy white or pale yellowish, outermost strongly reflexed, greenish. Spring. **FRUIT** Conelike aggregate of follicles; oblong, cucumber-like in outline, 2–7 cm long, to about 3 cm diam.; individual follicles split at maturity to reveal red or orange-red seeds; matures late summer to early autumn.

HABITAT/RANGE Native. Deep, rich soils on moist slopes, deciduous woodlands, along riverbanks, 0–1,500 m. Widespread in the East, from N.Y., Ohio, and s. Ind. south to nw. Fla. and west to La. and Ark.

SIMILAR SPECIES Fraser Magnolia and Pyramid Magnolia have similar-sized leaves but lack Umbrella Magnolia's furrowed brownish bark.

Notes: Several varieties of this species have been described, underscoring its morphological variability. The most common is var. *subcordata* (Spach) Dandy, ostensibly distinguished by its consistently yellowish flowers and abruptly pointed leaf tip.

FRASER MAGNOLIA *Magnolia fraseri* Walt.
A.K.A. MOUNTAIN MAGNOLIA

QUICKID Identified by the combination of grayish trunk, leaves eared at the base and grayish but not silvery or chalky white beneath, and twigs and buds hairless.

Deciduous tree to about 25 m tall, 30–45 cm diam. Erect, single trunk, or often multiple trunks; crown spreading, irregular, often high-branching. **BARK** Gray, grayish brown, or slightly greenish brown, smooth or slightly roughened and reminiscent of concrete, lacking furrows. **TWIG** Stout or slender, hairless, reddish brown or greenish brown, becoming gray with age; bud 3–5 cm long, torpedo-shaped, purple or greenish purple, tapering to a blunt point. **LEAF** Produced in whorl-like clusters near the branch tip, simple, thin, obovate or nearly spatulate, usually broadest near or slightly above the middle, base eared, margins entire. Upper surface green, hairless; lower surface paler, often with a whitish bloom; entire leaf turns coppery brown at maturity. Blade 20–30 cm long, 8–20 cm broad; petiole 3–8 cm long. **FLOWER** 16–22 cm diam., fragrant, showy; tepals usually 9, innermost creamy white, outermost greenish. Late spring. **FRUIT** Conelike aggregate of follicles; oblong, cucumber-like in outline, 6–13 cm long, to about 5 cm diam., green at first, turning pinkish; individual follicles split at maturity to reveal bright red seeds 7–10 mm long; matures late summer to early autumn.

CUCUMBER-TREE

FRASER MAGNOLIA

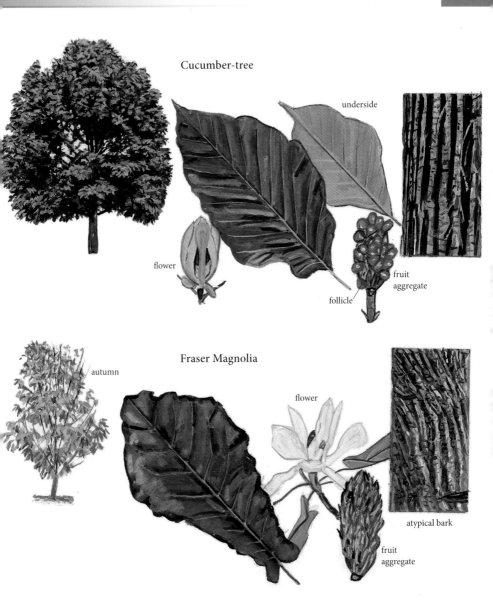

Cucumber-tree

underside

flower

follicle

fruit aggregate

Fraser Magnolia

autumn

flower

atypical bark

fruit aggregate

HABITAT/RANGE Native. Rich woods, cove forests, 300–1,520 m; confined mostly to the s. Appalachians, Va. and W. Va. south to Ky., Tenn., and n. Ga.

SIMILAR SPECIES Very similar to Pyramid Magnolia, which is sometimes treated as a variety; the two are morphologically very similar, most easily distinguished by range and habitat. The leaves of Fraser Magnolia are usually longer than 25 cm and the fruiting cones longer than 6 cm; those of Pyramid Magnolia are usually shorter than 25 cm and 6 cm, respectively.

PYRAMID MAGNOLIA *Magnolia pyramidata* W. Bartram

QUICK ID The eared leaves that are whitish beneath and borne in whorl-like clusters are diagnostic.

Deciduous tree, 10–17 m tall, to about 35 cm diam., usually smaller. Erect, single trunk, often leaning; crown more or less dense, pyramidal. **BARK** Gray or whitish gray, smooth or minutely roughened. **TWIG** Stout, hairless. **LEAF** Usually produced in whorl-like clusters near ends of branches; simple, obovate or nearly spatulate, widest toward the tip and tapering to an eared base (base of young leaves may lack ears); margins entire. Upper surface yellow-green or dull green; lower surface hairless, often with a whitish bloom. Blade 18–25 cm long, 7–14 cm broad; petiole 2–7 cm long, subtended by large stipules to about 7 cm long. **FLOWER** 12–18 cm diam., fragrant, showy; tepals 9, creamy white or yellowish white. Late spring. **FRUIT** Conelike aggregate of follicles; oblong or narrowly ellipsoid in outline, 4–9 cm long, about 3 cm diam., turning pinkish with age; individual follicles split at maturity to reveal bright red seeds 7–8 mm long; matures late summer to early autumn.

HABITAT/RANGE Native. Moist to dryish bluffs, slopes, and woodlands, sometimes along small streams at the bottom of ravines, 0–120 m; largely restricted to the coastal plains, rarely the outer Piedmont, S.C. south to n. Fla., west to e. Tex., more common in the central part of this distribution.

SIMILAR SPECIES The leaves of Ashe's Magnolia are chalky white beneath, and those of Bigleaf Magnolia are typically well over 25 cm long. Fraser Magnolia is similar, but does not overlap in range with Pyramid Magnolia.

ASHE'S MAGNOLIA *Magnolia ashei* Weath.

QUICK ID Easily distinguished by the combination of large leaves that are chalky white beneath and its restricted range.

Deciduous small tree or shrub, usually not exceeding 6–9 m tall and about 11 cm diam. Erect, usually single trunk, sometimes with several trunks; crown irregular, often branching low to the ground, the branches stout, often contorted. **BARK** Smooth, gray. **TWIG** Silky-hairy; bud large, silky-hairy. **LEAF** Often borne in a crowded whorl-like arrangement at the tip of the branch; simple, obovate, conspicuously widest toward the tip, base conspicuously eared; margins entire, usually undulate. Upper surface dull green, hairless; lower surface silvery or chalky white, hairy. Blade 20–60 cm long, 10–30 cm broad; petiole 2–8 cm long. **FLOWER** 25–40 cm diam., fragrant, usually borne singly near the end of the branch; tepals usually 9, creamy white, innermost often blotched purple near the base. Late spring. **FRUIT** Conelike aggregate of follicles; cylindric, 4–5 cm long, about 3 cm diam., turning rosy red with age; individual follicles splitting at maturity to reveal red or orange-red seeds 8–10 mm long; matures late summer.

HABITAT/RANGE Native. Moist, rich slopes in shady woodlands, 0–50 m; endemic to the Fla. panhandle; widely cultivated beyond this region.

SIMILAR SPECIES The similar Bigleaf Magnolia does not overlap with Ashe's Magnolia in range, and Bigleaf's conelike fruit is more rounded than cylindric.

PYRAMID MAGNOLIA

ASHE'S MAGNOLIA

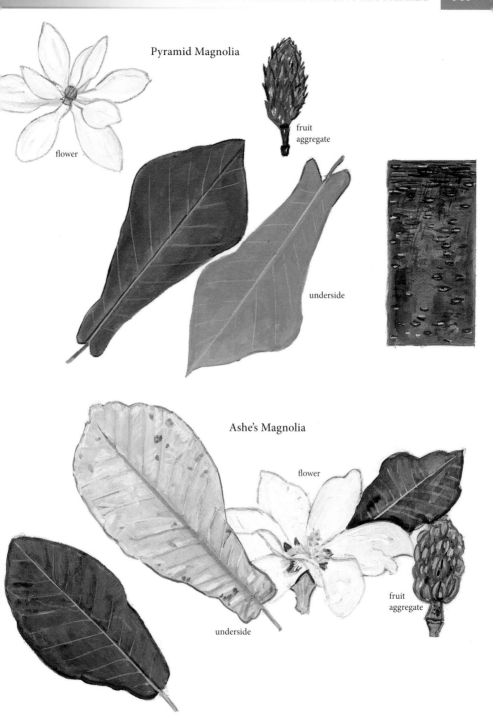

Pyramid Magnolia

flower

fruit aggregate

underside

Ashe's Magnolia

flower

underside

fruit aggregate

BIGLEAF MAGNOLIA *Magnolia macrophylla* Michx.

QUICK ID Easily recognized by the very large, eared leaves that are chalky white beneath, huge flowers, and rounded, conelike fruit.

Deciduous tree to about 18 m tall and 50 cm diam. Erect, single trunk, rarely leaning; crown pyramidal or rounded, with spreading branches. **BARK** Smooth or minutely bumpy with inconspicuous plates, pale gray or yellowish brown. **TWIG** Stout, grayish, silky-hairy. **LEAF** Borne in whorl-like clusters near the branch tips; simple, obovate to more or less broadly elliptic, usually conspicuously widest above the middle; margins entire, undulate. Upper surface dark green, hairless; lower surface chalky white, hairy. Blade 20–100 cm long, 15–30 cm broad; petiole 2–8 cm long. **FLOWER** 35–50 cm diam., fragrant, showy; tepals 9, inner 6 creamy white, often with a purple blotch at the base, outer 3 greenish; stamens numerous, borne at the base of a central axis and subtending numerous stigmas. Spring. **FRUIT** Conelike aggregate of follicles, round or slightly egg-shaped, 5–8 cm long, equally broad, turning reddish with age; individual follicles split at maturity to reveal orange-red seeds 10–12 mm long; matures late summer.

HABITAT/RANGE Native. Moist, rich woods and slopes, 150–300 m; Piedmont, w. N.C. and e. Ky. south to s. Ga. and s. Ala., west to La.; cultivated for ornament outside of its natural range.

SIMILAR SPECIES The similar Ashe's Magnolia does not overlap with Bigleaf Magnolia in range, and its conelike fruit is cylindric rather than round.

BIGLEAF MAGNOLIA

UMBRELLA MAGNOLIA *Magnolia tripetala* (L.) L.
A.K.A. UMBRELLA-TREE

QUICK ID A magnolia easily recognized by the large leaf with a tapering base.

Deciduous tree or very large shrub to about 15 m tall, 30–45 cm diam. Erect or ascending, sometimes with a single trunk, more often with several trunks, or branching near the base. Crown with numerous stout, contorted branches that often turn upward near the tip; upper branches usually borne at right angles to the stem. **BARK** Smooth, light gray. **TWIG** Stout, brittle, green at first, becoming light brown. Bud 3–4 cm long, terminal, pointed or blunt at the tip, purplish, hairless, sometimes with a whitish bloom. **LEAF** Often crowded near the branch tip and appearing whorled; simple, obovate, oblong, or oblanceolate, usually widest toward the tip, tapering to an elongated base, margins entire. Upper surface dark green, hairless; lower surface paler, densely hairy, especially on the veins. Blade 25–60 cm long, 10–30 cm broad; petiole 2–4 cm long, subtended by a large, conspicuous stipule 4–10 cm long. **FLOWER** 5–11 cm diam., with a rank aroma, tepals 9–11, the outer 3 smaller, greenish, reflexed, sepal-like, the inner creamy white, more or less spreading; stamens about 100, pistils about 55, borne along a cylindric axis. Late spring. **FRUIT** Conelike aggregate of follicles, slender, oblong, 8–12 cm long, to about 4 cm broad; individual follicles with a pink or reddish covering; matures late summer.

HABITAT/RANGE Native. Rich woods, ravine slopes, margins of mountain streams, typically upland, 0–1,065 m; s. Pa. and Ohio south to nw. Fla., west to e. La. and e. Miss., disjunct to Ark.

SIMILAR SPECIES In Bigleaf Magnolia the leaf is of a similar size but has an eared base and chalky lower surface.

UMBRELLA MAGNOLIA

Bigleaf Magnolia

follicle

fruit aggregate

flower

underside

Umbrella Magnolia

fruit aggregate

follicle

flower

SOUTHERN MAGNOLIA *Magnolia grandiflora* L.
A.K.A. BULLBAY MAGNOLIA

QUICK ID Easily recognized by the combination of thick, lustrous, dark green leaves, dark green pyramidal crown, and large creamy-white flowers.

Evergreen tree, to 37 m tall, 60–120 cm diam. Erect, single trunk; crown pyramidal, dense, with a lustrous appearance. Branches ascending or spreading, produced low on the trunk and drooping to ground level in open-grown trees. **BARK** Dark gray or bluish gray, smooth at first, becoming scaly, roughened, and splitting into irregular furrows and plates at maturity. **TWIG** Stout, gray, with reddish or whitish hairs. **LEAF** Alternate, simple, thick, leathery, very stiff; typically elliptical, sometimes wider toward the tip; margins entire, often slightly rolled under. Upper surface dark, lustrous green, hairless; lower surface paler green, sometimes hairless, often densely felty-hairy with reddish or orangish hairs. Blade 10–30 cm long, 6–10 cm broad; petiole 2–5 cm long, rusty-hairy. **FLOWER** Typically 15–25 cm diam., tepals 6–15, thick, fleshy, creamy white, forming an urnlike shape prior to opening fully. Late spring to summer. **FRUIT** Conelike aggregate of follicles, ellipsoid or oblong, 5–10 cm long, becoming pinkish with age; seeds with a bright red covering; matures midsummer to late summer.

HABITAT/RANGE Native. Upland woods, inland and coastal dunes, moist slopes, ravines, 0–120 m; confined chiefly to the southeastern coastal plains, established from plantings but not technically native to the lower Piedmont, N.C. south to Fla., west to e. Tex. and s. Ark.

SIMILAR SPECIES Sweetbay is also evergreen, but its leaves are smaller, paler green above, and silvery white beneath.

Notes: Southern Magnolia has become an important landscape plant; more than 100 cultivars are available in the garden trade. Plants established in deciduous woodlands in the Piedmont have become problematic, potentially shading the forest floor and reducing available light for wildflowers in early spring.

SWEETBAY *Magnolia virginiana* L.

QUICK ID Recognized by the combination of smooth grayish-white bark, bicolored leaves, fleshy creamy-white flowers, conelike fruit, and typically wetland habitat.

Evergreen tree or shrub, sometimes partially or completely deciduous, primarily in the northern parts of the range, 10–30 m tall, to about 1 m diam. Erect, single trunk or multiple, often suckering from the base and forming a clump of erect or ascending trunks; crown pyramidal, lower branches mostly laterally spreading, upper branches often ascending. **BARK** Pale grayish to grayish white, smooth when young, becoming slightly roughened and darker with age. **TWIG** Silvery silky-hairy; terminal buds to about 2 cm long, silky-hairy, lustrous. **LEAF** Alternate, simple, leathery; narrowly long-elliptic, margins entire. Upper surface dull green, silky-hairy when first emerging, hairless at maturity; lower surface silvery gray, silky-hairy. Blade 6–15 cm long, 2–6 cm broad; petiole to about 2 cm long, silky-hairy. **FLOWER** 4–8 cm diam., smaller than those of other native magnolias, tepals 6–15, the outer 3 smaller and reflexed; stamens 60–90, pistils 20–40. Spring. **FRUIT** Conelike aggregate of follicles, more or less rounded or egg-shaped, 2–5 cm long; seeds with a bright red covering; matures late summer to autumn.

HABITAT/RANGE Native. Swamps, low woods, bays, margins of wet savannas and flatwoods,

SOUTHERN MAGNOLIA

SWEETBAY

Southern Magnolia

underside

flower

follicle

fruit aggregate

Sweetbay

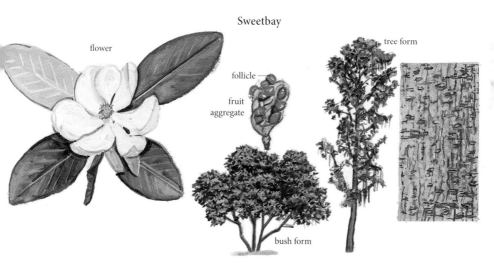

flower

follicle

fruit aggregate

tree form

bush form

0–540 m; chiefly southeastern coastal plains and Piedmont, ranging from coastal Mass. and N.Y. (where rare) south to s. Fla., west from S.C. to s. Ark. and e. Tex.

SIMILAR SPECIES The bays (*Persea*, Lauraceae) have similar-shaped leaves, but Sweetbay is easily distinguished by the silvery-gray lower leaf surface, which imparts a 2-toned appearance to the crown, especially in a breeze.

STAR MAGNOLIA *Magnolia stellata*
(Siebold & Zucc.) Maxim.

Deciduous shrub or small tree. **LEAF** Obovate or elliptic, tapering toward the base, dull, dark green above, paler and hairy beneath; blade 4–10 cm long. **FLOWER** About 8 cm diam., fragrant; tepals 12–18, white, sometimes suffused with pink, narrow, spreading, becoming reflexed. **HABITAT/RANGE** Introduced from Japan; widely planted in North America.

KOBUS MAGNOLIA *Magnolia kobus*
DC.

Deciduous tree to 10 m tall, often shrubby. **LEAF** Broadly obovate, abruptly pointed at the tip, tapering toward base; blade 15–25 cm long. **FLOWER** About 10 cm diam., fragrant; petals 6, narrow, white, sometimes faintly tinged purple or pink; sepals 3, smaller than the petals. **HABITAT/RANGE** Introduced from Japan; cultivated in North America.

SAUCER MAGNOLIA *Magnolia ×*
soulangeana Soul.-Bod.

Deciduous shrub or very small tree. **LEAF** Obovate, dark green above, paler and hairy beneath; blade 13–20 cm long. **FLOWER** 10–15 cm diam., bell-shaped; tepals purple, lavender, or white. *Notes:* A hybrid of *M. denudata* Desr. (China) and *M. liliiflora* Desr. (Japan).

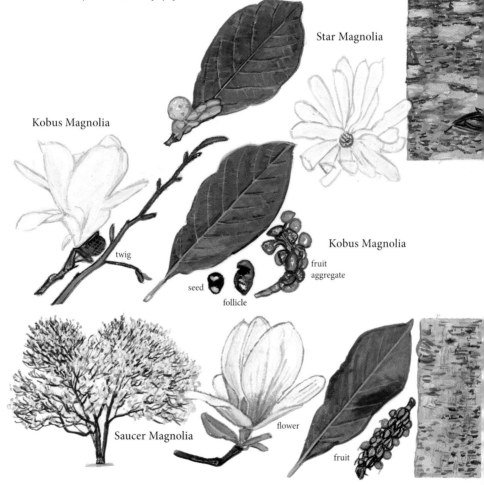

Star Magnolia

Kobus Magnolia

Kobus Magnolia

twig

seed

follicle

fruit
aggregate

Saucer Magnolia

flower

fruit

MALPIGHIACEAE: MALPIGHIA FAMILY

This is a mostly tropical family of about 66 genera and approximately 1,200 species of trees, shrubs, woody vines, and a few herbs. Two tree-size species occur in North America, 1 native and 1 introduced.

LONG KEY LOCUSTBERRY *Byrsonima lucida* (Mill.) DC.

QUICK ID The combination of multicolored flowers with conspicuous oil glands, opposite leaves, jointed twigs, and clasping petioles is diagnostic.

Evergreen large shrub or small shrubby tree to about 6 m tall. Erect or leaning, usually with multiple trunks or branches arising from near the base; crown of tree-size plants open, with spreading branches. **BARK** Smooth, light brown. **TWIG** Jointed. **LEAF** Opposite, simple, leathery, oblanceolate or spatulate; tip acuminate or rounded. Upper

LONG KEY LOCUSTBERRY

surface lustrous, dark green; lower surface paler. Blade 2–6 cm long, 0.5–2 cm broad; petiole short, thick, clasping the stem. **FLOWER** Bisexual, petals 5, white at first, becoming pink, then crimson at maturity, with all 3 colors usually represented on a single plant; sepals 5, each with a conspicuous pair of oil glands that are green at first but become yellow; stamens 10. Mainly spring but potentially any time of year. **FRUIT** Reddish-brown drupe, 5–8 mm diam. Year-round.

HABITAT/RANGE Native. Pine rocklands, hammocks; extreme s. Fla. including Fla. Keys.

BARBADOS CHERRY *Malpighia emarginata* Sessé & Moc. ex DC.

Evergreen shrub or small tree. **LEAF** Opposite, elliptic, with a rounded or short-pointed tip, margins often wavy, to about 7 cm long and 4 cm broad, petiole short. **FLOWER** Bisexual, reddish pink, about 12 mm diam., petals 5, sepals 5, with oil glands similar to those of Long Key Locustberry (*Byrsonima lucida*). **FRUIT** Lustrous, dark to bright red drupe. **HABITAT/RANGE** Introduced from tropical America; naturalized in s. Fla. and s. Tex.

flowers

Barbados Cherry

fruit section

seeds

fruit

Long Key Locustberry

flower

MALVACEAE: MALLOW FAMILY

The mallow (or hibiscus) family consists of about 243 genera and 4,225 species of herbs, shrubs, and trees distributed mostly in tropical regions; less common in temperate regions. About 250 native and naturalized species occur in North America, mostly herbs; 14 small to large trees occur in the East, 2 native. Recent molecular genetic studies have revealed this family to be broader than once construed, and it now includes the chocolate (Sterculiaceae), kapok (Bombacaceae), and linden or basswood (Tiliaceae) families.

Several morphological features are characteristic of the family. Mucilage canals are present in soft tissue, resulting in a viscous sap when stems are cut or broken. Hairs are usually branched, often in a treelike pattern (dendritic), sometimes starlike (stellate), or they may form a flattened, ragged-edged disk attached by a central stalk (peltate). Recognition of species is aided by the combination of palmate leaves, branched hairs, and stamens fused by their filaments. **LEAF** Usually alternate, simple, often palmately veined or lobed, the major veins often ending at the tip of a marginal tooth. **FLOWER** Usually bisexual, sometimes unisexual, radially symmetric, usually with 5 sepals, 5 petals, and 5 to many stamens, the filaments usually fused at the base, sometimes forming a tube surrounding the superior ovary, which has 2 to many chambers. Beneath the flower there is often a whorl of several bracts called an epicalyx, which resembles a 2nd calyx. **FRUIT** Variable; most eastern species produce capsules or follicles.

The family is economically important, contributing chocolate, okra, durian fruit, balsa wood and other valuable timber, cotton and kapok, and many ornamentals including *Hibiscus* species, which are often planted in tropical and subtropical regions.

UPLAND COTTON *Gossypium hirsutum* L.
A.K.A. WILD COTTON

QUICK ID Distinguished by the combination of creamy yellowish-white flowers, leaves with 3–5 lobes, and fruit a 3-valved capsule.

Evergreen shrub or small tree to about 4 m tall, to about 6 cm diam. Vase-shaped or shrubby with 1 or more trunks; crown spreading, usually broader than tall. **TWIG** Hairy. **LEAF** Opposite, simple, usually with 3, occasionally 5, conspicuous lobes; base usually heart-shaped, rarely rounded; tips of lobes acute; margins not toothed. Upper surface medium green, the veins palmate, conspicuous; lower surface paler, conspicuously hairy with branched hairs. Blade 5–15 cm long, 5–15 cm broad; petiole 6–11 cm long, hairy. **FLOWER** Bisexual, petals 5, 3–6 cm long, whitish or yellow, aging purplish or pinkish, usually with a reddish or purplish spot inside near the base; stamens numerous, fused at the base into a staminal column that surrounds the style. Year-round. **FRUIT** Three-valved triangular, ellipsoid, or ovoid capsule, 2–3 cm long; seeds have a dense covering of whitish cottony hairs that aid dispersal. Year-round.

HABITAT/RANGE Native. Subtropical coastal hammocks, dunes, disturbed sites; native to s. Fla., especially Fla. Keys, cultivated for commercial production in the Southeast and occasionally established. Once more common and widespread in s. Fla., but now reduced and considered endangered

UPLAND COTTON

boll

flower

seed

flower

unripe cotton boll

Upland Cotton

flowers

flower

seeds

fruit

Whiteflower Kurrajong

owing to intentional efforts to eradicate various diseases associated with commercial cotton cultivars.

Notes: *Gossypium* is a genus of 20–40 species; 2 are native to the U.S., 1 to the East. Species are similar in many respects to species of introduced *Hibiscus*, *Thespesia*, and *Talipariti*. Upland Cotton is closely related to commercially grown cotton, most of which in the U.S. has been developed from this native species, but the hairs of its seed coat remain rigid when dried and cannot be spun.

WHITEFLOWER KURRAJONG
Brachychiton populneum (Schott. & Endl.) R. Br.

Evergreen tree 6–20 m tall. **LEAF** Alternate, simple, lobed, tips of lobes pointed, base rounded; blade 2–6 cm long. **FLOWER** Unisexual, showy, calyx bell-shaped, 1–2 cm long. **FRUIT** Elliptic, flattened brown follicle, 4–6 cm long, with yellow seeds. **HABITAT/RANGE** Introduced from Australia; reportedly naturalized in se. La., in several of the so-called Florida parishes.

■ *HIBISCUS*: HIBISCUSES

A genus of 200–600 species of tropical and subtropical regions, very popular as garden plants and widely planted. The actual number of species in this genus remains unclear, as taxonomists continue to assess molecular data and revise phylogenetic relationships. Shrubs, trees, or herbs. **LEAF** Alternate, simple, palmately lobed and veined, or unlobed, with 3 or more primary veins. **FLOWER** Bisexual, usually solitary in the leaf axils, occasionally clustered; corolla usually large, showy, variously colored, often with a dark base inside; petals 5; stamens many, fused into a staminal tube surrounding the style; stigmas 5. **FRUIT** Five-valved cylindric or rounded capsule; seeds kidney-shaped, often hairy or warty.

ROSE-OF-CHINA *Hibiscus rosa-sinensis* L.
A.K.A. CHINESE HIBISCUS, SHOEBLACK PLANT

Popular ornamental; characterized by unlobed leaves and pendent flowers with a hairless stalk, entire or slightly incised petals, and the stamen column longer than the corolla. **HABITAT/RANGE** Introduced from China; reported in s. Fla.

DIXIE ROSEMALLOW *Hibiscus mutabilis* L.
A.K.A. CONFEDERATE ROSE

QUICK ID Recognized by the large, low-branching, shrubby habit; showy, brightly colored flowers that vary from white to red; capsule fruit; and palmately veined leaves.

Deciduous, usually a large shrub, sometimes forming a small tree to 5 m tall. Usually with multiple stems arising at or near ground level. **LEAF** Alternate, simple, broadly ovate, with 5–7 lobes; base rounded or heart-shaped; tip acute or abruptly short-pointed; margins bluntly toothed. Upper surface medium or dark green or yellow-green, sparsely and minutely hairy, venation palmate with 7–11 primary veins; lower surface paler, densely hairy with branched, starlike hairs. Blade 10–15 cm long, 10–15 cm broad; petiole 5–20 cm long, subtended by lanceolate stipules 5–8 mm long. **FLOWER** Corolla white or reddish, becoming dark red; calyx densely hairy; petals 5, nearly circular, 4–5 cm broad; stamens numerous, fused into a column to about 3 cm long. Summer to autumn. **FRUIT**

Rounded, hairy yellowish capsule to about 2.5 cm diam.; matures autumn.

HABITAT/RANGE Introduced from China; widely planted in southern gardens, rarely naturalized.

SIMILAR SPECIES See Shrubby Althea and Rose-of-China.

SHRUBBY ALTHEA *Hibiscus syriacus* L.
A.K.A. ROSE-OF-SHARON

Shrub or small single-trunked tree to about 3 m tall. Popular ornamental that sometimes escapes cultivation. Its leaves have 3–5 veins and are wedge-shaped at the base. **HABITAT/RANGE** Introduced from Asia; widely cultivated throughout the East, reported as established in most eastern states.

SEA HIBISCUS *Talipariti tiliaceum* (L.) Fryxell **var. *tiliaceum***
A.K.A. MAHOE

QUICK ID Recognized by large circular leaves, a spreading habit, and showy flowers that progress to deep red by the end of the day.

Evergreen large shrub or small tree to about 6 m tall, 15 cm diam. Trunk short, crooked or contorted, low-branched; crown broad, spreading, rounded. **LEAF** Alternate, simple, more or less circular; base deeply heart-shaped; tip abruptly short-pointed to moderately long-pointed; margins entire or shallowly toothed. Upper surface dark lustrous green, lower surface whitish gray. Blade 10–30 cm long, 10–30 cm broad; petiole 5–12 cm long, stout. **FLOWER** Corolla 5–8 cm long, yellow with a red throat early in the day, becoming red by evening and dropping during the night. Year-round. **FRUIT** Five-valved capsule, 2 cm broad; seeds numerous, dark brown or black, 3–5 mm long. Year-round.

HABITAT/RANGE Introduced from tropical Asia; disturbed hammocks and roadsides, naturalized in s. Fla.

SIMILAR SPECIES The variety *T. tiliaceum* var. *pernambucense* (Arruda) Fryxell, also naturalized in s. Fla., is distinguished by completely yellow flowers that lack a red throat. See also Upland Cotton (*Gossypium hirsutum*) and Portia Tree (*Thespesia populnea*).

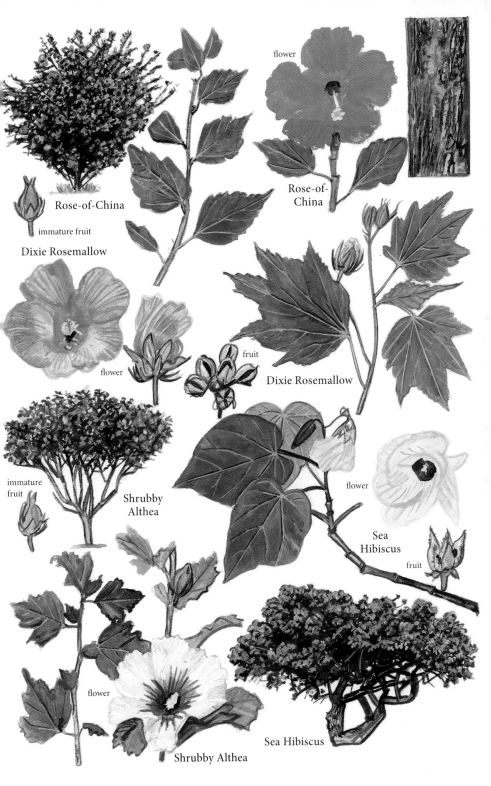

Rose-of-China

immature fruit

Dixie Rosemallow

flower

Rose-of-China

flower

Dixie Rosemallow

fruit

immature fruit

Shrubby Althea

flower

Sea Hibiscus

fruit

flower

Shrubby Althea

Sea Hibiscus

PORTIA TREE *Thespesia populnea* (L.)
Sol. ex Corrêa
A.K.A. SEASIDE MAHOE

QUICK ID Recognized by the combination of heart-shaped leaves with margins entire, creamy-yellow flowers with a red center, and leathery capsule.

Evergreen shrub or small bushy tree, 3–9 m tall. Erect, single trunk or multiple, often low-branching; crown spreading, rounded or vertically compressed. **BARK** Smooth, brown with grayish mottling. **LEAF** Alternate, simple, ovate, base heart-shaped, tip long-pointed, margins entire. Upper surface lustrous, dark green, palmately veined; lower surface paler. Blade 7–18 cm long, 5–12 cm broad; petiole 4–10 cm long. **FLOWER** Corolla yellow with a red or maroon base inside, bell-shaped, about 8 cm diam.; staminal column about 2.5 cm long. Year-round. **FRUIT** Flattened or rounded leathery capsule, yellow, becoming black; seeds brown, hairy. Year-round.

HABITAT/RANGE Introduced, native to Old and New World tropics; escaped from cultivation and established in disturbed sites, coastal hammocks, beaches in s. Fla., where it has become a troublesome weed and is listed as invasive.

SIMILAR SPECIES The leaves of Sea Hibiscus (*Talipariti tiliaceum*) are more or less circular, while those of Upland Cotton (*Gossypium hirsutum*) are usually 3-lobed.

Notes: Thespesia is a genus of about 17 species distributed in tropical parts of Africa, the Americas, Asia, and Australia.

▪ *TILIA*: LINDENS OR BASSWOODS

A genus of about 23 species distributed in temperate and subtropical regions, formerly treated within the monotypic family Tiliaceae. Some species in this genus are very similar and are distinguished by small differences in leaf size and hairiness.

Deciduous trees. **LEAF** Alternate, simple, 2-ranked, ovate; base usually asymmetric, rounded, cordate, or truncate; tip abruptly and sharply pointed; margins usually coarsely toothed. **FLOWER** Bisexual, radially symmetric, fragrant; sepals 5; petals 5, creamy white or yellowish; stamens many,

free or fused at base into several groups; pistil 1, ovary superior with 5 locules; usually insect-pollinated. **FRUIT** Dry, hard ovoid or rounded nut or capsule, usually dangling and subtended by a conspicuous bract.

AMERICAN BASSWOOD *Tilia americana* L.

QUICK ID Recognized by the combination of 2-ranked, alternate, heart-shaped leaves that are asymmetric at the base, the narrowly ridged and furrowed bark, and the leafy bract subtending the flowers and fruit.

Deciduous tree, 18–30 m tall, 40–150 cm diam. Erect, single straight trunk, often clear of branches for at least ½ its height; crown ovoid or rounded with numerous slender branches. **BARK** Smooth and dark gray on young trees, becoming finely to deeply furrowed with numerous narrow, vertically disposed ridges. **TWIG** Round in cross section, stout, reddish gray, hairy at first, becoming nearly hairless. **LEAF** Alternate, simple, 2-ranked, ovate; base heart-shaped, asymmetric; tip abruptly short-pointed; margins coarsely toothed. Upper surface dark yellowish green, hairless, veins conspicuous; lower surface paler, hairy or nearly hairless, hairs grayish, brownish, or tan. Blade 12–15 cm long, 7–10 cm broad; petiole 2.5–5 cm long, slender. **FLOWER** Yellowish white, sepals 5, petals 5; inflorescence a drooping cyme, the stalk attached for about ½ its length to a conspicuous leaflike bract. Late spring to summer. **FRUIT** Rounded, thick-shelled gray nut about 6 mm broad; matures autumn.

HABITAT/RANGE Native. Rich, deciduous woods, 50–1,500 m; widespread across the East, N.B. and Sask. south to c. Fla. and c. Tex.

AMERICAN BASSWOOD

Portia Tree

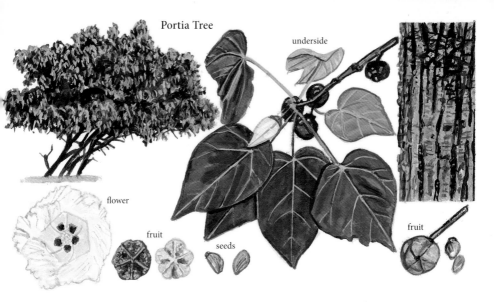

flower

fruit

seeds

underside

fruit

American Basswood

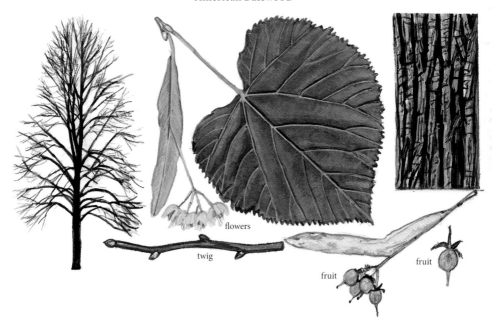

flowers

twig

fruit

fruit

SIMILAR SPECIES Red Mulberry and White Mulberry (*Morus rubra* and *M. alba*, Moraceae) have similarly shaped leaves but the petiole exudes milky sap when broken.

Notes: Some experts recognize 2 varieties of American Basswood, distinguishing var. *americana* by the lower surface of the leaf being nearly hairless or the hairs rusty or tawny, and var. *caroliniana* (Mill.) Castigl. by the lower surface of the leaf being densely white-hairy. However, there is significant intermediacy between these distinguishing characters, even on the same tree.

PENDENT SILVER LINDEN *Tilia petiolaris* DC.

Deciduous tree to about 21 m tall, with a vertically elongated crown and low branches. **LEAF** Ovate, 5–12 cm long; lower leaf surface hairy with branched hairs (distinguishing it from Littleleaf Linden); petiole longer than ½ the blade length (that and the pendent branches distinguish it from Silver Linden). **HABITAT/RANGE** Introduced from se. Europe and w. Asia; reported naturalized in Mass.

SILVER LINDEN *Tilia tomentosa* Moench

QUICK ID A linden recognized by the densely white-hairy lower surface of the leaf.

Deciduous tree 15–30 m tall. Erect, single trunk (sometimes multiple on cultivated plants), low branching; crown pyramidal, oval, or vertically elongated, branches upright. **BARK** Smooth, light gray, beechlike on young trees, becoming gray-brown and furrowed. **TWIG** Densely hairy. **LEAF** Alternate, simple, ovate or nearly circular; base heart-shaped or somewhat flattened, asymmetric; tip abruptly short-pointed; margins coarsely toothed. Upper surface lustrous, dark green; lower surface silvery-hairy. Blade 5–11 cm long, nearly as broad; petiole 2–3.5 cm long, densely hairy. **FLOWER** Yellowish white; inflorescence a pendent cyme, the stalk bearing a single conspicuous bract. Summer. **FRUIT** Ovoid nut 8–10 mm long, whitish-hairy, minutely warty, slightly 5-angled; matures autumn.

HABITAT/RANGE Introduced from se. Europe and w. Asia; cultivated, reportedly naturalized in Ont.

SIMILAR SPECIES Littleleaf Linden has tufts of orange or buff-colored hairs in the vein axils of the lower surface of the leaf.

LARGELEAF LINDEN *Tilia platyphyllos* Scop.

A.K.A. BIGLEAF LINDEN

QUICK ID A linden recognized by the combination of leaves 6–12 cm long, predominantly 3-flowered inflorescences, and 5-ribbed, hairy fruit 8–10 mm long.

Deciduous tree, potentially to about 40 m tall, usually not exceeding about 25 m where cultivated in North America. Erect, single trunk; crown oval, vertically elongated. **BARK** Brown, smooth at first, developing irregular ridges and furrows and flaking somewhat with age. **TWIG** Reddish brown, stout, with raised lenticels. **LEAF** Alternate, simple, ovate; base more or less heart-shaped; tip abruptly short-pointed; margins coarsely toothed. Upper surface dark green, hairy or nearly hairless; lower surface paler, usually hairy, especially on the veins, rarely nearly hairless. Blade 6–12 cm long, to about 10 cm broad; petiole 1.5–5 cm long, hairy. **FLOWER** Yellowish white; borne in predominantly 3-flowered pendent cymes. Summer. **FRUIT** Hairy, rounded or pear-shaped, 5-ribbed nut, 8–10 mm long; matures autumn.

HABITAT/RANGE Introduced from Europe; cultivated, rarely naturalized from Maine and N.B. to Ont., potentially south to Conn.

SIMILAR SPECIES The leaves of Silver Linden are similar in size but are whitish beneath, and the fruit is less hairy and not distinctly 5-ribbed.

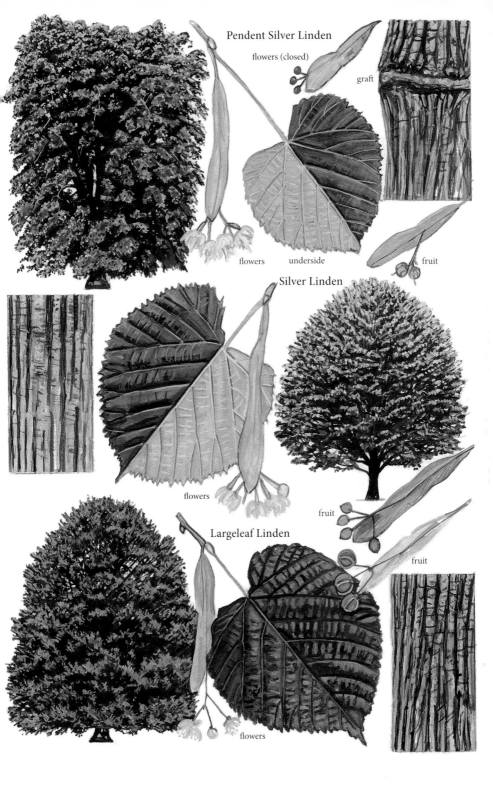

Pendent Silver Linden

flowers (closed)

graft

flowers

underside

fruit

Silver Linden

flowers

fruit

fruit

Largeleaf Linden

flowers

flowers

COMMON LINDEN *Tilia × europea* L.
A.K.A. EUROPEAN LINDEN

QUICK ID A linden distinguished by the upper surface of its toothed, broadly asymmetric leaf dull, dark green, and hairless, and flowers and fruit borne in a dangling cyme subtended by a leaflike bract.

Deciduous tree, 12–40 m tall, 1–2 m diam. Erect, single trunk; crown rounded or pyramidal, with several large, ascending branches. **BARK** Dull gray, becoming rough and fissured with age. **TWIG** Hairless; buds hairless. **LEAF** Alternate, simple, broadly ovate; base asymmetric, slightly heart-shaped or flattened; tip abruptly short-pointed; margins coarsely toothed. Upper surface dull, dark green, hairless; lower surface bright green, tufts of hairs in the vein axils, otherwise hairless. Blade 6–10 cm long, about as broad; petiole 3–5 cm long. **FLOWER** Produced in pendent cymes 7–8 cm long, the stalk with a conspicuous leaflike bract. Spring to early summer. **FRUIT** Rounded or ovoid nut, hairy, faintly ribbed; matures autumn.

HABITAT/RANGE Introduced from Europe; cultivated and rarely established from N.S. to Ont., south to Conn. and Ohio.

Notes: Common Linden is considered to be a hybrid between Littleleaf Linden and Largeleaf Linden.

LITTLELEAF LINDEN *Tilia cordata* Mill.

QUICK ID Recognized by the combination of small, nearly circular leaves and the distinctive bract subtending the flowering and fruiting cyme.

Deciduous tree, 10–18 m tall, 25–40 cm diam. Erect, single slender trunk, usually low-branching; crown pyramidal or conical. **BARK** Smooth, gray or pale brown on young trees, becoming dark gray or brown and broken into shallow platelets. **TWIG** Stout, smooth, reddish brown, with raised buff-colored lenticels. **LEAF** Alternate, simple, 2-ranked, broadly ovate or nearly circular; base heart-shaped, asymmetric; tip abruptly short-pointed; margins coarsely toothed. Upper surface lustrous green or yellow-green; lower surface bluish green or whitish green, with tufts of orange or buff-colored hairs in

the vein axils. Blade 4–7 cm long, 3–5 cm broad; petiole 2–4 cm long, slender, yellowish green. **FLOWER** White, about 2 cm diam., sepals 5, petals 5, stamens numerous, with bright yellow anthers; produced in an erect or pendent cyme, the stalk bearing a conspicuous leaflike bract. Summer. **FRUIT** Rounded nut, sometimes slightly ribbed, about 6 mm broad; matures autumn.

HABITAT/RANGE Introduced from Europe and w. Asia; cultivated and planted as a street tree in the Northeast, rarely and irregularly naturalized from s. Canada south to about Md.

SIMILAR SPECIES American Basswood has much larger leaves.

CHINESE PARASOLTREE *Firmiana simplex* (L.) W. Wight
A.K.A. VARNISH TREE

QUICK ID Easily distinguished by the large circular, deeply palmately lobed leaves with long, stout petioles.

Deciduous tree to about 20 m tall. Erect, single slender trunk; crown of branches mostly clustered at the top, umbrella-like. **BARK** Smooth, green or grayish green. **TWIG** Smooth, green. **LEAF** Alternate, simple, deeply palmately lobed, lobes usually 3 or 5, their tips abruptly short- and sharp-pointed; base deeply heart-shaped. Upper surface dark or bright green, hairless; lower surface paler, softly and densely hairy with branched hairs. Blade 10–30 cm long, equally broad; petiole 20–50 cm long, stout. **FLOWER** Unisexual, male and female flowers borne in various proportions in a compound paniculate inflorescence, some panicles mostly male, others mostly female, 15–60 cm long, to about 12 panicles per cluster; petals absent; sepals 5, 7–8 mm long; male flower with an erect, thick, columnlike filament topped with a hoodlike cluster of fused anthers; female flower with a stalked ovary of 5 pistils and 5 fused stigmas. Late spring to early summer. **FRUIT** Cluster of 5 follicles, all radiating from a single point and opening before maturity into distinct leaflike structures, each exposing up to 4 seeds that remain attached to the follicle wall; matures late summer to autumn.

HABITAT/RANGE Introduced from subtropical China; cultivated, established in the East from Md. south to n. Fla., west to Ark. and c. Tex.

Common Linden

flower

flowers

fruit

fruit

underside
flowers

Littleleaf Linden

fruit

Chinese Parasoltree

flowers

fruit

MELASTOMATACEAE: MELASTOME FAMILY

The melastome family is a moderately large collection of about 200 genera and 4,500 species distributed mostly in the tropics. The family is probably best known to plant lovers for an assorted collection of herbaceous wildflowers. A single woody species is native to North America.

TETRAZYGIA *Tetrazygia bicolor* (Mill.) Cogn.
A.K.A. FLORIDA CLOVER ASH

QUICK ID Distinct longitudinal leaf veins that are depressed above and prominent below distinguish this species.

Evergreen shrub or small tree, to about 10 m tall, 6–10 cm diam.; usually shrubby, occasionally becoming arborescent in hammocks. Erect, single trunk or multiple. **LEAF** Opposite, simple, lanceolate, often somewhat curved; margins entire. Upper surface lustrous, dark green with 2 conspicuously depressed longitudinal veins near the margins that are joined by numerous depressed lateral veins, giving the blade a quilted appearance; lower surface whitish-scaly with raised veins. Blade 7–12 cm long, 2–4 cm broad; petiole 1.5–2 cm long. **FLOWER** Bisexual; petals 5, white, falling readily if touched; stamens 10, yellow; pistil 1, often protruding while the flower is still in bud. Spring to summer. **FRUIT** Rounded black berry; matures late summer to autumn.

HABITAT/RANGE Native. Everglades pinelands and hammocks; s. Fla.

TETRAZYGIA

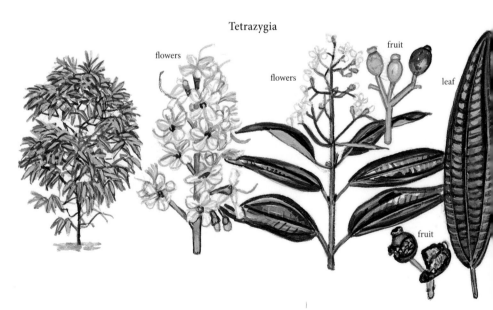

Tetrazygia

flowers

flowers

fruit

leaf

fruit

MELIACEAE: MAHOGANY FAMILY

The mahogany family includes about 50 genera and 550–615 species of trees and shrubs distributed mostly in lowlands of the New and Old World tropics; 4 genera and 4 species occur in North America, 1 native.

LEAF In most species alternate and pinnately or bipinnately compound. **FLOWER** Unisexual or bisexual; when unisexual, male and female flowers may be borne on the same (monoecious) or separate (dioecious) trees. Sometimes unisexual and bisexual flowers are intermixed on the same tree. Male flowers usually have residual, non-functional pistils; female flowers have residual, non-functional stamens. Stamens usually 4–10, occasionally more, the filaments fused and forming a tube around the pistil; ovary superior. **FRUIT** A capsule, drupe, or berry, the seeds dry and winged or with a fleshy coat.

Members of the family are important economically, chiefly as a source of high-quality timber, especially the mahoganies. Neem Tree (*Azadirachta indica* A. Juss) is important medicinally and as the source of insecticides, and Chinaberry-tree is an important ornamental. Most species are pollinated by bees or moths.

AUSTRALIAN REDCEDAR *Toona ciliata* M. Roem.

Deciduous tree to about 30 m tall, with a rounded, spreading crown. **LEAF** Alternate, pinnately compound; leaflets usually 9–15 pairs, each 9–13 cm long, 3–5 cm broad, with tip abruptly and conspicuously tapering to a narrow, elongated point. **FLOWER** Unisexual, 3.5–6 mm diam., fragrant; inflorescence about 55 cm long, pendent, the axis hairy. **FRUIT** Capsule, 1.5–2.5 cm long. **HABITAT/RANGE** Introduced from Asia and Australia; cultivated, reportedly naturalized in Md. *Notes:* *Toona* is a genus of about 5 species distributed in Asia and Australia.

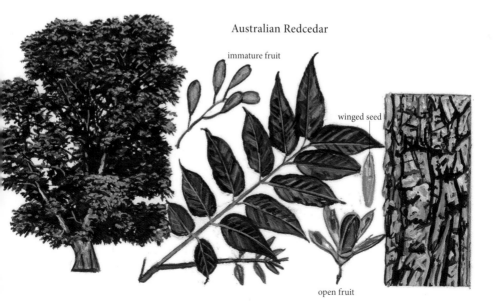

Australian Redcedar

immature fruit

winged seed

open fruit

WEST INDIAN MAHOGANY *Swietenia mahagoni* (L.) Jacq.

QUICK ID Recognized by the combination of fissured brownish bark, leaves with recurved leaflets, and the large fruit capsule.

Evergreen or semideciduous tree, 15–25 m tall, 30–140 cm diam. Erect, single trunk, low-branching; crown broad, rounded when open-grown, narrower in hammocks. **BARK** Brown, smooth at first, with small plates, becoming reddish brown and fissured at maturity. **TWIG** Reddish brown, slightly angled, becoming gray. **LEAF** Alternate, pinnately compound, terminal leaflet absent; blade 6–8 cm long, to about 9 cm broad; petiole 4–5 cm long, slender. Leaflets usually 4–8, rarely to 20, each 2–6 cm long, 1–2.5 cm broad, ovate or lanceolate, usually recurved; base usually asymmetric; tip abruptly sharp-pointed; margins entire. Upper surface dark green; lower surface yellowish green or brownish. **FLOWER** Unisexual, 5–7 mm diam.; sepals 5; petals 5, orange-yellow or greenish; male and female flowers produced on the same tree; sexes similar, male flowers with long non-functional pistils, female flowers with short pistils; stamens 10, filaments fused into a tube around the pistil. Year-round. **FRUIT** Large egg-shaped brown capsule, 6–13 cm long, 3–7 cm broad, splitting into 5 parts and releasing numerous more or less flat, winged seeds. Year-round.

HABITAT/RANGE Native. Subtropical hammocks, commonly cultivated in yards, roadsides, and highway medians; s. Fla.

SIMILAR SPECIES Gumbo Limbo (*Bursera simaruba*, Burseraceae) has somewhat similar leaves but is easily distinguished by its lustrous reddish-brown, often peeling bark.

Notes: Swietenia is a small genus of 3 species distributed in tropical w. Africa and tropical America.

WEST INDIAN MAHOGANY

AFRICAN MAHOGANY *Khaya senegalensis* (Desr.) A. Juss.
A.K.A. SENEGAL MAHOGANY

Evergreen or semideciduous tree to about 25 m tall, usually not exceeding about 12 m tall in the U.S. **LEAF** Alternate or opposite, pinnately compound, blade 25–60 cm long; leaflets 8–32, oblong, dark green above, greenish white below, margins entire but wavy. **FRUIT** Round, thick-walled capsule containing numerous thinly winged seeds. **HABITAT/RANGE** Introduced from tropical Africa; cultivated and rarely established in s. Fla. *Notes: Khaya* is a genus of about 6 species distributed in tropical Africa and Madagascar.

CHINABERRY-TREE *Melia azedarach* L.

QUICK ID Recognized by dark brown bark, large bipinnately or tripinnately compound leaves, and numerous purple or lilac flowers.

Deciduous tree to about 15 m tall, about 60 cm diam. Erect, single often low-branching trunk; crown spreading, somewhat rounded, especially when open-grown. **BARK** Smooth, purplish brown, becoming dark reddish brown and slightly fissured with age. **TWIG** Smooth, greenish. **LEAF** Alternate, bipinnately or tripinnately compound; blade to about 50 cm long, equally broad; petiole 6–9 cm long. Leaflets numerous, 2–7 cm long, 1–2 cm broad, stalks absent or 1–2 cm long; ovate, base rounded or wedge-shaped, sometimes deeply incised and lobed, tip abruptly long-pointed, margins toothed. Upper surface dark green, lower surface paler. **FLOWER** Bisexual, radially symmetric, fragrant; sepals 5 or 6, green; petals 5–6, 8–12 mm long, pinkish purple or lilac; stamens 10–12, filaments fused into a dark purple tube about 8 mm long; inflorescence a loose, stalked, many-flowered panicle to about 20 cm long. Spring. **FRUIT** Rounded, fleshy, multistoned yellowish or greenish-yellow drupe, 1–1.5 cm diam.; matures autumn, persisting throughout the winter.

HABITAT/RANGE Introduced from Asia; widely cultivated, naturalized in woodlands, floodplains, disturbed sites across much of the se. U.S., Va. south to s. Fla., west to e. Tex.

Notes: Melia is a genus of 3 species distributed in tropical Africa and tropical and temperate Asia. Chinaberry-tree is considered an invasive species across much of the s. U.S.

West Indian Mahogany

fruit

open fruit

seeds

African Mahogany

fruit

open fruit

flowers

Chinaberry-tree

fruit

fruit

MORACEAE: MULBERRY FAMILY

The mulberries, figs, and breadnuts compose a family of about 39–50 genera and 1,100–1,500 species of trees, shrubs, vines, and a few herbs, distributed mostly in tropical and warm temperate regions. Eight genera and about 25 species occur in North America, including 5 native and 12 non-native trees in the East. Members of the family have latex-bearing cells in the green tissue that excrete a milky sap when broken, a characteristic that is especially evident when the petiole is severed.

LEAF Alternate, simple, and 2-ranked (in our species). **FLOWER** Unisexual, individually inconspicuous, lacking a corolla, often highly modified and become part of the fruit. Male and female flowers produced on the same or separate plants; pollination is effected by wind or wasps. **FRUIT** Drupe, cluster of drupelets, achene produced inside a fleshy syconium (a fig), or achene embedded in a fleshy receptacle.

The family is economically important for the fruits of the mulberries, figs, breadfruit (*Artocarpus*), and breadnut, all of which are sources of food for both humans and wildlife. The wood of some species is used for timber. Figs are grown ornamentally, often as houseplants.

■ *MORUS*: MULBERRIES

A genus of about 10 species, widespread in tropical and temperate regions; 4 occur in North America, 2 native in the East, 2 introduced.

Deciduous shrubs and trees with milky sap. **LEAF** Alternate, simple, often deeply lobed, the margins entire or toothed. **FLOWER** Tiny, borne in unisexual catkins, the sexes on the same or separate plants; corolla absent, male flowers with 4 thin tepals and 4 inflexed stamens; pistillate flowers with 4 thickish tepals, 2 large, 2 smaller, the ovary superior, with 2 styles. **FRUIT** Aggregate of achenes (a syncarp), each achene enclosed in a juicy, fleshy calyx; syncarp cylindric, somewhat reminiscent of a blackberry. However, blackberries are formed of individual drupelets from a single flower, whereas mulberries are derived from many small flowers.

Mulberries are edible, though often rather insipid. Birds relish them. Several species are grown as vigorous ornamentals. Silkworms feed upon mulberry leaves.

RED MULBERRY *Morus rubra* L.

QUICKID Recognized by the combination of alternate, toothed and often lobed leaves that are rough to the touch above, and the elongated blackberry-like fruit, typically 3 cm long or more.

Deciduous tree to about 20 m tall, 1.5 m diam. Erect or slightly leaning, single straight, typically low-branching trunk; crown broad, rounded, even when growing in hammocks and temperate woodlands. **BARK** Dark brown or dark reddish brown; finely and irregularly fissured and scaly with age. **TWIG** Smooth, hairless, rarely finely hairy when very young, green, becoming reddish brown or tan, with scattered lenticels. **LEAF** Alternate, simple, ovate, broadly oblong, or nearly circular; unlobed or with 2–9 lobes, the lobing more prevalent on young trees, many or all leaves of mature trees often lacking lobes; base rounded, flattened, or heart-shaped; tip conspicuously and abruptly short-pointed; margins coarsely and sharply toothed. Upper surface dark green, rough to the touch due to copious stiff, forward-pointing hairs; lower surface paler, duller, softly-hairy or shaggy-hairy on the veins and sometimes the tissue. Blade 10–24 cm long, 6–20 cm broad; petiole 1.5–12 cm long, exuding milky sap when broken. **FLOWER** Greenish, borne in catkins, male and female in separate inflorescences on the same or separate plants; sepals 4, male flowers with 4 stamens, female flowers with 2 stigmas. Spring. **FRUIT** Achene surrounded by a juicy calyx, the individual units coalesced into a dark red or purplish-red ellipsoid cluster, 2.5–5 cm long, somewhat resembling a blackberry; matures summer.

HABITAT/RANGE Native. Floodplains, low ridges in bottomlands, slopes, rich moist woods,

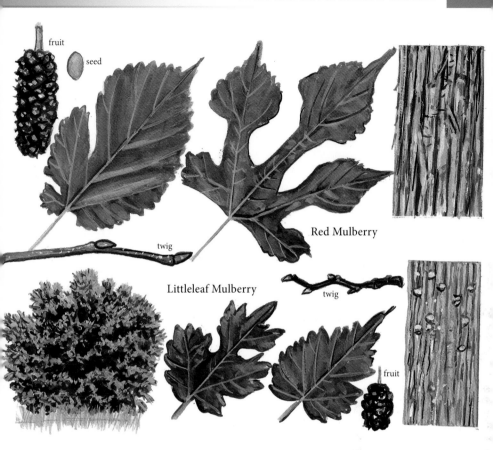

fruit

seed

Red Mulberry

twig

Littleleaf Mulberry

twig

fruit

0–700 m; Vt. and N.Y. west to Minn. and Nebr., south to sw. Tex. and c. Fla.

SIMILAR SPECIES White Mulberry is distinguished by the upper surface of its leaf being lustrous, medium green, and smooth to the touch. See also Littleleaf Mulberry.

RED MULBERRY

LITTLELEAF MULBERRY

LITTLELEAF MULBERRY *Morus microphylla* Buckley
A.K.A. TEXAS MULBERRY

QUICK ID A western mulberry with rough, small, coarsely toothed leaves and a short petiole.

Shrub or small tree to 7–8 m tall. Differs from Red Mulberry and White Mulberry by having leaves less than 7 cm long and harshly rough to the touch on both surfaces, a petiole to about 1.5 cm long, and a fruit cluster to about 1.5 cm long.

HABITAT/RANGE Native; predominantly a western species, ranging into the East in e. Tex. and s. Okla.

WHITE MULBERRY *Morus alba* L.

QUICK ID **Recognized by the combination of alternate, coarsely toothed and often lobed leaves that are lustrous above, and white to dark purple blackberry-like fruit.**

Deciduous tree to about 25 m tall, 1.5 m diam. Erect, single straight, typically low-branching trunk; crown broad, spreading. **BARK** Gray or brownish, shallowly and irregularly furrowed. **TWIG** Smooth, hairless, rarely finely hairy when very young, green, becoming reddish brown or tan, with scattered lenticels. **LEAF** Alternate, simple, ovate, broadly oblong, or nearly circular; unlobed or with 2–9 lobes, the lobing more prevalent on young trees; base rounded, flattened, or heart-shaped; leaf tip and lobe tips abruptly short-pointed; margins coarsely and sharply toothed. Upper surface lustrous, medium or yellowish green, smooth to the touch; lower surface paler, duller, hairy along the veins or just in tufts in the axils of major veins. Blade 6–16 cm long, 6–10 cm broad; petiole 3–5 cm long; exudes milky sap when broken. **FLOWER** Greenish, borne in catkins, male and female in separate inflorescences on the same or separate plants; sepals 4, male flowers with 4 stamens, female flowers with 2 stigmas. Spring. **FRUIT** Achene surrounded by a juicy calyx, the individual units coalesced into an ellipsoid whitish, pinkish, pale purple, or nearly black cluster, 1–2 cm long, somewhat resembling a blackberry; matures summer.

HABITAT/RANGE Introduced from East Asia; cultivated, naturalized in second-growth woodlands, stream banks, river bottoms, disturbed sites, fencerows; throughout the U.S. and s. Canada.

SIMILAR SPECIES Red Mulberry is distinguished by the upper surface of its leaf being dark green, rough to the touch, and not lustrous.

Dark-fruited forms of White Mulberry (sometimes referred to as *M. alba* var. *tatarica* [L.] Seringe) are easily misidentified as Black Mulberry, which can be distinguished by its uniformly hairy lower leaf surface.

BLACK MULBERRY *Morus nigra* L.

Deciduous, often a shrub, sometimes a small, slender, many-branched tree 6–9 m tall. Easily confused with other mulberries, but distinguished by the hairier lower leaf surface. **LEAF** Rough above, uniformly hairy below; blade 7–12 cm long, 7–11 cm broad, variably shaped, usually with 1 or more lobes. **FLOWER** Borne in greenish catkins in the leaf axils of new growth. Late spring. **FRUIT** Similar to other mulberries; 1.3–2.5 cm long; matures late summer. **HABITAT/RANGE** Introduced from Iran; cultivated and rarely established, Ohio, Ky., La., perhaps elsewhere.

BREADNUT *Brosimum alicastrum* Sw.

Deciduous tree to about 30 m tall, with smooth gray branches and trunk. **LEAF** Alternate, simple, with a short petiole, 3–14 cm long, to about 7 cm broad, lustrous green above with yellowish veins. **FLOWER** Unisexual, produced on the same tree. **FRUIT** Fleshy, compound, 1.5–2 cm diam., green, turning yellow; coalesced from the ovaries of several flowers, the achenes embedded in a fleshy syncarp. **HABITAT/RANGE** Introduced from tropical America; reported in s. Fla and Fla. Keys. *Notes: Brosimum* is a genus of about 41 species of the New World tropics, none native to North America.

WHITE MULBERRY

White Mulberry

fruit

Black Mulberry

fruit

Breadnut

fruit

fruit

opened fruit

STOREHOUSEBUSH *Cudrania tricuspidata* (Carrière) Bureau ex Lavallée
A.K.A. CHINESE MULBERRY, SILKWORM THORN

Deciduous slow-growing tree, to about 6 m tall, often shrublike. **LEAF** Alternate, simple, similar to the mulberries. **FRUIT** Round collection of calyx-covered achenes, 2.5–5 cm diam.; red, tasty when ripe. Somewhat similar to mulberries and Osage Orange (*Maclura pomifera*). **HABITAT/ RANGE** Introduced from Asia; cultivated, reportedly rarely established in Ga.

PAPER MULBERRY *Broussonetia papyrifera* (L.) Vent.

QUICK ID Recognized by the combination of toothed leaves that are alternate, opposite, and whorled on a single plant, and the elongated, cylindric male catkin.

Deciduous, fast-growing tree, 10–20 m tall, to about 1.25 m diam. Erect, often with the form of a large shrub, single stem or multiple, often producing root sprouts and branching near the ground; crown broad, rounded. **BARK** Smooth, tan, sometimes becoming slightly furrowed. **TWIG** Brown, with scattered, slightly raised corky lenticels and long, spreading, glassy-transparent hairs. **LEAF** Alternate, opposite, or whorled with 3 to the node, simple, ovate, unlobed or with 2–5 lobes; base rounded, flattened, heart-shaped, or broadly wedge-shaped; tip long-tapering and pointed; margins regularly or irregularly toothed, usually above the base. Upper surface dark brownish green or green at maturity, rough to the touch from persistent bases of hairs; lower surface hairy, velvety at maturity. Blade 6–28 cm long, 4–19 cm broad; petiole 3–17 cm long, conspicuously variable in length, hairy, oozing milky sap when broken. **FLOWER** Unisexual, tiny, male and female flowers produced on separate trees; female inflorescence a rounded cluster, male inflorescence an elongated, cylindric catkin 3–8 cm long. Spring. **FRUIT** Rounded, ball-like cluster of fleshy calyces 2–3 cm diam., each calyx enclosing a red or orange achene that protrudes and is visible on ripe fruit; matures summer.

HABITAT/RANGE Introduced from Asia in the mid-1700s; cultivated and established mostly near plantings; widespread but irregular across the East, Del. to s. Ill., south to Fla. and e. Tex.

SIMILAR SPECIES Red Mulberry (*Morus rubra*) and White Mulberry (*M. alba*) have alternate leaves and hairless or softly short-hairy new twigs.

Notes: *Broussonetia* is a genus of 4 species, all from East Asia or the Pacific islands.

OSAGE ORANGE *Maclura pomifera* (Raf.) C.K. Schneid.

QUICK ID Distinguished by the combination of spiny branches, ovate leaves, and lumpy green, orange-like fruit clusters.

Deciduous shrub or tree to about 25 m tall, to 2.3 m diam.; erect, single trunk or several; often thicket-forming from the production of root sprouts; crown open, rounded. **BARK** Dark yellowish brown or orange-brown, thickly and irregularly furrowed with interlacing ridges, peeling into strips. **TWIG** Smooth, becoming hairless, greenish or orange-brown, with axillary spines to 3.5 cm long. **LEAF** Alternate (sometimes closely clustered at the branch tips), simple; ovate, elliptic, or broadly lanceolate; base rounded, flattened, or broadly tapered; tip abruptly and conspicuously long-pointed; margins entire. Upper surface dark green, lustrous, hairless; lower surface paler, dull, sparsely hairy. Blade 7–15 cm long, 5–8 cm broad; petiole 3–5 cm long, slender, exuding milky sap when broken. Turns yellow in autumn. **FLOWER** Unisexual, male and female borne on separate trees; male inflorescence rounded or oblong, 2.5–3.5 cm long, produced on short spur shoots; female inflorescence rounded, 2–2.5 cm long, produced on long stalks from the leaf axils. Spring. **FRUIT** Compact round green collection of calyces 7–15 cm diam., each calyx containing an achene; resembles an immature orange, surface rind-like; matures late summer to autumn.

OSAGE ORANGE

HABITAT/RANGE Native. Produces thickets in river valleys, ravines, field margins, and hedgerows, 0–1,500 m; native to the lower Midwest, including sw. Ark., se. Okla., and Tex., planted and naturalized far beyond this range, as far north as Mass., Pa., Wis., and S.D., south to n. Fla. and La.

Storehousebush

fruit

Paper Mulberry

fruit

flowers

immature fruit

Osage Orange

autumn

fruit

autumn

◼ *FICUS*: FIGS

Ficus is a genus of about 750 species of the tropics and subtropics, most numerous in Asia. Thirteen species occur in N. America, including 2 native and 7 non-native trees in the East. Here, the native species are treated first.

Deciduous or evergreen trees, shrubs or woody vines, often epiphytic as seedlings. Buds subtended and enclosed by conspicuous stipules that fall as the leaf emerges, leaving an encircling scar. **LEAF** Alternate, simple, margins usually entire (in most of ours) or irregularly toothed, veins pinnate or palmate/pinnate; exuding milky sap when crushed or broken. **FLOWER/FRUIT** Minute, male and female flowers produced within and scattered across the inside wall of the developing fig, the fig being the inflorescence (technically a syconium). Female flowers are of 2 types, one long-stalked with a short style, the other short-stalked with a long style. Pollination is effected by tiny egg-laden female wasps that wriggle their way into the fig and pollinate and deposit eggs in the female flowers. Subsequently, short-styled flowers develop as gall flowers, essentially serving as the incubator for a new crop of male and female wasps; long-styled flowers develop seed. Male flowers and new wasps mature at about the same time. The new, wingless male wasps impregnate the new female wasps, which gather pollen, often by biting into the anthers, and exit the fig through tiny holes chewed by the males, and fly to a new fig and renew the cycle. The ripe figs are important to wildlife.

SHORTLEAF FIG *Ficus citrifolia* Mill.
A.K.A. WILD BANYANTREE

QUICKID Recognized by the combination of lustrous green leathery leaves with conspicuous venation, pinkish stipules, and stalked fruit.

Evergreen tree to about 15 m tall, often producing aerial roots from the branches; sometimes arises as an epiphyte on the trunks of other trees. Erect, single trunk or multiple; crown broad, rounded. **BARK** Smooth, gray or grayish brown. **TWIG** Greenish and finely hairy at first, becoming reddish brown and mostly hairless. **LEAF** Alternate, simple, thick, leathery, ovate or elliptic; base rounded or heart-shaped; tip bluntly or abruptly short-pointed; margins entire. Upper surface lustrous, medium green, veins pinnate, yellowish; lower surface pale green. Blade 5–11 cm long, 3.5–9 cm broad; petiole 1.5–4 cm long, stout, usually longer than ½ the width of the blade; stipules pink, hairy. **FRUIT** Rounded leathery fig, 8–20 mm diam., changing from green to yellow to red at maturity; stalks 7–15 mm long; matures summer to autumn, potentially present year-round.

HABITAT/RANGE Native. Subtropical hammocks; s. Fla. and Fla. Keys.

SIMILAR SPECIES Florida Strangler Fig is distinguished by its stalkless or very short-stalked fruit, greenish stipules, and petiole length less than ½ the width of the blade.

FLORIDA STRANGLER FIG *Ficus aurea* Nutt.

QUICKID Recognized by the combination of stalkless fruit, lustrous green leathery leaves with yellowish venation, green stipules, and a grayish trunk that often forms lattices on supporting trees.

Evergreen tree potentially to about 20 m tall, often producing aerial roots from the branches; usually arising as an epiphyte on other trees, the developing trunk becoming latticelike, eventually encircling and killing its host and becoming a single trunk; crown broad, rounded. **BARK** Smooth, gray. **TWIG** Green at first, becoming yellowish brown or grayish brown. **LEAF** Alternate, simple, thick, leathery, ovate or elliptic; base rounded or more often wedge-shaped; tip bluntly or abruptly short-pointed; margins entire. Upper surface lustrous, dark green, hairless, veins pinnate, yellowish; lower surface pale green. Blade 5–15 cm long,

SHORTLEAF FIG   FLORIDA STRANGLER FIG

Shortleaf Fig

fruit

fruit

Florida Strangler Fig

fruit

4–8 cm broad; petiole usually 1–4 cm long, stout, shorter than ½ the width of the blade; stipules green, hairless. **FRUIT** Hairless, rounded leathery fig, 6–20 mm diam., changing from green to yellow or red at maturity; stalks typically absent, not exceeding about 5 mm long. Matures summer to autumn, potentially present year-round.

HABITAT/RANGE Native. Subtropical hammocks, swamps, cypress strands, margins of mangrove wetlands, 0–10 m; s. Fla.

SIMILAR SPECIES Shortleaf Fig is distinguished by the stalked fruit, pinkish stipules, and petiole length exceeding ½ the width of the blade.

EDIBLE FIG *Ficus carica* L.
A.K.A. COMMON FIG

QUICK ID The leaves with 3–5 lobes and distinctive fruit (the fig of commerce) are diagnostic.

Deciduous large shrub or small tree, 3–10 m tall. Erect, usually with multiple trunks; crown spreading, irregular. **BARK** Grayish brown, smooth or slightly roughened. **TWIG** Green, hairy. **LEAF** Alternate, simple, ovate or circular, deeply incised, with 3–5 broad lobes; base flattened to more often deeply heart-shaped; tip bluntly pointed; margins undulate or coarsely and bluntly toothed. Upper surface dark or medium green, 3–5 palmately arranged main veins and secondary pinnate venation conspicuous; lower surface paler; both surfaces rough to the touch from the presence of stiff, persistent hairs. Blade 15–30 cm long, equally broad; petiole 8–20 cm long, stout. **FRUIT** Hairy, pear-shaped leathery fig, green, yellow, reddish brown, or purplish, 3–8 cm long; the fig of commerce, maturing in autumn.

HABITAT/RANGE Introduced from Asia, the precise origin location obscure; widely planted, probably naturalized in Ala., La., Tex., Va., W. Va., potentially elsewhere.

SIMILAR SPECIES All other figs growing in North America, native or introduced, have unlobed leaves.

COUNCIL TREE *Ficus altissima* Blume

QUICK ID Recognized among Florida's native and naturalized figs by the combination of large leaves, large fruit, and distinctive V-shaped basal veins on at least some leaves.

Evergreen tree, 25–30 m tall, individual trunks to about 90 cm diam., fused trunks potentially much larger; erect, usually producing numerous aerial roots and secondary trunks that often appear as buttresses; crown wide-spreading, flat-topped, wider than tall. **BARK** Smooth, grayish green. **TWIG** Grayish, stout. **LEAF** Alternate, simple, leathery; ovate, oval, or broadly elliptic. Upper surface

lustrous, medium or dark green, venation pinnate, conspicuous, veins yellowish, the basal pair of lateral veins arising from the base of the midvein, often at a greater angle than those above, and extending ⅓ or more the length of the blade. Blade 8–27 cm long, 8–14 cm broad; petiole 2–6 cm long, stout. **FRUIT** Fleshy, stalkless, rounded or egg-shaped fig, yellow tending toward orange or red, to about 2 cm diam. Year-round.

HABITAT/RANGE Introduced from Asia; cultivated, naturalized in s. Fla., and included on Florida's list of invasive species.

SIMILAR SPECIES Florida Strangler Fig and Indian Laurel also have sessile fruit. The basal pair of leaf veins in Florida Strangler Fig arises at about the same angle as the pair above and extends only about 1/16 the length of the blade. The leaves and fruit of Indian Laurel are smaller.

WEEPING FIG *Ficus benjamina* L.

QUICK ID Recognized by the combination of comparatively small leaves with finely parallel lateral veins and a hairless fig.

Evergreen tree to about 10 m tall; most plants produce aerial roots, in some plants these form secondary trunks; crown dense, of numerous slender, weeping branches. **BARK** Smooth, gray. **TWIG** Brownish, hairless. **LEAF** Alternate, simple, leathery; lanceolate, narrowly ovate, or elliptic; base rounded or wedge-shaped; tip abruptly tapering to a long or short point; margins entire, somewhat thickened. Upper surface lustrous, dark green, usually with 1 or 2 pairs of basal veins and numerous straight, finely parallel lateral veins; lower surface paler. Blade 4–14 cm long, 1.5–6 cm broad; petiole 1–3 cm long. **FRUIT** Round or nearly so, hairless red or yellow fig, about 1 cm diam.

HABITAT/RANGE Introduced from Asia; cultivated and naturalized in s. Fla.

SIMILAR SPECIES Indian Banyan can be distinguished by its hairy fig.

Edible Fig

fruit

Council Tree

fruit

Weeping Fig

fruit

fruit

INDIAN LAUREL *Ficus microcarpa* L. f.
A.K.A. CHINESE BANYAN

QUICK ID Recognized by the combination of stalkless fruit, comparatively short leaves, and small, dark-colored figs.

Evergreen tree potentially to about 30 m tall, usually only to about ½ this height in North America; usually with numerous aerial roots, many forming secondary trunks; crown dense, spreading, broader than tall. **BARK** Smooth, gray. **TWIG** Brown, hairy. **LEAF** Alternate, simple, leathery; oval or narrowly elliptic; base wedge-shaped; tip blunt, narrowly rounded, or abruptly short-pointed; margins entire. Upper surface lustrous green, hairless; lower surface paler, hairless. Blade typically 3–10 cm long, rarely longer, 1.5–5 cm broad; petiole 5–20 mm long. **FRUIT** Stalkless egg-shaped or rounded fig, 9–11 mm long, 5–6 mm diam.; green, becoming purple or reddish black; usually borne in pairs.

HABITAT/RANGE Introduced from Asia; cultivated, naturalized in s. Fla.; included on Florida's invasive species list.

SIMILAR SPECIES Florida Strangler Fig and Council Tree have stalkless but larger fruit and larger leaves.

JAMAICAN CHERRY FIG *Ficus americana* Aubl.
A.K.A. WEST INDIAN LAUREL FIG

Evergreen tree to about 12 m tall, with aerial roots. Recognized by the combination of leaves with short petioles and 10 or fewer lateral veins, and stalked fruit. **LEAF** Leathery; elliptic, ovate, or obovate, hairless, lustrous green above; blade 2–8 cm long, 1–4 cm broad, petiole to about 1 cm long. **FRUIT** Hairless, stalked, fleshy, rounded red fig, 3–7 mm

diam. **HABITAT/RANGE** Introduced from the West Indies and tropical America; cultivated and established in hammocks; s. Fla.

INDIAN BANYAN *Ficus benghalensis* L.
A.K.A. BANYAN TREE

Evergreen tree, potentially to about 30 m tall, usually shorter in North America; branches with aerial roots, often forming stout secondary trunks from the lower branches. Recognized by the combination of hairy fig and leaves with a blunt or rounded tip, 3 or 4 pairs of basal veins, and entire margins. **LEAF** Leathery, ovate, base rounded or heart-shaped, tip rounded; upper surface lustrous green, hairless, with 3 or 4 pairs of basal veins; lower surface paler, finely hairy; blade 10–30 cm long, 7–20 cm broad; petiole 1.5–7 cm long. **FRUIT** Hairy, stalkless, rounded or slightly vertically compressed orange or red fig, 1.5–2 cm long, 2–2.5 cm diam. **HABITAT/RANGE** Introduced from Asia; cultivated and established in subtropical hammocks; s. Fla.

SACRED FIG *Ficus religiosa* L.
A.K.A. PEEPUL TREE, BO TREE

Evergreen or deciduous tree, potentially to 30 m tall, usually to only about ½ this height in North America; often begins life as an epiphyte. Easily recognized by the ovate, narrowly long-pointed leaf. **LEAF** Ovate or nearly circular, the tip abruptly, narrowly, and conspicuously long-pointed, the narrow tip to about 9 cm long; base rounded to nearly flattened; margins entire or wavy; surfaces yellowish green or light green, hairless. Blade 3–17 cm long; petiole 5–14 cm long. **FRUIT** Hairless, stalkless, rounded, dark purple fig, 1–1.5 cm diam. **HABITAT/RANGE** Introduced from Asia; cultivated and established in subtropical hammocks and disturbed sites; Fla.

Indian Banyan

fruit

new leaf

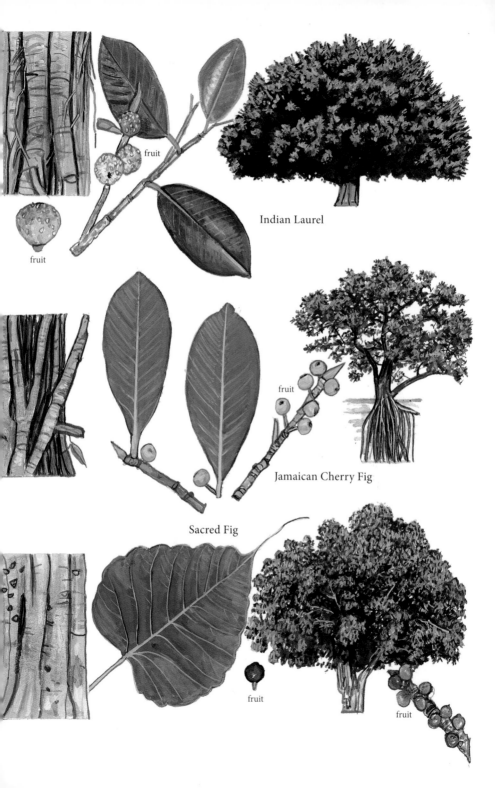

fruit

fruit

Indian Laurel

fruit

Jamaican Cherry Fig

Sacred Fig

fruit

fruit

MORINGACEAE: HORSERADISH-TREE FAMILY

This is a small family with 1 genus and 13 species, distributed naturally in Asia, Africa, and Madagascar; 1 species is naturalized in s. Fla.

HORSERADISH-TREE *Moringa oleifera* Lam.

QUICKID Recognized by the combination of tripinnately compound leaves, stalked glands at the leaf base, elongated 3-parted capsules, and the horseradish aroma of crushed foliage.

Evergreen shrub or tree, to about 12 m tall, 40 cm diam. Erect, single trunk; crown rounded, somewhat irregular. **BARK** Gray or greenish gray, smooth or slightly roughened. **LEAF** Alternate, tripinnately compound, with 4–6 lateral segments and a terminal segment; blade 30–60 cm long, exuding a strong aroma of horseradish when crushed or bruised. Ultimate leaflets 75–150 in number, 10–20 mm long, 5–12 mm broad, more or less rounded at base and tip. **FLOWER** Creamy white or yellowish, pea-like, to about 2.5 cm broad; petals 5, each about 1 cm long; borne in drooping, many-flowered panicles. Spring. **FRUIT** Three-angled, 3-parted beanlike capsule, 15–45 cm long, about 3 cm diam.; matures spring to autumn.

HABITAT/RANGE Introduced from India and Sri Lanka; cultivated and rarely naturalized in disturbed sites, s. Fla.

SIMILAR SPECIES The leaves of species in the bean (Fabaceae) and bignonia (Bignoniaceae) families lack a horseradish-like aroma, and the fruits are not 3-angled and typically lack 3-winged seeds.

MUNTINGIACEAE: MUNTINGIA FAMILY

This small family includes 3 genera and 3 species, all of which are trees distributed in Mexico and w. South America. One introduced species is naturalized in the U.S., mostly in s. Fla. **LEAF** Species in this family are characterized by 2-ranked toothed leaves with asymmetric bases, and reduced, variously shaped stipule-like leaves at the bases of axillary shoots. **FLOWER** In clusters or solitary, near and usually slightly above the leaf axil; petals usually 5, fused at the base. **FRUIT** Many-seeded berry.

STRAWBERRYTREE *Muntingia calabura* L.
A.K.A. JAMAICA CHERRY

QUICKID Recognized by the 2-ranked, coarsely toothed leaves with oblique, asymmetric bases.

Evergreen shrub or tree, 5–7 m tall; more often shrubby where naturalized in North America. Erect, single trunk; crown flat-topped, with laterally spreading branches. **BARK** Gray. **TWIG** Densely covered with soft glandular hairs, often slightly sticky. **LEAF** Alternate, simple; lanceolate, oblong, or narrowly ovate; base oblique, asymmetric; tip abruptly pointed; margins coarsely toothed. Upper surface green, smooth; lower surface grayish white, with a dense covering of stellate hairs. Blade 5–14 cm long, 1.5–5 cm broad; petiole 2–6 mm long. **FLOWER** Bisexual, about 2 cm diam., radially symmetric; petals 5, white, crinkled, about 1 cm long, nearly as broad; sepals 5, green, about 1 cm long, 3 mm broad, usually reflexed at anthesis; stamens many, about 6 mm long. Year-round. **FRUIT** Fleshy, many-seeded reddish berry, 1–1.5 cm diam.; seeds numerous; potentially year-round.

HABITAT/RANGE Introduced from the West Indies and tropical Americas; cultivated, and naturalized in hammocks and pinelands of s. Fla. Also reported in Calif., but apparently not naturalized there.

Horseradish-tree

flowers

fruit

Strawberrytree

fruit

MYOPORACEAE: MYOPORUM FAMILY

This small family of about 5 genera and 100 species is distributed mainly in Australia. Two species are naturalized in North America, 1 in the West and 1 in s. Fla. Some experts include the family within the figwort or snapdragon family (Scrophulariaceae). Members of the myoporum family usually have gland-dotted iso-bilateral leaves, in which the upper and lower surfaces are not clearly distinguishable from each other, and bilaterally symmetric flowers with united petals.

WHITE ALLING *Bontia daphnoides* L.

QUICK ID The combination of narrow leaves, long-stalked fruit, and tubular yellow and purple flowers is distinctive.

Evergreen shrub or small tree to about 8 m tall, 15 cm diam. Erect, single trunk or multiple; crown narrowly vertical, densely foliaged. **BARK** Pale brown, thick, furrowed. **LEAF** Alternate, simple, oblong to narrowly lanceolate or nearly linear; base and tip evenly tapering; margins entire. Upper and lower surfaces pale green. Blade 3–11 cm long, 1–3 cm broad; petiole 2–10 mm long. **FLOWER** Tubular, about 2 cm long, yellow and purple, flaring at the tip into 2 lobes, the lower conspicuously marked with a line of purplish hairs. Year-round. **FRUIT** Fleshy, single-stoned, long-stalked drupe, to about 1 cm long, greenish or yellowish, becoming dark after maturing; stalk to about 2 cm long; matures year-round.

HABITAT/RANGE Introduced from the West Indies; sparingly naturalized in s. Fla.

MYRICACEAE: WAX MYRTLE FAMILY

This is a family of evergreen or deciduous shrubs or small trees, often with aromatic leaves and resinous exudate on the twigs and leaf surfaces. There are 3 genera and 57 species in the family, 55 of which are in the genus *Myrica*. Species are distributed in temperate and subtropical regions; 2 genera and 8 species occur in North America, all native. Only the genus *Myrica* includes arborescent species in the East.

■ *MYRICA*: BAYBERRIES

Some authorities include several species of *Myrica* within the genus *Morella*, differentiating the 2 genera on the position of the catkin, size of the bracts subtending male flowers, and appearance of the fruit. Here we have retained the traditional classification. **LEAF** Alternate, simple. **FLOWER** Unisexual, produced on separate plants, lacking sepals and petals. **FRUIT** Rounded waxy nutlike drupe that is often bumpy on the outer surface from the presence of warty protuberances. Species of *Myrica* are the source of bayberry candles.

WAX MYRTLE *Myrica cerifera* L.

QUICK ID Recognized by its aromatic oblanceolate leaves, usually toothed toward the tip, and with numerous brown glandular dots on both surfaces.

Evergreen shrub or small tree, to about 12 m tall, potentially to about 32 cm diam., usually not exceeding about 15 cm; often forms colonies from underground rhizomes. Erect, leaning, or ascending, usually with multiple trunks or branching close to the ground; crown dense, oblong, the branches often upright or ascending. **BARK** Smooth, splotched light and dark gray. **TWIG** Reddish brown, hairless or densely hairy, usually with yellow scaly-glandular dots. **LEAF** Alternate, simple, aromatic when crushed, narrowly oblanceolate, base narrowly tapered; tip acute, blunt, or

White Alling

fruit

Wax Myrtle

underside

fruit

fruit

rounded; margins entire or more often toothed, at least near the tip. Upper surface dark green, lower surface paler, both with numerous brown or amber dots of glandular exudate. Blade 3–15 cm long, 1–2 cm broad; petiole to about 5 mm long. **FLOWER** Male and female flowers on separate plants; petals and sepals absent; inflorescence an erect catkin at the leaf axil. Late winter to spring. **FRUIT** Rounded whitish-gray waxy nutlike drupe, 2–4 mm diam.; matures summer to autumn.

HABITAT/RANGE Native. Inhabits a wide array of habitats, including bog margins, banks of fresh- or brackish-water ponds and inlets, swamps, wet hammocks, interdune swales, mixed upland woods, disturbed sites, pine flatwoods, 0–450 m; largely restricted to the southeastern coastal plains; Md. and Del. south throughout Fla., west to s. Ark. and e. Tex.

SIMILAR SPECIES The leaves of Southern Bayberry and Northern Bayberry have amber or brown dots only on the lower surface.

Notes: Widely cultivated, especially for hedges and to conceal unsightly foundations.

WAX MYRTLE

ODORLESS BAYBERRY *Myrica inodora*
W. Bartram
A.K.A. SCENTLESS BAYBERRY

QUICK ID Recognized by the dark green leaves with rolled, entire margins and oblong or rounded bumpy fruit on long stalks.

Evergreen shrub or small tree, to about 7 m tall. Erect or vase-shaped, usually with multiple trunks, sometimes with a single very low-branching trunk; crown dense, rounded. **BARK** Smooth, gray. **TWIG** Rust-colored, hairless, and glandular-scaly when young, becoming smooth and gray. **LEAF** Alternate, simple, leathery, not aromatic when crushed, dark green above; elliptic or elliptic-oblanceolate, base narrowly wedge-shaped, tip rounded or bluntly pointed; margins entire, usually rolled under. Blade 4–8 cm long, 2–3 cm broad; petiole 0–3 mm long, more or less winged. **FLOWER** Male and female flowers on separate plants; sepals and petals absent; produced in catkins at the leaf axils. Late winter to spring. **FRUIT** Oblong to rounded black drupe, 6–8 mm diam.; outer wall bumpy with warty protuberances; matures summer to autumn.

HABITAT/RANGE Native. Shrub bogs, bays, acid swamps, pine flatwoods, margins of cypress ponds, 0–10 m diam.; uncommon in East Gulf Coastal Plain (extreme s. Ga., s. Ala., s. Miss., and se. La.), slightly more common in nw. Fla.

SIMILAR SPECIES The leaves of other species of *Myrica* are aromatic when crushed and usually lack rolled margins.

SOUTHERN BAYBERRY *Myrica caroliniensis* Mill.

QUICK ID A southern bayberry, recognized by its evergreen habit and more or less flat, coarsely toothed leaves with glandular dots only on the lower surface.

Evergreen shrub, rarely a small gray-barked tree to about 3 m tall; branches blackish. **LEAF** Oblanceolate, coarsely toothed or notched near the tip, 6–12 cm long, to about 5 cm broad, larger and somewhat thicker on average than leaves of Wax Myrtle, only the lower surface with brown or amber glandular dots, aromatic when crushed. **FLOWER** Similar to that of Wax Myrtle; spring. **FRUIT** Drupe, 2–4.5 mm diam.

HABITAT/RANGE Native; range similar to that of Wax Myrtle but tending to occupy wetter sites.

NORTHERN BAYBERRY *Myrica pensylvanica* Mirb.

QUICK ID A northern bayberry recognized by its deciduous habit, white-gray branches, and more or less flat, coarsely toothed leaves with glandular dots only on the lower surface.

Deciduous shrub or small tree, usually not exceeding about 2 m tall, rarely to about 4 m. Similar in many respects to Southern Bayberry; some authorities recognize these 2 entities as a single species. Northern Bayberry differs by the combination of its deciduous habit, whitish-gray branches, and slightly larger fruit, 3.5–5.5 mm diam.

HABITAT/RANGE Native. Occurs north of Southern Bayberry's range; Del. and Md. north to P.E.I.

ODORLESS BAYBERRY

SOUTHERN BAYBERRY

NORTHERN BAYBERRY

fruit

fruit

Odorless Bayberry

Southern Bayberry

fruit

fruit

Northern Bayberry

fruit

MYRSINACEAE: MYRSINE FAMILY

The myrsine family has traditionally included 40–50 genera and about 1,435 species of trees, shrubs, and herbs distributed nearly worldwide. We have retained this traditional grouping, but recent classifications have included the Myrsinaceae within the Primulaceae, a family of 58 genera and 2,590 species worldwide, or have moved certain genera of Primulaceae into the Myrsinaceae. Most temperate species of myrsines are herbaceous; 30–35 species occur in North America, including 6 woody species, 5 of which form trees, 2 native. Most species are characterized by secretory resin canals in the tissue, evidenced by dark dots visible on the surfaces of leaves and flower parts.

■ *ARDISIA*: MARLBERRIES

A genus of 400–500 species, 5 in North America, 1 native. Distributed in the subtropical U.S., Mexico, the West Indies, Central and South America, Asia, Indian Ocean islands, Pacific islands, Australia.

Evergreen shrubs or trees. **LEAF** Alternate, simple; surfaces hairless or with glandular dots; margins toothed or entire. **FLOWER** Bisexual, white to pink; sepals 4 or 5, green; petals usually 5, white or pinkish; produced in terminal, subterminal, or axillary panicles, racemes, cymes, or umbels. **FRUIT** Single-seeded, rounded fleshy drupe, 4–8 mm diam., red, white, or black.

MARLBERRY *Ardisia escallonoides*
Schltdl. & Cham.

QUICK ID Recognized by the lustrous, dark green leaves, twigs with a brownish growing tip, and showy terminal flower and fruit panicles.

Evergreen large shrub or small tree, usually not exceeding about 3 m tall, potentially 11–15 m, 5–8 cm diam. Erect, usually with multiple trunks or branching close to the ground; crown dense, narrowly oblong. **BARK** Gray or whitish, often mottled or splotched greenish; smooth, with horizontal lenticels. **TWIG** Growing tip brownish. **LEAF** Alternate, simple, leathery; lanceolate, the blade often reflexed upward from the midrib and curved downward lengthwise; base wedge-shaped; tip bluntly pointed; margins entire. Upper surface lustrous, dark green; lower surface paler. Blade 7–15 cm long, 3–5 cm broad; petiole 5–12 mm long, bronze-colored. **FLOWER** Fragrant; sepals 5 or 6; petals 5 or 6, white or pinkish, punctate, densely clothed with yellow dots at the base; produced in

showy, many-flowered terminal panicles. Year-round, predominantly spring to early summer. **FRUIT** Lustrous rounded drupe, 7–9 mm diam.; red at first, maturing black; surface punctate. Year-round, predominantly winter.

HABITAT/RANGE Native. Hammocks, 0–10 m; s. Fla.

SIMILAR SPECIES Myrsine can be distinguished by the branches with green growing tips and the flowers and fruits produced along the branches below the leaves.

MARLBERRY

SHOEBUTTON ARDISIA *Ardisia elliptica* Thunb.

QUICK ID An *Ardisia* recognized by the combination of axillary inflorescences and reddish petioles.

Evergreen, usually a shrub 1–2 m tall, potentially a small tree to about 5 m tall. **LEAF** Alternate, simple, leathery; elliptic, oblong, oblanceolate, or obovate; base wedge-shaped; tip broadly pointed; margins entire, often rolled under. Surfaces hairless, lower surface with glandular dots. Blade 6–20 cm long,

Marlberry

flowers

stem

fruit

flower

fruit

Shoebutton Ardisia

flowers

fruit

flower

3–5 cm broad; petiole 4–10 mm long, reddish.
FLOWER Petals 5, punctate, white or pinkish;
produced in a flat-topped axillary cluster. Spring.
FRUIT Rounded or nearly rounded 1-seeded
drupe, about 8 mm diam.; red at first, becoming
black; matures autumn.

HABITAT/RANGE Introduced from Asia; cultivated, established in hammocks and disturbed sites
in s. Fla., where it is treated as an invasive species.

SIMILAR SPECIES Marlberry is distinguished
by its terminal rather than axillary inflorescence.

Three other species of *Ardisia* are naturalized in
North America, 2 of them large shrubs that rarely
reach tree stature. Coralberry (*A. crenata* Sims) is
typically a shrub to about 1.5 m tall, potentially
to 3 m tall, with bluntly toothed, lustrous green
leaves and bright red drupes. Cultivated and naturalized from Ga. and Fla. west. to Tex., it is an
aggressive, troublesome weed that is considered
invasive in several states. China Shrub (*A. solana-
cea* Roxb.) is also typically a shrub, potentially to
6 m tall, with vertically compressed fruits that are
copiously black-spotted. It is cultivated and established in s. Fla.

MYRSINE *Myrsine cubana* A. DC.

QUICKID Recognized by the combination of lustrous leaves with revolute margins, twigs with green growing tips, and fruit and flowers produced along the branch below the leaves.

Evergreen shrub or small tree, 6–15 m tall. Erect or leaning, single trunk or multiple; crown usually irregular and sparsely branched. **BARK** Light gray, more or less smooth. **TWIG** Hairless, growing tips green. **LEAF** Alternate, simple, closely set, especially near the branch tips; thick, leathery, obovate; base narrowly tapered; tip rounded, often notched; margins entire, usually rolled under. Upper surface hairless, lustrous green, lower surface paler, both surfaces with tiny dotlike depressions (punctate). Blade 6–13 cm long, 1–6 cm broad; petiole 4–7 mm long. **FLOWER** Unisexual, occasionally bisexual, male and female flowers produced in separate inflorescences, usually on separate plants, but similar, to about 7 mm diam., sepals and petals 5, whitish, virtually all parts punctate. Autumn to spring. **FRUIT** Round green to dark blue or black single-stoned drupe, 4–7 mm diam., usually produced in clusters along the branch well below the leaves. Year-round.

HABITAT/RANGE Native.   Hammocks   and coastal pinelands, 0–10 m; peninsular Fla., more common in s. Fla.

SIMILAR SPECIES Potentially mistaken for Marlberry (*Ardisia escallonoides*), which is distinguished by the combination of twigs with brownish growing tips and lustrous black fruit in terminal panicles.

Notes: Myrsine is a tropical genus of about 300 species, 1 native to North America.

MYRSINE

MYRTACEAE: MYRTLE FAMILY

This family of about 3,000 trees and shrubs is distributed primarily in the Southern Hemisphere, reaching north into the subtropics of Mexico, Eurasia, and s. Fla. About 33 species occur in North America, including 20 trees in the East, 8 native.

Mostly evergreen trees and shrubs. **LEAF** Usually opposite, simple, leathery, the margins entire, emitting a spicy or medicinal scent when crushed. **FLOWER** Radial and bisexual, usually white, cream, pink, lilac, or red, usually with numerous stamens joined together in bundles opposite the petals. A hypanthium forms the base of the flower; attached near the rim are 4 or 5 sepals, 4 or 5 separate petals, and many stamens. **FRUIT** A berry, drupe, nutlike structure, or capsule, which is often woody and hard.

■ *CALYPTRANTHES*: LIDFLOWERS

A genus of about 100 evergreen trees and shrubs distributed in the American tropics and subtropics. **LEAF** Opposite, simple, usually leathery. **FLOWER** Bisexual, petals absent; calyx cuplike, forming a circular, lidlike cap at the summit that dehisces but remains partially attached as the stamens expand; ovary inferior; stamens numerous; inflorescence a many-flowered panicle. **FRUIT** Berry with 1 to few seeds, the basal part of the calyx remaining attached at maturity.

PALE LIDFLOWER *Calyptranthes pallens* Griseb.

QUICKID Recognized by the combination of forked, longitudinally ridged twigs, capped, cuplike flowers, and a finely hairy inflorescence.

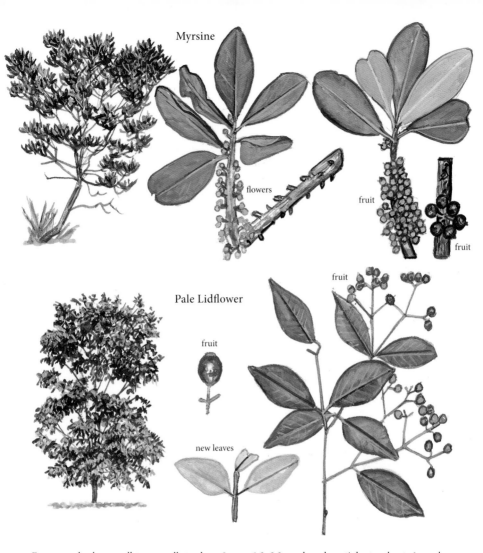

Myrsine

flowers

fruit

fruit

fruit

Pale Lidflower

fruit

new leaves

Evergreen shrub or small tree, usually to about 8 m tall in Fla. Usually shrubby, single trunk or multiple; crown dense or open. **BARK** Smooth or scaly, gray. **TWIG** Slender, smooth, gray, longitudinally ridged, produced in pairs at each node. **LEAF** Opposite, simple, aromatic when crushed; lanceolate or elliptic; base narrowly or broadly wedge-shaped; tip abruptly short-pointed; margins entire. Upper surface dark green, gland-dotted, midvein grooved toward the base; lower surface medium green, usually hairy. Blade 3–8 cm long,

PALE LIDFLOWER

1.2–2.2 cm broad; petiole to about 1 cm long. **FLOWER** Tiny, greenish or whitish; corolla absent, stamens numerous, calyx cuplike, forming a lidlike cap at the summit that conceals the stamens; buds somewhat fruitlike and resembling a capsule; inflorescence finely hairy. Early summer. **FRUIT** Round, juicy berry, 5–12 mm diam.; purplish black at maturity in summer to autumn.

HABITAT/RANGE Native. In coastal subtropical hammocks; s. Fla.

MYRTLE-OF-THE-RIVER
Calyptranthes zuzygium (L.) Sw.

QUICK ID Recognized by combination of forked, longitudinally ridged twigs, capped, cuplike flowers, and hairless inflorescence.

Evergreen shrub or small tree, to about 12 m tall, 15 cm diam. Erect, usually shrubby; crown irregularly spreading, with forking branches. **BARK** Smooth, gray. **TWIG** Longitudinally ridged; produced in pairs at the node, each twig terminating at the next pair of leaves. **LEAF** Opposite, simple, leathery, thick; elliptic or obovate, base rounded or wedge-shaped, tip bluntly or abruptly short-pointed. Upper surface dark green, lateral venation obscure, midvein slightly raised; lower surface usually hairless; both surfaces finely gland-dotted. Blade 3–7 cm long, 1.8–3.8 cm broad; petiole to about 5 mm long. **FLOWER** Tiny, greenish white, corolla lacking, calyx cuplike and forming a cap over the numerous stamens; inflorescence hairless. Early summer. **FRUIT** Round black berry, 7–10 mm diam., often with a whitish blush; matures summer to autumn.

HABITAT/RANGE Native. Subtropical hammocks, rare and endangered; s. Fla.

SIMILAR SPECIES Distinguished from Pale Lidflower by the finely hairy lower leaf surface and inflorescence.

MYRTLE-OF-THE-RIVER

■ *EUCALYPTUS:* EUCALYPTUSES

A genus of 450–500 species, almost all confined to Australia; a few in Malaysia. More than 200 have been introduced throughout the world; about 14 are naturalized in North America, 4 in s. Fla.

Evergreen dwarf shrubs to massive trees, vying with redwoods as the tallest plants. **BARK** Varying from hard, persistent, dark, and furrowed, to smooth and peeling or flaking; usually varicolored, white, cream, salmon, tan, or gray, and helpful for identification. **LEAF** Variable in arrangement; leaves initiated from opposite buds, and juvenile leaves usually opposite and often proportionately broader than adult leaves; unequal elongation of the stem results in alternate arrangement in adult leaves. Adult leaves are described in the species entries. Blade simple, leathery, often stiff; adult leaves usually lanceolate or curved; margins entire. **FLOWER** Small, often showy, bisexual, radially symmetric, borne singly or in umbellate clusters, the clusters in some arranged in branched panicles. Flower subtended at base by a leathery hypanthium; in bud the hypanthium has a cap made from completely fused petals and sepals that is shed as the flower opens, exposing the many stamens, which give color to the flower. Ovary inferior. **FRUIT** The fruit is a woody capsule, smooth, ribbed or warty, dehiscing to release numerous seeds.

Species of *Eucalyptus* are valued for timber, wood pulp, and fuel. Oils are extracted from the foliage of some species. Many are grown as ornamentals, often becoming weedy and invasive.

RIVER REDGUM *Eucalyptus camaldulensis* Dehnh. subsp. *acuta* Brooker & M.W. McDonald

QUICK ID Recognized by the combination of shredding bark, lanceolate leaves, umbels with 7–11 flowers, and 4-toothed, bowl-shaped woody capsules, 5–10 mm long.

Evergreen tree, 20–30 m tall, 1–2 m diam. Erect, single short trunk, low-branching, the branches often hanging in clumps. **BARK** Exfoliates in strips or flakes; mottled gray, white, and buff. **TWIG** Reddish. **LEAF** Leathery, lanceolate; margins entire. Surfaces light green, hairless. Blade 6–20 cm long, 1.5–4 cm broad; petiole 1–2 cm long. **FLOWER** Small, white, borne in axillary umbels of 7–11 flowers; hypanthium hemispheric, 2–3 mm long. Summer. **FRUIT** Smooth, bowl-shaped capsule, 5–10 mm long, with 4 broad teeth at the apex.

HABITAT/RANGE Introduced from Australia; established in disturbed areas, s. Fla.

Myrtle-of-the-river

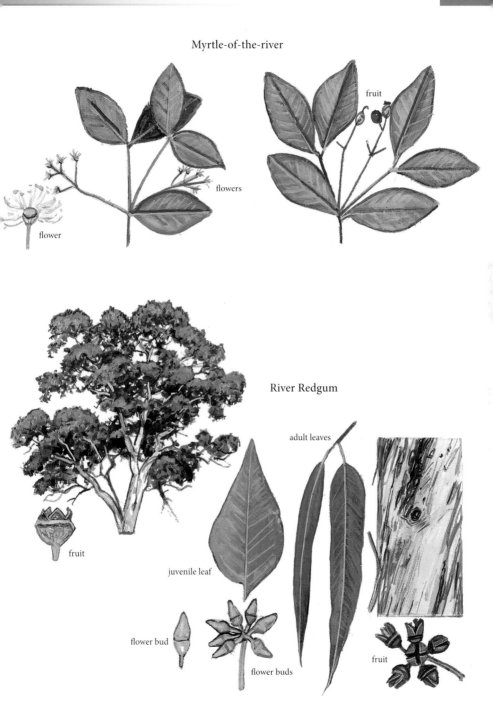

flowers

flower

fruit

River Redgum

fruit

adult leaves

juvenile leaf

flower bud

flower buds

fruit

GRAND EUCALYPTUS *Eucalyptus grandis* W. Hill ex Maiden
A.K.A. ROSE GUM

QUICK ID Recognized by the lanceolate or ovate leaves, fruit a capsule to about 8 mm long, and shredding, mottled bark.

Evergreen large tree, to at least 55 m tall, 1.8 m diam. in its native range, usually much smaller in Fla. Erect, single straight trunk; crown narrowly oblong. **BARK** Mottled, shredding to reveal smooth whitish, grayish, or greenish inner bark. **LEAF** Broadly lanceolate to ovate; base rounded or heart-shaped; tip evenly tapering to an elongated point; margins entire. Upper surface dark green, semi-lustrous; lower surface paler, grayish; both surfaces hairless, glandular. Blade 12–20 cm long, 2–3.5 cm broad; petiole to about 2 cm long. **FLOWER** Buds vase-shaped and covered with a pointed, conical cap that falls as the flower develops, leaving a puffy mass of about 20 whitish stamens. Summer. **FRUIT** Capsule to about 8 mm long, opening to release about 25 seeds.

HABITAT/RANGE Introduced from Australia; established in disturbed sites, c. and s. Fla.

SIMILAR SPECIES Swamp-mahogany has similar-size leaves, but its capsule is greater than 10 mm long.

SWAMP-MAHOGANY *Eucalyptus robusta* Sm.

QUICK ID Recognized by the combination of stiff, leathery leaves, flower buds 1.5–2 cm long, and fruit a capsule 10–15 mm long.

Evergreen tree, to about 40 m tall and 1.2 m diam. in its native range, smaller in Fla. Erect, single straight trunk; crown with several large, ascending branches topped with clumps of leaves. **BARK** Furrowed, grayish brown or reddish brown. **LEAF** Thick, stiff, leathery, broadly lanceolate to nearly elliptic; base rounded, sometimes asymmetric; tip abruptly tapered to a narrow point; margins entire. Upper surface dark green, hairless; lower surface

light green. Blade 10–18 cm long, 3–6 cm broad; petiole 2–3.5 cm long. **FLOWER** Bud 1.5–2 cm long, hypanthium cone-shaped, covered with a pointed cap that falls to reveal numerous creamy-white stamens to about 1.2 cm long. Summer. **FRUIT** Brown capsule, 10–15 mm long, narrow at base, abruptly flaring and cuplike above.

HABITAT/RANGE Introduced from Australia; sparingly naturalized in c. Fla. peninsula.

SIMILAR SPECIES The leaves of Grand Eucalyptus are similar in size, but the capsule is less than 10 mm long.

TORREL'S EUCALYPTUS *Eucalyptus torelliana* F. Muell.
A.K.A. CADAGA

QUICK ID Recognized by the combination of leathery leaves, greenish bark, and reddish hairs on twigs, petioles, and the midveins of the leaves.

Evergreen large tree, 20–30 m tall and 1 m diam. in its native range; smaller in Fla. Erect, single straight trunk; crown rounded when open-grown, narrower, oblong, and somewhat irregular when forest-grown. **BARK** Smooth, exfoliating, greenish, becoming gray or blackish on old trees. **TWIG** Slender, covered with reddish hairs. **LEAF** Leathery, broadly lanceolate to ovate; base rounded; tip evenly tapering to a blunt point; margins entire, wavy. Upper surface green, sometimes pinkish, the midvein finely hairy with reddish-orange hairs, at least when young. Blade 7–15 cm long, 4–9 cm broad; petiole 1–2 cm long. **FLOWER** Buds to about 1 cm long, hypanthium rounded, to about 6 mm long, topped with a cap 4 mm wide that falls to reveal about 10 creamy stamens, 8–10 mm long. Summer. **FRUIT** Rounded capsule to about 1.3 cm diam.

HABITAT/RANGE Introduced from Australia; established in disturbed sites, sc. Fla.

SIMILAR SPECIES The twigs, petioles, and leaf midveins of Grand Eucalyptus and Swamp-mahogany are not covered with reddish hairs.

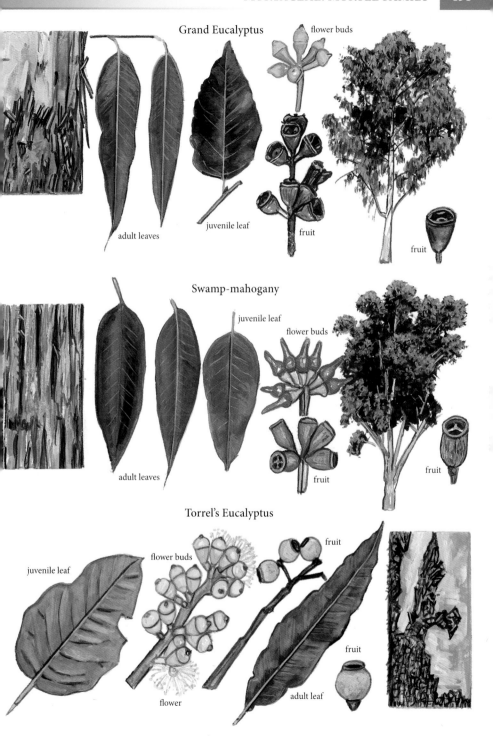

Grand Eucalyptus

flower buds

adult leaves

juvenile leaf

fruit

fruit

Swamp-mahogany

juvenile leaf

flower buds

adult leaves

fruit

fruit

Torrel's Eucalyptus

juvenile leaf

flower buds

fruit

flower

adult leaf

fruit

■ *EUGENIA*: STOPPERS

A genus of 500–1,000 species with a worldwide tropical distribution; 6 species occur in North America, 4 native, with 5 species in the East, 4 native.

Evergreen shrubs or trees. **LEAF** Opposite, simple, usually leathery and pinnately veined. **FLOWER** Bisexual, sepals and petals 4, stamens numerous; clustered or solitary in the leaf axils, sometimes in opposite pairs at the lower nodes on leafy branches. **FRUIT** Rounded berry with 1 or 2 seeds, usually crowned with the remains of the calyx.

WHITE STOPPER *Eugenia axillaris* (Sw.) Willd.

QUICK ID Recognized by the combination of opposite leaves greater than 3 cm long with an acute tip, short flower and fruit stalks less than 5 mm long, and a fine covering of black dots on the lower leaf surface.

Evergreen shrub or small tree, to about 8 m tall, about 12 cm diam. Erect, usually single trunk, often low-branching; crown narrow. **BARK** Smooth or slightly scaly, grayish white. **TWIG** Moderately stout, grayish. **LEAF** Opposite, simple, thick, leathery, with a strong musty odor when crushed; ovate, broadly lanceolate, or elliptic, widest at or below the middle; base wedge-shaped to nearly rounded; tip abruptly tapered to a narrow, blunt point; margins entire. Upper surface semi-lustrous or dull, dark green; lower surface paler, finely black-dotted. Blade 3–7 cm long, 1.5–4 cm broad; petiole 5–12 mm long, often reddish. **FLOWER** Fragrant, 5–10 mm diam.; sepals 4; petals 4, white; stamens numerous. Produced in clusters in the leaf axils, stalks stout, to about 5 mm long. Predominantly summer, potentially year-round. **FRUIT** Rounded, juicy berry, 8–12 mm diam., nearly stalkless; reddish, becoming black at maturity, likely present year-round.

HABITAT/RANGE Native. Coastal hammocks, nc. Fla. south to Fla. Keys.

SIMILAR SPECIES Boxleaf Stopper has stout fruit stalks less than 5 mm long, but the leaf is widest above the middle and has a rounded tip.

Notes: This species is the most commonly encountered stopper in s. Fla.

BOXLEAF STOPPER *Eugenia foetida* Pers.

A.K.A. SPANISH STOPPER

QUICK ID A stopper, recognized by the combination of opposite, predominantly oblanceolate or obovate leaves with a tapering base and rounded tip.

Evergreen shrub or small tree to about 6 m tall, 10 cm diam. Erect, single trunk or multiple, usually with a slender aspect; crown narrow, dense, especially in hammocks. **BARK** Smooth, gray, often mottled, becoming slightly fissured and divided into plates. **TWIG** Gray, slender, usually finely hairy, or hairless. **LEAF** Opposite, simple, leathery, aromatic when crushed; oval, elliptic, or obovate, more often widest above the middle but varying considerably in shape even on the same tree; base narrowly tapered; tip rounded or bluntly pointed; margins entire, slightly thickened, often curled under. Upper surface dull, dark green, hairless; lower surface paler, finely dotted with blackish glands. Blade 2–6 cm long, 1.4–4 cm broad; petiole 0–5 cm long, often appearing winged. **FLOWER** Mildly fragrant, less than 1 cm diam.; sepals 4, rounded; petals 4, white, gland-dotted; stamens numerous, threadlike; ovary inferior; produced in clusters at the leaf axils. Summer. **FRUIT** Rounded berry with 1 or 2 seeds, 5–8 mm diam., reddish orange or yellowish

WHITE STOPPER

BOXLEAF STOPPER

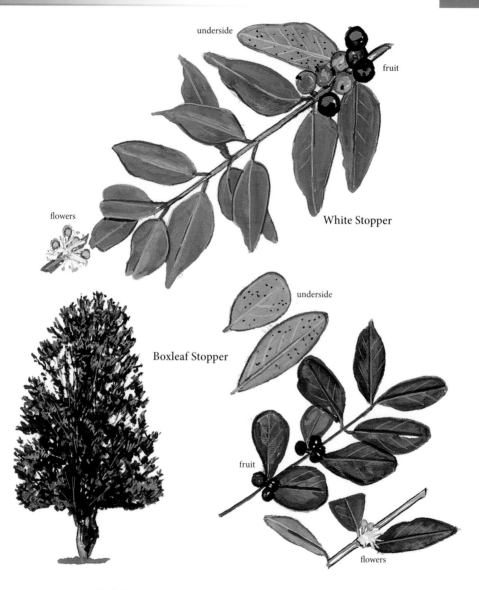

underside

fruit

flowers

White Stopper

Boxleaf Stopper

underside

fruit

flowers

orange, turning blackish brown, stalk less than 4 mm long; matures in autumn but often remains on the tree well into winter.

HABITAT/RANGE Native. Subtropical hammocks, pinelands, often where limestone is present; s. Fla.

SIMILAR SPECIES White Stopper has stout leaf stalks less than 5 mm long, but the leaves are widest at or below the middle and have an abruptly pointed tip. The leaves of Long-stalked Stopper (*Mosiera longipes*) are predominantly less than 2 cm long.

Notes: This species is widespread in the tropics and grows to larger proportions outside of Florida. It is one of the more common stoppers in s. Fla.

REDBERRY STOPPER *Eugenia confusa* DC.

QUICK ID A stopper, recognized by the combination of bright red fruit and opposite, stiff, lustrous, long-pointed leaves with drooping tips.

Evergreen small tree, to about 6 m tall and 8 cm diam. in Fla., potentially to 18 m tall and 30 cm diam. Erect, single straight trunk; crown rounded, spreading. **BARK** Light gray, rough, scaly, becoming deeply furrowed. **TWIG** Slender, hairless, green at first, becoming gray. **LEAF** Opposite, simple, stiff, leathery, broadly lanceolate or ovate; base rounded or broadly wedge-shaped; tip abruptly narrowed to an elongated point, often curved downward; margins entire. Upper surface lustrous, dark or yellowish green; lower surface paler, finely and minutely gland-dotted. Blade 3–7 cm long, 2–4 cm broad; petiole 5–10 mm long. **FLOWER** Fragrant, about 6 mm diam.; sepals 4, less than 4 mm long; petals 4, white; stamens numerous, threadlike, spreading. Spring to autumn. **FRUIT** Rounded, 1-seeded scarlet berry, 5–8 mm diam., stalk 8–16 mm long; matures late summer to autumn.

HABITAT/RANGE Native. Rare, subtropical hammocks; an endangered species in s. Fla., more common in the West Indies.

SIMILAR SPECIES The upper surface of the leaf of Red Stopper is dull.

RED STOPPER *Eugenia rhombea* (O. Berg) Krug & Urb.
A.K.A. SPICEBERRY EUGENIA

QUICK ID Recognized by the combination of opposite, dull green leaves not exceeding about 6 cm long and red-orange berries that turn black at maturity.

Evergreen shrub or small upright tree, to about 8 m tall, 5–20 cm diam. throughout much of its range, to about 3 m tall in Fla. Erect, single slender trunk. **BARK** Smooth, brownish gray or clay-colored, peeling off in flakes to reveal light brown inner bark. **TWIG** Slender, whitish gray, often drooping. **LEAF** Opposite, simple, leathery, ovate or nearly rhombic; base wedge-shaped or slightly rounded; apex abruptly long-pointed, the tip blunt; margins entire. Upper surface dull, dark green, lower surface yellow-green, both surfaces finely gland-dotted. Blade 3–6 cm long, 1.5–4 cm broad; petiole 3–6 mm long. **FLOWER** Fragrant, about 9 mm diam.; sepals 4, less than 4 mm long; petals 4, white. Produced solitarily or in clusters of 2–8. Year-round. **FRUIT** Rounded berry, scarlet or orange-red, becoming black, 7–9 mm diam.; stalk 8–15 mm long. Year-round.

HABITAT/RANGE Native. Hammocks, endangered in s. Fla. and the Fla. Keys.

SIMILAR SPECIES See Redberry Stopper.

SURINAM CHERRY *Eugenia uniflora* L.

QUICK ID Recognized by the combination of opposite leaves not exceeding about 7 cm long, short petioles, and ribbed red fruit.

Evergreen shrub or small tree, to about 5 m tall and 10 cm diam. Erect, single trunk; crown narrowly spreading, more or less rounded. **BARK** Grayish brown or reddish brown, smooth, mottled, peeling. **TWIG** Slender, light brown. **LEAF** Opposite, simple, leathery, ovate or broadly lanceolate; base rounded, sometimes slightly notched; apex abruptly short-pointed, the tip blunt; margins entire. Upper surface lustrous green, lower surface paler, both surfaces finely gland-dotted. Blade 3–7 cm long, to about 3.5 cm broad; petiole 3–4 mm long. **FLOWER** Fragrant, about 1.5 cm diam.; sepals 4, 4–8 mm long; petals 4, white; stamens about 60, to about 7 mm long; stalk 5–20 mm long. Year-round. **FRUIT** Vertically depressed, bright red berry with vertically ribbed and grooved sides; 2–3 cm diam.; stalk 4–8 mm long. Year-round.

HABITAT/RANGE Introduced; established in hammocks in s. Fla, considered invasive.

REDBERRY STOPPER   RED STOPPER

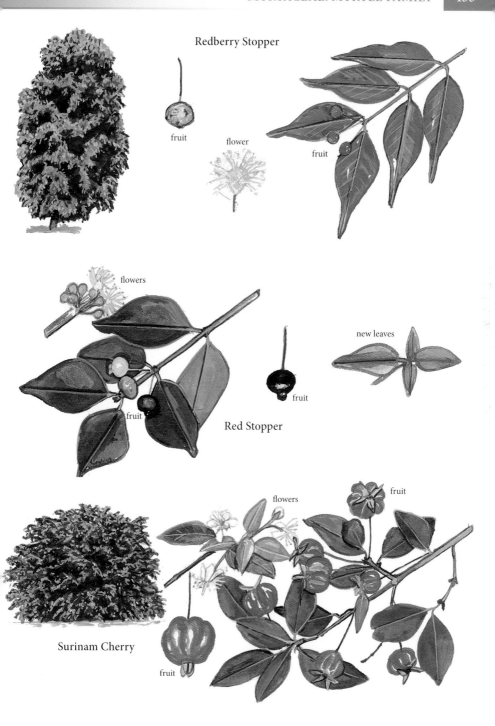

Redberry Stopper

fruit

flower

fruit

flowers

new leaves

fruit

fruit

Red Stopper

flowers

fruit

Surinam Cherry

fruit

◼ *MELALEUCA*: BOTTLE-BRUSHES AND CAJEPUTS

A genus of about 280 species distributed mainly in Australia, but also in Indonesia, New Caledonia, and New Guinea. Treated here as a single genus but formerly separated into the genera *Melaleuca* and *Callistemon*. Widely cultivated in the U.S. and elsewhere; 4 species naturalized in North America, all in the East, none native. Evergreen shrubs or trees. **LEAF** Alternate, simple, usually somewhat leathery, veins linear, sometimes only the midvein evident. **FLOWER** Bisexual; sepals 5; petals 5, white, pinkish, reddish, or yellowish; stamens numerous, 1–2.5 cm long; inflorescence a densely flowered terminal spike, 5–15 cm long, the central axis of the spike continuing to elongate and produce leaves after flowering. **FRUIT** Cup- or pot-shaped capsule about 6 mm broad; produced in more or less dense, elongate clusters that encircle the branch between leaf nodes; seeds brown, 1–2 mm long.

WEEPING BOTTLEBRUSH *Melaleuca viminalis* (Sol. ex Gaertn.) Byrnes

QUICK ID Recognized by the combination of the red bottlebrush-like inflorescence, narrow grayish-green leaves, and weeping crown.

Evergreen shrub or small tree, to about 6 m tall. Erect, single trunk or multiple, often crooked; crown graceful, drooping, more or less rounded. **BARK** Brown or grayish brown, ridged and furrowed at maturity. **TWIG** Silky-hairy. **LEAF** Alternate, simple, aromatic, narrowly lanceolate or linear; base tapering; tip pointed, often with a tiny knoblike protrusion; margins entire. Surfaces pale grayish green. Blade 5–13 cm long, usually less than 1 cm broad; petiole 2–3 mm long. **FLOWER** Bisexual, small, calyx cuplike; sepals 5; petals 5, deltoid, to about 3 mm long; stamens numerous, scarlet, to about 2.5 cm long; pistil red. Produced in a bottlebrush-like spike to about 10 cm long. Spring to summer. **FRUIT** Small, hard, persistent cuplike capsule, to about 6 mm long, containing numerous angular brown seeds. Maturing summer to autumn.

HABITAT/RANGE Introduced from Australia; escaped and common along roadsides in s. Fla.

SIMILAR SPECIES Melaleuca and Snow in Summer have white flowers and whitish papery bark. See also Lemon Bottlebrush.

LEMON BOTTLEBRUSH *Melaleuca citrina* (Curtis) Dum. Cours.
A.K.A. CRIMSON BOTTLEBRUSH

Shrub or small tree to about 3 m tall, easily mistaken for Weeping Bottlebrush, but the flower has conspicuous yellow anthers and the leaves are narrow. **HABITAT/RANGE** Introduced from Australia; reportedly naturalized in La.

MELALEUCA *Melaleuca quinquenervia* (Cav.) S.T. Blake
A.K.A. PUNKTREE, CAJEPUT

QUICK ID Easily recognized by the combination of whitish peeling bark, white bottlebrush-like inflorescence, and narrow, 5-veined leaves.

Evergreen tree, 15–30 m tall, 30–180 cm diam. Erect, single straight trunk; crown narrow, often open, irregularly branched. **BARK** Soft, whitish, papery, peeling in large curly plates to reveal numerous pinkish fibrous layers. **TWIG** Slender, often drooping, light brown and hairy at first, becoming gray. **LEAF** Alternate, simple, slightly thickened and stiffish, with a resinous odor when crushed; lanceolate, narrowly elliptic, or oblanceolate; base evenly tapered; tip evenly tapered, often abruptly short-pointed; margins entire. Upper surface grayish green, with 3–7 (usually 5) conspicuous longitudinal veins; lower surface paler, finely hairy. Blade 4–12 cm long, 1.8–2.5 cm broad; petiole to about 5 mm long, thick, light green, finely hairy. **FLOWER** Bisexual; sepals 5, tiny; petals 5, white, circular, 2–3 mm broad; stamens numerous, white, filaments white. Produced in closely set, or sometimes interrupted, internodal clusters, giving the appearance of a bottlebrush, 5–15 cm long. Nearly year-round. **FRUIT** Rounded or squarish capsule, about 6 mm diam.; the capsules stalkless, crowded, and encircling the stem between leaf nodes; seeds brown. Nearly year-round.

HABITAT/RANGE Introduced from Australia, Melanesia; well established in hammocks, pinelands, disturbed woodlands, and along roadsides, mostly in s. Fla., sparsely naturalized in se. La.

Notes: Melaleuca quinquenervia is among Florida's top 3 invasive species, covering thousands of hectares in tropical and subtropical regions. Eradication efforts have been largely unsuccessful owing to its aggressive growth and rapid establishment.

Weeping Bottlebrush

flowers

fruit

fruit

Lemon Bottlebrush

flowers

fruit

fruit

Melaleuca

leaf

flowers

fruit

fruit

SNOW IN SUMMER *Melaleuca linariifolia* Sm.
A.K.A. CAJEPUT

Similar to Melaleuca; differs in having much narrower leaves that do not exceed about 1 cm broad. **HABITAT/RANGE** Introduced from Australia; sparsely established in 1 county in c. Fla. peninsula.

LONG-STALKED STOPPER *Mosiera longipes* (O. Berg) Small
A.K.A MANGROVEBERRY

QUICKID Recognized by the combination of long-stalked flowers and fruits, opposite, oval to nearly circular leaves with a rounded tip, and multicolored white and pinkish flowers.

Evergreen shrub or small tree, to about 4 m tall; more often treelike where it invades hammocks. Erect, single short, slender trunk, or multiple trunks; crown diffuse, spreading or ascending, branches wiry, slender. **BARK** Smooth, grayish, mottled. **TWIG** Slender, finely hairy or hairless. **LEAF** Opposite, simple, somewhat stiff and leathery; ovate, oval, or elliptic to nearly circular; base rounded or wedge-shaped; tip rounded or bluntly pointed; margins entire. Upper surface lustrous green or yellow-green, lower surface paler, veins reddish; both surfaces hairless. Blade 1–5 cm long (often less than 2 cm), 1–3.5 cm broad; petiole 2–4 mm long. **FLOWER** Bisexual, 10–12 mm diam.; sepals 4; petals 4, nearly circular, white or pinkish; stamens numerous, style about 5 mm long. Produced in fascicled, several-flowered clusters, each flower borne singly at the terminus of a stalk 2 cm long or more. Year-round. **FRUIT** Rounded berry, 6–10 mm diam.; reddish at first, turning black or blue-black; produced on a long stalk. Year-round.

HABITAT/RANGE Native. Pinelands, subtropical hammocks; s. Fla., classified as endangered.

SIMILAR SPECIES White Indigoberry (*Randia aculeata*, Rubiaceae) has forked branches, closely clustered leaves, and white fruit. Stoppers (*Eugenia*) do not have long-stalked flowers. Twinberry (*Myrcianthes fragrans*) produces a cluster of several flowers at the end of a long stalk.

Notes: Mosiera is a genus of about 30 species, distributed mostly in Cuba; 1 is native to Florida. Formerly included within the genus *Psidium*.

TWINBERRY *Myrcianthes fragrans* (Sw.) McVaugh
A.K.A SIMPSON'S STOPPER

QUICKID Recognized by multibranched, long-stalked inflorescences, fruits usually in pairs, and opposite leaves, some with a notched tip.

Evergreen shrub or small tree, 8–15 m tall, potentially to about 20 cm diam., usually smaller. Erect, often dense and shrubby; crown rounded or diffusely spreading, branches slender. **BARK** Smooth, whitish or reddish, often flaking. **TWIG** Slender, gray, finely hairy or hairless. **LEAF** Opposite, simple, leathery, stiffish, aromatic when crushed; elliptic, oblong, obovate, or ovate, base wedge-shaped, tip rounded or bluntly pointed, often notched; margins entire. Upper surface lustrous green, lower surface paler, both surfaces densely covered with minute, often black glandular dots. Blade 2–6 cm long, 1–4 cm broad; petiole about 5 mm long, usually finely hairy. **FLOWER** Bisexual, about 12 mm diam., sepals 4, unequal; petals 4, white; stamens numerous, about as long as the petals. Produced in a multibranched cluster, the main stalk 2–4 cm long, terminated by a cluster of 3–7 flowers, individual flowers on subsidiary stalks 5–15 mm long. Year-round. **FRUIT** Typically a 1-seeded, rounded red or black berry, 6–10 mm diam., usually produced in pairs.

HABITAT/RANGE Native. Hammocks, c. and s. Fla.

SIMILAR SPECIES The sepals of Long-stalked Stopper (*Mosiera longipes*) are closed in bud, Twinberry's are spreading.

Notes: Myrcianthes is a genus of about 40 species distributed in South America and Fla.

LONG-STALKED STOPPER

TWINBERRY

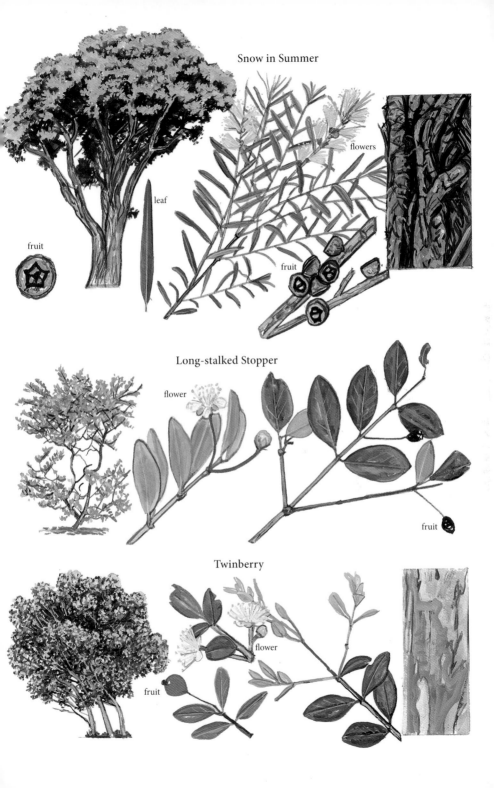

Snow in Summer

leaf

flowers

fruit

fruit

Long-stalked Stopper

flower

fruit

Twinberry

flower

fruit

■ *PSIDIUM*: GUAVAS

A genus of about 150 species distributed mostly in tropical America, introduced and cultivated elsewhere; 2 species introduced to, and cultivated in, North America, both considered to be invasive species in Fla. Long-stalked Stopper (*Mosiera longipes*) was formerly included within this genus.

Evergreen shrubs or small trees. **LEAF** Opposite, simple, pinnately veined, stalked. **FLOWER** Bisexual, hypanthium cup- or urn-shaped; sepals 4 or 5; petals 4 or 5, white; stamens numerous, conspicuous; style 1, ovary inferior. **FRUIT** Many-seeded rounded or pear-shaped berry, the seeds hard-coated.

STRAWBERRY GUAVA *Psidium cattleianum* Sabine

QUICK ID Recognized by the combination of opposite leaves that lack hairs or prominent veins beneath, white flowers with numerous stamens, and distinctive reddish or yellow fruit.

Evergreen shrub or small tree, to about 8 m tall. Erect, usually single trunk; crown rounded, dense. **BARK** Smooth, gray or reddish-brown, mottled, often peeling. **TWIG** Stout, round in cross section, finely hairy. **LEAF** Opposite, simple, leathery, elliptic to obovate; base broadly wedge-shaped; tip blunt or abruptly short-pointed; margins entire. Upper surface lustrous, dark green; lower surface paler, usually hairless. Blade 4–10 cm long, 2–4 cm broad; petiole about 1 cm long. **FLOWER** About 2.5 cm diam.; petals 4 or 5, white, to about 1 cm long; stamens numerous, about as long as the petals. Year-round. **FRUIT** Many-seeded rounded purplish-red or yellow berry, 2–6 cm diam., the remains of the calyx usually protruding at the apex; whitish inside. Year-round.

HABITAT/RANGE Introduced from South America (chiefly Brazil); cultivated for its fruit, established in prairies, hammocks, bottomland forests, flatwoods, and swamps in s. Fla., where it is treated as an invasive species.

SIMILAR SPECIES Guava has angled twigs and larger leaves with prominent raised veins on the lower surface.

GUAVA *Psidium guajava* L.

QUICK ID Recognized by the combination of stiff opposite leaves with prominent venation, scaly bark, distinctive fruit, and angled twigs.

Evergreen shrub or small tree, usually not exceeding about 5 m tall, potentially to 11 m, to about 14 cm diam. More or less erect; crown spreading. **BARK** Smooth, reddish or greenish, shedding in thin plates. **TWIG** Slender, hairy, scaly, 4-angled. **LEAF** Opposite, simple, thick, leathery, coarse, elliptic or oblong, base wedge-shaped, tip bluntly or abruptly pointed; margins entire. Upper surface dark, lustrous green; lower surface paler, with a covering of soft grayish hairs and glandular dots, lateral veins prominent. Blade 4–15 cm long, 3–6 cm broad; petiole to about 1 cm long. **FLOWER** 3–4 cm diam.; sepals 5, to about 1.5 cm long; petals 5, white, 1.5–2 cm long; solitary in the leaf axils. **FRUIT** Greenish, yellowish, or pinkish berry, rounded or pear-shaped, 2–6 cm long, edible.

HABITAT/RANGE Introduced from tropical America; established in hammocks, disturbed sites, primarily in s. Fla., also reported for La. Treated as invasive in Fla.

SIMILAR SPECIES Distinctive in s. Fla. Perhaps confused with Deviltree (*Alstonia macrophylla*, Apocynaceae), which also has prominent leaf venation but produces milky sap from the broken petiole.

Strawberry Guava

fruit

fruit section

flowers

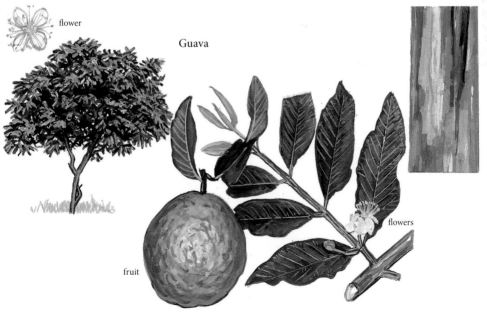

flower

Guava

flowers

fruit

■ *SYZYGIUM*: ROSE-APPLES

A tropical genus of 300–1,200 species distributed in Southeast Asia, Africa, Australia, New Caledonia, New Zealand, and Pacific islands; 2 species are introduced and established in North America.

Usually evergreen shrubs or trees. **LEAF** Opposite (in ours) or whorled, simple, usually pinnately veined, the veins usually numerous and closely set; margins usually entire. **FLOWER** Bisexual; sepals 4 or 5; petals 4 or 5, distinct and spreading or fused and cuplike and falling as a unit; stamens numerous, anthers minute; style 1, ovary inferior. **FRUIT** Drupelike berry with 1 or 2 seeds.

JAVA PLUM *Syzygium cumini* (L.) Skeels

QUICKID Recognized by the opposite, lustrous green leaves, fused flower petals, and a reddish, pinkish, or purplish, apparently single-seeded berry to 2.5 cm long.

Evergreen fast-growing tree, 10–25 m tall, 40–100 cm diam. Erect, single short, straight or crooked trunk; crown irregular, more or less rounded, dense, with numerous branches. **BARK** Smooth or rough, brown or grayish white, thick, scaly. **TWIG** Slender, green or gray, slightly flattened, hairy. **LEAF** Opposite, simple, thick, leathery; elliptic, oblong, or broadly obovate; base rounded or broadly wedge-shaped; tip rounded, blunt, or tapering to a long point; margins entire, usually with a visible and sometimes transparent marginal vein. Upper surface lustrous, dark green, lateral veins yellowish and closely set; lower surface yellowish green, duller; both surfaces hairless. Blade 7–18 cm long, 3–10 cm broad; petiole 5–25 mm long, light yellow. **FLOWER** Individually small, to about 7 mm long; petals 4, fused into a rounded cap that opens to expose a mass of white or pinkish threadlike stamens about 5 mm long. Produced in clusters 5–6 cm long on wood of the previous year. Year-round. **FRUIT** Fleshy 1-seeded oblong or ellipsoid berry, 1–2.5 cm long, about 2 cm diam.; green at first, becoming pink or red then purplish black. Matures year-round.

HABITAT/RANGE Introduced from Asia; established in maritime hammocks, flatwoods, rockland hammocks, lake margins, in c. and s. peninsula Fla., where it is treated as an invasive species.

SIMILAR SPECIES Malabar Plum is distinguished by its separate flower petals and its larger leaves and fruit.

MALABAR PLUM *Syzygium jambos* (L.) Alston
A.K.A. ROSE APPLE

QUICKID Recognized by the combination of the large opposite, long-tapering leaves, distinctive pale yellow fruit, and comparatively large flower with a conspicuous mass of long white stamens.

Evergreen shrub or, more often, a tree, 7.5–12 m tall, 10–20 cm diam. Erect, usually single trunk; crown dense, broad, of slender, wide-spreading, and often drooping branches. **BARK** More or less smooth and finely fissured. **TWIG** Green at first, becoming brown. **LEAF** Opposite, simple, moderately leathery, lanceolate or narrowly elliptic, base rounded or wedge-shaped, tip long-tapering to a sharp point; margins entire. Upper surface rosy red at first, becoming dark, lustrous green; lower surface dull green. Blade 8–22 cm long, 2–6 cm broad; petiole to about 1 cm long. **FLOWER** About 3 cm diam. across the petals; sepals 4, broad, rounded; petals 4, not fused, white, oblong with a rounded apex, to about 1.5 cm long; pistil 1; stamens numerous, 4–5 cm long, densely massed and forming the conspicuous part of the flower. Commonly produced in clusters of 4 or 5 flowers. Year-round. **FRUIT** Firm, rounded or ellipsoid, pale yellow or greenish berry with 1 or 2 seeds, 2.5–5 cm diam.; matures year-round.

HABITAT/RANGE Introduced from Southeast Asia; widely established in tropical and subtropical ecosystems far beyond its native range; well established in hammocks and disturbed sites in s. Fla., where it is treated as an invasive species.

SIMILAR SPECIES Java Plum has fused flower petals and smaller fruit and leaves.

Java Plum

flowers

fruit

fruit

Malabar Plum

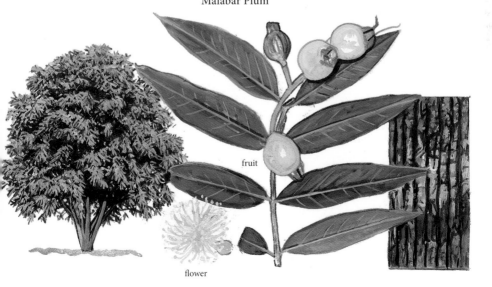

fruit

flower

NYCTAGINACEAE: FOUR-O'CLOCK FAMILY

The four-o'clock family includes about 30 genera and 300–350 species of herbs, shrubs, and trees distributed primarily in tropical and subtropical regions worldwide; 88 species occur in North America, including 3 trees native to s. Fla.

LEAF Opposite, sub-opposite, rarely alternate, simple, stalked or not, margins entire or sinuate. **FLOWER** Unisexual or bisexual; sepals usually 5 and joined, petal-like; petals absent; stamens usually equaling the sepals in number; style 1, ovary superior but appearing inferior. **FRUIT** Achene or nut, enclosed in the basal portion of a fleshy, leathery, or woody perianth tube that is often decorated with longitudinal ribs, wings, or lines of sticky, gland-tipped hairs or teeth; usually referred to as an anthocarp.

COCKSPUR *Pisonia rotundata* Griseb.
A.K.A. PISONIA, SMOOTH DEVIL'S-CLAWS

QUICK ID Recognized within its U.S. range by opposite oval leaves with conspicuous, deeply impressed yellowish veins.

Deciduous, nearly evergreen, quickly replacing fallen leaves; shrub or small spreading tree, 4–5 m tall (potentially to 8.6 m), potentially to 30 cm diam., usually much smaller in Fla. Erect, single trunk or multiple, often low-branching; crown dense, rounded or oval with numerous ascending, unarmed branches. **BARK** Ashy gray, with conspicuous leaf scars. **TWIG** Yellowish green, stout, densely or finely hairy, becoming hairless or nearly so. **LEAF** Opposite or sub-opposite, youngest leaves often produced singly at a node, simple, leathery, stiffish, oval or broadly elliptic; base rounded or broadly wedge-shaped; tip rounded, often notched; margins entire, sometimes slightly revolute. Upper surface lustrous or dull green, the veins yellowish, conspicuous, and deeply impressed; lower surface paler, veins raised, conspicuous. Blade 2–10 cm long, 2–5 cm broad; petiole to about 1.5 cm long, stout, often brownish. **FLOWER** Unisexual, male and female on separate plants, greenish white; male flowers tubular or urn-shaped, 2–3 mm long, stamens 10, about twice the length of the perianth; female flowers cuplike, 3–4 mm long, often blushed with red. Mid-spring to late spring, coinciding with leaf expansion. **FRUIT** An achene or nutlet enclosed within a sticky, persistent perianth 7–10 mm long, 3–4 mm broad; matures summer, ripening quickly.

HABITAT/RANGE Native. Hammocks, scrub; restricted in North America to lower Fla. Keys.

SIMILAR SPECIES *Pisonia* is a genus of 10–50 pantropical species; Pull-and-hold-back (*P. aculeata* L.), also of s. Fla., is a vinelike shrub armed with stout, recurved spines.

BLOLLY *Guapira discolor* (Spreng.) Little
A.K.A. BEEFTREE, BEEFWOOD

QUICK ID Recognized within its U.S. range by the combination of opposite leaves with a translucent midvein and bright red fruit.

Evergreen, scraggly shrub to about 4 m tall, or a tree 5–10 m tall, 10–50 cm diam. Erect, single

COCKSPUR   BLOLLY   BROADLEAF BLOLLY

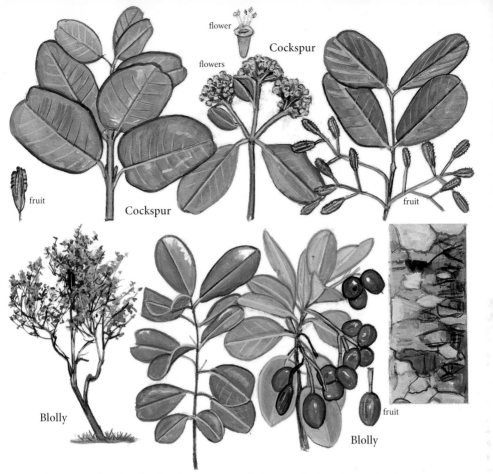

flower

flowers

Cockspur

Cockspur

Cockspur

fruit

fruit

fruit

Blolly

Blolly

trunk or multiple, often low-branching; crown of hammock-grown plants narrow, upright, with ascending branches; crown of open-grown trees irregular, spreading. **BARK** Smooth, gray or reddish gray, mottled. **TWIG** Stout, green or yellowish green. **LEAF** Opposite, sub-opposite, rarely alternate, simple, leathery, obovate, less often elliptic; base tapering, narrowly wedge-shaped; tip rounded or bluntly pointed, often notched; margins entire, thickened. Upper surface yellowish green, lateral veins obscured; midvein conspicuous, yellowish, translucent; lower surface paler; both surfaces more or less hairless. Blade averages 1–7 cm long and 2.5 cm broad, potentially larger; petiole to about 1.5 cm long, slender, grooved. **FLOWER** Unisexual, male and female flowers produced on separate plants; male flower yellow or light green, tubular or trumpet-shaped, 3–4 mm long, stamens 6–8; female flower about 3 mm long, green; produced in a branched inflorescence 3–7 cm long. Spring to summer. **FRUIT** Achene, enclosed within an oval,

fleshy, juicy, bright red perianth tube and resembling a berry or drupe, becoming weakly 10-ribbed upon drying; matures summer to autumn.

HABITAT/RANGE Native. Hammocks, coastal scrub; along the Atlantic coast from c. Fla. peninsula south to Fla. Keys.

SIMILAR SPECIES Dahoon (*Ilex cassine*, Aquifoliaceae), a holly, also has red fruit but is easily distinguished by its alternate leaves. *Guapira* is a genus of as many as 60 species distributed in the American tropics. **Broadleaf Blolly** or Corcho Prieto (*G. obtusata* [Jacq.] Little) is rare in tropical hammocks of the Fla. Keys. It is a shrub or small tree 2.5–8 m tall with smooth, light gray bark; the leaves are leathery, more often broadly elliptic, and usually broader than those of Blolly, with stout petioles. The flower buds and inflorescence are densely rusty-hairy, whereas those of Blolly are sparsely rusty-hairy.

NYSSACEAE: TUPELO FAMILY

This family of deciduous trees and shrubs includes 5 genera and 22–30 species distributed mostly in Asia. The family is represented in North America by the genus *Nyssa*. Nyssaceae is often included within the dogwood family (Cornaceae), but is treated separately owing to morphological distinctions.

■ *NYSSA*: TUPELOS

The tupelos genus includes 5 species, all native and essentially eastern in distribution. Species of *Nyssa* are deciduous trees or shrubs with furrowed, blocky grayish bark. **LEAF** Alternate, simple. **FLOWER** Usually unisexual, produced on separate trees (rarely some trees predominantly with bisexual flowers). **FRUIT** Single-stoned drupe.

Several trees of this genus are well known as the source of tupelo honey, a product of the Deep South, where expansive tupelo-dominated swamps are abundant. The common name "gum" is used for several species, an apparent misnomer as none produces gumlike latex. At least 2 species (Sour Gum and Blackgum) are used horticulturally.

WATER TUPELO *Nyssa aquatica* L.

QUICK ID Recognized by the combination of wetland habitat; large, long-stalked leaves, the margins often with a few large teeth; and long-stalked purplish drupes.

Deciduous tree to 32 m tall, usually not exceeding about 1.2 m diam., potentially to about 2.6 m diam. Erect, single trunk, the base often conspicuously and broadly swollen or buttressed, especially on old trees in undisturbed swamps. **BARK** Gray, furrowed, the ridges divided into squarish or rectangular, blocky plates. **TWIG** Reddish brown, moderately stout, usually hairless. **LEAF** Alternate, simple, obovate, ovate, or oblong; base broadly or narrowly wedge-shaped or heart-shaped; tip abruptly short-pointed; margins entire or with a few large, irregularly spaced teeth, especially toward the tip. Upper surface lustrous, dark green, hairless or nearly so; lower surface paler, usually downy-hairy. Blade 6–30 cm long (usually exceeding 15 cm), 6–8 cm broad; petiole 3–6 cm long. **FLOWER** Usually male and female flowers on separate trees; produced in stalked, rounded, compact clusters, 1–1.5 cm diam. Spring. **FRUIT** Oblong, dark blue to purple drupe, 1.5–4 cm long, borne singly on a conspicuous stalk to about 5 cm long; the stone ribbed, lacking papery wings; matures summer to autumn.

HABITAT/RANGE Native. River swamps, floodplains, lake margins; Va. south to n. Fla., west to s. Ill., se. Mo., Ark., and e. Tex.

SIMILAR SPECIES Ogeechee Tupelo can be distinguished by its shorter leaf stalks and fruit stalks, reddish drupe, and the seed with papery wings along the ribs.

OGEECHEE TUPELO *Nyssa ogeche* W. Bartram ex Marshall
A.K.A. OGEECHE-LIME

QUICK ID Recognized by the combination of wetland habitat, leaning habit, short-stalked leaves, and short-stalked, reddish drupes with papery-winged seeds.

Deciduous tree, to 18 m tall, usually not exceeding about 77 cm diam., potentially larger in undisturbed swamps. Erect or leaning, often with multiple crooked trunks, base usually conspicuously and broadly swollen or buttressed, especially on large old trees in still-water swamps. **BARK** Gray or brown, furrowed, the ridges divided into

WATER TUPELO

OGEECHEE TUPELO

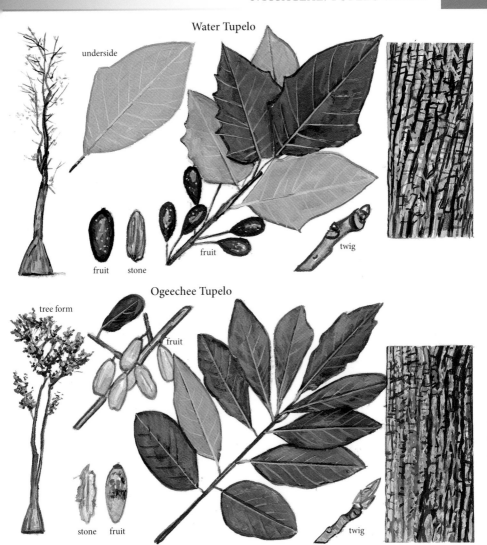

Water Tupelo

underside

fruit stone

fruit

twig

Ogeechee Tupelo

tree form

fruit

stone fruit

twig

squarish or rectangular, blocky plates. **TWIG** Reddish brown, slender, usually hairy. **LEAF** Alternate, simple, obovate or elliptic; base broadly or narrowly wedge-shaped or heart-shaped; tip rounded or bluntly pointed; margins entire. Upper surface lustrous, dark green; lower surface paler, velvety. Blade 8–15 cm long, 5–8 cm broad; petiole less than 2 cm long. **FLOWER** Usually unisexual, male and female usually on separate trees; produced in stalked, rounded, compact clusters, 1–1.5 cm diam. Spring. **FRUIT** Oblong or obovoid reddish drupe, 2.5–4 cm long, often widest above the middle, borne singly on a comparatively short stalk to about 1.25 cm long; the stone ribbed, the ribs decorated with conspicuous papery wings; matures summer.

HABITAT/RANGE Native. River swamps, floodplains, lake margins; southeastern coastal plains, se. S.C., se. Ga., n. Fla., sw. Ala.

SIMILAR SPECIES Water Tupelo has longer leaf stalks, longer fruit stalks, and a purplish drupe, and the ribbed seed lacks papery wings.

SOUR GUM *Nyssa sylvatica* Marshall
A.K.A. BLACK TUPELO, BLACK GUM

QUICK ID **Distinguished by the combination of upland habitat, typically obovate leaves, horizontally spreading branches, and single-seeded purplish-black drupes borne in clusters of 2 or 3 at the end of a long stalk.**

Deciduous tree to about 35 m tall, 50–150 cm diam. Erect, single straight trunk, lacking a bulging or buttressed base; crown broad, layered, the lateral branches usually spreading at right angles to the trunk. **BARK** Grayish, becoming furrowed and blocky, the blocks rectangular or oblong. **TWIG** Slender or moderately stout, reddish brown or greenish brown, hairless or not, with pale lenticels; pith solid, with cross partitions. **LEAF** Alternate, simple, often clustered near the tips of branches; thin and papery, elliptic to obovate, usually widest above the middle; base broadly wedge-shaped; tip bluntly pointed; margins entire, or with 1–3 large teeth near the tip. Upper surface lustrous dark green; lower surface paler, dull green. Blade 3–15 cm long, 2.5–10 cm broad; petiole 1.5–3 cm long. Turns scarlet in autumn. **FLOWER** Unisexual, male and female flowers produced on separate trees; greenish yellow, tiny, borne at the tip of an elongated stalk. Spring. **FRUIT** Single-stoned purplish-black drupe, 6–13 mm long, the stone with 10–12 faint ribs; usually 2 or 3 at the end of an elongated stalk; matures summer to autumn.

HABITAT/RANGE Native. Well-drained upland woods and rich deciduous forests, to about 1,250 m; widespread and common in the East, N.Y. south to n. Fla., west to se. Wis., s. Mo., and e. Tex.

SIMILAR SPECIES Sour Gum is our only *Nyssa* species that occurs in a predominately upland habitat. The fruit of Common Persimmon (*Diospyros virginiana*, Ebenaceae) is vertically depressed, 4–5 cm diam., and yellowish to orange at maturity, and the leaves are usually at least slightly hairy beneath. The fruit of Bigleaf Snowbell (*Styrax grandifolius*, Styracaceae) is a nutlike capsule and the leaves are hairy beneath.

BLACKGUM *Nyssa biflora* Walter
A.K.A. SWAMP BLACKGUM, SWAMP BLACK TUPELO

QUICK ID **Recognized by the combination of wetland habitat; narrowly elliptic, often purplish-spotted leaves; and paired purplish-black drupes at the end of a long stalk.**

Deciduous shrub or tree, to about 34 m tall, 1.2 m diam. Erect, single trunk, the base often swollen and conspicuously buttressed; crown narrow, oblong, especially when forest-grown. **BARK** Grayish, furrowed, divided into oblong or squarish, blocky plates. **TWIG** Slender, grayish brown. **LEAF** Alternate, simple, thin and papery to somewhat leathery, narrowly elliptic to sometimes widest above the middle; base narrowly wedge-shaped; tip usually bluntly pointed; margins entire. Upper surface of young leaves usually soft, dull green, becoming lustrous, dark green and often developing purplish spots as the season progresses; lower surface paler. Blade usually 3–10 cm long, 1.2–3 cm broad; petiole 5–15 mm long. **FLOWER** Usually unisexual, male and female flowers on separate trees; tiny, greenish yellow. Spring. **FRUIT** Single-stoned purplish-black drupe, 6–13 mm long, the stone prominently ribbed; usually 1 or 2 at the end of an elongated stalk; matures summer to autumn.

HABITAT/RANGE Native. Often forms dense colonies in freshwater swamps, usually in standing water; distributed predominantly in the southeastern coastal plains, Va. south to sc. Fla., west to s. Ark. and e. Tex.

SIMILAR SPECIES Water Tupelo and Ogeechee Tupelo have larger leaves and fruit. **Bear Tupelo** (*N. ursina* Small), sometimes considered a distinct species, grows to about 1.5 m tall in fire-maintained savannas, bogs, and wet pinelands in the Fla. panhandle. Sour Gum is an upland species with broadly elliptic or obovate leaves.

SOUR GUM

BLACKGUM

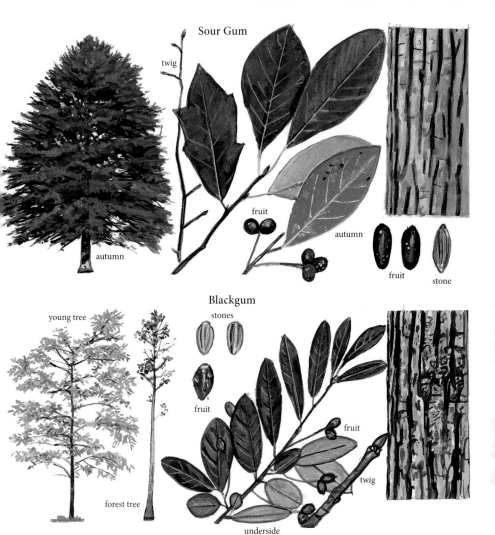

Sour Gum

twig

fruit

autumn

autumn

fruit   stone

Blackgum

young tree

stones

fruit

fruit

twig

forest tree

underside

Bear Tupelo

autumn

fruit

OLEACEAE: OLIVE FAMILY

The olive family includes about 24 genera and more than 600 species of trees, shrubs, and a few vines distributed in tropical, subtropical, and temperate regions. The family is particularly abundant and diverse in Asia and Australasia. Members of the family occur in a wide range of habitats. Eight genera and about 28 arborescent species occur in the East, including 4 native genera containing 19 native species.

LEAF Opposite (rarely alternate or whorled) and simple, pinnately compound, or trifoliolate, the margins entire or toothed. **FLOWER** On a worldwide basis, most species in the family have bisexual flowers. Notable North American exceptions include the genera *Chionanthus*, *Forestiera*, *Fraxinus*, and *Osmanthus*, the species of which have unisexual or functionally unisexual flowers, with male and female flowers usually borne on separate trees. Petals are usually 4 (or none); stamens 2, arising from near the base of the petals; pistil 1, ovary superior. White or yellow is the most common flower color in North American species. **FRUIT** Diverse; on a worldwide basis, the fruit of most species is a 1-seeded drupe, less often a capsule, berry, or samara. The fruit of the family's largest genus in North America, the ashes, is a samara.

The family is probably best known for *Olea europaea* L., the source of the edible olive and the cooking oil extracted from its fleshy pulp. The ash trees are economically important as timber trees, touted for the hardness, strength, and durability of the wood. The family is also noted for several ornamentals, including forsythia, lilacs, Fringetree, Tea Olive, privets, and Madagascar Olive. The privets (genus *Ligustrum*) are non-native species well known for their invasive tendencies throughout the Southeast.

■ *CHIONANTHUS:* FRINGETREES

Chionanthus is a largely tropical and subtropical genus of about 80 shrubs and trees with 2 species in the e. U.S.

FRINGETREE *Chionanthus virginicus* L.
A.K.A. WHITE FRINGETREE, GRANDSIE-GRAY-BEARD, OLD-MAN'S BEARD

QUICK ID Easily identified by the opposite leaves, fringelike flowers, and dark, olive-like fruit.

Deciduous small tree or large shrub to about 10 m tall, 20 cm diam. Erect, single trunk or multiple, often branching very near or at ground level; crown rounded. **BARK** Grayish when young, becoming reddish brown and slightly scaly with age. **TWIG** Reddish brown when young, becoming gray, hairless, decorated with widely scattered circular, slightly elevated tan lenticels that are interspersed with numerous dark dots. **LEAF** Opposite, simple, broadly lanceolate, elliptic, oval, or oblong; base and tip tapered; margins entire. Upper surface medium or dark green, hairless; lower surface paler, softly hairy when new, becoming sparsely hairy or hairless. Blade 10–20 cm long, 2–10 cm broad; petiole 2–2.5 cm long, stout, slightly winged, often with a reddish blush. **FLOWER** Functionally unisexual (a few bisexual flowers may be present), male and female flowers on separate trees; 1.5–3 cm long, petals 4, linear and narrowly

FRINGETREE

PYGMY FRINGETREE

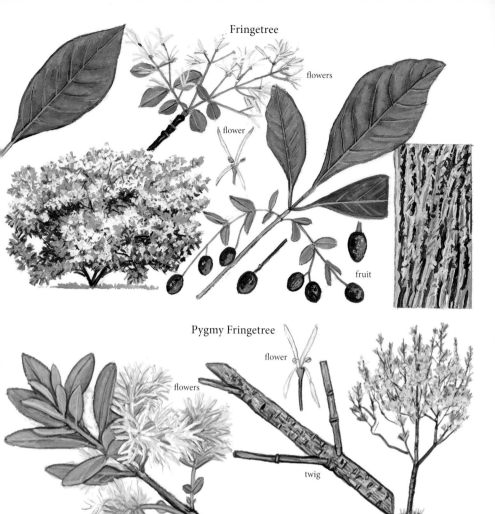

Fringetree

flowers

flower

fruit

Pygmy Fringetree

flower

flowers

twig

straplike, borne in a conspicuous long-stalked, dangling, fringelike inflorescence 10–15 cm long. Spring. **FRUIT** Ellipsoid or egg-shaped, dark blue or nearly black olive-like drupe, 1–1.7 cm long, with a single stone; matures midsummer to late summer.

HABITAT/RANGE Native. Upland woodlands, pine forests, pine–oak scrub, margins of savannas, rocky glades, flatwoods, dunes, sandhills, 0–1,350 m; widespread in the East, Mass., N.Y., and Ohio, south to c. Fla., west to Mo., e. Okla., and e. Tex. A popular landscape and garden tree, increasingly used in roadside plantings.

SIMILAR SPECIES See Pygmy Fringetree.

PYGMY FRINGETREE *Chionanthus pygmaeus* Small

QUICK ID A shrub of sc. Fla. very similar to Fringetree.

Closely related and similar to Fringetree, typically a shrub to about 2 m tall, but may reach heights of 4 m. **LEAF** Similar to Fringetree but smaller, usually only 3–10 cm long. **FLOWER** Also similar but smaller, with petals usually not exceeding about 1 cm long. Early spring. **FRUIT** Drupe 2–2.5 cm long; matures late summer.

HABITAT/RANGE Endemic to sand scrub of sc. Fla.

■ *FORESTIERA*: SWAMPPRIVETS

This is a small genus of 10–15 species distributed in Central America, North America, and the West Indies; 8 species occur in the U.S., 6 in the East, all native. Deciduous shrubs or small trees, the trunk often strongly leaning. **LEAF** Opposite, simple; margins toothed or entire. Blade typically flat, venation pinnate, petiole usually conspicuous, rarely absent. **FLOWER** Individually small, produced in round, dense yellowish axillary clusters; unisexual, or structurally bisexual and then female. Petals absent; sepals 4, minute, quickly deciduous. **FRUIT** Drupe with 1 or 2 stones.

EASTERN SWAMPPRIVET *Forestiera acuminata* (Michx.) Poir.

QUICK ID Distinguished by the clump-forming habit, wetland habitat, elongated leaf tip, and wrinkled fruit.

Deciduous, usually a large shrub, occasionally forming a small tree to about 10 m tall, 25 cm diam. Usually leaning and clumplike, with short, closely set multiple trunks ascending from a single base; crown ascending, vase-shaped. **BARK** Dark brown, roughened or slightly furrowed at maturity. **TWIG** Grayish brown, hairless or finely hairy, usually with conspicuous lenticels. **LEAF** Opposite, simple, occasionally lanceolate, more often widest at or just below the middle, somewhat diamond-shaped; tip long-tapering to a sharp, elongated point; margins finely and inconspicuously toothed. Upper surface dark green or yellowish green, usually hairless; lower surface paler. Blade 4–12 cm long, 2–3.5 cm broad; petiole 5–20 mm long. **FLOWER** Functionally unisexual, male and female on separate trees, individually tiny, yellow, petals absent, borne in a conspicuous rounded inflorescence. Early spring to mid-spring. **FRUIT** Wrinkled, oblong pinkish or reddish-purple drupe, 10–15 mm long, 7–10 mm diam.; matures summer.

HABITAT/RANGE Native. Swamps, alluvial woodlands, floodplains, bottoms; widely scattered in the East, more common along the floodplain of the Mississippi, Chattahoochee/Apalachicola, and Savannah rivers; S.C. south to n. Fla., west to e. Kans., e. Okla., and e. Tex.

SIMILAR SPECIES Five other species of *Forestiera* occur in the East, all of which are typically spring-flowering shrubs; none has Eastern Swampprivet's long-tapering, sharply-pointed leaf tip. **Desert Olive** (*F. angustifolia* Torr.), a.k.a. Texas Elbow Bush, a shrub of Mexico, has a few locations in e. Tex.

FLORIDA SWAMPPRIVET *Forestiera segregata* (Jacq.) Krug & Urb.

QUICK ID A southeastern coast swampprivet with untoothed leaf margins.

Similar to Eastern Swampprivet; distinguished by the leaf margin being entire. **HABITAT/RANGE** Native; occurs chiefly along the Ga. and Fla. coasts

GODFREY'S SWAMPPRIVET *Forestiera godfreyi* L.C. Anderson

QUICK ID A southern swampprivet with finely hairy leaves and twigs.

LEAF 5–8 cm long, 2.3–4 cm broad, ovate to broadly elliptic, with finely toothed margins; twigs and lower leaf surfaces finely and evenly hairy. **HABITAT/RANGE** Native; calcareous woods, n. Fla. and se. Ga.

EASTERN SWAMPPRIVET   FLORIDA SWAMPPVIVET   GODFREY'S SWAMPPRIVET

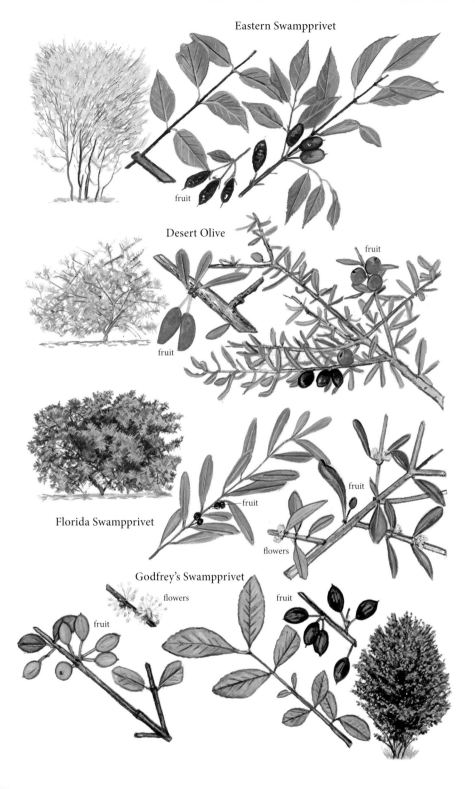

Eastern Swampprivet

fruit

Desert Olive

fruit

fruit

Florida Swampprivet

fruit

fruit

flowers

Godfrey's Swampprivet

flowers

fruit

fruit

■ *FRAXINUS*: ASHES

The genus *Fraxinus* includes 45–65 species distributed mostly in the temperate and subtropical regions of the Northern Hemisphere. About 20 species occur in North America north of Mexico, 20 native, 2 naturalized; 13 occur in the East. Members of the genus occupy diverse habitats, from upland forests to riverine bottoms and from low to moderate elevations.

Deciduous trees or rarely large shrubs, 2.5–40 m tall, 30–200 cm diam. Often erect, with a single trunk, sometimes forming clumps with several trunks. Crown rounded, pyramidal, narrow or broad, sometimes with drooping lower branches. **BARK** Usually gray, sometimes blotchy, occasionally reddish brown, sometimes smooth, especially when young, more often roughened with numerous interlacing furrows and narrow ridges. **TWIG** Usually gray, sometimes green at first, orange on 1 species, usually hairless, sometimes densely hairy, at least 1 species with purplish lenticels. **LEAF** Opposite, pinnately compound, with a terminal leaflet; leaflets usually 5–11, sometimes to 15. **FLOWER** Unisexual (in ours); petals usually 4 (in ours), sometimes 0 or 2; stamens usually 2; pistils 1, ovary superior. Spring. **FRUIT** Winged samara, usually with 1 hard, indehiscent, flat or swollen seed body (rarely 2 seeds), the wing usually flattened, arising at the base, near the middle, or near the tip of the seed body; the wing sometimes with a vertical vane down the middle, separating the wing into 2 sections, the fruit then called "3-vaned." The width and point of origin of the wing on the seed body, and the presence of a 3rd vane, are important to identification. Fruit usually matures in late summer to autumn.

Ashes are easily recognized by the combination of opposite, pinnately compound leaves and winged samaras. They are sometimes confused with the hickories (*Carya*, Juglandaceae), which also have pinnately compound leaves and furrowed bark with interlacing fissures, but the leaves of hickories are alternate and the fruit is a husk-covered nut. Ashes are important timber trees. The wood is hard, resilient, and shock-resistant and has been used in the manufacture of baseball bats, boat paddles, and high-quality veneer.

WHITE ASH   *Fraxinus americana* L.
A.K.A. AMERICAN ASH

QUICK ID The opposite, compound leaves with 5–9 leaflets that are whitish beneath distinguish White Ash. The more or less evenly parallel furrows in the upper bark are a helpful winter identification character.

Deciduous large tree 15–30 m tall, 1–2 m diam. Erect, single trunk; crown rounded or pyramidal. **BARK** Grayish, scaly, distinctly narrowly ridged and furrowed, the lowermost furrows often interlacing to form diamond-like patterns, those higher on the trunk more or less evenly parallel. **TWIG** Light gray, hairless. **LEAF** Opposite, pinnately compound, blade 15–30 cm long, rachis 5–10 cm long, not winged; leaflets 5–9, more or less ovate; margins bluntly toothed. Upper surface dark green; lower surface usually whitish, hairy when new, becoming hairless. Leaflet blade 6–15 cm long, 2–7.5 cm broad, stalk 5–15 mm long. Red, maroon, or yellow in autumn. **FRUIT** Narrowly elliptic or linear samara, 2.5–3.2 cm long, 3–6 mm broad, the wing arising from the upper ¼ or less of the seed body; often minutely notched at the apex; matures late summer to autumn.

HABITAT/RANGE Native. Upland woods, floodplains, alluvial terraces, cove forests, dry hills, hammocks, 50–1,500 m; widespread in the East, Ont., Que., and N.B., south to n. Fla., west to e. Nebr. and e. Tex.

SIMILAR SPECIES Three variations formerly treated as forms of White Ash are now recognized

WHITE ASH

TEXAS ASH

BILTMORE ASH

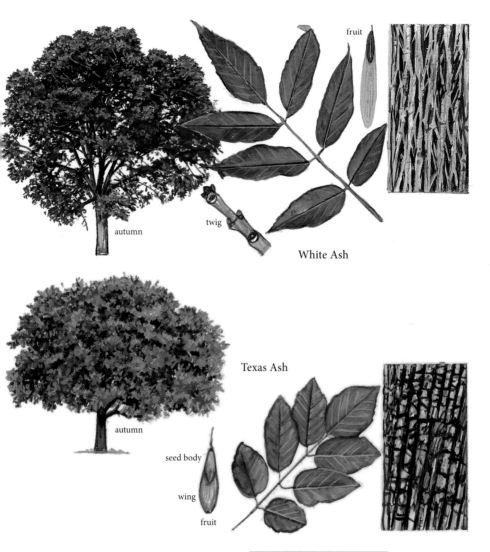

fruit

twig

autumn

White Ash

Texas Ash

autumn

seed body

wing

fruit

as distinct species. In **Texas Ash** (*F. albicans* Buckley), distributed mostly along the e. Edwards Plateau of Tex. into sc. Okla., the leaflet blades are mostly 3–6 cm long and the rachis mostly 2–6 cm long. In the **Biltmore Ash** (*F. biltmoreana* Beadle) the samaras are usually longer than 3.2 cm and broader than 5 mm, and the twig, petiole, leaflet stalk, and rachis are sparsely to densely hairy. In *F. smallii* Britton the samaras are also longer and wider than those of White Ash, but the twig, petiole, leaflet stalk, and rachis are hairless.

Fraxinus smallii

CAROLINA ASH   *Fraxinus caroliniana* Mill.

A.K.A. POP ASH, WATER ASH

QUICK ID The multitrunked habit and rhomboid or diamond-shaped samara distinguish Carolina Ash.

Deciduous small tree or large shrub, 2.5–15 m tall, to about 30 cm diam. Leaning or ascending, usually clump-forming, with several often short trunks; crown open, rounded. **BARK** Gray or light gray, often blotchy, more or less smooth when young, becoming shallowly furrowed and scaly with age. **TWIG** Slender, round in cross section, green at first, becoming gray. **LEAF** Opposite, pinnately compound, blade 12–40 cm long, rachis 3–9 cm long; leaflets 5–7, rarely 9, ovate, oblong, or broadly elliptic, the terminal one often nearly circular, base often rounded, margins shallowly toothed. Upper surface dark green, hairless; lower surface paler, hairless or hairy mostly along the veins, the tissue often beset with minute scales. Leaflet blade 2.5–12 cm long, 2–6 cm broad, stalk 2–15 mm long. Turns dingy yellow or brown in autumn. **FRUIT** Samara, 35–46 mm long, 12–22 mm broad, often diamond-shaped, the wing arising at or below the base of the seed body, with 11–19 lateral veins; wing rarely bears a 3rd vane; matures summer.

HABITAT/RANGE Native. Swamps, alluvial woods, floodplains, river- and stream banks, margins of gum ponds, sometimes in standing water, 3–100 m; southeastern coastal plains, se. Va. south to s. Fla., west to s. Ark. and e. Tex.

SIMILAR SPECIES Several closely similar variants constitute a group known as the water ashes, two others of which are sometimes considered distinct species. *F. cubensis* Griseb. is similar to Carolina Ash in virtually all features except the fruit; the samaras of *F. cubensis*, distributed mostly in the c. and s. Fla. peninsula and ostensibly not overlapping in range with Carolina Ash, are usually less than 12 mm broad, with wings that have 5–9 lateral veins. In **Swamp White Ash** (*F. pauciflora* Nutt.), distributed in n. Fla. and adjacent s. Ga., the lower surface of the leaflet lacks scales but is beset with tiny protuberances or projections held within shallow depressions that require at least 20× magnification to see clearly; the lower surface of the leaflets of Carolina Ash have scales, but lack protuberances.

BLACK ASH   *Fraxinus nigra* Marshall

QUICK ID The corky bark and opposite, pinnately compound leaves with stalkless lateral leaflets distinguish this species.

Deciduous tree, 12–20 m tall, 30–60 cm diam. Erect, often leaning or crooked, single trunk; crown of forest-grown trees open, narrow, with coarse, ascending branches, crown of open-grown trees usually more or less rounded. **BARK** Gray, roughened with soft, corky ridges that flake off when rubbed with the hand, especially when young, becoming scaly and shallowly furrowed on older trees. **TWIG** Stout, hairless; green with raised purplish lenticels when young, becoming gray with age. Terminal bud egg-shaped, pointed at the apex, 4–10 mm long, bluish black or dark brown. **LEAF** Opposite, pinnately compound, blade 15–40 cm long; leaflets 7–11, elliptic, narrowly oval, or lanceolate, margins finely and sharply toothed. Upper surface dark green; lower surface slightly paler, hairless except in the leaflet axils. Leaflet blade 7–14 cm long, 2.5–5 cm broad, stalkless or nearly so. Red-brown in autumn. **FRUIT** More or less oblong samara, 2.5–4.5 cm long, wing arising from near the base of the seed body; matures late summer to early autumn.

CAROLINA ASH   *Fraxinus cubensis*   SWAMP WHITE ASH

Carolina Ash

fruit

underside

Black Ash

fruit

HABITAT/RANGE Native. Saturated organic soils of swampy woodlands and saturated flood-plains where not regularly inundated, to about 1,100 m; e. Man. and e. N.D. east to N.F., south to Ill., Ky., and Va.

SIMILAR SPECIES The lateral leaflets of our other ashes are stalked.

Notes: The wood of this species was used for basket weaving by Native Americans.

BLACK ASH

PUMPKIN ASH *Fraxinus profunda*
(Bush) Bush
A.K.A. SWELL-BUTT ASH

QUICK ID The combination of buttressed trunk base; large, pinnately compound leaves with 7–9 large, dark green leaflets; and samara fruit helps distinguish this species.

Deciduous tree, 12–30 m tall, 30–60 cm diam. Erect, single straight or sometimes crooked trunk, usually with a swollen or buttressed base; crown narrow, open, branches small, spreading. **BARK** Light gray with interlacing ridges. **TWIG** Stout, densely hairy or hairless. **LEAF** Opposite, pinnately compound, blade 20–45 cm long, rachis 8–15 cm long; leaflets 7–9, ovate, narrowly oblong, or elliptic, margins entire or sparsely and bluntly toothed. Upper surface dark green, hairless; lower surface hairy, at least along the midvein. Leaflet blade 8–20 cm long, 5–8 cm broad, stalks 5–12 mm long. **FRUIT** Samara, 4–7 cm long, to 14 mm broad, varying from narrowly linear to oblanceolate or narrowly elliptic, wing arising near the base of the seed body; matures early autumn.

HABITAT/RANGE Native. Swamps, old lake beds, freshwater tidal wetlands, calcareous wetlands, floodplains, wet woodlands, to about 150 m; sporadically distributed, mainly along the Mississippi and Ohio rivers, Mich. south to La., eastern seaboard from N.J. south to n. Fla.

SIMILAR SPECIES Often confused with water ashes of the Carolina Ash complex; those and Green Ash differ in having the largest leaflets, averaging less than 11 cm long.

Notes: The swollen or pumpkin-like trunk base is readily apparent on some trees, especially those inhabiting deep swamps in the southern part of the range.

GREEN ASH *Fraxinus pennsylvanica*
Marshall
A.K.A. RED ASH

QUICK ID The combination of wetland habitat; opposite, pinnately compound leaves with leaflets usually not exceeding 11 cm long; samara fruit; and hairy twig, petiole, and lower surface of the leaflet helps distinguish this species.

Deciduous tree, 12–25 m tall, 30–60 cm diam. Usually erect, with a single straight trunk, sometimes shrubby or leaning; crown usually compact, rounded, with numerous lateral branches. **BARK** Grayish brown, shallowly furrowed with interlacing ridges, sometimes with a reddish tinge. **TWIG** Stout, densely hairy (rarely hairless), becoming grayish or reddish brown, the reddish color especially apparent in winter. Terminal bud rounded, 3–8 mm long, rusty brown, hairy. **LEAF** Opposite, pinnately compound, blade 25–40 cm long, rachis 7–14 cm long, petiole 4–11 cm long, hairy; leaflets 5–9 (usually 7), oval or oblong-lanceolate, margins bluntly toothed, primarily above the middle of the leaflet blade. Upper surface yellow-green, hairless; lower surface slightly paler, often downy-hairy. Leaflet blade 7–11 cm long, 2.5–4.5 cm broad; short-stalked. Yellowish brown in autumn. **FRUIT** Samara, 2.5–6 cm long, narrowly linear, narrowly elliptic, or oblanceolate; wing arising about the middle of the seed body, often notched at the apex; matures late summer to early autumn.

HABITAT/RANGE Native. Bottomlands, floodplains, riverbanks, tolerant of moving water, often in the wettest areas where inundated for long periods, 0–900 m; throughout the East, N.S. west to Man., south to c. Fla., west to e. Tex.

SIMILAR SPECIES The leaflets of Black Ash are stalkless, while those of White Ash are whitish beneath. In Pumpkin Ash the wing of the samara arises at or near the base of the seed body. See also Mexican Ash.

Notes: Pubescence on this species is quite variable, ranging from very hairy to hairless, even within a single population. Distinguishing between this and other wetland ashes can be difficult.

PUMPKIN ASH

GREEN ASH

Pumpkin Ash

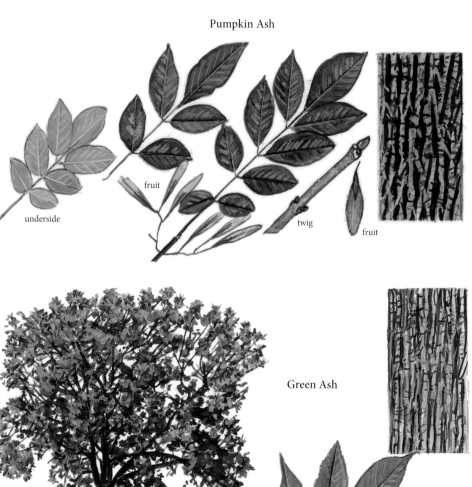

underside

fruit

twig

fruit

Green Ash

twig

fruit

MEXICAN ASH *Fraxinus berlandieriana*
DC.

QUICK ID A western ash with 3–5 leaflets usually 3–7 mm long, and a flat or 3-vaned samara with the wing originating in the lower 3rd of the seed body.

Closely related to Green Ash, distinguished by leaves with fewer leaflets (3–5) and by most trees producing at least a few 3-vaned samaras.

HABITAT/RANGE   Native; a western species that extends into the East along the margins of Edwards Plateau in Tex. and in s. Okla.

BLUE ASH *Fraxinus quadrangulata*
Michx.

QUICK ID An ash, recognized by the combination of distinctly 4-angled or narrowly 4-winged twigs and scaly, shaggy bark.

Deciduous tree, 10–15 m tall, 30–50 cm diam. Erect, single trunk; crown narrow, smaller branches often appearing 4-sided. **BARK** Light gray, often tinged reddish, smooth on young trees, becoming irregularly divided into large shaggy plates, reminiscent of the bark of Pecan (*Carya illinoinensis*, Juglandaceae). **TWIG** Stout, rusty-hairy, with 4 conspicuous wings or ridges, more or less orange when young, becoming brownish or gray with age; winter buds gray or reddish brown. **LEAF** Opposite, pinnately compound, blade 13–38 cm long; leaflets 5–11, usually 7, narrowly ovate or lanceolate; margins coarsely toothed. Upper surface yellowish green, hairless; lower surface paler, hairless. Leaflet blade 7–14 cm long, 2.5–5 cm broad, short-stalked. **FRUIT** Samara, broadly oblong to obovate, 2.5–5 cm long, wing 8–10 mm broad, often twisted, arising below the seed body; matures early autumn.

HABITAT/RANGE   Native. Floodplains, moist woodlands, slopes, limestone outcrops, 125–600 m; Ont. and Minn. south to Va. and Ga., west to se. Kans. and ne. Okla.

SIMILAR SPECIES   European Ash also has only slightly 4-angled twigs, stalkless leaflets, and blackish or blackish-brown buds.

Notes: Crushed twigs of Blue Ash color water blue and were used by early settlers for fabricating dyes.

EUROPEAN ASH *Fraxinus excelsior* L.
A.K.A. COMMON ASH

QUICK ID An ash recognized by the combination of opposite, pinnately compound leaves with nearly stalkless leaflets and black buds.

Deciduous tree, 20–40 m tall. Erect, single straight trunk; crown rounded, broad, lower branches usually ascending (drooping in some cultivars). **BARK** Gray, scaly when young, becoming finely ridged and furrowed with age. **TWIG** Light greenish gray or grayish brown, hairless, dotted, twigs slightly 4-angled. Terminal winter buds black, hairy. **LEAF** Opposite, pinnately compound, blade 25–30 cm long, rachis usually hairy; leaflets 9–15, ovate, oblong, or broadly lanceolate; margins toothed. Upper surface dark green, hairless; lower surface paler, usually hairy along the midvein. Leaflet blade 5–8 cm long, 2.5–3.5 cm broad, stalkless or nearly so. Turns yellow in autumn. **FRUIT** Samara, 2.5–4 cm long, narrowly oblong, wing 5–8 mm broad; matures autumn.

HABITAT/RANGE   Introduced from Europe; established from plantings in North America, primarily from N.S. and Ont. south to Ohio and Ky.

SIMILAR SPECIES   The twigs of Blue Ash are strongly 4-angled, the samara wings are 8–10 mm broad, and the winter buds are gray or reddish brown.

Notes: There are numerous cultivars of this non-native ash, making precise description difficult. Popular cultivated forms include selections for yellow bark, yellow fall color, simple leaves, dense crown, and drooping lower branches, among others.

MEXICAN ASH   BLUE ASH

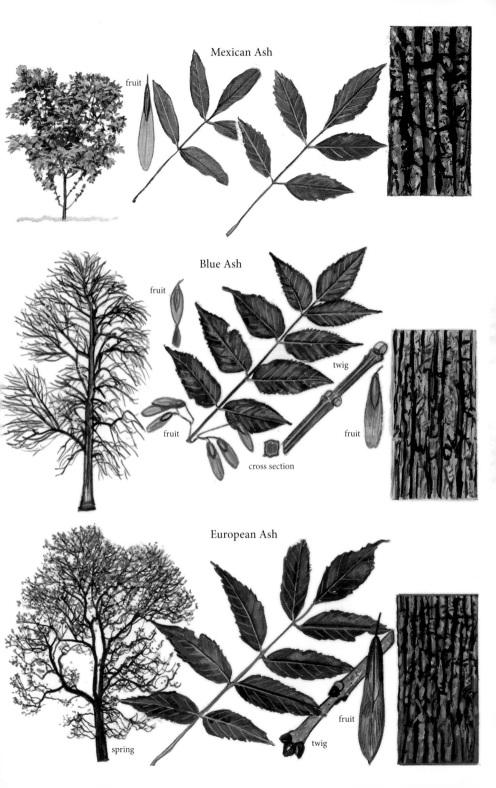

Mexican Ash

fruit

Blue Ash

fruit

fruit

twig

fruit

cross section

European Ash

spring

twig

fruit

■ *LIGUSTRUM*: PRIVETS

Ligustrum is a genus of about 45 species, introduced from Asia, Australia, and Europe.

Evergreen or deciduous shrubs or small trees to about 10 m tall. Erect or ascending, single trunk or multiple; crown rounded or vase-shaped, often with ascending or spreading branches. **BARK** Gray or greenish gray, smooth or slightly roughened. **TWIG** Grayish, usually hairy, often decorated with conspicuous lenticels. **LEAF** Opposite, simple, thick or moderately so, often leathery; margins entire; petioles short. **FLOWER** Bisexual, white or creamy white, radially symmetric, corolla 4-lobed, stamens 2; borne in conspicuous terminal panicles or cymes to about 15 cm long. **FRUIT** Blue-black drupe to about 12 mm long with 1–4 seeds.

Privets are most easily identified by a combination of opposite, simple leaves (which distinguish them from most other arborescent shrubs or small trees, with the exception of Fringetree, *Chionanthus virginicus*, and Wild Olive, *Osmanthus americanus*), conspicuous inflorescences of creamy-white flowers, and branched clusters of blue-black fruit. The 3 species treated here are naturalized from cultivation. At least 2 (*Ligustrum lucidum*, *L. sinense*) have spread into natural areas, especially in the Southeast, and have become pernicious and destructive weeds, displacing native flora and altering the integrity of natural woodlands.

GLOSSY PRIVET *Ligustrum lucidum* Ait.
A.K.A. Wax-leaf Ligustrum

QUICK ID Recognized by its shrubby habit, lustrous, V-shaped leaf blade, large inflorescence, and branching clusters of blue-black drupes.

Evergreen large shrub or small shrubby tree, to about 6 m tall and 8 cm diam. Leaning or ascending, usually with multiple trunks; crown ascending or spreading, more or less vase-shaped, the branches arching or drooping. **BARK** Gray or greenish gray, smooth when young, becoming slightly roughened with corky outgrowths. **TWIG** Greenish gray, hairless, roughened with corky lenticels. **LEAF** Opposite, simple, thick, leathery, often reflexed upward from the midvein (V-shaped), tip narrowing to an elongated, tapered point; margins entire. Upper surface lustrous, dark green, hairless; lower surface paler. Blade 6–15 cm long, to about 5 cm broad; petiole 1–2 cm long. **FLOWER** Small, greenish white, tubular, 4-petaled, fragrant, borne in conspicuous branching panicles to about 15 cm long, 14 cm broad. Spring to early summer. **FRUIT** Black or blue-black drupe, 4–8 mm long; matures late summer to winter.

HABITAT/RANGE Introduced from Asia. Established from cultivation; southeastern coastal plains, S.C. south to c. Fla., west to e. Tex.

SIMILAR SPECIES The leaves of Japanese Privet average less than 10 cm long, while those of Glossy Privet average greater than 10 cm long.

JAPANESE PRIVET *Ligustrum japonicum* Thunb.

QUICK ID The opposite, usually blunt-tipped, dark green leaves; showy flowering panicles; and blue-black drupes distinguish this species.

Evergreen shrub or small tree, to about 6 m tall. Erect or ascending, usually with multiple trunks. **LEAF** Opposite, simple, thick, leathery; ovate, elliptic, to nearly circular, tip rounded or bluntly pointed; margins entire. Upper surface dark green, lustrous; lower surface paler, both surfaces finely dotted. Blade 3–8 cm long, 2.5–4 cm broad. **FLOWER** Numerous, small, white, 4-petaled with a tubular corolla, fragrant, borne in a large, conspicuous panicle 8–16 cm long, to about 10 cm broad. Spring. **FRUIT** Ellipsoid blue-black drupe, 8–12 mm long; matures late summer to winter.

HABITAT/RANGE Introduced from Asia. Sporadically established from cultivation; Md. and Tenn., south to n. Fla., west to e. Tex.

SIMILAR SPECIES Glossy Privet has smaller fruit and larger leaves with a narrow, elongated tip.

CHINESE PRIVET *Ligustrum sinense* Lour.

QUICK ID Recognized by its small opposite, oval leaves and branched terminal inflorescences of small greenish-white flowers, and typically shrubby habit.

Evergreen or late deciduous (in colder climes) shrub, occasionally a slender tree to about 10 m tall. Single trunk or more often multiple trunks, usually branching near the ground. **BARK** Greenish gray, smooth. **TWIG** Densely hairy when new,

Glossy Privet

flowers

underside

fruit

Japanese Privet

flowers

twig

fruit

Chinese Privet

fruit

flowers

becoming buff-colored, ridged, and decorated with numerous lenticels. **LEAF** Opposite, simple, thin, oval or elliptic; margins entire. Upper surface dull green or variegated cream and green, hairless at maturity; lower surface paler, usually hairy, at least on the midvein. Blade 1.5–3 cm long, 1–2 cm broad; petiole 2–4 mm long, hairy. **FLOWER** Numerous, small, white or greenish white, borne in a branched terminal inflorescence 4–10 cm long, to about 5 cm broad. Spring. **FRUIT** Blue-black drupe, 5–8 mm long; matures late summer to autumn.

HABITAT/RANGE Introduced from China. Invasive in woodlands; Mass. south to Fla., west to Mo., Okla., and e. Tex.

SIMILAR SPECIES Glossy Privet and Japanese Privet have larger leaves and longer inflorescences.

■ *OSMANTHUS:* OSMANTHUSES

Osmanthus is a genus of about 15 species, distributed largely in Asia. Two species are native to North America.

WILD OLIVE *Osmanthus americanus*
(L.) Benth. & Hook. f. ex A. Gray
A.K.A. DEVILWOOD

QUICK ID The opposite, dark green leathery leaves, small white flowers, and olive-like fruit are diagnostic.

Evergreen shrub or tree, to about 15 m tall, 25 cm diam. Erect, single trunk or multiple, usually short, branching near the ground, sometimes taller and distinctly arborescent with a longer trunk and narrow, rounded crown. **BARK** Gray or reddish gray when young, becoming roughened, scaly, and dark reddish brown with age. **TWIG** Gray or brownish gray, with small, inconspicuous scattered lenticels; hairless or finely hairy. **LEAF** Opposite, simple, thick, leathery; elliptic, oblong, oblanceolate, or narrowly obovate, the tip pointed, rounded, or occasionally notched; margins entire, often rolled under. Upper surface dark green, lustrous, hairless; lower surface paler, hairless. Blade 5–15 cm long, 1.8–5.5 cm broad; petiole 1–2 cm long. **FLOWER** Unisexual, male and female flowers on separate trees, small, creamy white; petals 4, fused into a tube 3–5 mm long; male flowers with only 2 stamens; produced in short axillary panicles. Early spring to mid-spring. **FRUIT** Oval or ellipsoid, 1-seeded, dark purple or nearly black drupe, 1–1.5 cm diam.; matures summer to autumn.

HABITAT/RANGE Native. In many habitats from upland woods, sandhills, and coastal dunes to rich forests, to about 150 m; confined chiefly to the southeastern coastal plains, se. Va. south to sc. Fla., east to La.

WILD OLIVE

SIMILAR SPECIES Fringetree (*Chionanthus virginicus*) has deciduous leaves that are thinner and lighter green. Common Sweetleaf (*Symplocos tinctoria,* Symplocaceae) and the several bays (*Persea,* Lauraceae) have alternate leaves. The shrubby, large-fruited Scrub Wild Olive (*O. megacarpus* [Small] Small ex Little), endemic to c. Fla. has larger, rounded drupes 2–2.5 cm diam. See also Tea Olive.

Notes: The alternate common name of this species, Devilwood, probably derives from the hard wood, which is "devilish" for woodworkers.

TEA OLIVE *Osmanthus fragrans* Lour.

A popular garden and landscape shrub or small tree with very fragrant flowers. **LEAF** 5–10 cm long. **HABITAT/RANGE** Introduced from Asia; planted throughout the se. U.S. but not known to naturalize.

MADAGASCAR OLIVE *Noronhia emarginata* (Lam.) Thouars

QUICK ID Naturalized only in s. Fla., where the notched, conspicuously veined leaves and usually greenish-yellow fruit distinguish it.

Evergreen small tree, to about 15 m tall. Erect or spreading, single trunk or usually multiple; crown irregularly rounded, oval, or vase-shaped, branches ascending. **BARK** Smooth, grayish brown. **TWIG** Stout, new twigs flattened, becoming rounded with age. **LEAF** Opposite, simple, thick, leathery; elliptic, oval, or obovate, with a notched tip; margins entire. Upper surface lustrous yellow-green or bluish green, with conspicuous lateral veins and a thick midvein; lower surface paler. Blade 10–20 cm long, 5–10 cm broad; petiole stout, light brown, 10–15 mm long. **FLOWER** Bisexual, 6–7 mm diam., petals 4, yellow, borne in panicles or racemes to 8 cm long. **FRUIT** Rounded, fleshy green, yellow, or purple drupe 1–2 cm long.

HABITAT/RANGE Introduced; native to Madagascar, rarely naturalized from plantings in s. Fla., cultivated mainly along the coast.

SIMILAR SPECIES The leaves are similar to those of Lipstick Tree (*Ochrosia elliptica,* Apocynaceae) but are distinguished by the notched tip. The leaves of Seven-year Apple (*Genipa clusiifolia,* Rubiaceae) are also obovate and dark green with conspicuous lateral veins but lack the notched tip.

Wild Olive

flowers

flowers

fruit

Tea Olive

flowers

flower

twig

Madagascar Olive

underside

fruit

flowers

JAPANESE TREE LILAC *Syringa reticulata* (Blume) H. Hara

QUICK ID Easily recognized during flowering by the abundant creamy-white to yellowish-white flowers, opposite long-stalked leaves, and reddish-brown cherry-like bark.

Deciduous large shrub or small tree, 2–10 m tall, to 25 cm diam. Erect, usually single trunk, sometimes with multiple trunks or branching near ground level; crown rounded or oval, with ascending or spreading branches. **BARK** Greenish with conspicuous tan lenticels when young, becoming reddish brown and somewhat resembling cherry bark with age. **TWIG** Lustrous red-brown at first, becoming lustrous gray, with conspicuous lenticels. **LEAF** Opposite, simple, elliptic, broadly oval, or ovate, tip pointed, base rounded or heart-shaped. Upper surface dark green, hairless; lower surface grayish green, hairless or finely hairy. Blade 5–13 cm long, 1–6 cm broad, petiole 1–3 cm long. **FLOWER** Bisexual, creamy or yellowish white, individually small, 3–5 mm diam., petals 4; borne in a showy, conspicuous, many-flowered terminal panicle, 10–30 cm long. Summer. **FRUIT** Narrowly ellipsoid leathery capsule, 1.5–2.5 cm long, lime green at first, becoming brown, smooth or somewhat warty; matures autumn.

HABITAT/RANGE Introduced; native to Japan. Cultivated in northern areas, naturalized in s. New England and Wyo.

SIMILAR SPECIES Other species of *Syringa* lack prominent lenticels on the trunk and twigs.

Notes: A genus of about 20 species, native mostly to Asia. Several species are used ornamentally in North America, especially the purple- or lavender-flowered Common Lilac (*S. vulgaris* L.).

PAULOWNIACEAE: PRINCESSTREE FAMILY

The princesstrees constitute a monotypic family of 1 genus and 7 species distributed largely in East Asia, with introductions to Europe and North America; 1 introduced species occurs in the East. *Paulownia* has traditionally been placed in the figwort family (Scrophulariaceae) and allied with the bignonia family (Bignoniaceae) based on morphological, anatomical, and embryological evidence, but modern molecular data suggest that it is more closely tied to the largely herbaceous broomrape (Orobanchaceae) and lopseed (Phrymaceae) families.

The paulownias have long held mythical, spiritual, cultural, and economic significance in China and Japan. The wood of some species is highly prized, including the wood of the species grown in the U.S., which has been exported to Japan.

PRINCESSTREE *Paulownia tomentosa* (Thunb.) Siebold & Zucc. ex Steud.
A.K.A. EMPRESSTREE

QUICK ID Recognized by the combination of large heart-shaped leaves, large lavender to purplish flowers, and large egg-shaped capsule fruit.

Deciduous tree, 18–20 m tall, to 60 cm diam. Erect, single trunk; crown rounded, spreading, moderately dense, with thick, often contorted branches. **BARK** Grayish brown, thin, slightly roughened and fissured. **TWIG** Stout, usually sticky, at least when young, with a hollow pith and conspicuous white lenticels. **LEAF** Opposite, simple, moderately thick, broadly ovate, base usually heart-shaped, tip pointed, often abruptly so; margins usually entire, often 3–5 lobes, sometimes coarsely toothed, especially on young plants. Upper surface dark green, sparsely hairy; lower surface paler, sparsely to more often densely hairy. Blade 14–40 cm long, 8–30 cm broad (potentially larger); petiole averaging 5–21 cm long, usually hairy. **FLOWER** Bisexual, fragrant; calyx tube cup-shaped, 7–9 mm long; corolla 4–6 cm long, bilabiate, lavender, pinkish purple, or purple outside, whitish or yellowish inside and marked with reddish-purple spots; externally hairy; produced in large, erect, showy panicles. Spring. **FRUIT** Large, hard, sticky, egg-shaped capsule, 2.5–5 cm long, 1.5–2.6 cm broad; green at first, turning brown then black; matures winter, splitting in ½ to release numerous winged seeds 3–4 mm long.

flowers

underside

Japanese Tree Lilac

fruit

Princesstree

flowers

fruit

fruit

flower

HABITAT/RANGE Introduced from plants grown in Europe. Planted as a shade and ornamental tree throughout the East; naturalized along roadsides, in wetlands, and forest margins; an aggressive weed, treated as an invasive species in many states.

SIMILAR SPECIES Southern Catalpa (*Catalpa bignonioides*, Bignoniaceae) has similar leaves but is easily distinguished by its mostly white flower and the long, bean-podlike fruit.

PICRAMNIACEAE: BITTERBUSH FAMILY

A family of 2 or 3 genera and about 50 species of dioecious trees and shrubs with bitter bark, distributed in Central and South America, the Caribbean, and Fla.; 2 native species in the East. Some members were formerly placed in the Simaroubaceae.

MEXICAN ALVARADOA *Alvaradoa amorphoides* Liebm.

QUICK ID Recognized by alternate, pinnately compound leaves with small oval, alternate and opposite leaflets.

Evergreen tree, 5–15 m tall, to about 20 cm diam. **TWIG** Hairy, jointed. **LEAF** Alternate, pinnately compound, blade 10–30 cm long, 4–5 cm broad; petiole to about 3 cm long. Leaflets 19–41, alternate and opposite along the rachis, each 1–2.5 cm long, less than 1 cm broad; oval or oblong; margins entire. Upper surface hairless; lower surface silky-hairy. **FLOWER** Unisexual, small, green or yellowish; male racemes to 20 cm long; female racemes to 13 cm long. Winter to spring. **FRUIT** Flattened, lanceolate, samara-like capsule, 1–1.5 cm long, hairy, reddish. **HABITAT/RANGE** Native. Hammocks; Miami-Dade County, Fla.

FLORIDA BITTERBUSH *Picramnia pentandra* Sw.

QUICK ID Recognized by alternate, pinnately compound leaves with 5–9 alternate and opposite leaflets, and dangling panicles of red fruit.

Evergreen shrub, or rarely a small tree to about 6 m tall, 10 cm diam. **BARK** Smooth, gray. **LEAF** Alternate, pinnately compound, blade 20–36 cm long, to about 20 cm broad; petiole 2–4 cm long. Leaflets 5–9, alternate or opposite along a sometimes zigzag rachis, papery, 5–10 cm long, 2–5 cm broad; elliptic, ovate, or lanceolate; margins entire. Upper surface lustrous green; hairless. **FLOWER** Unisexual, minute, green with a reddish tinge, less than 3 mm diam.; in a dangling panicle 7–15 cm long. Primarily summer. **FRUIT** Fleshy, round scarlet berry, 9–15 mm long. **HABITAT/RANGE** Native. Hammocks; Miami-Dade County, Fla.

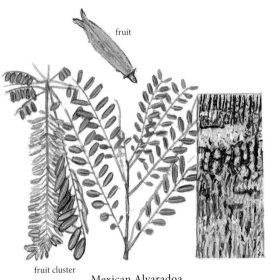

fruit

fruit cluster

Mexican Alvaradoa

Florida Bitterbush

fruit

flowers

fruit

PITTOSPORACEAE: CHEESEWOOD FAMILY

A family of evergreen trees and shrubs with 6–9 genera and 200–250 species, distributed in tropical and subtropical regions of Africa, Asia, Australia, and the Pacific islands. The genus *Pittosporum* has naturalized in the East.

JAPANESE CHEESEWOOD *Pittosporum tobira* (Thunb.) Aiton

QUICK ID Recognized by its obovate leaves, 4–9 cm long, usually clustered whorl-like at branch tips, upper surface variegated or dark green, tip rounded, and margins rolled under.

Evergreen shrub or small tree, to about 12 m tall. **BARK** Gray or grayish brown, roughened by conspicuous horizontal lenticels. **TWIG** Stout with grayish, longitudinal lenticels. **LEAF** Alternate, rarely opposite, usually produced at the tips of branches and appearing whorled; leathery, simple, obovate, tip rounded, sometimes slightly notched; margins entire, rolled under. Upper surface lustrous, dark green or variegated creamy white and medium green; both surfaces hairy. Blade 4–9 cm long,

1.5–4 cm broad; petiole 12–20 mm long. **FLOWER** Bisexual, white, fading to yellow, fragrant, to about 2.5 cm diam.; petals 5. Spring. **FRUIT** Ovoid, angular, hairy, many-seeded, pale yellow woody capsule, about 1.2 cm diam.; splitting into 3 valves to reveal red seeds; matures summer to autumn.

HABITAT/RANGE Introduced from Japan, Korea, Taiwan; a popular garden plant, especially in the coastal Southeast, escaped and rarely established in Fla. and N.C. and perhaps other southeastern states, also established in Calif.

SIMILAR SPECIES Taiwanese Cheesewood (*P. pentandrum* [Blanco] Merr.), a tree to about 12 m tall, is established in s. Fla., where it is treated as an invasive species; it is distinguished from Japanese Cheesewood by its oblong to ovate leaves with flat margins. The fruit is a yellowish or orange-red compressed capsule, 6–9 mm diam., that splits into 2 valves at maturity.

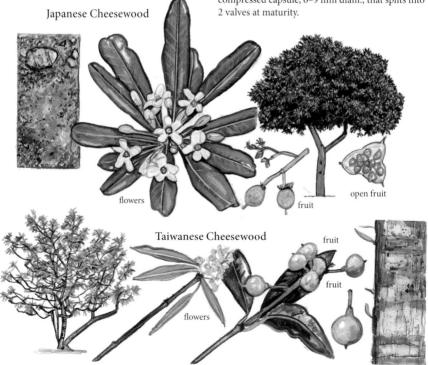

Japanese Cheesewood

flowers

fruit

open fruit

Taiwanese Cheesewood

fruit

fruit

flowers

PLATANACEAE: PLANETREE FAMILY

This small, monotypic family consists of a single genus, *Platanus*, distributed in temperate regions of North America, sc. Europe, and w. Asia to Indochina. Members of the family are cultivated for large shade trees in urban and suburban landscapes. The wood is hard, difficult to split, and has been used in the fabrication of butcher blocks.

▪ *PLATANUS*: SYCAMORES

The genus includes 7–10 species worldwide. Four species occur in North America, 3 native, 1 a horticultural hybrid; 2 are present in the East, 1 native.

Usually large deciduous trees. **BARK** Smooth, eventually exfoliating in thin plates to reveal buff, creamy-white, or green inner bark, thus often appearing mottled. **LEAF** Alternate, simple, usually palmately or subpalmately veined and lobed (1 species pinnately veined), the margins entire or coarsely toothed. **FLOWER** Unisexual, male and female on the same plant, borne in rounded heads; usually wind-pollinated. **FRUIT** More or less linear achene subtended by long bristles and produced in dense, rounded, often pendent heads.

AMERICAN SYCAMORE *Platanus occidentalis* L.

QUICK ID **Easily recognized by the combination of mottled, exfoliating bark that is conspicuously white on the trunk and branches in the crown; subpalmately lobed leaves; and dangling, ball-like fruit clusters.**

Deciduous, sometimes massive tree, to at least 50 m tall, 1–4 m diam. Erect, single straight trunk, rarely multiple trunks; crown of forest-grown trees spreading, open, with large, crooked branches; crown of open-grown trees pyramidal, often densely foliaged and low-branched. **BARK** Smooth, brown, mottled, peeling in thin plates and sloughing off to reveal buff, green, or creamy-white inner bark; often very whitish in the crown. **TWIG** Brown, becoming gray with the development of a waxy covering; occasionally zigzag. **LEAF** Alternate, simple, ovate or circular in outline, subpalmately lobed, tips of lobes abruptly short-pointed; base deeply cordate or more or less flat; margins more or less entire or coarsely toothed. Upper surface lustrous green, palmately or subpalmately veined, the major veins raised, with 2 major lateral veins arising from or slightly above the base of the midvein; lower surface usually hairy, at least along the veins and in the vein axils. Blade 6–20 cm long, 6–25 cm broad; petiole 1–5 cm long, dilated at the base, usually hairy, subtended by a conspicuous, often toothed stipule. **FLOWER** Minute, borne in a stalked, many-flowered rounded head, each with only male or female flowers; male inflorescences on stiff, erect stalks; female inflorescences on lax, often pendent stalks. Spring. **FRUIT** Achene to about 8 mm long; produced in a dense, spherical tan or brownish fruiting head, about 2.5 cm diam. and dangling on stalks 8–15 cm long; matures late autumn.

HABITAT/RANGE Native. Usually along streams, lakes, and large alluvial rivers, occasionally in uplands, 0–950 m; widespread in the East from se. Maine to n. Fla., west to e. Nebr., Okla., and sc. Tex.

SIMILAR SPECIES See London Planetree, below. The leaves of some maples are similar in shape and lobing, but are alternate.

Notes: American Sycamore is one of the tallest and most massive trees in North America. It is well known as a pioneer species along large alluvial rivers, where it soon occupies and stabilizes newly formed banks and sandbars.

AMERICAN SYCAMORE

American Sycamore

twig

fruit cluster

fruit section   achene

achene   fruit cluster

twig

London Planetree

LONDON PLANETREE *Platanus hybrida* Brot.

Large tree, easily confused with American Syca-more, but distinguished by its greener bark, nar-rower and longer leaf lobes (especially on larger leaves), and fruiting heads often produced 2 to the stalk. **HABITAT/RANGE** Horticultural hybrid; cultivated as a street tree and rarely established in the Northeast.

POLYGONACEAE: BUCKWHEAT FAMILY

The buckwheat family includes 43–48 genera and 1,100–1,200 species of trees, shrubs, vines, and perennial, biennial, or annual herbs. About 35 genera and 442 species occur in North America, at least 376 of which are native. Although this widespread family is especially well represented in the north temperate zone, only 2 tree species occur in North America, both native and confined to subtropical Fla.

LEAF Usually alternate, simple, with entire margins and pinnate venation. The stipules are often fused into a thin sheath (ocrea) around the stem, which provides an excellent identification feature. **FLOWER** Usually bisexual, sometimes bisexual and unisexual, and rarely unisexual and dioecious. Individual flowers are usually small, radial, and individually inconspicuous, with 5 or 6 usually undifferentiated sepals and petals (tepals). The inflorescence is a terminal or axillary cyme, spike, raceme, or panicle, or a headlike or umbellate cluster. **FRUIT** Achene or nutlet, often angled or winged, usually associated with an enlarged fleshy or dry perianth (sepals and petals collectively). The achenes are dispersed by wind, water, birds, and other wildlife.

The family is probably best known in North America for several herbaceous genera, including *Erigonum* (buckwheat) and *Rumex* (sorrel). Several genera have been used medicinally or for food by Native Americans, and the 2 North American species of *Coccoloba* are widely used as ornamental plants in s. Fla.

■ *COCCOLOBA*: SEAGRAPES AND PIGEON PLUMS

About 120 species of tropical trees distributed in Mexico, Central and South America, the West Indies, and Fla. Evergreen, erect or spreading trees or shrubs. **LEAF** Alternate, simple, thin or leathery, stipule usually forming a sheath at the base of the petiole but often quickly deciduous. **FLOWER** Unisexual, male and female usually produced on separate plants, tiny, greenish or whitish; produced in a stalked, terminal spike or few-flowered cyme. **FRUIT** Achene, usually embedded in a fleshy perianth tube; often resembling a drupe.

PIGEON PLUM *Coccoloba diversifolia*
Jacq.
A.K.A. TIETONGUE

QUICK ID Recognized by the combination of thick, variably shaped leathery leaves with margins rolled under and the fleshy fruit surrounding a single achene.

Evergreen tree, 10–20 m tall, to about 65 cm diam., usually smaller. Erect, single trunk, usually low-branching and appearing multitrunked; crown dense, rounded, with several large, spreading or ascending branches. **BARK** Smooth, gray or bluish gray, mottled, often exfoliating in small flakes. **TWIG** Green or gray-green, becoming grayish; hairless. **LEAF** Alternate, simple, leathery, oval, ovate, elliptic, or obovate; base rounded or broadly wedge-shaped; tip rounded, blunt, or short-pointed; margins entire, usually rolled under. Upper surface lustrous or dull dark or medium green, surface often appearing quilted, veins conspicuous; lower surface pale green. Blade varying greatly in size, those of juvenile trees and of shaded locations much the largest, crown leaves often smaller, typically 6–10 cm long, 3–5 cm broad; petiole 5–15 mm long, those lower on the branch often subtended by a persistent sheath. **FLOWER** Unisexual, greenish white, with a fused cuplike tube; tepals 5; stamens usually 8, conspicuous; styles 3; produced in an upright or dangling raceme. Year-round. **FRUIT** Achene, 6–10 mm long, embedded within a more or less egg-shaped, dark red drupelike persistent floral tube, 10–13 mm long. Year-round.

HABITAT/RANGE Native. Subtropical and coastal hammocks, 0–10 m; s. Fla.

SIMILAR SPECIES The leaves of Seagrape are more or less circular in outline.

fruit

Pigeon
Plum

fruit

flowers

Seagrape

fruit

SEAGRAPE *Coccoloba uvifera* (L.) L.

QUICK ID Easily identified by the circular leaves and dangling clusters of drupelike fruit.

Evergreen large shrub or small tree, to 2–7 m tall, 30–120 cm diam. Erect or sprawling, rarely single trunk, more often with multiple trunks, often very low-branched, the crown dense, rounded, often with several large, contorted branches; sometimes nearly prostrate. **BARK** Smooth or slightly roughened, reddish or gray, peeling in whitish, gray, or brownish flakes. **TWIG** Green and hairy at first, becoming gray and hairless. **LEAF** Alternate, simple, circular or broadly transversely elliptic, thick, leathery; base rounded or more often heart-shaped; tip rounded, sometimes notched; margins entire, flat or rolled under. Upper surface lustrous, medium green with reddish veins; lower surface pale green, lustrous or not. Blade 10–27 cm long, equally broad; petiole 5–15 cm long, hairy, usually subtended by a conspicuous persistent sheath that encircles the stem. **FLOWER** Unisexual, greenish white, with a fused cuplike tube; tepals 5; stamens usually 8, conspicuous; styles 3; produced in an upright or dangling raceme. Year-round. **FRUIT** Achene, enclosed within an egg-shaped or rounded drupelike persistent floral tube, 1.8–2.5 cm long, 1–2 cm broad, green at first, turning red then dark purple; dangling in elongated grapelike clusters. Year-round.

PIGEON PLUM

SEAGRAPE

HABITAT/RANGE Native. In coastal hammocks, dunes, often seen adorning roadsides and suburban and urban landscapes, 0–10 m; s. Fla.

Notes: Stabilizes dunes and shorelines, sometimes forming an almost continual mat to about 1 m tall. The fleshy "fruit" is used in seagrape jelly.

PROTEACEAE: PROTEA FAMILY

This mostly Southern Hemisphere family includes 80 genera and about 1,770 species of trees and shrubs, distributed mostly in tropical regions of Australia, Africa, Southeast Asia, and Central and South America. The family is closely allied with the Platanaceae and is placed taxonomically in the group "basal eudicots," which are considered by many systematists to represent the earliest evolutionary lineages of plants with tricolpate pollen (pollen grains with 3 pores). Only a single species is naturalized in North America. The family is probably best known for species of *Protea* and *Banksia*, which have interesting, showy, and complicated flowers and are sometimes grown as ornamentals in the warmer regions of the s. U.S.

SILKOAK *Grevillea robusta* A. Cunn. ex R. Br.

QUICK ID Easily recognized by the deeply divided fernlike leaves, which are olive green above and silvery white beneath.

Evergreen tree, 10–25 m tall, to about 50 cm diam. in North America. Erect, single straight trunk; crown narrow, upright. **BARK** Gray, finely fissured with narrow ridges. **LEAF** Alternate, pinnately compound or simple and deeply incised, somewhat fernlike; leaflets or major divisions 7–19, usually connected by a narrow band of tissue along the midrib, opposite or alternate, 3–12 cm long, themselves usually divided into several narrow lobes. Upper surface dark olive green, lower surface silvery white,

especially on new growth. Blade 15–33 cm long, to about 20 cm broad; petiole 4–6 cm long. **FLOWER** Bisexual, sepals 1.5–2 cm long, orange, yellow, or golden yellow, fused at first, becoming free; petals absent; style conspicuous, 1–2.5 cm long; produced in a showy, cylindric, elongated raceme 5–15 cm long. Spring. **FRUIT** Two-seeded silvery-gray or green follicle, about 1 cm long; splits along 1 side at maturity; seeds broadly winged, 10–15 mm long; matures late summer to autumn.

HABITAT/RANGE Introduced from Australia, cultivated and established in c. and s. Fla.

Notes: Grevillea is the largest genus in the Proteaceae, including about 200 species of trees. No other tree in Fla. has similar leaves.

Silkoak

flowers

fruit

PUNICACEAE: POMEGRANATE FAMILY

This is a small family of opposite-leaved, sometimes spiny shrubs and small trees distributed in Asia and the island of Socotra in the Indian Ocean. It includes a single genus with 2 species, 1 naturalized in North America. Recent systematists have included the Punicaceae within the loosestrife family (Lythraceae). As treated here, the family is characterized by opposite or sub-opposite leaves that are sometimes closely clustered on short shoots and lack stipules; showy bisexual radial flowers with 5–7 free petals, numerous free stamens, a simple style with a single stigma, and an inferior ovary; and the large, distinctive berry that is conspicuously crowned by the remains of the calyx.

POMEGRANATE *Punica granatum* L.

QUICK ID Distinguished by the often spiny branches, opposite and clustered leaves, large, showy flowers, and large, distinctive fruit.

Deciduous shrub or small tree, 2–8 m tall. Upright, often densely branched from the ground, sometimes with a single short trunk, branches sometimes spiny; crown rounded. **BARK** Brownish gray, thin, smooth, becoming slightly roughened. **TWIG** Angled at first, becoming round. **LEAF** Opposite and clustered, simple, lanceolate, elliptic, oblong, or oblanceolate; base narrowly wedge-shaped; tip bluntly pointed; margins entire. Upper surface lustrous green, hairless; lower surface paler. Blade 2–9 cm long, 1–2.5 cm broad; petiole 2–10 mm long. **FLOWER** Bisexual; sepals fused, forming a tube, calyx to about 2 cm long, fleshy, reddish; petals 5–9, red-orange, yellow, or white, circular, margins crinkly. Spring to summer. **FRUIT** Rounded red, yellowish, red-brown, or white leathery berry, 5–12 cm diam., with the remains of the calyx forming a distinctive crown at the summit; matures autumn.

HABITAT/RANGE Introduced from Asia. Cultivated, sparingly established in scattered states in the southern U.S. from about N.C. to Calif. Perhaps more often persisting from cultivation than strictly naturalized.

Notes: Pomegranate has been grown for ornament and food for centuries and is mentioned in both the Bible and the Quran; the persistent calyx on the fruit was apparently the inspiration for King Solomon's crown.

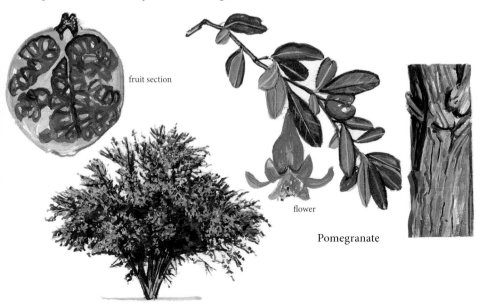

fruit section

flower

Pomegranate

RHAMNACEAE: BUCKTHORN FAMILY

The buckthorn family includes 50–60 genera and about 900 species of trees, shrubs, and a few vines that climb by twining stems or tendrils or gain support by hooks. The family is widely distributed in temperate and tropical regions. North of Mexico there are about 14 genera, 2 introduced, and about 115 species, 13 introduced, including 20 trees or large, often arborescent shrubs.

Deciduous or evergreen trees and shrubs. **LEAF** Usually alternate, sometimes opposite, simple, petiolate, with the margins entire or toothed; venation is often prominently pinnate or palmate. Stipules are often developed into a pair of unequal spines. **FLOWER** Bisexual or unisexual, radially symmetric, small, with a hypanthium and often a thick nectar disk; sepals, petals, and stamens number 4 or 5; or sometimes petals absent. Stamens are opposite the petals (when petals are present) and often enfolded by them in young flowers. **FRUIT** The ovary is superior or inferior, developing into a drupe or a dry fruit that splits into several sections.

■ *COLUBRINA*: NAKEDWOOD

A genus of 20–30 species distributed in tropical and subtropical regions of Africa, s. Asia, Australia, the Pacific islands, South America, and North America.

Deciduous or evergreen shrubs or trees. **TWIG** Lacks spines. **LEAF** Alternate, rarely opposite, simple, thin or leathery, toothed or not. **FLOWER** Bisexual; sepals usually 5, often fused; petals usually 5, often shorter than the sepals; stamens 5; central nectar-producing disk conspicuous, fleshy, green at first, turning yellow; the stigma becomes receptive after the stamens have dehisced and become reflexed. **FRUIT** Drupe or drupelike, 3-lobed, fleshy at first, becoming hard and capsule-like, splitting at maturity to reveal the seeds.

GREENHEART *Colubrina arborescens*
(Mill.) Sarg.
A.K.A. SNAKEBARK

QUICK ID Recognized within its s. Fla. range by the rusty-red hairs on young stems and twigs and the alternate, lustrous leaves that are reddish-hairy beneath and lack marginal glands.

Evergreen shrub or small tree, to about 8 m tall, usually not exceeding about 5 cm diam. in Fla., potentially to 25 m tall and 30 cm diam. Erect, usually a single trunk, sometimes a shrub with multiple trunks; crown of open-grown trees broad, spreading, that of hammock-grown trees narrower. **BARK** Gray or brownish, smooth or slightly fissured. **TWIG** Brownish, finely and moderately or densely hairy. **LEAF** Alternate, simple, leathery, ovate or elliptic; base rounded, broadly wedge-shaped, or nearly heart-shaped; tip acute or abruptly long- or short-pointed; margins entire, lacking glands. Upper surface lustrous, dark green, hairy at first, becoming mostly hairless, veins not impressed; lower surface paler, permanently finely and densely hairy with reddish hairs. Blade 5–14 cm long, 3–8 cm broad; petiole 5–20 mm long, hairy. **FLOWER** Tiny, greenish yellow; sepals 4 or 5, fused, ovate; petals 4 or 5, shorter than the sepals, notched at the tip; produced in axillary clusters. Year-round. **FRUIT** Three-lobed, dark purple to nearly black drupe, 8–9 mm diam., fleshy at first, becoming hard and capsule-like, splitting at maturity to reveal lustrous black seeds 4 mm long. Year-round.

HABITAT/RANGE Native. Subtropical hammocks, s. Fla., most common in Fla. Keys; also distributed in Mexico, Central America, and the West Indies. Treated as an endangered species in Fla.

GREENHEART

Greenheart

split fruit and seeds

flowers

flower

SIMILAR SPECIES The upper surface of the leaves in Cuban Nakedwood are distinctly hairy and have impressed veins. The leaves of Soldierwood are nearly hairless, the hairs on the lower surface, when present, are not reddish, and the leaf margins have 2 conspicuous glands near the base.

CUBAN NAKEDWOOD *Colubrina cubensis* (Jacq.) Brongn. **var.** *floridana* M.C. Johnst.

QUICK ID Recognized in its s. Fla. range by the alternate oblong or elliptic, dull medium green leaves with deeply impressed veins, wavy, bluntly toothed margins, and velvety-hairy lower surface.

Evergreen shrub or small tree, to about 9 m tall, 15–20 cm diam. Erect, usually a single trunk; shrubby plants are dense, rounded, and branched to the ground; arborescent plants are irregularly branched, with a somewhat spreading and contorted crown. **TWIG** Slender, reddish, hairy. **LEAF** Alternate, simple, thick and somewhat leathery, oblong or elliptic; base rounded or broadly wedge-shaped; tip rounded, acute, or bluntly pointed; margins more or less wavy, appearing bluntly toothed. Upper surface lustrous, medium green, hairy, lateral veins deeply impressed, parallel; lower surface paler, velvety-hairy. Blade 4–10 cm long, 1–5 cm broad; petiole 5–15 mm long. **FLOWER** Tiny, with a disk-like center and

Cuban Nakedwood

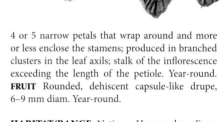

fruit

flowers

CUBAN NAKEDWOOD

4 or 5 narrow petals that wrap around and more or less enclose the stamens; produced in branched clusters in the leaf axils; stalk of the inflorescence exceeding the length of the petiole. Year-round. **FRUIT** Rounded, dehiscent capsule-like drupe, 6–9 mm diam. Year-round.

HABITAT/RANGE Native. Hammocks, Everglades tree islands; s. Fla. Rare and uncommon in Fla., treated as an endangered species; also distributed in Cuba and Hispaniola.

SIMILAR SPECIES The leaves of Soldierwood are hairless or inconspicuously hairy; those of Greenheart are reddish-hairy beneath. Neither has leaves with conspicuously impressed veins on the upper surface.

SOLDIERWOOD *Colubrina elliptica*
(Sw.) Brizicky & W.L. Stern

QUICKID Recognized in its s. Fla. range by orange-brown exfoliating bark and leaf margins with conspicuous glands near the base of the blade.

Evergreen, often a shrub, sometimes a tree 6–15 m tall, usually not exceeding about 20 cm diam., reportedly to about 1 m diam. in Fla. Keys. Erect, single trunk or multiple; crown of hammock-grown trees narrow, irregularly branched, branches slender. **BARK** Orange-brown, dark outside, exfoliating in thin sheets to reveal orange or buff inner bark. **TWIG** Slender, reddish-hairy at first, becoming mostly hairless and gray or light brown, marked with lenticels. **LEAF** Alternate, simple, soft to the touch, elliptic, ovate, or broadly lanceolate; base rounded or broadly wedge-shaped; tip abruptly long-pointed; margins entire, with 2 conspicuous glands near the attachment to the petiole. Upper surface lustrous, dark green, hairless; lower surface sparsely hairy or hairless. Blade 4–12 cm long, 4–6 cm broad; petiole to about 2.5 cm long. **FLOWER** Small, greenish; sepals 5, fused; petals 5, shorter than the sepals, hooded, more or less enclosing the stamens; produced in branched clusters at the leaf axils. Year-round. **FRUIT** Rounded orange-red drupe, 6–10 mm diam., becoming hard, capsule-like, and splitting at maturity to reveal lustrous blackish seeds about 5 mm long. Year-round.

HABITAT/RANGE Native. Subtropical hammocks, s. Fla. and Fla. Keys; widespread in the West Indies, treated as an endangered species in Fla.

SIMILAR SPECIES The leaves of Greenheart are similar but lack marginal glands and are reddish-hairy beneath.

SOLDIERWOOD

■ *FRANGULA* AND *RHAMNUS*: BUCKTHORNS

The genera *Frangula* and *Rhamnus* form a closely related group of tropical and temperate shrubs and trees distributed in Africa, Europe, East Asia, and North America. *Frangula* includes about 50 mostly temperate species, *Rhamnus* about 150 mostly tropical or subtropical species. About a dozen species of *Rhamnus* occur in North America, 7 native and 4 introduced, including 6 in the East, 1 native; about 7 species of *Frangula* occur in North America, 6 native, including 2 in the East, 1 native. Here we treat 4 arborescent species of *Rhamnus*, all introduced, and 2 arborescent species of *Frangula*. The taxonomic rank of these 2 groups—whether they should be treated as separate genera or separate subgenera—has long been a subject of debate, with species being traditionally treated within the genus *Rhamnus*.

Species of *Frangula* have alternate leaves with conspicuous straight, parallel lateral veins; the twigs not thorny (in all of those included here); naked winter buds that lack scales; bisexual flowers, usually with 5 sepals and 5 petals; and the stone remains intact within the fruit, and the seeds are smooth on the back. Species of *Rhamnus* usually have mostly opposite or nearly opposite leaves with curving lateral veins; twigs often transformed into thorns; buds with scales; unisexual flowers, usually with 4 sepals and 4 petals; and the stone splits open within the fruit, and the seed is grooved.

GLOSSY BUCKTHORN *Frangula alnus*
Mill.
A.K.A. ALDER BUCKTHORN

QUICKID Recognized by the typically shrubby habit, conspicuous parallel leaf veins, and clusters of reddish to purplish-black drupes.

Deciduous shrub or small tree to about 7 m tall. Often shrubby, with several trunks, sometimes with a single trunk and arborescent; crown with stout, usually erect branches, naturalized plants often showing signs of having originated from strongly fastigiate cultivars. **BARK** Smooth, grayish brown, usually with conspicuous horizontal lenticels. **TWIG** Thornless, slender, reddish brown, usually hairy. **LEAF** Alternate, simple, oblong, oval, or broadly elliptic; base rounded; tip usually abruptly short-pointed; margins entire, often somewhat wavy. Upper surface lustrous green with 5–9 pairs of conspicuously parallel lateral veins that curve

flower

flowers

fruit

Soldierwood

fruit

stone

flowers

autumn

fruit

Glossy Buckthorn

and follow the margin, lower surface dull green. Blade 5–10 cm long, to about 5 cm broad; petiole 6–14 mm long. **FLOWER** Bisexual, small, creamy green or yellowish green, produced in clusters at the leaf axils. Late spring. **FRUIT** Rounded, usually 2-seeded drupe 5–10 mm diam., red at first, becoming purplish black; matures late summer.

HABITAT/RANGE Introduced from Europe. Established and weedy in bogs, fens, and other wetlands; naturalized from Que. to Sask., south to W. Va., Tenn., Idaho, and Colo.; established from cultivation and treated as an invasive species, especially in Midwestern wetlands.

SIMILAR SPECIES The leaves of Carolina Buckthorn also have conspicuous parallel veins, but the margins are usually at least obscurely toothed and plants of the species more often form trees.

CAROLINA BUCKTHORN *Frangula caroliniana* (Walter) A. Gray

QUICK ID Recognized by the combination of leaves with conspicuous straight, parallel lateral veins that become fainter and strongly curved only as they near the margin, leaf margins obscurely toothed, thornless twigs, and usually 3-stoned reddish to blackish drupes.

Deciduous shrub or small tree, 10–14 m tall, 15–30 cm diam. Erect, usually a single trunk; crown open, spreading, the branches sometimes arching or drooping near the tips. **BARK** Smooth and brown at first, usually with conspicuous lenticels, becoming gray with brownish vertical markings and slightly roughened or finely fissured. **TWIG** Thornless, reddish brown and hairy, becoming gray and hairless; buds axillary and lacking scales. **LEAF** Alternate, simple, those lowest on the branchlet usually noticeably smaller than those above; thin, papery, broadly oblong, elliptic, or slightly obovate; base broadly wedge-shaped or rounded; tip blunt, broadly pointed, or abruptly short-pointed; margins obscurely and irregularly toothed. Upper surface lustrous, dark green, lateral veins conspicuous, parallel, curving at and running for some distance along the margin; lower surface lighter green, usually at least somewhat hairy. Blade 5–12 cm long, 3–5 cm broad; petiole 8–14 mm long, usually hairy. **FLOWER** Bisexual, small, the floral tube cuplike; sepals 5, erect, triangular, greenish yellow; petals 5, shorter than the sepals, notched at the tip, yellowish or whitish; stamens 5, about as long as the petals; produced in branched clusters in the leaf axils. Spring. **FRUIT** More or less rounded, 3-stoned drupe to about 1 cm long, red at first, becoming black and juicy at maturity, in summer to early autumn.

HABITAT/RANGE Native. Calcareous woods, glades, shell middens, rich uplands, 0–600 m; throughout much of the East, Md. west to s. Ill. and s. Mo., south to c. Fla. and c. Tex.

SIMILAR SPECIES The leaves of American Beech (*Fagus grandifolia*, Fagaceae) have parallel veins but the margins are distinctly toothed and the tip pointed. Glossy Buckthorn is similar, but its leaf margins are entire or wavy.

EUROPEAN BUCKTHORN *Rhamnus cathartica* L.

A.K.A. COMMON BUCKTHORN, PURGING BUCKTHORN

QUICK ID A buckthorn, recognized by the combination of mostly opposite, toothed leaves not exceeding about 2 times longer than broad, usually about 3 lateral veins on either side of the midvein, lateral veins strongly curving toward the blade tip, and black drupes with 2 or 3 stones.

Deciduous shrub or small tree to about 8 m tall, 36 cm diam. Erect, single short, crooked trunk; crown irregular, rounded, bushy, the branches crooked, with stout axillary, lateral, and terminal thorns 5–55 mm long. **BARK** Gray-brown, smooth, becoming dark brown or blackish and scaly. **TWIG** Gray, hairless, thorn-tipped, with conspicuous lenticels. **LEAF** Opposite or subopposite, rarely alternate, simple, persisting on the branch and remaining green well into winter; thin, papery, broadly elliptic or ovate; base rounded, flattened, or broadly wedge-shaped; tip abruptly short- and sharp-pointed; margins distinctly toothed. Upper surface dull green, lateral veins 2–4 pairs, strongly curving toward the tip of the blade; lower surface yellow-green; both surfaces usually hairless. Blade 4–9 cm long, 3–5 cm broad; petiole 1–4 cm long. **FLOWER** Unisexual or bisexual, about 5 mm diam., yellowish green, fragrant; male and female usually produced on separate trees; sepals 4, 2–3 mm long; petals 4, tiny; stamens 4; style 1 with 4 stigmatic branches. Late spring. **FRUIT** Rounded black drupe, 6–10 mm diam., with 2 or 3 stones; reportedly poisonous and nauseating to humans; matures late summer to early autumn.

HABITAT/RANGE Introduced from Europe. Cultivated, naturalized, widespread across n. U.S. and Canada; N.S. west to Que. and Man., south to N.C. and Utah.

SIMILAR SPECIES Dahurian Buckthorn is distinguished by the leaves being 2 or 3 times longer than wide and having 4–6 pairs of lateral veins.

Notes: Shade-tolerant, fast-growing, and widely regarded as an aggressive invasive species in several northern states and Canada, where its dense shade prevents the establishment of native trees and shrubs.

CAROLINA BUCKTHORN

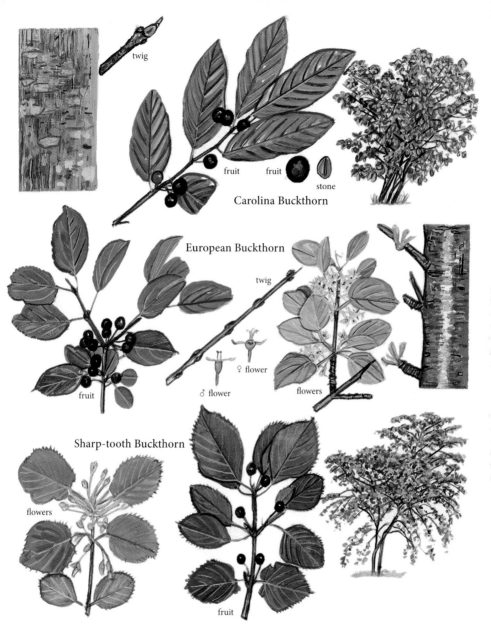

twig

fruit   fruit   stone

Carolina Buckthorn

European Buckthorn

twig

♀ flower

♂ flower   flowers

fruit

Sharp-tooth Buckthorn

flowers

fruit

SHARP-TOOTH BUCKTHORN
Rhamnus arguta Maxim.

Similar to European Buckthorn, but its leaf blades are more consistently rounded or heart-shaped at the base and usually have 4 or 5 pairs of lateral veins. **HABITAT/RANGE** Introduced; reportedly naturalized in Ind.

DAHURIAN BUCKTHORN *Rhamnus davurica* Pall.

QUICK ID Recognized by the combination of opposite leaves, impressed and strongly curved leaf venation, thorn-tipped twigs and short shoots, and 2-stoned black drupe.

Deciduous shrub or small tree, to about 10 m tall, 30 cm diam. Erect or vase-shaped, single trunk or multiple; crown dense, vase-shaped, of many ascending branches. **BARK** Yellowish brown or reddish brown, smooth, peeling in small flakes. **TWIG** Stout, gray, usually thorn-tipped. **LEAF** Opposite or clustered on short shoots, simple, thin, papery, usually broadly elliptic or ovate; base broadly wedge-shaped or nearly rounded; tip usually abruptly short-pointed; margins toothed, the teeth gland-tipped. Upper surface lustrous, dark green, hairless or hairy, lateral veins 4–6 pairs, conspicuous, impressed, strongly curving toward the blade tip; lower surface usually hairy on the veins. Blade 4–13 cm long, 2–6 cm broad; petiole 1.5–4 cm long. **FLOWER** Unisexual, male and female produced on separate plants, yellowish green, small, sepals and petals 4. Late spring to early summer. **FRUIT** Rounded or egg-shaped, 2-stoned black drupe, 5–6 mm diam.; matures midsummer to autumn.

HABITAT/RANGE Introduced from Asia. Cultivated and escaped in the East, mostly from Conn. and S.D. south to N.C.; treated as invasive in some states.

SIMILAR SPECIES European Buckthorn is distinguished by its predominantly shorter, broader leaves with 2–4 pairs of lateral veins.

JAPANESE BUCKTHORN *Rhamnus japonica* Maxim.

Deciduous shrub to about 3 m tall, rarely treelike. **TWIG** Yellowish brown or grayish brown, lustrous, usually thorny. **LEAF** Opposite or subopposite, simple, oblong or oblanceolate; tip rounded or abruptly pointed; margins finely toothed. Upper surface lustrous dark green, lateral veins 3–5 pairs. Blade 5–8 cm long, 4 cm broad; petiole 8–25 mm long. **FLOWER** Greenish, small, produced in dense clusters. Late spring to early summer. **FRUIT** Black drupe, 6–8 mm diam.; matures summer to autumn.

HABITAT/RANGE Introduced from Asia; cultivated, rarely naturalized, reported in Ill.

JAPANESE RAISINTREE *Hovenia dulcis* Thunb.

QUICK ID Recognized by its showy flowering panicles, rounded purplish-black drupes, and coarsely toothed leaves that are often flat at the base and decorated above with conspicuously impressed veins.

Deciduous tree, rarely shrubby, to about 10 m tall. Erect, single trunk; crown oval. **BARK** Grayish brown, finely ridged and furrowed. **TWIG** Brown or purplish black, hairless, lenticels inconspicuous. **LEAF** Alternate, simple, papery to somewhat thickened, ovate, oblong, or elliptic; base rounded or nearly flattened; tip abruptly short-pointed; margins coarsely and sharply toothed. Upper surface lustrous, dark green, hairless, veins impressed, conspicuous; lower surface paler, hairless or hairy on the veins. Blade 7–17 cm long, 4–11 cm broad; petiole 2–4.5 cm long, hairless. **FLOWER** Bisexual, yellow-green, 6–8 mm diam.; produced in dense, showy, paniculate terminal clusters. Late spring to midsummer. **FRUIT** Rounded, juicy, 3-stoned purplish-black drupe, about 7 mm diam.; matures late summer to autumn.

HABITAT/RANGE Introduced from China; cultivated and rarely naturalized, reportedly in Tex. and N.C.

Notes: Hovenia is a genus of 3 species distributed in Bhutan, China, India, Japan, Korea, Myanmar, and Nepal; only this species has naturalized in North America.

flowers

fruit

Dahurian Buckthorn

Japanese Buckthorn

flowers

flower

fruit

Japanese Raisintree

flowers

fruit

LEADWOOD *Krugiodendron ferreum*
(Vahl) Urb.
A.K.A. BLACK IRONWOOD, STRONG BACK

QUICK ID Recognized in its southernmost Fla. range by the lustrous, oval, opposite leaves with a notched tip.

Evergreen shrub or small tree. to about 9 m tall, about 50 cm diam. Erect, single or multiple trunks; crown dense, leafy, with numerous spreading branches. **BARK** Brownish gray, usually ridged and shallow furrowed, the ridges with horizontal partitions, becoming dark gray and deeply furrowed. **TWIG** Stout, gray, finely hairy. **LEAF** Opposite, rarely subopposite or nearly alternate, simple, thick, leathery; oval, ovate, or broadly elliptic; base rounded or broadly wedge-shaped; tip rounded or blunt, usually conspicuously notched; margins entire, flat. Upper surface lustrous, dark green; lower surface paler, dull. Blade 2.5–4 cm long, 2–2.6 cm broad; petiole 3–6 mm long. **FLOWER** Bisexual, about 4 mm diam., yellowish green, fragrant; sepals 5, triangular, fused; petals absent; stamens 5, style short, with 2 stigmas; produced in clusters in the leaf axils. Spring. **FRUIT** Rounded or ovoid, usually 1-seeded black drupe, 5–10 mm diam.; matures summer to autumn.

HABITAT/RANGE Native. Subtropical hammocks, 0–10 m; coastally from c. Fla. peninsula south to Fla. Keys.

SIMILAR SPECIES The leaves of Darlingplum (*Reynosia septentrionalis*) are also notched at the tip, but are stiff, more often yellowish green, and the margins are conspicuously rolled under.

Notes: The genus *Krugiodendron* includes only this species, distributed in s. Fla., s. Mexico, Central America, and the West Indies. Its wood has a specific gravity of 1.3, weighs about 1,300 kg per cubic meter, and is among the heaviest woods in the U.S.

DARLINGPLUM *Reynosia septentrionalis* Urb.
A.K.A. RED IRONWOOD

QUICK ID Recognized by the evergreen medium-green leaves with conspicuously rolled margins and a notched tip.

Evergreen shrub or small tree, to about 10 m tall, 20 cm diam. Erect or leaning, usually a single short, low-branching trunk; crown dense, spreading. **BARK** Reddish brown, stripping off in thin plates or strips. **TWIG** Slender, grayish. **LEAF** Opposite, simple, stiff; oval, obovate, or narrowly elliptic; base rounded, wedge-shaped, or nearly flattened; tip rounded, notched; margins distinctly and conspicuously rolled under. Upper surface dark green or yellowish green; lower surface paler and duller; both surfaces usually hairless. Blade 1.5–4 cm long, to about 1.5 cm broad; petiole 1.5–3 mm long. **FLOWER** Bisexual, yellowish green, about 5 mm diam., sepals 5, about 2 mm long, fused, petals absent, stamens 5; produced in small axillary or terminal clusters. Spring to summer. **FRUIT** Rounded or egg-shaped, 1-seeded purplish-black drupe, 1–2 cm long, usually with the remains of the style protruding at the apex; matures summer to early autumn.

HABITAT/RANGE Native. Coastal subtropical hammocks, 0–10 m; s. Fla.

SIMILAR SPECIES The leaf margins of Leadwood (*Krugiodendron ferreum*) are more or less flat.

Notes: *Reynosia* is a genus of 10–20 species distributed in Fla. and the West Indies. The close-grained wood of Darlingplum is heavy, hard, and strong.

LEADWOOD

DARLINGPLUM

Leadwood

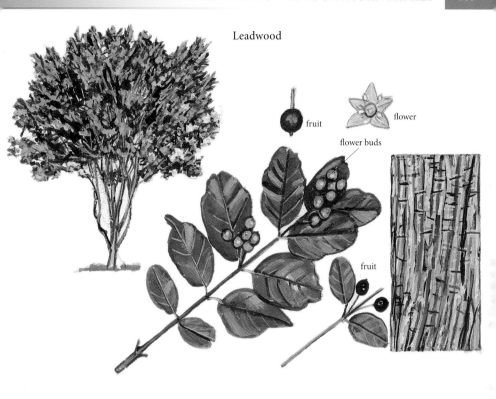

fruit

flower

flower buds

fruit

fruit

Darlingplum

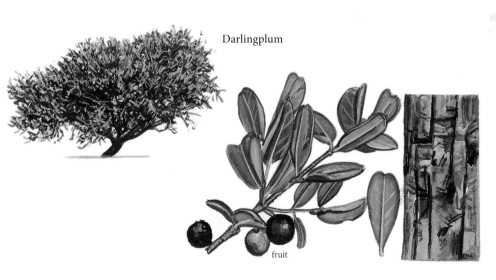

fruit

◼ *ZIZIPHUS*: JUJUBES

A genus of about 100 species, distributed mostly in subtropical or tropical regions of Asia, Africa, and the Americas; a few temperate species. Deciduous or evergreen shrubs or small to medium trees; usually armed with stipular spines. **LEAF** Alternate, simple, usually with 3 primary longitudinal veins. **FLOWER** Bisexual, yellow-green, usually with 5 petals and 5 sepals; nectar-producing disk surrounding the ovary thick and fleshy with 5–10 lobes; ovary superior, rounded. **FRUIT** Rounded or oblong, 1-stoned drupe.

COMMON JUJUBE *Ziziphus jujuba* Mill.

QUICK ID Recognized by the combination of alternate ovate leaves with 3 main longitudinal veins, lower surface of leaf mostly hairless, pairs of spines often subtending the petiole, and conspicuous, fleshy red or purplish fruit.

Deciduous shrub or small tree, to about 10 m tall, 15–30 cm diam. Erect, single trunk or multiple; crown dense, with usually drooping and often zigzag greenish branches. **BARK** Grayish brown, usually flaking in strips or small plates. **TWIG** Purplish red, smooth, flexuous, usually zigzag. **LEAF** Alternate, simple, ovate, ovate-elliptic, or oblong; base rounded; tip abruptly long- or short-pointed; margins bluntly toothed. Upper surface lustrous, dark green, with 3 conspicuous longitudinal veins arising from the base of the blade; lower surface hairless, or finely hairy along the midvein. Blade 3–7 cm long, 1.5–4 cm broad; petiole about 1 cm long, often subtended by a pair of spines, 1 short and hooked, the other long, needlelike, to about 3 cm long. **FLOWER** Less than 1 cm diam., yellowish green; sepals and petals 5; produced in clusters of 1–8 flowers in the leaf axils. Spring to summer. **FRUIT** Rounded, juicy, edible drupe, 2–3.5 cm long, about 2 cm diam., with 1 or 2 stones; red or purplish red at maturity, in autumn.

HABITAT/RANGE Introduced from Europe and Asia; irregularly established from cultivation in the East, including locations in Ala., Fla., Ga., La., and Tex.

SIMILAR SPECIES Indian Jujube is distinguished by the densely hairy lower surface of the leaves.

Notes: Common Jujube has long been cultivated for its fruit, which usually has a tart taste and is also attractive to small mammals. It is often referenced under the synonymous name *Z. zizyphus* (L.) Karst.

INDIAN JUJUBE *Ziziphus mauritiana* Lam.

QUICK ID Recognized by oblong to nearly circular leaves with hairy lower surfaces and 3 primary longitudinal veins, paired axillary spines, and orange-red to black fruit.

Evergreen (to deciduous in Fla.) shrub or tree, 9–15 m tall, to about 40 cm diam. Erect, single trunk or multiple, often a spiny shrub; crown rounded, with numerous often drooping branches armed with sharp spines. **BARK** Grayish to reddish brown, thick, irregularly and shallowly ridged and furrowed. **TWIG** Slender, pinkish, zigzag, hairy. **LEAF** Alternate, simple, leathery, firm, elliptic, ovate, or nearly circular; base rounded; tip rounded, often notched; margins finely toothed. Upper surface lustrous, dark green, with 3 conspicuous primary longitudinal veins, each giving rise to several lateral veins; lower surface paler, yellowish- or grayish-hairy. Blade 2–4.5 cm long, 1.5–2 cm broad; petiole 5–13 mm long, subtended by a pair of unequal sharp spines, one short and hooked, the other 5–10 mm long, straight and angling from the leaf node. **FLOWER** Greenish yellow; sepals 5; petals 5, wrapping around and more or less enclosing the stamens; produced in axillary clusters. Summer to autumn. **FRUIT** Rounded or ellipsoid, fleshy drupe with 1 or 2 stones, 1–1.2 cm long; orange-red at first, becoming black at maturity, in autumn.

HABITAT/RANGE Introduced, probably native to Southeast Asia but widely naturalized in tropical regions; cultivated, established in rockland hammocks in s. Fla., reportedly naturalized in Calif.

SIMILAR SPECIES Common Jujube is distinguished by the lower surface of the leaf hairless or with hairs confined mostly along the central vein.

Common Jujube

fruit

fruit

flower

Indian Jujube

fruit

RHIZOPHORACEAE: RED MANGROVE FAMILY

This family of 12 genera and 84 species is distributed in tropical and subtropical regions worldwide. Two genera and 2 species occur in North America, 1 native. **LEAF** Opposite, simple, often diverging from the stem at an angle of less than 90°, with the petiole subtended by a pair of interpetiolar stipules that fall as the leaf grows, leaving the stipular scar encircling the twig. **FLOWER** Usually bisexual, with 5 thick leathery sepals and 5 fringed or hairy petals that enclose 1 or a group of stamens in bud; stamens 8–10. **FRUIT** Capsule or berry.

RED MANGROVE *Rhizophora mangle* L.

QUICK ID Recognized by the combination of saltwater habitat; lustrous, dark green opposite leaves; and the unique elongated seedlings that develop while the fruit is still on the tree.

Evergreen large shrub or medium-size tree, 10–25 m tall, to 19 cm diam. Erect, contorted, with a single low-branching trunk that produces adventitious prop roots; crown spreading, often vertically flattened, the branches often twisted or contorted. **BARK** Smooth, reddish, becoming gray. **TWIG** Smooth, terminal bud covered by conspicuous stipules, 2.5–4 cm long. **LEAF** Opposite, simple, leathery, thick, elliptic tending toward obovate, base wedge-shaped, tip rounded or bluntly pointed, margins entire. Upper surface lustrous, dark green; lower surface pale green, covered with numerous tiny black dots. Blade 4–15 cm long, 2–6 cm broad; petiole to about 2 cm long, subtended by conspicuous interpetiolar stipules or stipular scars. **FLOWER** Bisexual, calyx thick, fleshy, cup- or turban-shaped; sepals 4, 1–1.5 cm long; petals 4, pale yellow, narrow, 8–10 mm long; stamens 8; style 1. Year-round. **FRUIT** Brown, egg-shaped, pendent, leathery, 2–3 cm long, with 1 seed, viviparous (germinating while still attached to the

parent tree), producing a narrow green pendent seedling to 25 cm long, usually persisting for some time, eventually falling, capable of floating great distances before becoming lodged in the substrate and growing into a new plant; seedlings evident all year.

HABITAT/RANGE Native. Coastal wetlands and shallow saltwater bays; common in s. Fla., rarely established along the Gulf Coast to n. Fla. and the Atlantic Coast to N.C., usually not persisting in these temperate locations.

SIMILAR SPECIES Red Mangrove grows with White Mangrove (*Laguncularia racemosa*, Combretaceae), the fruit of which is a ribbed drupe, and Black Mangrove (*Avicennia germinans*, Acanthaceae), which produces an asymmetric, laterally flattened capsule; neither produces a similarly elongated seedling. Large-leaved Mangrove (*Bruguiera gymnorhiza* [L.] Savigny), also in the family Rhizophoraceae, is escaped and established in s. Fla. from plantings made in the 1940s. Efforts have been instituted to remove these trees to prevent their spread. The leaves of Large-leaved Mangrove are usually reflexed upward from the midrib.

Notes: *Rhizophora* is a genus of about 8 species.

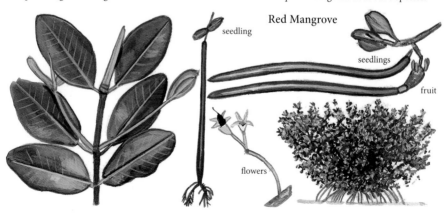

Red Mangrove

seedling

seedlings

fruit

flowers

ROSACEAE: ROSE FAMILY

The large and economically important rose family (Rosaceae) comprises about 120 genera and 3,300 species of herbs, shrubs, and trees worldwide. The family is most diverse in north temperate regions. Species are found in all habitats, from deserts to forests, and from sea coasts to alpine tundra. Fifteen genera and more than 70 species of trees of Rosaceae occur in North America north of Mexico, most in the eastern forests, several introduced from Eurasia. The hawthorn genus (*Crataegus*), in which delimitation of species is arguable, constitutes the family's largest woody genus native to North America. It is particularly complex in the East, much less so in the West.

LEAF Usually alternate, simple or compound, the margins entire, toothed, or lobed. **FLOWER** Most species in the family have bisexual flowers that are insect-pollinated. Flowers are often large and showy or may be small but showy en masse or, in some cases, inconspicuous. White is the most common flower color in the wild, but pink and yellow are also common. Flowers are radially symmetric and have a hypanthium, or floral cup, on the rim of which are borne 5 sepals, 5 separate petals (sometimes no petals), and 2 to several times as many stamens as petals. The hypanthium may be free from the ovary, or it may be fused to it, when the ovary is inferior in position. **FRUIT** Especially diverse, fruits provide distinctive characteristics for classification within the family. Fruit types of eastern arborescent Rosaceae include drupes (cherries, plums) and pomes (apples, serviceberries, hawthorns, quince, pears, mountain ash).

The fruits of the Rosaceae are among the most important of temperate woody plants and include strawberries, blackberries, raspberries, cherries, apricots, peaches, nectarines, plums, almonds, loquats, apples, pears, and quinces. Numerous cultivars are excellent for human food, and wild-grown plants are important as wildlife food.

■ *AMELANCHIER*: SERVICEBERRIES

Amelanchier includes about 25 taxa distributed in North America, Europe, East Asia, and North Africa; as many as 20 species are reported for North America, all native. Members of the genus grow naturally on stream banks, river and lake shores, dry uplands, rocky and grassy slopes, mountainsides, bogs, wet thickets, swamps, and fields, 0–2,000 m. Serviceberries are usually easily identified to genus by the combination of distinctive dull green leaves with a comparatively long petiole, white flowers with narrow petals, and reddish, purplish, or blackish pomes. Discriminating among species within the genus is often difficult. Distinctions are slight, and hybridization between species is common, often leading to an array of overlapping characteristics.

Deciduous shrubs or small trees, 1–20 m tall, 40 cm diam. Sometimes erect with a single trunk, more often with several trunks, some species with up to 100 trunks; often rhizomatous and colony-forming. **BARK** Smooth, grayish, brown, or dark brown, often ridged and furrowed on older trees. **TWIG** Slender, hairy or not at maturity, with a faint odor of bitter almond when crushed. **LEAF** Alternate, simple, lanceolate, elliptic, or obovate, pinnately veined, lateral veins often appressed to the midvein for about 1 mm before diverging, ending in marginal teeth or not; base tapering, rounded, or heart-shaped; margins entire or finely toothed. On most species turns yellow in autumn. **FLOWER** Bisexual, radially symmetric, 1–5 cm diam., with 5 usually narrow white petals; in terminal inflorescences, erect or drooping, of up to 20 flowers. Late winter to spring. **FRUIT** A pome, rounded or ellipsoid, 5–10 mm diam.; red, purple, or nearly black; matures summer.

DOWNY SERVICEBERRY *Amelanchier arborea* (F. Michx.) Fernald
A.K.A. SHADBUSH, SARVISBERRY, COMMON SERVICEBERRY

QUICK ID Distinguished among arborescent serviceberries by its drooping inflorescence, relatively large, finely toothed leaves that are widest above the middle and densely hairy beneath when young, flowers appearing before leaves, petals 10–20 mm long, and the bland-tasting reddish-purple pome.

Deciduous small tree or shrub, to about 20 m tall, to 40 cm diam. Erect or angling and ascending; single trunk or several. **BARK** Smooth, gray, and sometimes vertically streaked when young, becoming darker, almost black, and narrowly and shallow furrowed between thin, scaly ridges at maturity. **TWIG** Slender, brown and hairy at first, becoming ashy gray and hairless or only slightly hairy. **LEAF** Alternate, simple, thin, pliable; oval, ovate, oblong, or obovate, usually widest above the middle, base rounded or heart-shaped, tip pointed; margins finely and regularly toothed, 6–10 teeth per cm. Upper surface dull green, hairy at first, becoming hairless; lower surface paler, hairy when young, the hairs persisting or sloughing off at maturity. Turns yellow in autumn. Blade 3–10 cm long, 2–4 cm broad; petiole 1–2.5 cm long. **FLOWER** 3–4 cm diam.; petals 5, white, narrow, spreading at maturity, 10–20 mm long; sepals 5, lance-shaped, often turning downward at anthesis; stamens 10–20. Inflorescence branched, arching or drooping at the branch tip, 3–5 cm long, with 4–11 flowers. Late winter to mid-spring, before leaf expansion. **FRUIT** Rounded reddish-purple pome, 5–8 mm diam.; remains of sepals evident at apex.

HABITAT/RANGE Native. Moist, well-drained slopes, stream banks, open upland woods, 0–1,960 m; throughout the East, s. Canada to n. Fla.

SIMILAR SPECIES Most similar to Canadian Serviceberry, which can be distinguished by its shrubby habit, erect inflorescence, and shorter flower petals.

CANADIAN SERVICEBERRY
Amelanchier canadensis (L.) Medik.

QUICK ID The combination of the plant's large, vase-shaped form, the erect inflorescence, and flower petals 6–10 mm long is distinctive.

Shrub to 8 m tall, plants usually vase-shaped, with up to 25 trunks. **LEAF** At flowering time less than halfway expanded and unfolded, green, densely hairy beneath. **FLOWER** Petals white, 6–10 mm long, 2–4 mm broad. Inflorescence erect, 2.5–6 cm long, with 4–10 flowers. **FRUIT** Reddish-purple pome, 7–10 mm diam., sweet to the taste.

HABITAT/RANGE Native. Swamps, bogs, wet thickets, moist woods, 0–200 m; Que. and N.S. south to n. Ga.

SIMILAR SPECIES Downy Serviceberry can be distinguished by its drooping inflorescence and longer petals.

RED-TWIGGED SHADBUSH
Amelanchier sanguinea (Pursh) DC.

QUICK ID The coarsely toothed leaves with veins extending into the tips of the marginal teeth are diagnostic.

Deciduous shrub or small tree, to 7 m tall. Erect or clumping, trunks 1–7. **LEAF** Alternate, simple, elliptic, oblong, or nearly round, rounded or heart-shaped at the base, rounded or bluntly pointed at the tip; margins coarsely toothed, 3–6 teeth per cm;

DOWNY SERVICEBERRY   CANADIAN SERVICEBERRY   RED-TWIGGED SHADBUSH

Downy Serviceberry

twig

fruit

flowers

spring

fruit

Canadian Serviceberry

fruit

flowers

autumn

fruit

Red-twigged Shadbush

spring

flowers

fruit

lateral veins conspicuous, terminating at the tips of the marginal teeth. Upper surface green; lower surface paler, densely hairy at flowering time. Blade 2.5–7 cm long, 2–5.5 cm broad; petiole 12–30 mm long. **FLOWER** White, 2.5–3.5 cm diam.; petals linear or narrowly spatulate, 11–18 mm long, 3–6 mm broad; stamens 20. Inflorescence arching or drooping, 4–8 cm long, with 4–10 flowers. Late spring to early summer. **FRUIT** Dark purple or black pome, 5–10 mm diam., sweet to the taste.

HABITAT/RANGE Native. Woodland margins, rocky slopes, open woods, 0–1,000 m; Ont., Que., west to Minn. and Iowa, south to n. Ala.

INTERMEDIATE SHADBUSH
Amelanchier intermedia Spach

Deciduous shrub or small tree 2–7 m tall; solitary or clump forming. Trunks 1–10, crown narrow. **SIMILAR SPECIES** Distinguished from Canadian Serviceberry by leaves at flowering time reddish, sparsely hairy beneath, and nearly fully developed, and petals 9–12 mm long.

HABITAT/RANGE Native. Swamps, bogs, wet thickets, lake shores, 0–500 m; Nfld. and Ont., south to Mich. and N.C.

SASKATOON SERVICEBERRY
Amelanchier alnifolia (Nutt.) Nutt. ex M. Roem.

QUICKID Distinguished by its round or truncate leaves, which are well developed and hairless at flowering.

Typically a rhizomatous, spreading, clump- or colony-forming shrub 1–7 m tall. Stems 1–20.

HABITAT/RANGE Native. Largely western in range, to about 1,850 m, extending into the East mostly in N.D., S.D., and Nebr.

ALLEGHENY SERVICEBERRY
Amelanchier laevis Wiegand
A.K.A. SMOOTH SHADBUSH

QUICKID Identified by the combination of tree size, leaves that are reddish and hairless at flowering, and comparatively long inflorescence.

Deciduous small tree or shrub, to 17 m tall, sometimes clump-forming. Erect, single trunk or several, crown narrow. **BARK** Smooth, brown to grayish brown. **TWIG** Hairless at flowering time. **LEAF** Elliptic or ovate; margins finely toothed, lateral veins not terminating in the tip of the marginal teeth. Upper surface hairless, conspicuously reddish or purplish when unfolding at flowering time. Blades 4–6 cm long, 2.5–4 cm broad; petiole 1–2.5 cm long. **FLOWER** White, 2–4 cm diam.; petals 10–20 mm long, 3–7 mm broad; stamens 20. Inflorescence drooping, 3–7 cm long, with 4–11 flowers. Spring to early summer. **FRUIT** Dark purple pome, 6–8 mm diam., sweet to the taste.

HABITAT/RANGE Native. Mixed forests, dry to moist woodlands, open woods, thickets, roadsides, 0–2,000 m; Nfld. to Ont., south to Ala. and Ga.

WIEGAND'S SHADBUSH *Amelanchier interior* E.L. Nielsen

QUICKID Distinguished by the combination of its occasionally arborescent form, sparsely hairy young leaves that are usually reddish as they emerge, and conspicuously hairy ovary.

Deciduous shrub or small tree, to 10 m tall, usually with 1–10 arching trunks.

HABITAT/RANGE Native. Dry woods, bluffs, rocky slopes, riverbanks, fields, 0–300 m; Nfld. to Ont., south to Mich., Wis., and Minn.

INTERMEDIATE SHADBUSH

SASKATOON SERVICEBERRY

ALLEGHENY SERVICEBERRY

WIEGAND'S SHADBUSH

Saskatoon Serviceberry

spring

fruit

flowers

fruit

autumn

Allegheny Serviceberry

fruit

flowers

spring

Wiegand's Shadbush

flowers

spring

fruit

CRATAEGUS: HAWTHORNS

The hawthorn genus contains 150–280 species or more, all from the Northern Hemisphere, some now introduced to the Southern Hemisphere. As many as 150 occur in the East, in open woods, limestone glades, mountain slopes, rich woodlands, and xeric pinelands, 0–2,000 m. See "Hawthorn Identification," p. 498, for more information.

Deciduous shrubs or small trees, branches usually armed with conspicuous piercing thorns; trunk also sometimes armed with branched thorns. Trunk single or many, often erect in arborescent species. Crown spreading, open, in some species strongly drooping. **BARK** Thin, brownish or grayish, varying from smooth, scaly and flaking in plates or peeling in strips, to more or less blocky and corrugated. **BRANCH/TWIG** Branches and twigs are straight or zigzag. Buds are blunt, the scales overlapping. **LEAF** Alternate, simple, narrowly elliptic to broadly ovate, diamond-shaped, or nearly circular, often lobed, the margins frequently toothed, the teeth sometimes gland-tipped, often entire near the base of the blade. The foliage of many species contributes rich yellows, reds, or burgundies to fall color. In the accounts that follow, statements of leaf measurements and morphology are applied to mature leaves, not those on new shoot growth unless specifically stated. **FLOWER** Showy en masse, in few-branched, rounded, often drooping clusters at ends of branches; flowers bisexual, radial, the parts in 5s, the sepals, petals, and stamens borne near the rim of a hypanthium; petals 5, separate, usually white and circular; stamens 5–45; styles 1–5, protruding from the opening of the hypanthium. **FRUIT** A small pome, usually more or less globose, containing 1–5 very hard nutlets (technically pyrenes, including the inner wall of the ovary and the seed). The color of mature fruits of hawthorns is important for identification. As the fruit matures it may pass from green through yellows and reds to purples or ultimately black (the mature color, red, purple or black, is given in this book, unless otherwise specified). Sculpturing of the pyrenes, particularly the back and sides, is also important for identification, but is left for more technical sources.

Fruits are edible and those from some species are used in jellies. Others are not especially palatable. The fruits are the "haws," tracing back to very old European words referring to "hedge" or "pasture." Cultivated forms are prized ornamentals because of the showy spring bloom and the clusters of small red or purple pomes in autumn. Some may persist in plantings or around old homesteads. Among them are *C. marshallii*, *C. mollis*, *C. phaenopyrum*, and *C. viridis*.

Series *Aestivales*

A fairly distinct series of 3 species, ranging predominately in the se. U.S. Two species are treated here. Rusty Mayhaw (*C. rufula* Sarg.) is intermediate between them, ranging mostly in the Fla. panhandle and adjacent Ga. and Ala.

WESTERN MAYHAW *Crataegus opaca*
Hook. & Arn.

QUICK ID The wavy-lobed leaves, early summer fruit, and wetland habitat distinguish Western Mayhaw.

Deciduous tree to about 10 m tall, to 30 cm diam. Erect, single trunk, crown diffuse, spreading. **BARK** Gray, smooth on young trees, becoming scaly and flaking. **BRANCH** Gray or dark gray, armed with few to many straight, stout, sharp thorns 2–4 cm long. **TWIG** Reddish, densely hairy. **LEAF** Alternate, simple, elliptic, long-elliptic, or broadly lanceolate; margins unlobed and bluntly toothed to more often wavy-lobed from base to tip. Upper surface dull yellow-green, usually rough to the touch; lower surface usually conspicuously reddish-hairy, especially along the veins and in the vein axils. Blade 5–7 cm long, 1–2.5 cm broad; petioles 4–7 mm long. **FLOWER** 12–18 mm diam.; petals white or tinged with rose, about 7 mm long; stamens 20. Early spring. **FRUIT** Red pome, occasionally yellow, 12–15 mm diam.; matures May–June.

HABITAT/RANGE Native. Wet woods, swamp margins, river-bottom wetlands, often in standing water, to 75 m; nw. Fla. to Tex. and s. Ark.

SIMILAR SPECIES The wavy-lobed leaves distinguish Western Mayhaw from Eastern Mayhaw. The flowers of Eastern Mayhaw emerge at flowering time, while those of Western Mayhaw follow flowering.

EASTERN MAYHAW *Crataegus aestivalis* (Walter) Torr. & A. Gray

QUICK ID Easily identified by the combination of wetland habitat, lustrous leaves, and fruit ripening in May.

Deciduous, usually a tree, sometimes a shrub, 3–12 m tall, about 20 cm diam. Usually erect with

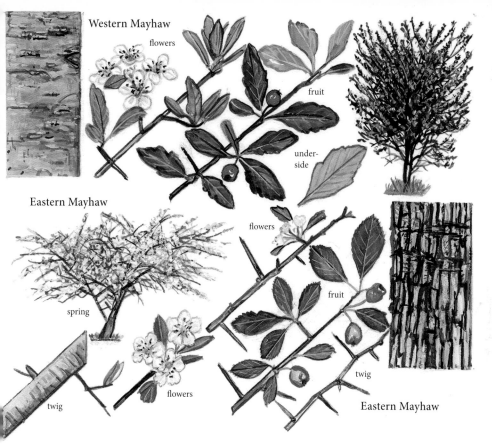

Western Mayhaw

flowers

fruit

under-
side

Eastern Mayhaw

flowers

spring

fruit

twig

twig

flowers

Eastern Mayhaw

a single trunk, crown dense, rounded, compact, especially when growing in open sun along pond margins. **BARK** Grayish brown, scaly at maturity. **BRANCH** Gray, armed with stout, sharp thorns 2–4 cm long; thorns more numerous on younger branches. **TWIG** Gray, becoming brown. **LEAF** Alternate, simple, elliptic or oblanceolate, those on new growth usually the largest; margins usually not lobed, entire near base, finely or bluntly toothed on the outer half, marginal teeth sometimes tipped with a tiny black gland. Upper surface dark green,

usually lustrous, rough or smooth to the touch; lower surface paler, with tufts of grayish hairs in the vein axils and sometimes along the midrib. Blade 2–5 cm long, 1.5–2 cm broad; petiole 3–15 mm long. **FLOWER** 12–30 mm diam., petals white, stamens 20. Early spring. **FRUIT** Red pome, somewhat translucent, 8–20 mm diam., sweet to the taste; matures May.

HABITAT/RANGE Native. Pond margins, edges of pineland depressions, floodplain pools, swampy woods, usually where water stands much of the time, 0–100 m; extreme se. Va., south to n. Fla., west to se. Ala.

SIMILAR SPECIES The leaf of Rusty Mayhaw is dull above and rusty-hairy beneath.

Notes: This is the species from which mayhaw jelly is made.

WESTERN MAYHAW

EASTERN MAYHAW

Series *Apiifoliae*

A distinctive series composed of a single, easily identified species in the U.S. Similar to the European series *Crataegus* in leaf shape, relatively small flowers, and small number of nutlets per pome.

PARSLEY HAWTHORN *Crataegus marshallii* Eggl.

QUICKID The deeply dissected, parsley-like leaves are diagnostic among the hawthorns.

Deciduous, typically a small understory tree, potentially to about 11 m tall, 20 cm diam., often shorter; sometimes flowering when of small stature and appearing shrubby. Erect, usually a single trunk, crown broad, open, with slender branches. **BARK** Smooth, mottled, exfoliating to reveal reddish inner bark. **BRANCH** Sometimes thornless, more often with slender, sharp-tipped chestnut-brown thorns 1–3 cm long. **TWIG** Slender, woolly-pubescent, and purplish brown when young, becoming gray and roughened with persistent bases of sloughed hairs. **LEAF** Alternate, simple, triangular to somewhat ovate, slightly stiff or more often thin and pliable, usually about as wide as long, the base of most leaves truncate, occasionally broadly tapered; margins usually deeply incised into several lobes, the lobes conspicuously toothed. Upper surface dull green, slightly to moderately hairy; lower surface paler, hairy. Blade 1–3 cm long, 1–3 cm broad; petiole 1.5–3 cm long; often turns red in autumn. **FLOWER** 12–20 mm diam.; petals white, elliptic; stamens 20, anthers usually red at maturity. Spring. **FRUIT** Bright red pome, lustrous, ellipsoid, 4–7 mm long, about 5 mm diam., usually with 3 nutlets; matures autumn.

HABITAT/RANGE Native. Woodland slopes, bottomlands, floodplain forests, moist or wet banks along small streams or rivers, ravine slopes, 0–1,500 m; chiefly the coastal plains and Piedmont from se. Va., s. Ill., and s. Mo., south to n. Fla. and e. Tex.

SIMILAR SPECIES No other species of *Crataegus* has similar leaves, making this the easiest to identify of the native eastern hawthorns. The bark of Littlehip Hawthorn (series *Microcarpae*) is similar; the two are easily distinguished by their leaves.

Notes: A popular garden plant valued for its numerous flowers, ornamental leaves, and the bright red fruits, which are eaten by birds.

Series *Apricae*

A series of approximately 12 species in the East, distributed primarily in the Southeast. The series is not clearly understood and it is likely that at least some so-called species within the complex may be hybrids or apomictic offspring (genetic copies of the parent plant produced asexually from the development of an unfertilized seed). Members of series *Lacrimatae* are very similar. Species of series *Apricae* usually produce distinctive reddish glands along the petioles and at the tips of the marginal teeth. Sunny Hawthorn, the species treated here, is representative of the variation within this difficult to distinguish group.

SUNNY HAWTHORN *Crataegus aprica* Beadle

QUICKID Distinguished with difficulty by the combination of ascending and crooked crown branches, flowers with 10 stamens, acutely pointed leaf tip, reddish marginal glands, and 1 or 2 lobelike points on either leaf margin.

Deciduous, usually a shrub, sometimes a small tree to about 3 m tall. Trunk single or multiple. Crown branches sometimes drooping, usually ascending, moderately zigzag. **BRANCH** Flexuous when young, usually armed with slender, straight or slightly curved gray-brown thorns 3–4 cm long. **TWIG** Olive green at first, becoming reddish brown and hairy during the 1st year, eventually becoming dark gray and hairless. **LEAF** Alternate, simple, elliptic, broadly elliptic, or ovate, thick

PARSLEY HAWTHORN

SUNNY HAWTHORN

Parsley Hawthorn

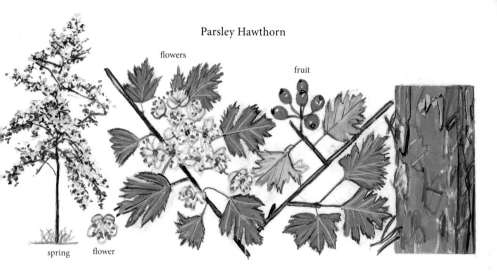

flowers

fruit

spring   flower

Sunny Hawthorn

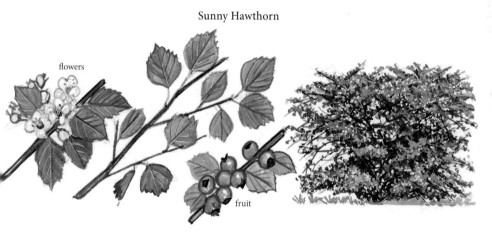

flowers

fruit

and stiff at maturity; margins unlobed or shallowly lobed, toothed, the teeth usually tipped by tiny reddish glands; tip wedge-shaped or abruptly short-pointed, base tapering and forming a narrow wing along part of the petiole. Upper surface slightly hairy at first, becoming mostly hairless, lower surface hairless except on midvein. Blade 1.5–4 cm long, 1.5–3.5 cm broad; petiole 3–8 mm long. **FLOWER** 13–15 mm diam.; petals white, more or less circular; stamens 10, anthers creamy white to pinkish. Late spring. **FRUIT** Red or reddish-orange pome, round, 9–15 mm diam.; matures autumn.

HABITAT/RANGE Native. Open sites, roadsides, upland pine forests, mixed hardwood forests, pine–oak forests, 0–2,000 m; N.C. south to n. Fla., west to Miss., most common in the s. Appalachians.

SIMILAR SPECIES Distinguished from others in this series and from most species of the series *Lacrimatae* by the combination of crown branches not strongly drooping, flowers with 10 stamens, and leaves mostly hairless at maturity.

HAWTHORN IDENTIFICATION

Hawthorns are recognized by the combination of alternate leaves, usually spiny branches, showy spring flowers, and pome fruit. But see the apples (*Malus*). Identification and classification of hawthorns are notoriously difficult, sometimes arbitrary, and often subjective, as suggested by the estimated number of species. Hawthorns may reproduce sexually or asexually. By varying in chromosome number they may be reproductively isolated from one another without much genetic exchange. Most easily hybridize with others and many produce viable seeds in the absence of pollination. This all leads to a complicated array of populations, some widespread and different from other hawthorn species, some hybrids and intergrades, and some forming uniform local clones barely different from others. Given this complexity, species are often arranged in series (a taxonomic category between genus and family) of closely related species. This approach has been adopted in this guide to facilitate identification.

Series Bracteatae

A series of 2 or 3 species, of which Harbison's Hawthorn is the rarest but most often treelike. Some authorities consider all species in this series to be morphological variations of *C. harbisonii*, not distinct species. Ashe Hawthorn (*C. ashei* Beadle), a large, multistemmed shrub to about 5 m tall, is the most commonly accepted second member of the series.

HARBISON'S HAWTHORN *Crataegus harbisonii* Beadle

QUICK ID The relatively large flowers with usually 20 stamens, borne on wood several years old, in conjunction with the single erect trunk, help distinguish this species.

Deciduous, usually a small tree to 8 m tall, 25–30 cm diam., sometimes shrubby. Erect, single trunk. **BARK** Gray to brown, scaly, furrowed. **BRANCH** Chestnut brown, armed with lustrous, straight brown or nearly black thorns 3–5 cm long. **TWIG** Hairy at first, becoming hairless at the end of the 1st year. **LEAF** Alternate, simple, elliptic, ovate, or broadly obovate; margins

slightly lobed, conspicuously and unevenly double-toothed, the teeth gland-tipped, the glands extending onto the petiole. Upper surface hairy when young, roughened at maturity; lower surface hairy. Blade 4–7 cm long, 3–5 cm broad; petiole 5–10 mm long. **FLOWER** 2–2.5 cm diam.; petals white, circular; stamens usually 20, anthers cream or yellowish. Spring. **FRUIT** Red or orange-red pome, spotted, round, 12–22 mm diam.; matures autumn.

HABITAT/RANGE Native. Sparse hardwood forests on calcareous soils, 100–400 m; Tenn.

Series Brainerdianae

A series of approximately 4 species. Closely related and similar to species of the series *Macracanthae*, and distinguished from them (at least in the East) by the leaf stalks bearing tiny glands along their margins.

BRAINERD'S HAWTHORN *Crataegus brainerdii* Sarg.

QUICK ID Distinguished by the leaf with 4–6 pairs of marginal lobes, petioles obscurely glandular, and upper surface bluish green and rough to the touch.

Deciduous shrub or small tree, to 5 m tall, about 20 cm diam. Erect, usually single trunk, crown open, with slender, ascending branches. **BARK** Gray, scaly. **LEAF** Alternate, simple, ovate or broadly elliptic, somewhat thick and firm at maturity, tip acute or acuminate, base wedge-shaped, tissue of lower blade extending slightly onto the obscurely glandular petiole; margins finely and usually double-toothed, the teeth straight or curving upward and tipped by a small gland. Upper

HARBISON'S HAWTHORN

BRAINERD'S HAWTHORN

Harbison's Hawthorn

flowers

fruit

Brainerd's Hawthorn

fruit

surface of young leaves rough to the touch, becoming dark bluish green; lower surface paler. Blade 4–7 cm long, 2–5 cm broad; petiole about 2 cm long, obscurely glandular. **FLOWER** About 1.8 cm diam.; petals white; stamens 20, anthers usually pinkish. Late May. **FRUIT** Bright red pome,

1–1.2 cm long; matures September, usually falling before winter.

HABITAT/RANGE Native. Open, upland woods, pastures; Que. and Ont. south to Pa. and Mich.

Series *Macracanthae*

A series of 3 or 4 mostly western and northern montane species, distinguished in the East by relatively large leaves, more or less winged, nonglandular petioles, and fruit with 2 or 3 nutlets. Two widespread eastern species are included here.

PEAR HAWTHORN *Crataegus calpodendron* (Ehrh.) Medik.

QUICK ID The comparatively large leaves, late flowering, and horizontally disposed branches help distinguish the species.

Deciduous shrub to about 5 m tall, or small tree to 7 m tall, 20 cm diam. Erect or clump-forming, with a single trunk or multiple, often leaning. Crown broad, vertically flattened, often lacking a terminal stem. **BARK** Smooth when young, becoming scaly and furrowed. **BRANCH** Usually horizontally spreading, unarmed or armed with slender, straight grayish thorns 3–6 cm long. **TWIG** Hairy when young, remaining hairy or becoming hairless at maturity. **LEAF** Alternate, simple, thin, pliable, obovate, oblong, or broadly elliptic; margins sharply double-toothed, except near the base, occasionally shallowly lobed. Upper surface dull green, hairy at first, becoming hairless; lower surface paler, hairy. Blade 5–12 cm long, 3–7 cm broad; petiole winged, 1–3 cm long. **FLOWER** 1–1.5 cm diam.; petals white, circular; stamens 20, anthers red, pink, or purple. Late spring, early summer. **FRUIT** Red, orange-red, or yellowish pome, ellipsoid, about 1 cm long, 7–9 mm diam.; matures autumn.

HABITAT/RANGE Native. Rich slopes, streamsides, often in association with calcareous soils; Ont. and Minn., south to nw. Ga. and ne. Tex.

PEAR HAWTHORN

FLESHY HAWTHORN *Crataegus succulenta* Schrad. ex Link

QUICK ID The combination of narrowly winged, nonglandular petiole, thick double-toothed leaves, and comparatively long, stout thorns is characteristic.

Deciduous, thicket-forming shrub 4–6 m tall, or small tree to 7 m tall, 20 cm diam. Erect or clump-forming, single trunk or multiple, older trunks often with stout, compound thorns. **BARK** Gray, scaly. **BRANCH** With numerous lustrous, stout, straight or curved blackish-brown thorns 3–6 cm long. **TWIG** Hairy when young, hairless at maturity. **LEAF** Alternate, simple, thick, firm, predominately obovate, ovate, or broadly elliptic; margins distinctly and often double-toothed, except near the base, usually shallowly lobed. Upper surface lustrous, usually hairless at maturity, with conspicuously impressed lateral veins; lower surface paler. Blade 4–8 cm long, 3–6 cm broad; petiole narrowly winged, 1–2 cm long. **FLOWER** 1.2–1.7 cm diam.; petals white, circular; stamens 20, anthers reddish or pink, rarely white. Late spring, early summer. **FRUIT** Bright red pome, lustrous, 6–12 mm diam.; matures autumn.

HABITAT/RANGE Native. Streamsides, pastures, open woodlands, mountain slopes, ridges; Minn. and Man. south to Iowa, Mo., and Ohio, along the Appalachians to N.C.

Notes: This is the most widespread hawthorn in North America.

FLESHY HAWTHORN

Pear Hawthorn

dried fruit

immature fruit

flowers

Fleshy Hawthorn

flowers

fruit

autumn

nutlets

Series *Brevispinae*

This series is represented by a single species endemic to the se. U.S., distinctive for its large size and blue fruit.

BLUEBERRY HAWTHORN *Crataegus brachyacantha* Sarg. & Engelm.

QUICK ID The combination of blue or black fruit, flowers turning orange with age, and restricted range is distinctive.

Deciduous tree, 6–12 m tall, to about 45 cm diam. Erect, single trunk; crown rounded, compact. **BARK** Dark gray to brown, scaly, furrowed. **BRANCH** Slender, nearly straight, unarmed or armed with short, curved thorns 1–2 cm long. **LEAF** Alternate, simple, leathery, elliptic; margins bluntly toothed, usually unlobed on reproductive shoots, often deeply lobed on vegetative shoots. Upper surface lustrous, hairy on midrib; lower surface paler, hairy on midrib. Blade 2–3 cm long on spur shoots, to 6 cm long on vegetative shoots, 1–2 cm broad; petiole winged, to about 1 cm long; often turns red in autumn. **FLOWER** About 12 mm diam.; petals white, becoming yellowish orange at maturity, circular; stamens 20, anthers creamy yellow. Spring. **FRUIT** Blue, becoming almost black, often with a whitish cast, round to obovoid, 8–14 mm diam.; matures late summer.

HABITAT/RANGE Native. Wet prairies, moist soils of woodlands and thickets, alluvial flats, mesic woods; predominately La., adjacent Ark., e. Tex., se. Okla., and sw. Miss.

Notes: This is the tallest species of hawthorn found in the U.S.

BLUEBERRY HAWTHORN

Series *Crataegus*

A series of about 20 species, distributed naturally in Europe, Asia, North Africa. Represented in the East by a single introduced species. Its single-seeded pome is unique among North American hawthorns.

ONESEED HAWTHORN *Crataegus monogyna* Jacq.

QUICK ID The single-seeded fruit separates this species from our native hawthorns.

Deciduous shrub or small tree to about 10 m tall. **BARK** Brown, often with shallow furrows and spiraling ridges. **TWIG** Greenish or reddish brown, densely hairy or hairless; thorns stout, to about 2.5 cm long. **LEAF** Alternate, simple, ovate or triangular; margins deeply divided into several narrow lobes, cut at least halfway to the midrib. Upper surface lustrous, dark green, hairless; lower surface distinctly hairy, at least on the main veins. Blade 1.25–6 cm long, nearly as broad; petiole 1–3 cm long. **FLOWER** 8–16 mm diam.; petals white, sometimes fading to reddish at maturity; stamens 15–20, anthers pinkish purple. Late spring. **FRUIT** Dark or bright red pome, round, 6–11 mm diam., with a single nutlet.

HABITAT/RANGE Introduced from Europe. Found near plantings; naturalized from Ont. and N.B. south to Ill., Ky., N.C., and in the Pacific Northwest.

SIMILAR SPECIES Somewhat similar to Parsley Hawthorn (series *Apiifoliae*) but with fewer, broader lobes; Parsley Hawthorn is a southern species, barely overlapping in distribution.

Notes: Numerous horticultural forms and cultivars have been selected from this species, several of which are planted in the U.S. and Canada.

Blueberry Hawthorn

flowers

fruit

thorn

old
flowers

flowers

fruit

fruit section

twig

Oneseed Hawthorn

spring

Series *Coccineae*

A series of 4 species in e. North America, 1 of which has not been seen in the wild for many years. Members of the series are similar to those of series *Molles*. The leaves on species of series *Coccineae* are thin and usually hairless on their lower surfaces when fully expanded; those of series *Molles* are thicker and their lower surfaces are usually hairy at full expansion.

SCARLET HAWTHORN *Crataegus coccinea* L.

QUICK ID The combination of relatively large flowers with 5–10 stamens, pink anthers, hairy inflorescences, scarlet fruit, and comparatively large leaves helps distinguish Scarlet Hawthorn.

Deciduous large shrub or small tree, 7–12 m tall, to about 35 cm diam. Erect, single straight trunk or multiple trunks; crown open. **BARK** Gray, scaly. **BRANCH** Armed with dark, lustrous, stout, straight or curved thorns 2–4 cm long. **TWIG** Greenish, varying to golden or tan, hairless or sparsely hairy. **LEAF** Alternate, simple, thin, firm, ovate, elliptic, oblong, or narrowly ovate; margins with 4 or 5 shallow lobes and coarsely double-toothed, the teeth sometimes 2 mm long. Upper surface hairless or nearly so at maturity, rough to the touch, lower surface hairy on the veins. Blade 4–12 cm long, to about 7 cm broad; petiole 2–3 cm long. **FLOWER** 15–22 mm diam.; petals white, circular; stamens usually 5–10, anthers pink, rose, or rose-purple. Late spring. **FRUIT** Scarlet or orange-red pome, ellipsoid or nearly round, 10–18 mm long; matures autumn.

HABITAT/RANGE Native. Woodland margins, fencelines, upland woods, pastures, along small streams; Maine west to Minn., south along the Appalachians at high altitudes to N.C.

SCARLET HAWTHORN

HOLMES' HAWTHORN *Crataegus holmesiana* Ashe

QUICK ID The lobed, relatively large, usually double-toothed leaf with a rough upper surface, deep red ellipsoid fruit, and comparatively long thorns help distinguish this species.

Deciduous large shrub or small tree, 4–7 m tall. Erect, single trunk. **BRANCH** Armed with slightly curved thorns 4–5 cm long. **TWIG** Greenish or reddish during the 1st year, becoming golden or pale tan, finally light gray. **LEAF** Alternate, simple, ovate or narrowly ovate, acute or acuminate at the tip, rounded at the base; margins with 4 or 5 lobes, conspicuously toothed or double-toothed, the teeth to 2 mm long. Upper surface of young leaves rough to the touch with persistent hairs, sometimes becoming hairless at maturity; lower surface hairless except along the major veins. Blade 6–9 cm long, to about 7 cm broad; petiole 2–3 cm long. **FLOWER** 16–22 mm diam.; petals white, circular; stamens 5–10, anthers pink or rose-purple, occasionally red. Late spring. **FRUIT** Bright red pome, ellipsoid or pear-shaped, about 12 mm long; matures autumn.

HABITAT/RANGE Native. Woodland margins, fencerows, thickets, fertile ground near streams; Que. and Ont., south to Ill. and W.Va.

SIMILAR SPECIES Distinguished from Scarlet Hawthorn by the ellipsoid fruit, longer thorns, and leaves usually greater than 1.5 times longer than broad.

HOLMES' HAWTHORN

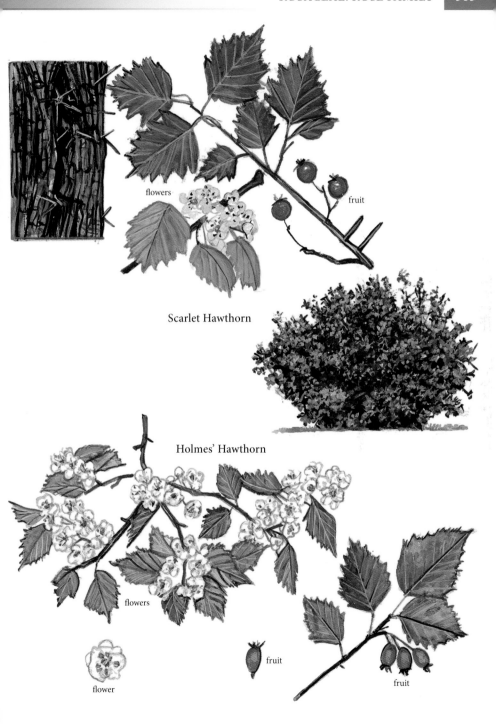

flowers

fruit

Scarlet Hawthorn

Holmes' Hawthorn

flowers

flower

fruit

fruit

Series *Cordatae*

A series of 1 easily identified tree characterized by a thorny trunk and maplelike leaves. The base of the leaf is usually heart-shaped (cordate), which explains the series name. This is 1 of 3 native series in which the lateral leaf veins terminate in the tips of the marginal teeth or lobes and in the sinuses between them.

WASHINGTON HAWTHORN *Crataegus phaenopyrum* (L. f.) Medik.

QUICK ID The only eastern hawthorn with the combination of maplelike leaves and thorny trunk.

Deciduous small tree, 4–10 m tall, to about 30 cm diam. Erect, single trunk, armed with branched thorns. Crown moderately dense, rounded or cylindric, with slender, upright branches. **BARK** Brownish gray, scaly, sometimes forming small platelets. **BRANCH** Armed with slender, straight, sharp-pointed thorns 2–5 cm long. **TWIG** Lustrous, reddish brown, becoming gray; hairless. **LEAF** Alternate, simple, more or less triangular; margins with 3–5 lobes, coarsely toothed, the lobes often somewhat drooping at the tip; smaller leaves often 3-lobed, similar in outline to the leaves of Red Maple (*Acer rubrum*, Sapindaceae); base truncate or heart-shaped. Upper surface lustrous, dark green, usually hairless at maturity; lower surface paler, hairy or hairless. Blade 2–6 cm long, nearly as broad; petiole slender, reddish purple, 1–2 cm long; turns red in autumn. **FLOWER** 10–12 mm diam.; petals white, occasionally tinged pink, circular; stamens 10–20, anthers yellowish white or rose. Late spring. **FRUIT** Scarlet pome, lustrous, round, 4–8 mm diam.; matures autumn, persisting into winter.

HABITAT/RANGE Native.   Pastures,   open woods, woodland margins, streamsides, wet woods along small rivers, often in association with rich soils; Ont. and Maine, south to nw. Fla., west to Mo. and La.

SIMILAR SPECIES Potentially confused at a glance with small-leaved forms of Red Maple, the two differ markedly in flowers and fruit, and the trunk of Red Maple is never adorned with branched thorns.

Notes: Washington Hawthorn is a popular ornamental tree that graces gardens and arboreta throughout the East. It is probably native only from Pa. south to nw. Fla. and west to Ark., Mo. and Ill., but has escaped cultivation and naturalized extensively, mostly northward of its largely southern range. Several cultivars have been selected, varying mostly in habit and fruit size.

Series *Crus-galli*

A series of 4 highly variable species with several varieties and more than 80 recognized forms. Members of the series are usually easily identified by their unlobed, short-stalked, lustrous, dark green leathery leaves with a rounded tip and strongly tapered, more or less wedge-shaped base.

REVERCHON'S HAWTHORN
Crataegus reverchonii Sarg.

QUICK ID Distinguished from other species in this series by the combination of hairless rounded or broadly elliptic leaves and fruit with 3–5 seeds.

Deciduous, typically a shrub to about 4 m tall, potentially a tree to 7 m tall, 10 cm diam. Crown rounded with slender branches. **LEAF** Obovate to

WASHINGTON HAWTHORN

REVERCHON'S HAWTHORN

Washington Hawthorn

fruit

autumn

flowers

autumn

Reverchon's Hawthorn

flowers

fruit

nearly round, firm, stiff; margins sharply toothed except near base. Blade 3–4 cm long, nearly as broad; petiole 2–12 mm long. **FLOWER** 8–17 mm diam.; petals white, circular; stamens 10–20, anthers yellow, pink, rose, or red. Late spring, early summer. **FRUIT** Rounded or oblong red or orange-red pome, 12–22 mm diam.; nutlets 3–5; matures autumn.

HABITAT/RANGE Native. Rocky prairies or hillsides, along streams; Del. south to Ga., west to Kans., Okla., and Tex.

COCKSPUR HAWTHORN *Crataegus crus-galli* L.

QUICK ID Distinguished by the combination of typically unlobed, hairless, short-stalked, lustrous, dark green leaves; a pome with 1–3 seeds and usually larger than 8 mm diam.; and mostly entire sepals.

Deciduous small tree, to about 10 m tall, 30 cm diam., occasionally shrubby northward. Typically erect, single trunk. Crown broad, rounded, with spreading, rigid branches. **BARK** Dark gray or brownish gray, scaly, armed with stout, branched thorns to 15 cm long. **BRANCH** Armed with stout, straight or curved brown, gray, or nearly black thorns 3–10 cm long. **TWIG** Pale brown at first, becoming gray, usually hairless. **LEAF** Alternate, simple, oblanceolate, narrowly obovate, or spatulate, thick, leathery; margins finely toothed at least toward the tip, the teeth often blunt, occasionally slightly lobed; tip rounded, base wedge-shaped. Upper surface dark green, lustrous, hairless; lower surface paler, hairy on the midvein. Blade 2–8 cm long, 1–3 cm broad; petiole 0–5 mm long. **FLOWER** 10–15 mm diam.; petals white, circular; stamens usually 10, sometimes 20, anthers creamy white, yellowish, pink, or rose. Mid-spring. **FRUIT** Greenish pome, becoming dull red, rarely yellow, rounded or oblong, 8–15 mm long, nutlets 1–3; matures autumn.

HABITAT/RANGE Native. Thickets, thin woodlands, upland woodland openings, bottomlands along spring runs and small streams, pastures, 0–1,500 m; Ont. and N.S., south to c. Fla., e. Kans., and e. Tex.; among the most common and more widespread of the eastern hawthorns, occurring in the U.S. in all but 3 eastern states.

SIMILAR SPECIES Not easily confused with hawthorns in other series. Barberry Hawthorn is distinguished by its young leaves being hairy above, while Cockspur's are nearly hairless; Reverchon's Hawthorn has fruit with 3–5 seeds, compared to Cockspur's 1–3 seeds.

Notes: Plants with very narrow leaves have been called *C. crus-galli* var. *pyracanthifolia* Aiton. Cockspur Hawthorn is quite variable; numerous forms and varieties have been recognized based largely on leaf shape and color, and hairiness of the inflorescence. This is a popular garden tree and has been widely used in residential and roadside plantings.

BARBERRY HAWTHORN *Crataegus berberifolia* Torr. & Gray

QUICK ID The somewhat smaller leaves that are hairy above when young and become sandpapery at maturity distinguish this species from others in the series.

Deciduous small tree to about 8 m tall, 15–25 cm diam., often a shrub on poorer sites. Erect, single trunk or multiple. Crown broad, open, flat-topped, with tough, spreading branches. **BARK** Gray to nearly black, scaly. **BRANCH** Armed with straight or slightly curved thorns 2–6 cm long, thorns at first orange-brown or greenish, becoming lustrous brown or black. **TWIG** Hairy at first, becoming hairless. **LEAF** Alternate, simple, obovate or oblanceolate, thick, leathery; margins toothed, often entire below the middle. Upper surface sandpapery, lower surface hairy along the veins. Blade 2–7 cm long, to about 3 cm broad; petiole 4–6 mm long. **FLOWER** 10–20 mm diam.; petals white, circular; stamens 10–20, anthers cream, yellow, or pinkish. Mid- to late spring. **FRUIT** Red, greenish red, or yellow pome, 6–10 mm diam.; nutlets 2 or 3; matures autumn.

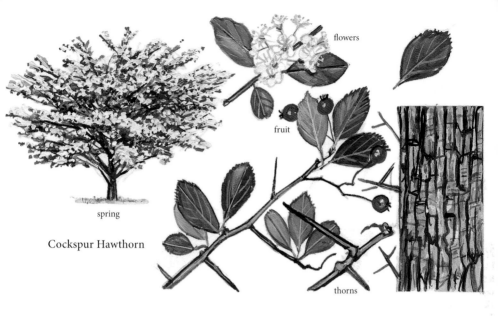

spring

Cockspur Hawthorn

flowers

fruit

thorns

flowers

Barberry Hawthorn

fruit

twig

HABITAT/RANGE Native. Dry limestone ridges, moist or wet lowlands; Va. south to Fla., west to Tex. and Mo.

SIMILAR SPECIES The young leaves of Cockspur Hawthorn are generally hairless on the upper surface, while those of Barberry Hawthorn are usually hairy, at least until fully mature.

Series *Dilatatae*

A series of 1 or 2 species, typically referred to as the broadleaf hawthorns. Species of this series are similar to species of series *Pruinosae*, but are distinguished from them by the hairy flower stalks, deeply cut sepals, and typically larger leaves that are hairy above.

KANSAS HAWTHORN *Crataegus coccinioides* Ashe

QUICK ID Distinguished by the combination of large leaves, large fruit, and comparatively long, typically glandular petioles.

Deciduous shrub or small tree, 4–8 m tall, to 30 cm diam. Erect, single or multiple trunks; crown comparatively wide, spreading, rounded, dense, with slender, flexuous branches. **BARK** Gray or brown, scaly. **BRANCH** Armed with lustrous, stout, straight or curved thorns 2–6 cm long. **TWIG** Reddish at first, hairy or hairless, becoming lustrous tan or dark brown, eventually gray. **LEAF** Alternate, simple, deltoid or egg-shaped, base rounded, heart-shaped, or truncate; margins sharply toothed, with 4–5 pairs of short lobes. Upper surface dull green, usually hairy at maturity, sometimes hairless, veins impressed, lower surface paler, usually hairless, or hairy on the veins. Blade 3–11 cm long, those of new vegetative shoots sometimes to 15 cm, often broader than long; petiole 2–5 cm long, sometimes to about ½ the length of the blade, often bearing stalked glands. **FLOWER** 20–25 mm diam.; petals white, circular; stamens 20, anthers yellow-white, rose, pink, or red. Mid- to late spring. **FRUIT** Dark red, crimson, or bright pink pome, lustrous, more or less spherical, 10–25 mm diam.; matures autumn.

HABITAT/RANGE Native. Old fields, pastures, woodland margins, streamsides, open calcareous

woods; s. Que., N.Y., Pa., and Mass., west to Kans. and n. Ark.

SIMILAR SPECIES Distinguished from Waxy-fruit Hawthorn (series *Pruinosae*) by the overall larger leaves and fruit, and more glandular petiole.

Notes: Crataegus dilatata Sarg. (Broadleaf Hawthorn) is sometimes treated as a distinct species but is included here within *C. coccinioides*.

Series *Douglasianae*

A series of 4 species restricted largely to the northwestern U.S. and adjacent Canada. Only *C. douglasii* extends into the East, primarily to the Great Lakes region. Species in this series are noted for their short thorns, laterally pitted nutlets, and black or dark purple pomes. In this latter character they are reminiscent of Blueberry Hawthorn (series *Brevispinae*).

BLACK HAWTHORN *Crataegus douglasii* Lindl.

QUICK ID The black or dark purplish mature fruits that usually do not exceed about 8 mm diam. are diagnostic.

Deciduous, usually a shrub 4–6 m tall, rarely tree-like to about 8 m tall. Erect or vase-shaped, single trunk or multiple. **BRANCH** Dark gray, armed with lustrous, short, stout, straight or slightly curved thorns 1.5–3.5 cm long. **TWIG** Lustrous tan or dark brown at first, becoming gray. **LEAF** Alternate, simple, elliptic or broadly elliptic; margins coarsely and sharply toothed, sometimes with 2–4 lobes per side, the teeth usually gland-tipped. Upper surface dark green, usually with short hairs; lower surface hairless except for the veins. Blade 4–7 cm long, 2–3 cm broad; petiole 7–15 mm long. **FLOWER**

KANSAS HAWTHORN

BLACK HAWTHORN

Kansas Hawthorn

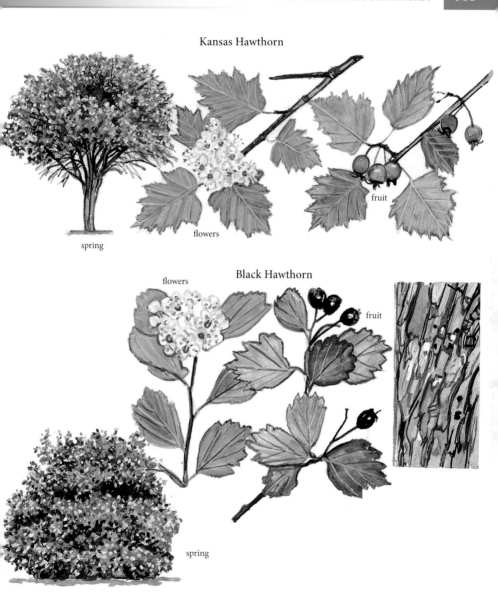

spring

flowers

fruit

Black Hawthorn

flowers

fruit

spring

12–15 mm diam.; petals white, circular; stamens 10, anthers pink. Late spring to early summer. **FRUIT** Dull black or purplish pome at maturity, ellipsoid, 6–8 mm diam.; matures autumn.

HABITAT/RANGE Native. Old pastures and fencelines, sometimes near water; Que. and Mich., west to N.D. and S.D.

SIMILAR SPECIES The black or dark purple fruit distinguishes this species from most other eastern hawthorns; the leaves of Blueberry Hawthorn (series *Brevispinae*) usually do not exceed about 5 cm long, and the fruit is typically 8–14 mm diam.

Series *Intricatae*

A series with 10–12 species in North America, restricted in range mostly to the East, and predominately the Southeast. The flowers of most members of the series have 10 stamens, in contrast to mostly 20 stamens in flowers of the very similar series *Pulcherrimae*. Species of the series *Pruinosae* are also similar, but generally have flowers with 20 stamens and greenish to crimson fruits that are often blushed with pink or purple. The species of series *Intricatae* are among the most difficult to identify of eastern hawthorns.

INTRICATE HAWTHORN *Crataegus intricata* Lange
a.k.a. COPENHAGEN HAWTHORN

QUICK ID **Most easily recognized by the shrub-by form, dull yellow or orange fruit, flowers usually with 10 stamens, and hairless, glandular petiole.**

Deciduous, usually a dense shrub, rarely a bushy tree to about 5 m tall, 15 cm diam. Erect or arching and shrublike, usually with multiple trunks. Crown dense, rounded. **BARK** Gray, scaly. **BRANCH** Unarmed, or more often armed with slender, straight or slightly curved grayish-black thorns 3–5 cm long. **TWIG** Reddish, hairy, becoming reddish black, then gray. **LEAF** Alternate, simple, broadly elliptic or egg-shaped, usually firm, stiff, with a broadly wedge-shaped base; margins toothed nearly to the base with coarse, blunt, gland-tipped teeth, often shallowly lobed. Upper surface dull green or yellow-green, usually hairless or with hairs on the veins; lower surface paler. Blade 3–8 cm long, to about 5 cm broad; petiole 15–30 mm long, stout, glandular, often slightly winged nearest the blade. **FLOWER** 15–20 mm diam.; petals white, circular; stamens usually 10, anthers ivory, creamy white,

yellowish, or pinkish. Mid-spring, concurrent with the developing leaves. **FRUIT** Dull yellow or orange pome, often with darker spots, sometimes rounded, usually oblong, 8–15 mm diam.; matures autumn.

HABITAT/RANGE Native. Rocky woods, sparse woodland, slopes, hills, forest gaps; Ont., N.H., and Wis. south to n. Ga., ostensibly west to Ark. and Mo., common in the Appalachians; the western range limits are not well understood.

Notes: The alternate name Copenhagen Hawthorn derives from an early description of this or a similar species from a garden specimen in Copenhagen, Denmark. The plant is native to North America.

Series *Lacrimatae*

This series encompasses a complex group of shrubs and small trees, many of which are challenging to distinguish from one another. As many as 22 species are said to occur in North America, a number with which all experts do not agree. Species in this series are characterized by conspicuously pendulous ultimate branches that form a drooping or "weeping" crown. Most species in the series have firm, stiff leaves, zigzag twigs, occur in sandy, xeric uplands, and are similar to species of the series *Apricae* and *Intricatae*.

WEEPING HAWTHORN *Crataegus lacrimata* Small
a.k.a. PENSACOLA HAWTHORN

QUICK ID The combination of small leaves, yellow fruit, upright form, and strongly pendulous crown is distinctive.

Deciduous shrub or small tree, to about 6 m tall, 10–15 cm diam. Erect or slightly leaning, usually a single trunk. Crown usually rounded at top, branches slender and strongly pendulous. **BARK** Gray or blackish gray, furrowed and divided into small blocks. **BRANCH** Armed with short, straight thorns 1–3 cm long. **TWIG** Strongly zigzag at the nodes, hairy at first, becoming gray or purple-gray in the 2nd year. **LEAF** Alternate, simple, obovate or spatulate, usually widest toward the tip, stiff, firm, rounded at the tip, gradually

INTRICATE HAWTHORN

WEEPING HAWTHORN

Intricate Hawthorn

flowers

fruit

Weeping Hawthorn

flowers

fruit

tapering to a narrow base; margins entire below the middle, toothed at or near the tip, usually with conspicuous red glands that resemble teeth to the unaided eye. Upper surface green or grayish green. Blade 1–2 cm long, less than 1 cm broad; petiole 2–6 mm long, hairy. **FLOWER** About 15 mm diam.; petals white, circular; stamens 20, anthers cream or pale yellow. Mid-spring. **FRUIT** Yellow or brownish-yellow pome, often blushed with red, round or oblong, 8–10 mm diam., usually with 3 nutlets; matures late summer.

HABITAT/RANGE Native. Dry, sandy pinelands, scrub, usually in association with deep sands, 0–200 m; S.C. south to nw. Fla., west to Ala.

SIMILAR SPECIES The several species in series *Lacrimatae* are similar; the relatively large size, small leaves and flowers, and the yellow pomes help distinguish Weeping Hawthorn.

Series *Microcarpae*

A distinctive series with 1 easily identified species characterized by small fruit, spatulate or narrowly obovate leaves, and smooth, attractive, exfoliating bark.

LITTLEHIP HAWTHORN *Crataegus spathulata* Michx.

QUICKID The combination of spatulate leaves, exfoliating bark, and small fruit is distinctive.

Deciduous small tree to about 8 m tall, 20–25 cm diam. Erect or slightly leaning, single or several trunks. Crown broad, open, of crooked branches. **BARK** Smooth, grayish, peeling to reveal mottled orange-brown inner bark. **BRANCH** Unarmed, or armed with short, stout, straight brown thorns 2–5 cm long. **TWIG** Purplish brown, becoming gray. **LEAF** Alternate, simple, spatulate or narrowly obovate, stiff, firm, apices of many leaves 3-lobed; margins bluntly toothed, rarely shallowly lobed. Upper surface lustrous, usually hairless; lower surface paler. Blade 1–4 cm long, 1–3 cm broad; petiole winged nearly to the base. **FLOWER** Strongly aromatic, 7–12 mm diam.; petals white, circular; stamens 20, anthers pale yellow or rose. Mid-spring. **FRUIT** Bright red, orange, or rarely yellow pome, rounded, 3–7 mm diam.; matures autumn.

HABITAT/RANGE Native. Bottomlands, moist hammocks, stream banks, rich slopes, to 200 m; Va., N.C., Tenn., Ky., and Mo., south to nw. Fla., west to Tex. and Ark.

Series *Molles*

Series *Molles* consists of eastern species ranging from the Great Plains and Appalachians northward. Six species are included in the series, 4 of which are wide-ranging. Species of series *Molles* are similar to those of series *Punctatae* and *Coccineae* but are distinguished by their hairiness.

DOWNY HAWTHORN *Crataegus mollis* (Torr. & A. Gray) Scheele

QUICKID The comparatively large flowers, relatively broad leaves, and glandless petioles are important identification features.

Deciduous tree to 12 m tall, to 45 cm diam.; one of the largest hawthorns. Erect, single trunk. Crown broad, rounded, of spreading, horizontal branches. **BARK** Brown or brownish gray, deeply and thickly furrowed, sometimes exfoliating in the north. **BRANCH** Armed with stout brown thorns 2–6 cm long. **TWIG** Hairy at first, becoming tan, then pale gray and hairless. **LEAF** Alternate, simple, broadly ovate, elliptic, or nearly triangular; margins coarsely toothed and lobed. Upper surface hairy, rough; lower surface densely hairy to nearly hairless. **FLOWER** 15–25 mm diam.; petals white, circular; stamens 20, anthers creamy white, yellow, pink, or rose. Mid-spring. **FRUIT** Bright red, or rarely orange or yellow pome, rounded, 8–25 mm diam.; matures late summer to early autumn.

HABITAT/RANGE Native. Lowlands, alluvial bottoms, often in association with rich or calcareous soils; N.S., Ont., N.D., south to n. Ala. and e. Tex.

LITTLEHIP HAWTHORN

DOWNY HAWTHORN

Littlehip Hawthorn

flowers

fruit

leaf variation

Downy Hawthorn

flowers

fruit

Series *Parvifoliae*

A small series of 2 species, 1 rare, 1 common and widespread. Plants of the series are characterized by their small stature, unlobed leaves, single-flowered inflorescences, small flowers, and relatively long, conspicuous sepals. Members of the series share similar characters with those of series *Triflorae*, from which they are distinguished by their smaller size and more or less unlobed leaves. They are most often confused with species of series *Lacrimatae*, but lack the latter's zigzag twigs.

DWARF HAWTHORN *Crataegus uniflora* Münchh.

QUICK ID The single-flowered inflorescence and long, conspicuous sepals are distinctive.

Deciduous shrub or small tree, to 5 m tall, 10 cm diam. Erect or shrubby, single or multiple trunks. **BARK** Gray, scaly. **BRANCH** Armed with slender, sharp, straight thorns 1–6 cm long. **TWIG** Hairy, rough, brown, becoming gray. **LEAF** Alternate, simple, obovate or elliptic, sometimes narrowly so, stiff; margins bluntly toothed, mostly above the middle, the teeth tipped with black glands. Upper surface lustrous, dark green, hairless or not, often roughened; lower surface paler, usually hairy. Blade 1–6 cm long, 1–3 cm broad; petiole short or absent, less than 5 mm long. **FLOWER** 10–15 mm diam., usually 1 per inflorescence; petals white, circular; stamens 20, anthers white or pale yellow; sepals often longer than the petals, conspicuous. Mid-spring. **FRUIT** Dull red, greenish yellow, or ruddy orange, rounded, 8–12 mm diam.; matures late summer to autumn.

HABITAT/RANGE Native. Sandy or rocky soils, xeric woodlands; N.Y. south to c. Fla., west to Ohio and Tex.

Series *Pruinosae*

A series of 7 shrubs or small trees distributed in North America mostly in the East. Species in this series are characterized by medium to large leaves that are hairless and blue-green, numerous thorns, and comparatively hard fruit with a whitish waxy covering that can be rubbed off.

WAXYFRUIT HAWTHORN *Crataegus pruinosa* (H.L. Wendl.) K. Koch
A.K.A. FROSTED HAWTHORN

QUICK ID Recognized by the comparatively large blue-green leaves, branched thorns on the trunk, and waxy fruit.

Deciduous, often a shrub 2–3 m tall in the North, more often treelike and 5–9 m tall in the South, to about 30 cm diam. Erect, single trunk or densely shrubby with multiple trunks; trunk of mature plants often armed with branched thorns. Crown open, rounded. **BRANCH** Slender, armed with stout, straight, dark purple or black thorns 3–6 cm long. **TWIG** Hairless, purplish brown, becoming gray. **LEAF** Alternate, simple, ovate or broadly elliptic; firm, thick, stiff at maturity; margins toothed and coarsely lobed, the teeth often gland-tipped. Upper and lower surfaces blue-green, hairless. Blade 2.5–7 cm long, to about 6 cm broad; petiole 2–6 cm long, usually with a few glands. **FLOWER** 17–25 mm diam.; petals white, circular; stamens 10–20, anthers pink, white, yellow, or rose. Mid-spring. **FRUIT** Rounded greenish pome, becoming bright red, often with pinkish spots and a whitish waxy coating, 10–20 mm diam.; matures autumn.

HABITAT/RANGE Native. Thin woods, early successional forests, mountains; Ont., Que., south through New England and the Great Lakes to n. Ga. and n. La., mostly outside the coastal plains.

DWARF HAWTHORN

WAXYFRUIT HAWTHORN

flowers

Dwarf Hawthorn

twig

fruit

spring

Waxyfruit Hawthorn

flowers

fruit

fruit

Series *Pulcherrimae*

A series of 10–15 species distributed largely in the Southeast from S.C. to Miss. Members of the series are similar in appearance and characterized by a combination of deeply corrugated brown bark, hairless plant parts, usually about 20 stamens, glandular inflorescences, and a usually moist to dry understory habitat.

BEAUTIFUL HAWTHORN *Crataegus pulcherrima* Ashe

QUICK ID Distinguished by the combination of comparatively long petioles; blocky, deeply corrugated bark; hairless plant parts; and a preference for rich upland, mixed hardwood forests.

Deciduous, usually a small tree to 8 m tall, 10–15 cm diam. Erect, usually a single trunk, sometimes multiple trunks; crown open, rounded. **BARK** Brownish or grayish, usually darkest near the base, thick, blocky. **BRANCH** Armed with straight, slender, lustrous brown or blackish thorns 2–4 cm long. **TWIG** Hairless, green with a reddish tinge, becoming reddish black, then gray. **LEAF** Alternate, simple, ovate, oval, or broadly elliptic, thin, papery; margins usually with 2–4 lobes, toothed, the teeth tipped with dark red or nearly black glands. Upper surface dull green, hairless; lower surface usually hairless, sometimes sparsely hairy, lacking hairs in the vein axils. Blade usually 3–6 cm long, 3–5 cm broad; petiole 1–2 cm long, often with dark red to nearly black glands. **FLOWER** 15–25 mm diam.; petals white, often tinged with pink, circular; stamens usually 20, anthers rose-pink. Mid- to late spring. **FRUIT** Rounded pome, often bright red at maturity, sometimes yellow blushed with red, rarely purplish red, 7–14 mm diam.; matures early autumn, often persisting into mid-autumn.

HABITAT/RANGE Native. Mixed upland hardwood and pine forests, often in association with rich, sandy soils, 0–100 m; nw. Fla. west to Miss.

SIMILAR SPECIES Similar to Green Hawthorn (series *Viridis*), which is distinguished by the presence of tufts of grayish hairs in the vein axils on the lower surface of the leaf.

Series *Punctatae*

A series of 5 species, 4 in the East, 1 in Mexico; 3 species are widespread and common, 2 are restricted and local in distribution. The series is characterized by narrow, mostly unlobed leaves, flowers with usually 20 stamens and 5 pistils, and pomes with 5 nutlets.

DOTTED HAWTHORN *Crataegus punctata* Jacq.

QUICK ID The dull green leaves with impressed veins, pale ashy-gray bark, and spotted pomes are distinctive.

Deciduous small tree, to about 10 m tall, 45 cm diam. Erect, single trunk, often with branched thorns; crown broad, flat-topped. **BARK** Pale ashy gray, with plate-like scales. **BRANCH** Pale gray, armed with straight, gray thorns 2–8 cm long. **TWIG** Hairy, gray. **LEAF** Alternate, simple, obovate or elliptic, thin, firm, with 7–10 pairs of lateral veins, narrowed at the base to a winged petiole; margins toothed on outer half, mostly entire near the base. Upper surface dull green, hairy when young, becoming hairless, veins impressed; lower surface hairy on the blade tissue. Blade 4–10 cm long, 3–5 cm broad; petiole 5–15 mm long. **FLOWER** 13–20 mm diam.; petals white, circular; stamens usually about 20, anthers pink, red, or yellow. Early summer. **FRUIT** Red, burgundy, or yellow pome, usually white-spotted, 11–22 mm diam.; matures early autumn.

HABITAT/RANGE Native. Old fields, fencelines, sunny openings near streams, moderately shaded woodlands; N.B. and Minn., south to Ind., Ill., along the Blue Ridge Mountains to N.C.; usually forms large colonies and is among the more common hawthorns in the Northeast.

BEAUTIFUL HAWTHORN

DOTTED HAWTHORN

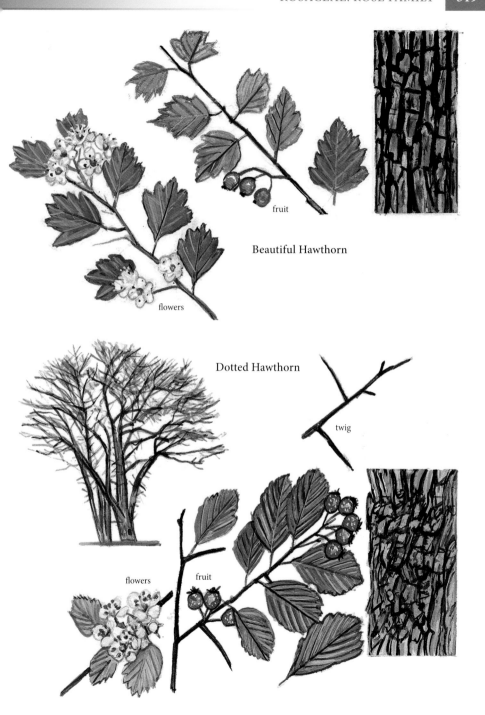

fruit

Beautiful Hawthorn

flowers

Dotted Hawthorn

twig

flowers   fruit

HILL THORN *Crataegus collina* Chapm.

QUICK ID Distinguished from Dotted Hawthorn by its differing range, leaves with 5–7 pairs of lateral veins, inflorescences usually with 10 or fewer flowers, and typically orange pomes.

Deciduous shrub or small tree, 6–8 m tall. Flowers in mid-spring; fruit matures in early autumn.

HABITAT/RANGE Native. Not overlapping with Dotted Hawthorn; ranging from Va. and s. Ga. to s. Ill., Kans., and Okla.

Series *Rotundifoliae*

A series of about 10 species native to Canada and the n. U. S.; the most northerly ranging of eastern hawthorns. Most species in the series are large or small shrubs. Those that reach tree size are distinguished from similar species by the elliptic to broadly elliptic, shallowly lobed or unlobed leaves 2.5–5 cm long.

DODGE'S HAWTHORN *Crataegus dodgei* Ashe

QUICK ID Distinguished from Fireberry Hawthorn by the more often yellowish fruit and hairless leaves.

Deciduous shrub or small tree, to 5 m tall. **BRANCH** Armed with curved, lustrous brown or grayish thorns 2.5–7 cm long. **TWIG** Reddish brown, hairless. **LEAF** Alternate, simple, ovate, obovate, or nearly round; margins shallowly lobed or unlobed, toothed. Upper and lower surfaces hairless. Blade 3–6 cm long, about as broad; petiole 15–30 mm long, usually with minute glands. **FLOWER** 13–18 mm diam.; petals white, circular; stamens usually about 10, anthers ivory. Mid-spring. **FRUIT** Red, orange, or yellow pome, 7–12 mm diam.; matures early autumn.

HABITAT/RANGE Native. Thickets, old fields; Conn. and Wis. south to Va. and n. Ill.

MARGARET'S HAWTHORN *Crataegus margaretta* Ashe

QUICK ID Similar to Dodge's Hawthorn; distinguished from it by flowers with 20 stamens and petioles lacking glands.

Deciduous large shrub or small tree, to about 7 m tall. **LEAF** Variable in outline, 2–5 cm long, margins toothed. **FRUIT** Yellow, orange-red, or red pome, rounded, 7–12 mm diam.; matures early to mid-autumn.

HABITAT/RANGE Native. Woodland margins, hedgerows, usually in dry soils; sw. Ont., Pa., and Wis., south to W.Va., Iowa, and Mo.

HILL THORN

DODGE'S HAWTHORN

MARGARET'S HAWTHORN

Hill Thorn

flowers

fruit

thorn

Dodge's Hawthorn

flowers

fruit

thorn

spring

Margaret's Hawthorn

fruit

flowers

autumn

FIREBERRY HAWTHORN *Crataegus chrysocarpa* Ashe

QUICK ID The northern range and leaves that are about as broad as long help distinguish this species.

Deciduous shrub or small tree to about 8 m tall, 15 cm diam. Erect, single straight trunk or multiple trunks. Crown narrow, open, ascending. **BARK** Gray brown, scaly. **BRANCH** Slender, often crooked, armed with slender, straight or slightly curved, lustrous, dark brown or nearly black thorns 3–10 cm long. **TWIG** Usually hairy, yellowish or greenish brown, becoming gray-brown. **LEAF** Alternate, simple, firm at maturity, obovate, rhombic, or broadly elliptic; margins with 2–4 shallow lobes and conspicuous teeth. Upper surface often hairy on young leaves, sometimes becoming hairless at maturity; lower surface hairy on the veins. Blade typically small, varying in size, 2–6 cm long, often at least as broad; petiole 1–2.5 cm long, narrowly winged. **FLOWER** 1–2 cm diam.; petals white, circular; stamens 10–20, anthers creamy white, yellowish, or pink. Mid-spring. **FRUIT** Rounded red or dark red pome, rarely yellow, often dark-spotted, 6–12 mm diam.; matures and falls early autumn.

HABITAT/RANGE Native. Open woods, hillsides, stream margins, usually in association with rocky, calcareous soils; largely western in distribution, ranging in the East to Nfld. and n. New England, south to Mo. North America's most northern-ranging and cold-adapted hawthorn.

Series *Silvicolae*

A series of 8 species, restricted in distribution to the e. U.S. and adjacent s. Canada. Difficult to distinguish from Bigfruit Hawthorn (series *Tenuifoliae*) and species in series *Pruinosae*. The non-glandular petioles that are 20–30% as long as the blade, leaf blade sparsely hairy on the upper surface, and flowers having mostly 10 stamens are helpful distinguishing characters.

RED HAWTHORN *Crataegus iracunda* Beadle
A.K.A. STOLONBEARING HAWTHORN

QUICK ID The rounded fruit, ovate or triangular leaves, 10-stamened flowers, and hairless inflorescence are important recognition characters in distinguishing Red Hawthorn from species in this and other series.

Deciduous tall shrub or small tree, to about 9 m tall, 20 cm diam. Erect, single trunk or multiple. Crown broad, open, irregular. **BARK** Gray, scaly. **BRANCH** Tough, flexuous, armed with stout, straight or curved, lustrous, dark gray or blackish thorns 2.5–5 cm long. **TWIG** Greenish, hairless, becoming reddish brown, then gray. **LEAF** Alternate, simple, ovate or triangular, firm but thin and papery at maturity, base abruptly narrowed and rounded or nearly flat; margins with 2–5 pairs of shallow triangular lobes, toothed, the teeth sharp-pointed and gland-tipped. Upper surface dull green or blue-green, finely hairy and somewhat sandpapery when young, usually becoming hairless at maturity; lower surface hairless except along the veins. **FLOWER** 12–18 mm diam.; petals white, circular; stamens 10, anthers pink or purplish. Early or mid-spring. **FRUIT** Green pome, usually blushed with red or orange, rounded or slightly oblong, 8–14 mm diam.; matures mid-autumn.

HABITAT/RANGE Native. Open woods, thickets, swamps, margins of limestone glades, flat lowlands and adjacent uplands; sporadically distributed in the Piedmont and upper coastal plain, infrequent and local from S.C. and Ga. to La.

FIREBERRY HAWTHORN

RED HAWTHORN

autumn

Fireberry Hawthorn

flowers

fruit

Red Hawthorn

flowers

fruit

Series *Tenuifoliae*

A series of about 6 species distributed mostly in the e. U.S. and Canada from the Maritimes west to Minn., south to Ga., Ala., and Ark. A single species occurs in Mexico. The series is characterized by thin, hairless leaves and mostly ellipsoid, bright red fruit.

BIGFRUIT HAWTHORN *Crataegus macrosperma* Ashe

QUICK ID The large, thin leaves and oblong fruit are helpful for identification.

Deciduous shrub or small tree, to 8 m tall, 15 cm diam. Erect, single trunk or several. **LEAF** Alternate, simple, thin, comparatively large, broadly ovate; margins with 3–6 shallow lobes, sharply toothed. Upper surface rough at first, hairless at maturity; lower surface hairless. Blade 3–8 cm long, to 12 cm long on new shoots, 3–8 cm broad; petiole 15–30 mm long, slender, hairless, often glandular. **FLOWER** 13–18 mm diam.; petals white, circular; stamens 5–10, anthers pink or red. Mid-spring to early summer. **FRUIT** Bright red, mostly oblong, 6–15 mm diam.; matures early autumn.

HABITAT/RANGE Native. Old fields, fencelines, open woods, 0–2,000 m; Nfld. and Minn., south along the Appalachians to n. Ala.

FANLEAF HAWTHORN *Crataegus flabellata* (Bosc ex Spach) K. Koch

QUICK ID Distinguished from Bigfruit Hawthorn by the margins of the sepals being conspicuously glandular and usually toothed.

Deciduous shrub or small tree, 4–5 m tall. Often confused with Bigfruit Hawthorn owing to similarities in habit and leaf, but the sepals of Bigfruit lack glands.

HABITAT/RANGE The ranges of Fanleaf Hawthorn and Bigfruit Hawthorn overlap significantly.

SCHUETTE'S HAWTHORN *Crataegus schuettei* Ashe

QUICK ID Flowers have 20 stamens and the sepal margins do not have conspicuous glands.

Distinguished from Bigfruit Hawthorn by flowers usually with 20 stamens, and from Fanleaf Hawthorn by the sepals lacking conspicuous glands.

HABITAT/RANGE Native; Ont. and Que., south to Ky. and S.C.

BIGFRUIT HAWTHORN

FANLEAF HAWTHORN

SCHUETTE'S HAWTHORN

Bigfruit Hawthorn

flowers

fruit

spring

Fanleaf Hawthorn

flowers

fruit

Schuette's Hawthorn

flowers

spring

fruit

Series *Triflorae*

A small, distinctive series of 2 species, 1 common, 1 rare, distributed in the se. U.S. The series is characterized by comparatively large flowers borne in few-flowered inflorescences, in combination with conspicuous glands on the petioles, leaf margins, fruit stalks, and sepal margins.

THREEFLOWER HAWTHORN
Crataegus triflora Chapm.

QUICK ID **The predominately 3-flowered inflorescence, which is sometimes borne directly from new wood rather than at the tips of short shoots, is distinctive among the hawthorns.**

Deciduous, usually a shrub, rarely arborescent and to about 6 m tall, 13 cm diam. Usually vase-shaped with multiple trunks, rarely erect with a single trunk; trunk often with compound thorns. Crown open, with slender ascending branches, the leaves clustered near the branch tips. **BARK** Gray or brown, scaly. **BRANCH** Armed with straight, dark gray or blackish thorns 2–5 cm long. **TWIG** Hairy, becoming brown, then gray. **LEAF** Alternate, simple, ovate or elliptic, thin, base rounded or wide-angled; margins shallowly lobed, toothed, the teeth gland-tipped. Upper surface hairy at first, becoming hairless; lower surface hairy only on the veins at maturity. Blade usually 2–8 cm long, occasionally longer, to about 5 cm broad; petiole to about 2 cm long, glandular. **FLOWER** 25–30 mm diam.; petals white, circular; stamens 20–45, anthers cream or yellow. Usually borne in inflorescences of 1–3 flowers. Mid- to late spring. **FRUIT** Deep or bright red pome, rounded, 12–15 mm diam.; matures early to mid-autumn.

HABITAT/RANGE Native. Pine forests, sunny gaps in hardwood forests, margins of rocky glades, blackbelt prairies, prairie margins; Ga. west to La., Ark., and Tenn.

Notes: The relatively large flowers make this species among the showiest of the hawthorns.

Series *Virides*

Series *Virides* consists of a single variable, largely wetland species distributed in the coastal plains and lower Piedmont from Va. to Tex. Early botanists recognized as many as 42 species in this group.

GREEN HAWTHORN   *Crataegus viridis* L.

QUICK ID **Recognized by the combination of its wetland habitat, comparatively long petiole, and tufts of hairs in the axils of the lower surface of the leaf.**

Deciduous, typically a small tree, sometimes a tall shrub, 8–15 m tall, to about 50 cm diam. Erect, typically a single trunk, this often fluted at the base and usually armed with sharp, straight, branched thorns to at least 5 cm long; crown generally dense, rounded, sometimes vertically compressed. **BARK** Mottled reddish, gray, and yellow-brown, often exfoliating in strips, flakes, or small plates to reveal the orange-brown inner bark. **BRANCH** Gray, short, slender, thorny, larger ones often lacking thorns. **TWIG** Reddish and hairless at first, becoming grayish brown, armed with few to many straight, unbranched, often blackish thorns 3–4 cm long. **LEAF** Alternate, simple, elliptic, oblong, or rhombic, sometimes nearly circular, usually widest near the middle; margins unlobed or usually with 3–5 lobes, toothed. Upper surface usually dull green, rarely lustrous, hairless; lower surface paler, usually with tufts of grayish hairs in the major vein axils. Blade 2–7 cm long, 2–5 cm broad;

THREEFLOWER HAWTHORN

GREEN HAWTHORN

Threeflower Hawthorn

flowers

fruit

leaf variation

Green Hawthorn

flowers

fruit

autumn

petiole 1–5 cm long. **FLOWER** 13–15 mm diam.; petals white, 4–8 mm long; stamens 15–20. Early to mid-spring. **FRUIT** Red or orange pome, rounded or ellipsoid, 5–8 mm diam.; matures late autumn, often remaining on the tree well into winter after all the leaves have fallen.

HABITAT/RANGE Native. Floodplain woods, levees along alluvial rivers and streams, wet bottomlands, 0–500 m; Piedmont and southeastern coastal plains, coastal Md. south to n. Fla., west to Ill., Mo., Kans., and Tex.

SIMILAR SPECIES Green Hawthorn's leaves are similar to those of Beautiful Hawthorn (series *Pulcherrimae*), which is easily separated by its upland rather than wetland habitat and by the lack of tufts of hairs in the vein axils on the lower leaf surface.

Notes: Several varieties are described for this species, underscoring its morphological variation. This is one of several hawthorns that have found wide use in landscaping and gardening. The cultivar 'Winter King' is readily available in the nursery trade and is often encountered in arboreta.

QUINCE *Cydonia oblonga* Mill.

QUICK ID The large, fuzzy yellow apple-like fruit is diagnostic.

Deciduous shrub or small tree, 4–6 m tall. Erect, single trunk or multiple. Crown rounded, with crooked, lateral or ascending branches. **BARK** Blackish. **LEAF** Alternate, simple, ovate or oblong, slightly heart-shaped at the base; margins entire. Upper surface dark green, lower surface densely hairy. Blade 5–10 cm long, about 5 cm broad; petiole 8–20 mm long, hairy, subtended by a conspicuous stipule. **FLOWER** 4–5 cm diam.; petals 5, white, pale pink, often blushed pink near the apex; stamens 20; styles 5. Mid- to late spring. **FRUIT** Yellow pome, pear-shaped, fragrant, many-seeded, conspicuously hairy, 8.5–12 cm long, about 8 cm diam.; matures autumn.

HABITAT/RANGE Introduced from the Middle East. Naturalized near plantings; Ont. and Vt., south to Md. and Ill.

Notes: Cydonia is a monotypic genus, meaning that Quince is its only representative. Quince has been cultivated for its fruit since biblical times, predating the cultivation of apples. It may have been the apple of temptation referenced in the biblical story of Adam and Eve.

LOQUAT *Eriobotrya japonica* (Thunb.) Lindl.
A.K.A. JAPANESE PLUM

QUICK ID Easily recognized by the combination of the large, coarsely toothed, distinctly veined, dark green leaves; large flowering panicles; and yellow or orange fruit.

Evergreen shrub, or more typically a small tree where naturalized, 3–7 m tall, to about 15 cm diam. Crown dense, rounded or somewhat vase-shaped. **BARK** Brownish gray, smooth, woolly-hairy. **TWIG** Stout, densely rusty-hairy. **LEAF** Alternate, simple, stiff, leathery, obovate or elliptic; margins coarsely toothed, each tooth terminated by a conspicuous lateral vein; lateral veins parallel, often appearing impressed. Upper surface lustrous, dark green, hairless; lower surface paler, densely rusty-hairy and feltlike. Blade 15–25 cm long, 7–12 cm broad; petiole about 7 mm long, conspicuously hairy. **FLOWER** 10–15 mm diam.; petals 5, oval or nearly

circular, white or creamy white; sweetly fragrant; borne in conspicuous branched, hairy terminal panicles. Autumn to early winter. **FRUIT** Yellow, orange, or whitish pome, pear-shaped or oblong, 3–4 cm long, with 1 or 2 large seeds; matures spring to early summer.

HABITAT/RANGE Introduced from East Asia. Disturbed sites; escaped from cultivation and established from s. Fla. to s. La., but cultivated and cold-hardy to at least the s. Piedmont. Potentially invasive in s. Fla.

Notes: Eriobotrya is a genus of nearly 30 species of evergreen shrubs or trees, restricted in natural distribution mostly to Asia.

■ *MALUS*: APPLES AND CRAB APPLES

A genus of 25–55 species native to the temperate zones of Europe, Asia, and North America; 9 species occur in the East, 3 native. They are found in dry woodlands, old fields, roadsides, and the understory of open upland woods. The combination of mostly unarmed branches, showy clusters of spring-blooming 5-petaled flowers, and apple fruit distinguishes the genus. Numerous cultivars are available and are widely planted, making identification difficult. See also the hawthorns (*Crataegus*), which are similar but usually spiny and typically have much smaller fruit.

Deciduous shrubs or, more often, small to medium-size trees, to about 12 m tall, 60 cm diam.; crown usually dense, rounded. Single or occasionally multiple trunks, usually erect, sometimes angling-ascending on shrubby forms. **BARK** Often rough, scaly and flaking at maturity, sometimes somewhat smooth when young. **TWIG** Hairy or hairless, often reddish brown, usually unarmed, sometimes with sharp-tipped, thornlike spur branches. **LEAF** Alternate, simple, ovate, toothed, to about 10 cm long. **FLOWER** To about 3 cm diam.; stalked, showy, produced in small clusters on short shoots; sepals and petals 5, borne at the rim of the hypanthium; petals white, pink, or reddish, color often darker in bud; stamens numerous, anthers usually 5, protruding from the hypanthium. Mid- to late spring. **FRUIT** Rounded pome, 1–8 cm diam., yellow, red, orange, green, or maroon, produced by the expansion of the hypanthium, with 3–5 locules (chambers) containing 1 or 2 seeds. Species of this genus with mature pomes 5 cm or

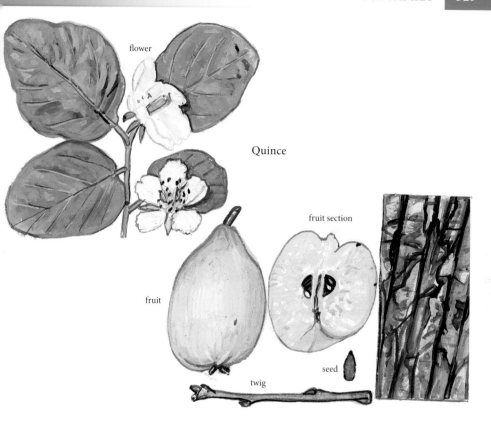

flower

Quince

fruit section

fruit

seed

twig

Loquat

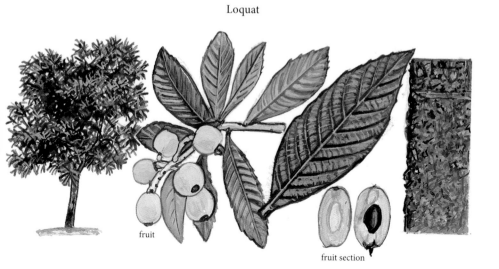

fruit

fruit section

less diam. are usually called crab apples. The fruit is an important food for wildlife, which serve as an important vector in seed distribution.

SOUTHERN CRAB APPLE *Malus angustifolia* (Aiton) Michx.

QUICK ID Distinguished from most other apples by the hairless, predominately bluntly toothed leaves.

Deciduous thicket-forming shrub or small, fast-growing tree, 8–14 m tall, to about 45 cm diam. Crown dense, rounded, branches spreading at nearly right angles to the trunk. **BARK** Grayish, breaking into scaly plates to reveal reddish inner bark. **TWIG** Stiff, reddish brown, hairy at first, becoming essentially hairless; branches often produce sharp-tipped, thorny, twiglike leafy short shoots. **LEAF** Alternate, simple, ovate, elliptic, or oblong, firm and stiff at maturity; margins entire or bluntly or sharply toothed, sometimes lobed. Upper surface medium or yellowish green, hairy when unfurling, hairless at maturity; lower surface paler, hairless at maturity. Blade 2.5–5 cm long, to 2.5 cm broad; petiole 3–15 mm long, hairy. **FLOWER** 2.5 cm diam.; petals 5, white or pink, deep pink in bud, distinctly and abruptly narrowed at the base; stamens numerous; pistils 1, styles 5. Spring. **FRUIT** Pale yellow or yellowish-green pome, rounded, about 2.5 cm diam., with persistent sepals at the apex; matures late summer to autumn.

HABITAT/RANGE Native. Open, well-drained woodlands, thickets, hedges, fencelines, old fields, moist habitats, sometimes in association with limestone, to about 600 m; N.J. and Pa., west to Iowa, south to n. Fla. and e. Tex.

SIMILAR SPECIES The hawthorns (*Crataegus*) have smaller pomes and usually distinctly spiny branches.

Notes: Leaves of Southern Crab Apple trees growing near Eastern Redcedar (*Juniperus virginiana*, Cupressaceae) often display the reddish-orange spots associated with cedar-apple rust, caused by the fungus *Gymnosporangium juniperi-virginianae*; trees with heavy infestations may succumb.

SWEET CRAB APPLE *Malus coronaria* (L.) Mill.
A.K.A. WILD CRAB APPLE

QUICK ID The more or less triangular leaf blade, red bud, comparatively small fruit, and roughened thorns are important identification characters.

Deciduous small tree or thicket-forming shrub, 4–7 m tall, 20–30 cm diam. Crown broad, rounded; branches rigid, contorted, with numerous short, roughened, thornlike shoots. Erect, single trunk. **BARK** Reddish brown, scaly and flaking, vertically fissured. **TWIG** Grayish and densely hairy at first, becoming reddish brown and hairless; buds red, hairy. **LEAF** Alternate, simple, ovate or triangular; margins sharply and deeply double-toothed or lobed, the larger teeth increasing in size from tip to base. Upper surface lustrous green, hairless; lower surface paler, hairy at first, becoming essentially hairless. Blade 3–10 cm long, to about 8 cm broad; petiole to about 5 cm long, often with 2 glands near the middle. **FLOWER** 3–5 cm diam., very fragrant; sepals 5, hairy; petals 5, white, tinted or streaked with rose; stamens 10–20; styles 5. Mid-spring to early summer. **FRUIT** Pale yellow or green pome, rounded, 2–4 cm diam., waxy, sour-tasting; matures autumn.

HABITAT/RANGE Native. Open woods, stream margins, fencelines, roadsides, old fields, clearings, pastures, 100–1,000 m; nearly throughout the East from N.Y. and Ont. south to n. Ga. and ne. Ark.

SOUTHERN CRAB APPLE

SWEET CRAB APPLE

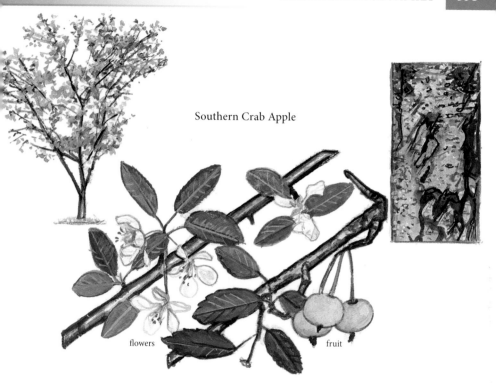

Southern Crab Apple

flowers

fruit

Sweet Crab Apple

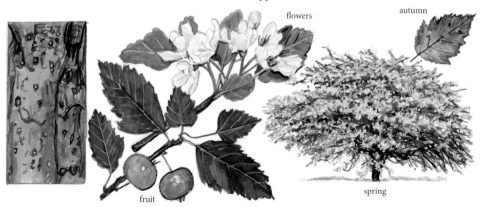

flowers

autumn

fruit

spring

SIMILAR SPECIES The extremely similar Prairie Crab Apple can be distinguished by having mature leaves usually persistently hairy beneath. Hawthorns bear smooth spines rather than roughened thorns.

Notes: This slow-growing native crab apple is shade-tolerant and widely used for ornamental plantings. It is very susceptible to cedar-apple rust (caused by the fungus *Gymnosporangium juniperivirginianae*), which produces orange spots on the leaves and can disfigure the tree.

COMMON APPLE *Malus pumila* Mill.
A.K.A. PARADISE APPLE

QUICK ID The non-thorny twigs, unlobed leaves, densely hairy buds, hairy lower surface of the leaf, and large fruit are diagnostic.

Deciduous tree, 6–13 m tall, 30–140 cm diam. Erect, single short trunk, usually branching low to the ground; crown dense, broad, rounded; branches crooked, spreading or ascending, often with an abundance of short spur shoots. **BARK** Usually smooth when young, becoming grayish and peeling to reveal a smooth reddish inner bark; young and mature bark are sharply contrasted. **TWIG** Stout, lacking thorns, finely hairy, especially when young; terminal bud egg-shaped, densely hairy. **LEAF** Alternate, simple, typically more or less oval or elliptic, with a bluntly or sharply pointed tip, varying to broadly elliptic or ovate, thick, firm, typically borne clustered near the ends of spur shoots; margins finely toothed. Upper surface dark green, hairy at first, becoming hairless; lower surface paler, persistently hairy. Blade 4–10 cm long, 3–6 cm broad; petiole 1.5–3 cm long, stout, hairy. **FLOWER** 2.5–4 cm diam.; sepals 5, green, hairy; petals 5, pinkish white or white; stamens numerous; styles 5. Mid- to late spring. **FRUIT** Round or slightly ellipsoid pome, green at first, becoming red, 7–10 cm long, 5–9 cm diam.; matures summer to early autumn.

HABITAT/RANGE Probably introduced from Europe and Asia; cultivated widely and now sporadically naturalized in fields, along roadsides and fencelines, and near old homesteads, to 1,500 m; essentially throughout the East, except the Gulf Coast region.

SIMILAR SPECIES Other apples and crab apples have smaller fruit and thorny twigs.

Notes: This is the apple of commerce. Numerous cultivars have been selected based on fruit color, taste, and size. Fruits of escaped seedlings and untended plants are often of lesser quality.

SIBERIAN CRAB APPLE *Malus baccata* (L.) Borkh.

QUICK ID The combination of thornless, hairless twigs and small fruit is diagnostic among the crab apples.

Deciduous tree, 4–15 m tall. Erect, usually with multiple trunks, sometimes with a single low-branching trunk; crown dense, spreading, rounded, branches drooping with age. **TWIG** Slender, reddish brown, hairless, lacking thorns; terminal bud egg-shaped, reddish brown, hairy along the margins. **LEAF** Alternate, simple, elliptic or ovate with a rounded base; margins toothed. Surfaces hairy at first, becoming essentially hairless. Blade 3–8 cm long, 2–3.5 cm broad; petiole 2–5 cm long, finely hairy. **FLOWER** 3–4 cm diam., very fragrant; petals 5, pink in bud, opening white. Spring to early summer. **FRUIT** Yellow or red pome, round, to about 1 cm diam.; matures early autumn.

HABITAT/RANGE Introduced from East Asia; cultivated in the East, rarely naturalized; potentially established from Nfld. and Ont. south to Md., W.Va., Ky., and Mo.

SIMILAR SPECIES Plumleaf Crab Apple can be distinguished by its hairy twigs and the larger fruit, averaging about 2–2.5 cm diam.

Notes: A commonly cultivated crab apple with numerous named cultivars.

JAPANESE FLOWERING CRAB APPLE
Malus floribunda (Siebold) ex Van Houtte

QUICK ID The deep pink or red flower buds with flowers that fade to white upon opening are distinctive.

Deciduous small tree, 4–8 m tall. Erect, single trunk or multiple; crown broad, rounded, densely branched, branches arching and ascending, often drooping with age. **BARK** Reddish brown, scaly, flaking. **TWIG** Brown, hairy at first, becoming hairless. **LEAF** Alternate, simple, ovate, ovate-elliptic, or oblong-ovate; margins sharply and coarsely toothed. Upper surface lustrous, dark green; lower surface hairy at first, becoming hairless. Blade 4–8 cm long, to about 4 cm broad; petiole 1.5–2.5 cm long. **FLOWER** 2.5–4 cm diam., fragrant; petals 5, deep pink or nearly red in bud, opening white or pale pink; stamens numerous; styles 5. Spring. **FRUIT** Yellowish, often blushed red, round, about 1 cm diam.; matures late summer to autumn.

HABITAT/RANGE Probably introduced from China; cultivated, sporadically escaped in the U.S.

Common Apple

flowers

fruit

spring

Siberian Crab Apple

flowers

fruit

spring

Japanese Flowering Crab Apple

flowers

fruit

spring

PRAIRIE CRAB APPLE *Malus ioensis*
(Alph. Wood) Britton

QUICK ID The hairy inflorescences and hairy lower surface of the leaf are important identification features.

Deciduous shrub or small tree to about 10 m tall, 25 cm diam. Crown rounded, spreading, branches often with numerous short, lateral, sharp-tipped thornlike shoots. Erect, single trunk. **BARK** Reddish brown or gray, separating into narrow scales. **TWIG** Reddish brown or gray, hairy. **LEAF** Alternate, simple, elliptic, oblong, tending toward ovate, base more or less rounded, tip blunt or rounded; margins sometimes lobed, single- or double-toothed, the teeth blunt or sharp. Upper surface dark green, lustrous, hairless; lower surface hairless or, more often, whitish-hairy. Blade 4–13 cm long, 2–10 cm broad; petiole to about 5 cm long, usually white-hairy. **FLOWER** 3.5–5 cm diam.; petals 5, pink in bud, opening white or pink, borne on white-hairy stalks 2.5–4 cm long. Spring. **FRUIT** Yellow-green pome, rounded, 2–4 cm diam., waxy; matures early autumn.

HABITAT/RANGE Native. Stream margins and woodland borders, usually on moist soil, 100–450 m; mostly Midwestern in distribution, Mich. and Ohio west to Minn. and S.D., south to La. and e. Tex.

SIMILAR SPECIES Extremely similar to Sweet Crab Apple, which has hairless mature leaf blades. Prairie Crab Apple is distinguished from it and other eastern crab apples by having mature leaves usually persistently hairy beneath. Distinguished from hawthorns by the mostly thick, roughened thorns rather than thin, smooth spines.

PRAIRIE CRAB APPLE

PLUMLEAF CRAB APPLE *Malus prunifolia* (Willd.) Borkh.

Deciduous tree, 3–8 m tall. Recognized by the combination of persistent sepals longer than the hypanthium, sharply toothed leaves, and small fruit. **TWIG** Hairy when young, becoming hairless at maturity. **LEAF** 5–9 cm long, 4–5 cm broad; petiole 1–5 cm long. **FLOWER** 4–5 cm diam.; petals pink in bud, opening white. **FRUIT** Yellow or red pome, ovoid, 2–2.5 cm diam.

HABITAT/RANGE Introduced from China, sporadically established in the East from N.S. and Minn., south to S.C. and Ill.

ASIATIC APPLE *Malus spectabilis*
(Aiton) Borkh.

Deciduous tree to about 8 m tall. Recognized by the combination of persistent sepals shorter than or about as long as the floral cup; narrow, finely toothed leaves; and petiole length. **LEAF** Elliptic or narrowly elliptic; blade 5–8 cm long, 2–3 cm broad; petiole 1.5–2 cm long. **FLOWER** 4–5 cm diam.; petals pink in bud, opening white; hypanthium often white-hairy. **FRUIT** Yellow pome, about 2 cm diam.

HABITAT/RANGE Introduced from China, cultivated in the East.

Prairie Crab Apple

spring

flowers

fruit

Plumleaf Crab Apple

flowers

fruit

spring

Asiatic Apple

flowers

fruit

spring

■ *PHOTINIA*: PHOTINIAS OR CHOKEBERRIES

There are about 60 *Photinia* species worldwide, more than half endemic to China. About 5 species occur in e. North America, including 1 native shrub and 2 introduced trees. Several species or hybrids are used in landscaping and gardening, a few of which are naturalized. Some experts combine the genera *Photinia* and *Aronia*, in which case the appropriate name is *Aronia*. Of the 2 groups, only species of *Aronia*, all of which are shrubs for the purposes of this book (and thus not included), are native to North America. Plants are mostly escaped from cultivation in North America and established in disturbed areas.

Deciduous or evergreen ornamental trees or shrubs with dense, broad crowns. **BARK** Gray or nearly black. **TWIG** Slender, round in cross section, usually with conspicuous lenticels. **LEAF** Alternate, simple, obovate or elliptic, papery or leathery; margins finely or coarsely toothed, rarely entire. **FLOWER** White, petals 5, often strongly and unpleasantly aromatic, usually borne in a showy terminal cluster. **FRUIT** Red pome, rounded or egg-shaped, with 1 or 2 seeds; usually matures late summer, sometimes turning black in autumn.

TAIWANESE PHOTINIA *Photinia serratifolia* (Desf.) Kalkman

QUICK ID A photinia, recognized by the petiole 2–4 cm long and the lower surface of the leaves lacking black glands.

Evergreen, very large shrub or small tree, 4–12 m tall; crown broad, dense; often with multiple trunks. **BARK** Black, attractive, often exfoliating in large plates. **TWIG** Hairless, greenish brown, conspicuously spotted with brownish lenticels. **LEAF** Alternate, simple, leathery, firm; narrowly elliptic, narrowly obovate, or obovate-elliptic; margins entire or inconspicuously and finely toothed. Upper surface lustrous green, hairless at maturity, the central veins impressed; lower surface dull green, hairy along the veins when young, becoming hairless, central vein raised. Blade 9–22 cm long, 3–6.5 cm broad; petiole 2–4 cm long. **FLOWER** 6–8 mm diam.; petals 5, white; inflorescence a showy terminal corymb, 10–18 cm wide. Mid-spring. **FRUIT** Rounded red pome, 5–6 mm diam.; matures late summer.

HABITAT/RANGE Introduced from Asia. Escaped from cultivation; se. U.S., Ga. to La.

ORIENTAL PHOTINIA *Photinia villosa* (Thunb.) DC.

Deciduous shrub or small tree, 2–5 m tall. **TWIG** Twigs and young branches white-hairy at first, becoming hairless. **LEAF** Obovate or elliptic; margins sharply toothed, tip abruptly narrowed, extended, often somewhat tail-like. Blade 3–8 cm long, 2–4 cm broad; petiole 2–6 mm long, densely hairy. **FRUIT** Red or yellowish-red pome, egg-shaped or ellipsoid. **HABITAT/RANGE** Introduced from Asia; escaped from cultivation, established in se. N.Y., se. Pa., Del. and D.C.

■ *PRUNUS*: CHERRIES, PLUMS, PEACHES, AND APRICOTS

A genus of at least 200 species worldwide, distributed in North, Central, and South America, Mexico, Eurasia, Africa, and Australia; most abundant in north temperate regions. Members favor open woods, woodland margins, stream banks, bottomlands, dunes, pastures, old fields, and roadside thickets; especially common in disturbed sites. *Prunus* has traditionally been divided into several sections, including the cherries, plums, apricots, peaches, nectarines, and almonds, based largely on fruit morphology. However, there is no consistent agreement about these sections, and recent molecular and DNA data do not precisely support these divisions. In general, the cherries have true terminal buds projecting from the ends of the twigs and usually lack sharp-tipped spur branches; plums have offset or axillary buds and usually sharp-tipped spur branches. The combination of glandular petiole, toothed leaves, showy flowers, abundant fruit, and crushed twigs with the odor of bitter almond helps distinguish the genus.

Deciduous or evergreen shrubs or trees to 40 m tall; mostly erect with a single trunk or often with multiple trunks, sometimes up to 20 or more; several species suckering from the roots or base and forming distinctive clonal thickets. **BARK** On young trees smooth, occasionally finely fissured, reddish brown or grayish; at maturity often becoming scaly, furrowed, or broken into small plates, often darker, sometimes blackish, a few species exfoliating in curly plates; several species with horizontal lenticels, especially evident on young trees. **TWIG** Reddish brown or grayish, hairy or not, often with a skinlike grayish covering that peels off; usually with the odor of bitter almond when crushed. Branches often with short and long shoots, thorny

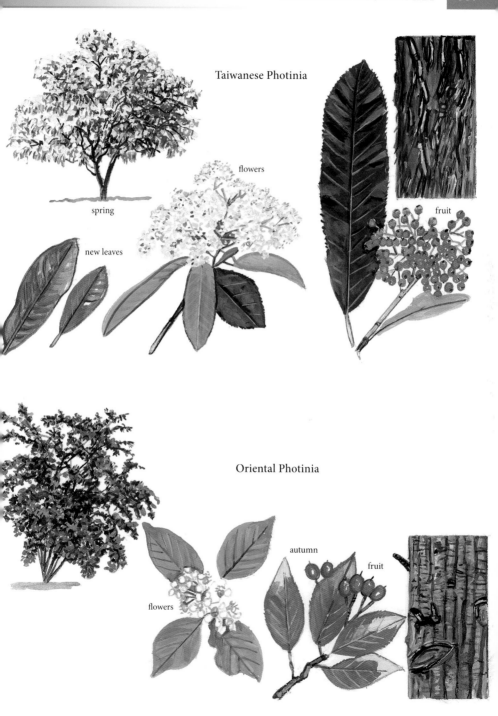

Taiwanese Photinia

spring

new leaves

flowers

fruit

Oriental Photinia

flowers

autumn

fruit

or not. **LEAF** Alternate, simple, thin or leathery, linear or lanceolate, often clustered near the tips of short shoots; margins usually toothed, the teeth often glandular; petiole hairy or not, usually with 1 or more glands near the point of attachment to the blade, these glands also sometimes on adjacent blade margins. **FLOWER** 4–40 mm diam., usually bisexual, sometimes unisexual and plants dioecious; petals 5, white, pink, or dark pink, circular, elliptic, or obovate; stamens 10–30; typically opens in spring, with or before leaf emergence; inflorescence a raceme, corymb, or umbellate fascicle of 1–100 flowers. **FRUIT** Rounded or egg-shaped drupe, 0.5–3 cm diam., hairy or not; yellowish, reddish, dark purple, or black, in many species progressing from green to red to purple to black at maturity.

AMERICAN PLUM *Prunus americana*
Marshall

QUICK ID Recognized by the combination of scaly, flaking bark, sharply toothed leaf margins, glandless marginal teeth, glandless petioles, and red or yellow fruit.

Deciduous shrub or small tree, usually to 8 m tall and 30 cm diam., potentially to 10 m tall and 90 cm diam. Usually erect, single trunk, sometimes with multiple trunks, often bearing thorn-tipped short shoots when young. **BARK** Smooth and reddish brown on very young plants, with conspicuous horizontal lenticels, becoming tan, buff, gray, or nearly black, conspicuously scaly, flaking off in curly plates. **TWIG** Grayish or reddish brown, hairy or hairless, sometimes thorn-tipped. **LEAF** Alternate, simple; elliptic, oblong, oval, obovate, or narrowly ovate, base rounded or wedge-shaped, tip abruptly and conspicuously pinched to a point; margins coarsely and sharply single- or double-toothed, the teeth broad at the base and abruptly pinched to a narrow, glandless tip. Upper surface

hairless, lower surface hairless or hairy along the midvein and lateral veins. Blade 4–12 cm long, 2–5.5 cm broad; petiole 4–19 mm long, usually hairy, rarely hairless, lacking glands. **FLOWER** 20–25 mm diam., petals 5, white, often becoming pink with age. Mid-spring to early summer. **FRUIT** Rounded or ellipsoid red, orange, or yellowish drupe, 1.5–3 cm diam., hairless, often glaucous, with a whitish waxy blush; matures late summer.

HABITAT/RANGE Native. Moist, rich, loamy soils, often where calcium is present; open woods and woodland margins, fencelines, stream banks, 10–2,100 m; throughout the East, west throughout the Rocky Mountains region.

SIMILAR SPECIES American Plum is similar to the closely related Canada Plum, but that has broader leaves with blunt, gland-tipped marginal teeth; predominantly lanceolate, sharply toothed leaves; non-glandular petioles; and sepal margins lacking hairs. It is also similar to Mexican Plum, which is distinguished by having twigs and flower stalks usually hairless or only sparsely hairy; American Plum has usually hairy twigs and flower stalks.

Notes: American Plum is sometimes reported as thicket-forming. It may be that such thickets develop mostly from seedlings rather than root suckers, with only a few seedlings reaching maturity. About 260 horticultural forms have been derived from American Plum, underscoring the variability across its expansive range.

MEXICAN PLUM *Prunus mexicana* S.
Watson

QUICK ID The combination of leaves coarsely and sharply toothed, twigs and flower stalks usually hairless, and lower surface of the leaf hairy, helps distinguish Mexican Plum.

Deciduous tree, 3–12 m tall, 45 cm diam. Erect, single trunk, rarely producing multiple trunks; crown open, irregular. **BARK** Gray to nearly black, exfoliating in curly plates, becoming furrowed at maturity. **TWIG** Slender, grayish brown, usually hairless, often hairy when young. **LEAF** Alternate, simple, somewhat thickish; elliptic, broadly elliptic,

AMERICAN PLUM

MEXICAN PLUM

American Plum

flowers

stone

fruit

Mexican Plum

flowers

fruit

spring

obovate, ovate, or oblong, base usually rounded, tip abruptly pinched to a point; margins coarsely double-toothed, the teeth sharp, not gland-tipped. Upper surface hairless, lustrous yellow-green, veins impressed; lower surface densely hairy. Blade 6–12 cm long, 3–7 cm broad; petiole 4–18 mm long, usually hairy, with 1–4 glands near the point of attachment to the blade. **FLOWER** 20–25 mm diam.; petals 5, white, sometimes fading to pink. Mid-spring. **FRUIT** Rounded or ellipsoid red or dark blue drupe 1.5–3 cm diam., usually glaucous; matures late summer to autumn.

HABITAT/RANGE Native. Open woods, bottomlands, woodland margins, 10–400 m; essentially Iowa, Ill., and Tenn., south and west to Ala., Kans., Okla., and Tex.

SIMILAR SPECIES Similar to American Plum, which is distinguished from it by its usually hairy twigs and flower stalks. The 2 forms hybridize where their ranges overlap, making identification difficult.

CANADA PLUM *Prunus nigra* Aiton

QUICK ID The combination of thornlike twigs, blunt and gland-tipped marginal teeth, red to yellow fruit, comparatively long leaf, and inflorescence with a pinkish cast helps distinguish this species.

Deciduous shrub or small tree, 3–9 m tall, 12–25 cm diam. Erect, usually a single short, crooked trunk, sometimes with multiple trunks; crown vase-shaped with a broad top, branches crooked. **BARK** Thin, smooth, and grayish brown at first, becoming darker and splitting vertically into thick plates. **TWIG** Slender, green at first, becoming dark brown to nearly black, usually hairless, rarely hairy, thornlike. **LEAF** Alternate, simple; elliptic, ovate, oblong, or obovate, thin, firm, base rounded; margins coarsely double-toothed, the teeth blunt, gland-tipped. Upper surface light green, hairless, veins prominent, impressed; lower surface paler, hairy on the veins. Blade 5–11 cm long, 3–6.5 cm broad; petiole 8–22 mm long, occasionally with 1–3 glands near the point of attachment to the blade. **FLOWER** 2–3 cm diam.; petals 5, white, fading to pink. Late spring to early summer. **FRUIT** Rounded or ellipsoid red, orange, or yellowish drupe, 1.5–3 cm diam., hairless; matures late summer.

HABITAT/RANGE Native. Woodland margins, disturbed open sites, roadside thickets, bottomland forests, margins of floodplains, 10–800 m; N.S. and Man. south to Ohio, Ill., and Iowa.

SIMILAR SPECIES The leaves with blunt, gland-tipped marginal teeth distinguish Canada Plum from American Plum, which has predominately lanceolate, sharply toothed leaves, non-glandular petioles, and the margins of the sepals lacking hairs. European Plum has mostly shorter leaves.

CHICKASAW PLUM *Prunus angustifolia* Marshall

QUICK ID The thicket-forming habit, folded leaves, relatively small size, and very early flowering are usually enough to identify Chickasaw Plum.

Deciduous shrub or small tree, to about 6 m tall, 50 cm diam. Erect, usually with multiple trunks and distinctly thicket-forming, the thickets often extensive and generally circular in outline. **BARK** Dark reddish brown or grayish, splitting but not exfoliating with age. **TWIG** Slender, rigid, slightly zigzag, hairless, the short lateral twigs typically sharply thorn-tipped. **LEAF** Alternate, simple, lanceolate, narrowly elliptic, or oblong, usually folded upward from the midrib, trough- or trowel-like; base wedge-shaped; margins finely and bluntly toothed, the teeth tipped with a tiny reddish or yellowish gland, the glands usually larger on new leaves, often shrinking in size and falling with age, leaving a callus. Upper surface lustrous, bright green, hairless; lower surface duller, usually sparsely hairy, at least along the veins. Blade 1.5–8 cm long, 1–2.5 cm broad; petiole 2–14 mm long, sparsely hairy, rarely hairless, usually lacking glands, or with 1–2 glands near the attachment to the blade. **FLOWER** 7–10 mm diam.; petals 5, white; stamens 10–20, filaments white, anthers yellow. Early to mid-spring. **FRUIT** Ovoid or ellipsoid red or yellow drupe, 1.5–2.5 cm diam., the fruit on a given plant often tending toward the larger or smaller extremes of this range; pleasant-tasting, matures summer.

HABITAT/RANGE Native. Roadsides, sandy clearings, old fields, rural home sites, fencelines, thickets, open woods, dunes, pastures, 0–600 m; N.J. and Pa. south to Fla., west to Nebr., Colo., and N.M.

CANADA PLUM

CHICKASAW PLUM

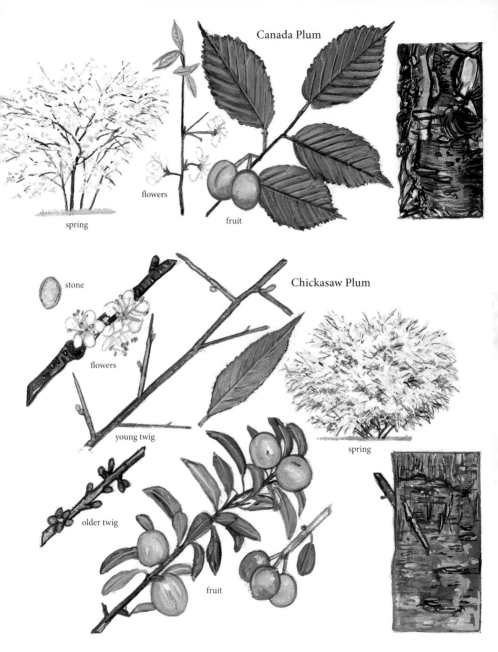

Canada Plum

flowers

spring

fruit

stone

flowers

Chickasaw Plum

young twig

spring

older twig

fruit

SIMILAR SPECIES Often confused with Hog Plum and virtually indistinguishable by flower when leaves are absent, except by Chickasaw Plum's suckering, thicket-forming habit; otherwise, Hog Plum is distinguished by the leaf blade being flat, rather than folded upward from the midvein, and the marginal teeth usually lacking glands.

HOG PLUM *Prunus umbellata* Elliott
A.K.A. FLATWOODS PLUM, ALLEGHENY PLUM, SLOE

QUICKID The fascicled flowers and fruit, flat leaf blade, non-glandular marginal teeth, and purple drupes help distinguish the species.

Deciduous shrub or small tree, to about 10 m tall, 30 cm diam. Erect, single, usually crooked trunk, rarely with multiple trunks; usually solitary, not thicket-forming; crown spreading and ascending with crooked branches. **BARK** Reddish and smooth when young, becoming grayish to blackish, splitting, and somewhat scaly. **TWIG** Slender, usually hairless, sometimes hairy, usually not thorn-tipped. **LEAF** Alternate, simple, flat, elliptic, oval, oblong, or oblanceolate, base wedge-shaped to nearly truncate, tip acute or pinched to a point; margins toothed, the teeth pointed, not gland-tipped. Upper surface dull green, hairless or scarcely hairy; lower surface paler, variously hairy. Blade 2–8 cm long, 1–4 cm broad; petiole 3–14 mm long, with 1–3 glands near the attachment to the blade. **FLOWER** 12–15 mm diam.; petals 5, white, fading pink; stamens 10–20, sometimes more, filaments white, anthers yellow; inflorescence a fascicle of 2–5 flowers. Early to late spring. **FRUIT** Rounded or egg-shaped drupe, at first red or yellow, maturing dark purplish or greenish, blotched purple, rarely remaining red, 1–2 cm diam.; bitter to taste; matures summer.

HABITAT/RANGE Native. Open pinelands, sandy pine–oak woods, mixed pine–hardwood forests, hammocks, limestone bluffs, rocky uplands, old fields, disturbed roadsides, 10–800 m; Mass. and Pa., south to Fla., west to e. Tex. and Ark., disjunct to Mich., more common in the southeastern coastal plains.

SIMILAR SPECIES Often confused with Chickasaw Plum, which is distinguished by some or many leaves folded upward from the midvein,

gland-tipped marginal teeth, and its thicket-forming habit. When Hog Plum forms thickets it colonizes by seedlings rather than root suckers.

Notes: As construed here, Hog Plum encompasses what has been called Allegheny Plum (*P. alleghaniensis* Porter), which has traditionally been reliably distinguished only by its more northerly distribution. Leaf size and shape between these 2 supposed species vary considerably, even on a single tree, suggesting that the 2 forms constitute a single species.

CREEK PLUM *Prunus rivularis* Scheele
A.K.A. HOG PLUM

QUICKID Recognized by the combination of leaf typically greater than 2 cm broad, petiole glandular, marginal teeth gland-tipped, leaves often trough-shaped, and flowers opening before or with leaf emergence.

Deciduous shrub or small tree, to 9 m tall, 30 cm diam. Erect, single trunk, often suckering and producing numerous trunks; crown of arborescent plants rounded, with erect branches. **BARK** Smooth and reddish brown on young trunks, becoming gray or grayish brown and splitting into plates with age. **TWIG** Reddish brown, hairless, with numerous lenticels. **LEAF** Alternate, simple, lanceolate, oblong, or narrowly elliptic, thin, usually folded upward troughlike from the midvein, base rounded or wedge-shaped, tip acute or pinched to a point; margins single- or double-toothed, the teeth blunt, gland-tipped. Upper surface light green, lustrous, hairless; lower surface paler, hairless or hairy along the veins. Blade 4–11 cm long, 1.5–5 cm broad; petiole 7–20 mm long, hairless or sparsely hairy, with 1–4 glands near the point of attachment to the blade. **FLOWER** 12–16 mm diam.; petals 5, white; in an inflorescence of 2–4 flowers. Mid-spring,

HOG PLUM

CREEK PLUM

WILD GOOSE PLUM

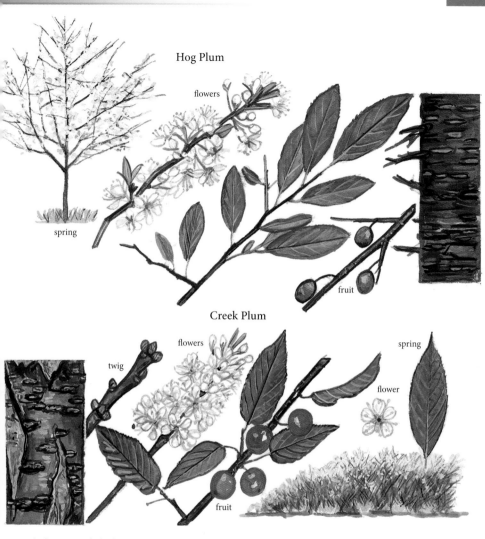

Hog Plum

flowers

spring

fruit

Creek Plum

flowers

twig

spring

flower

fruit

before or with leaf emergence. **FRUIT** Rounded, bright red, yellowish, or orange drupe 1.2–2.5 cm diam., hairless; matures summer.

HABITAT/RANGE Native. Thickets, woodland margins, stream banks, 200–1,000 m; N. J., Pa., south to Ga., west to Colo., Tex.

SIMILAR SPECIES The similar Hortulan Plum has leaves flat, rather than folded upward from the midrib, and rarely forms multiple trunks. In the very similar Chickasaw Plum the petiole usually lacks glands or has 1 or 2 glands near the attachment to the blade, while in Creek Plum the petiole often has more than 2 glands.

Notes: As treated here, Creek Plum also includes what has been called Wild Goose Plum (*P. munsoniana* W. Wight & Hedrick). The 2 forms have long been treated as separate species, distinguished mostly by relative differences in the size of the plants, leaves, and floral structures. Recent evidence suggests that Wild Goose Plum probably represents merely a larger form of Creek Plum. Traditionally, Wild Goose Plum has been reported to occupy a larger range than Creek Plum.

EUROPEAN PLUM *Prunus domestica* L.

QUICKID The combination of usually wrinkled leaves with coarsely toothed margins, relatively large fruit, and usually hairy twigs helps distinguish European Plum.

Deciduous shrub or small tree, 2–10 m tall. Usually erect, single trunk, sometimes producing multiple trunks. Crown dense, rounded, low-branching. **BARK** Purplish, finely furrowed when young, becoming more coarsely furrowed at maturity. **TWIG** Usually hairy, occasionally hairless. **LEAF** Alternate, simple, elliptic or obovate, more or less undulate or wrinkled, base wedge-shaped or bluntly rounded, tip acute or pinched to a point; margins coarsely single- or double-toothed, the teeth blunt, conspicuous, gland-tipped. Upper surface hairless or hairy on the midvein, lower surface hairy on the tissue and veins. Blade 2.5–9 cm long, 1.5–5 cm broad; petiole 6–20 mm long, hairy or hairless, sometimes lacking glands, sometimes with 1–3 glands near or at point of blade attachment or on adjacent leaf margin. **FLOWER** 1.5–2.5 cm diam.; petals 5, white. Mid- to late spring. **FRUIT** Rounded or ellipsoid, hairless blue-black, green, yellow, or red drupe, 1.5–3.5 cm diam.; matures late summer to early autumn.

HABITAT/RANGE Introduced from Europe. Roadsides, fencelines, home sites, disturbed sites, escaped from cultivation, 0–1,500 m; established in the East from Nfld. and Ont. south to Ohio and n. Va.

HORTULAN PLUM *Prunus hortulana* L.H. Bailey

QUICKID The combination of hairless twigs, usually lanceolate or narrowly elliptic leaf blades that are flat after expansion, and inflorescences of 2–4 flowers helps distinguish the species.

Deciduous small tree, 4–10 m tall, to about 27 cm diam. Erect, single trunk, rarely with multiple trunks. **BARK** Brown, thin, scaly. **TWIG** Hairless, becoming dark reddish brown, sometimes thorn-tipped. **LEAF** Alternate, simple, narrowly elliptic, lanceolate, oblanceolate, or oblong, thickish, folded in bud but flat after expansion, base rounded, tip long-tapering to a pinched point; margins single- or double-toothed, the teeth blunt, gland-tipped. Upper surface hairless or with a few hairs along the midvein, lower surface hairy along the midvein and lateral veins. Blade 5–7 cm long, 2–5.5 cm broad; petiole 6–25 mm long, hairy at least on 1 side, usually with 1–5 glands near the point of blade attachment. **FLOWER** 10–15 mm diam.; petals 5, white; inflorescence of 2–4 flowers. Mid- to late spring. **FRUIT** Red to yellowish drupe, often dotted white, rounded, hairless, 2–3 cm diam.; matures late summer.

HABITAT/RANGE Native. Open woods, roadsides, floodplains, moist lowlands, calcareous uplands, 50–500 m; mostly Midwestern, Mass., Md., and Va., west to Tenn., Ark., Nebr., Kans., and Okla.

SIMILAR SPECIES The similar Creek Plum has leaves folded upward from the midrib rather than flat, and plants often suckering and forming multiple trunks.

CHOKECHERRY *Prunus virginiana* L.

QUICKID Most easily identified by the combination of the bicolored bud scales and broad, elliptic leaves with sharply toothed margins, the teeth conspicuously spreading.

Deciduous shrub or small tree, 4–10 m tall, 10–15 cm diam.; crown narrow, irregular, more or less rounded. Erect or leaning, single or multiple, usually crooked trunks; typically suckering from the root crown and thicket-forming. **BARK** Smooth, dark brown when young, becoming almost black, slightly fissured, lenticels oriented more or less vertically. **TWIG** Slender, green or light brown at first, becoming dark brown, with an almond odor when crushed; buds hairless, 6–8 mm long, scales dark brown with paler margins. **LEAF** Alternate, simple, thin, papery; obovate, oblong-obovate, or oval, tip abruptly acuminate; margins finely and

HORTULAN PLUM

CHOKECHERRY

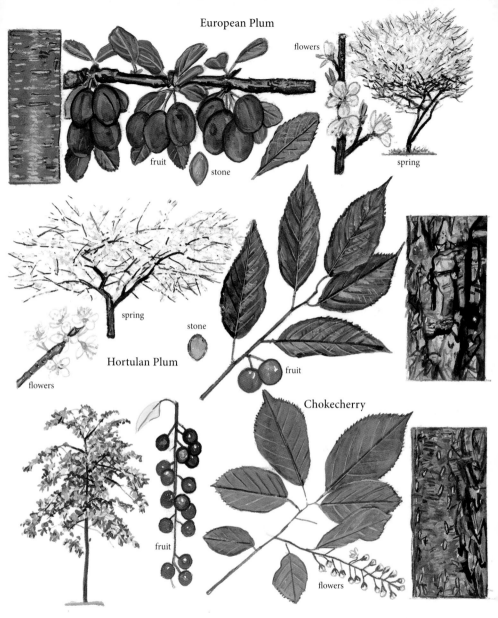

European Plum

flowers

fruit

stone

spring

spring

flowers

Hortulan Plum

stone

fruit

Chokecherry

fruit

flowers

sharply toothed, the teeth spreading. Upper surface dark green, hairless; lower surface paler. Turns yellow in autumn. Blade 5–10 cm long, 3–5 cm broad; petiole about 1 cm long, with 2 glands near its attachment to the blade. **FLOWER** 8–12 mm diam., petals 5, white; stamens 15–20; inflorescence a raceme 7–15 cm long. Mid-spring to early summer. **FRUIT** Rounded, juicy drupe 6–10 mm diam.; matures late summer to early autumn.

HABITAT/RANGE Native. Open woods, roadsides, usually on rich, moist soils, 0–2,600 m; Canada, south to n. Ga., west to the West Coast; absent from the southeastern coastal plains.

SIMILAR SPECIES Black Cherry has medium-width leaves with fine, incurved marginal teeth; Pin Cherry has longer, long-tapering, narrower leaves.

PIN CHERRY *Prunus pensylvanica* L. f.
A.K.A. FIRE CHERRY

QUICK ID Easily identified among the cherries by the red twig and long-tapering, lanceolate, finely toothed leaf.

Deciduous small tree, 8–12 m tall, 20–25 cm diam. Erect, usually with a single slender, straight trunk, often producing suckers from the root crown, especially following injury. Crown open, rounded, with slender, ascending or spreading branches. **BARK** Reddish brown, lustrous, with numerous well-spaced horizontal lenticels; fissured at maturity and peeling off in papery plates. **TWIG** Slender, lustrous reddish at first, becoming reddish brown; marked by orange lenticels; emits an almond odor when crushed. **LEAF** Alternate, simple, thin, lanceolate, often folded upward from the midvein; tip long, tapering, often curved at the apex; margins finely, sharply, and unevenly toothed. Upper surface lustrous yellow-green, hairless; lower surface paler, hairless. Turns red, maroon, or orange in autumn. Blade 7–15 cm long, to about 5 cm broad; petiole 1–2 cm with glands near the attachment to the blade. **FLOWER** 1–1.2 cm diam.; petals 5, white; stamens 15 or more, conspicuous. Late spring to early summer. **FRUIT** Rounded, bright red drupe, 6–8 mm diam.; stalk slender, 15–20 mm long; matures midsummer to late summer.

HABITAT/RANGE Native. Open, disturbed sites such as roadsides, fields, clearings, 0–2,800 m; Nfld. west to B.C., south to Colo. in the West, to n. Ga. in the East.

SIMILAR SPECIES The long-tapering, narrower leaf distinguishes Pin Cherry from Black Cherry, which has elliptic, medium-width leaves, and from Chokecherry, whose shorter, wider leaves have an abruptly pointed tip.

Notes: This is a fast-growing, short-lived cherry that favors disturbance. Seeds are dispersed widely by birds, remain viable for many years in the soil, and germinate quickly following fire or mechanical disturbance. Pin Cherry is intolerant of shade and is overtopped and soon displaced by canopy trees in a restored or maturing forest.

BLACK CHERRY *Prunus serotina* Ehrh.

QUICK ID The combination of hairy terminal bud, elongate inflorescence with 20 or more flowers, and incurved teeth along the leaf margin is diagnostic among the cherries and plums.

Deciduous tree, 15–40 m tall, 50–150 cm diam.; erect, single trunk, usually straight when forest-grown, sometimes crooked when open-grown. Crown cylindric, usually lustrous, with conspicuously drooping leaves. **BARK** Reddish brown, more or less smooth, with narrow, horizontal fissures when young, becoming gray or grayish black and conspicuously blocky at maturity. **TWIG** Slender, green at first, becoming reddish brown, usually hairless, with a bitter almond aroma when crushed; terminal bud 4–6 mm long, egg-shaped, hairy, reddish brown, darkest at the tip. **LEAF** Alternate, simple, more or less thick, waxy; narrowly elliptic, oval, or oblong; tip abruptly short-tapered; margins finely and conspicuously toothed with incurving teeth. Upper surface lustrous green, hairless; lower surface paler, hairless, the lower portion of the midvein often vested with reddish hairs. Turns yellow or salmon orange in autumn. Blade 5–15 cm long, 2.5–4 cm broad; petiole 5–20 mm long, usually with 1 or more glands. **FLOWER** To about 6 mm diam., petals 5, stamens 15 or more, inflorescence a raceme 10–12 cm long. Early to mid-spring. **FRUIT** Rounded, juicy drupe with 1 stone, red at first, turning lustrous purplish black, 7–10 mm diam.; matures late summer to early autumn.

PIN CHERRY

BLACK CHERRY

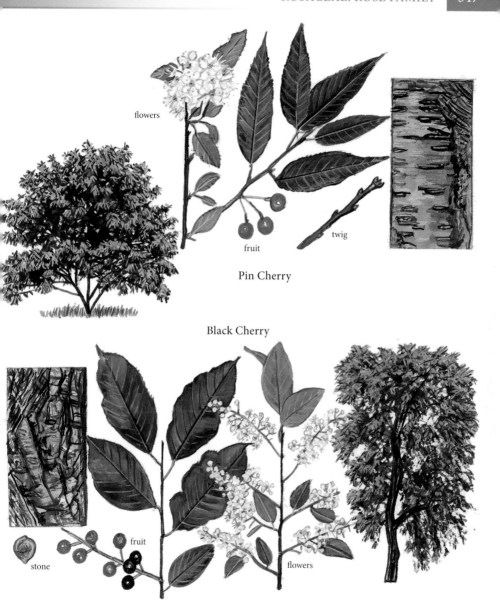

flowers

fruit

twig

Pin Cherry

Black Cherry

stone

fruit

flowers

HABITAT/RANGE Native. Occurs in numerous habitats, often in disturbed areas, mixed forests, fencerows, fields, 0–1,500 m; widespread across the East, s. Canada south to c. Fla., west to N.M. and N.D.

SIMILAR SPECIES Alabama Cherry is most similar, distinguished by its rounded leaf tip, distinctly hairy petiole, and hairier lower leaf surface; the similar Pin Cherry is distinguished by its long-tapering, narrower leaf, and Chokecherry by its sharp, spreading marginal teeth.

ALABAMA CHERRY *Prunus alabamensis* C. Mohr

QUICK ID Generally similar to Black Cherry; distinguished by the rounded leaf tip, distinctly hairy petiole, and more numerous hairs on the lower surface of the leaf.

Deciduous small tree, to about 10 m tall. **TWIG** Hairy. **LEAF** Lustrous above, tip usually more or less rounded with an abrupt point, lacking an extended tip; margins toothed; petioles hairy.

HABITAT/RANGE Native; longleaf pine–scrub oak forests, sand ridges, mixed woodlands on upper slopes bordering ravines, 0–150 m, coastal plain, N.C. to Miss., Fla. panhandle.

CAROLINA LAURELCHERRY *Prunus caroliniana* Aiton

QUICK ID Identified by the combination of the evergreen leaves with margins toothed or entire, and fruit and flowers often present at the same time.

Evergreen, very large shrub or medium-size tree to about 14 m tall, 1 m diam.; erect, single trunk or several, often thicket-forming. Crown dense, rounded or somewhat cylindric on erect trees, sometimes broadly rounded and branching nearly to the ground in thickets. **BARK** Dark gray, young trunks smooth, with conspicuous elongate, horizontal, dull orange lenticels; older trunks sometimes becoming vertically and horizontally fissured, often decorated with holes produced by Yellow-bellied Sapsuckers (*Sphyrapicus varius*). **TWIG** Slender, aromatic, marked with lenticels. **LEAF** Alternate, simple, elliptic, leathery and stiff; margins entire or with short, sharp, usually widely spaced teeth, the number of teeth varying from

tree to tree and from leaf to leaf on a single tree. Upper surface dark, lustrous green, lower surface paler. Blade 5–15 cm long, 1.5–4 cm broad; petiole 3–6 mm long, those of at least new leaves reddish. **FLOWER** About 5 mm diam.; petals 5, white or creamy white; stamens 10–15; inflorescence a short-stalked raceme 1–4 cm long. Early to mid-spring. **FRUIT** Firm, usually more or less egg-shaped, dull black drupe, 1–1.5 cm long, often longer than broad, the persistent style bases forming a short point at the apex; matures from summer into winter, often persisting for much of the year.

HABITAT/RANGE Native. Fencerows, open woodlands, fields, often forming dense thickets, 0–200 m; southeastern coastal plains, N.C. south to n. Fla., west to e. Tex.

SIMILAR SPECIES Distinguished from other cherries by the evergreen habit, variously toothed or entire leaves, and egg-shaped fruit.

SWEET CHERRY *Prunus avium* (L.) L.
A.K.A. MAZZARD

QUICK ID Distinguished by the combination of double-toothed leaves, glandular petiole, bright red fruit, and hairy lower surface of the leaf.

Deciduous tree, 9–18 m tall, 30–50 cm diam.; erect, single straight or crooked trunk; crown cylindric or pyramidal. **BARK** Grayish pink and lustrous on young trees, becoming dark purplish red, fissured, and marked with conspicuous lenticels on old trees, peeling in horizontal strips. **TWIG** Stout, pale reddish brown above, grayish beneath, with the odor of bitter almond when crushed. **LEAF** Alternate, simple, oblong, obovate, tip abruptly pinched to a distinctive point; margins double-toothed, the teeth sharp, ascending, and tipped with a gland. Upper surface bronze when young, becoming dark green, with impressed veins; lower surface hairy. Blade 8–15 cm long, 4–6 cm broad; petiole 2–4 cm long, with 2–5 reddish glands. **FLOWER** 2.5–3.5 cm diam.; petals 5, white; long-stalked; inflorescence an umbel. Mid-spring. **FRUIT** Bright red drupe, egg-shaped, about 2.5 cm diam.; matures late summer to early autumn.

ALABAMA CHERRY

CAROLINA LAURELCHERRY

Alabama Cherry

Carolina Laurelcherry

Sweet Cherry

fruit

fruit

flowers

flowers

stone

stone

fruit

fruit

flowers

underside

HABITAT/RANGE Introduced from Europe, North and West Africa. Escaped from cultivation; established in the East from N.S. and Ont. south to S.C. and Tenn.

SIMILAR SPECIES Similar to Sour Cherry, but that has smaller, less sweet fruit; overall smaller leaves, usually less than 8 cm long; and a petiole 10–24 mm long and lacking glands.

SOUR CHERRY *Prunus cerasus* L.
A.K.A. PIE CHERRY

Deciduous, shrub or small tree to about 6 m tall. Erect or vase-shaped, with a single trunk or multiple. Identified by the combination of double-toothed leaves, bright red fruit not exceeding about 2 cm diam., and a hairless and glandless petiole 10–24 mm long. **HABITAT/RANGE** Introduced from Eurasia. Escaped from cultivation and established in the East from N.S. and Ont. south to n. Ga., Ark., and Kans.; also established in scattered locations in the West. **SIMILAR SPECIES** Generally similar to Sweet Cherry, but that has sweeter fruit, and larger leaves with a petiole 20–40 mm long that has conspicuous glands near its attachment to the blade.

MAHALEB CHERRY *Prunus mahaleb* L.

QUICK ID The only cherry in the East with predominantly circular leaves.

Deciduous small tree, to about 10 m tall, 40 cm diam. **BARK** Dark brown with conspicuous lenticels, becoming shallowly fissured with age. **LEAF** Alternate, simple, oval to nearly circular, base rounded, truncate, or heart-shaped, tip pinched to a sharp point; margins finely toothed. Upper surface lustrous, dark green; lower surface paler, hairy on the midvein. Blade 2.5–5 cm long, nearly as broad; petiole 5–20 mm long, with reddish glands. **FLOWER** About 18 mm diam.; petals 5, white, circular; inflorescence a raceme 3–4 cm long with 10 or fewer flowers, arising from the leaf axils. Spring. **FRUIT** Black or reddish-black drupe, rounded, about 8 mm diam.

HABITAT/RANGE Introduced from Eurasia. Escaped from cultivation, naturalized along roadsides, fencerows, fields, and vacant lots, 0–1,100 m; established in the East from Mass., N.Y., and Ont., south to N.C. and Okla.; also established in scattered locations in the West.

EUROPEAN BIRD CHERRY *Prunus padus* L.

QUICK ID Identified by the combination of sharply toothed leaves, small black fruit, and smooth bark.

Deciduous large shrub or tree 9–12 m tall. **BARK** Gray, smooth to finely roughened. Erect, single trunk; crown rounded, low-branching, with ascending branches. **LEAF** Alternate, simple, obovate or elliptic, tip abruptly pinched to a point, base wedge-shaped; margins finely and sharply toothed. Upper surface dull, dark green; lower surface grayish, usually hairless on the tissue, often with tufts of hairs in the vein axils. Turns yellow or bronze in autumn. Blade 5–13 cm long, 2.5–5 cm broad; petiole 8–20 mm long, hairless or finely hairy, with 1–4 glands near the point of blade attachment. **FLOWER** 8–14 mm diam.; petals 5, white; inflorescence an erect or drooping raceme 8–15 cm long. Mid- to late spring. **FRUIT** Rounded black drupe, 4–8 mm diam.; matures summer.

HABITAT/RANGE Introduced from Europe and Asia. Escaped from cultivation, 0–1,700 m; established in the East, mostly in the North and Northeast, from N.B. and Ont. sparingly south to N.J., Pa., and Ill.; also the Pacific Northwest.

SIMILAR SPECIES Very similar to Chokecherry, but the petals of European Bird Cherry average 6–9 mm long, and the sepals are 1.2–2 mm long, with the length greater than width; petals of Chokecherry are 2.5–4 mm long, and the sepals are 0.7–1 mm, the length about equal to the width.

Sour Cherry

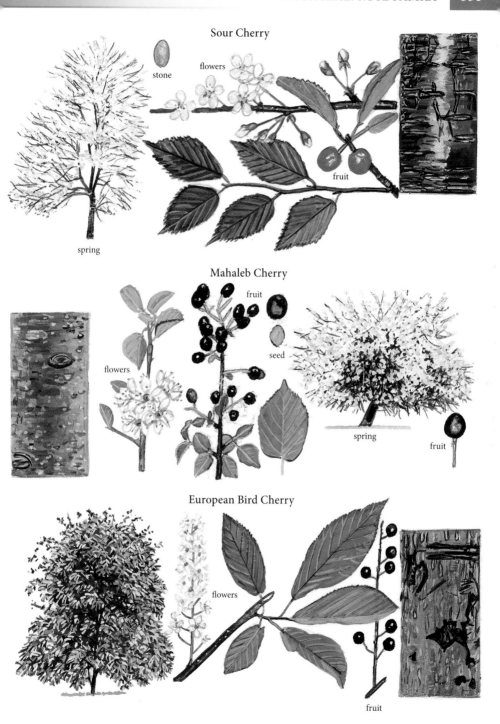

stone

flowers

fruit

spring

Mahaleb Cherry

fruit

flowers

seed

spring

fruit

European Bird Cherry

flowers

fruit

WINTER-FLOWERING CHERRY
Prunus subhirtella Miq.
A.K.A. HIGAN CHERRY

QUICK ID Distinguished by the combination of a hairy petiole 5–10 mm long, leaf base bluntly rounded, leaf margins sharply double-toothed, lower leaf surface hairy along the midvein and lateral veins, twigs and branches thornless, and fruit hairless.

Deciduous small tree, 3–10 m tall. Erect, single trunk; crown vase-shaped, spreading, with crooked branches. **BARK** Grayish brown, lenticels prominent. **TWIG** Hairy. **LEAF** Alternate, simple, elliptic, oblong, or ovate, base bluntly rounded, tip pinched to a point; margins double-toothed, the teeth sharp and gland-tipped. Upper surface hairless or hairy along the midvein; lower surface hairy along the midvein and lateral veins. Blade 3–8 cm long, 1.5–4 cm broad; petiole 5–10 mm long, hairy, with glands near or at the point of blade attachment. **FLOWER** 1.5–3 cm diam.; petals 5, pale pink. Mid-spring. **FRUIT** Rounded, hairless black drupe, to about 8 mm diam.; matures early summer.

HABITAT/RANGE Introduced from Asia. Disturbed sites, old plantings, rarely escaped from cultivation, 0–200 m; sparingly naturalized, Ohio, Va., D.C.

YOSHINO CHERRY *Prunus yedoensis*
Matsum.

QUICK ID Distinguished by the combination of a hairy petiole, 1–2 cm long; leaf with base rounded, tip abruptly tapered, and margins double-toothed, the blade hairy along the veins beneath; and flowers externally hairy and appearing before the leaves emerge.

Deciduous small tree, 4–8 m tall. **BARK** Gray, smooth, with brownish lenticels. **TWIG** Sparsely hairy. **LEAF** Alternate, simple, elliptic, ovate, or obovate, drooping, base rounded, tip abruptly tapering to a point; margins double-toothed, the teeth bristle-tipped and glandular. Upper surface dark green, hairless; lower surface hairy on the midvein and lateral veins. Blade 5–12 cm long, 2.5–7 cm broad; petiole 1–2 cm long, hairy, sometimes with 1 or 2 glands near the attachment to the blade. **FLOWER** 15–35 mm diam.; petals 5, white, pink, or white blushed with pink. Mid-spring. **FRUIT** Hairless, rounded black drupe, 7–12 mm diam.; matures late spring.

HABITAT/RANGE Introduced from Japan. Disturbed sites, abandoned plantings, very rarely escaped from cultivation, reported in Washington, D.C.

APRICOT *Prunus armeniaca* L.

QUICK ID Recognized by the combination of broadly ovate to nearly circular leaves, flowers pink in bud, and hairy fruit, the stone not pitted.

Deciduous small tree, 5–10 m tall. Erect, single trunk; crown rounded, dense, with crooked branches. **BARK** Gray, furrowed. **TWIG** Hairless. **LEAF** Alternate, simple, broadly ovate to nearly circular, base usually rounded, tip often abruptly pinched to a short point; margins single- or double-toothed, the teeth blunt, gland-tipped. Upper surface hairless, lower surface hairy along the veins. Blade 3–9 cm long, 2–8 cm broad; petiole 12–45 mm long, with 1–5 glands near the point of attachment to the blade or on the adjacent blade margins. **FLOWER** 1.5–2.5 cm diam.; petals 5, pink in bud, opening white. Mid-spring. **FRUIT** Hairy, rounded or ellipsoid yellow or orange drupe, 2–6 cm diam., surface of stone not pitted; the apricot of commerce, maturing in summer.

HABITAT/RANGE Introduced from China. Disturbed sites, roadsides, abandoned plantings, 20–1,600 m; occasionally established in the East, Pa., Ill., Mo., Kans., perhaps elsewhere.

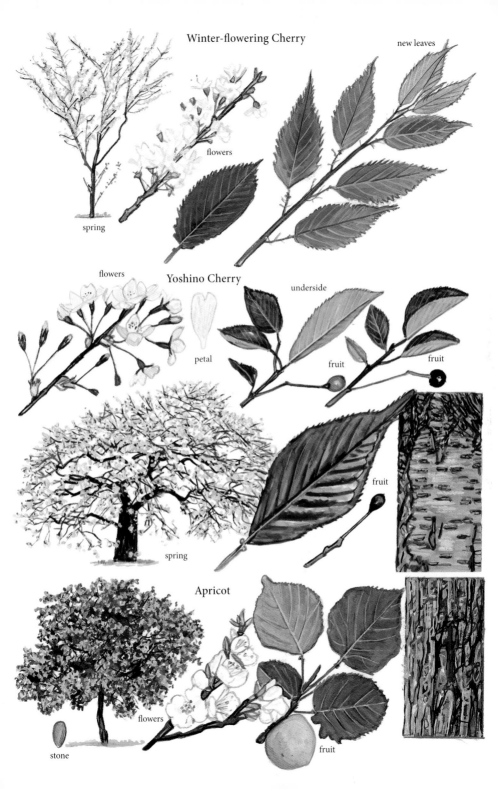

Winter-flowering Cherry

new leaves

flowers

spring

Yoshino Cherry

flowers

petal

underside

fruit

fruit

fruit

spring

Apricot

flowers

fruit

stone

CHERRY PLUM *Prunus cerasifera* Ehrh.
A.K.A. Myrobalan Plum

QUICK ID Identified by the combination of hairless, glandless petioles, purplish-red or yellow drupes, leaves usually less than 7 cm long and often purple in color, and inflorescences with only 1 or 2 flowers.

Deciduous small tree, 4–8 m tall, to 35 cm diam. Erect, single trunk, occasionally with multiple trunks; crown oval, dense, with ascending branches. **BARK** Dark gray, becoming furrowed with age. **TWIG** Purplish, hairless. **LEAF** Alternate, simple, ovate, elliptic, or obovate, base blunt, tip bluntly pointed; margins single- or double-toothed, the teeth blunt, gland-tipped. Upper surface hairless, lower surface hairy along the midvein and lateral veins; both surfaces sometimes purplish. Blade 3–7 cm long, 1.5–3.5 cm broad; petiole 5–20 cm long, hairless or with a few hairs, lacking glands. **FLOWER** 1.5–2.5 cm diam.; petals 5, white or pale reddish pink; inflorescence with 1 or 2 flowers. Early to mid-spring. **FRUIT** Hairless, egg-shaped or ellipsoid purplish-red or yellow drupe, 1.5–3 cm diam.; matures summer.

HABITAT/RANGE Introduced from Asia. Roadsides, stream banks, escaped from cultivation, 0–900 m; established in scattered locations throughout the East, Ont. to Ga.

PEACH *Prunus persica* (L.) Batsch

QUICK ID The combination of comparatively long, narrow leaves and the distinctive fruit is diagnostic.

Deciduous small tree, 3–10 m tall; commercially cultivated and escaped plants often shrubby. Erect, single trunk, crown usually open, with more or less ascending branches. **BARK** Reddish brown. **TWIG** Hairless. **LEAF** Alternate, simple, lanceolate, long-elliptic, or oblanceolate, often folded upward from the midrib, base wedge-shaped or bluntly rounded, tip long-tapering, often pinched to a point at the apex; margins finely and bluntly toothed, the teeth gland-tipped. Surfaces bright green, hairless. Blade 4–15 cm long, 2–4.5 cm broad; petiole 5–15 mm long, hairless, often bearing glands near the point of blade attachment or on the adjacent leaf margin. **FLOWER** 2–4 cm diam.; petals 5, dark pink. Early spring. **FRUIT** Rounded yellowish or orange drupe, often tinged red, usually hairy, 4–8 cm diam., stone pitted; the peach of commerce, maturing in summer.

HABITAT/RANGE Introduced from China. Fencerows, old fields, roadsides, abandoned plantings, escaped from cultivation, 0–2,300 m; established nearly throughout the East.

WEST INDIAN CHERRY *Prunus myrtifolia* (L.) Urb.
A.K.A. West Indies Cherry, Myrtle Laurel Cherry

QUICK ID The only cherry likely to be encountered in southernmost Florida.

Evergreen small tree, 6–12 m tall, about 30 cm diam. Erect, single trunk, not producing suckers as in some cherries. Crown rounded. **BARK** Reddish brown or grayish. **LEAF** Alternate, simple, thick, somewhat stiff, elliptic or broadly elliptic, tip pinched to an abrupt blunt point; margins entire, often wavy. Upper surface hairless, lower surface usually with 2 circular or oval glands near the base. Blade 4–10 cm long, 2–5 cm broad; petiole 8–16 mm long, glandless. **FLOWER** 1.5–2.5 cm diam.; petals 5, white, more or less circular or obovate; stamens 15–20. Midwinter. **FRUIT** Purplish-black drupe, rounded or egg-shaped, 8–12 mm long; matures mid-spring to early summer.

HABITAT/RANGE Native. Subtropical hammocks, pinelands, 0–10 m; restricted in the East to southernmost peninsular Fla.

SIMILAR SPECIES Somewhat similar to Carolina Laurelcherry, but the two do not overlap in range; West Indian Cherry is distinguished by the wider, more bluntly pointed leaves and earlier, mostly winter flowering period.

WEST INDIAN CHERRY

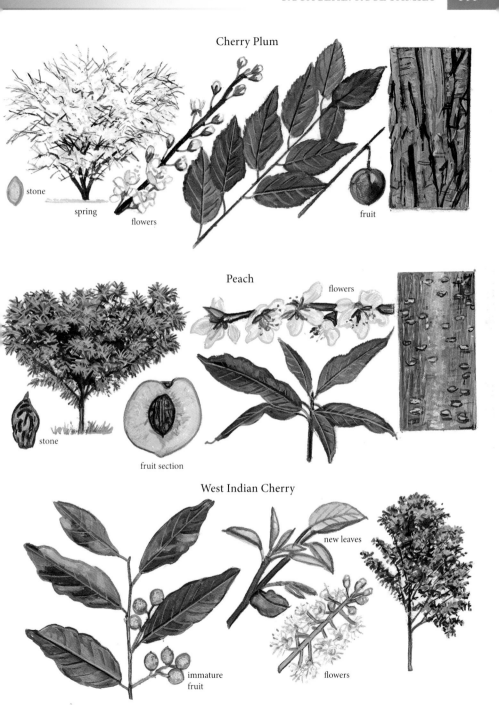

Cherry Plum

stone

spring

flowers

fruit

Peach

flowers

stone

fruit section

West Indian Cherry

new leaves

immature
fruit

flowers

◼ *PYRUS*: PEARS

The pears are introduced species native to Asia or Europe. All are cultivated in the East for ornament or fruit production. Callery Pear, often called Bradford Pear, in particular, has become an exceedingly popular landscape tree and is widely planted in residential and commercial settings and along roadways. Numerous cultivars are available for these species, making precise descriptions of them difficult.

CALLERY PEAR *Pyrus calleryana* Decne.
A.K.A. BRADFORD PEAR, RED SPIRE

QUICK ID The distinctly oval crown, rigidly ascending branches, and lustrous, dark green leaves that become scarlet or purplish in autumn make this tree easy to identify.

Deciduous tree, 9–15 m tall. Erect, single trunk; crown pyramidal when young, becoming more or less oval with rigidly ascending branches at maturity and a consistent form from tree to tree. **BARK** Lustrous brown and smooth when young, becoming grayish, scaly, and shallow-furrowed. **LEAF** Alternate, simple, leathery; oval, oblong, or nearly circular; margins wavy, toothed. Upper surface coppery at first, becoming lustrous, dark green in summer, changing to purplish or scarlet in autumn. Blade 4–8 cm long, nearly as broad; petiole 10–15 mm long. **FLOWER** 15–25 mm diam.; petals 5, white. Profuse in mid-spring. **FRUIT**

Coppery-russet pome, to about 15 mm long; matures late summer.

HABITAT/RANGE Introduced from Asia. Escaped from cultivation in disturbed sites; widely planted and established in the East; N.J. west to Ill., south to n. Fla., west to Tex. and Okla.

COMMON PEAR *Pyrus communis* L.

Deciduous tree, to about 15 m tall; crown columnar when young, becoming spreading, open, and somewhat contorted and drooping with age. **LEAF** Alternate, simple, oval or oblong, with bluntly toothed margins; 5–10 cm long. **FRUIT** Easily identified by the fruit, the pear of commerce; matures autumn. **HABITAT/RANGE** Introduced from Europe and w. Asia; cultivated and rarely established.

CHINESE PEAR *Pyrus pyrifolia* (Burm.) Nak.
A.K.A. CHINESE SAND PEAR

Deciduous tree to about 13 m tall. **LEAF** Alternate, simple, lustrous, dark green above with toothed margins, the marginal teeth conspicuously bristle-tipped, which aids identification; 7–12 cm long. **FRUIT** Spotted pome, 5–7 cm diam. **HABITAT/RANGE** Introduced from China; cultivated and rarely established, reported in mid-Atlantic.

Callery Pear

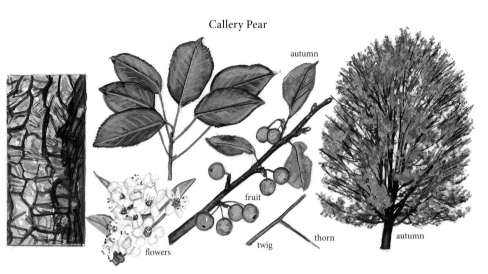

autumn

fruit

flowers

twig

thorn

autumn

Common Pear

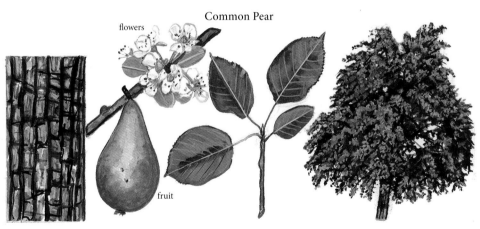

flowers

fruit

Chinese Pear

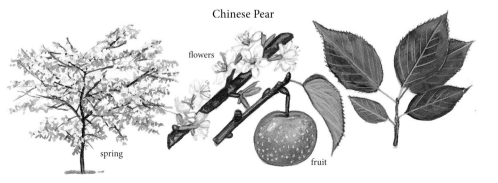

spring

flowers

fruit

▇ *SORBUS*: MOUNTAIN ASHES

Mountain ashes are confined to the Northern Hemisphere, mostly in cool, moist sites, often in poor soils. Conservative estimates include about 75 species in this genus but some experts recognize as many as 260 species; 3 species are native to e. North America.

Deciduous shrubs or small trees. **LEAF** Alternate, pinnately compound, mostly with 9–17 leaflets; rarely simple. **FLOWER** Usually white, 5-petaled. **FRUIT** Red pome, usually retained on the tree until at least mid-autumn.

Hybridization within the genus is common, as is the production of viable seeds in the absence of pollination. Species of *Sorbus* hybridize with species of serviceberry (*Amelanchier*) and chokeberry (*Aronia*, see *Photinia*) to produce the hybrid genera *Amelasorbus* and *Sorbaronia*. Several species are attractive ornamentals, appreciated for their leaves, flowers, and red fruits. Fruits provide food to wildlife when other foods are scarce.

AMERICAN MOUNTAIN ASH *Sorbus americana* Marshall

QUICK ID The combination of alternate compound leaves, showy clusters of bright red pomes, and grayish bark is diagnostic.

Deciduous shrub or small, contorted tree, to about 18 m tall, to about 50 cm diam. Erect, single trunk, sometimes with multiple trunks; crown spreading, with a more or less rounded top. **BARK** Grayish or reddish brown and smooth when young, becoming gray, scaly, furrowed, and exfoliating in plates at maturity. **TWIG** Hairless, reddish brown; terminal bud sticky. **LEAF** Alternate, pinnately compound, with a reddish rachis; blade 15–23 cm long; petiole 5–7.5 cm long, often twisted, orienting the leaf perpendicular to the ground. Leaflets 9–17,

opposite, coarse, stiff, 3–8 cm long, narrowly elliptic or lanceolate, tip tapering to a point; margins of leaflets finely and sharply toothed. Upper surface dull yellowish green or dark green; lower surface paler, hairless. **FLOWER** About 7 mm diam.; petals 5, white, circular; inflorescence a dense, showy, flat-topped cluster 8–15 cm wide. Early summer. **FRUIT** Rounded, bright red or orange-red pome, 4–8 mm diam.; matures and most showy late summer to autumn, often persisting into early winter.

HABITAT/RANGE Native. Cold swamps in the northern part of the range, open sites, rocky slopes above 1,000 m in s. Appalachians, 0–1,800 m; Nfld., Ont., and Minn., south to Tenn. and extreme ne. Ga.

SIMILAR SPECIES Similar and difficult to distinguish from Northern Mountain Ash, which has usually broader leaflets and lacks the twisted petiole. Potentially confused with the similar-leaved Staghorn Sumac and Smooth Sumac (*Rhus typhina* and *R. glabra*, Anacardiaceae) when flowers and fruits are absent, but neither of those species has scaly grayish bark, and the twigs of Staghorn Sumac are hairy, while the leaves of Smooth Sumac have up to 21 leaflets and are much longer.

NORTHERN MOUNTAIN ASH *Sorbus decora* (Sarg.) C.K. Schneid.
A.K.A. SHOWY MOUNTAIN ASH

QUICK ID The combination of bright red pomes mostly 8–10 mm diam., sticky terminal buds, and alternate compound leaves is diagnostic.

Deciduous small tree, to about 15 m tall, 25 cm diam. Erect, single straight trunk; crown short, rounded. **BARK** Grayish or grayish green, smooth when young; scaly and exfoliating, at least near the base when mature. **TWIG** Reddish brown or grayish, hairless; buds dark reddish brown, sticky. **LEAF**

AMERICAN MOUNTAIN ASH

NORTHERN MOUNTAIN ASH

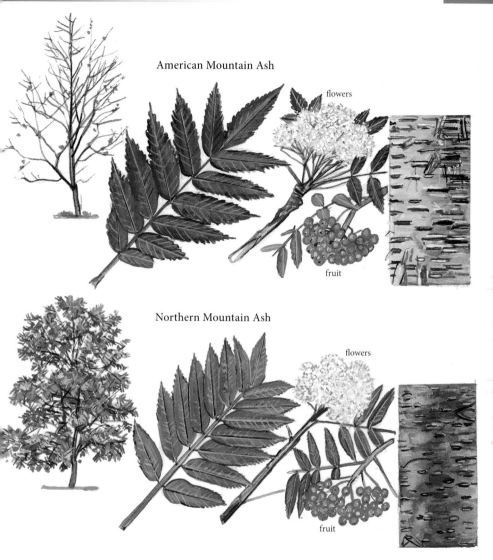

American Mountain Ash

flowers

fruit

Northern Mountain Ash

flowers

fruit

Alternate, pinnately compound, with a reddish rachis; blade to about 25 cm long; petiole to about 5 cm long. Leaflets 11–17, coarse, stiff, 3–8 cm long, narrowly elliptic, often broadest at the middle; leaflet margins finely toothed, occasionally entire toward the base. Upper surface bluish green; lower surface paler, hairy at first, becoming mostly hairless. **FLOWER** About 1 cm diam.; petals 5, circular; inflorescence a dense, flat-topped cluster. Late spring to early summer, slightly later than American Mountain Ash. **FRUIT** Rounded, bright red pome, 6–10 mm diam.; matures late summer to early autumn.

HABITAT/RANGE Native. Rocky shores of rivers and lakes, adaptable to many soils and conditions, 150–600 m; Pa., Ohio, Ind., Ill., and Iowa, north to Greenland.

SIMILAR SPECIES American Mountain Ash has narrower leaflets and a twisted petiole; European Mountain Ash lacks sticky buds.

EUROPEAN MOUNTAIN ASH *Sorbus aucuparia* L.

QUICK ID The bright red fruit, alternate compound leaves, and unsticky terminal buds help distinguish this species.

Deciduous small tree, to about 18 m tall, 80 cm diam. Erect, single short trunk; crown open, rounded. **BARK** Smooth on young trees, becoming scaly and gray at maturity. **TWIG** Slender, reddish, hairy at first, becoming hairless with age; buds not sticky. **LEAF** Alternate, pinnately compound, blade 12–25 cm long; petiole to about 2 cm long. Leaflets 9–17, each 2.5–7.5 cm long, narrowly elliptic or lanceolate, tip blunt or acute, margins sharply toothed. Upper surface green, lower surface paler. **FLOWER** About 1 cm diam.; petals 5, white, circular. **FRUIT** Rounded, bright red pome, 8–10 mm diam.

HABITAT/RANGE Introduced from Eurasia. Widely planted, escaped from cultivation in disturbed sites; Nfld., west to Ont., south to Iowa, Ill., W.Va., and Md.

SIMILAR SPECIES The buds of the American Mountain Ash and the Northern Mountain Ash are sticky.

GREENLAND MOUNTAIN ASH *Sorbus groenlandica* (C.K. Schneid.) Á. Löve & D. Löve

QUICK ID Uncommon, very small mountain ash found mainly in Maritime Canada.

Deciduous shrub or very small tree, 1–3 m tall. Closely related to Northern Mountain Ash and originally described as *S. decora* var. *groenlandica* (C.K. Schneid.) G. N. Jones. **TWIG** Buds are sticky, with reddish-brown outer scales and white-hairy inner scales. **LEAF** Compound, with 11–17 oblong, sharply toothed leaflets, each with an acute tip. **FRUIT** Lustrous red pome, sometimes with a whitish bloom.

HABITAT/RANGE Native. 150–600 m; this species ranges from Lab. and s. Greenland to Maine and N.H., but is nowhere common.

GREENLAND MOUNTAIN ASH

OAKLEAF MOUNTAIN ASH *Sorbus hybrida* L.

Deciduous tree, 10–15 m tall, to about 60 cm diam. **LEAF** With 6–9 lobes, only the lower 2 pairs of lobes cutting to the midrib; upper surface green, lower surface distinctly white-hairy. **FRUIT** Bright red pome, 12–15 mm diam. **HABITAT/RANGE** Introduced from Norway, Sweden, and Finland; sparingly naturalized from cultivation in e. Canada and New England from N.B. south to N.H. and Vt. *Notes:* A hybrid between *S. aucuparia* and the Swedish species *S. intermedia* (Ehrh.) Pers.

European Mountain Ash

flowers

fruit

Greenland Mountain Ash

fruit

fruit

Oakleaf Mountain Ash

underside

flowers

fruit

RUBIACEAE: MADDER FAMILY

The madder or coffee family includes about 550 genera and 9,000 species of woody and herbaceous plants worldwide, mostly from warm temperate and tropical regions (a few in colder climes); 11 genera with trees occur in North America, 9 with native species, all represented in the East.

LEAF Opposite or whorled, simple, the petioles subtended by conspicuous, fused stipules that are joined across the node. **FLOWER** Usually bisexual and radial, occasionally unisexual (sometimes by abortion), often aggregated into clusters. Sepals, petals, and stamens are 4 or 5 each, the petals joined into a usually funnel-shaped corolla. The ovary is inferior, usually 2-celled, with a superimposed nectar disk. **FRUIT** Capsule, berry, drupe, schizocarp, indehiscent podlike structure, or fleshy syncarp formed from the coalescence of several flowers.

The family is best known as the source of coffee (genus *Coffea*). The drugs quinine (*Cinchona*) and ipecac (*Psychotria*), and many ornamentals including gardenia (*Gardenia*), come from the family. A red dye from madder (*Rubia*) was important prior to the development of synthetic dyes.

COMMON BUTTONBUSH
Cephalanthus occidentalis L.
A.K.A. HONEY-BALLS, GLOBE-FLOWERS

QUICK ID Recognized by simple, opposite or whorled leaves and distinctive creamy-white globular heads of numerous tubular flowers.

Deciduous, usually a shrub, occasionally a small tree, 3–15 m tall, to 30 cm diam. Erect, a single main trunk, rarely multiple; crown open, vase-shaped, spreading or ascending. **BARK** Smooth at first, becoming ridged, furrowed, and roughened. **TWIG** Reddish brown, usually hairy at first, becoming nearly hairless; decorated with corky lenticels, leaf scars U-shaped. **LEAF** Opposite or in whorls of 3 or 4 per node, simple, lanceolate or elliptic; base wedge-shaped or nearly rounded, rarely heart-shaped; tip abruptly long- or short-pointed. Upper surface lustrous, dark green; lower surface paler, hairy or not, veins conspicuous. Blade 6–19 cm long, 1.5–10 cm broad; petiole 5–30 mm long, hairy or not. **FLOWER** Bisexual, creamy white, tubular, numerous, produced in a globular, pendent, ball-like head 2–4 cm diam.; corolla 5–10 mm long, with 4 short, rounded lobes; stamens 4. Spring to early summer. **FRUIT** Capsule (or capsule-like), 5–8 mm long, splitting from the base at maturity into indehiscent nutlets; matures summer to autumn.

HABITAT/RANGE Native. Swamps, lake and pond margins, wetland depressions, shallow ponds, banks of small streams, 0–550 m; widespread across the East, west to Nebr., Tex., Ariz., and Calif.

SIMILAR SPECIES Georgia Fevertree (*Pinckneya bracteata*) is vegetatively similar and also grows in wetlands; it is easily distinguished by its showy pink flower clusters and smoother fruit capsules.

Notes: Cephalanthus is a genus of about 6 species distributed in the Americas, Asia, Africa, and China.

BLACKTORCH *Erithalis fruticosa* L.

QUICK ID Recognized within its U.S. range by the combination of opposite leaves often clustered near the branch tips, jointed twigs, and dense crown.

COMMON BUTTONBUSH

Common Buttonbush

flower

flowers

Blacktorch

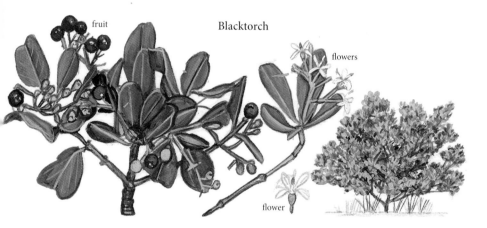

fruit

flowers

flower

Evergreen, usually a low, compact shrub, rarely a spindly tree, usually not exceeding about 3 m tall, rarely to 6 m. Erect, usually with a single short, low-branched trunk; crown dense, rounded, with numerous branches. **BARK** Dark and light brown. **TWIG** Stout, often appearing jointed. **LEAF** Opposite, often clustered near the branch tips, simple, thin, flat; oval, elliptic, broadly obovate, or circular; base wedge-shaped; tip rounded or bluntly pointed; margins entire. Upper surface lustrous, dark or medium green; lower surface paler. Blade 2–10 cm long, 2–6 cm broad; petiole 10–15 mm long. **FLOWER** Bisexual, small, 4–8 mm long; petals 3–8, usually 5, narrowly linear, spreading; stamens and stigma exerted beyond the corolla; produced in long-stalked cymes. Year-round. **FRUIT** Rounded, several-seeded, lustrous black drupe to about 1 cm long. Year-round.

HABITAT/RANGE Native. Subtropical hammocks, coastal scrub; s. Fla. including Fla. Keys.

Notes: Erithalis is a genus of about 10 species distributed largely in the West Indies.

BLACKTORCH

SNOWBERRY *Chiococca alba* (L.) Hitchc.

QUICK ID Recognized by the evergreen opposite leaves and hanging clusters of slightly flattened white drupes.

Somewhat similar to Blacktorch (*Erithalis fruticosa*). Usually a scraggly, vinelike shrub, with clusters of small tubular yellow to white flowers with reflexed petals, followed by round white fruits that are often laterally flattened.

HABITAT/RANGE Native; Fla. and extreme s. Tex.

CARIBBEAN PRINCEWOOD *Exostema caribaeum* (Jacq.) Roem. & Schult.

QUICK ID Recognized by the combination of opposite, crowded, lustrous leaves; comparatively large, showy whitish flowers; and jointed twigs with conspicuous encircling stipules.

Evergreen shrub or small tree, 6–8 m tall, to about 10 cm diam. Erect, single trunk; crown spreading. BARK Smooth, becoming fissured, dark gray, with conspicuous lenticels. TWIG Slender, gray, hairless, each node usually with a pair of fused stipules that encircle the stem. LEAF Opposite, often crowded at the branch tips and appearing whorled, simple, leathery; ovate, elliptic, or lanceolate; base wedge-shaped or broadly pointed; tip abruptly pointed; margins entire. Upper surface lustrous, dark green, hairless, usually reflexed upward from the midvein. Blade 3–11 cm long, 1–5 cm broad; petiole 5–10 mm long. FLOWER Bisexual; corolla tubular below, the tube 3–5 cm long; petals 5, white or pinkish, strap-shaped, flaring and recurved at the apex; stamens 5, anthers to about 2 cm long; pistil 1, extending well beyond the corolla. Spring to autumn, nearly year-round. FRUIT Upright, ovoid to ellipsoid, 2-valved, hard, lustrous, dark brown capsule, 1–1.5 cm long; seeds brown, winged, 3–6 mm long. Year-round.

HABITAT/RANGE Native. Subtropical hammocks, pinelands; s. Fla., more common in Fla. Keys. Treated as endangered in Fla.

SIMILAR SPECIES The leaves of Seven-year Apple (*Genipa clusiifolia*) are obovate.

SEVEN-YEAR APPLE *Genipa clusiifolia* (Jacq.) Griseb.

QUICK ID Recognized within its U.S. range by the combination of opposite, lustrous, obovate leaves with conspicuous lateral venation and a usually notched tip; star-shaped flowers; and large ovoid berries.

Evergreen shrub or small tree, to about 6 m tall. Erect or vase-shaped, single trunk or multiple; crown open, branches stout, largely leafless except near the tip. BARK Gray, smooth. TWIG Stout, appearing jointed, the nodes encircled by conspicuous fused stipules. LEAF Opposite, often crowded at the branch tip, simple, stiff, leathery; obovate, base wedge-shaped, tip rounded or notched; margins entire, slightly rolled under. Upper surface lustrous, dark green, midvein yellowish. Blade 5–15 cm long, 2.5–7.5 cm broad; petiole to about 1 cm long, slightly winged. FLOWER Unisexual, male and female produced on separate plants, about 2 cm diam.; corolla white or yellowish white, sometimes tinged pink, tubular below; petals 5 or 6, spreading to form a starlike pattern; stamens 5 or 6. Year-round. FRUIT Comparatively large, hard, fleshy, ovoid or obovoid berry, 5–10 cm long; green at first, becoming yellow, then black; seeds numerous, flat. Year-round.

HABITAT/RANGE Native. Coastal hammocks and adjoining ecotones; s. Fla. and Fla. Keys.

SNOWBERRY

CARIBBEAN PRINCEWOOD

SEVEN-YEAR APPLE

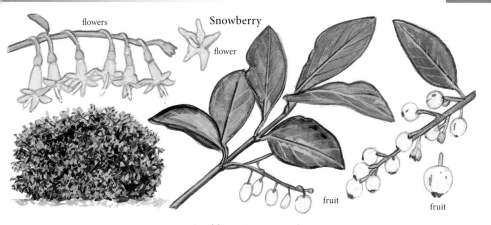

flowers

Snowberry

flower

fruit

fruit

Caribbean Princewood

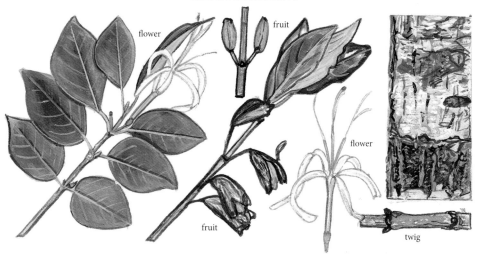

flower

fruit

flower

fruit

twig

Seven-year Apple

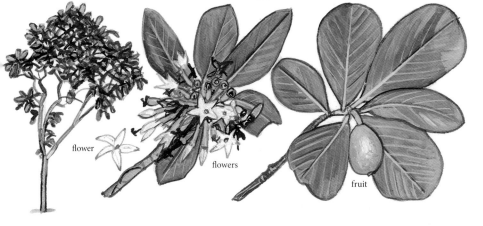

flower

flowers

fruit

■ *GUETTARDA*: VELVETSEEDS

A genus of 60–100 species distributed mostly in tropical America and the South Pacific, with 1 species in China and 1 along coasts of the Indian Ocean and e. Pacific. **LEAF** Opposite, or borne 3 to a node, simple, petiole conspicuous or nearly absent. **FLOWER** Borne in 2-parted or congested flat-topped clusters in the leaf axils; corolla funnel-like, usually white, sometimes tinged pink, flaring at the apex into 4–9 petal-like lobes; calyx tubular, with 4–9 teeth at the apex; stamens 4–9, usually concealed within the corolla; styles variable in length, very short and hidden within the corolla to elongated and exerted from the corolla. **FRUIT** Fleshy, often velvety (in ours), rounded to ovoid, oblong, or sometimes angular drupe.

HAMMOCK VELVETSEED *Guettarda elliptica* Sw.

QUICK ID Recognized in its U.S. range by the white to pinkish 4-petaled flowers, velvety-hairy red and black fruit, and oval or circular leaves that are soft to the touch above.

Evergreen shrub or small, spindly tree, to about 6 m tall, to about 28 cm diam. Erect, contorted, single main trunk; crown open, branches slender, arching. **BARK** Smooth, grayish. **TWIG** Slender, round, usually with conspicuous whitish lenticels. **LEAF** Opposite, simple, moderately stiff, usually thick, sometimes papery; oval, obovate, or nearly circular; base flattened or broadly pointed; tip rounded or broadly pointed, the central vein often extending slightly beyond the blade tip; margins entire. Upper surface dull, dark green, finely hairy or not, smooth, lateral veins conspicuous, usually somewhat impressed; lower surface paler, usually finely hairy. Blade 3–7.5 cm long, 1–4.5 cm broad;

petiole to about 12 mm long. **FLOWER** Bisexual, radial, about 6 mm diam.; corolla white, tinged pink, tubular below, flaring into 4 rounded or narrow, spreading, often crinkly lobes; inflorescence axillary, with 1–10 (usually 3) flowers, the main stalk to about 3 cm long. Year-round, predominantly spring to summer. **FRUIT** Rounded, velvety-hairy drupe, 4–10 mm diam.; red at first, turning black. Year-round.

HABITAT/RANGE Native. Subtropical hammocks, pinelands; s. Fla and Fla. Keys.

SIMILAR SPECIES Rough Velvetseed is distinguished by the upper surface of the leaf being very rough to the touch.

ROUGH VELVETSEED *Guettarda scabra* (L.) Vent.

QUICK ID Recognized in its U.S. range by its ovate or obovate leaves, the upper surface very rough to the touch, and the velvety reddish to black fruit.

Evergreen shrub or tree, potentially to 10 m tall and 4 cm diam. in hammocks; usually a shrub not exceeding about 1.5 m tall in pinelands. Erect or contorted, single main trunk; crown narrow, spreading, sparsely branched. **BARK** Smooth, dark brown, rarely scaly. **TWIG** Slender, densely hairy. **LEAF** Opposite, simple, stiff, thick; elliptic, obovate, or ovate; base broadly wedge-shaped, blunt, or heart-shaped; tip bluntly short-pointed, the main vein often extending slightly beyond the blade tip. Upper surface lustrous green, harshly rough to the touch, the veins conspicuously impressed; lower surface paler, finely hairy. Blade 3–15 cm long, 2–8 cm broad; petiole 5–20 mm long, stout. **FLOWER** Bisexual; corolla white, tinged pink, tubular below, flaring into 5–7 spreading lobes;

HAMMOCK VELVETSEED

ROUGH VELVETSEED

Hammock Velvetseed

fruit

developing flowers

fruit

Rough Velvetseed

flowers

fruit

fruit

inflorescence axillary, with 1–10 flowers, the main stalk 2–10 cm long. Year-round, predominantly spring to summer. **FRUIT** Rounded, velvety-hairy drupe, 6–12 mm diam., red at first, becoming black. Year-round.

HABITAT/RANGE Native. Subtropical hammocks, pinelands; s. Fla. and Fla. Keys.

SIMILAR SPECIES Distinguished from Hammock Velvetseed by the upper surface of the leaf soft to the touch.

TORCH TREE *Ixora arborea* Roxb. ex Sm.
A.K.A. SMALLFLOWER JUNGLEFLAME

QUICK ID Recognized in its naturalized U.S. range by the dense ball-like flower clusters, the flowers with narrow white or pinkish petals.

Evergreen small tree, 3–5 m tall, 3–10 cm diam. Erect, single trunk or multiple; crown densely branched, spreading. **BARK** Yellowish brown. **LEAF** Opposite, simple, narrowly elliptic, oblong, or slightly obovate; base rounded or broadly wedge-shaped; tip abruptly short-pointed; margins entire. Upper surface lustrous, dark green, midvein yellowish; lower surface paler. Blade 7–12 cm long, 3–5 cm broad; petiole 5–10 mm long. **FLOWER** Bisexual, fragrant; corolla white, sometimes tinged pink, about 1 cm long; petals 4, narrow, spreading; inflorescence a showy, rounded, many-flowered terminal cluster. Year-round. **FRUIT** Rounded green or black berry to about 6 mm diam. Year-round.

HABITAT/RANGE Introduced from Asia. Cultivated and naturalized; s. Fla.

Notes: A genus of 300–400 species distributed in tropical Africa, America, Asia, Madagascar, and Pacific islands. *Ixora coccinea* L., a shrub with red flowers, is also reported as naturalized in Fla.

SCARLETBUSH *Hamelia patens* Jacq.

QUICK ID Easily distinguished from other shrubs and trees in s. Fla. by the combination of the whorled leaves with reddish veins that fold upward from the midvein, the tubular orange-red flowers, and the reddish to purplish-black berry.

Evergreen or deciduous, usually a shrub, rarely a small tree, 3–5 m tall. Erect, vase-shaped, or rounded; crown dense, leafy, especially on shrubby plants. **BARK** Reddish brown, smooth, sometimes peeling. **TWIG** Slender, hairy, brownish. **LEAF** Whorled, 3–7 leaves per node; simple, elliptic, ovate, or oblong; base rounded or broadly wedge-shaped; tip abruptly short-pointed; margins entire. Upper surface lustrous green, veins reddish, conspicuous, finely hairy, usually reflexed upward from the midvein; lower surface pale green, finely densely hairy. Blade 5–15 cm long, 2–9 cm broad; petiole 1–5 cm long, reddish. **FLOWER** Bisexual; corolla tubular, 1.5–2 cm long, orange-red, finely hairy, minutely divided at the apex into 5 tiny, erect lobes; stamens

5, usually hidden within the corolla; inflorescence a many-flowered, branched terminal or axillary cluster. Year-round. **FRUIT** Finely hairy, oblong or ellipsoid, juicy reddish, purplish, or nearly black berry, 6–10 mm long, 4–6 mm diam. Year-round.

HABITAT/RANGE Native. Hammocks, roadsides, disturbed sites, often cultivated, to about 10 m; c. and s. Fla.

Note: The genus of about 40 species is distributed in tropical and subtropical America; only this species occurs in North America. Often a semi-woody shrub, it may die to the ground in cold winters.

SCARLETBUSH

INDIAN MULBERRY *Morinda citrifolia* L.

QUICK ID Distinguished in its naturalized U.S. range by the combination of large, fleshy, compound fruit; star-shaped flowers; and large elliptic leaves with conspicuous yellowish venation.

Evergreen shrub or small tree to about 6 m tall. Erect, single trunk or multiple, usually low-branched; vase-shaped or rounded, often shrubby in s. Fla.; crown dense. **BARK** Brownish, becoming furrowed. **TWIG** Brownish, angled. **LEAF** Opposite, simple, elliptic, base rounded or broadly wedge-shaped, tip abruptly short-pointed; margins entire. Upper surface lustrous, dark green, veins yellowish, conspicuous, usually impressed; lower surface paler. Blade 12–45 cm long, 7–25 cm broad; petiole to about 2 cm long, stout. **FLOWER** Bisexual, corolla white, tubular below, about 1 cm long, spreading at the summit into 5 lance-shaped lobes; stamens 5–7, hidden within the corolla; inflorescence a dense head of multiple flowers, usually with 1 open, or a few open simultaneously. Year-round. **FRUIT** Distinctive ellipsoid or cylindric, fleshy yellowish syncarp formed from the fusion of the fruits of several flowers; to about 10 cm long, 3 cm diam. Year-round.

Torch Tree

flowers

flower

fruit

fruit

Scarletbush

flowers

flowers

fruit

Indian Mulberry

fruit

fruit
section

seed

flower

HABITAT/RANGE Introduced from India. Cultivated and rarely established in s. Fla.

SIMILAR SPECIES *Morinda* is a genus of 80–100 subtropical and tropical trees and shrubs. Redgal (*M. royoc* L.), a shrub native to c. and s. Fla., has similar fruit, but the leaf blade does not exceed about 10 cm long.

WHITE INDIGOBERRY *Randia aculeata* L.

A.K.A. RANDIA, INDIGOBERRY

QUICKID Recognized by the combination of opposite branches, opposite leaves closely clustered along the twigs and branches, spiny leaf nodes, and white berries.

Evergreen, typically a spiny, densely branched shrub in open, sunny habitats, occasionally a small tree to about 3.5 m tall in hammocks. Erect, single trunk or multiple; crown of arborescent plants open; branches distinctly opposite. **BARK** Smooth, light gray, often splotched with darker spots. **TWIG** Stout, hairless, sharp-tipped and/or spiny at the nodes. **LEAF** Opposite, the leaves usually in dense clusters, simple, thick, stiff; elliptic or obovate; base narrowly wedge-shaped; tip rounded, often with a tiny point at the apex; margins entire. Upper surface medium green or light green, hairless, veins obscure; lower surface paler, hairless or hairy mostly along the midvein. Blade 1–6 cm long, 0.5–3 cm broad; petiole 2–5 mm long, often subtended by a pair of stout, sharp spines to about 1.5 cm long. **FLOWER** Functionally unisexual or bisexual, male and female flowers borne on separate plants, sometimes intermixed with functionally bisexual flowers; fragrant; corolla white; petals 4–6, usually 5, white, spreading. Spring. **FRUIT** Oval berry about 1 cm diam., green at first, becoming exteriorly white with a black pulp; matures summer to winter.

HABITAT/RANGE Native. Pinelands, dune thickets, hammocks, to about 5 m; c. and s. Fla., especially along the coast.

Notes: Randia is a genus of about 250 species distributed mostly in tropical and warm temperate regions of both hemispheres. Two occur in North America, both native, including Crucillo (*R. rhagocarpa* Standl.), a shrub distributed in extreme s. Tex.

GEORGIA FEVERTREE *Pinckneya bracteata* (W. Bartram) Raf.

A.K.A. FEVERTREE

QUICKID Recognized by the combination of wetland habitat; comparatively large, opposite, hairy leaves; flower with a single enlarged pinkish sepal; and capsule fruit 1–3 cm long.

Deciduous large shrub or small tree, to about 8 m tall (tallest in wooded streams and drainage bottoms), usually not exceeding about 10 cm diam. Erect, single trunk; crown open, spreading, more or less flat-topped, the branches often somewhat drooping. **BARK** Smooth, grayish, often with patches of lichens and raised lenticels. **TWIG** Stout, tawny, becoming reddish brown, densely soft-hairy, usually with raised corky lenticels. **LEAF** Opposite or whorled, often clustered near the branch tips; simple, oval, elliptic, or ovate; base broadly wedge-shaped, often extending onto the petiole; tip bluntly or sharply pointed; margins entire. Upper surface lustrous or dull green, usually sparsely hairy; lower surface paler, usually uniformly soft-hairy. Blade 4–20 cm long, 2.5–12 cm broad; petiole 1–3 cm long, subtended by interpetiolar stipules, the remains of which form a circle around the branch. **FLOWER** Bisexual; corolla greenish yellow with brownish markings, tubular, 1.5–2.5 cm long; petals 5, subtended by a 5-parted calyx; 1 sepal much enlarged, leaflike, 6–7 cm long, 4–5 cm broad, usually pinkish, sometimes yellowish or white, usually the showiest part of the flower. Spring to early summer. **FRUIT** Rounded or egg-shaped, 2-valved brown capsule, 1–3 cm long, splitting at maturity to reveal numerous flat tan winged seeds 5–8 mm long; matures summer to autumn.

HABITAT/RANGE Native. Swamps, swamp margins, wooded drainages, bottoms of small streams, pineland bogs, to about 50 m; restricted to the southeastern coastal plains, n. Fla., s. Ga., and se. S.C.

WHITE INDIGOBERRY

GEORGIA FEVERTREE

White Indigoberry

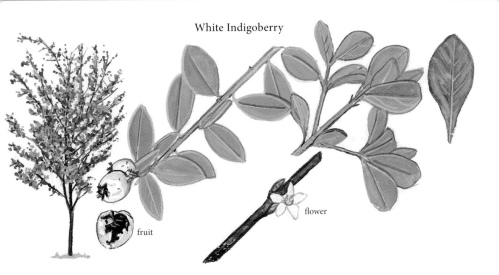

fruit

flower

Georgia Fevertree

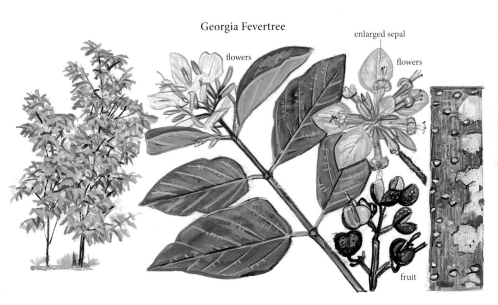

flowers

enlarged sepal

flowers

fruit

SIMILAR SPECIES The leaves of Common Buttonbush (*Cephalanthus occidentalis*) are more often whorled than opposite, and its flowers are whitish, tubular, and borne in pendent globular clusters.

Notes: The genus consists of this single species, native to and restricted to the se. U.S.

RUTACEAE: CITRUS OR RUE FAMILY

The citrus or rue family includes more than 150 genera and 900 species, mostly shrubs and trees, distributed in warm regions of the world; it is most diverse in the Southern Hemisphere. A few are native to the U.S. near its southern border and in s. Fla. Most species in North America are naturalized from cultivation.

LEAF Alternate or opposite, pinnately compound (with or without a terminal leaflet), trifoliolate, or simple by reduction and therefore unifoliolate. Petiole often conspicuously winged. Blade dotted with translucent amber glands that are visible when held up to transmitted light and are loaded with oily chemicals that impart a bitter taste and skunkish or citrusy odor. **FLOWER** Bisexual or unisexual; when unisexual, borne on separate plants or not. Flowers are radial, usually whitish, greenish yellow, or purplish, sepals and petals usually 4 or 5, stamens 4–10 or more, the ovary superior, with 4 or 5 chambers. There is usually a nectary disk beneath the stamens and ovary. Clusters are terminal, branched, with few to many flowers, or sometimes only a single flower. **FRUIT** Highly variable: a samara, schizocarp, drupe, cluster of more or less separate chambers (follicles), or a berry (often a hesperidium, a berry with a leathery rind, as in the citrus fruit).

The family is economically very important for it fruits, particularly those of the genus *Citrus*, but also kumquat (*Fortunella*) and white zapote (*Casimiroa*). The essential oils produced in all parts of the plant are used medicinally and in perfumery. A few species provide valuable lumber, and some are used as ornamentals, prized for their foliage or their showy and sometimes delightfully fragrant flowers.

■ *AMYRIS*: TORCHWOODS

A genus of about 30 species of the American tropics and subtropics. The wood of these species is very resinous, burns easily and fragrantly, and has been used in the West Indies as a torch and in the fabrication of medicine and varnish.

SEA TORCHWOOD *Amyris elemifera* L.

QUICKID Recognized by the opposite, predominantly trifoliolate leaves that are gland-dotted above; terminal clusters of tiny, fragrant white flowers; and blackish drupes.

Evergreen shrub or rarely a small tree to about 7 m tall, 14 cm diam. Erect, single trunk or multiple, often low-branching; crown dense, branches ascending. **BARK** Smooth, brownish. **TWIG** Smooth, slender, hairless or sparsely hairy. **LEAF** Opposite, compound, turgid or somewhat drooping; blade to about 10 cm long, 10 cm broad; petiole 3–4 cm long, slender. Leaflets usually 3, rarely 5; 2–7 cm long, 1–4.5 cm broad, firm; ovate, lanceolate, or somewhat diamond-shaped, base wedge-shaped; tip abruptly short-pointed; margins finely and bluntly toothed or nearly entire. Upper surface lustrous or dull, dark or medium green, usually hairless, covered with glandular dots; lower surface paler. **FLOWER** Bisexual, fragrant; corolla tiny, to about 5 mm diam.; petals 4, gland-dotted; sepals 4; inflorescence a showy, hairless terminal panicle. Year-round. **FRUIT** Rounded drupe, 5–8 mm long,

SEA TORCHWOOD

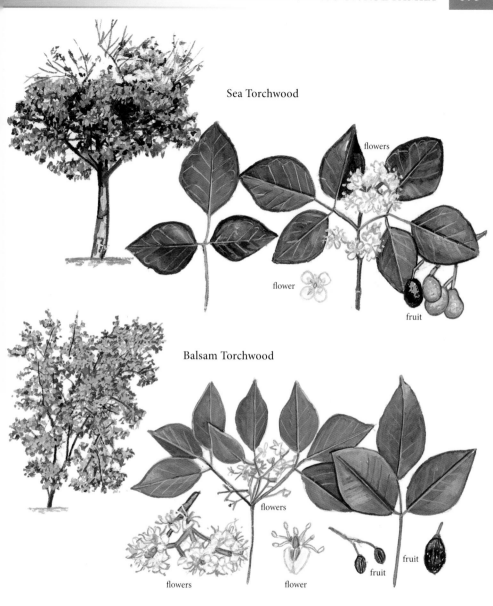

Sea Torchwood

flowers

flower

fruit

Balsam Torchwood

flowers

flowers

flower

fruit

fruit

flowers

black, gland-dotted, the surface gaining a whitish bloom at maturity. Year-round.

HABITAT/RANGE Native. Wet coastal hammocks; east coast from c. Fla. south to Fla. Keys.

SIMILAR SPECIES See Balsam Torchwood.

BALSAM TORCHWOOD *Amyris balsamifera* L.

Similar to but rarer than Sea Torchwood; distinguished by its hairy inflorescence. **HABITAT/RANGE** Native; restricted in its U.S. range to hammocks of extreme s. Fla.

■ *CITRUS*: CITRUS

A genus of 12–25 species distributed in Asia, Australia, and Pacific islands. Three species widely cultivated for their fruit are rarely naturalized in North America.

Evergreen (rarely deciduous) shrubs or trees. **LEAF** Alternate, compound, usually unifoliolate, sometimes trifoliolate; blade leathery, with conspicuous yellowish oil glands in the tissue visible when held against transmitted light; petiole usually conspicuously winged. **FLOWER** Bisexual or unisexual male; petals usually 4 or 5 (3–8), white, sometimes suffused with pinkish red; stamens usually 4, potentially to 10; ovary superior. **FRUIT** Hesperidium, usually with a thick, leathery rind enclosing several separate sections or cells, each from a single carpel; rind with numerous oil glands, fragrant; seeds usually several per cell.

CITRON *Citrus medica* L.

QUICK ID Recognized by the combination of large elliptic leaves, white flowers with numerous stamens enclosed within a white tube, purplish flower buds, and large yellow fruit with a bumpy rind.

Evergreen shrub or small aromatic tree to about 5 m tall, about 8 cm diam. Erect, single short trunk; crown rounded, with long, irregular branches. **BARK** Smooth, light brown, slightly bitter. **TWIG** Green, smooth, angled, the nodes usually with a stout, sharp-tipped green spine 1–4 cm long. **LEAF** Alternate, unifoliolate, oval or elliptic, thick, leathery; base wedge-shaped; tip usually rounded, sometimes bluntly pointed or notched; margins with rounded, blunt teeth. Upper surface lustrous, dark green; lower surface paler. Blade 6–18 cm long, 3–6 cm broad; petiole 3–7 mm long, not winged. **FLOWER** Bisexual or male, produced on the same or separate plants, buds purplish; sepals 5, fused into a cuplike calyx; petals 5, white or pinkish, 1.5–2 cm long; stamens 30–50, usually united below into a whitish tube; produced singly or in compact terminal or axillary clusters. Spring. **FRUIT** Large egg-shaped or ellipsoid hesperidium with a thick, firm, bumpy, slightly bitter rind, 15–25 cm long, to about 15 cm diam., yellow; matures autumn.

HABITAT/RANGE Introduced from n. India. Cultivated, rarely naturalized in s. Fla. and along the Gulf Coast of the nw. Fla. panhandle.

SIMILAR SPECIES Other naturalized citrus have smaller fruit.

TANGERINE *Citrus reticulata* Blanco
A.K.A. SATSUMA, MANDARIN ORANGE

QUICK ID Recognized by the narrowly winged petiole and the distinctive vertically compressed fruit with 8–15 sections.

Evergreen small tree, to about 5 m tall, 8 cm diam. Erect, single short, low-branched trunk or multiple trunks; crown dense, branches and twigs often spineless, those on some plants bearing sharp thorns. **LEAF** Alternate, unifoliolate; lanceolate or elliptic, margins with blunt, rounded teeth; upper surface lustrous, dark green; blade to about 10 cm long, 4 cm broad; petiole 7–10 mm long, narrowly winged. **FLOWER** White, petals 5, produced in terminal clusters. Spring. **FRUIT** Vertically compressed hesperidium, 5–10 cm diam., the rind loose and easily removed to reveal 8–15 easily separated sections; matures autumn to early winter. **HABITAT/RANGE** Introduced from China. Cultivated, rarely naturalized in Fla.

SOUR ORANGE *Citrus × aurantium* L., pro sp.
A.K.A. SEVILLE ORANGE

Evergreen shrub or small tree with green twigs, some bearing sharp-tipped green thorns. Petiole usually broadly and conspicuously winged. **HABITAT/RANGE** Naturalized in Fla., Ga., Tex., perhaps elsewhere. The most widely cultivated and naturalized citrus in Fla. *Notes:* A hybrid of Shaddock (*C. maxima* [Burm. f.] Merr.) and Tangerine; this complex has given rise to many cultivated citruses, the best known of which are Sour Orange, Sweet Orange, and Grapefruit.

Citron

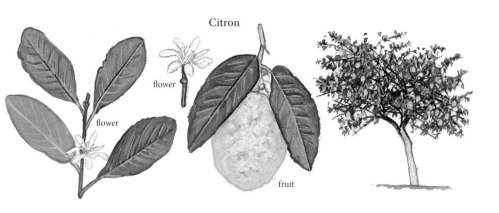

flower

flower

fruit

Tangerine

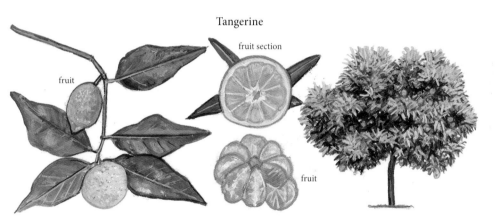

fruit

fruit section

fruit

Sour Orange

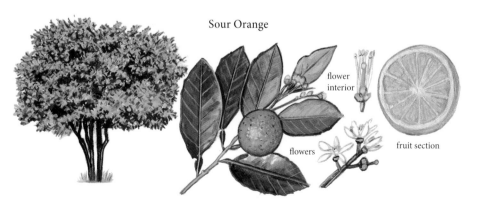

flower interior

flowers

fruit section

CHINESE BOX *Murraya paniculata* (L.) Jack

A.K.A. ORANGE JESSAMINE

QUICKID The pinnately compound leaves with alternate and opposite obovate leaflets along a hairy, zigzag rachis are usually enough to identify Chinese Box.

Evergreen, usually a large shrub, sometimes a tree, potentially to 12 m tall, 13 cm diam., usually not exceeding about 6 m tall where naturalized in Fla. Erect or rounded, single trunk or multiple; crown dense, spreading, broad and hedgelike. **BARK** Grayish or yellowish, becoming fissured and shredding. **TWIG** Green, finely hairy, becoming gray and fissured. **LEAF** Alternate, compound, aromatic, central rachis finely hairy, often zigzag; blade averaging about 5 cm long, to about 9 cm broad; petiole 1–2 cm long. Leaflets 3–11, opposite and alternate, usually obovate, 1.5–8 cm long, 1.5–4 cm broad, stalk to about 3 mm long; upper surface lustrous, dark green. **FLOWER** Bisexual, about 4 cm diam., strongly fragrant with the scent of orange blossoms; sepals 5; petals 5, white, narrowly elliptic or oblanceolate, to about 2 cm long; stamens 10; produced in a terminal or axillary cluster. Year-round. **FRUIT** Rounded red or orange berry, 1–2 cm long; skin with conspicuous glandular dots; matures year-round.

HABITAT/RANGE Introduced from tropical Asia. Naturalized in hammocks in s. Fla. Treated as an invasive species in Fla.

Notes: Murraya is a genus of about 12 species distributed in Asia, Australia, and Pacific islands.

■ *PHELLODENDRON*: CORKTREES

As treated here, *Phellodendron* is a genus of 2 species distributed in East and Southeast Asia, naturalized in the U.S. At least 16 species and 15 varieties were described between 1857 and 2005, all now treated as synonymous with either Amur Corktree or Chinese Corktree.

Deciduous, erect trees with spreading, rounded crowns and corky bark. **LEAF** Opposite, compound, leaflets 7–11, usually 9. **FLOWER** Unisexual, petals 5, male flowers with stamens longer than the petals; female flowers with staminodes and 1 very short or nearly absent style. **FRUIT** Black or purple drupelike berry with 5–10 seeds.

AMUR CORKTREE *Phellodendron amurense* Rupr.

QUICKID Recognized by the combination of opposite, pinnately compound leaves, usually with 9 leaflets; branched inflorescence; and conspicuously thickened, furrowed corky bark.

Deciduous tree, 25–35 m tall, 60–100 cm diam. Erect, single trunk; crown rounded, spreading. **BARK** Corky, dark gray, about 1.5 cm thick, the outer deeply fissured, 3–4 times as thick as the inner layer. **LEAF** Pinnate; blade 17–32 cm long, 13–16 cm broad; petiole 5.5–7.5 cm long. Leaflets 7–11, commonly 9, moderately thick, 6–11 cm long, 3.5–5 cm broad; elliptic or ovate-oblong, base narrowly wedge-shaped, tip abruptly short-pointed; margins entire to very finely and obscurely toothed. Upper surface bright green, hairless; lower surface pale green, usually hairy along the midvein, lateral veins conspicuous, usually curving toward the leaflet tip. **FLOWER** Unisexual, male and female flowers on separate plants; petals 5, yellow-green; inflorescence a panicle 8.5–13.5 cm long, 6.5–9 cm broad, stalk 5–8.5 cm long, secondary axes with branches to about 1 cm long. Late spring to early summer. **FRUIT** Rounded black drupe, 8–9 mm long, 7–9 mm diam., hairless; matures autumn.

HABITAT/RANGE Introduced from Asia. Rarely and spottily naturalized in the Midwest, the Northeast, and e. Canada.

SIMILAR SPECIES Similar to, and difficult to distinguish from, Chinese Corktree; see that species for differences.

CHINESE CORKTREE *Phellodendron chinense* C.K. Schneid.

Deciduous tree, 15–25 m tall, 40–60 cm diam. Similar in most respects to Amur Corktree. Distinguished by its smaller stature; shorter and narrower inflorescences, 6.5–9.5 cm long, 4–6.5 cm broad, with secondary inflorescence branches short, thick, the flowers and fruit appearing sessile; and the smooth, thin bark that lacks deep furrows. **HABITAT/RANGE** Introduced from China, the precise nativity obscure due to longtime cultivation; sparsely naturalized in the Midwest and the Northeast.

Chinese Box

fruit

seed

flowers

fruit

Amur Corktree

fruit

fruit

Chinese Corktree

fruit

flower

FLOWER AXISTREE *Glycosmis parviflora* (Sims) Little

Evergreen shrub or small tree, 1–3 m tall. **LEAF** Opposite or alternate, compound; leaflets usually 2–4, occasionally 1 or 5, lanceolate or oblong, each 5–19 cm long, 2.5–8 cm broad, base rounded, tip bluntly pointed, surfaces hairless, margins entire. **FLOWER** Bisexual, small, petals and sepals 4 or 5; produced in a terminal panicle to about 14 cm long. **FRUIT** Rounded or ellipsoid berry, 1–1.5 cm diam., yellowish white, turning pinkish. **HABITAT/ RANGE** Introduced from Asia; naturalized in hammocks in s. Fla.

HARDY ORANGE *Poncirus trifoliata* (L.) Raf.

QUICK ID Recognized by the combination of the green twigs with stout, basally flattened axillary thorns; 3-parted leaves; and winged petioles.

Deciduous shrub or small tree, to about 3.5 m tall. Erect, single trunk; crown open, branches green, often zigzag. **BARK** Green at first, eventually decorated with long, irregular green and brownish stripes. **TWIG** Stout, green, somewhat flattened, bearing stout, sharp, green axillary thorns that are flattened at the base. **LEAF** Alternate, compound, usually widely spaced; blade to about 6 cm long, 10 cm broad; petiole 5–30 cm long, usually with a broad, blade-like wing. Leaflets usually 3, rarely 2; 2–6 cm long, 1–2 cm broad; elliptic, rhombic, obovate, or nearly circular, base wedge-shaped, tip bluntly pointed or rounded, margins finely toothed above the middle. Upper surface dark green, finely hairy along the midvein; lower surface paler. **FLOWER** Bisexual, 3–6 cm diam., radial; sepals 4–7; petals 4–7, white, widest toward the apex, margins usually upturned; stamens numerous; pistils 1, style short, stout; produced singly or in pairs from the thorn axils. Spring. **FRUIT** Round yellow, orange-like hesperidium, 4–5 cm diam.; matures summer to autumn.

HABITAT/RANGE Introduced from China. Cultivated, sporadically naturalized in the East, Pa. to Fla., west to Okla. and e. Tex.

SIMILAR SPECIES The 3-parted leaves of Common Hoptree (*Ptelea trifoliata*) are larger.

Notes: Poncirus is a monotypic genus of n. China and Japan, sometimes included within *Citrus*.

COMMON HOPTREE *Ptelea trifoliata* L.
A.K.A. WAFER-ASH, STINKING-ASH, SKUNK-BUSH

QUICK ID Recognized by the combination of 3-parted leaves with a musky aroma when crushed, and flat, winged, waferlike samaras borne in ball-like clusters.

Deciduous colony-forming shrub or small tree, to about 7.5 m tall. Erect, single trunk or multiple; crown usually broad and spreading, somewhat vase-shaped. **BARK** Gray-brown, slightly scaly, usually with lenticels and corky ridges. **TWIG** Slender, round, light reddish brown, decorated with pustular spots. **LEAF** Alternate, compound, releasing a musky or fetid odor when crushed; blade 10–18 cm long, to about 20 cm broad; petiole 4–8 cm long. Leaflets 3, rarely 5, the lateral ones stalkless or nearly so, 1–10 cm long, to about 8 cm broad; elliptic, obovate, ovate, or broadly lanceolate, base wedge-shaped or slightly asymmetric, tip pointed, margins bluntly or sharply toothed. Upper surface lustrous, dark green; lower surface paler, varying from hairless to evenly soft-hairy. **FLOWER** Bisexual or functionally unisexual; sepals 4 or 5, tiny; petals 4 or 5, greenish white, 4–6 mm long; stamens usually 4 or 5; ovary superior; inflorescence a terminal panicle. Spring. **FRUIT** Flat, circular, waferlike samara, 1.5–2 cm diam., with 2 conspicuous wings and a body with 1 or 2 seeds; produced in ball-like clusters, maturing in autumn.

HABITAT/RANGE Native. Rich woods, slopes, bluffs, upland forests, to about 2,600 m; widespread across the East, west to at least Ariz. and Utah.

Notes: Ptelea is now considered to contain 2–4 species in North America, previously as many as 59 species; 1 is native in the East. Hoptree is North America's most northerly ranging member of the citrus family.

COMMON HOPTREE

Flower Axistree

fruit

Hardy Orange

flowers

fruit section

fruit

twig

Common Hoptree

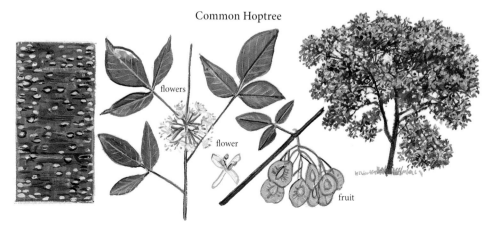

flowers

flower

fruit

CHINESE BOXORANGE *Severinia buxifolia* (Poir.) Ten.
A.K.A. BOXTHORN

Evergreen shrub or very small spiny tree, to about 4 m tall. Usually shrubby, branches green. **LEAF** Alternate, unifoliolate, leathery, obovate or oval, tip notched, dark green above, to about 4.5 cm long, 2.5 cm broad, petiole subtended by a sharp spine. **FLOWER** White, fragrant, petals 5, produced in axillary clusters. Spring. **FRUIT** Rounded, several-seeded black berry to about 7 mm diam. **HABITAT/RANGE** Introduced from China and Taiwan; sparsely established in s. Fla.

BEE-BEE TREE *Tetradium daniellii* (Benn.) T.G. Hartley

Evergreen shrub or small tree to about 20 m tall. **LEAF** Opposite, pinnately compound. Leaflets usually 5–9; 5–18.5 cm long, 2.5–10.5 cm broad; lanceolate to broadly ovate or elliptic, base narrowly or broadly wedge-shaped or nearly rounded, tip abruptly short-pointed, margins obscurely or bluntly toothed. **FLOWER** Functionally unisexual male and female on separate plants, or bisexual and female flowers on the same plant; petals usually 5, white, 3–5 mm long; produced in branched terminal clusters 3.5–19 cm long. Summer. **FRUIT** Pear-shaped pod, 5–11 mm long; matures late summer to autumn. **HABITAT/RANGE** Introduced from Asia; cultivated, reportedly naturalized in Pa. and Ohio.

■ *ZANTHOXYLUM*: PRICKLYASHES

A genus of about 200 species distributed mainly in the tropics of Mexico, Central and South America, the West Indies, Africa, Asia, Australia, and the Pacific islands, and in temperate regions of North America and East Asia.

Deciduous or evergreen shrubs or trees. **LEAF** Alternate, pinnately compound, with or without a terminal leaflet, the rachis winged or not; leaflets alternate, opposite, or sub-opposite, blade tissue usually punctate, margins entire or toothed. **FLOWER** Unisexual or bisexual, male and female on separate plants; sepals 0–5; petals 3–5; stamens 3–5. **FRUIT** Two-valved follicle, usually 1-seeded; seeds lustrous, black or reddish.

COMMON PRICKLYASH *Zanthoxylum americanum* Mill.
A.K.A. TOOTHACHE-TREE

QUICK ID Recognized by the combination of alternate pinnate leaves subtended by paired prickles, the leaf rachis sometimes bearing thin, paired prickles at the leaflet nodes, and small axillary clusters of greenish-yellow flowers.

Deciduous, typically a thicket-forming shrub, infrequently a small, slender tree, 6–10 m tall. Erect, usually a single trunk; crown narrow. **BARK** Smooth, becoming furrowed, with stout, flat-based prickles that usually fall off with age. **TWIG** Slender, dark brown, smooth, often with lighter streaking, usually armed at the nodes with pairs of prickles. **LEAF** Alternate, pinnately compound, blade 15–20 cm long, to about 12 cm broad; petiole 3–6 cm long. Leaflets 5–11, predominantly 7 or fewer; ovate, broadly lanceolate, or oval, 1.5–6 cm long, 1.5–2 cm broad; rachis often lacking prickles or prickles present, thin, and borne in pairs at the bases of the leaflets; the leaflets usually lacking prickles. Upper surface lustrous, medium or dark green; lower surface paler, usually hairy. **FLOWER** Unisexual or bisexual, male and female usually on separate plants, greenish yellow, petals usually 4 or 5, oblong, fringed at the tip, pistils 2–5; produced in small axillary clusters. Spring to summer. **FRUIT** Fleshy orange-brown pod with 1 or 2 seeds; seeds lustrous black, about 5 mm long; matures summer.

HABITAT/RANGE Native. Moist or dry woodlands, usually in rich soils, 0–600 m; widespread in the East, Que., Ont., and N.D., south to extreme nw. Fla., Okla., and La.

SIMILAR SPECIES The prickles on the branches and leaf rachis of Hercules' Club are stout and irregularly scattered instead of paired.

COMMON PRICKLYASH

Chinese Boxorange

flowers

fruit

Bee-bee Tree

flowers

fruit

fruit

fruit

seeds

open fruit

Common Pricklylash

fruit

fruit

twig

opening fruit
showing seed

HERCULES' CLUB *Zanthoxylum clava-herculis* L.

A.K.A. SOUTHERN PRICKLYASH, TICKLE-TONGUE

QUICK ID One of few species with the combination of alternate, pinnately compound leaves and stout, sharp prickles on the lower trunk, branches, and leaves.

Deciduous shrub or tree, 10–20 m tall, to about 70 cm diam. Erect, single trunk, often short and low-branched, sometimes leaning; branches stout, often conspicuously thorny with short, sharp, flat-based prickles; crown rounded. **BARK** Grayish, often with darker splotches, armed with stout sharp prickles, at least on the lower trunk; prickles becoming blunt, knoblike, and elevated with a mounded base on old trees; prickles of trunk, branches, and twigs not paired. **TWIG** Stout, gray, with prickles. **LEAF** Pinnate, rachis often bearing solitary prickles; blade 12–20 cm long, to about 14 cm broad; petiole 4–5 cm long. Leaflets 5–19, usually 9–13, 2.5–7 cm long, 2–3 cm broad; stalk short, stout, often with a fleshy wing; leaflet blade firm, stiff, lanceolate or ovate, usually strongly asymmetric on either side of the midvein, curved or sickle-shaped, base wedge-shaped or rounded, tip pointed, margins coarsely toothed, the teeth yellowish with glands between. Upper surface lustrous, dark green; lower surface paler, hairless. **FLOWER** Functionally unisexual or bisexual; petals 4 or 5, greenish yellow, 3–4 mm long; female flowers with 1–5 pistils and rudimentary stamens. Spring. **FRUIT** Follicle, 5–6 mm diam.; seeds lustrous black, 5–6 mm long; matures late spring to summer.

HABITAT/RANGE Native. Dunes, shell middens, coastal hammocks, disturbed sites, upland woodlands, 0–300 m; the Southeast, Va. to Fla., west to e. Tex. and Ark.

SIMILAR SPECIES The prickles on Common Pricklyash are thin and usually paired at the leaf or leaflet nodes.

BISCAYNE PRICKLYASH *Zanthoxylum coriaceum* A. Rich.

QUICK ID The only pricklyash in Fla. with predominantly evenly pinnate leaves.

Evergreen shrub or small tree to about 7 m tall. Erect, single trunk or multiple; crown dense; branches ascending, usually prickly. **LEAF** Pinnately compound, often lacking a terminal leaflet; blade to about 20 cm long, about 6 cm broad; petiole 2–6 cm long. Leaflets 4–13, stiff, 2–6.5 cm long, to about 2 cm broad; obovate, oblong, or elliptic, base wedge-shaped; tip rounded, bluntly pointed, often notched. Upper surface lustrous, dark green; lower surface pale green. **FLOWER** Unisexual; petals 4 or 5, yellowish white. Year-round. **FRUIT** Rounded or ellipsoid, 1-seeded pod, 5–6 mm long.

HABITAT/RANGE Native. Coastal hammocks, s. Fla.; endangered.

WEST INDIAN SATINWOOD *Zanthoxylum flavum* Vahl

QUICK ID A rare Fla. Keys pricklyash lacking prickles on its branches.

A small, essentially evergreen tree with alternate, pinnately compound leaves with 5–9 ovate leaflets, each 2.5–10 cm long; spineless twigs and branches; and nearly smooth grayish bark.

HABITAT/RANGE Native; occurs very rarely in Fla. Keys.

HERCULES' CLUB

BISCAYNE PRICKLYASH

WEST INDIAN SATINWOOD

Hercules' Club

fruit

seed

twig

Biscayne Pricklylash

fruit

West Indian Satinwood

flowers

flower

fruit

LIME PRICKLYASH *Zanthoxylum fagara* (L.) Sarg.
A.K.A. WILD LIME

QUICKID Recognized by the alternate, pinnately compound leaves with a winged rachis and petiole, and bluntly toothed leaflets.

Evergreen shrub or small tree, to about 10 m tall, 15 cm diam. Erect, single trunk; crown dense or open, branches armed with hooked prickles or unarmed. **LEAF** Alternate, pinnately compound, blade 2–10 cm long, 3–5 cm broad; petiole to about 2 cm long, usually winged, rachis grooved and distinctly winged. Leaflets 5–13, usually 7–9, each 7–20 mm long, to about 5–15 mm broad; obovate, elliptic, or nearly circular, base broadly or narrowly wedge-shaped; tip rounded, often notched; margins with blunt or rounded teeth. Upper surface medium green. **FLOWER** Unisexual; petals 4, 2–3 mm long, yellow-green; produced in axillary clusters. Year-round. **FRUIT** Rounded, bumpy red or yellow pod 3–4 mm diam.; seeds 1 per pod, lustrous black. Year-round.

HABITAT/RANGE Native. Hammocks; c. and s. Fla.

TEXAS HERCULES' CLUB *Zanthoxylum hirsutum* Buckley

QUICKID A pricklyash, distinguished in the East by its western range, leaflets mostly numbering 5–9, flowers in terminal panicles, each flower with 5 sepals, petals, and stamens.

Deciduous shrub or small tree, to 5 m tall, 15 cm diam. Erect, single trunk or multiple; crown rounded or oval, dense; branches and twigs gray, prickly. **BARK** Light gray or reddish brown, smooth, bearing sharp prickles. **LEAF** Pinnate, rachis often with at least a few prickles; leaflets 5–9, 1–4 cm long, to about 2 cm broad, finely hairy, at least on the primary veins, elliptic or ovate, base slightly asymmetric, margins bluntly toothed. **FLOWER** In terminal panicles to 7 cm long; petals, sepals, and stamens 5. Spring. **FRUIT** Follicle usually 1 per flower, globose, reddish brown, 6 mm diam., hairless.

HABITAT/RANGE Native. Dry bluffs, deciduous woods, often where limestone is present, 0–850 m; e. Tex. and reportedly adjacent Okla. and Ark.

SIMILAR SPECIES Similar to, and sometimes hybridizing with, Hercules' Club, which has usually 9–13 leaflets and the leaflet blade strongly asymmetric at the base.

LIME PRICKLYASH

TEXAS HERCULES' CLUB

Lime Pricklylash

flowers

open fruit

fruit

Texas Hercules' Club

fruit

flowers

open fruit

twig

prickles

SALICACEAE: WILLOW FAMILY

The willow family includes 50–60 genera and more than 1,000 species of woody plants distributed worldwide. Recent molecular genetic studies show that Flacourtiaceae is better placed within Salicaceae. As construed here, Salicaceae is represented by 5 genera in North America, 3 of which include native species.

Members of the family range from diminutive creeping shrubs of cold regions to massive, majestic trees in eastern forests and along southwestern rivers. **LEAF** Usually alternate, simple, and toothed. Stipules are often present, sometimes large and leafy. The teeth on the margins of leaves in *Salix* and *Populus* are usually tipped with a persistent spherical gland that arises as an extension of the vein that enters the tooth. **FLOWER** Unisexual or bisexual, borne in catkins or terminal or axillary clusters; male and female flowers usually on separate plants. Petals are absent, the perianth usually reduced to either a small disk or a glandular nectary. Stamens range from 1 to 60, the filaments free or partially fused, hairy or not near the base. **FRUIT** The single ovary bears 2 stigmas, and matures into a small capsule, berry, or drupe, the capsule sometimes splitting into 2 or 4 segments and releasing long-haired seeds that are carried by the wind.

The wood of larger species in the family is used for lumber, pulp, and occasionally for fuel. Salicaceae species are an important food source for many kinds of wildlife. Some genera soon revegetate moist disturbed areas, helping to control erosion. A number of species are also popular ornamentals.

SMOOTH HONEYTREE *Casearia nitida* (L.) Jacq.
A.K.A. SMOOTH CASEARIA

QUICK ID Recognized by the combination of finely toothed simple leaves with marginal glands, petalless flowers, and yellow fruit capsules.

Evergreen shrub or small tree, to about 5 m tall. Erect, rounded, or vase-shaped, single trunk or multiple; crown dense, with numerous branches. **TWIG** Slender, rounded. **LEAF** Alternate, simple, moderately leathery; elliptic, ovate, or obovate; base rounded or nearly heart-shaped; tip abruptly short-pointed or blunt; margins finely, evenly, and bluntly toothed, the teeth often gland-tipped. Upper surface lustrous, dark or medium green, midvein yellowish; lower surface paler. Blade 1.5–7 cm long, to about 3 cm broad; petiole 6–12 mm long, yellowish. **FLOWER** Bisexual, greenish yellow; sepals 4–6, fused, the calyx about 5 mm long; petals absent; produced in axillary clusters. Spring to summer. **FRUIT** Rounded yellowish capsule, 5–7 mm diam.; seeds 1–5, with a fleshy aril; matures summer.

HABITAT/RANGE Introduced from the West Indies. Established in disturbed sites, s. Fla.

Notes: *Casearia* is a genus of about 160 species distributed in the tropics and subtropics, with 1 species introduced to North America. Formerly treated within the flacourtia family (Flacourtiaceae).

GOVERNOR'S PLUM *Flacourtia indica* (Burm. f.) Merr.
A.K.A. MADAGASCAR PLUM

QUICK ID Recognized by the combination of simple, bluntly toothed leaves, pairs of sharp spines in the leaf axils, and round reddish fruit.

Evergreen shrub or small tree, 3–15 m tall, often shrubby. Vase-shaped or upright, single trunk or multiple; crown dense, rounded, branches produced from just below a withered terminal bud. **LEAF** Alternate, simple, stiff, leathery; ovate, elliptic, or nearly circular; base rounded; tip rounded or pointed; margins usually bluntly toothed, the teeth often rounded. Upper surface lustrous, dark green, hairy or not; lower surface paler, usually

Smooth Honeytree

flowers

immature fruit

open capsule
with seed

Governor's Plum

seed

flowers

fruit section

fruit

hairy. Blade 3–8 cm long, 2–3 cm broad; petiole to about 1 cm long, usually subtended by sharp axillary spines. **FLOWER** Unisexual or bisexual, male and female on separate plants, the bisexual flowers sometimes on branches with female flowers; sepals 4 or 5, scalelike; petals absent; produced in few-flowered terminal or axillary racemes. Year-round. **FRUIT** Rounded, fleshy, several-seeded edible drupe, 1–2 cm diam.; green at first, becoming red to red-purple. Year-round.

HABITAT/RANGE Introduced from Asia. Cultivated, naturalized, weedy; s. Fla., where it is considered an invasive species.

Notes: Flacourtia is a genus of about 8 species distributed in the Old World tropics.

■ *POPULUS*: POPLARS, COTTONWOODS, ASPENS

A genus of 30–35 species native to the Northern Hemisphere, and now spread throughout cooler regions of the world from sea-level to the tree-line; 8 species are native to North America, 7 occurring in the East. Several introduced as ornamentals have escaped and persist clonally, often as hybrids with native species.

Deciduous medium, large, or massive trees. **BARK** Smooth and pale on young trees, in aspens often white; older bark usually darker, thick, and deeply furrowed between flat, often cracked ridges. **TWIG** Hairy or hairless, the buds conspicuous, often resinous, usually fragrant in poplars and cottonwoods, but not fragrant in aspens. **LEAF** Alternate, simple, usually toothed, sometimes lobed. Usually heterophyllous, the leaves from different parts of the season's twig expressing varying forms. **FLOWER** Wind-pollinated, very small, unisexual, the sexes borne on separate trees in pendulous catkins that expand before the leaves emerge, the perianth modified into a cup- or saucer-shaped disk at the base of the flower. Stamens 6–12 in aspens, 12–60 in cottonwoods and poplars. Female flowers have a lobed ovary topped by a short stigma and 2 spreading styles. **FRUIT** Ovoid or globose capsule, splitting into 2–4 segments to release the seeds, covered by long white down, which waft by the thousands in the air after the leaves mature; capsules are thin-walled in aspens, thick-walled in cottonwoods and poplars.

Members of the genus provide wood for paper pulp, pallets, boxes, matches, and small utilitarian items. Hybrids are bred for rapid production of biomass, and are planted in large plantations to supply the pulp industry; once carved for farm implements, water troughs, oxen yolks, and doors, and used as building material. The bark has been used in tanning, and the resin of the buds was used medicinally. Cultivated, but troublesome as ornamentals owing to the tendency of roots to invade sidewalks, foundations, and sewage lines.

WHITE POPLAR *Populus alba* L.
A.K.A. EUROPEAN WHITE POPLAR

QUICK ID Recognized by bark whitish on upper parts of the trunk; lower surface of leaf whitish-hairy; petiole hairy, generally round in cross section, potentially laterally flattened near the point of attachment to the blade; and a usually crooked trunk.

Deciduous tree, 16–24 m tall, 50–100 cm diam.; sometimes forms clones from root suckers. Erect, single crooked, leaning, often forked trunk; crown large, spreading, usually rounded; branches large, crooked, with few stout branchlets. **BARK** Smooth and creamy white or grayish on young trees, becoming blackish, furrowed, and deeply pitted, especially on the lower trunk. **TWIG** Stout, green, white-hairy, becoming brownish; buds covered with whitish hairs. **LEAF** Alternate, simple, ovate or palmately lobed to nearly circular; base truncate or broadly rounded; tip bluntly pointed; margins wavy or deeply 5-lobed with large, bluntly pointed teeth (then resembling a maple leaf). Upper surface lustrous, dark green, hairless; lower surface white-hairy, becoming nearly hairless. Blade 4–10 cm long, nearly as broad; petiole to about 6 cm long, densely hairy, flattened. **FLOWER** Unisexual, male and female in catkins on separate plants; male catkins 4–8 cm long, stamens 6–16; female catkins 2–5 cm long. Spring. **FRUIT** Two-valved, narrowly egg-shaped capsule, 3–6 mm long, produced in a drooping catkin 4–8 cm long; seeds whitish or light brown, hairy; matures late spring to summer.

HABITAT/RANGE Introduced from Europe. Among the most widely cultivated trees in North America, escaped and established essentially throughout, less common in southern climes. Considered weedy and invasive in several states, especially in the North.

BALSAM POPLAR *Populus balsamifera* L.
A.K.A. HACKMATACK

QUICK ID Recognized by the combination of the large ovate, bluntly toothed leaves, rounded petiole, dangling or drooping catkins, and strongly fragrant buds with the odor of balsam.

Deciduous tree, 18–40 m tall, 30–200 cm diam. Erect, single, often slender trunk, sometimes forming multitrunked clones; crown narrow, open, pyramidal, usually with numerous branches. **BARK** Reddish gray, smooth and thin at first, becoming thick and furrowed. **TWIG** Stout, smooth, reddish brown, becoming dark orange then gray; winter buds reddish, hairless, resinous; resin fragrant, resembling balsam. **LEAF** Alternate, simple, thin, flexible, ovate or broadly lanceolate, base rounded, tip narrowing to a long point; margins toothed,

White Poplar

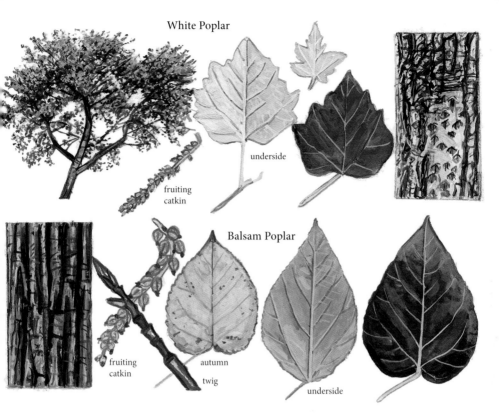

fruiting
catkin

underside

Balsam Poplar

fruiting
catkin

autumn
twig

underside

teeth mostly rounded. Upper surface lustrous, dark green; lower surface whitish or silvery, usually stained with reddish-brown resin, often with 2 glands near the leaf base; both surfaces hairless. Blade 5–15 cm long, 3–6 cm broad; petiole 1–5 cm long, round in cross section, or slightly flattened at the leaf attachment. Turns yellow in autumn. **FLOWER** Unisexual, male and female in catkins on separate trees; disk 2–4 mm wide; male flowers with 20–30 stamens, produced in catkins 8–10 cm long, with 50–70 flowers; female catkins 10–13 cm long. Spring. **FRUIT** Two-valved, egg-shaped capsule, 3–8 mm long; produced in drooping catkins 10–15 cm long; seeds light brown with a tuft of whitish hairs; matures late spring to early summer.

HABITAT/RANGE Native. Wet, cool lowlands; stream banks, floodplains, bog margins, moist rocky slopes, dry sands where the water table is high; boreal regions, 0–3,700 m; throughout Canada, Maine and Mass., west to Mont., Wyo., Colo., and Alaska.

SIMILAR SPECIES Swamp Cottonwood also has round petioles, but it lacks rusty-brown resin on the lower leaf surface.

Notes: Sometimes referred to as Balm-of-Gilead owing to the alleged healing properties of the fragrant resin on its leaves and buds. However, this name is more appropriately ascribed to *P. × jackii*.

BALSAM POPLAR

EASTERN COTTONWOOD *Populus deltoides* W. Bartram ex Marshall

QUICK ID Recognized by the combination of broadly ovate, coarsely toothed leaves with a truncate base, laterally flattened petiole, cottony seeds, and colonizing habit.

Deciduous tree, 18–55 m tall, to about 50–350 cm diam. Erect, forest-grown trees with a single straight trunk and producing a broad, open, symmetric crown, usually wider than tall; trunk of open-grown trees often forking into 2 or more main stems, branching low, the crown taller, broader, more or less pyramidal. **BARK** Smooth and light brown or yellowish gray on young trees, becoming darker gray and irregularly and roughly furrowed. **TWIG** Stout, yellowish green, hairless or sparsely hairy, angled in cross section, usually with narrow longitudinal ridges. Terminal buds 8–15 mm long, yellow-green, hairless or stiffly hairy, moderately fragrant. **LEAF** Alternate, simple, thin, flaccid at first, becoming leathery; more or less triangular, base truncate or somewhat heart-shaped, tip narrowly long-pointed; margins coarsely and bluntly toothed, the teeth usually 15–25 per side. Upper surface lustrous, dark green, hairless; lower surface paler, hairless or sparsely hairy, with 0 or 3–6 glands near the base. Blade 3–12 cm long, 3–9 cm broad; petiole 3–13 cm long, flattened, often at a right angle to the plane of the blade, often dilated at the leaf attachment. Turns yellow in autumn. **FLOWER** Unisexual; male and female in catkins on separate plants; male catkins 8–10 cm long, stamens 30–60, anthers red; female catkins usually 15–20 cm long. Spring. **FRUIT** Egg-shaped capsule 6–11 mm long with 2–4 valves, produced in a catkin 15–25 cm long; seeds whitish or light brown, with a tuft of whitish hairs; matures late spring to early summer.

HABITAT/RANGE Native. Floodplains, colonizing wet fields, open river margins, ditches, 0–2,200 m; widespread in the East, Maine and Ont. south to n. Fla., west to B.C., Wash., and Ore.

SIMILAR SPECIES The petiole of Swamp Cottonwood is round in cross section, and the base of its leaf is rounded or heart-shaped. Three subspecies of Eastern Cottonwood are recognized, subsp. *deltoides* in the East, subsp. *monilifera* (Aiton) Eckenwalder in the East and West,

EASTERN COTTONWOOD

and subsp. *wislizeni* (S. Watson) Eckenwalder in the West. Subsp. *monilifera* is distinguished from subsp. *deltoides* by usually having 2 glands at the base of the leaf blade (vs. 0 or 3–6 in *deltoides*).

Notes: This is a shade-tolerant, fast-growing, short-lived, aggressively colonizing tree best known for the abundance of cottony, wind-dispersed seeds that are shed in late spring and early summer.

BALM-OF-GILEAD *Populus × jackii* Sarg.

A sterile female clone (cultivar) of Jack's Hybrid Poplar (*P. × jackii* Sarg.), a cross between *P. balsamifera* and *P. deltoides* that is distinguished by the combination of large heart-shaped leaves to about 17 cm long; hairy petiole and lower veins; broadly ovoid, hairless ovary; and flower disk 1–3.5 mm diam. **HABITAT/RANGE** Cultivated in e. Canada and U.S., persisting in disturbed areas, woodland edges.

LOMBARDY POPLAR *Populus nigra* L.

QUICK ID Recognized by the combination of its tapering-columnar form and alternate, often strongly rhombic leaves with toothed margins.

Deciduous tree, 10–20 m tall, 30–80 cm diam. Erect, single straight, slender trunk; crown low-branching, narrow, columnar, tapering, branches strongly ascending. **BARK** Smooth at first, grayish brown or gray-green, becoming blackish and deeply and irregularly furrowed. **TWIG** Slender, hairless, lustrous yellow-brown, becoming gray; terminal buds slender, conical. **LEAF** Alternate, simple, thick, firm, ovate or more often somewhat diamond-shaped, conspicuously widest at the center of the blade; base broadly wedge-shaped; tip abruptly narrowing to a sharp point; margins toothed with blunt or somewhat curved teeth. Upper surface lustrous, dark green; lower surface lighter, lustrous green. Blade 5–7 cm long, about as broad or broader; petiole 2–5 cm long, slender, laterally flattened. Turns yellow in autumn. **FLOWER** Unisexual, male and female catkins on separate plants; male catkins to

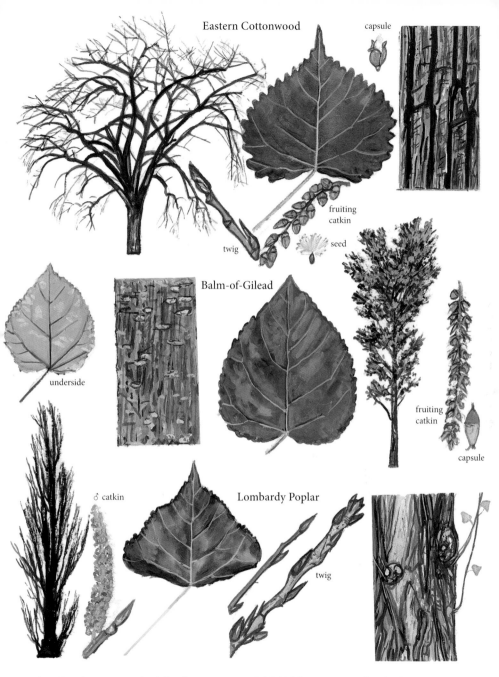

Eastern Cottonwood

capsule

fruiting
catkin

twig

seed

Balm-of-Gilead

underside

fruiting
catkin

capsule

♂ catkin

Lombardy Poplar

twig

about 8 cm long, stamens 8–10; female trees scarce or absent in North America. Spring. **FRUIT** Most representatives in North America are male cultivars, hence no fruit is produced.

HABITAT/RANGE Introduced from Europe. Usually represented in North America by 1 of 4 main cultivars, some of which produce only male flowers and no fruit; widely cultivated, occasionally escaped, nearly throughout.

BIGTOOTH ASPEN *Populus grandidentata* Michx.

QUICK ID Recognized by the combination of smooth yellowish to orange-tinted bark; broadly ovate leaves with large, broad marginal teeth; a long, slender, hairless, laterally flattened petiole; and a tendency for the leaves to tremble in even the slightest breeze.

Deciduous tree, 18–35 m tall, 30–140 cm diam. Erect, single slender trunk; crown open, short, ovoid or rounded, usually with few spreading branches. **BARK** Smooth, yellowish green, gray, or tan, often with an orange cast, smooth at first, becoming dark gray and developing deep interlacing ridges and furrows. **TWIG** Stout, greenish- or brownish gray, white-hairy at first, becoming lustrous orange-brown or reddish brown, eventually greenish with orange lenticels. Terminal bud 2–10 mm long, reddish, hairy on the bottom half. **LEAF** Alternate, simple, thin, firm, ovate or nearly circular; base rounded, broadly wedge-shaped, rarely heart-shaped; tip pointed; margins wavy or coarsely toothed with broad, pointed teeth, usually 6–15 per side. Upper surface dark green; lower surface densely white-hairy at first, becoming greenish white, often with a pair of glands near the base. Blade 4–13 cm long, 3–9 cm broad; petiole 1.5–11 cm long, laterally flattened near the point of attachment to the blade, the plane at a right angle to the plane of the blade. Turns yellow or orange in autumn. **FLOWER** Unisexual, male and female produced in catkins on separate plants; male catkins 3–8 cm long, stamens 6–13; female catkins 3–8 cm long. Spring. **FRUIT** Narrowly egg-shaped, 2-valved capsule, to about 6 mm long, produced in a drooping catkin 8–15 cm long; seeds minute, brown, with a tuft of hairs; matures early summer.

HABITAT/RANGE Native. Moist or dry forests, reaching its greatest size in moist, fertile soils, 0–1,000 m; P.E.I. and Nfld., west to Sask., south to N.C., Tenn., and Mo.

SIMILAR SPECIES The leaves of Quaking Aspen also tremble in the breeze, but the leaf margins are finely toothed.

SWAMP COTTONWOOD *Populus heterophylla* L.
A.K.A. DOWNY POPLAR, SWAMP POPLAR

QUICK ID Recognized by the combination of the rounded petiole and large ovate leaf that is not stained below with rusty resin.

Deciduous medium or large tree, 12–28 m tall, 30–120 cm diam. Erect, single slender, straight, or crooked trunk; crown open, short, more or less oblong. **BARK** Smooth, yellowish brown or reddish brown to gray tinged with red, smooth at first, becoming deeply furrowed and breaking into long, narrow plates. **TWIG** Stout, hairy at first, becoming reddish brown, hairless, and longitudinally ridged or fluted; buds slightly resinous. **LEAF** Alternate, simple, broadly ovate to nearly triangular; base broadly rounded or heart-shaped; tip pointed; margins bluntly or moderately sharply toothed. Upper surface dark green, hairy and grayish at first, becoming hairless or retaining hairs along the veins; lower surface paler, hairy, usually with 2 glands near the base, not stained with rusty-resinous glands. Blade 8–25 cm long, 6–20 cm broad; petiole usually 4–8 cm long, rounded, not dilated near the leaf attachment. **FLOWER** Unisexual, male and female flowers produced in catkins on separate plants; male catkins 3–8 cm long, stamens 12–20; female catkins 3–6 cm long. Spring. **FRUIT** Egg-shaped capsule 8–14 mm long with 2 or 3 valves; seeds whitish or light brown, with a tuft of whitish hairs; matures early summer.

HABITAT/RANGE Native. In river swamps, wet depressions, bottomlands, 0–400 m; R.I. and N.Y., west to Ill. and s. Ont., south to Mo., La., and nw. Fla.

SIMILAR SPECIES The Eastern Cottonwood has a flattened petiole, and the leaf base is truncate.

BIGTOOTH ASPEN

SWAMP COTTONWOOD

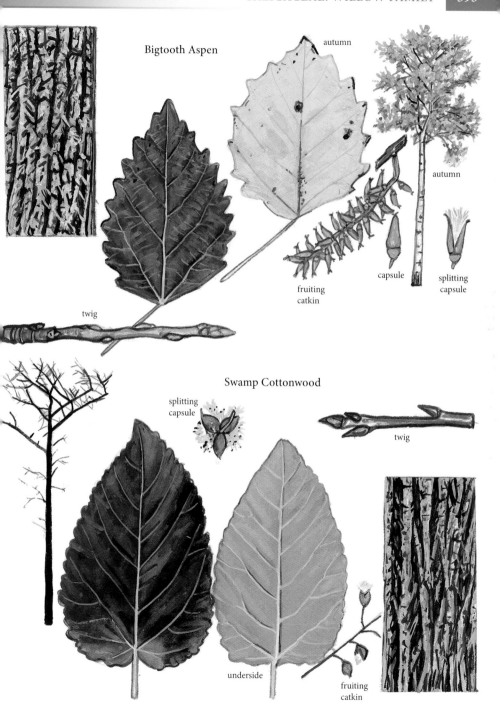

Bigtooth Aspen

autumn

autumn

fruiting
catkin

capsule

splitting
capsule

twig

Swamp Cottonwood

splitting
capsule

twig

underside

fruiting
catkin

QUAKING ASPEN *Populus tremuloides*
Michx.

QUICK ID Recognized by the combination of alternate ovate, finely toothed leaves with a laterally flattened petiole that tremble in the slightest breeze; smooth, yellowish- or creamy-white bark; and colony-forming habit.

Deciduous tree, 16–35 m tall, 30–100 cm diam. Erect, single slender, straight or crooked, usually high-branching trunk, often producing clonal thickets from the roots; crown open, rounded, with slender branches. **BARK** Smooth, yellowish white or creamy white on young trees, becoming grayish and fissured, sometimes developing long, flat ridges. **TWIG** Slender, lustrous reddish brown, hairless, becoming grayish and roughened; winter buds reddish brown, hairless. **LEAF** Alternate, simple, firm, ovate to circular; base truncate, heart-shaped, or broadly wedge-shaped; tip broadly tapering to an elongate point or abruptly short-pointed; margins finely toothed with 25–40 teeth per side. Upper surface lustrous dark green; lower surface paler and duller, often whitish, usually with 1 or 2 glands near the base. Blade 3–7 cm long, 3–7 cm broad; petiole 1–6 cm long, laterally flattened near the leaf attachment. Turns yellow and orange in autumn. **FLOWER** Unisexual, male and female in catkins on separate plants; male catkins 4–8 cm long, stamens 6–12; female catkins 4–8 cm long. Spring to early summer. **FRUIT** Cylindric or oblong, 2-valved capsule, to about 6 mm long; seeds light brown, with a tuft of whitish hairs; matures late spring to summer.

HABITAT/RANGE Native. Wet or moist forests, open woodlands, stream and swamp margins, 0–4,000 m; nearly throughout North America, Nfld. south to Va., west to Calif. and Alaska. Quaking Aspen is the most widely distributed tree in North America, absent only from the Southeast; it is more common and widespread in northern climes.

SIMILAR SPECIES The bark is reminiscent of several of the birches, which can be distinguished by their coarsely and double-toothed leaf margins and slender, densely flowered catkins. See also Eurasian Aspen.

EURASIAN ASPEN *Populus tremula* L.

Closely related and similar to Quaking Aspen, but its leaves usually have slightly larger marginal teeth, and the winter buds are usually minutely hairy. **HABITAT/RANGE** Introduced from Europe and Asia; sometimes cultivated in North America, and perhaps naturalized in Mo.

■ *SALIX*: WILLOWS

A genus of about 450 species, mostly in the Northern Hemisphere; about 113 occur in North America, with about 30 tree-size species in the East. Often in wetland habitats, occurring from sea-level to beyond the timberline; one of the few woody genera to survive on the treeless tundra and at very high elevations.

Deciduous, or rarely evergreen, shrubs and trees; individual species often display both arborescent and shrubby forms. **BARK** Generally smooth except on older trunks, then variously furrowed, often with scaly ridges. **TWIG** Usually very flexible, hairy or glabrous, often brittle at the base, sometimes breaking away and rooting on sandy banks, often at some distance from the parent plant; a single scale envelops the bud, the scale margins overlapping or fused. **LEAF** Alternate, simple, margins flat or rolled under, entire or toothed. Upper surface usually dull or lustrous, dark green; lower surface often bluish white or pale. Petiole often with glands near the point of attachment to the blade. **FLOWER** Unisexual, male and female usually produced in erect or drooping catkins on separate plants. Early spring to early summer, before, with, or after the emergence of new leaves. Lacks petals and sepals, the perianth present only as a nectary; flowers are both insect- and wind-pollinated. Male flowers have 1–10 stamens; female flowers are borne in the axil of a deciduous or persistent, usually hairy bract, each flower with 1 usually pear-shaped ovary. **FRUIT** Tiny capsule that splits at the top to release the hairy seeds.

QUAKING ASPEN

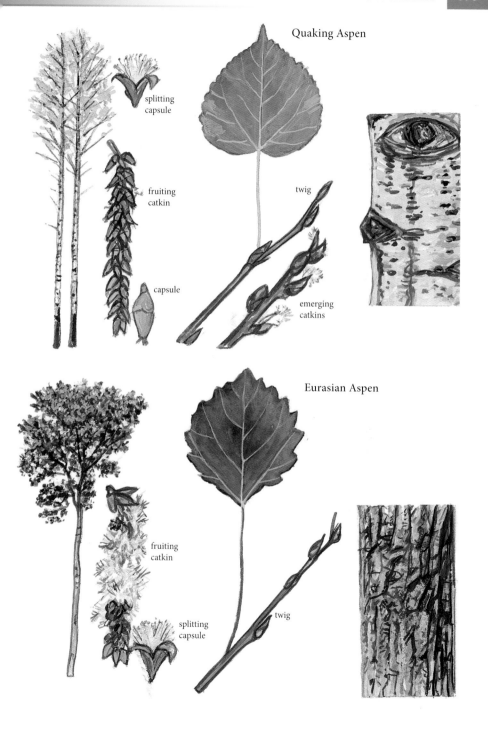

Quaking Aspen

splitting
capsule

fruiting
catkin

twig

capsule

emerging
catkins

Eurasian Aspen

fruiting
catkin

twig

splitting
capsule

Willows are often pioneer species and important in conservation, soon colonizing disturbed habitats. Salicin, a component of aspirin, occurs in the bark, and extracts from willow were used by indigenous people to treat toothache, gastrointestinal problems, and dandruff. Twigs were woven into baskets, and split branches were woven into watertight containers, scoops, and fish traps. Slender, straight stems were used for arrow shafts. Willows are important browse for deer, elk, moose, and domestic livestock. Buds, young shoots, and catkins are consumed by songbirds, ducks, and small mammals. Willow stems and branches are the preferred building material of beavers. Several introduced species have numerous horticultural variants, among them Corkscrew Willow (*S. matsudana* Koidz.) and the ever-popular Weeping Willow (*S. babylonica*).

Although the genus is usually easy to recognize, willow species are notoriously difficult to separate, often taxing the patience of even the specialist. Willows are variable and they hybridize, resulting in a plethora of forms that makes delimitation of species tenuous. A combination of flowers, leaves, and fruits is often needed for certain identification. Important features include characteristics of the petiole; the shape, color, and distribution of hairs on the leaf blade; characteristics of the leaf margin; whether the flowers appear before, with, or following leaf emergence; and the length of the catkin.

FELTLEAF WILLOW *Salix alaxensis*
(Andersson) Coville

QUICK ID Recognized by the strongly rolled leaf margins and a dense, feltlike covering of whitish hairs on the lower leaf surface.

Deciduous shrub, 1–3 m tall, rarely a small tree to about 7 m tall. Usually vase-shaped, with multiple trunks, sometimes with a single crooked trunk;

FELTLEAF WILLOW

crown ascending, irregular, open. **BARK** Reddish brown or grayish, furrowed, scaly, often with a diamond-like pattern. **TWIG** Reddish brown, densely white-hairy or nearly hairless, bud usually densely hairy. **LEAF** Alternate, simple, narrowly elliptic, oblong, or oblanceolate; base wedge-shaped; tip tapering or abruptly short-pointed; margins strongly rolled under, entire or bluntly toothed. Upper surface dull, densely hairy with whitish hairs (especially on young leaves) or nearly hairless; lower surface usually densely whitish-hairy, feltlike, sometimes the blade tissue bluish white in var. *longistylis*. Blade 5–12 cm long, 2–4 cm broad; petiole 3–20 mm long, hairy, subtended by conspicuous linear, leafy stipules 6–20 mm long. **FLOWER** Unisexual, male and female in catkins on separate plants; male catkins 3–5 cm long; female catkins 5–15 cm long. Spring to summer, before the new leaves. **FRUIT** Hairy capsule, 4–5 mm long; matures summer.

HABITAT/RANGE Native. Calcareous gravel, wet sand plains, terraces, stream and lake margins, 0–2,000 m; boreal Canada, Que., north and west to Alaska.

Notes: Feltleaf Willow is among the tallest plants in the Canadian Arctic. Two varieties are recognized: var. *alaxensis*, distributed throughout the range; and var. *longistylis* (Rydb.) Schneider, distributed mostly in w. Canada and Alaska.

WHITE WILLOW *Salix alba* L.

QUICK ID Recognized by its drooping branch tips, comparatively large size, and silvery-white appearance when viewed from a distance.

Deciduous fast-growing tree, 10–25 m tall. Erect, single trunk or multiple; crown somewhat conical, many-branched, the branches drooping at their tips. **BARK** Brown, becoming deeply furrowed with corky ridges. **TWIG** Slender, flexuous, pendent, yellowish, gray-brown, or red-brown, usually densely hairy. **LEAF** Alternate, simple, narrow, oblong, elliptic or lanceolate; base narrowly wedge-shaped; tip long-tapering, pointed; margins finely or bluntly toothed. Upper surface silky at first, becoming hairless and bluish white; lower surface silky-hairy, bluish white. Blade 4–12 cm long, 4–7 cm broad; petiole 3–13 mm long, grooved above, bearing a pair of glands near the point of leaf attachment. **FLOWER** Unisexual, male and female in erect

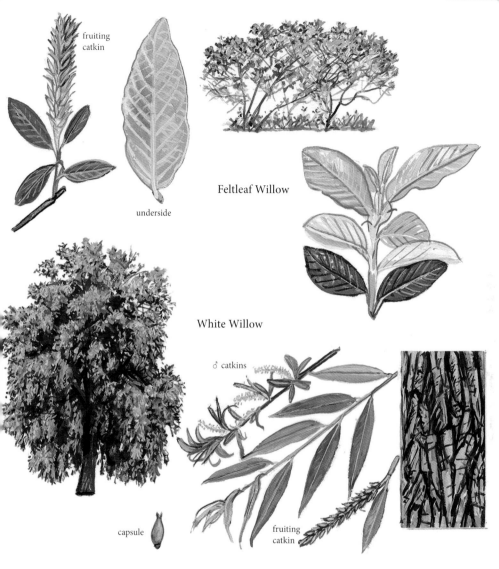

fruiting catkin

underside

Feltleaf Willow

White Willow

♂ catkins

capsule

fruiting catkin

catkins on separate plants; male catkins 27–60 mm long, 6–10 mm diam., stamens 2; female catkins 31–51 mm long, 4–8 mm diam. Spring to early summer. **FRUIT** Capsule, 3–5 mm long; matures summer.

HABITAT/RANGE Introduced from Europe in colonial times. Widely cultivated; naturalized from N.B. to n. Ga., west in the East to Sask., Minn., Nebr., and Ark.; also naturalized in the West.

SIMILAR SPECIES White Willow forms hybrids with several native and introduced species, including Crack Willow (*S. euxina*), Black Willow (*S. nigra*), Shining Willow (*S. lucida*), and Sandbar Willow (*S. interior*).

Notes: This popular ornamental has given rise to numerous cultivars that vary in size, crown shape, and foliage; many are from hybrids resulting from crosses with native species.

PEACHLEAF WILLOW *Salix amygdaloides* Andersson

QUICK ID Recognized by the hairless branches, twigs, and leaf tissue, and usually hairless or finely hairy petioles, and the leaf with a long-tapering tip, dull upper surface, and bluish-white lower surface.

Deciduous large shrub or small tree, 4–20 m tall, to about 40 cm diam. Erect, single trunk or a cluster of several leaning or ascending trunks; crown ascending, the branches gray-brown and arching, often with drooping tips. **BARK** Brown, becoming grayish brown, irregularly furrowed, with broad, flat, shaggy ridges. **TWIG** Smooth, slender, flexible, hairless, lustrous yellow or reddish brown with pale lenticels and lustrous buds. **LEAF** Alternate, simple, lanceolate or narrowly elliptic; base narrowly wedge-shaped or tapered, rarely heart-shaped; apex long-tapering to a sharp tip; margins finely toothed. Upper surface dull green, hairless, or sparsely hairy along the midvein; lower surface bluish white, hairless. Blade 5–14 cm long, 2–4 cm broad; petiole 7–21 mm long, hairless or finely hairy, with or without glands near the point of leaf attachment. **FLOWER** Unisexual, male and female in catkins on separate plants; male catkins 23–80 mm long, 5–12 mm diam.; female catkins 41–110 mm long, 8–16 mm diam. Spring to early summer, with the new leaves. **FRUIT** Reddish or yellowish capsule, 3–7 mm long; matures summer.

HABITAT/RANGE Native. Floodplains, lake margins, marshes, wet sand dunes, often in association with sandy, silty, or gravelly sites, 60–2,400 m; widespread, Que., N.Y., and Pa., southwest to Tex., west to B.C.; absent from the Southeast.

SIMILAR SPECIES The branches, twigs, petioles, and leaves of Carolina Willow (*S. caroliniana*) are more likely to be hairy, and the upper surfaces of the leaves lustrous green.

LITTLETREE WILLOW *Salix arbusculoides* Andersson

QUICK ID Recognized by the combination of lustrous reddish-brown twigs, leaf margin finely toothed and slightly rolled under, the upper surface of the leaf conspicuously lustrous, and the lower surface silky white-hairy.

Deciduous small thicket-forming shrub or tree, to about 9 m tall. Erect, usually multiple trunks, often crowded together and low-branching; crown ascending, the branches lustrous, sometimes exfoliating. **BARK** Smooth, becoming ridged and furrowed, usually forming a diamond-like pattern. **TWIG** Slender, reddish brown or gray, sparsely hairy. **LEAF** Alternate, simple, narrowly elliptic; base tapering, narrowly wedge-shaped; tip pointed or abruptly short-pointed; margins slightly rolled under, finely toothed, the teeth gland-tipped. Upper surface lustrous green, hairless; lower surface usually silvery-hairy with silky hairs, the tissue bluish white. Blade 4–8 cm long, 1–2 cm broad; petiole 3–11 mm long. **FLOWER** Unisexual, male and female in catkins on separate trees; male catkins 17–43 mm long, 5–10 mm diam.; female catkins 20–46 mm long, 6–15 mm diam. Spring to summer, with the new leaves. **FRUIT** White-hairy capsule, 4–6 mm long; matures summer.

HABITAT/RANGE Native. Stream and lake margins, clearings in White Spruce forests, bogs, fens, tundra margin, 0–2,000 m; a Canadian species distributed from Que. to Alaska.

SIMILAR SPECIES Bebb Willow (*S. bebbiana*) and Feltleaf Willow (*S. alaxensis*) have similar bark, but their leaf margins are entire or only slightly toothed.

PEACHLEAF WILLOW

LITTLETREE WILLOW

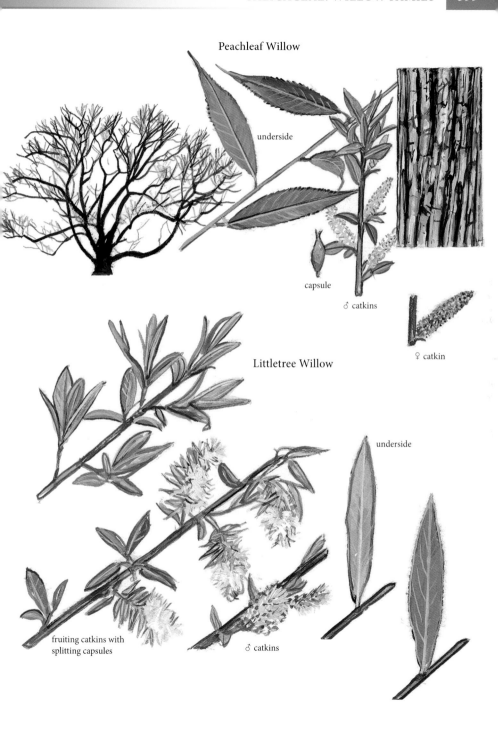

Peachleaf Willow

underside

capsule

♂ catkins

♀ catkin

Littletree Willow

underside

fruiting catkins with
splitting capsules

♂ catkins

DIAMONDLEAF WILLOW *Salix planifolia* Pursh

QUICKID Recognized in the East by the lustrous upper leaf surface with closely set, parallel veins, and the typically alpine or boreal habitat.

Deciduous shrub or small tree, 1–9 m tall, sometimes forming clones by layering. Ascending or spreading, sometimes with the trunk reclining and branch tips ascending; branches yellowish, reddish, or violet, sometimes slightly glaucous. **TWIG** Yellow, red-brown, or violet, varying from densely hairy to hairless. **LEAF** Alternate, simple, elliptic, oblong, or obovate; base wedge-shaped; tip acutely pointed; margins entire (especially toward the petiole) or bluntly toothed, the teeth gland-tipped. Upper surface lustrous green, hairless or sparsely hairy, lateral veins closely set and regularly spaced; lower surface bluish white, hairless or sparsely silky-hairy. Blade 2–6 cm long, 1–2 cm broad; petiole 2–13 mm long. **FLOWER** Unisexual, male and female in stout catkins on separate plants; male catkins 12–41 mm long, 10–20 mm diam.; female catkins 15–67 mm long, 8–18 mm diam. Late spring to early summer, before the new leaves. **FRUIT** Capsule, 5–6 mm long; matures summer.

HABITAT/RANGE Native. Alpine, subalpine, and boreal meadows and riverbanks, streams, bogs, fens, seepages, usually in association with sandy loam or rocky substrates, 100–4,000 m; ne. U.S. and Canada, N.S. and Nfld., south to N.H., west to Sask. and S.D. in the East; throughout the West.

SIMILAR SPECIES The leaves of Pussy Willow (*S. discolor*) are duller on the upper surface, and the veins are widely and irregularly spaced and curve upward.

PUSSY WILLOW *Salix discolor* Muhl.

QUICKID Recognized by the densely hairy catkins that appear in early spring and the conspicuous color contrast between the upper and lower surfaces of the leaf.

Deciduous, normally a shrub not exceeding about 4 m tall, rarely a small, clumping tree 6–8 m tall. Erect or leaning, usually with multiple trunks; crown open, branches upright. **BARK** Grayish brown or reddish. **TWIG** Stout, lustrous, red-brown, hairy at first, becoming hairless, with pale lenticels. **LEAF** Alternate, simple, stiff, narrowly elliptic or somewhat obovate; base wedge-shaped; tip pointed; margins entire or toothed, especially toward the tip. Upper surface dull or slightly lustrous, the lateral veins raised, irregularly spaced, curving toward the leaf margin; lower surface conspicuously bluish white, contrasting sharply with the upper surface, hairless or hairy, the hairs sometimes long and silky. Blade 3–10 cm long, 1–3 cm broad; petiole 6–17 mm long. **FLOWER** Unisexual, male and female in catkins on separate plants; male catkins 23–52 mm long, 12–22 mm diam., appearing fuzzy and sometimes resembling a small bottlebrush; female catkins 25–108 mm long, 12–33 mm diam. Mid-spring, before the new leaves. **FRUIT** Hairy capsule, 6–12 mm long.

HABITAT/RANGE Native. Pond and stream margins, alluvial woods, fens, seepages, 0–2,400 m; Nfld. and N.S., south to N.C., west to B.C. and Idaho.

SIMILAR SPECIES Rusty Willow (*S. atrocinerea*) and Large Gray Willow (*S. cinerea*) can usually be distinguished from Pussy Willow by their lateral leaf veins, which are parallel and closely spaced as opposed to irregular.

RUSTY WILLOW *Salix atrocinerea* Brot.

A shrub or small tree, 3–12 m tall, very similar to Pussy Willow (*S. discolor*). It has yellow-, gray-, or red-brown branches, and its leaves are densely hairy on the lower surface and have parallel, closely spaced lateral leaf veins. **HABITAT/RANGE** Introduced from Europe; most conspicuously naturalized in New England, N.Y., and Pa.; in some areas is considered invasive.

DIAMONDLEAF WILLOW

PUSSY WILLOW

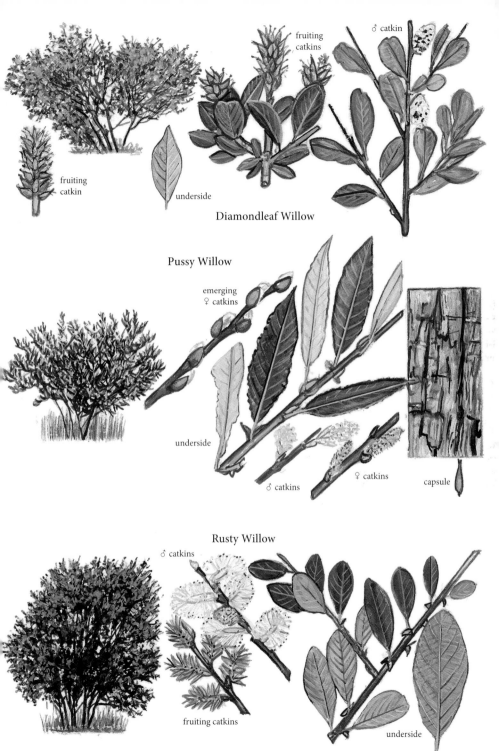

fruiting
catkin

underside

fruiting
catkins

♂ catkin

Diamondleaf Willow

Pussy Willow

emerging
♀ catkins

underside

♂ catkins

♀ catkins

capsule

Rusty Willow

♂ catkins

fruiting catkins

underside

LARGE GRAY WILLOW *Salix cinerea* L.

Typically a multistemmed shrub, 3–7 m tall, with hairy brownish branches and densely hairy yellowish-brown twigs. Its lateral leaf veins are parallel and closely spaced. **HABITAT/RANGE** Introduced from Eurasia; well established in the East from Ont. and N.Y. south to Ga., Ala., and La.; sometimes treated as an invasive species.

BEBB WILLOW *Salix bebbiana* Sarg.
A.K.A. DIAMOND WILLOW, BEAKED WILLOW

QUICK ID Recognized by the combination of long-beaked capsules, and dull green leaves that are quilted above and whitish hairy beneath.

Deciduous shrub or shrubby tree, 1–10 m tall, to about 15 cm diam. Erect or spreading, usually with multiple closely set, upright trunks; branches upright or ascending, forming an arching or spreading crown. **BARK** Dark reddish brown to yellowish brown or grayish brown, becoming furrowed, often with diamond-shaped fungal patches. **TWIG** Reddish purple to yellow- or orange-brown, hairy at first, usually becoming hairless. **LEAF** Alternate, simple, elliptic, oblong, or obovate, sometimes narrowly so; base broadly wedge-shaped or rounded; tip acute or abruptly short-pointed; margins usually entire, or bluntly or sharply glandular-toothed, primarily toward the base. Upper surface dull or moderately lustrous green, hairy or nearly hairless, usually with conspicuously depressed veins, quiltlike; lower surface bluish white, white-hairy. Blade mostly 3–10 cm long, 2–4 cm broad; petiole 2–13 mm long. **FLOWER** Unisexual, male and female in catkins on separate trees; male catkins 10–42 mm long, 7–16 mm diam.; female catkins 16–85 mm long, 9–32 mm diam. Spring to early summer, just before the leaves. **FRUIT** Long-tipped (beaked), sparsely hairy capsule, 5–9 mm long; matures summer.

HABITAT/RANGE Native. Moist conifer forests, often in association with Jack Pine, 0–3,300 m; n. and w. U.S. and throughout Canada; Nfld. south to Md. and west to Nebr. in the East; widespread in the West. Among the more widespread boreal willows.

SIMILAR SPECIES Balsam Willow (*S. pyrifolia*) and Goat Willow (*S. caprea*) also have relatively broad leaves; see those species for distinguishing characters.

SATINY WILLOW *Salix pellita*
(Andersson) Bebb

QUICK ID Recognized in part by the narrow leaves, strongly bluish white below and lustrous above, and the bluish-gray branches.

Deciduous, usually a shrub, occasionally a small tree, 3–6 m tall. Erect or ascending, usually with multiple trunks, branches often brittle at base, reddish brown or yellowish brown, usually obscured with a bluish-gray powdery covering, hairy or hairless. **LEAF** Alternate, simple, linear, narrowly elliptic, or narrowly lanceolate; base narrowly wedge-shaped; tip abruptly short-pointed; margins usually rolled under, entire, wavy, or finely blunt-toothed. Upper surface lustrous, usually glossy, hairless or sparsely hairy; lower surface strongly bluish white, usually densely hairy, sometimes slightly so. Blade 4–12 cm long, 6–20 mm broad; petiole 3–14 mm long, flattened or grooved. **FLOWER** Unisexual, male and female in catkins on separate plants; male catkins 20–39 mm long, 7–20 mm diam.; female catkins 19–65 mm long, 7–17 mm diam., becoming longer in fruit. Spring to early summer, before the leaves. **FRUIT** Capsule, 3–6 mm long.

HABITAT/RANGE Native. River and stream banks, floodplain forests, moist thickets, forested swamps, lake and pond margins, usually associated with rich alluvial soils, 0–800 m; ne. U.S. and e. Canada, Nfld. south to N.H., west to Sask. and Minn. Considered threatened in some northeastern states.

SIMILAR SPECIES Diamond-leaf Willow (*S. planifolia*) also has branches that are bluish gray but not as strongly colored as those of Satiny Willow.

BEBB WILLOW   SATINY WILLOW

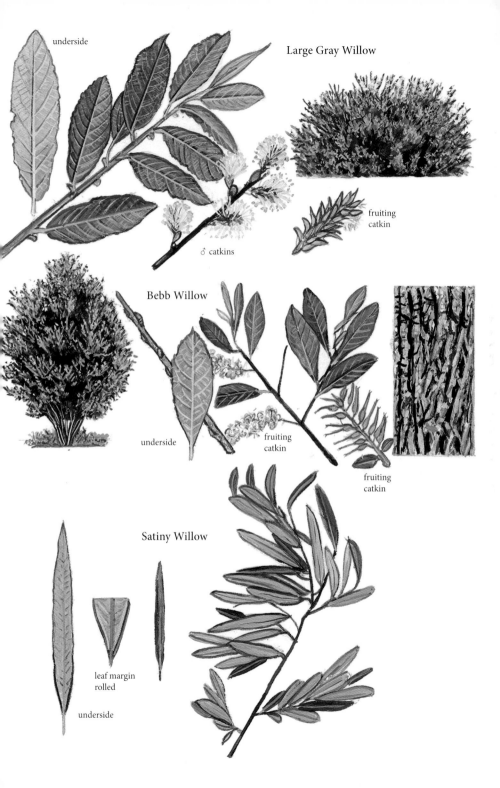

underside

Large Gray Willow

♂ catkins

fruiting catkin

Bebb Willow

underside

fruiting catkin

fruiting catkin

Satiny Willow

leaf margin rolled

underside

BLACK WILLOW *Salix nigra* Marshall

QUICKID Recognized among eastern willows by its combination of mature size; the deeply furrowed dark brown to nearly black bark with broad, interconnected ridges that become plate-like; and leaves that are green and semi-lustrous beneath, with hair in the axils and along main veins.

Deciduous, relatively large tree, 12–20 m tall, 30–100 cm diam. Erect or leaning, single trunk, often dividing near the base into 2 main trunks; crown irregular, broadly rounded, the branches red-brown or dark gray-brown, stout, spreading, the smaller branches often breaking off. **BARK** Thick, becoming dark brown or nearly black and deeply furrowed into flat, scaly, plate-like ridges, eventually shaggy. **TWIG** Slender, hairy or hairless, bright reddish brown, becoming darker; brittle at the base and easily breaking. **LEAF** Alternate, simple, narrowly lanceolate or nearly linear; base narrowly wedge-shaped; tip long-tapering; margins finely glandular-toothed. Upper surface green, moderately lustrous; lower surface duller, semi-lustrous, hairy on the veins and in the vein axils. Blade 5–18 cm long, 5–20 mm broad; petiole 2–10 mm long. **FLOWER** Unisexual, male and female in catkins on separate trees; male catkins 35–83 mm long, 7–13 mm diam.; female catkins 23–74 mm long, 5–10 mm diam. (slightly longer in fruit). Early to late spring, with the emergence of new leaves. **FRUIT** Egg- or cone-shaped capsule, 3–5 mm long.

HABITAT/RANGE Native. Floodplains, swamps, marshes, river sandbars, pond and lake margins, ditches, canals, Atlantic White Cedar bogs, wet meadows, open fields, 10–1,400 m; widespread in the East, N.B. to Ont., south to Fla. and Tex.

BLACK WILLOW

SIMILAR SPECIES The leaves of Crack Willow (*S. euxina*) and Carolina Willow (*S. caroliniana*) are grayish beneath.

GOODDING'S BLACK WILLOW *Salix gooddingii* C.R. Ball

QUICKID Twigs usually yellowish and often brittle, leaves green beneath, margins toothed.

Closely related and similar to Black Willow (*S. nigra*), with which it is sometimes considered conspecific. It has yellow-brown or pale gray-brown branches, and capsules 6–7 mm long.

HABITAT/RANGE Native; a western species ranging into the East in Okla. and Tex.

GOODDING'S BLACK WILLOW

CRACK WILLOW *Salix euxina*
V. Belyaeva
A.K.A. BRITTLE WILLOW

Formerly recognized as *S. fragilis* L., this willow forms a tree 6–18 m tall and is marked by its lustrous, extremely brittle branches. **HABITAT/RANGE** Introduced from Asia; Que., Ont., and perhaps elsewhere.

Black Willow

♂ catkin

fruiting catkin

capsule

Goodding's Black Willow

spring

fruiting catkins

capsule

fruiting catkin

Crack Willow

♂ catkins

twig

fruiting catkin

capsule

CAROLINA WILLOW *Salix caroliniana*
Michx.
A.K.A. COASTAL PLAIN WILLOW

QUICKID Recognized among the willows by its combination of narrowly lanceolate leaves that are bluish white beneath and finely toothed along the margins, the development of leaflike stipules in late-developing leaves, and the mostly southern distribution.

Deciduous medium tree, 5–10 m tall, 30–40 cm diam. Erect, single trunk, often low-branching and leaning; crown irregular, branches ascending and spreading, brittle, easily breaking. **BARK** Brown, becoming fissured into large, broad, scaly ridges. **TWIG** Slender, dull yellowish brown, reddish brown, grayish, or light brown, densely hairy, sometimes hairless. **LEAF** Alternate, simple, narrowly lanceolate; base wedge-shaped or nearly rounded; tip long-tapering, narrowly pointed; margins finely toothed. Upper surface lustrous green, hairless or hairy along the veins; lower surface bluish white, hairless or hairy along the veins. Blade 5–22 cm long, usually 1–3 cm broad, rarely broader; petiole 3–22 mm long, on early- or late-developing leaves sometimes subtended by conspicuous rounded, non-persistent stipules. **FLOWER** Unisexual, male and female in catkins on separate plants; male catkins 28–97 mm long, 5–11 mm diam.; female catkins 33–93 mm long, 7–15 mm diam. Late winter to early summer, before the new leaves. **FRUIT** Capsule, 4–7 mm long.

HABITAT/RANGE Native. Floodplains, swamps, marshes, river sandbars, pond and lake margins, interdune swales, ditches, canals, wet clearings, calcareous flats, 0–600 m; widespread in the East, Pa. and Ill., south to Fla., Kans., and Tex.

SIMILAR SPECIES The leaves of Florida Willow (*S. floridana*) are much broader and those of Black Willow (*S. nigra*) are dull green and semi-lustrous beneath. Peachleaf Willow (*S. amygdaloides*) is more northerly in distribution.

SILKY WILLOW *Salix sericea* Marshall

QUICKID Recognized by the combination of leaves bearing white silky hairs, capsules not exceeding about 4 mm long, and branches brittle at the base.

Deciduous, typically a large shrub, occasionally a small tree, to 4 m tall, sometimes forming clones; branches brittle. **BARK** Smooth, grayish, usually with conspicuous raised lenticels. **TWIG** Slender, purplish, finely hairy at first, becoming hairless. **LEAF** Alternate, simple, narrowly elliptic, narrowly oblong, or lanceolate; base wedge-shaped or rounded; tip evenly or abruptly tapering to a narrow point; margins flat, minutely bluntly toothed. Upper surface silky-hairy at first, becoming sparsely hairy or nearly hairless, the blade tissue dull green; lower surface densely silky-hairy, the blade tissue bluish white. Blade 5–12 cm long, 1–3 cm broad; petiole 3–21 mm long. **FLOWER** Unisexual, male and female in catkins on separate plants; male catkins 13–40 mm long, 4–9 mm diam.; female catkins 18–43 mm long, 5–12 mm diam. Late winter to spring, with or just before the new leaves. **FRUIT** Capsule, 2.5–4 mm long.

HABITAT/RANGE Native. Wet banks, boggy shores and stream banks, low woods, wet meadows, sandy terraces, 5–1,300 m; widespread in the East, Que. and N.S., west to Wis. and Iowa, south to n. Ga., Ala., and Ark.

SIMILAR SPECIES Meadow Willow (*S. petiolaris*) is distinguished by its stout, non-brittle branches, less hairy leaves, and longer capsules.

CAROLINA WILLOW   SILKY WILLOW   MEADOW WILLOW

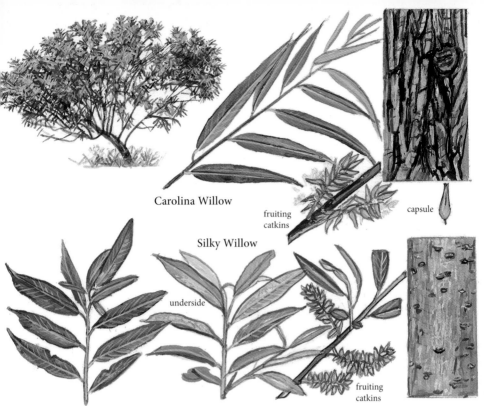

Carolina Willow

Silky Willow

fruiting catkins

capsule

underside

fruiting catkins

Meadow Willow

fruiting catkins

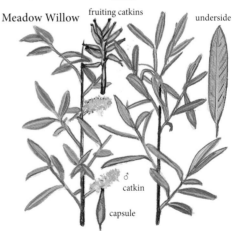

underside

♂ catkin

capsule

MEADOW WILLOW *Salix petiolaris*
Smith

QUICK ID The long, slender, arching purplish stems and branches and open wetland habitat help distinguish Meadow Willow.

Deciduous large shrub or multitrunked tree, 1–7 m tall, the branches slender, arching, red-brown, purple, or violet, finely hairy, becoming hairless. **BARK** Grayish green or reddish brown, becoming dark brown. **TWIG** Yellow-green or olive brown at first, becoming dark brown. **LEAF** Alternate, simple, narrowly elliptic or lanceolate; base wedge-shaped or acute; tip often abruptly pointed; margins entire or finely toothed. Upper surface dull or lustrous, hairless or sparsely hairy; lower surface densely silky-hairy, becoming hairless, the blade tissue bluish white. Blade 4–15 cm long, 1–3 cm broad; petiole 3–11 mm long, usually hairy. **FLOWER** Unisexual, male and female in catkins on separate plants; male catkins 12–29 mm long, 6–17 mm diam.; female catkins 12–39 mm long, 6–18 mm diam. Spring to early summer, with the new leaves. **FRUIT** Finely silky-hairy capsule, 5–9 mm long.

HABITAT/RANGE Native. Meadows, openings in low, moist deciduous woods, lake margins, wet sandy prairies, 10–2,700 m; N.S. and N.B., west to B.C., Minn., Nebr., and Colo., south to Pa. and Ill.

SIMILAR SPECIES Silky Willow (*S. sericea*) is distinguished by its brittle branches, young leaves with whitish hairs throughout, and shorter capsules.

PURPLEOSIER WILLOW *Salix purpurea* L.

QUICK ID Recognized among the willows by the alternate and opposite leaves with comparatively short petioles.

Deciduous clone-forming shrub or shrubby tree, 1.5–5 m tall. Erect, upright, or arching, usually with numerous branches and multiple trunks, branches yellow- or olive-brown, hairless. **BARK** Pale gray, smooth, hairless. **TWIG** Purplish or yellowish-brown, hairless. **LEAF** Alternate or opposite, simple, narrowly oblong or oblanceolate, often widest near the tip; base rounded or wedge-shaped; tip sharply pointed; margins entire or obscurely toothed toward the tip. Upper surface dull or slightly lustrous, dark green, hairless; lower surface bluish white, hairless. Blade 2–10 cm long, 1.5–3 cm broad; petiole 2–7 mm long. **FLOWER** Unisexual, male and female in catkins on separate plants; male catkins 25–33 mm long, 6–10 mm diam.; female catkins 13–35 mm long, 3–7 mm diam. Spring, before the new leaves. **FRUIT** Egg-shaped capsule, 2–5 mm long.

HABITAT/RANGE Introduced from Europe. Cultivated, naturalized in various wetlands throughout much of the East, south to about Ga., west to Minn. and Iowa; also scattered in the West.

MISSOURI RIVER WILLOW *Salix eriocephala* Michx.
A.K.A. HEART-LEAF WILLOW

QUICK ID Recognized by its lanceolate leaves, which are bluish gray below and subtended by conspicuous, persistent rounded, leaflike stipules to about 15 mm broad.

Deciduous shrub or small shrubby tree, 3–6 m tall. Erect or leaning, usually with multiple trunks or

low-branching; crown rounded. **BARK** Reddish brown, scaly, slightly furrowed. **TWIG** Reddish brown, hairy at first, becoming hairless. **LEAF** Alternate, simple, lanceolate or oblanceolate; base rounded and inconspicuously heart-shaped; tip tapering to a long point; margins finely toothed, the teeth gland-tipped. Upper surface dark green, hairless; lower surface bluish gray. Blade 6–12 cm long, 2–3 cm broad; petiole 3–18 mm long, subtended by conspicuous, persistent rounded or kidney-shaped, leaflike clasping stipules, 8–15 mm broad, usually broader than long. **FLOWER** Unisexual, male and female in catkins on separate plants; male catkins 19–44 mm long, 7–14 mm diam.; female catkins 22–65 mm long, 7–14 mm diam. Spring to early summer. **FRUIT** Yellowish-brown capsule, 3.5–7 mm long.

HABITAT/RANGE Native. Gravelly or rocky stream banks, marshy fields, ditch banks, moist upland woods, alluvial plains, 0–1,200 m; widespread in the East, Nfld. to Ont., N.D., and Kans., south to nw. Fla., Ala., and Ark.

SIMILAR SPECIES Silky Willow (*S. sericea*) lacks the conspicuous, persistent leaflike stipules. Young or growing branches of Carolina Willow (*S. caroliniana*) also sometimes produce enlarged stipules, but they are not persistent.

FLORIDA WILLOW *Salix floridana* Chapm.

QUICK ID Recognized in its restricted distribution by the comparatively broad leaves, which are bluish white beneath.

Deciduous few-branched shrub or small tree, to about 4 m tall. Erect, usually a single trunk or multiple; crown open, irregular, branches usually brittle at the joints. **BARK** Dark reddish brown or gray-brown, scaly. **TWIG** Brittle, yellow-brown or red-brown, densely hairy at first, becoming nearly hairless. **LEAF** Alternate, simple, broadly lanceolate, narrowly ovate, elliptic, or oblong; base rounded, rarely heart-shaped; tip bluntly or sharply pointed; margins toothed or entire, glandular. Upper surface dark green, hairy along the midvein and lateral veins; lower surface bluish white, usually with brownish veins. Blade 8–16 cm long, 3–5 cm

MISSOURI RIVER WILLOW

FLORIDA WILLOW

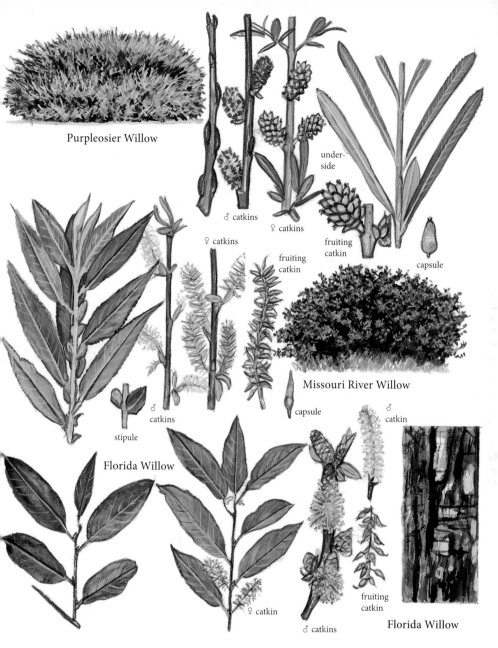

Purpleosier Willow

under-side

♂ catkins

♀ catkins

♀ catkins

fruiting catkin

fruiting catkin

capsule

Missouri River Willow

capsule

♂ catkins

stipule

Florida Willow

♂ catkin

♀ catkin

♂ catkins

fruiting catkin

Florida Willow

broad; petiole 1–2 cm long, stout, on mature leaves often subtended by conspicuous rounded, clasping stipules. **FLOWER** Unisexual, male and female in catkins on separate plants; male catkins 29–72 mm long, 12–15 mm diam.; female catkins 50–81 mm long, 17–27 mm diam. Spring, with the new leaves. **FRUIT** Yellowish-brown capsule, 6–7 mm long.

HABITAT/RANGE Native. Wet, swampy woodlands, margins of spring runs, 0–40 m; Fla. and Ga., considered endangered.

SIMILAR SPECIES Potentially confused with broad-leaved forms of Carolina Willow (*S. caroliniana*).

GOAT WILLOW *Salix caprea* L.

QUICK ID Recognized among the northern willows by the comparatively large, broad leaves.

Deciduous shrub or small tree, 8–15 m tall. Upright, vase-shaped, usually with multiple trunks or very low-branching; crown oblong; branches ascending, brownish, hairy or not. **BARK** Grayish, becoming fissured. **TWIG** Yellow- or gray-brown, sparsely or densely hairy. **LEAF** Alternate, simple, narrowly or broadly elliptic or obovate; base wedge-shaped or rounded; tip abruptly short-pointed; margins entire or bluntly toothed. Upper surface dull, sparsely hairy; lower surface bluish white, hairy. Blade 5–13 cm long, 2–8 cm broad; petiole 7–25 mm long, often flattened. **FLOWER** Unisexual, male and female in catkins on separate plants; male catkins 16–39 mm long, 12–30 cm diam.; female catkins 27–64 mm long, 10–25 mm diam. Spring, before the leaves. **FRUIT** Capsule, 6–12 mm long.

HABITAT/RANGE Introduced from Europe. Cultivated and established in scattered locations throughout the East.

SIMILAR SPECIES Distinguished from most native willows by the broad leaves. Balsam Willow (*S. pyrifolia*) also has broadly elliptic leaves, but it flowers later.

BALSAM WILLOW *Salix pyrifolia*
Andersson

QUICK ID Recognized by the typically oval leaves, late flowering, and northern distribution.

Deciduous large, vigorous shrub or small tree, to 9 m tall. **BARK** Reddish brown. **TWIG** Yellowish green, becoming glossy, lustrous, dark red or reddish brown, hairless. **LEAF** Alternate, simple, thick, elliptic, oval, or broadly ovate; base rounded, usually heart-shaped; tip short-pointed, sometimes abruptly so; margins bluntly or sharply toothed, often wavy. Upper surface lustrous, hairless; lower surface bluish white, hairless. Blade 3–10 cm long, 2–5 cm broad; petiole 7–20 mm long, usually grooved. **FLOWER** Unisexual, male and female in catkins on separate plants; male catkins 18–63 mm long, 7–15 mm diam.; female catkins 25–85 mm long, 8–20 mm diam. Late spring to summer, just before or with the new leaves. **FRUIT** Capsule, 7–8 mm long.

HABITAT/RANGE Native. Lake and pond margins, fens, forested bogs, 0–300 m; ne. U.S. and Canada, Nfld. and N.Y., west to Minn., B.C., and Y.T.

SIMILAR SPECIES Goat Willow (*S. caprea*) is similar in leaf size and shape, but the lower surface of its leaf is usually hairy and plants flower earlier.

BALSAM WILLOW

ELAEAGNUS WILLOW *Salix elaeagnos*
Scop.
A.K.A. HOARY WILLOW

QUICK ID Recognized by the combination of the narrowly linear leaves, bluish white below, and the slender catkins.

Deciduous tall shrub or small tree, 1–15 m tall. Erect, often with multiple trunks; crown irregular, branches yellow- or red-brown, long, spreading, erect or gracefully arching. **TWIG** Slender, lustrous, dark brown, grayish-hairy, becoming hairless. **LEAF** Alternate, simple, narrowly linear; base rounded or narrowly pointed; tip acute or bluntly pointed; margins finely toothed, especially toward the tip. Upper surface lustrous or dull, hairy or hairless; lower surface bluish white, densely whitish-hairy. Blade 5–20 cm long, usually not exceeding about 1 cm broad; petiole 2–6 mm long. **FLOWER** Unisexual, male and female in catkins on separate plants; male catkins 26–34 mm long, 6–10 mm diam.; female catkins 19–40 mm long, 3–10 mm diam. Spring, slightly before or with the emergence of new leaves. **FRUIT** Capsule, 3–5 mm long.

HABITAT/RANGE Introduced from Europe. Cultivated, established in scattered locations in e. Canada and U.S., mostly in the north.

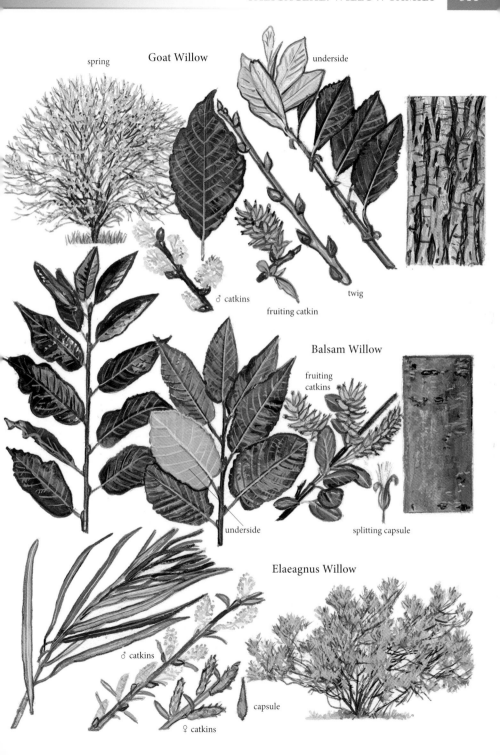

Goat Willow

spring

underside

♂ catkins

fruiting catkin

twig

Balsam Willow

fruiting catkins

underside

splitting capsule

Elaeagnus Willow

♂ catkins

♀ catkins

capsule

SHINING WILLOW *Salix lucida* Muhl.

QUICK ID Recognized by the combination of its broad, glossy, dark green leaves with an extended tip; usually hairy twigs; and golden anthers on male flowers.

Deciduous shrub or tree, 4–6 m tall, 15–20 cm diam. Upright, single short trunk or often multiple; crown rounded and dense, sometimes open and spreading on arborescent plants. **TWIG** Yellowish brown, reddish brown, or orange-brown, lustrous and glossy, usually hairy (sometimes nearly hairless). **LEAF** Alternate, simple, elliptic or lanceolate; base rounded; tip abruptly narrowing to an extended point; margins entire (especially on the lower ½ of the blade), glandular, or finely toothed. Upper surface lustrous, dark green, hairy or not; lower surface paler, hairless or densely hairy. Blade 6–14 cm long, 1–4 cm broad; petiole 5–13 mm long, young leaves subtended by leaflike stipules. **FLOWER** Unisexual, male and female in catkins on separate plants; male catkins 19–69 mm long, 4–14 mm diam., anthers golden; female catkins 23–56 mm long, 8–12 mm diam. Summer, after the new leaves. **FRUIT** Capsule, 5–7 mm long.

HABITAT/RANGE Native. Floodplains, lake margins, meadows, fens, bogs, 0–600 m; Nfld. and Lab., south to Va. (where introduced) and Ill., west to Sask., N.D., and S.D.

SIMILAR SPECIES Similar to Laurel Willow (*S. pentandra*), in which the tip of the leaf is slightly less drawn out, the twigs are hairless, and young leaves are not subtended by leaflike stipules.

SHINING WILLOW

LAUREL WILLOW *Salix pentandra* L.
A.K.A. BAY-LEAF WILLOW

QUICK ID Recognized by the combination of its broad, glossy, dark green leaves; lustrous, hairless twigs; golden anthers on male flowers; and densely rounded form.

Deciduous shrub or tree, 5–15 m tall, usually a tall shrub in the wild, taking on the stature of a tree in cultivation. Erect, single short, low-branching trunk or multiple trunks; crown rounded, the branches flexible, lustrous brown or yellow-brown, spreading or ascending. **BARK** Gray, shallowly fissured. **TWIG** Hairless, lustrous reddish brown. **LEAF** Alternate, simple, narrowly elliptic or linear; base rounded or broadly wedge-shaped, the blade tissue usually extending onto the petiole; tip abruptly narrowed to a moderately extended point; margins entire or finely toothed. Upper surface lustrous, dark green, hairless; lower surface paler, hairless. Blade 5–13 cm long, 2–5 cm broad; petiole 5–15 mm long, glandular near the attachment to the blade, stipules rudimentary. **FLOWER** Unisexual, male and female in catkins on separate plants; male catkins 27–81 mm long, 9–13 mm diam., anthers golden; female catkins 29–68 mm long. Early summer, with the new leaves. **FRUIT** Capsule, 6–9 mm long.

HABITAT/RANGE Introduced from Eurasia. Cultivated and established in much of the East, from about N.C. and Ky. northward.

SIMILAR SPECIES Similar to Shining Willow (*S. lucida*), in which the leaf is more drawn out to a narrow, extended tip. Shining Willow is further distinguished by its often hairy twigs and leaflike stipules subtending young leaves.

LAUREL WILLOW

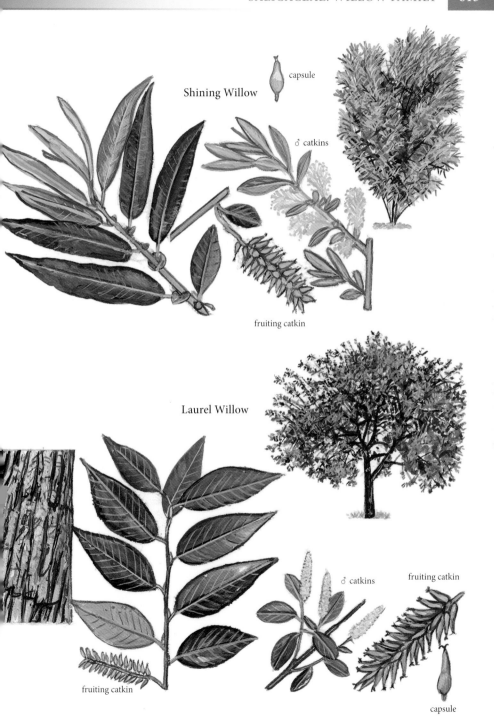

capsule

Shining Willow

♂ catkins

fruiting catkin

Laurel Willow

♂ catkins

fruiting catkin

fruiting catkin

capsule

SANDBAR WILLOW *Salix interior*
Rowlee

QUICK ID Recognized by its sprawling, thicket-forming habit and narrowly linear leaves that are only slightly bluish white beneath.

Deciduous thicket-forming shrub or small tree, 4–9 m tall. Usually shrubby and sprawling, with multiple clonal trunks arising from wide-ranging surface roots; sometimes erect, with a single trunk; crown dense, rounded on shrubby plants, erect, ascending, or columnar on arborescent plants. **BARK** Smooth, thin, reddish brown. **TWIG** Yellowish brown to reddish brown, densely hairy or nearly hairless. **LEAF** Alternate, simple, narrowly linear; base wedge-shaped; tip abruptly pointed; margins remotely toothed. Upper surface moderately lustrous, hairy or nearly hairless; lower surface paler, slightly bluish white, densely hairy or nearly hairless. Blade 6–16 cm long, 4–11 mm broad; petiole 1–9 mm long. **FLOWER** Unisexual, male and female in catkins on separate plants, or rarely with male and female flowers intermixed on the same catkin; male catkins 20–61 mm long, 4–10 mm diam.; female catkins 20–67 mm long, 5–9 mm diam. Spring to summer, after the new leaves. **FRUIT** Capsule, 4–10 mm long.

HABITAT/RANGE Native. Riverine sandbars, sandy and silty floodplains, lake and pond margins, sand hills in prairies, disturbed sites, 10–1,800 m; widespread, the range forming a broad triangle from Que. and N.B., southwest through Va. and Tenn. to La. and Tex., thence northwest through Colo. and B.C. to Alaska.

SIMILAR SPECIES Elaeagnus Willow (*S. eleagnos*) also has narrow, linear leaves often not exceeding about 1 cm broad, but it flowers just before or with new leaf emergence.

SANDBAR WILLOW

HYBRID WHITE WILLOW *Salix × jesupii* Fernald

Deciduous shrub or small tree 7–10 m tall with red-brown twigs and branchlets. **LEAF** Alternate, simple, bluish white and moderately to sparsely hairy beneath. Origin unknown, probably a hybrid between the native Shining Willow (*S. lucida*) and introduced White Willow (*S. alba*). **HABITAT/RANGE** Planted, sometimes naturalized, on stream and lake margins, sand dunes, and railroad rights of way, and in wet woods; in the East in Canada and n. U.S., from P.E.I. south to Va., west to Sask., Wis., and Ill.

WISCONSIN WEEPING WILLOW *Salix × pendulina* Wender.

Deciduous shrub or small tree to about 12 m tall, with a pendulous crown and very brittle branches. **LEAF** Alternate, simple, narrowly elliptic, linear, or narrowly lanceolate; margins coarsely or finely toothed, the teeth often minutely spine-tipped; lower surface bluish white. A hybrid of Weeping Willow (*S. babylonica*) and Crack Willow (*S. euxina*). **HABITAT/RANGE** Cultivated in the East, Ont. south to Ga., west to Nebr. and Tex.

HYBRID WHITE WILLOW *Salix × fragilis* L.

Deciduous tree to 20 m tall with a single or several erect, drooping, or strongly ascending trunks, branches often yellowish, brittle at the base. **LEAF** Alternate, simple, narrowly or very narrowly elliptic, margins regularly toothed, surfaces silky-hairy to nearly hairless, lower surface bluish white, petiole densely hairy on the lower side, glandular near the leaf attachment. A hybrid of White Willow (*S. alba*) and Crack Willow (*S. euxina*), and intermediate in size between the parents. **HABITAT/RANGE** Widely cultivated across Canada and the U.S.

Sandbar Willow

bud

fruiting catkin

capsule

autumn

twig

♂ catkins

Hybrid White Willow
(*Salix × jesupii*)

underside

♂ catkin

young twigs

fruiting catkin

capsule

shrubby form

Wisconsin Weeping
Willow

stipule

underside

♀ catkins

Hybrid White Willow
(*Salix × fragilis*)

fruiting catkin

WEEPING WILLOW *Salix babylonica* L.

QUICK ID Easily recognized by its narrow leaves and pendulous form.

Deciduous small tree, 4–20 m tall. Erect, single slender trunk, often low-branching; crown usually broad, rounded, the branches strongly and dramatically drooping, the tips often reaching or nearly reaching the ground. **BARK** Gray, rough, furrowed. **TWIG** Slender, yellowish green or brown, sparsely to moderately hairy. **LEAF** Alternate, simple; lanceolate, narrowly oblong, or narrowly elliptic; base narrowly wedge-shaped; tip narrowly long-tapering to an extended point; margins finely toothed, the teeth sometimes tipped with small spines. Upper and lower surfaces dull, grayish, silky-hairy or hairless. Blade 9–16 cm long, 5–20 mm broad; petiole 7–9 mm long, hairy on the lower side. **FLOWER** Unisexual, male and female in catkins on separate trees; male catkin 13–35 mm long; female catkin 9–27 mm long, 2–5 mm diam. Late spring, with the new leaves. **FRUIT** Capsule, 2–3 mm long.

HABITAT/RANGE Introduced, origin uncertain, originally described from a garden plant; thought to have originated in China, but it no longer occurs in the wild. Cultivated in North America primarily in the Southeast, naturalized from Md., Del., and Ky., south to Fla., west to Ark. and La.

SIMILAR SPECIES Several cultivars or hybrids of Weeping Willow are cultivated and easily confused, including **S. × sepulcralis** Simonk. (also called **Weeping Willow**), an introduced and widely planted hybrid of White Willow (*S. alba*) and *S. babylonica*. It is naturalized in the East from Que. south to N.C. and Tenn., and west to Ill. There is confusion about the proper identification of many plants referred to as Weeping Willow.

■ *XYLOSMA*: XYLOSMAS

Xylosma is a genus of 80–90 species distributed in Tex., Mexico, West Indies, Central and South America, Southeast Asia, and the Pacific islands; 2 species are native to North America, 1 in the East (the second occurs outside our region in s. Tex.), and 1 species is introduced.

MUCHA-GENTE *Xylosma buxifolia* A. Gray

QUICK ID Recognized in s. Fla. by the combination of notched leaves, thorny trunk, small greenish flowers in axillary bundles, and stipular spines at the base of the petiole.

Evergreen tree, potentially to about 15 m tall in parts of its range, usually shorter and shrublike in Fla. Erect, single trunk or multiple; the trunk, branches, and stems often armed with sharp, several-branched spines. **BARK** Gray, smooth, becoming slightly roughened. **TWIG** Slender, often armed with sharp spines. **LEAF** Alternate, simple, obovate, oblanceolate, or elliptic; base wedge-shaped; tip abruptly narrowed to a short, sharp, extended toothlike projection; margins variable, entire, or with notchlike teeth, especially near the apex. Upper surface lustrous green, lower surface paler. Blade 2.5–7 cm long, 1–3 cm broad; petiole 1–2 mm long, often subtended by short, sharp, axillary spines. **FLOWER** Unisexual or bisexual, male and female on the same or separate plants; sepals 4 or 5, yellow-green; petals absent; produced in few-flowered axillary clusters. Summer. **FRUIT** Rounded or ellipsoid reddish or black berry about 5 mm diam., with 2–5 seeds; matures summer to autumn.

HABITAT/RANGE Native. Hammocks; Fla. Everglades, rare.

MUCHA-GENTE

DENSE LOGWOOD *Xylosma congestum* (Lour.) Merr.

Evergreen shrub or small tree, similar to Mucha-gente. Branches spiny only when young. **HABITAT/RANGE** Introduced from Asia; reported as naturalized in Ga.

Weeping Willow (*Salix babylonica*)

♂ catkins

underside

fruiting
catkin

Weeping Willow (*Salix × sepulcralis*)

capsule

♂
catkins

twig

seeds

flowers

Mucha-gente

fruit

flowers

Dense Logwood

SAPINDACEAE: SOAPBERRY FAMILY

The soapberry family is a tropical and warm temperate collection of about 150 genera and 2,200 species of lianas, shrubs, and trees. Recent studies have demonstrated that maples (formerly Aceraceae) and buckeyes (formerly Hippocastanaceae) are best placed within the Sapindaceae. As treated here, approximately 15 genera and 54 species occur in North America, about 38 of which are native, including 34 arborescent species in the East, 25 native.

LEAF Compound, often unifoliolate and appearing simple, alternate or opposite. **FLOWER** Usually unisexual or functionally unisexual, rarely bisexual; radial or slightly bilateral, with 4 or 5 sepals and usually 4 or 5 petals, 8 or fewer stamens attached to a nectary disk, and a pistil with 2 or 3 chambers. **FRUIT** Diverse: Fleshy or dry capsules, drupes, berries, nuts, or samaras. Toxic chemicals such as saponins are frequently present in the fruit.

■ *ACER*: MAPLES

A genus of about 130 species worldwide, encompassing nearly 100 subspecies and varieties. About 20 species occur in North America, 14 native; 15 occur in the East, 9 native.

Deciduous, usually trees, a few shrubs. **TWIG** Lateral buds opposite; terminal and lateral buds usually with 2–8 pairs of overlapping scales, sometimes clamlike, with 2 opposite scales meeting at their margins. **LEAF** Opposite, usually unifoliolate and appearing simple, rarely compound (Boxelder), the margins usually lobed and sometimes toothed (a few species in China have unlobed leaves with entire margins), the lobes often sharp-pointed. **FLOWER** Unisexual, functionally unisexual, or bisexual, all types occurring on the same or separate plants, sometimes within the same inflorescence; tiny, individually inconspicuous, radially symmetric; usually produced in the leaf axils as racemes, fascicles, or reduced panicles, with or before leaf emergence; usually wind-pollinated. **FRUIT** Winged samara, usually produced in joined pairs and uniquely designed to be carried by the wind; the paired samaras often referred to collectively as a "key," the size and shape of which assist with identification.

Maples grow in a wide range of cool, moist habitats distributed throughout temperate North America and Europe, extending eastward through the Balkans to Pakistan, across the Himalayas into China, southward into Southeast Asia, Korea, and Japan, and crossing the Equator into Indonesia; also in the mountains of the Philippines, Sumatra, Borneo, and Malaysia. They are among the more commonly known trees in e. North America, easily recognized by their uniquely proportioned leaves and revered for their splendid autumn foliage. Few trees add more color to the Appalachian Mountains' autumn display. Maples have fine-grained wood that is usually divided into "hard" and "soft." Hard maples, such as Sugar Maple and Black Maple, are highly regarded for the fabrication of fine furniture, veneer, and flooring.

SUGAR MAPLE *Acer saccharum* Marshall
A.K.A. HARD MAPLE, ROCK MAPLE

QUICK ID Distinguished by its large size, comparatively large leaves with usually 5 squarish lobes, and distinctive winged fruit.

Deciduous tree, 18–35 m tall, 60–120 cm diam. Erect, single trunk; open-grown trees with stout, large branches from near the ground; forest-grown trees free of branches on the lower ⅓–⅔ of the elongate trunk and with a narrow, rounded crown. **BARK** Smooth and gray on young trees, becoming irregularly furrowed, scaly, and dark gray on older trees. **TWIG** Smooth, lustrous, reddish brown, becoming gray with age, hairless. **LEAF** Opposite, appearing simple, thin, firm, usually broader than long; margins with usually 5 (rarely 3) squarish lobes, each lobe with 1 to several sharp-pointed tips. Upper surface dark yellowish green, palmately veined; lower surface pale green to whitish, hairless or hairy along the veins. Blade 7–20 cm long and broad; petiole 4–8 cm long, slender, hairless. Turns red, yellow, or orange in autumn. **FLOWER** Tiny, sepals 5, greenish yellow, clustered at the leaf axils and borne on threadlike, hairy stalks 3–7 cm

♂ flower

Sugar Maple

fruit

♀ flower

autumn

long; male and female on the same or separate trees. Mid- or late spring. **FRUIT** Paired samaras, 2–3 cm long, the margins of the individual samaras more or less parallel or only slightly diverging from a common point of attachment, the paired unit U-shaped, the margins of the wings forming a more or less 90° angle with the base of the seed cavity; matures early autumn.

HABITAT/RANGE Native. Deep, fertile, moist, well-drained soils of mesic forests, 50–1,600 m; throughout much of the East, N.S. to Ont., and N.D., south to n. Ga., n. Ala., n. La., and e. Okla.

SIMILAR SPECIES Similar to, but only marginally overlapping in range with, Southern Sugar Maple, and distinguished from it by leaf size: leaves of Sugar Maple average about 15 cm broad, those of Southern Sugar Maple about 8 cm broad. The undersurface of the leaves of Black Maple is yellowish green and that of Chalk Maple medium green;

the lobe tips of the leaves of Black Maple droop. The margins of Red Maple leaves are toothed.

Notes: This is a slow-growing, long-lived tree persisting to nearly 400 years old. It is a common component in several eastern forest types, including beech–sugar maple, hemlock–northern hardwoods, sugar maple–basswood, red spruce–sugar maple–beech, and black cherry–maple.

SUGAR MAPLE

SOUTHERN SUGAR MAPLE *Acer floridanum* (Chapm.) Pax

QUICKID Recognized in its mostly southern distribution by the squarish-lobed leaves that are whitish beneath.

Deciduous tree, to 30 m tall, usually to about 60 cm diam., potentially 1 m diam. Erect, single straight trunk; crown of open-grown trees spreading, of forest-grown trees narrow, rounded. **BARK** Gray, smooth on young trees, becoming shallowly ridged and somewhat scaly with maturity. **TWIG** Green at first, becoming reddish brown with conspicuous lenticels, hairless. **LEAF** Opposite, appearing simple, thin, about as broad as long; margins usually with 5 (rarely 3) squarish lobes, the lobe tips sharp-pointed. Upper surface lustrous, dark green, palmately veined; lower surface whitish, hairy. Blade 3–9 cm long and broad; petiole 2.5–5 cm long, slender. Turns red or yellow in autumn. **FLOWER** Tiny, sepals 5, greenish, clustered in the axils of developing leaves on slender stalks 2–4 cm long; male and female flowers borne in the same fascicle or on separate trees. Spring. **FRUIT** Paired samaras, 2.5–3 cm long, widely angled from the point of the pair's attachment; matures midsummer.

HABITAT/RANGE Native. Moist woods, bluffs, ravine slopes, calcareous woodlands, stream banks, largely coastal plains and lower Piedmont, to about 200 m; Va. west to s. Ill. and s. Mo., south to c. Fla. peninsula, west to e. Tex. and e. Okla.

SIMILAR SPECIES Similar to, but only marginally overlapping in range with, Sugar Maple, from which it is distinguished by its smaller leaves, averaging about 8 cm broad. The undersurface of the leaf of the very similar Chalk Maple is green.

CHALK MAPLE *Acer leucoderme* Small

QUICKID Distinguished by its small size and relatively small, squarish-lobed leaves that are green beneath.

Deciduous small tree or large shrub to about 12 m tall, 25 cm diam. Erect, single slender trunk or multiple; crown open, spreading, of slender branches. **BARK** Smooth, gray, often reported as having whitish streaks, these perhaps mostly lichens rather than a character of the bark. **TWIG** Reddish brown, lustrous, smooth, hairless. **LEAF** Opposite, appearing simple, thin, about as broad as long; margins with 3–5 (commonly 3) lobes, these squarish, each with several pointed tips. Upper surface lustrous yellowish green; lower surface yellowish green, hairy, not at all whitish. Blade 3–9 cm long and broad; petiole 1–7 cm long, slender. Turns salmon orange, yellow, or purplish red in autumn. **FLOWER** Tiny, sepals 5, greenish yellow. Mid-spring. **FRUIT** Paired samaras, 2.5–3 cm long, widely angled from the point of attachment; matures midsummer to autumn.

HABITAT/RANGE Native. Well-drained upland woods, stream terraces, calcareous woodlands, 10–300 m; generally restricted to the Piedmont, sparingly in coastal plains, N.C. and Va. south to Fla., west to e. Okla. and Tex.

SIMILAR SPECIES Very similar to, and overlapping in range with, Southern Sugar Maple, which is distinguished by its larger stature and the whitish lower surface of the leaf.

SOUTHERN SUGAR MAPLE

CHALK MAPLE

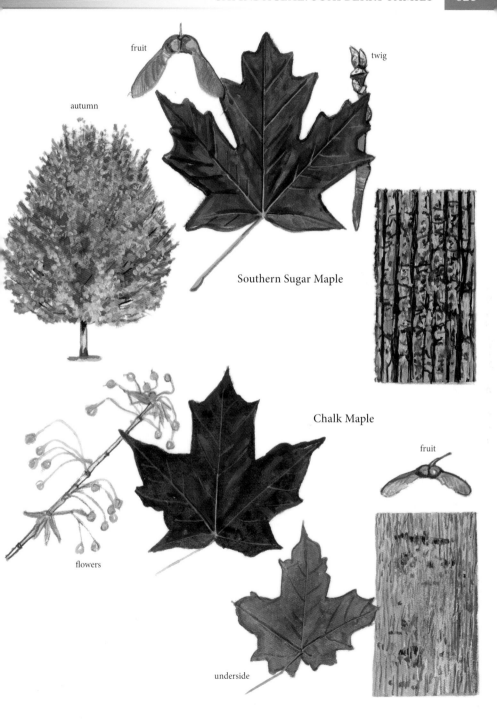

fruit

twig

autumn

Southern Sugar Maple

Chalk Maple

fruit

flowers

underside

BLACK MAPLE *Acer nigrum* F. Michx.

QUICK ID Leaves that are green beneath and have 3–5 lobes with drooping tips help identify this maple.

Deciduous tree, 18–35 m tall, 0.5–1.5 m diam. Erect, single straight trunk; crown broad, rounded, symmetric, of stout branches. **BARK** Gray, smooth at first, soon becoming deeply furrowed, with long, narrow, vertical, irregular blackish ridges, the ridges often scaly. **TWIG** Straw-colored, moderately stout, usually hairy and with conspicuous lenticels. **LEAF** Opposite, appearing simple, thick, firm, broader than long; margins usually 3-lobed, less often 5-lobed, the points of the lobes often demonstrably drooping. Upper surface dark green, hairless; lower surface yellowish green, with dense velvety hairs. Blade 10–16 cm long, slightly broader than long; petiole 6–12 cm long, stout, hairy. Turns yellow or brownish yellow in autumn. **FLOWER** Tiny, sepals 5, greenish yellow, in clusters and borne on slender, hairy stalks 5–7 cm long; male and female on the same or separate trees. Mid- to late spring. **FRUIT** Paired samaras, the individual samaras hairless, more or less parallel or only slightly diverging, the paired unit U-shaped, the margins of the wings forming a more or less 90° angle with the base of the seed cavity; matures autumn.

HABITAT/RANGE Native. Floodplains, bottomlands, river terraces, cove forests, usually in moist, fertile soils, 100–1,600 m; Que. west to Ont., Minn. and extreme e. S.D., south to extreme nw. Ga., west to n. Ark. and e. Kans.

SIMILAR SPECIES Similar to Sugar Maple, but its leaves more often have 5 lobes, the tips of the lobes do not droop, and the lower leaf surface is pale; it also has drier habitat requirements.

Notes: Black Maple has been considered a subspecies of Sugar Maple owing to the range of intermediate forms between the 2 species. Black Maple is a mostly wetland tree that survives periodic flooding much better than Sugar Maple; the microhabitats of the 2 seldom overlap. Black Maple is also said to produce better syrup than Sugar Maple.

STRIPED MAPLE *Acer pensylvanicum* L.

QUICK ID Easily recognized by the broad, 3-lobed papery leaves and striped bark.

Deciduous small tree or large shrub, 6–12 m tall, 12–25 cm diam. Trunk short, often divided into several branches from near the base, branches ascending or arching to form an irregular flat-topped or rounded crown. **BARK** Smooth, grayish green or brownish green, distinctively marked with narrow, vertical creamy-white stripes; stripes especially evident on older bark, but noticeable on very young trees. **TWIG** Stout, smooth, greenish, hairless; 2nd-year twigs with vertical creamy-white stripes. **LEAF** Opposite, appearing simple, somewhat thin, papery, base rounded or heart-shaped; margins shallowly 3-lobed, the terminal lobe more or less triangular, and finely and uniformly double-toothed, usually with more than 3 teeth per cm. Upper surface yellow-green, conspicuously palmately 3-veined, hairless; lower surface slightly paler, usually hairless. Blade 10–18 cm long, equally broad or slightly broader; petiole stout, grooved, 3–8 cm long. Turns clear yellow in autumn. **FLOWER** Unisexual, comparatively large for a maple, about 6 mm diam., bell-shaped, bright yellow, petals and sepals 5; inflorescence a slender, drooping raceme; male and female flowers on separate trees; individual trees may produce male flowers one year, female flowers the next. Late spring to early summer, after

BLACK MAPLE

STRIPED MAPLE

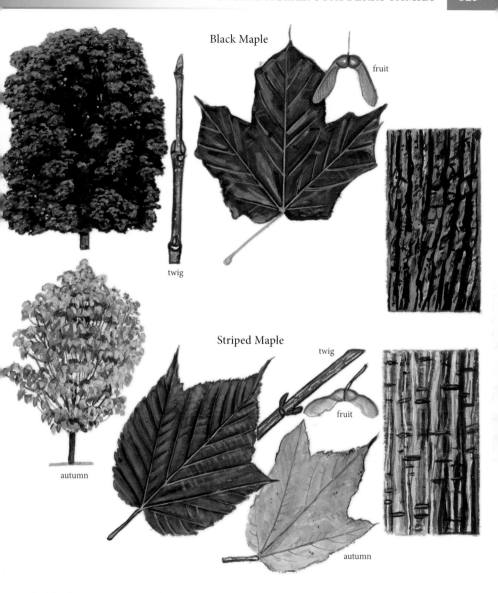

Black Maple

fruit

twig

Striped Maple

twig

fruit

autumn

autumn

leaf development. **FRUIT** Paired samaras, 2–3.5 cm long, widely angled from the point of attachment; matures summer.

HABITAT/RANGE Native. Understory of cool, moist, deciduous forests, stream banks, 100–1,700 m; N.S. to Ont. and Minn., south to Tenn. and Ga.

SIMILAR SPECIES No other eastern maple has the combination of broad, 3-lobed, toothed leaves and striped bark. Mountain Maple has similar leaves (sometimes with 5 lobes) but lacks the striped bark.

Notes: This is a very shade-tolerant, short-lived tree. Deer and other wildlife browse the leaves, the damage from which may be conspicuous on young trees.

MOUNTAIN MAPLE *Acer spicatum* Lam.

QUICK ID Distinguished by leaves with 3–5 shallow lobes and the erect terminal inflorescence.

Deciduous, usually a bushy shrub, potentially a small tree, 5–9 m tall, 8–18 cm diam. Trunk short, crooked, usually branching from near the base into several slender, straight, ascending branches; crown open, irregularly rounded. **BARK** Reddish brown, smooth at first, sometimes becoming slightly furrowed; sometimes blotched gray, without conspicuous vertical striping. **TWIG** Reddish or yellow-green, hairy with grayish hairs. **LEAF** Opposite, appearing simple, somewhat thin and papery; 3–5 shallow lobes, the terminal 3 lobes arising above the midpoint of the blade; base rounded or heart-shaped; margins coarsely toothed, usually 2 or 3 teeth per cm. Upper surface yellow-green, hairless; lower surface paler, usually hairy. Blade 6–12 cm long, slightly narrower; petiole to about 8 cm long. Turns orange to brilliant red in autumn. **FLOWER** Unisexual or bisexual, small, yellow-green, petals 5; inflorescence an erect terminal raceme or panicle, the flowers produced in fascicles along the axis. Male, female, and bisexual flowers on the same or separate trees. Early summer, following leaf development. **FRUIT** Paired samaras, 1–2 cm long, often bright red at first, becoming yellowish, widely angled from the point of attachment; matures summer.

HABITAT/RANGE Native. Cool, moist deciduous forests, swamp margins, often along streams, 300–1,800 m; Nfld. and N.S. west to Sask., south to n. Ala., n. Ga., and w. N.C.

SIMILAR SPECIES The leaves of Striped Maple are similar in shape but are more finely toothed, on average slightly larger, and are usually hairless beneath; Mountain Maple lacks striped bark.

RED MAPLE *Acer rubrum* L.

QUICK ID Recognized by leaves with 3–5 lobes and coarsely toothed margins, the terminal lobe wider at its base than at its midsection (or equal in width).

Deciduous tree, 18–37 m tall, 20–160 cm diam. Erect, single trunk; forest-grown trees usually free of branches for at least ½ their height, open-grown trees branching lower; branches usually stocky, ascending, forming a more or less dense, narrow, rounded crown. **BARK** Smooth, light gray when young, becoming darker gray; shallowly and irregularly ridged, furrowed, and scaly at maturity, the scales loose along the edges. **TWIG** Purplish red or bright red, lustrous, hairless, becoming gray with age. **LEAF** Opposite, appearing simple, thin; 3–5 lobes, the tips narrowly pointed, the base of the terminal lobe equal to or wider than the middle of the lobe; base rounded or heart-shaped; margins sharply, irregularly, and usually doubly toothed. Upper surface green or yellow-green, hairless; lower surface whitish, hairless, hairy along the veins, or felty-hairy throughout. Blade 5–15 cm long, equally broad; petiole 4–14 cm long, slender, reddish. Turns scarlet, yellow, or orange in autumn. **FLOWER** Unisexual, tiny, red or orange, sepals and petals 4 or 5, male and female flowers usually on separate trees, occasionally on the same tree; buds forming long before new shoot growth, usually becoming evident during midwinter. Late winter to early spring. **FRUIT** Paired samaras, 1.5–3 cm long, often bright red, usually maturing and shedding before or with leaf emergence.

HABITAT/RANGE Native. Among the most widely distributed trees in e. North America, occurring in a diverse array of ecological conditions, from swamps and wetlands to dry uplands, mountain slopes, and rich deciduous forests, 0–1,800 m; throughout e. U.S. and Canada.

MOUNTAIN MAPLE

RED MAPLE

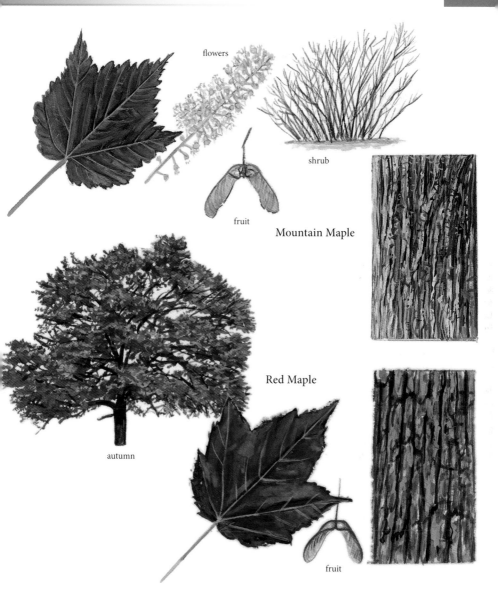

flowers

shrub

fruit

Mountain Maple

Red Maple

autumn

fruit

SIMILAR SPECIES Large-leaved Red Maples of the mountains can be confused at a distance with Sugar Maple, but are easily distinguished by the toothed leaves. The terminal leaf lobe of Silver Maple is narrower at its base than at its middle.

Notes: Red Maple expresses perhaps the widest latitudinal range of any eastern tree, growing from the Fla. Everglades to southernmost Canada. At least 2 varieties have been recognized: Swamp Red Maple (var. *drummondii* [Hook. & Arn. ex Nutt.] Sarg.) and Carolina or Trident Red Maple (var. *trilobum* Torr. & A. Gray ex. K. Koch). If these varieties are accepted, the leaves of Swamp Red Maple are felty-hairy beneath, while those of Carolina Red Maple are smaller and predominantly 3-lobed.

SILVER MAPLE *Acer saccharinum* L.

QUICKID Recognized by the coarsely toothed leaves, silvery beneath, with 5–7 lobes, the terminal lobe narrower at the base than at the middle.

Deciduous fast-growing tree, 18–30 m tall, 60–120 cm diam. Erect, single trunk or multiple; forest-grown trees clear of branches for at least ½ their height, crown more or less open, branches ascending; open-grown trees branching low, usually with a short trunk, the branches ascending and spreading, forming a broad, rounded crown. **BARK** Smooth and gray when young, becoming reddish brown at maturity and shaggy, breaking into long, loose, scaly plates; base often buttressed with large, rounded root crowns. **TWIG** Hairless, lustrous, green at first, becoming reddish brown with conspicuous lenticels; unpleasantly fragrant when bruised. **LEAF** Opposite, appearing simple, thin; 5–7 lobes, the terminal lobe narrower at the base than at the middle of the lobe; margins coarsely and sharply toothed. Upper surface light yellow-green, lower surface silvery white. Blade 6–15 cm long, equally broad; petiole 4–12 cm long, slender. Turns yellow in autumn. **FLOWER** Unisexual or bisexual, male, female, and bisexual on the same or different trees, yellowish green, sepals 5. Spring, prior to leaf emergence. **FRUIT** Paired samaras, 3–6 cm long, samaras widely angled; matures late spring to early summer.

HABITAT/RANGE Native. River bottoms, floodplains, bottomlands, often where periodically inundated, 0–600 m; throughout e. North America, west to N.D., S.D., Nebr., Kans., Okla., and La.; naturalized in the West.

SIMILAR SPECIES The base of the terminal lobe of Red Maple leaves is equal to or wider than its middle.

Notes: Silver Maple is a widely planted ornamental, often used in parks, along roadsides, in residential yards, and along fencelines and parking lots. Numerous horticultural cultivars are known, most of which are only rarely seen in the garden trade owing to their brittle, easily shed branches, which make for a messy landscape.

BOXELDER *Acer negundo* L.

QUICKID Recognized by the combination of opposite, pinnately compound leaves and paired samara fruit.

Deciduous fast-growing tree, 12–25 m tall, 40–90 cm diam. Erect, single trunk or multiple; forest-grown trees usually with a single undivided trunk and a narrow crown of ascending branches; open-grown trees often divided near the ground into several stout ascending and spreading branches, crown broad, irregularly rounded. **BARK** Smooth, pale gray or brownish on young trees, becoming darker gray with scaly ridges at maturity. **TWIG** Green, hairless, developing brownish, rounded lenticels with age. **LEAF** Opposite, pinnately compound, thin, petiole slender, 3–7 cm long; leaflets commonly 3, sometimes 5, rarely 7–9; margins nearly entire or remotely few-toothed. Upper surface light green, lower surface grayish green. Leaflet blade 5–12 cm long, 2.5–6 cm broad; stalk of terminal leaflet 0.75–1.5 cm long, stalks of lateral leaflets 2–5 mm long. Turns yellow in autumn. **FLOWER** Unisexual, rarely with a few bisexual flowers, male and female on separate trees, yellow-green, sepals 5, petals absent. Late spring, before or with the new leaves. **FRUIT** Paired samaras, 3–4 cm long, pale brown or tan, the pair more or less V-shaped; matures autumn.

HABITAT/RANGE Native. Stream banks, floodplains, bottomlands, swamp margins, usually

SILVER MAPLE

BOXELDER

fruit

winter

Silver Maple

Boxelder

underside

fruit

where wet, 0–600 m; essentially throughout North America, south to c. Fla. peninsula.

SIMILAR SPECIES Poison Ivy (*Toxicodendron radicans* [L.] Kuntze) has similar leaves but it is usually a vinelike shrub, its fruit a cluster of green to grayish-white drupes.

Notes: Boxelder is among the most widespread trees in North America, ranging throughout the U.S. and most of Canada. At least 6 varieties are recognized, 3 predominately eastern and 3 mostly western.

JAPANESE MAPLE *Acer palmatum* Thunb.

QUICKID The deeply palmately lobed leaves and small form help distinguish Japanese Maple.

Deciduous small tree or large shrub, 12–15 m tall within its natural range, about ½ this height in cultivation in North America, the trunk to about 20 cm diam. Erect, usually a single short, very low-branching trunk, often with a twisted or somewhat contorted aspect; crown rounded, spreading, the outline of the tree usually about as broad as tall. **BARK** Smooth, usually reddish-brown or greenish brown on young trees, becoming gray-brown with age. **TWIG** Slender, hairless, green, turning red by autumn, often with a whitish bloom; buds small, reddish, produced in pairs. **LEAF** Opposite, appearing simple; 5–9 (usually 7) deeply palmately lobes, these narrowly ovate or lanceolate, with a long-tapering, sharp-pointed tip; margins double-toothed. Surfaces hairless, emerging reddish orange, becoming green in summer, turning various shades of yellow, red, purple, or orange in autumn. Blade 5–10 cm long, 5–10 cm broad; petiole 1.5–5 cm long. **FLOWER** Unisexual, 6–8 mm diam.; petals creamy white; sepals purple, reddish purple, or red; borne in dangling corymbs. Late spring. **FRUIT** Paired samaras, 1 cm long, red, hairless, the pair forming a wide angle from the point of attachment; matures late summer to early autumn.

HABITAT/RANGE Introduced; native to Japan, e. China, Taiwan, and Korea. Widely cultivated throughout the East; occasionally naturalized in North America, mainly from Ont. south to Pa. and Ohio.

SIMILAR SPECIES Sweetgum (*Liquidambar styraciflua*, Altingiaceae) has similar leaves, usually with fewer lobes, but the fruit is a spiky, dangling ball, and it is a large tree, while Japanese Maple is always a small tree or shrub.

Notes: This is a popular ornamental, widely cultivated in Europe and North America. At least 150 cultivars and horticultural selections are available in the garden trade, varying in flower color, foliage color and morphology, maximum size, and habit. Japanese Maple is easily propagated from seed, but cultivated forms are usually propagated by grafting or from cuttings. Natural seedlings regularly spring up near or under plantings.

TATARIAN MAPLE *Acer tataricum* L.

QUICKID Most easily distinguished by the combination of opposite unlobed leaves and paired samaras.

Deciduous, usually a shrub, sometimes a small tree, 5–10 m tall. Erect, single trunk or multiple, often low-branching and somewhat bushy; crown rounded, spreading. **BARK** Gray-brown, smooth at first, becoming somewhat shaggy at maturity. **TWIG** Slender, hairless, reddish brown with numerous lenticels. **LEAF** Opposite, appearing simple, usually unlobed or irregularly and shallowly lobed (especially on young trees), oval or broadly ovate, heart-shaped at the base; margins irregularly double-toothed. Upper surface bright green, hairless; lower surface paler, hairy along the veins when new, becoming hairless. Blade 5–10 cm long, 3.5–7 cm broad; petiole 1.5–5 cm long. Turns yellow in autumn. **FLOWER** Unisexual, creamy or greenish white, borne in upright panicles 5–8 cm long. Late spring. **FRUIT** Paired samaras, 2–3 cm long, red, joined at the base, inner margins of samaras nearly parallel; matures late summer.

HABITAT/RANGE Introduced; native to Europe and w. Asia. Cultivated in the East, rarely naturalized.

HEDGE MAPLE *Acer campestre* L.

Deciduous, densely twiggy shrub or small tree, 12–25 m tall. **BARK** Grayish black, somewhat ridged and furrowed. **TWIG** Often corky. **LEAF** Opposite, appearing simple, 3–5 lobes, margins entire; somewhat similar to the leaf of Southern Sugar Maple and Chalk Maple. Dark green in summer, turning yellow in autumn. Blade 5–10 cm long and broad. **FRUIT** Paired samaras, 3–4.5 cm long, greenish, joined at the base and forming a wide angle; matures late summer. **HABITAT/RANGE** Introduced from Europe; widely cultivated, rarely naturalized, mostly in the north from Ont. south to Ind. and N.J.

Japanese Maple

fruit

autumn

flowers

Tatarian Maple

fruit

Hedge Maple

twig

fruit

AMUR MAPLE *Acer ginnala* Maxim.

Deciduous large shrub or small, shrubby, multi-stemmed tree, to about 7 m tall. **BARK** Smooth, grayish brown, often with dark streaks. **LEAF** Opposite, appearing simple; 3-lobed, the middle lobe much the longest; margins double-toothed. Upper surface dark green, hairless; lower surface paler, hairless. Blade 4–8 cm long, 3–6 cm broad; petiole 1.5–4.5 cm long. **HABITAT/RANGE** Introduced from East Asia; cultivated, naturalized from N.B. and Sask. south to Pa., Ky., and N.D. *Notes:* Amur Maple has been considered both a variety and subspecies of Tatarian Maple.

NORWAY MAPLE *Acer platanoides* L.

QUICK ID The sycamore- or Sugar Maple-like leaves in combination with the widely angled samaras are usually enough to identify this species.

Deciduous tree, to 30 m tall. Erect, single large trunk; crown broad, rounded or cylindric. **BARK** Dark gray-brown, smooth on young trees, becoming increasingly fissured with age, the ridges narrow and often interlacing to form diamond patterns. **LEAF** Opposite, appearing simple; usually 5–7 lobes, these often acuminate at the tip; margins with large, well-spaced, sharp-tipped teeth. Upper surface lustrous green, hairless; lower surface paler, hairy in the vein axils. Blade 10–20 cm long, 10–20 cm broad; petiole 8–15 cm long, slender, reddish, usually exuding milky sap when broken. Turns yellow in autumn. **FLOWER** Bisexual, about 8 mm diam., yellow or greenish yellow, borne in erect terminal umbels. Spring. **FRUIT** Paired

samaras, each 3–4 cm long, joined at the base and forming a wide angle; matures early autumn.

HABITAT/RANGE Introduced from Europe. Cultivated and naturalized across much of the East, from N.B. and Ont., south to N.C. and Tenn. Now considered invasive in the Northeast.

SIMILAR SPECIES Leaves of the similar Sycamore Maple have more coarsely toothed margins, while those of Sugar Maple are smaller on average and the petiole does not exude milky sap.

SYCAMORE MAPLE *Acer pseudoplatanus* L.

QUICK ID The coarsely toothed, 5-lobed leaves help distinguish this species.

Deciduous tree, usually 12–24 m tall. Erect, single trunk, potentially massive; crown oval or rounded. **BARK** Grayish or reddish brown; flaking into regular scalelike plates that often curl up at the margins to reveal the orange inner bark. **LEAF** Opposite, appearing simple, usually 5-lobed, heart-shaped at the base, margins coarsely toothed. Upper surface dark green, wrinkled with depressed veins; lower surface paler, with raised veins. **FLOWER** Unisexual, male and female on the same tree, about 15 mm diam., borne in upright panicles 6–15 cm long. Late spring. **FRUIT** Paired samaras, 3–5 cm long, joined at the base and forming a narrow angle; matures early autumn.

HABITAT/RANGE Introduced from Europe. Cultivated in the East, naturalized from about N.S. and Ont. south to Ill., Ky., and N.C.

Amur Maple

autumn

fruit

Norway Maple

spring

fruit

fruit

Sycamore Maple

■ *AESCULUS*: BUCKEYES AND HORSE CHESTNUTS

A genus of 13 temperate species distributed mainly in North America and Asia, with a single species in Europe. Deciduous shrubs or small to medium trees. Generally easily recognized by the long-stalked, palmately compound leaves, usually with 5–7 toothed leaflets. **TWIG** Stout, brownish with pale lenticels; winter buds comparatively large, conspicuous, with several pairs of overlapping scales. **LEAF** Opposite, palmately compound; leaflets 5–11, margins toothed; petiole stout, usually comparatively long. **FLOWER** Bisexual or functionally unisexual, the unisexual ones usually male, both types produced in the same inflorescence, often with only the upper flowers in the inflorescence bearing pollen, the lower flowers often functionally female; sepals fused, bell-shaped or tubular; petals 4 or 5, often unequal; stamens 6–8, rarely 5, usually protruding beyond the corolla; pistil 1, ovary superior. Produced in a conspicuous elongate, often cone-shaped terminal cluster, usually after the new leaves. Insect- or hummingbird-pollinated. **FRUIT** Depressed, pear-shaped or rounded green or brown leathery capsule, often produced in conspicuous clusters; usually with 1–3 seeds, rarely 4–6; commonly splits into 3 parts at maturity; seeds pear-shaped or rounded, comparatively large. The common name "buckeye" derives from the seeds, which resemble the eyeball of a deer.

BOTTLEBRUSH BUCKEYE *Aesculus parviflora* Walter

QUICK ID A mound-forming shrub with palmately compound leaves of 5–7 leaflets and large, erect, showy white inflorescences.

Deciduous, mounding or sprawling, single- or multitrunked shrub to about 3 m tall and 3 m wide. Like Horse Chestnut, it produces a columnar terminal cluster of tubular white flowers with protruding stamens.

HABITAT/RANGE Native primarily to Ala. and Ga., but a popular and widely cultivated garden shrub throughout the Southeast, north to at least Pa.

YELLOW BUCKEYE *Aesculus flava* Sol.

QUICK ID Recognized by the combination of opposite, palmately compound leaves with 5–7 leaflets, leaflets with stalks not exceeding about 3 mm long, yellow flowers with petals of 2 different lengths, and stamens 15–20 mm long.

Deciduous tree, 20–30 m tall, to about 1.5 m diam. Erect, single trunk; crown rounded or oblong, branches mostly ascending. **BARK** Brownish gray when young, becoming gray, furrowed, and divided into large scaly plates and numerous smaller plates. **TWIG** Orange-brown, becoming gray, hairless or densely gray-hairy. Buds with 10 or more overlapping scales, lateral buds opposite, somewhat spreading, terminal buds about 1.5 cm long. **LEAF** Opposite, palmately compound; blade to about 40 cm long and broad; petiole 8–19 cm long. Leaflets 5–7, each 10–21 cm long, 4–8 cm broad, on a stalk 2–3 mm long; obovate, oblong, or elliptic, base wedge-shaped, tip usually abruptly short-pointed. Upper surface dark green, hairless or nearly so; lower surface paler, hairless or moderately to densely hairy, especially along the veins. Turns yellowish orange or yellowish brown in autumn. **FLOWER** Bisexual or functionally unisexual, both types appearing on the same plant; sepals 5, fused into a cuplike calyx 7–10 mm long; petals 5, unequal in length, longer ones 20–30 mm long, shorter ones 16–25 mm long, pale or deep yellow, the lower portion becoming deep yellow or red-brown; stamens 7 or 8, 15–20 mm long; inflorescence 8–19 cm long, more or less cylindric. Late spring. **FRUIT** Rounded,

BOTTLEBRUSH BUCKEYE

YELLOW BUCKEYE

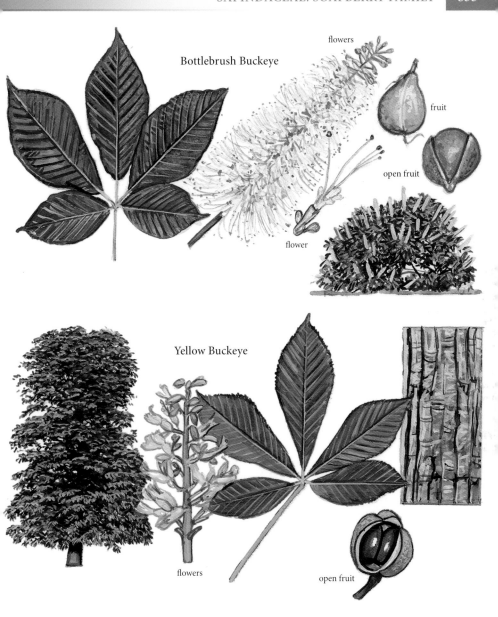

Bottlebrush Buckeye

flowers

fruit

open fruit

flower

Yellow Buckeye

flowers

open fruit

smooth or pitted brownish leathery capsule, 5–8 cm diam.; 1–3 seeds, about 5 cm long, lustrous chestnut-brown with a large, pale scar; matures autumn.

HABITAT/RANGE Native. Moist deciduous forests, to 1,900 m; central portions of the East, chiefly Va. and W.Va. to Ky., south to n. Ala. and n. Ga.

SIMILAR SPECIES Painted Buckeye has leaflet stalks 3–12 mm long and stamens up to 30 mm long. Other buckeyes lack the yellow flowers with petals of unequal length.

OHIO BUCKEYE *Aesculus glabra* Willd.
A.K.A. FETID BUCKEYE

QUICKID Recognized by the combination of palmate, 5-parted leaves, prickly capsule, and terminal clusters of greenish-yellow flowers, the petals equal in length.

Deciduous tree, averaging 9–15 m tall, 20–40 cm diam. Erect, single trunk; crown broad, rounded, with slender, spreading branches. **BARK** Smooth, yellowish brown or gray, becoming dark gray-brown, scaly, roughly and irregularly furrowed, divided into thin, flat plates. **TWIG** Stout, smooth, reddish brown, becoming gray and hairless with orange lenticels; unpleasantly aromatic when crushed or bruised; terminal buds 15–18 mm long, expanding to 3–5 cm long in spring, powdery-resinous but not sticky, brownish with a bluish-white bloom. **LEAF** Opposite, palmately compound; blade 5–15 cm long and broad; petiole 10–15 cm long. Leaflets usually 5, rarely 7, each 6–16 cm long, 2–6 cm broad, on a stalk 0–11 mm long; oblanceolate or obovate, evenly and gradually tapered to the base, margins finely and irregularly toothed, often entire near the base. Upper surface yellowish green, hairless, conspicuously pinnately veined; lower surface paler or dark green, hairless or densely hairy. Turns orange-yellow in autumn. **FLOWER** Bisexual or functionally unisexual, male and bisexual on some trees, female and bisexual on other trees; sepals 5, fused; petals 4, 10–19 mm long, equal in length, greenish yellow or pale yellow; stamens 7; inflorescence a conspicuous terminal panicle 10–15 cm long, 5–7 cm broad. Spring, after the new leaves. **FRUIT** Ovoid, prickly, light brown or tan leathery capsule, 2–5 cm diam.; usually with 1–3 (rarely 4–6) smooth, lustrous seeds, 2–4 cm diam., dark reddish brown, marked with a light brown scar; matures autumn.

HABITAT/RANGE Native. Moist deciduous woods, floodplains, bottomlands, stream banks,

OHIO BUCKEYE

0–600 m; widespread in the East, Maine and Ont., south to W.Va., Tenn., n. Ga., west to Minn., Nebr., and e. Tex.

SIMILAR SPECIES The non-native Horse Chestnut also has prickly capsules, but its leaves usually have 7 (and up to 9) leaflets, and its terminal buds are larger and sticky to the touch.

HORSE CHESTNUT *Aesculus hippocastanum* L.

QUICKID Recognized by the combination of prickly fruit; opposite, palmately compound leaves predominantly with 7 (5–9) toothed leaflets; and sticky terminal buds.

Deciduous tree, 10–25 m tall, 30–65 cm diam. Erect, single trunk; crown broadly rounded or dome-shaped, with ascending and spreading branches that curve up at the tip. **BARK** Dark brown, shallowly furrowed and divided into thin, irregular plates. **TWIG** Stout, smooth, reddish brown, with whitish lenticels; terminal buds 2–4 cm long, purplish brown, covered with glistening, resinous scales, sticky to the touch. **LEAF** Opposite, palmately compound; blade about 40 cm long and broad; petiole to about 10 cm long. Leaflets usually 7–9, occasionally 5, each 12–25 cm long, 3–6 cm broad, stalkless; thick, obovate, base evenly tapering and wedge-shaped, tip abruptly short-pointed, margins irregularly and bluntly toothed. Upper surface lustrous, dark green, conspicuously pinnately veined; lower surface paler. **FLOWER** Bisexual or functionally unisexual, all types in the same inflorescence; male above, female below, bisexual in the middle; sepals 5, fused into a bell-shaped calyx; petals 5, white with red or yellow spots; stamens 7, protruding beyond the corolla; inflorescence an upright terminal panicle, 20–30 cm long, 10–20 cm broad. Early summer. **FRUIT** Leathery capsule, 5–6 cm diam., green at first, turning brown, covered with flexible prickles; 1–3 smooth, lustrous seeds, 2–4 cm diam., mahogany brown, with a pale, circular scar; matures early autumn.

HABITAT/RANGE Introduced from Europe. Widely cultivated in the East, N.B. to Ont., south to Ill. and Ga., west to Minn. and Iowa.

SIMILAR SPECIES Ohio Buckeye also has prickly capsules, but its terminal buds are not sticky, and most of its leaves have 5 leaflets.

Ohio Buckeye

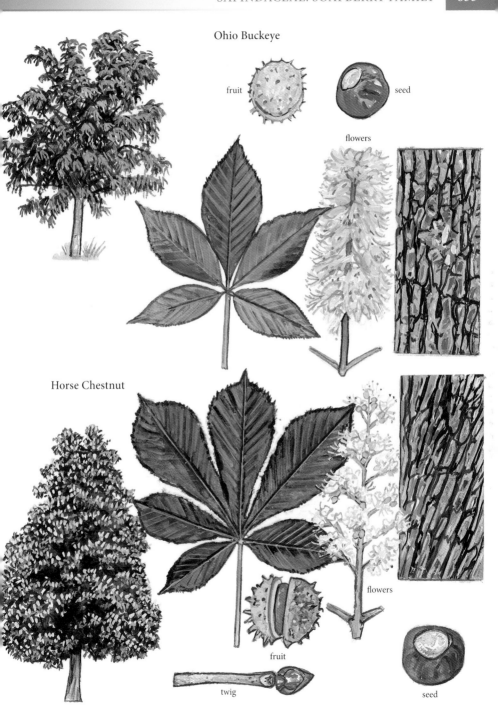

fruit

seed

flowers

Horse Chestnut

flowers

fruit

twig

seed

RED BUCKEYE *Aesculus pavia* L.

QUICKID Recognized by the combination of opposite, palmately compound leaves with 5–7 leaflets, each on a stalk potentially to nearly 2 cm long, and red flowers with petals of 2 unequal lengths and stamens 23–36 mm long.

Deciduous, often a shrub or small tree, 1–4 m tall, rarely to 12 m and 20 cm diam. Erect, usually a single trunk, often low-branching; crown rounded or oblong, with numerous slightly ascending branches. **BARK** Smooth, light gray or brownish gray. **TWIG** Stout, reddish brown; buds broad, to about 1 cm long, with rounded scales. **LEAF** Opposite, palmately compound; blade about 36 cm long and broad; petiole 3–17 cm long. Leaflets 5–7, each 6–17 cm long, 3–6 cm broad, on a stalk 1–19 mm long; moderately thick, oblong, oblanceolate, or narrowly elliptic, base narrowly wedge-shaped, tip abruptly short-pointed, margins irregularly and often bluntly toothed. Upper surface lustrous, dark green, hairless or with scattered hairs along the veins; lower surface slightly paler, hairy or not, the veins usually reddish. **FLOWER** Bisexual or functionally unisexual, both types on the same plant; sepals 5, fused into a cuplike calyx 8–18 mm long; petals usually 4, red, varying to yellowish red, unequal in length, the longer ones 25–40 mm long, the shorter ones 20–31 mm long; stamens 6–8, 23–36 mm long. Early to mid-spring. **FRUIT** Rounded, light brown leathery capsule, 3.5–6 cm diam.; 1–3 (rarely 4–6) seeds, 2–3 cm diam., lustrous chestnut brown or yellowish brown, with a pale scar; matures summer to autumn.

HABITAT/RANGE Native. Lowland and upland woods of various mixtures, including rolling pinelands, mixed pine and hardwood forests, oak–hickory woodlands, floodplains, moist slopes, hammocks, natural levees, to about 450 m; chiefly in the Southeast, N.C. to s. Ill. and Mo., south to n. Fla. and e. Tex.

SIMILAR SPECIES No other buckeye has red flowers.

PAINTED BUCKEYE *Aesculus sylvatica* W. Bartram

QUICKID Recognized by the combination of opposite, palmately compound leaves with 5–7 leaflets, each on a stalk not exceeding about 12 mm long, and yellow flowers with petals of 2 unequal lengths and stamens 20–30 mm long.

Deciduous, usually a shrub 1–3 m tall, sometimes a small tree to 15 m tall, 5–25 cm diam. Erect, single, often crooked trunk or multiple trunks; crown oblong or rounded, branches spreading. **BARK** Dark or light gray, often splotched, dividing into small, thin plates. **TWIG** Light reddish brown, hairless; buds light brown, 7–8 mm long. **LEAF** Opposite, palmately compound, blade to about 40 cm long and broad; petiole 8–18 cm long. Leaflets 5–7, each 8–20 cm long, 3–7 cm broad, on a stalk 3–12 mm long; lanceolate, oblanceolate, elliptic, or oblong, base gradually tapered and narrowly wedge-shaped, tip abruptly short-pointed; margins single- or double-toothed, the teeth sometimes blunt. Upper surface lustrous yellow-green or dark green, hairless or with a few hairs along the veins; lower surface green. **FLOWER** Bisexual or functionally unisexual, male and bisexual in same cluster; sepals 5, fused into a cuplike calyx 7–15 mm long; petals yellow, often tinged with red, usually 4, of 2 lengths, the longer ones 25–37 mm long, the shorter ones 20–30 mm long; stamens 6 or 7, usually 18–30 cm long, rarely shorter. Spring. **FRUIT** Rounded, light brown leathery capsule, 2.5–4 cm diam.; 1–3 (rarely 4–6) rounded seeds, lustrous,

RED BUCKEYE

PAINTED BUCKEYE

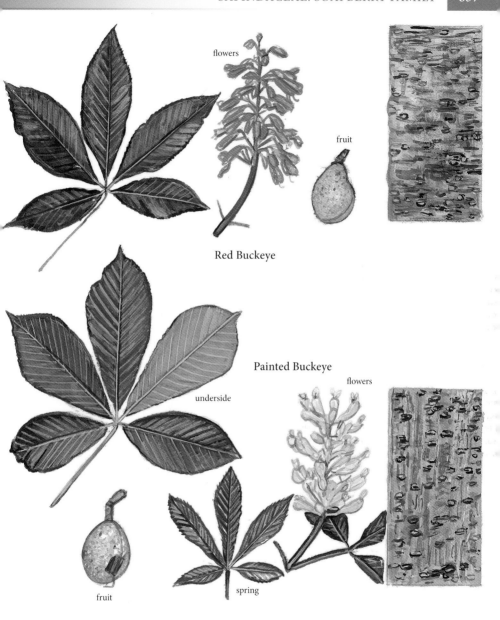

flowers

fruit

Red Buckeye

Painted Buckeye

flowers

underside

fruit

spring

medium or dark chestnut brown; matures summer to autumn.

HABITAT/RANGE Native. Deciduous and pine woodlands, rocky hillsides, red clay slopes, river- and stream banks, poorly drained flatwoods, to about 400 m; distributed primarily in the Piedmont, s. Pa. south to Va. and N.C., southwest to s. Ill. and n. Ala.

SIMILAR SPECIES Yellow Buckeye also has yellow flowers with petals of 2 different lengths, but its leaflet stalk does not exceed about 3 mm long and the stamens do not exceed about 20 mm long.

CARROTWOOD *Cupaniopsis anacardioides* (A. Rich.) Radlk.

QUICK ID Recognized by the combination of relatively large, pinnately compound leaves with alternate and opposite leaflets, pendent inflorescences, and yellowish fruit.

Evergreen slender tree, to about 10 m tall. Erect, single trunk, crown rounded. **BARK** Grayish brown with darker grayish mottling, inner bark with an orange tint. **TWIG** Brownish, smooth, stout. **LEAF** Alternate, pinnate, usually with an even number of mostly alternate leaflets, blade to about 21 cm long, 20 cm broad; petiole 3–7 cm long. Leaflets 4–12, each 7–10 cm long, 2.5–4 cm broad, oblong to elliptic or obovate, leathery, tip notched or rounded. Upper surface green or yellowish green, often with a yellowish midvein; lower surface paler. **FLOWER** Unisexual, white or greenish; sepals 5; petals 5, to about 3 mm long; produced in a pendent axillary panicle, 8–25 cm long. Spring to summer. **FRUIT** Three-sided, pear-shaped yellowish capsule, 1.5–2.5 cm diam., with 3 lustrous black seeds, covered at first with a red aril; matures summer to autumn.

HABITAT/RANGE Introduced from Australia, where it is endemic. Widely established and invasive in s. Fla.

Notes: A genus of about 60 species distributed mostly in Australia and Polynesia; 1 non-native species occurs in North America.

FLORIDA TOADWOOD *Cupania glabra* Sw.
A.K.A. FLORIDA CUPANIA, AMERICAN TOADWOOD

QUICK ID The only tree in the Fla. Keys with the combination of alternate compound leaves, the leaflets alternate with coarsely toothed margins.

Evergreen shrub or small tree, to about 10 m tall, 15–25 cm diam. Erect or leaning, single trunk. **BARK** Dark brown or splotchy gray and brown, smooth, becoming scaly. **TWIG** Slender, brown, finely hairy, with minute buds. **LEAF** Alternate, pinnately compound; blade 15–25 cm long, about as broad; petiole 1–2.5 cm long. Leaflets 5–15, alternate, 6–18 cm long, 2.5–8 cm broad, oblong, tip rounded, margins coarsely toothed, usually reflexed upward from the rachis, thus forming a V. Upper surface lustrous, dark green, lateral veins conspicuous; lower surface paler, hairy. **FLOWER** Unisexual, tiny, white, male and female borne on the same tree, often with 1 sex predominating, produced in short axillary panicles. Autumn. **FRUIT** Three-parted leathery capsule, 1–2 cm long, splitting to reveal flesh-covered greenish seeds; matures summer.

HABITAT/RANGE Native. Tropical hammocks; rare in Fla. Keys, more common in West Indies and Central America.

Notes: Cupania is a genus of about 60 mostly tropical species, only this one native to North America.

FLORIDA HOPBUSH *Dodonaea viscosa* (L.) Jacq.
A.K.A. VARNISH LEAF

QUICK ID Recognized by the 2-winged capsule and lustrous leaf with a varnished appearance.

Evergreen shrub or very small tree to about 3 m tall. Erect, shrubby in pinelands, sometimes becoming arborescent in hammocks. **BARK** Gray, shaggy, usually exfoliating in strips. **LEAF** Alternate, appearing simple, leathery; narrowly obovate or oblanceolate; tip rounded, pointed, or notched; margins entire. Upper surface lustrous green with a scaly texture, appearing varnished, midvein prominent, lateral veins obscure; lower surface paler. Blade 7–15 cm long, 1.5–4 cm broad; petiole to about 1.5 cm long, narrowly winged. **FLOWER** Unisexual or apparently bisexual, male and female usually on separate plants, sometimes male and apparently bisexual on the same plant, female flowers remain closed, male and bisexual flowers open widely. Tiny, reddish or yellowish green; sepals usually

Carrotwood

fruit

Florida
Toadwood

fruit

open fruit

fruit

Florida Hopbush

fruit

♂ flowers

4 or 5; petals absent; stamens usually 8. Autumn to spring. **FRUIT** Two-winged pinkish to yellowish papery capsule, 1.5–2.5 cm long; matures spring to summer.

HABITAT/RANGE Native. Hammocks, pinelands, s. Fla. and Fla. Keys; also in Ariz., where it is a shrub.

SIMILAR SPECIES The genus *Dodonaea* contains about 60 species, distributed mostly in Australia, with 2 species native to North America. Smallfruit Varnish Leaf (*D. elaeagnoides* Rudolphi ex Ledeb. & Alderstam) has predominantly 3-winged capsules and is restricted to Fla. Keys. It is considered endangered in Fla.

INKWOOD   *Exothea paniculata* (Juss.) Radlk.
A.K.A. Butterbough

QUICKID Distinguished by its evenly compound leaves with predominantly 4 leaflets.

Evergreen shrub or tree, to about 15 m tall and 30 cm diam. Erect, single trunk; crown narrow, rounded. **BARK** Bright reddish brown when young, becoming dark gray with age; fissured, forming large, irregular scales. **LEAF** Alternate, pinnately compound, with an even number of leaflets; blade about 7 cm long, to about 12 cm broad; petiole 1–3.5 cm long. Leaflets 2–6, usually 4, firm, each 5–12.5 cm long, to about 3 cm broad; elliptic or oblong, tip rounded, blunt, or slightly notched. Upper surface lustrous, dark green, hairless; lower surface paler. **FLOWER** Unisexual, white, male and female usually on separate plants, occasionally both sexes on the same plant; sepals 5, reflexed; petals 5, spreading; stamens usually 8. Late winter to spring. **FRUIT** Fleshy berry, red at first, turning purplish black at maturity, 8–12 mm diam.; matures summer.

HABITAT/RANGE Native. Hammocks, shell mounds; s. Fla. and Fla. Keys.

SIMILAR SPECIES Leaves of Spanish Lime (*Melicoccus bijugatus*) and Wingleaf Soapberry (*Sapindus saponaria*) are similar but have a winged rachis.

Notes: *Exothea* is a genus of 3 species, Caribbean in distribution, with 1 species in North America.

WHITE IRONWOOD   *Hypelate trifoliata* Sw.
A.K.A. Inkwood

QUICKID The only tree in subtropical Fla. with palmately trifoliolate leaves.

Evergreen shrub or small tree, to about 13 m tall, 15–40 cm diam. Erect, usually single trunk. **BARK** Smooth, reddish gray or pale brown with irregular depressions. **TWIG** Gray-green at first, becoming brown, lustrous. **LEAF** Alternate, palmately compound; blade 3.5–4 cm long, 3–6 cm broad; petiole 2.5–4 cm long. Leaflets 3, each 2.5–4 cm long, to about 2.5 cm broad, stalkless, leathery; obovate, base wedge-shaped; tip flattened, notched; margins entire, rolled downward. Both surfaces lustrous, green; lower surface paler. **FLOWER** Unisexual, white or greenish white, male and female produced on the same tree; sepals 5; petals 5; male flowers with 8 elongate stamens. Spring to summer. **FRUIT** Rounded, fleshy, single-seeded black drupelike berry, to about 1 cm diam.; matures summer to autumn.

HABITAT/RANGE Native. Hammocks, Everglades National Park and Fla. Keys., rare in the wild and considered endangered in Fla.

Notes: This monotypic genus is distributed in the West Indies and southernmost Fla.

TULIP-WOOD TREE   *Harpullia arborea* (Blanco) Radlk.

QUICKID Recognized by the comparatively large compound leaves with alternate leaflets and showy orange-red fruit.

Evergreen tree, 20–30 m tall, 60–70 cm diam. Erect, single trunk, often buttressed at the base; crown dense, often expansive, rounded or spreading. **BARK** Greenish gray, smooth or slightly roughened with irregular lenticels. **LEAF** Alternate, pinnately compound, with an even number of leaflets, the outermost leaflet often appearing terminal; blade to about 34 cm long, to about 20 cm broad; petiole 5–7 cm long, grooved. Leaflets 2–10, alternate, 8–20 cm long, 5–8 cm broad, oblong, tip pointed. Upper surface lustrous green, veins conspicuous, impressed; lower surface paler. **FLOWER** Unisexual, male and female borne on the same plant, 10–15 mm diam., about 15 mm long; sepals 5; petals 5, green or pinkish; stamens 5. Spring to early summer. **FRUIT** Fleshy orange-red capsule to about 2.5 cm long, typically with 2 black seeds; matures summer to early autumn.

INKWOOD   WHITE IRONWOOD

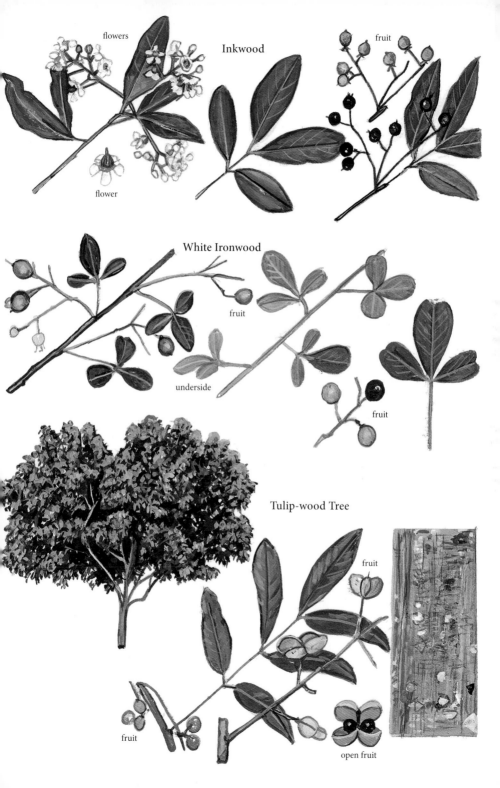

flowers

Inkwood

fruit

flower

White Ironwood

fruit

underside

fruit

fruit

Tulip-wood Tree

fruit

fruit

open fruit

TULIP-WOOD TREE *continued*

HABITAT/RANGE Introduced from Asia, Australia, and the Philippines. Escaped and naturalized in s. Fla., mainly near Miami.

Notes: Harpullia is a genus of 26 species, distributed mainly in the eastern part of the Malay Archipelago and the w. Pacific, with many species endemic to New Guinea. None is native to North America.

SPANISH LIME *Melicoccus bijugatus* Jacq.

QUICK ID **Recognized by the evenly pinnate leaves with only 4 leaflets and a winged rachis.**

Evergreen tree, 10–25 m tall, to about 1 m diam. Erect, single trunk; crown spreading. **BARK** Smooth, gray or grayish white with horizontal markings. **TWIG** Reddish, hairless, round in cross section. **LEAF** Alternate, pinnately compound, with an even number of leaflets, the rachis usually winged; blade to about 10 cm long, to 20 cm broad; petiole 2.5–7 cm long. Leaflets usually 4, opposite, 4–14 cm long, 2–6 cm broad, stalkless; ovate or elliptic, often asymmetric at base, tip abruptly tapered and pointed, margins entire. Upper and lower surfaces hairless. **FLOWER** Unisexual, male and female in the same inflorescence, a terminal panicle 5–12 cm long; sepals usually 4, greenish; petals 5, cream to yellowish, 2–2.5 mm long; stamens 8. Spring to summer. **FRUIT** Rounded yellowish-green drupe, 2–3 cm diam.; seeds 1.5–2.5 cm long; matures autumn, potentially later.

HABITAT/RANGE Introduced from South America. Sparsely established in southernmost Fla.

SIMILAR SPECIES The leaves of Wingleaf Soapberry (*Sapindus saponaria*) usually have more than 4 leaflets.

Notes: Melicoccus is a genus of 10 species native to South America and Hispaniola; only this non-native species is established in North America.

■ *KOELREUTERIA*: GOLDENRAIN TREES

All 3 species of this Asian (mainly Chinese) genus of deciduous trees and shrubs are introduced in North America, 2 established.

GOLDENRAIN TREE *Koelreuteria paniculata* Laxm.

QUICK ID **Recognized by the combination of its compound leaves with many coarsely toothed leaflets and showy yellow flowers.**

Deciduous shrub or, more often, a small tree to about 15 m tall, to about 50 cm diam. Erect, single trunk; crown rounded with spreading or ascending branches. **BARK** Grayish brown, becoming fissured with age. **TWIG** Brownish with conspicuous raised lenticels. **LEAF** Alternate, compound, pinnate to bipinnate; blade to about 50 cm long, to about 36 cm broad; petiole 1–4 cm long. Leaflets 7–18, opposite, 5–10 cm long, 3–6 cm broad, the longer leaflets usually near mid-blade, the terminal leaflets sometimes fused; ovate or broadly lanceolate, with a short stalk, tip sharply or abruptly pointed, base often flattened, margins coarsely toothed. Upper surface dull green; lower surface often densely yellowish hairy. **FLOWER** Unisexual, pale yellow, produced in branched clusters 25–40 cm long; petals 4, reflexed, 5–9 mm long; stamens 8. Summer. **FRUIT** Three-ridged, cone-shaped papery capsule, 4–6 cm long, usually drooping; matures autumn.

HABITAT/RANGE Introduced from China. Widely naturalized in the East, N.Y., Mass., Kans., south to Ala. and Tex. Aggressive, potentially invasive.

SIMILAR SPECIES See Flamegold.

FLAMEGOLD *Koelreuteria elegans* (Seem.) A.C. Sm. **subsp.** *formosana* (Hayata) F.G. Mey.

Very similar to Goldenrain Tree, and distinguishable by the combination of its consistently bipinnately compound leaves, 5-petaled flowers, and ellipsoid capsules. **HABITAT/RANGE** Introduced from Taiwan; sparingly established from Fla. to e. Tex.

Spanish Lime

fruit

fruit section

fruit

Goldenrain Tree

seed fruit

flowers flower

Flamegold

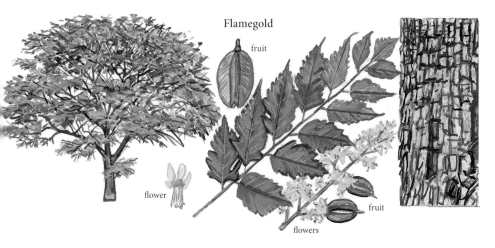

fruit

flower

flowers fruit

■ *SAPINDUS*: SOAPBERRIES

The soapberries constitute a taxonomically confusing genus of as many as 13 species distributed in temperate and tropical regions of Asia, Australia, and North and South America. Some authorities recognize 2 or 3 species native to North America. Others reduce these entities to 1 or 2 varieties of a single polymorphic species. The broader view for North America is taken here, recognizing 3 species for the East.

The genus is best known for the saponins in its fruit, which when mixed with water can produce a cleansing, soaplike lather, but have also been used by Native Americans to kill fish. The seeds are poisonous when consumed.

FLORIDA SOAPBERRY *Sapindus marginatus* Willd.

QUICK ID Recognized by alternate, pinnately compound leaves with up to about 18 alternate and opposite leaflets.

Deciduous tree, to about 10 m tall, 13–14 cm diam. Erect, usually single trunk, damaged trees sometimes producing suckers from the base; crown rounded or somewhat vase-shaped with ascending or spreading branches. **BARK** Smooth, gray with darker gray mottling, becoming roughened. **TWIG** Green with raised whitish to pale brown lenticels. **LEAF** Alternate, pinnately compound, the rachis usually unwinged, or rarely with a very narrow wing; blade 15–32 cm long, to about 30 cm broad; petiole 5–12 cm long. Leaflets often 10–18, opposite and alternate, 5–15 cm long, 2–7 cm broad; lanceolate or narrowly elliptic, often curved like the blade of a sickle, margins entire but often appearing wavy. Upper surface dark or medium green, hairless; lower surface paler, hairless or finely hairy. Turns yellow in autumn. **FLOWER** Unisexual, creamy

yellow, male and female borne in the same inflorescence, a loosely branched terminal panicle to about 15 cm long. Early summer. **FRUIT** Rounded, leathery, drupelike, 1–2 cm diam., green with paler creamy spots, becoming yellowish, then black; as many as 3 developing from a single flower, usually 1 reaching maturity, the undeveloped ones usually forming wartlike projections at the base of the developed fruit; matures late summer to autumn.

HABITAT/RANGE Native. Hammocks, shell middens, calcareous woodlands, often where limestone is present, 0–50 m; coastal S.C. south to c. Fla., west to Miss.

SIMILAR SPECIES The leaves of Wingleaf Soapberry usually have 10 or fewer leaflets and a wide wing along the rachis. Western Soapberry is very similar and may not be distinct from Florida Soapberry.

WESTERN SOAPBERRY *Sapindus drummondii* Hook. & Arn.

QUICK ID Recognized by the combination of alternate, pinnately compound leaves with up to about 18 alternate and opposite leaflets, and its western range.

Deciduous shrub or small tree, 3–15 m tall, with a single trunk or multiple trunks. Crown more or less vase-shaped or rounded, with ascending branches. **BARK** Yellowish gray or pale reddish brown, becoming gray and fissured into scaly plates. The leaf, flower, and fruit are very similar to those of Florida Soapberry.

HABITAT/RANGE Native; low spots in prairies, hardwood forests near bottomlands, along streams, sometimes forming colonies in abandoned fields, 0–1,900 m; sw. U.S., east to Mo., Ark., and La. Difficult to distinguish and perhaps not distinct from Florida Soapberry; differs mostly in its range.

FLORIDA SOAPBERRY   WESTERN SOAPBERRY

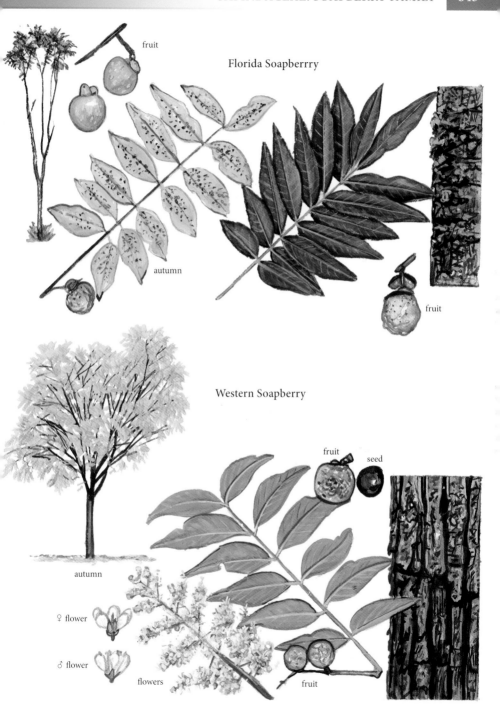

fruit

Florida Soapberrry

autumn

fruit

Western Soapberry

fruit

seed

autumn

♀ flower

♂ flower

flowers

fruit

WINGLEAF SOAPBERRY *Sapindus saponaria* L.
A.K.A. TROPICAL SOAPBERRY

QUICK ID Recognized by the alternate compound leaves predominantly with 4–8 leaflets and a winged rachis.

Evergreen shrub or small tree, to about 15 m tall, 30 cm diam. Erect, single trunk; crown broad, rounded. **BARK** Pale gray or brown, smooth, with conspicuous lenticels, becoming finely fissured and scaly. **TWIG** Stout, light gray with raised reddish-brown lenticels. **LEAF** Alternate, pinnately compound, predominantly with a conspicuous broadly winged rachis; blade 20–45 cm long, to about 40 cm broad; petiole about 5 cm long, usually winged. Leaflets usually 10 or fewer, odd or even in number, opposite or nearly alternate, elliptic tending toward widest above the middle, base wedge-shaped, tip bluntly pointed, margins entire. Upper surface dark or medium green, hairless; lower surface paler, often finely hairy. **FLOWER** Unisexual or bisexual, male and female or bisexual borne in the same inflorescence; petals 5, white, hairy, round, smaller than the sepals; stamens 8. Year-round. **FRUIT** Rounded, leathery, yellowish, drupelike, potentially

3 from a single flower, usually only 1 reaching maturity, the remaining 2 developing into appendages near the base of the mature fruit. Year-round.

HABITAT/RANGE Native. Subtropical hammocks; s. Fla. and Fla. Keys.

SIMILAR SPECIES Florida Soapberry and Western Soapberry usually have more leaflets and the leaves predominantly lack a broadly winged rachis. Spanish Lime (*Melicoccus bijugatus*) leaves usually have only 4 leaflets. Chinese Soapberry (*S. mukorossi* Gaertn.) is reportedly naturalized in Ga.; it is considered by some authorities to be conspecific with *S. saponaria*.

WINGLEAF SOAPBERRY

SAPOTACEAE: SAPODILLA FAMILY

This is a family of 53 genera and about 1,100 species of trees and shrubs distributed in North America, Mexico, West Indies, Central and South America, Asia, Africa, Atlantic islands, Indian Ocean islands, Pacific islands, and Australia; 4 or 5 genera and 14–16 species occur in North America, 11 native.

Deciduous or evergreen trees or shrubs characterized by twigs with milky sap. **LEAF** Alternate or whorled, on short shoots, margins entire. **FLOWER** Inflorescence usually fasciculate and axillary (in most of ours), flowers bisexual (rarely functionally unisexual). **FRUIT** Fleshy berry (in ours).

The family is widespread in the tropics and is economically important for Sapodilla, from which chicle, used in chewing gum, is extracted; for the edible fruits of Star-apple, Mamey (*Mammea americana* L.), and Canistel; and for several ornamental species used in gardening.

SATINLEAF *Chrysophyllum oliviforme* L.
A.K.A. SAFFRON-TREE

QUICK ID Easily recognized in s. Fla. by the oval leaves, which are coppery brown on 1 side and lustrous dark green on the other.

Evergreen shrub or small, delicate tree to about 15 m tall, about 58 cm diam. Erect, usually single straight trunk; crown oval or rounded, moderately dense. **BARK** Smooth, reddish brown. **LEAF** Alternate, simple, stiff; oval, ovate, or elliptic, base rounded, tip abruptly short-pointed, margins entire. Upper surface lustrous, dark green, hairless at

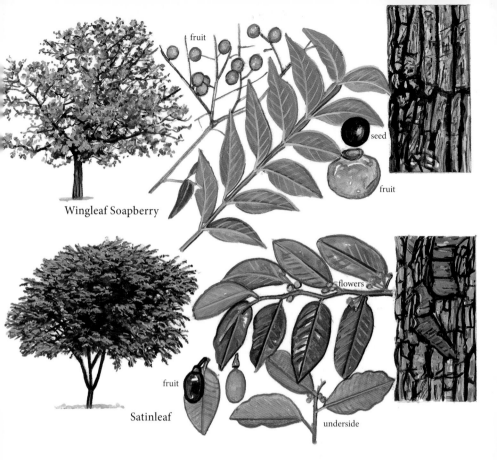

Wingleaf Soapberry

fruit

seed

fruit

flowers

fruit

Satinleaf

underside

maturity, lateral veins parallel and closely spaced; lower surface coppery brown from a covering of densely matted, feltlike coppery or rusty-brown hairs. Blade 1.5–13 cm long, 1–7 cm broad; petiole 8–12 mm long. **FLOWER** Bisexual; sepals 5, fused into a silky cuplike calyx less than 2 mm long; petals 5, fused, the tube about 2.5 mm long, spreading into reflexed lobes less than 2 mm long; stamens 5, within the corolla; stigma 5-lobed; produced in short-stalked axillary clusters of 3–10 flowers.

Year-round. **FRUIT** Fleshy, ovoid or ellipsoid, dark purple berry, 1–2 cm long, about 1 cm diam., with 1 or 2 seeds. Year-round.

HABITAT/RANGE Native. Coastal and inland hammocks, east coast of c. Fla. south to the Everglades and Fla. Keys, often in association with limestone or calcareous soils.

SIMILAR SPECIES Star-apple (*C. cainito* L.) is cultivated in Fla. and is similar, but its fruits are many-seeded and larger, 5–8 cm diam.

Notes: Chrysophyllum is a genus of about 70 species distributed mainly in tropical America, including Mexico, West Indies, Central and South America; also Asia, Afric, Australia, and Indian Ocean islands. The only species native to North America, Satinleaf has become a popular garden plant owing to its size and attractive leaves, which alternately show their lustrous green and coppery surfaces in even a mild breeze.

SATINLEAF

■ *MANILKARA*: DILLIES

A genus of about 65 species, mostly tropical, in Mexico, West Indies, Central and South America, Asia, Africa, Indian Ocean islands; 2 occur in North America, 1 native.

Evergreen shrubs or trees. **LEAF** Alternate, simple. **FLOWER** Bisexual; sepals 6, in 2 whorls of 3; petals 6–9, white or yellow; stamens 6–12. **FRUIT** Rounded brownish berry with 2–10 seeds.

WILD DILLY *Manilkara jaimiqui* (C. Wright ex Griseb.) Dubard **subsp. *emarginata*** (L.) Cronquist

QUICK ID Recognized in s. Fla. by the stiff, oval grayish-green leaves that are notched at the tip and often clustered near the branch tips.

Evergreen low, dense, salt-tolerant shrub or small tree, to about 13 m tall, potentially to 30 cm diam., often smaller. Erect, single usually low-branching trunk or multiple trunks; crown dense, rounded or vase-shaped, the branches usually ascending. **BARK** Gray, more or less smooth. **LEAF** Alternate, often densely clustered at the tips of the twigs, simple, stiff; elliptic, base rounded, tip rounded, usually notched; margins entire. Upper surface grayish green, finely hairy at first, becoming mostly hairless; lower surface pale green, often with brownish hairs or nearly hairless. Blade 5–10 cm long, 2–5 cm broad; petiole 1–2 cm long. **FLOWER** Bisexual; sepals 6, hairy, 6–8 mm long; corolla tubular, light yellow, dividing into 6 linear lobes 6–7 mm long; produced in pendent axillary clusters, stalk 1–3 cm long. Winter to spring. **FRUIT** Rounded, scaly brownish berry, to about 3 cm diam. Predominantly summer to autumn, but potentially present year-round.

HABITAT/RANGE Native. Hammocks, Fla. and Fla. Keys. Treated as a threatened species in Fla.

WILD DILLY

SAPODILLA *Manilkara zapota* (L.) P. Royen

QUICK ID Recognized by the combination of leaves to 13 cm long and clustered at the branch tips, and rounded brownish fruit 5–8 cm diam.

Evergreen tree, to about 15 m tall, to 1 m diam. Erect, single stout, low-branching trunk; crown upright, dense, usually with numerous ascending branches. **BARK** Dark brown, finely furrowed, with narrow ridges. **TWIG** Stout, gray, more or less smooth, brownish-hairy when young. **LEAF** Alternate, clustered near the tips of branches, simple, leathery; elliptic or widest at the apex; base wedge-shaped; tip rounded, bluntly pointed, or abruptly short-pointed; margins entire. Upper surface lustrous, medium or dark green, midvein yellowish; lower surface paler, brownish-hairy. Blade 5–13 cm long, to about 5 cm broad; petiole to about 3 cm long. **FLOWER** Bisexual; sepals 6, of 2 sizes; corolla white, tubular below, spreading into 6 lobes that are 4–6 mm long, 3–4 mm broad; produced in the leaf axils at the end of a stalk 2.5 cm long. Year-round. **FRUIT** Rounded, roughened, sometimes speckled, light or dark brown berry, 5–8 cm diam. Year-round.

HABITAT/RANGE Introduced from Mexico and Central America. Cultivated and naturalized in s. Fla.

SIMILAR SPECIES Wild Dilly has smaller fruit and grayish-green leaves.

CANISTEL *Pouteria campechiana* (Kunth) Baehni
A.K.A. EGG-FRUIT

QUICK ID Recognized by the combination of large leaves with conspicuous impressed veins and large yellowish fruit.

Evergreen tree, to about 25 m tall, 1 m diam., usually smaller where established in Fla. Erect, single slender trunk or multiple; crown open, broad, spreading. **BARK** Grayish, becoming loose, scaly, and irregularly and deeply furrowed. **LEAF** Alternate, closely set and sometimes appearing opposite, simple; narrowly elliptic or wider near the tip; base gradually tapered and narrowly wedge-shaped; tip rounded or bluntly short-pointed; margins entire. Upper surface yellow-green, central and lateral veins conspicuous, impressed, surface appearing

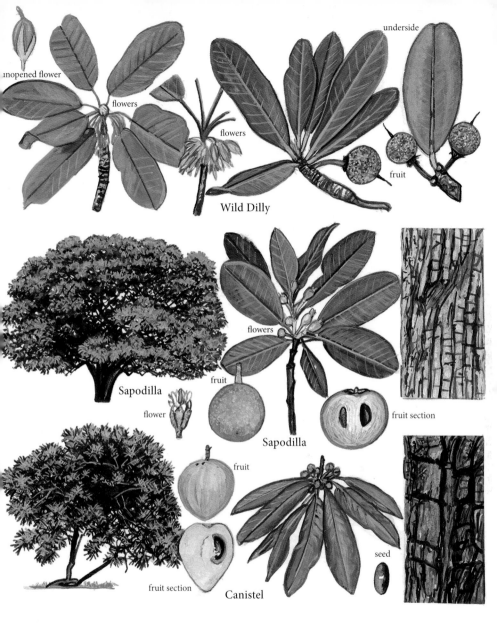

inopened flower

flowers

flowers

fruit

underside

Wild Dilly

flowers

fruit

flower

fruit

fruit section

Sapodilla

Sapodilla

fruit

fruit section

seed

Canistel

slightly quilted, often reflexed upward from the midvein; lower surface slightly paler. **FLOWER** Bisexual; sepals 4–6, 4–12 mm long; corolla white or greenish white, cylindric, 6–15 mm long, with 4–7 lobes; produced in axillary clusters of 1–9 flowers. Year-round. **FRUIT** Large, mostly pear-shaped or oval yellow, brown, or nearly orange berry, 5–13 cm long, with 1–4 hard, lustrous brown seeds 2–4 cm long; matures mostly in winter.

HABITAT/RANGE Introduced from Mexico, Central America, and the West Indies. Cultivated and sparsely naturalized in s. Fla.

Notes: Pouteria is a genus of about 325 species distributed in Mexico, West Indies, Central and South America, Asia, Africa, Pacific islands, Australia; 1 species introduced and established in North America.

■ *SIDEROXYLON*: BULLIES

A genus of about 69 species, distributed in tropical and warm temperate regions in Mexico, West Indies, Central and South America, Africa, and Indian Ocean islands; 11 occur in North America, all native, 9 reaching tree stature.

Evergreen or deciduous shrubs or trees, often with milky sap. **TWIG** Often a thorn-tipped short shoot arising from a leaf node or leaf cluster. **LEAF** Alternate, often in dense fascicles and appearing opposite, simple, margins usually entire. **FLOWER** Bisexual; sepals 4–6; petals 4–6, usually white, creamy yellow, or yellow; usually produced in dense multiflowered clusters in the leaf axils or along leafless parts of the branch. **FRUIT** Ovoid, obovoid, or rounded berry, varying from yellow to orange, purplish black, or black, with 1 or 2 seeds; usually produced on a long stalk and clustered in the leaf axils or along leafless parts of the stem.

ALACHUA BULLY *Sideroxylon alachuense* L.C. Anderson
A.K.A. SILVER BUCKTHORN, SILVER BULLY, CLARK'S BUCKTHORN

QUICK ID A buckthorn recognized by leaves that are lustrous green above and silvery gray beneath with a dense covering of matted hairs.

Deciduous (leaves often persisting well into winter) shrub or small tree to about 9 m tall, 13 cm diam. Erect or upright, single trunk or multiple; crown irregular, with thorny, thick, crooked grayish-white branches. **TWIG** Bright green or silvery, with scattered pale hairs, thorny at the nodes, the thorns to about 2 cm long; sometimes takes the form of a short, sharp-tipped branchlet. **LEAF** Alternate, simple; ovate-elliptic, rhombic, or broadly obovate; base narrowly wedge-shaped; tip rounded or bluntly pointed, sometimes notched; margins entire. Upper

surface lustrous, dark green; lower surface silvery-gray with matted hairs that obscure the blade tissue. Blade 3–9 cm long, 3–4 cm broad; petiole to about 5 mm long. **FLOWER** Bisexual; sepals 5 or 6; corolla white, 4–6 mm long; petals 3-pronged; produced in axillary clusters of 10–20 flowers along spur shoots. Spring to early summer. **FRUIT** Oblong or ovate, 1-seeded berry, 11–13 mm long, about 1 cm diam., tipped with a persistent style about 1 mm long; seed light brown, smooth, about 1 cm long, 6 mm diam.; matures late summer to autumn.

HABITAT/RANGE Native. Mesic hardwood forests, islands in the Okefenokee Swamp, and coastal shell middens, often in association with limestone, 0–200 m; nc. Fla., se. Ga. Considered endangered in Fla. and of special concern in Ga.

SIMILAR SPECIES The lower surface of the leaves of Gum Bully are covered with rusty brownish hairs.

TOUGH BULLY *Sideroxylon tenax* L.
A.K.A. TOUGH BUCKTHORN, TOUGH BUMELIA

QUICK ID Recognized by the zigzag branches, thorn-tipped twigs, tight clusters of brownish buds and white flowers, and clusters of predominantly oblanceolate leaves that are dark green above and coppery brown beneath.

Evergreen, usually a shrub, potentially a small tree 8–12 m tall, to 30 cm diam. Erect or upright, single low-branched trunk or multiple trunks; crown of irregular, crooked or zigzag branches. **BARK** Reddish brown, smooth at first, quickly becoming fissured, scaly, with flat ridges. **TWIG** Dark reddish brown, often thorn-tipped, densely hairy. **LEAF** Alternate, usually in crowded fascicles and appearing opposite; simple, stiff, predominately oblanceolate; base tapered, narrowly wedge-shaped; tip blunt or rounded; margins entire. Upper surface

ALACHUA BULLY

TOUGH BULLY

Alachua Bully

flowers

underside

fruit

flowers

Tough Bully

underside

flowers

flowers

fruit

fruit

semi-lustrous, dark green; lower surface densely covered with a tightly appressed mat of brownish or coppery hairs, contrasting conspicuously with the upper surface. Blade 2–7 cm long, 5–30 mm broad; petiole 0–1 cm long, densely hairy. **FLOWER** Bisexual, tiny, buds coppery brown, corolla white; produced in axillary clusters of 10–50 flowers. Late spring to early summer. **FRUIT** Obovoid blackish berry, 10–14 mm long; matures early autumn.

HABITAT/RANGE Native. Coastal scrub, dry maritime hammocks, sand pine–oak scrub, 0–100 m; southeastern coastal plains, se. N.C. south to peninsular Fla.

SIMILAR SPECIES The leaves of Saffron Plum are also small, but lack the covering of coppery hairs on the lower surface.

SAFFRON PLUM *Sideroxylon celastrinum* (Kunth) T.D. Penn.

QUICKID Recognized by the combination of thorn-tipped twigs; fascicled, blunt-tipped leaves with the lower surface hairless and the veins obscure; and small creamy-white flowers borne in clusters at the nodes.

Evergreen small tree, to about 6 m tall, to about 25 cm diam. Erect, somewhat crooked, single trunk or multiple; crown dense, with slender, spreading, usually thorny branches. **BARK** Dark, nearly black, becoming divided into small, regular blocks and appearing checkered. **TWIG** Grayish, thorn-tipped and producing sharp thorns at the leaf nodes. **LEAF** Alternate, usually closely set in regularly spaced clusters and appearing opposite; simple, leathery, firm, oblanceolate, obovate, rarely elliptic; base narrowly or broadly wedge-shaped; tip rounded or blunt; margins entire, thickened. Upper surface dull green; lower surface pale green, tissue hairless, veins obscure. Blade 1–4 cm long, 5–30 mm broad; petiole to about 1 cm long. **FLOWER** Bisexual; sepals 5, fused; corolla creamy white, about 4 mm long; functional stamens 5, non-functional stamens 5; produced in axillary clusters of 3–15 flowers. Year-round. **FRUIT** Ellipsoid, 1-seeded blue-black berry, 10–25 mm long. Year-round.

HABITAT/RANGE Native. Coastal hammocks, salt flats, saltmarshes, gravelly hills, 0–100 m; c. and s. Fla., s. Tex.

SIMILAR SPECIES The lower surface of the leaves of Tough Bully are densely covered with a mat of coppery hairs.

FALSE MASTIC *Sideroxylon foetidissimum* Jacq.

QUICKID Recognized by its comparatively large size, large leaves with wavy margins and a yellow central vein, and flowers and fruit usually borne on leafless portions of the branch.

Evergreen tree, to about 25 m tall, 50–150 cm diam. Erect, single stout trunk; crown rounded, dense, with ascending and spreading branches. **BARK** Reddish brown, scaly, splitting into regular flakes; with an unpleasant aroma when bruised. **TWIG** Stout, brown, smooth, becoming somewhat roughened by the remains of old leaf bases, thornless. **LEAF** Alternate (sometimes closely set), often more abundant near the branch tips; simple, elliptic, oblong, or narrowly ovate; base broadly wedge-shaped; tip blunt, acute, or abruptly short-pointed; margins entire, usually wavy. Upper surface lustrous, dark green or yellow-green, the central vein yellowish, lateral veins conspicuous, distinctly curved toward the blade tip; lower surface paler, yellow-green, hairy at first, becoming hairless. Blade 5–20 cm long, 4–6 cm broad; petiole to about 7 cm long, yellowish green. **FLOWER** Bisexual, buds greenish yellow, sepals and petals 5, corolla yellow or greenish yellow, about 7 mm diam.; produced in crowded, several-flowered clusters along the naked branch, below the leaves. Spring to summer. **FRUIT** Ellipsoid, ovoid, or pear-shaped, bright yellow to orange-yellow berry, about 2.5 cm long, often produced along leafless portions of the branch; matures summer to autumn.

HABITAT/RANGE Native. Coastal hammocks, 0–50 m; s. Fla. and Fla. Keys.

SIMILAR SPECIES The leaves of White Bully are not as large and lack a yellowish central vein.

SAFFRON PLUM

FALSE MASTIC

Saffron Plum

fruit

False Mastic

flowers

flowers

flowers

fruit

fruit

GUM BULLY *Sideroxylon lanuginosum* Michx.

QUICK ID Recognized by often thorn-tipped branchlets, usually felty-hairy lower leaf surface, rounded leaf tip, and fascicle-like clusters of flowers and fruits.

Deciduous, irregularly shaped shrub or small tree, 6–15 m tall, about 20 cm diam. Erect or upright, single often low-branching trunk or multiple trunks. Crown of open-grown trees dense, rounded; that of forest-grown trees narrower, open, irregularly branched and spreading, the branches unarmed or armed with short, stout or slender thorn-tipped branchlets. **BARK** Reddish brown, narrowly ridged and furrowed, usually with flaky reddish-brown scales; becomes deeply furrowed on old trees. **TWIG** Grayish brown, often thorn-tipped, usually rusty-hairy. **LEAF** Alternate, often in closely set clusters; simple, oblanceolate, obovate, rarely elliptic; base evenly tapered or broadly wedge-shaped; tip usually rounded, sometimes acutely pointed; margins entire. Upper surface lustrous or semi-lustrous, dark green, hairy at first, soon becoming mostly hairless; lower surface usually conspicuously hairy and feltlike, the hairs rusty brown, especially on young leaves, the hairs sometimes becoming sparse on older leaves. Blade predominately 2–8 cm long, 1–4 cm broad; petiole 2–5 mm long, usually hairy. **FLOWER** Bisexual; sepals usually 5, the lobes erect, 2–3 mm long; corolla white or creamy yellow; petals usually 5, usually divided into 3 segments, only slightly longer than the calyx; produced in axillary clusters of up to 40 flowers. Spring to summer. **FRUIT** Obovoid or ellipsoid, lustrous black berry, 6–12 mm long, the style usually persistent at the tip; seed 6–11 mm long; matures summer to autumn.

HABITAT/RANGE Native. Rich, moist upland woods, well-drained sandy woods, sandy old fields, sand pine–oak scrub, longleaf pine ridges, rarely bottomland woods, 0–400 m; S.C., Ky., and Ill., south to n. Fla., west to Ariz.

SIMILAR SPECIES The leaves of Georgia Bully are similar, but usually have only tufts of hairs in the vein axils on the lower surface. Distinguished from other *Sideroxylon* species by the felty lower leaf surface and thornlike twigs and branchlets.

Notes: Several subspecies are recognized; the leaf hairs of *S. lanuginosum* subsp. *oblongifolium* (Nutt.) T.D. Penn., more common in the western part of our region, Ky. and La. to e. Tex. and e. Kans., become grayish white with age.

BUCKTHORN BULLY *Sideroxylon lycioides* (L.)

QUICK ID Recognized by the combination of scaly reddish-brown bark that peels in strips, thorny twigs, and leaves mostly hairless beneath and tapering to both ends.

Deciduous shrub 1–2 m tall or small tree to 20 m tall, 35 cm diam. Erect, single trunk on arborescent plants; crown usually somewhat columnar, especially on forest-grown plants, somewhat more rounded and slightly spreading on open-grown plants; branches spiny, often crooked and spine-tipped. **BARK** Grayish brown with reddish-brown overtones, eventually breaking into irregularly scaly strips or small plates to expose the reddish-brown inner bark; not unlike the bark of Hophornbeam (*Ostrya virginiana*, Betulaceae). **TWIG** Grayish or reddish brown, thorny, often thorn-tipped. **LEAF** Alternate, simple, papery; elliptic, oblong-elliptic, or somewhat oval, rarely widest near the tip; base tapering or narrowly wedge-shaped; tip long-pointed, narrowly acute, or rounded; margins entire. Upper surface dull, soft green or yellowish green,

GUM BULLY

BUCKTHORN BULLY

Gum Bully

twig

flowers

thorn

flowers

fruit

fruit

Buckthorn Bully

twig

thorn

fruit

fruit

flowers

with moderately dense silky hairs when young; lower surface more densely hairy with blond hairs; both surfaces eventually becoming nearly hairless at maturity. Blade 8–15 cm long, 1–5 cm broad; petiole 5–15 mm long, usually hairless. **FLOWER** Bisexual, tiny, corolla white, produced in clusters in the leaf axils. Late spring to summer. **FRUIT** Ovoid black berry, 10–15 mm long, 10–12 mm diam.; matures midsummer to autumn.

HABITAT/RANGE Native. Wooded floodplains, riverine levees, wooded slopes and bluffs, hammocks, 10–1,500 m, usually in association with neutral soils; Va. south to n. Fla., west to Ill. and Mo., south to e. Tex.

SIMILAR SPECIES The lower surface of Gum Bully leaves is usually copiously covered with rusty-brown hairs. Florida Bumelia (*S. reclinatum* Michx.) is typically a shrub that sometimes reaches 5 m tall; it differs by its overall shorter leaves and smaller fruit, 4–9 mm diam. Despite its common name, Florida Bumelia is distributed from S.C. south throughout Fla., west to Miss. and La.

GEORGIA BULLY *Sideroxylon thornei*
(Cronquist) T.D. Penn.
A.K.A. THORNE'S BUCKTHORN

QUICK ID Recognized by the simple leaves with tufts of hairs in the leaf axils beneath, small veins on the upper leaf surface not significantly different in color than the enclosing tissue, tiny whitish flowers, and purplish-black berries in fascicled clusters.

Deciduous, often spindly shrub to about 1.5 m tall, sometimes a small tree 1.5–6 m tall. Erect or upright, single trunk or multiple; crown open, sparsely few-branched or somewhat bushy. **TWIG** Hairy at first, becoming mostly hairless, often thorn-tipped, exuding milky sap when broken. **LEAF** Alternate, simple; oblanceolate, elliptic, or obovate; base tapered and narrowly wedge-shaped; tip rounded or bluntly pointed; margins entire. Upper surface dull green, with a few hairs along the midvein, veins of the upper surface not impressed, networked veinlets not significantly different in color from the tissue; lower surface paler, with tufts of grayish or rusty hairs in the vein axils. Blade 1–7 cm long, 5–25 mm broad; petiole 1–3 cm long. **FLOWER** Bisexual, petals 5, corolla white; produced in many-flowered axillary clusters. Summer. **FRUIT** Oval or ovoid black or purplish-black berry, 8–11 mm long, with slender stalks 6–8 mm long; seeds 6–8 mm long; matures autumn.

HABITAT/RANGE Native. Low woods, bottomlands, floodplains, 10–80 m; s. Ga., nw. Fla., se. Ala.

SIMILAR SPECIES The lower leaf surface of Gum Bully is usually covered throughout with rusty-brown hairs.

WHITE BULLY *Sideroxylon salicifolium*
(L.) Lam.

QUICK ID Recognized by the alternate, simple, mostly hairless leaves in combination with flowers and fruits in dense, closely adjacent clusters usually on leafless portions of the branch.

Deciduous or evergreen small tree, to about 17 m tall, 42–60 cm diam. Erect, single slender trunk; crown of open-grown trees pyramidal, branched nearly to ground level, hammock-grown trees few-branched, the branches ascending or spreading. **BARK** Grayish or reddish brown, scaly, shallowly fissured with flat ridges, sometimes with horizontal lenticels. **TWIG** Lacking thorns, rusty-hairy at first, becoming mostly hairless. **LEAF** Alternate, simple, moderately leathery; ovate, narrowly elliptic, or lanceolate; base narrowly long-tapered; tip abruptly short-pointed; margins entire. Upper surface lustrous green, hairless, veins evident; lower surface paler, hairless or nearly so. Blade 7–13 cm long, 1–4 cm broad; petiole 6–14 mm long, hairless or nearly so. **FLOWER** Bisexual, sepals 5, petals 5, corolla creamy white, stamens 5; produced in dense clusters of 5–14 flowers along naked portions of the branch, the clusters often very close together. Early spring to summer. **FRUIT** Ellipsoid or nearly rounded, usually 1-seeded purplish-black berry, 6–10 mm long, 5–10 mm diam.

HABITAT/RANGE Native. Hammocks, margins of pinelands, 0–100 m; s. Fla.

SIMILAR SPECIES Myrsine (*Myrsine cubana*, Myrsinaceae) also flowers and fruits in elongate clusters on naked wood, but its leaves are usually revolute and have obscure veins.

GEORGIA BULLY

WHITE BULLY

Georgia Bully

flowers

fruit

White Bully

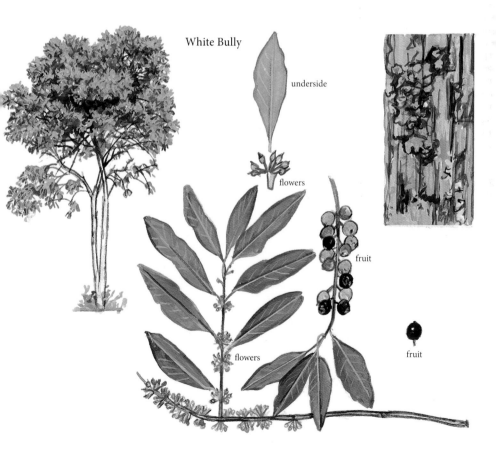

underside

flowers

flowers

fruit

fruit

SCHOEPFIACEAE: SCHOEPFIA FAMILY

This is a small family of 3 genera and about 55 species distributed mostly in the tropics; 1 species is native to North America and restricted to s. Fla. Schoepfiaceae was formerly included within Olacaceae, a family that has now been mostly dissolved based on recent phylogenetic advances.

GULF GRAYTWIG *Schoepfia chrysophylloides* (A. Rich.) Planch.
A.K.A. GRAYTWIG

QUICK ID Recognized by the combination of smooth, zigzag whitish branchlets and orange flowers.

Evergreen shrub or small tree, to about 10 m tall. Erect, single stem or multiple; crown of crooked grayish branches. **BARK** Pale gray, smooth or slightly roughened. **TWIG** Smooth, zigzag, whitish. **LEAF** Alternate, simple, thick, leathery; ovate, elliptic, or broadly lanceolate, base wedge-shaped, tip abruptly pointed; margins entire, often wavy. Upper surface dull green, lower surface paler. Blade 3–7.5 cm long, 2–5 cm broad; petiole 3–8 mm long; exudes a strong aroma when crushed. **FLOWER** Bisexual, reddish or orange, sweetly fragrant, calyx with 4 or 5 lobes, corolla bell-shaped; petals 4 or 5, tips strongly recurved at anthesis. Autumn to spring. **FRUIT** Single-seeded egg-shaped drupe, 8–12 mm long; red at first, becoming black; retains and is nearly enclosed by the calyx at maturity, in summer.

HABITAT/RANGE Native. Hammocks; s. Fla., more common in Fla. Keys.

SIMILAR SPECIES The leaves of several of the stoppers (*Eugenia*, Myrtaceae) are similar but are opposite.

Notes: Gulf Graytwig is hemiparasitic: Its roots produce haustoria that attach themselves to at least 10 host-plant species.

GULF GRAYTWIG

Gulf Graytwig

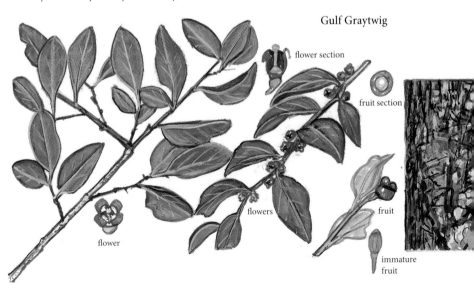

flower section

fruit section

flowers

fruit

flower

immature fruit

SIMAROUBACEAE: QUASSIA FAMILY

The quassia family encompasses about 20 genera and 100 species distributed mostly in tropical or subtropical regions but extending into warm temperate regions. As treated here, the family includes 3 genera and 4 species in North America, 1 species native to the East, 1 introduced. Most modern systematists also include Corkwood (*Leitneria floridana*) within Simaroubaceae; here it is retained in Leitneriaceae. See also the family Picramniaceae, several species of which were formerly included within Simaroubaceae.

Deciduous or evergreen shrubs or trees. **LEAF** Alternate, pinnately compound, the leaves sometimes reduced to a single leaflet. **FLOWER** Small, bisexual or unisexual (male and female on the same or separate plants), radial, stamens usually 10, styles united above the base. **FRUIT** Clusters of samaras or dry to fleshy drupes.

TREE-OF-HEAVEN *Ailanthus altissima* (Mill.) Swingle

QUICKID Recognized by the large compound leaves with opposite and sub-opposite leaflets, the lowermost leaflets toothed near the base, with a flat, circular gland on the lower surface.

Deciduous, often colony-forming tree, to about 25 m tall, 1 m diam. Erect, single straight trunk; crown dense, branches ascending and spreading. **BARK** Smooth, light or medium brown, developing whitish lenticels, eventually becoming shallowly vertically fissured, the furrows visible as pale, discontinuous lines. **TWIG** Stout, smooth, reddish brown, hairy at first, soon becoming hairless. **LEAF** Alternate, pinnately compound; blade 15–90 cm long, to about 30 cm broad; petiole 2–15 cm long. Leaflets opposite, sub-opposite, to slightly alternate, up to about 41 in number, each 2–15 cm long, 4–7 cm broad, lanceolate to broadly ovate, often curved and sickle-shaped, base rounded or truncate, often with 1 or 2 toothlike lobes, the tips of which often bear a conspicuous flattened, circular gland on the lower surface; leaflet tip narrowly pointed or abruptly short-pointed; margins otherwise entire or minutely wavy. Upper surface medium green, sometimes purplish when first unfurling; lower surface paler, densely hairy at first, a few hairs usually remaining, at least along the veins.

Tree-of-heaven

fruit

fruit

TREE-OF-HEAVEN *continued*

FLOWER Bisexual and unisexual, male and female on separate plants, sometimes mixed with bisexual flowers; sepals united, cuplike, with 5 minute lobes; petals 5, folded inward and boatlike, greenish yellow, 2–3 mm long; stamens 10, in 2 series of 5; pistils 5, fused at anthesis and appearing as 1. Spring. **FRUIT** Winged samara, 4–5 cm long, the wings narrowed to both ends; matures summer to autumn.

HABITAT/RANGE Introduced from Asia. Treated as a troublesome invasive; nearly throughout the U.S., e. Canada.

SIMILAR SPECIES At first glance this species might be confused with sumacs (*Rhus*, Anacardiaceae), ashes (*Fraxinus*, Oleaceae), or members of the walnut family (Juglandaceae). However, none of these shares with Tree-of-heaven the combination of colonial habit, alternate leaf arrangement, teeth confined to the lower portion of the leaflet margins, and samaras with the wing elongate at each end.

Notes: The genus contains about 10 species distributed largely in Asia. This hardy tree, the only *Ailanthus* naturalized in North America, withstands dust, smog, poor soil, and lack of care, and is often found crowded against abandoned buildings or sprouting from sidewalk cracks in urban situations. The common and genus names apparently refer to the tree's height.

PARADISETREE *Simarouba glauca* DC.

QUICK ID Easily recognized by the large, pinnately compound leaves with more than 10 hairless, round-tipped, lustrous green leaflets that are arranged both alternately and oppositely along the rachis.

Evergreen small tree, 10–15 m tall, 30–90 cm diam., usually smaller than 30 cm diam. Erect, single straight, slender trunk. Crown of hammock-grown trees open, sparsely branched; crown of open-grown trees oblong or moderately pyramidal, with stout, ascending branches. **BARK** Smooth, reddish brown or grayish, sometimes with orangish overtones, becoming finely and very shallowly fissured. **LEAF** Alternate, pinnately compound; blade 15–40 cm long, to about 18 cm broad; petiole to about 7 cm long. Leaflets 10–20, alternate or opposite, each 4–10 cm long, 2–4 cm broad; stiff,

oblong, obovate, or elliptic; base broadly or narrowly wedge-shaped, often asymmetric; tip rounded; margins entire, usually conspicuously rolled under. Upper surface lustrous, dark green, hairless; lower surface paler, brownish, grayish, or pale green. **FLOWER** Unisexual, small, radial, male and female on separate plants; sepals 5; petals 5, yellow or creamy; produced in open, lax, showy panicles that usually equal or exceed the leaf in length. Late winter to spring. **FRUIT** Single-seeded oval drupe, red or purplish-black, 2–2.5 cm long; seed orange-brown, roughened, oily; matures summer.

HABITAT/RANGE Native. Dry coastal and inland hammocks; s. Fla. and Fla. Keys.

SIMILAR SPECIES Florida Bitterbush (*Picramnia pentandra*, Picramniaceae) is superficially similar; it also has pinnately compound leaves, but usually with fewer than 10 leaflets.

Notes: Paradisetree has been the source of resins and oils, and the roots provide pharmaceutical compounds used in the treatment of dysentery. It belongs to a genus of about 6 species of the American tropics and subtropics.

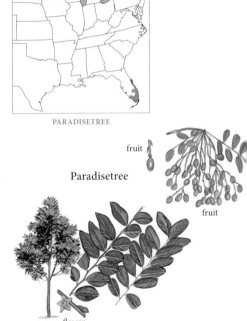

PARADISETREE

fruit

Paradisetree

fruit

flower

SOLANACEAE: NIGHTSHADE FAMILY

The nightshades constitute a family of 102 genera and about 2,500 species of herbs, shrubs, trees, and vines. The family is globally widespread, often due to introduction, but is most diverse in the neotropics. About 31 genera and 175 species occur in North America, including about 105 native species. The largest of the North American genera include *Solanum*, with more than 60 species, and the herbaceous genus *Physalis*, with nearly 30 species.

LEAF Alternate and simple, lobed, or compound. **FLOWER** Usually bisexual and radial, usually with 5 fused sepals and 5 fused petals; the corolla is tubular, funnel-shaped, or bell-shaped, the tips of the petals often curving inward, or it is spreading and star-shaped. There are usually 5 stamens. **FRUIT** Berry or capsule, the latter sometimes splitting into several compartments at maturity.

Most members of the family are poisonous. Even so, the family is well known for a variety of important foods, including peppers, tomatoes, eggplants, and potatoes. Several genera are important for ornamental and garden plants, including *Brunfelsia* (raintrees), *Cestrum* (jessamines), *Brugmansia* (angel's-trumpets), *Petunia* (petunias), *Physalis* (ground-cherries), and *Solanum* (nightshades).

◼ *BRUGMANSIA:* ANGEL'S-TRUMPETS

This is a small genus of shrubs or small trees of 5–7 species native to South America; popular ornamental plants, several species have escaped or naturalized in North America. The trumpet-shaped flowers are pendent rather than erect.

ARBORESCENT ANGEL'S-TEARS
Brugmansia versicolor Lagerh.

Shrub or small tree to about 5 m tall. Very similar to Angel's-tears with larger flowers, 30–50 cm long, which open white but may turn peach or pink with age. **HABITAT/RANGE** Introduced from Ecuador. Cultivated in the Southeast; reported as naturalized in Ga.

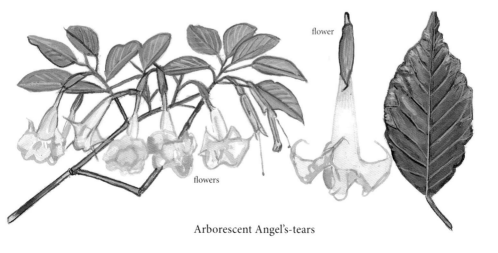

flower

flowers

Arborescent Angel's-tears

ANGEL'S-TEARS *Brugmansia suaveolens* (Humb. & Bonpl. ex Willd.) Bercht. & J. Presl

A.K.A. ANGEL'S-TRUMPETS

QUICKID Immediately recognized by the combination of large leaves and large, pendent, trumpet-shaped flowers.

Evergreen or deciduous, semi-woody, large shrub or small tree, to about 5 m tall in tropical climes, dying back to the ground and usually not exceeding about 3 m tall north of c. Fla. Erect, usually single trunk; crown spreading, vertically flattened, usually densely foliaged. **LEAF** Alternate, simple, usually borne closely adjacent and crowded; ovate, elliptic, or oval; base rounded or very bluntly pointed; tip broadly pointed or abruptly short-pointed; margins entire. Upper surface dull yellow-green, lower surface paler, both surfaces hairy. Blade 15–30 cm long, 8–16 cm broad; petiole 2–8 cm long. **FLOWER** Bisexual; large, showy, pendent, trumpet-shaped; calyx tubular, 9–12 cm long, 3–4 cm broad, 5-lobed, the lobes to about 2 cm long; corolla tubular below, 25–30 cm long, to about 20 cm across, flaring at the apex into 5 narrowly pointed lobes with conspicuously wavy margins; petals white, blushed yellowish or pinkish; anthers conspicuous, 25–35 mm long. Summer to autumn. **FRUIT** Indehiscent, spindle-shaped woody capsule to about 20 cm long; seeds 8–12 mm long, roughened; matures autumn.

HABITAT/RANGE Introduced from South America. Cultivated and sparsely naturalized in s. Fla.

SIMILAR SPECIES Arborescent Angel's-tears has large flowers, the corolla to 50 cm long.

TREE TOBACCO *Nicotiana glauca* Graham

QUICKID Recognized by the combination of the grayish foliage and the narrowly tubular yellow or greenish-yellow flowers with a bulge just below the apex.

Evergreen shrub or small tree, 2–8 m tall. Erect, single slender semi-woody trunk; crown open, sparsely branched. **BARK** Grayish. **LEAF** Alternate, simple, moderately leathery; ovate or lanceolate-oblong; base rounded, acute, broadly wedge-shaped, nearly truncate, or heart-shaped; tip acute or bluntly pointed; margins entire, often wavy. Upper surface grayish green, hairless, veins obscure; lower surface paler, hairless. Blade 5–25 cm long, 2–7 cm broad; petiole 3–12 cm long. **FLOWER** Bisexual, sepals 5, fused into a cuplike calyx 8–12 mm long; corolla tubular, 35–45 mm long, yellow or greenish yellow, bulging near the apex then flaring into a 5-parted orifice to reveal the stigma and anthers; produced in drooping, many-flowered panicles. Year-round. **FRUIT** Egg-shaped, 4-valved capsule, 10–15 mm long; seeds reddish brown. Year-round.

HABITAT/RANGE Introduced from South America. Escaped and established in sandy and clayey soils and along stream banks, 10–300 m; mostly s. U.S., from Ga. and n. Fla. to Calif. and Nev.

Notes: Nicotiana is a genus of about 95 species of annuals, perennials, and, less commonly, shrubs or small trees distributed mainly in Africa, Australia, and the South Pacific; about 5 species are native to North America. It is widely cultivated, including for the tobacco of commerce. All parts of this plant are extremely poisonous.

Angel's-tears

immature
fruit

flowers

Tree Tobacco

flowers

flower

fruit

fruit

fruit

■ *SOLANUM*: NIGHTSHADES

This is a large genus of 1,200–1,400 herbs, shrubs, and trees distributed mostly in the American tropics; about 65 occur in North America, about 35 of them native.

POTATOTREE *Solanum erianthum* D. Don
A.K.A. MULLEIN NIGHTSHADE

QUICK ID Recognized by the combination of soft, velvety-feeling hairs on the branches, leaves, and twigs; large ovate or elliptic grayish-green leaves; 5-parted white flowers; and round yellow berries.

Evergreen shrub or small tree, to about 5 m tall. Erect, usually single trunk; crown dense, rounded, usually low-branching, the branches ascending or spreading. **TWIG** Densely grayish-hairy with star-shaped hairs; velvety. **LEAF** Alternate, simple, thick; ovate, oval, or elliptic, base rounded, tip acute or abruptly short-pointed, margins entire. Upper surface grayish green, densely hairy with star-shaped hairs; lower surface similar, velvety. Blade 10–30 cm long, 4–14 cm broad; petiole to

about 4 cm long. **FLOWER** Bisexual, 15–18 mm diam.; sepals 5; petals 5, white, lanceolate, spreading; stamens 5, anthers yellow, to about 3 mm long; produced in a many-flowered, branched terminal or axillary cluster. Year-round. **FRUIT** Round yellow berry, 1–2 cm diam. Year-round.

HABITAT/RANGE Native. Hammock margins, open woods, thickets, disturbed sites; peninsular Fla., se. Tex.

SIMILAR SPECIES Turkeyberry (*S. torvum* Sw.) is also naturalized in s. Fla. (where it is treated as invasive) and sometimes becomes a small tree to about 5 m tall and 8 cm diam. It is distinguished by bearing recurved prickles and broad, lobed leaves 8–20 cm long and 2–18 cm broad. **Earleaf Nightshade** (*S. mauritianum* Scop.) is a shrub or small tree, 2–4 m tall, with a rounded crown, elliptic leaves to 30 cm long, and 12 cm broad, purple or lilac flowers, and rounded, dull yellowish berries 1–1.5 cm diam. It is introduced from South America and scarcely naturalized in the East, only in Fla.; it is distinguished from Potatotree by flower color.

POTATOTREE

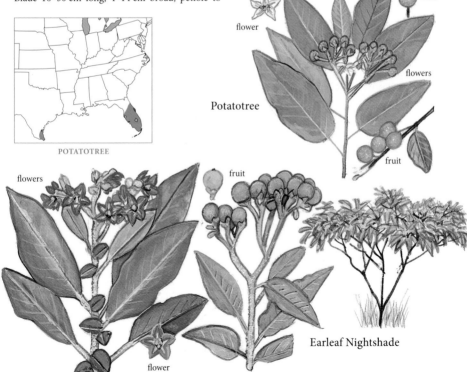

flower

flowers

fruit

Potatotree

flowers

fruit

flowers

fruit

flower

Earleaf Nightshade

STAPHYLEACEAE: BLADDERNUT FAMILY

The bladdernut family encompasses 3 genera and 40–50 species of evergreen or deciduous shrubs or trees distributed largely in tropical and subtropical parts of the Northern Hemisphere; 1 genus and 2 native species occur in North America, 1 widespread in the East. Plants in this family have opposite, compound leaves, often with only 3 leaflets. The fruit is an inflated capsule (in ours), follicle, or several-stoned drupe.

AMERICAN BLADDERNUT *Staphylea trifolia* L.

QUICK ID Recognized by the long-petioled, 3-parted leaf with a long-stalked terminal leaflet, bell-shaped flowers, bladderlike fruit, and striped trunk.

Deciduous, usually a thicket-forming shrub spreading by underground runners, occasionally a small tree to about 8 m tall, 15 cm diam. Erect, single slender trunk; crown loosely branched, open. **BARK** Grayish green, smooth, usually with light creamy-white vertical stripes. **TWIG** Greenish, smooth, becoming reddish brown. **LEAF** Opposite, trifoliolately compound (rarely with 5 leaflets); leaflets 3–10 cm long, 2–5 cm broad, lateral leaflets stalkless, stalk of terminal leaflet 1.5–3 cm long; leaflet blade elliptic, base broadly wedge-shaped, tip abruptly short-pointed, margins finely and regularly toothed. Upper surface medium to dark green; lower surface paler, hairy. Blade to about 13 cm long, to about 18 cm broad; petiole 4–9 cm long, slender. Turns yellow in autumn. **FLOWER** Bisexual; sepals 5, fused, lobes erect, greenish white; petals 5, greenish white, slightly longer than the sepals; corolla bell-shaped; produced in a drooping, loosely branched cluster 5–10 cm long in the axils of the uppermost leaves of a branch. Spring. **FRUIT** Inflated, 3-parted, bladder-like creamy or pale brown papery capsule, 3–6 cm long, with 1–3 seeds; matures summer to autumn.

HABITAT/RANGE Native. Floodplains, stream banks, moist upland woods, 5–600 m; nearly throughout the East, from Que. and Ont. south to nw. Fla., west to Nebr., Kans., and Okla.

SIMILAR SPECIES The leaves of Common Hoptree (*Ptelea trifoliata*, Rutaceae) are reminiscent but alternate rather than opposite, and the fruit is a disk-like winged samara.

Notes: *Staphylea* is a genus of about 13 species distributed in Asia, Europe, and North America.

AMERICAN BLADDERNUT

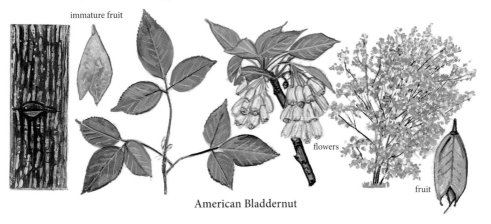

immature fruit

flowers

fruit

American Bladdernut

STYRACACEAE: STORAX FAMILY

This is a family of about 11 genera and 160 species of shrubs and trees distributed in warm temperate regions of Mexico, West Indies, Central and South America, s. Europe, and Southeast Asia. Two genera and 7–9 species are represented in North America; 6 occur in the East, 5 native, 1 introduced. Recent evidence suggests that the genus *Halesia* includes only 2 species, but some taxonomists recognize 3 or 4 species.

LEAF Alternate, simple, petiolate, and lacking stipules. **FLOWER** Bisexual, typically with 4–6 sepals; petals number 4–6 and are fused at the base and sometimes well above it. Corolla usually white (in ours) and bell-shaped, the flowers borne in conspicuous, showy clusters. Stamens number usually 10, commonly twice the number of petals. **FRUIT** Flattened, pear-shaped, or more or less round, with 1–4 seeds, and capsule-, nut-, or drupelike.

■ *HALESIA*: SILVERBELLS

A genus of 2–4 species distributed in warm temperate regions of North America and Asia; 3 native species are treated here. *Halesia* is among a well-studied group of genera with East Asian–North American affinities.

Deciduous shrubs or small trees. **TWIG** Pith diaphragmed, chambered between the partitions. **LEAF** Alternate, simple, more or less thin and papery to slightly thickened, margins entire or usually at least somewhat toothed. **FLOWER** Bisexual; sepals 4, distinct; petals 4, white, fused at least at the base, sometimes more extensively fused and forming a bell-shaped corolla; stamens 7–16, the filaments fused for about ⅓ their length; pistil 1, ovary inferior, with 2–4 chambers. **FRUIT** Dry, indehiscent, nutlike or capsule-like, with 2–4 wings and 1–4 seeds, the remains of the persistent style usually forming a beaklike projection at the apex.

CAROLINA SILVERBELL *Halesia carolina* L.
A.K.A. LITTLE SILVERBELL

QUICK ID Recognized by the combination of alternate, simple elliptic leaves; bell-shaped white flowers; and the diaphragmed and chambered twig pith.

Deciduous shrub or small tree, 10–24 m tall, to 1.3 m diam. Erect, single often low-branching trunk; crown irregular or rounded, branches spreading or ascending, sometimes drooping at the tips. **BARK** Brownish or greenish gray, shallowly and finely furrowed at first, the furrows becoming deeper with age. **TWIG** Pith diaphragmed and chambered. **LEAF** Alternate, simple; ovate, elliptic, or obovate, base usually rounded, tip abruptly long-pointed or evenly tapered to an elongate point; margins entire, inconspicuously and bluntly toothed, or finely toothed. Upper surface medium or dark green, sparsely hairy or hairless; lower surface paler, grayish green, sparsely hairy throughout. Blade 7–18 cm long, 3–7 cm broad; petiole 1–3 cm long. **FLOWER** Bisexual; sepals 4; petals 4, fused; corolla white, bell-shaped, 1.2–3 cm long; produced in pendent clusters. Early or mid-spring. **FRUIT** Pear-shaped, greenish, greenish yellow, or somewhat creamy green, 2–5 cm long, 1–2.5 cm broad, with 4 narrow, equal-sized papery wings and 1–3 seeds; matures late summer to autumn.

HABITAT/RANGE Native. Sandy bluffs, wooded slopes and riverbanks, elevated floodplains, hammocks, swamp margins, rich deciduous woodlands, mountain slopes, 0–1,600 m; throughout the East, N.Y. and Mich. south to nw. Fla., La., and Okla.

SIMILAR SPECIES Carolina Silverbell has been the subject of significant taxonomic controversy; at least 2 additional closely similar species have been recognized. Recent molecular data suggests that **Mountain Silverbell** (*H. tetraptera* Ellis) and Little Silverbell (*H. parviflora* Michx.) are best recognized within the concept of *H. carolina*. In the strict sense, Carolina Silverbell is a small tree usually not exceeding about 10 m tall with the corolla usually less than 13 mm long. Mountain Silverbell is a much larger plant, reaching at least 24 m tall, with larger flowers and a mountain habitat. The 2 are treated as a single species here and incorporated into the above description.

spring

Mountain Silverbell

flowers

fruit

Carolina Silverbell

Two-wing
Silverbell

flowers

fruit

TWO-WING SILVERBELL *Halesia diptera* Ellis

QUICK ID Recognized by broad, obovate to nearly circular leaves; 4-petaled white flowers that are divided to the base and are produced in drooping clusters; and essentially 2-winged fruit.

Deciduous small tree, 10–15 m tall, 40 cm diam.; often flowering and fruiting when of small stature. Erect, single often low-branching trunk. Crown of open-grown plants usually rounded; crown of forest-grown plants more often loosely branched, with ascending or spreading branches. **BARK** Brown, shallowly furrowed, ridges sometimes flaking off in narrow, elongate strips. **TWIG** Brown or reddish brown, somewhat zigzag, pith diaphragmed and chambered. **LEAF** Alternate, simple; broadly oval, elliptic, or nearly circular, base broadly rounded or wedge-shaped or short-tapered, tip abruptly short-pointed; margins toothed, the teeth glandular. Upper surface medium green, lower surface paler, both surfaces sparsely hairy. Blade 8–17 cm long, 4–12 cm broad; petiole 15–35 mm long. **FLOWER** Bisexual; sepals 4; petals 4, white, fused only near the base; corolla bell-shaped, 1–1.5 cm long, the petals spreading toward the tip; produced in several-flowered clusters. Spring. **FRUIT** More or less flattened, oval in outline, dry, indehiscent, hard, greenish yellow, with 1–3 seeds and 2 conspicuous wings and 2 narrow, ridgelike wings; matures late spring to autumn.

HABITAT/RANGE Native. Floodplain woodlands, ravines, swamp margins, hammocks, sandy upland woods, 0–100 m; southeastern coastal plains, S.C. south to n. Fla., west to Ark., La., and e. Tex.

Notes: A large-flowered variety occurs in the western half of the Fla. panhandle and sw. Ga. It is virtually indistinguishable from the nominate variety except by corolla length, which can be to about 3 cm long.

CAROLINA SILVERBELL

TWO-WING SILVERBELL

■ *STYRAX*: SNOWBELLS

This is the largest genus in Styracaceae, containing about 130 species, including 5 in North America, 4 native; 3 occur in the East, 2 native. Otherwise distributed in warm temperate and tropical regions of n. Mexico, South America, s. Europe, and Asia.

Deciduous shrubs or small trees. **TWIG** Pith homogeneous and continuous, not chambered. **LEAF** Alternate, simple, margins entire or toothed. **FLOWER** Bisexual; sepals usually 4 or 5, fused, forming a tube tipped with minute teeth; petals 5 (rarely 6 or 7), distinct or fused; corolla white, usually flaring at the apex; stamens usually 10, joined to the tube of the corolla; pistil 1, exceeding the stamens in length. **FRUIT** Rounded, indehiscent, capsule-like, nutlike, or drupelike, with 1–3 seeds, the remains of the pistil usually (not always) forming a beak at the apex.

AMERICAN SNOWBELL *Styrax americanus* Lam.

QUICK ID Recognized by the combination of leaves usually green beneath and hairless to sparsely hairy, small white flowers with strongly recurved flower petals, and trunk with pale vertical stripes.

Deciduous, usually a shrub, sometimes a small tree, to about 5 m tall, to about 9 cm diam. Erect, upright, usually with multiple trunks or a single very low-branched trunk; crown spreading or ascending, often sparsely branched, the branches often forming a spraylike pattern. **BARK** Brown, smooth or slightly roughened, on larger trunks marked with pale vertical stripes. **TWIG** Round in cross section, brown; pith solid. **LEAF** Alternate, simple; elliptic, narrowly obovate, or oval; base broadly or narrowly wedge-shaped; tip rounded or blunt; margins entire or obscurely bluntly toothed, often wavy. Upper surface dark green, hairless or sparsely hairy; lower surface

pale green, hairless or sparsely to densely hairy. Blade 2–10 cm long, 1–6 cm broad; petiole 2–6 mm long, hairy or not. **FLOWER** Bisexual; sepals 5; petals usually 5, white, narrow, 10–12 mm long, strongly and conspicuously recurved; corolla tube 1.5–3 mm long; stamens usually 10, conspicuously protruding from the corolla; commonly produced singly (occasionally 2–4) in the leaf axils, stalk of the inflorescence to 14 mm long. Spring to early summer. **FRUIT** Rounded or obovoid capsule, 6–10 mm diam., with 1–3 seeds; matures summer to autumn.

HABITAT/RANGE Native. Swamps and swamp margins, wet woods, stream banks, floodplains, and hammocks, usually associated with acidic soils, 0–300 m; Ohio, Ill., and se. Mo., south to c. Fla. peninsula, se. Okla., and e. Tex.

SIMILAR SPECIES Bigleaf Snowbell usually occurs in drier habitats and has broader leaves and a longer flower tube; the stalk of the inflorescence of Japanese Snowbell usually exceeds 15 mm long.

BIGLEAF SNOWBELL *Styrax grandifolius* Aiton

QUICK ID Recognized by the combination of broad leaves that are grayish-hairy beneath and elongate clusters of bell-shaped white flowers.

Deciduous shrub or small tree to about 6 m tall, about 10 cm diam. Erect, usually single low-branching trunk, or multiple trunks; crown spreading, somewhat flat-topped. **TWIG** Round, brownish, pith solid. **LEAF** Alternate, simple; oval, ovate, obovate, or nearly circular, conspicuously broad in relation to length; base rounded or broadly wedge-shaped; tip rounded, blunt, or abruptly short- or very short-pointed; margins entire or occasionally obscurely toothed. Upper surface dark green, hairless or sparsely hairy, especially along

AMERICAN SNOWBELL

BIGLEAF SNOWBELL

American Snowbell

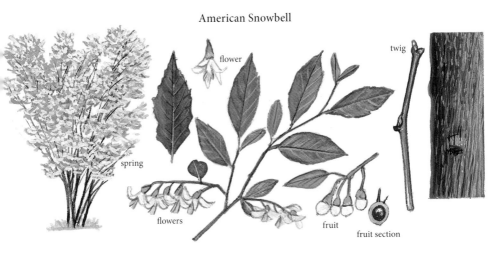

spring

flower

flowers

fruit

fruit section

twig

Bigleaf Snowbell

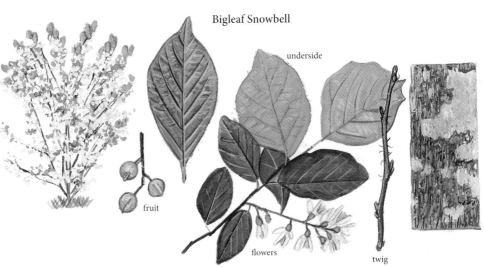

underside

fruit

flowers

twig

the veins; lower surface pale grayish green, hairy throughout. Blade 7–20 cm long, 4–15 cm broad; petiole 4–12 mm long. **FLOWER** Bisexual; sepals 5; petals 5, white, elliptic or oblong, 15–22 mm long; corolla tube 3–5 mm long; stamens 10, conspicuous, about equaling the corolla in length; inflorescence a drooping, elongate raceme of 2–19 flowers, to about 15 cm long, growing from the tips of new branchlets. Spring. **FRUIT** Nutlike, rounded, 8–12 mm long, 6–9 mm diam., hairy with star-shaped grayish hairs; matures summer to autumn.

HABITAT/RANGE Native. Moist upland forests, slopes and bluffs, ravines, rocky outcrops, elevated portions of river floodplains, usually where well drained, 0–300 m; Va. to Ill., south to nw. Fla., Ark., and e. Tex.

SIMILAR SPECIES Nonflowering plants of American Snowbell can be distinguished by the combination of habitat and the green lower leaf surface lacking a grayish cast.

JAPANESE SNOWBELL *Styrax japonicus*
Siebold & Zucc.

QUICK ID Recognized by the combination of alternate simple leaves that are dark green above and hairy beneath, numerous white flowers produced in late spring and early summer, and the stalk of the inflorescence 15–50 mm long.

Deciduous shrub or small tree, 8–10 m tall. Erect, single straight or low-branched trunk; crown narrow, becoming broad and flat-topped at maturity. **BARK** Grayish brown, shallowly furrowed at maturity. **TWIG** Slender, reddish brown, somewhat zigzag, slightly roughened. **LEAF** Alternate, simple; narrowly or broadly ovate or oblong, or somewhat diamond-shaped; base wedge-shaped; tip tapered to a sharp point or abruptly short-pointed; margins nearly entire or finely toothed, especially toward the tip. Upper surface lustrous, dark green; lower surface paler, hairy with star-shaped hairs. Blade 3–11 cm long, 2–7 cm broad; petiole 2–10 mm long. **FLOWER** Bisexual; sepals 5; petals 5, bright white, spreading, 8–23 mm long; corolla tube 3–5 mm long; stamens conspicuous, protruding; inflorescence a cluster of 2–5 flowers on a stalk 15–50 mm long. Late spring to early summer. **FRUIT** Ovoid or ellipsoid capsule, 8–15 mm long, with grayish or grayish-yellow hairs; matures autumn.

HABITAT/RANGE Introduced from Asia. Cultivated and sparingly established in the Northeast, essentially Conn., N.Y., and Pa.

SIMILAR SPECIES The leaves of Bigleaf Snowbell are grayish beneath. The flowers of American Snowbell have strongly recurved petals.

SYMPLOCACEAE: SWEETLEAF FAMILY

The sweetleaf family includes 2 genera and about 320 species of shrubs and trees distributed in tropical, subtropical, and temperate regions of the se. U.S., West Indies, South America, Asia, Pacific islands, and Australia; 1 genus with 2 species occurs in the U.S., 1 native.

■ *SYMPLOCOS*: SWEETLEAF

A genus of 318 species; 2 in the East, 1 native. Deciduous shrubs or trees. **LEAF** Alternate, simple, midvein on the lower surface usually prominent and sweet to the taste. **FLOWER** Bisexual, fragrant; sepals usually 5, overlapping; petals 5, overlapping, usually creamy white or yellowish. **FRUIT** Bluish or blue-black drupe, the remains of the calyx forming a crown at the apex.

SWEETLEAF *Symplocos tinctoria* (L.) L'Hér.
A.K.A. HORSE SUGAR

QUICK ID Recognized by the combination of alternate simple leathery leaves with obscurely toothed margins; dense, ball-like clusters of yellowish-white flowers appearing prior to the new leaves; and oblong greenish fruit with the toothlike remains of the calyx conspicuous at its summit.

Deciduous, potentially semi-evergreen in southern parts of the range. Shrub or small tree, 2–15 m tall, to about 36 cm diam. Erect, usually single trunk; crown open, usually sparsely branched, branches commonly ascending. **BARK** Grayish with pinkish overtones, usually slightly roughened and warty. **TWIG** Round, slender, grayish and hairy at first, becoming waxy with an ashy-gray bloom, then brown; pith chambered. **LEAF** Alternate, simple, usually elliptic or narrowly elliptic, leathery; base tapered, wedge-shaped; tip evenly or abruptly pointed; margins entire or more often with low, blunt, obscure teeth. Upper surface lustrous, dark green at first, becoming yellowish green, hairy or hairless; lower surface pale green, usually hairy. Blade 5–15 cm long, 2–7 cm broad; petiole 8–12 mm long. **FLOWER** Bisexual, fragrant; sepals 5, fused, represented by short, toothlike points at the tip of the vaselike calyx; petals 5, yellow or creamy white, 6–8 mm long; stamens numerous, conspicuous; pistil 1; closely set in a crowded, ball-like cluster on wood of the previous season. Early spring, prior to the new leaves. **FRUIT** Oblong or ellipsoid, usually 1-seeded drupe, to about 1 cm long, the summit with teethlike points from the remains of the calyx; green at first, becoming darker with age; matures summer to autumn.

Japanese Snowbell

twig

flowers

fruit

Sweetleaf

flowers

fruit

fruit

fruit

fruit

underside

flower

underside

HABITAT/RANGE Native. Upland mixed woods, longleaf pinelands and moist pine flatwoods, ravine slopes, maritime and inland hammocks, stream banks, floodplain forests, 0–1,400 m; the Southeast, Long Island, Del., and Tenn., south to c. Fla., west to e. Okla., Ark., and e. Tex.

SIMILAR SPECIES Similar to several species of Lauraceae, which can be distinguished vegetatively by the leaves having margins always entire, never obscurely toothed. Also potentially confused with Carolina Silverbell (*Halesia carolina*, Styracaceae), which differs in its dangling, bell-shaped white flowers and winged, pear-shaped fruits; and Loblolly Bay (*Gordonia lasianthus*, Theaceae), which has darker green leaves with more conspicuously toothed margins and showy white flowers.

SWEETLEAF

SAPPHIRE-BERRY *Symplocos paniculata* (Thunb.) Miq.

QUICK ID Recognized by the combination of alternate simple, finely toothed leaves, the central vein on the upper surface impressed; an elongate, branched inflorescence with creamy-white or yellowish flowers; and an ovoid or rounded bluish-black drupe

Deciduous shrub or small tree, 1–10 m tall. Erect or ascending, single trunk or often multiple trunks; crown vase-shaped or somewhat rounded, branches usually ascending. **BARK** Gray, shallowly or moderately vertically fissured, somewhat scaly. **LEAF** Alternate, simple, thin; ovate, obovate, or slightly rhombic; base broadly wedge-shaped or nearly rounded; tip abruptly pointed; margins finely, evenly, and conspicuously toothed. Upper surface dark green, hairy or not, midvein impressed; lower surface light green, hairy or not. Blade 4–9 cm long, 2–5 cm broad; petiole 3–9 mm long. **FLOWER** Bisexual; corolla white or yellow, to about 5 mm long; inflorescence a branched, elongate panicle of 4–20 flowers. Spring. **FRUIT** Ovoid or nearly rounded blue or bluish-black drupe, 3–8 mm long; matures summer to autumn.

HABITAT/RANGE Introduced from East Asia. Established in disturbed sites and floodplains in the Northeast, Conn., D.C., N.Y., and Pa.

SIMILAR SPECIES Sweetleaf can be distinguished by the entire or obscurely toothed leaf margins and the ball-like inflorescence.

TAMARICACEAE: TAMARISK FAMILY

Tamaricaceae is a small family of about 5 genera and about 80 species of shrubs, subshrubs, and trees distributed in salty or dry areas of steppes, deserts, sandy shores, and along rivers, chiefly in Africa and Eurasia. The family is represented in North America by the genus *Tamarix*, one of the most taxonomically challenging genera among the angiosperms. Species cannot be identified without flowers and fruit, and the morphological characters used for identification often vary from plant to plant, or even on the same plant from season to season. In addition, species of *Tamarix* are thought to hybridize, producing intermediate forms with intermediate characters. Given this complexity, here we describe the genus and include an accounting of the 4 species thought to be naturalized in the East.

■ *TAMARIX*: TAMARISKS OR SALTCEDARS

A genus of about 55 species, perhaps 9 in North America, 4 in the East. Deciduous shrubs or small trees, 2–12 m tall, with a distinctly redcedar-like appearance and usually a deep root system with a long taproot. Erect or upright, single low-branching trunk or multiple; crown with numerous ascending or spreading branches, appearing wispy. **BARK** Brownish or reddish brown, smooth at first, eventually becoming thick and furrowed. **TWIG** Red at first, becoming reddish brown. **LEAF** Alternate, scalelike, 1–7 mm long, grayish, covered with salt-excreting glands and often salt-encrusted; petiole absent. **FLOWER** Usually bisexual; if unisexual, male and female on separate plants; pinkish or pinkish white; sepals and petals usually 4 or 5; stamens 4 or 5 or numerous; pistil 1, with 3 or 4 carpels, ovary superior; inflorescence a raceme or panicle. Spring, potentially year-round. **FRUIT** Many-seeded cone-shaped capsule; seeds dispersed by wind or water.

Tamarisks were imported from Europe and Asia in the 1800s for use in erosion control and as shade plants; virtually all are aggressive, invasive species, especially in the West, where they have overtaken more than half a million hectares of riparian habitat and are expanding at an estimated rate of 16,000 hectares per year. Distributed in the East primarily along the Atlantic coast from ne. Fla. to N.C., and along the Gulf of Mexico coast from nw. Fla. to Tex. Plants can produce flowers within 4 months of germination in warm temperate climates. The salt-encrusted fallen foliage changes soil chemistry under dense stands, killing or preventing establishment of native species.

Sapphire-berry

flowers

fruit

leaves

Canary Island Tamarisk

nectar disk

flower

leaves

French Tamarisk

nectar disk

flower

Smallflower Tamarisk

nectar disk

flower

leaves

Saltcedar

flower

salt glands

nectar disk

leaves

FRENCH TAMARISK *Tamarix gallica* L.

Similar to Canary Island Tamarisk in all respects except petals elliptic and the central axis of the raceme lacking protuberances. **HABITAT/RANGE** Currently reported from S.C. and the Gulf Coast of La. and Tex. Many early reports of this species in the East were probably examples of Canary Island Tamarisk.

CANARY ISLAND TAMARISK *Tamarix canariensis* Willd.

Distinguished by leaves linear to ovate; sepals, petals, and stamens 5; petals obovate; lobes on the nectar disk at the base of the corolla distinctly longer than wide; flowering raceme 4–5 mm wide, the central axis with tiny protuberances. **HABITAT/RANGE** Perhaps the most widespread and commonly encountered tamarisk in the East, ranging from ne. Fla. to N.C., chiefly along the coast.

SMALLFLOWER TAMARISK *Tamarix parviflora* DC.

Distinguished by leaves linear; sepals, petals, and stamens usually 4. **HABITAT/RANGE** Reported from Miss. and N.C.

SALTCEDAR *Tamarix ramosissima* Ledeb.

Distinguished by leaves linear; sepals, petals, and stamens 5; lobes on the nectar disk at the base of the corolla wider than long; racemes 3–4 mm wide. **HABITAT/RANGE** Mostly western in distribution, occurring in the East in Tex. and La.

French Tamarisk

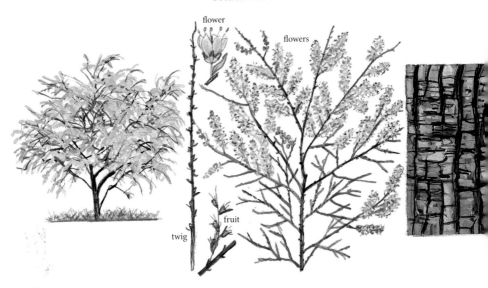

flower

flowers

twig

fruit

Canary Island Tamarisk

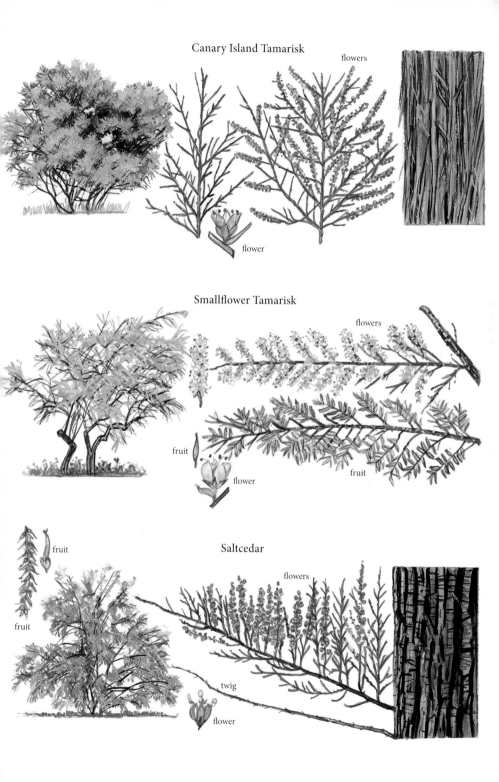

flowers

flower

Smallflower Tamarisk

flowers

fruit

fruit

flower

Saltcedar

fruit

fruit

flowers

twig

flower

THEACEAE: TEA FAMILY

This moderately sized family encompasses 9 genera and 300–450 species distributed in North America, South America, Central America, Mexico, the West Indies, and Asia; 3 genera and 4 species are represented in North America, all of which are native trees restricted in range to the se. U.S.

Evergreen or deciduous trees or shrubs. **LEAF** Alternate, simple. **FLOWER** The North American species are especially noted for their showy flowers with 5 white petals (often with wrinkled margins), 5 sepals, and numerous showy stamens that in some species are joined at the base into a ring or into 5 distinct bundles, each bundle appressed to the base of a petal. Flowers are typically insect-pollinated. **FRUIT** Few-seeded, hard, more or less "woody" capsule. The seeds are usually flat, sometimes winged, and are dispersed primarily by wind or water.

The family is probably best known for the Asian genus *Camellia*. The Tea Plant (*C. sinensis* [L.] Kuntze) is the source of commercial tea, and many members of the genus are widely used ornamentally for their attractive form and abundant showy flowers.

BEN FRANKLIN TREE *Franklinia alatamaha* W. Bartram ex Marshall
A.K.A. FRANKLINIA, FRANKLIN TREE

QUICK ID Recognized by combination of showy 5-petaled flowers, rounded capsular fruit, and deciduous obovate leaves that turn red in autumn.

Deciduous tree or shrub, 3–7 m tall, 10–25 cm diam. Erect or leaning, often with multiple trunks, sometimes with a single trunk; crown rounded. **BARK** Smooth, brown or reddish brown. **LEAF** Alternate, simple, obovate, with a long-tapering base; margins toothed, at least above mid-blade. Upper surface lustrous, dark green, veins conspicuous; lower surface paler. Blade 6–15 cm long, 4–5 cm broad; petiole absent or indistinct, winged and appearing as an extension of the blade. Turns an attractive red in autumn. **FLOWER** 7–10 cm diam.; sepals 5; petals 5, slightly joined at base, white, margins wrinkled; stamens 75–150. Late summer. **FRUIT** Rounded brown capsule, about 2 cm diam., splitting to release 6–12 angled or narrowly winged seeds; matures late autumn.

HABITAT/RANGE Native. Originally known from the Altamaha River, near Savannah, Ga.; knowledge of the exact location of the original plants is lost, and no plants have been seen in nature since 1773. Cultivated in arboreta and botanical gardens.

SIMILAR SPECIES Loblolly Bay (*Gordonia lasianthus*) has evergreen elliptic leaves with the margins toothed throughout.

LOBLOLLY BAY *Gordonia lasianthus* (L.) Ellis

QUICK ID Distinguished in its swampy habitat by the bluntly toothed, dark green leaves and deeply ridged and furrowed bark.

Evergreen tree, to about 25 m tall, usually 30–40 cm diam., potentially to 60 cm diam. Erect, single straight trunk; crown dense, compact, pyramidal, dark green. **BARK** Grayish or reddish brown, somewhat smooth at first, rugged at maturity, developing thick, interlacing ridges between narrow furrows, the furrows 2 cm deep or more. **TWIG** Smooth, grayish or whitish at first, becoming brown; hairless or minutely hairy. **LEAF** Alternate, simple, leathery, stiff; oblong or elliptic, margins shallowly and bluntly toothed. Upper surface lustrous, dark green, hairless, veins conspicuous; lower surface paler, sparsely hairy, the hairs in scattered tufts. Blade 8–18 cm long, 3–5 cm broad; petiole about 1 cm long, hairy near the base. **FLOWER** About 8 cm diam.; sepals 5; petals 5, creamy white, fused at the base, margins crinkled; stamens 50–150, joined at the base into 5 bundles, each bundle appressed to the base of a petal; anthers yellow. Summer. **FRUIT** Hard, silky-hairy, rounded capsule about 1.5 cm long, splitting at the base into

Ben Franklin Tree

flower

autumn

mature fruit

fruit

Loblolly Bay

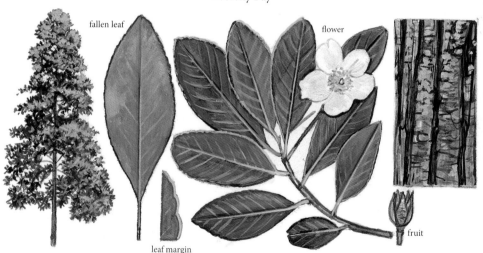

fallen leaf

flower

leaf margin

fruit

5 segments, each with 4–8 flat winged seeds to about 1 cm long; matures autumn.

HABITAT/RANGE Native. In bogs, bay swamps, pond cypress depressions, pine flatwood depressions, pocosins, seepage areas in pine savannas, 0–200 m; southeastern coastal plains, S.C. to peninsular Fla., west to Miss.

LOBLOLLY BAY

SIMILAR SPECIES Often intermixed with Sweetbay (*Magnolia virginiana*, Magnoliaceae) and Swamp Bay (*Persea palustris*, Lauraceae); both of those species have leaves with margins entire, rather than shallowly toothed.

■ *STEWARTIA*: STEWARTIAS

Approximately 20 species of deciduous or evergreen shrubs or small trees, predominantly from China, Japan, and Korea; 2 species are native to the southeastern U.S.

SILKY CAMELLIA *Stewartia malacodendron* L.

A.K.A. VIRGINIA STEWARTIA

QUICK ID The spraylike branches, exquisite creamy-white flowers with purple stamens, and capsular fruit are usually enough to identify Silky Camellia.

Deciduous small tree or shrub, to about 6 m tall, potentially to 25 cm diam., usually not exceeding about 10 cm diam. Erect or leaning, usually a single trunk, sometimes multiple; crown rounded, the branches and branchlets often 2-ranked, laterally spreading, often oriented in a single plane and spraylike. **BARK** Mottled dark and light brown, smooth, breaking into thin, longitudinal, flaking strips. **TWIG** Brown or gray, silky-hairy at first, becoming nearly hairless; terminal bud visible before leaf-fall, not enveloped and obscured by the petiole, about 5–9 mm long, silvery-hairy. **LEAF** Alternate, simple, oval or elliptic; margins minutely toothed and finely hairy. Upper surface yellow-green, primary veins conspicuous, in 7 or 8 lateral pairs, arching toward the apex prior to reaching the margins; lower surface paler, that of young blade silky-hairy. Blade 5–12 cm long, 3–6 cm broad; petiole 2–5 mm long. **FLOWER** 7–10 cm diam.; sepals 5; petals 5, hairy, surfaces rippled, margins crinkled; stamens 50–125, filaments purple, anthers typically bluish. Late spring to early summer. **FRUIT** Rounded or slightly egg-shaped capsule, 1–1.8 cm diam., surface hairy; seeds brown, unwinged, 5–7 mm long; matures late summer to early autumn.

HABITAT/RANGE Native. Ravine slopes, rich wooded bluffs, creek banks, infrequently inundated floodplain terraces, 0–200 m; primarily in the southeastern coastal plains, Va. to nw. Fla., west to extreme e. Tex. An uncommon species throughout its range. It is listed as endangered in Ark. and Fla., and rare in Ga.

SIMILAR SPECIES At least some of the leaves of Sour Gum (*Nyssa sylvatica*, Nyssaceae) are broadest above the middle, sometimes with 1–3 large, coarse marginal teeth nearer the apex. The flowers of Mountain Camellia have yellow anthers and the leaves usually have 5–7 pairs of main lateral veins. Mountain Camellia and Silky Camellia overlap only slightly in range.

MOUNTAIN CAMELLIA *Stewartia ovata* (Cav.) Weath.

QUICK ID Most easily distinguished from other trees of the s. Appalachians by the finely toothed leaves and showy flowers with creamy-white or yellow stamens and yellow anthers.

Deciduous shrub or small tree, usually 4–6 m tall (potentially to 10 m), 3–13 cm diam. Erect, usually a single trunk, sometimes multiple; crown rounded. **BARK** Thin, brown or grayish brown, fissured with narrow ridges, usually not forming strips as in Silky Camellia. **TWIG** Red-brown, terminal and lateral buds nearly enclosed and obscured by the petiole prior to leaf-fall; terminal bud 2–5 mm long, silvery-hairy. **LEAF** Alternate, simple, ovate or broadly elliptic; base wedge-shaped, rounded, or slightly tapered; margins finely toothed. Upper surface dark green, mostly hairless, primary veins conspicuous, in 5–7 lateral pairs, arching toward the apex prior to reaching the margins; lower surface paler, hairy. Blade 6–15 cm long, 4–7 cm broad; petiole 2–15 mm long, winged, the wing

SILKY CAMELLIA

MOUNTAIN CAMELLIA

Silky Camellia

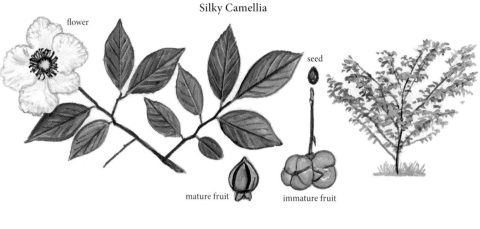

flower

seed

mature fruit

immature fruit

Mountain Camellia

flower

fruit

usually curved upward, troughlike. **FLOWER** 6–10 cm diam.; sepals 5; petals usually 5 (rarely more), creamy white, surfaces rippled, margins crinkled; stamens 100–150, filaments yellow, white, rose, or purple, anthers yellow. Early or midsummer. **FRUIT** Egg-shaped capsule, 1.5–2.2 cm long, hairy; seeds reddish brown, winged, 7–10 mm long; matures autumn.

HABITAT/RANGE Native. Moist ravines, gorges, shaded mountain slopes, usually in rich soils, 200–1,100 m; mostly concentrated in the s. Appalachians and interior plateau of Ky., less common in the Piedmont; Va. and Ky. south to Miss., Ala., and Ga. Uncommon and of conservation concern.

SIMILAR SPECIES The flowers of Silky Camellia have bluish anthers, the leaves usually have 7 or 8 pairs of main lateral veins, and the terminal buds are slightly larger; the 2 species only barely overlap in range. Potentially confused with immature Carolina Silverbell (*Halesia carolina*, Styracaceae), but that has smaller, bell-shaped flowers and predominantly elliptic leaves.

THEOPHRASTACEAE: JOEWOOD FAMILY

This small family of 7 genera and about 100 species of herbs, shrubs, and trees is distributed mainly in the New World tropics. Members of the family are closely related to the myrsine (Myrsinaceae) and primrose (Primulaceae) families. Several modern taxonomists combine these families, including Theophrastaceae and Myrsinaceae within Primulaceae. Here we keep the traditional view.

LEAF Alternate, often appearing clustered at the branch tips, simple. **FLOWER** Bisexual, usually radial, produced in axillary or terminal racemes or branched inflorescences. **FRUIT** Hard-coated berry or capsule.

■ *JACQUINIA*: JACQUINIAS

Jacquinia is a genus of about 13 species distributed in tropical portions of Mexico, the West Indies, Central and South America; 3 occur in the U.S., 1 native. The genus *Bonellia* was previously included within *Jacquinia*.

JOEWOOD *Jacquinia keyensis* Mez

QUICK ID Recognized by the combination of contorted habit, coastal scrub habitat, stiff leaves with rolled margins and a rounded or notched tip, and orange-red berries.

Evergreen, typically a shrub, sometimes a small tree to about 6 m tall, to about 18 cm diam. Erect or upright, often contorted, single low-branching trunk or multiple trunks; crown open or dense. **BARK** Smooth, varying light gray to tan, thin. **TWIG** Gray, smooth, round in cross section, stout, often spotted with conspicuous scales. **LEAF** Alternate on lower parts of the branch, densely clustered near the branch tip, slightly obovate, simple, thick, stiff, leathery; base narrowly tapered; tip rounded, often notched or with a tiny toothlike extension; margins entire, usually strongly rolled under. Upper surface medium or yellow-green, lower surface slightly

paler. Blade 1–4 cm long, 1–2.5 cm broad; petiole to about 5 mm long, hairy. **FLOWER** Bisexual, sepals 5, 2–4 mm long; petals 5, white, 6–9 mm long, the free portion as long as or longer than the tube; inflorescence a raceme of 4–30 flowers, to 6 cm long. Year-round. **FRUIT** Hard-coated rounded or oblong berry, 8–10 mm diam.; green at first, becoming yellowish to orange-red. Year-round.

HABITAT/RANGE Native. Coastal scrub, 0–10 m; extreme s. Fla. and Fla. Keys, treated as a threatened species in Fla.

SIMILAR SPECIES Cudjoewood (*Bonellia macrocarpa* [Cav.] Ståhl & Källersjö), formerly included within *Jacquinia* and usually a shrub, sometimes arborescent, is naturalized in Miami-Dade County, Fla. Its leaf tips lack a notch and the flowers are red or orange.

BRACELETWOOD *Jacquinia arborea* Vahl*

A shrub or tree to about 5 m tall. **LEAF** Crowded in pseudo-whorls. Blade 3–8 cm long, up to 5 cm broad. **HABITAT/RANGE** Introduced from the West Indies and Central America. Naturalized and potentially invasive in se. Fla. and Fla. Keys.

JOEWOOD

Joewood

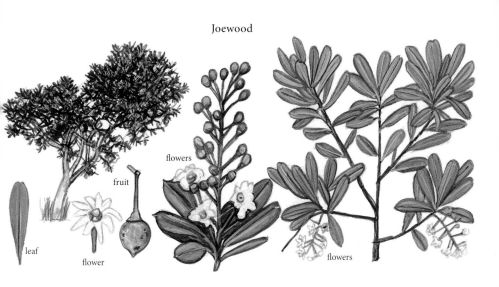

leaf

flower

fruit

flowers

flowers

Braceletwood

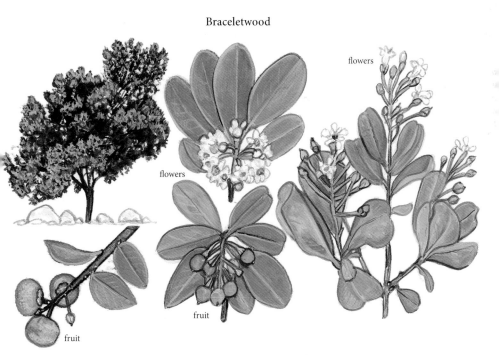

flowers

flowers

fruit

fruit

fruit

ULMACEAE: ELM FAMILY

The elm family (Ulmaceae) includes about 6 genera and 40 species of shrubs and trees distributed nearly worldwide, especially well represented in temperate and warm regions of the Northern Hemisphere. As previously perceived, the family included several genera now placed in Cannabaceae (*Celtis*, *Trema*). As circumscribed here, the family includes 3 genera and 12 species in the East, 7 native.

LEAF Alternate, mostly in 2 rows; simple, margins toothed or entire, the leaf base often asymmetric. Venation is prominent, consisting of a single midrib with prominent parallel lateral veins that sometimes fork near the leaf margin. **FLOWER** Tiny and wind-pollinated; sepals united, 3–9; petals absent; stamens opposite the sepals and equaling them in number; pistil 1 with 2 styles or stigmas. **FRUIT** Samara or drupe.

JAPANESE ZELKOVA *Zelkova serrata* (Thunb.) Makino

QUICK ID Recognized by the alternate simple leaves, with margins toothed, the tip an elongate point, and usually hairless above; new branches purplish brown, hairless or sparsely hairy; and the fruit a small drupe, the surface with a fine network of ridges.

Deciduous tree, to 30 m tall, 1 m diam. Erect, single short, low-branching trunk; crown vase-shaped at first, becoming broad and rounded; branches ascending or spreading, purplish brown or brown. **BARK** Grayish white or grayish brown, with horizontal lenticels, exfoliating in plates revealing the orange inner bark. **LEAF** Alternate, simple, papery; elliptic or broadly lanceolate; base rounded or heart-shaped, slightly asymmetric; tip abruptly long-pointed; margins coarsely and bluntly toothed. Upper surface dark green, hairless; lower surface paler, sparsely hairy along the veins. Blade 3–10 cm long, 1.5–5 cm broad; petiole 2–6 mm long, hairy. **FLOWER** Unisexual or bisexual, both types on the same plant; petals and sepals virtually indistinguishable from one another; male flowers usually with 7 parts, female flowers usually with 4 or 5 parts. Spring. **FRUIT** Nearly stalkless green drupe, 2.5–4 mm diam., the surface with a network of low ridges; matures autumn.

HABITAT/RANGE Introduced from Japan and adjacent parts of Asia. Cultivated, sparsely established in the East.

PLANERTREE *Planera aquatica* (Walter) J.F. Gmel.

A.K.A. WATERELM

QUICK ID Recognized by the combination of the scaly, flaking bark; alternate, 2-ranked, stiffish ovate to kite-shaped leaves with toothed margins, the base only slightly if at all asymmetric; and the soft drupes with fleshy, tentacle-like projections.

Deciduous shrub or small to moderate-size tree, usually not exceeding about 18 m tall, potentially to about 1 m diam.; typically much smaller than these dimensions. Erect or leaning, single usually short, low-branched trunk, or multiple trunks from a common base; trunk of old trees often sprouting near or at ground level. Crown of forest-grown trees spreading, with several lateral branches; crown of open-grown trees rounded. **BARK** Reddish brown and grayish, conspicuously scaly, somewhat shaggy, peeling in long grayish-brown plates. **TWIG** Rounded, slender, brittle, hairy at first, becoming mostly hairless. **LEAF** Alternate, simple, stiff, distinctly 2-ranked, the

PLANERTREE

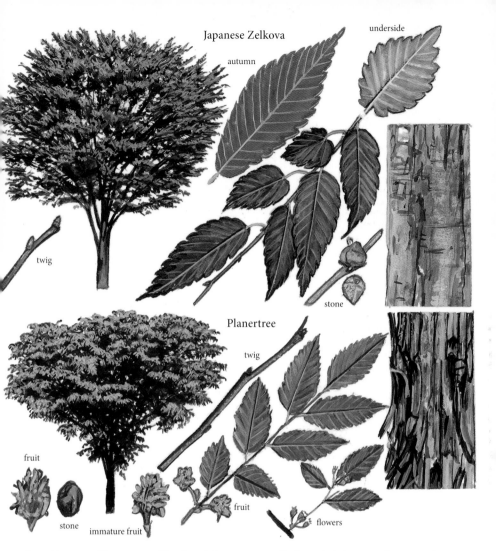

Japanese Zelkova

autumn

underside

twig

stone

Planertree

twig

fruit

stone

immature fruit

fruit

flowers

branchlets spraylike; ovate or kite-shaped, base rounded or broadly wedge-shaped, occasionally asymmetric; tip evenly tapered to a sharp point, occasionally abruptly tapered; margins finely and irregularly toothed, the teeth usually of 2 sizes, often obscure. Upper surface dark green, usually hairless, veins parallel, curving toward the leaf margin; lower surface paler, veins usually brownish. Blade 2–3.5 cm long, 2–4 cm broad; petiole 3–5 mm long **FLOWER** Bisexual or unisexual, small, male and female produced on the same plant, often in the same cluster; sepals 2–5, fused; petals absent; produced in clusters in the leaf axils; overwintering buds often infested with insects and forming a velvety-hairy, ball-shaped gall. Spring.

FRUIT Single-seeded drupe to about 1 cm long, the surface producing conspicuous fleshy projections; matures summer.

HABITAT/RANGE Native. River bottoms and floodplains, pond and swamp margins, backwaters, to 650 m; the Southeast, N.C., Ky., and Ill., south to n. Fla. and e. Tex.

SIMILAR SPECIES Distinguished from Winged Elm and Cedar Elm by the conspicuously shaggy bark.

Notes: *Planera* is a monotypic genus, distributed only in the southeastern U.S.

■ *ULMUS*: ELMS

Deciduous single-trunked trees, some reaching stately proportions. **LEAF** Alternate, simple, venation usually prominent, margins toothed, base often asymmetric. **FLOWER** Bisexual, small; sepals 3–9, the number and hairiness helpful with identification; petals absent; stamens 3–9, usually matching the sepals in number; inflorescence a fascicle, raceme, or cyme, usually subtended by 2 bracts. **FRUIT** Flattened, winged samara.

WINGED ELM *Ulmus alata* Michx.

QUICK ID Recognized by the combination of the alternate, 2-ranked, lanceolate or narrowly elliptic leaves with double-toothed margins and a mostly symmetric base; and samara margins fringed with whitish hairs.

Deciduous tree, 10–18 m tall, about 1 m diam. Erect, single straight trunk. Crown of forest-grown trees open, the branches ascending or spreading; crown of open-grown trees rounded. **BARK** Grayish brown, with irregular flat ridges divided by shallow furrows, often scaly, that of young trees sometimes corky. **TWIG** Slender, often decorated with flat, laterally spreading corky wings 1.5–2 cm broad; wings becoming less obvious on older trees, absent on others. **LEAF** Alternate, simple, somewhat firm, lanceolate or elliptic; base wedge-shaped, usually symmetric, occasionally asymmetric; tip sharply pointed; margins distinctly and coarsely toothed, the teeth of 2 sizes. Upper surface dark green, hairless, sometimes rough to the touch; lower surface paler, softly hairy at least on the veins. Blade 1.5–10 cm long, 1–4 cm broad; petiole to about 3 mm long, hairy. **FLOWER** Sepals 5, hairless. Late winter to early spring. **FRUIT** Stalked, narrowly ovate or narrowly elliptic, 1-seeded grayish or reddish-tinged

samara, about 5–8 mm long; margins and stalks copiously and conspicuously lined with short whitish hairs; the face sparsely hairy; matures late spring to early summer.

HABITAT/RANGE Native. Well-drained upland woods, slopes, moist hammocks, margins of floodplains, 0–600 m; the Southeast, Va., west to Mo., south to c. Fla., e. Okla., and e. Tex.

SIMILAR SPECIES Cedar Elm, which may also have corky-winged twigs, has flowers with 6–9 hairy sepals, overall smaller leaves, some rounded at the tip, and flowers and fruits in late summer to autumn.

AMERICAN ELM *Ulmus americana* L.

QUICK ID Recognized by the combination of alternate leaves with coarsely double-toothed margins and a strongly asymmetric base; yellowish-white hairs lining samara margins; and narrow, flange-like buttresses at base of trunk.

Deciduous tree, 21–35 m tall, 50–120 cm diam. Erect, single straight trunk, often buttressed at the base with narrow, flange-like buttresses; usually dividing 6–9 m above ground into several large ascending branches that form an open, vase-shaped or broadly spreading crown. **BARK** Smooth and grayish brown at first, becoming ashy gray and scaly with narrow ridges and furrows. **TWIG** Slender, light green at first, becoming grayish or grayish brown. **LEAF** Alternate, simple, moderately stiff; oblong, obovate, oval, or elliptic, base moderately or strongly asymmetric, tip usually abruptly pointed; margins coarsely toothed, the teeth usually of 2 sizes. Upper surface dark green, moderately lustrous, usually hairless, sometimes rough to the touch, especially on young trees or vigorous new branches; lower surface paler, duller, with tufts of hairs in the vein axils. Blade 2–15 cm long, 1–8 cm broad; petiole to about 5 mm long. Turns yellow in autumn. **FLOWER** Sepals 7–9, hairy; inflorescence a pendent cluster. Late winter to early spring, prior to the new leaves. **FRUIT** Stalked, 1-seeded samara, 10–12 mm long; sparsely hairy on the surfaces, hairy along the margins, the hairs often yellowish white; matures spring to early summer.

WINGED ELM

AMERICAN ELM

Winged Elm

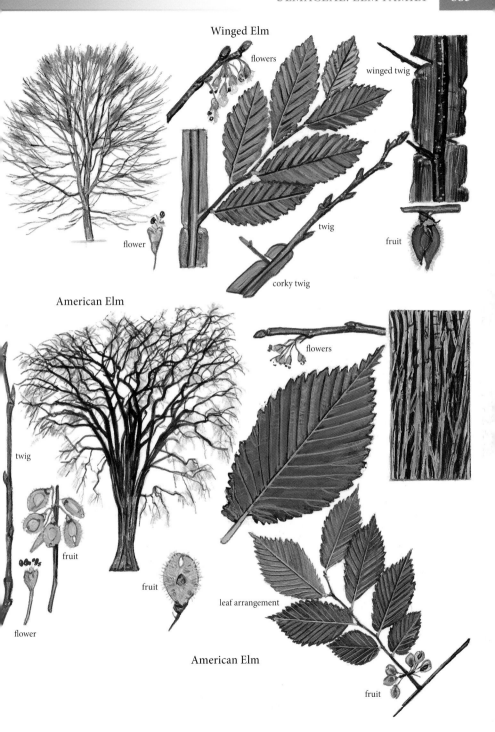

flowers

winged twig

flower

twig

corky twig

fruit

American Elm

flowers

twig

fruit

fruit

fruit

leaf arrangement

flower

American Elm

fruit

AMERICAN ELM *continued*

HABITAT/RANGE Native. Floodplains, swamp margins, alluvial woods, wet hammocks, 0–1,400 m; widespread in the East, N.S. to Man., south to c. Fla. and e. Tex.

SIMILAR SPECIES The leaves of Slippery Elm usually have mostly symmetric bases, the upper leaf surface is duller and consistently hairy and finely rough to the touch, and the margins of the samaras lack hairs.

Notes: American Elm, a favored street and landscape tree throughout the East, is subject to several blights, most famously Dutch elm disease.

CEDAR ELM *Ulmus crassifolia* Nutt.

QUICK ID Recognized by the combination of small alternate leaves that are usually symmetric at the base and have toothed margins, and the late-summer and autumn flowering period, the flowers with 6–9 hairy sepals.

Deciduous, the leaves often retained until very late in the season; tree 24–27 m tall, to about 90 cm diam. Erect, single straight trunk; crown with crooked limbs and interlacing branches that often have corky wings, the wings usually interrupted at the leaf nodes. **BARK** Light brown, irregularly and moderately ridged and furrowed, shedding in scalelike plates. **TWIG** Reddish brown, hairy, stiffish, on some trees with brown corky wings. **LEAF** Alternate, simple; elliptic, ovate, or oblong, those at the base of the branch often nearly circular; base rounded or moderately asymmetric; tip rounded to bluntly or sharply pointed; margins sharply or bluntly toothed, sometimes the teeth of 2 sizes. Upper surface dark green, rough to the touch; lower surface shaggy-hairy throughout or

only along the veins. Blade 1–5 cm long, 1–3 cm broad; petiole 0–2 mm long, hairy. **FLOWER** Sepals 6–9, hairy. Late summer to early autumn. **FRUIT** Stalked, more or less oval samara, 7–10 mm long; surfaces and margins hairy; matures autumn.

HABITAT/RANGE Native. River and stream banks, low woods, often where limestone is present, 0–500 m; primarily distributed in Ark., La., se. Tex., and se. Okla., disjunct to the Suwannee River drainage basin in n. Fla.

SIMILAR SPECIES Winged Elm has overall larger leaves, the tips consistently sharply pointed, and flowers with 5 hairless sepals that appear in late winter to early spring, and are followed shortly by the fruit.

SLIPPERY ELM *Ulmus rubra* Muhl.
A.K.A. RED ELM

QUICK ID Recognized by the combination of alternate, often obovate, double-toothed leaves that are rough to the touch above; new twigs that are rough to the touch; stiff hairs on the petiole; and samara fruit that lacks hairs on the margins.

Deciduous tree, 15–24 m tall, 30–60 cm diam. Erect, single straight, high-branching trunk, the branches few and well separated, forming an irregular, open, spreading, flat-topped crown. **BARK** Dark reddish brown to grayish, with flat, nearly parallel, interlacing ridges divided by shallow furrows; inner bark mucilaginous and slippery. **TWIG** Moderately stout, widely spaced, green at first, young twigs covered with short, stiff hairs and rough to the touch. **LEAF** Alternate, simple; obovate, oval, oblong, or elliptic, those nearest the base of the twig more nearly ovate; base rounded, occasionally asymmetric; tip abruptly short-pointed; margins conspicuously toothed, the teeth of 2 sizes. Upper surface dark, dull green, very rough to the touch from the presence of stiff, erect hairs, veins parallel, forked near the margin; lower surface paler, hairs softer. Blade 3–18 cm long, 4–8 cm broad; petiole 5–7 mm long, hairy with stiff hairs. **FLOWER** Sepals 5–9, greenish red, reddish-hairy. Late winter, spring. **FRUIT** Oval to nearly circular, 1-seeded yellow-green or

CEDAR ELM   SLIPPERY ELM

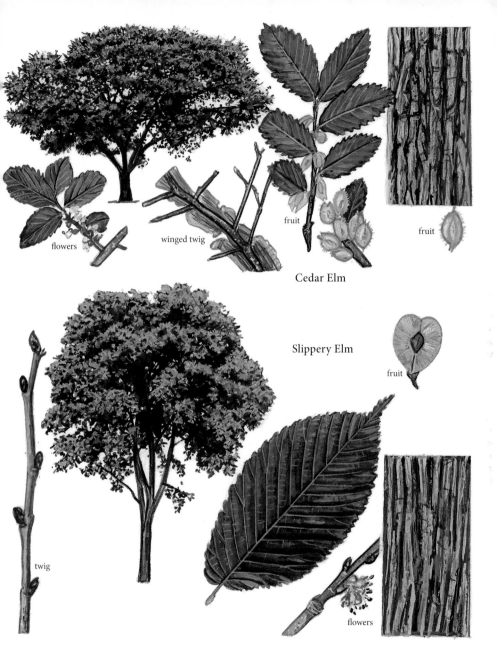

flowers

winged twig

fruit

fruit

Cedar Elm

Slippery Elm

fruit

twig

flowers

creamy-white samara, 8–20 mm long; margins and faces lack hairs; matures mid- to late spring.

HABITAT/RANGE Native. Upland woods, mixed forests, moist bluffs and slopes, often in association with clay or limestone, 0–900 m; widespread in the East, Maine and e. N.D., south to nw. Fla. and e. Tex.

SIMILAR SPECIES American Elm has leaves that are regularly asymmetric at the base, with a moderately lustrous, usually hairless upper surface, only sometimes rough to the touch; and yellowish-white hairs line the margins of the samara.

SEPTEMBER ELM *Ulmus serotina* Sarg.
A.K.A. RED ELM

QUICK ID Recognized by the combination of alternate simple, double-toothed leaves; mature branches with corky wings; autumn flowering and fruiting, the fruit often present after the leaves have fallen; and the margins of the samaras lined with hairs 1 mm long.

Deciduous tree to about 21 m tall, 80 cm diam. Erect, single trunk; crown spreading, broadly rounded, the branches often with corky wings at maturity. **BARK** Light brown or reddish brown, with shallow furrows and low ridges. **TWIG** Brown or gray, hairy or not, usually with scattered whitish lenticels; buds about 5 mm long. **LEAF** Alternate, simple; base usually strongly asymmetric; tip abruptly short-pointed; margins conspicuously toothed, the teeth of 2 sizes. Upper surface yellow-green, hairless, veins parallel, distinctly forking near the margins; lower surface yellowish gold, softly hairy, vein axils lacking hairs. Blade 5–10 cm long, 3–4.5 cm broad; petiole about 6 mm long. **FLOWER** Sepals 5 or 6. Summer to autumn. **FRUIT** Ovoid to elliptic, 1-seeded, light brown samara, 1–1.5 cm long, apex notched; margins densely hairy, the hairs about 1 mm long; matures autumn, sometimes after the leaves have fallen.

HABITAT/RANGE Native. Rare and uncommon on limestone bluffs, bottomlands, and hillsides, 0–400 m; restricted primarily to Tenn., also ranging from ne. Ga. and n. Ala. west to e. Okla. and ne. Tex.; disjunct to Ill.

SIMILAR SPECIES Hybridizes with Cedar Elm, the offspring of which are often difficult to assign to species.

ROCK ELM *Ulmus thomasii* Sarg.
A.K.A. CORK ELM

QUICK ID Recognized by the combination of alternate simple, double-toothed leaves; twigs with corky wings; flowers produced in spring; and faces of the samara hairy, the margins lined with short hairs.

Deciduous tree, 15–30 m tall, 30–60 cm diam. Erect, single high-branching trunk; crown slender, oblong or cylindrical; side branches short, drooping; older branches usually with corky wings or outgrowths. **BARK** Gray, thick, with broad furrows and broad, flat-topped, scaly ridges. **TWIG** Light brown and hairy at first, becoming lustrous reddish brown, then grayish brown, usually with corky wings or winglike ridges. **LEAF** Alternate, simple, obovate to oblong-oval, stiffish; base usually asymmetric; tip abruptly short-pointed; margins coarsely toothed, the teeth of 2 sizes. Upper surface lustrous, dark green, hairless, veins parallel, closely set, usually not forking near the margin; lower surface paler, white-hairy, the hairs not tufted in the vein axils. Blade 7–14 cm long, 2.5–5 cm broad; petiole about 5 mm long, hairy. **FLOWER** Sepals 7 or 8. Spring. **FRUIT** Elliptic or oval, 1-seeded samara, 1.5–2.2 cm long; apex shallowly notched; faces hairy, margins lined with short hairs; matures spring to summer.

HABITAT/RANGE Native. Moist or poorly drained hardwood forests, limestone outcrops, rocky slopes, floodplains, stream banks, 30–900 m; scattered in the n. U.S., N.H. and Vt. west to Minn. and S.D., south to W.Va., Tenn., ne. Nebr., and nw. Ark.

SIMILAR SPECIES Distinguished from Slippery Elm and American Elm by the irregular corky wings on the branches and essentially undivided trunk.

SIBERIAN ELM *Ulmus pumila* L.

QUICK ID Recognized by the combination of alternate simple, single-toothed leaves; hairless sepals; and hairless samaras.

Deciduous shrub or small to medium tree, 15–30 m tall, introduced from Asia and widespread in N. America. English Elm, Wych Elm, and Slippery Elm have hairy sepals, as opposed to hairless sepals in Siberian Elm; Winged Elm has corky wings along the twigs.

SEPTEMBER ELM   ROCK ELM

September Elm

flowers

fruit

fruit

winged twig

Rock Elm

twig

corky twig

flowers

fruit

Siberian Elm

twig

fruit

fruit

WYCH ELM *Ulmus glabra* Huds.
A.K.A. SCOTCH ELM

QUICK ID Recognized by the combination of alternate simple, double-toothed leaves, often with 3 small lobelike points at the tip; and samaras hairy only along the central vein of the wing.

Deciduous tree, to about 40 m tall. Erect, single trunk; crown spreading, broadly rounded. **BARK** Gray, smoothish, becoming shallowly furrowed. **TWIG** Grayish or reddish brown, hairy when young. **LEAF** Alternate, simple, elliptic to ovate, base conspicuously asymmetric; tip abruptly short-pointed, sometimes with 3 lobelike points; margins coarsely toothed, the teeth of 2 sizes. Upper surface dark green, conspicuously rough to the touch; lower surface hairy, especially in the vein axils. Blade 7–16 cm long, 3–10 cm broad; petiole 2–7 mm long, densely hairy. **FLOWER** Sepals 4–8, reddish-hairy. Spring to summer. **FRUIT** Winged, elliptic to obovate, pale greenish-brown samara, 15–25 mm long; apex blunt or rounded; hairy only along the central vein of the wing; matures summer.

HABITAT/RANGE Introduced from Europe and w. Asia. Established along woodland margins in the Northeast, 0–300 m; Maine and Vt. to Mass., N.Y., and R.I.

SIMILAR SPECIES The samaras of Slippery Elm are hairy only on the body; those of English Elm are hairless except near the apex.

CHINESE ELM *Ulmus parvifolia* Jacq.
A.K.A. DRAKE ELM

QUICK ID Recognized by the combination of alternate simple, mostly single-toothed leaves; elliptic or ovate samara; and mottled greenish, tan, and brownish flaking bark.

Deciduous tree, to about 25 m tall. Erect, single low-branched trunk; crown open, rounded, more or less flat-topped. **BARK** Mottled olive green, brown, and tan, flaking into small orange or tan plates. **TWIG** Light or medium brown, hairless or not. **LEAF** Alternate, simple, elliptic to ovate or obovate, base moderately to strongly asymmetric, tip abruptly short- and sharp-pointed; margins finely toothed, the teeth usually of 1 size, sometimes of 2 sizes.

Upper surface lustrous, dark green, hairless; lower surface paler. Blade 3.5–6 cm long, 1.5–2.5 cm broad; petiole 2–8 mm long. **FLOWER** Sepals 3–5, hairless. Late summer to autumn. **FRUIT** Elliptic or ovate, hairless, 1-seeded green to light brown samara, about 1 cm long; matures autumn.

HABITAT/RANGE Introduced from Asia. Widely planted in parking lots, along city streets, and in urban and suburban landscapes, 0–400 m; sparsely established from Maine to Fla., west to Ky.

SIMILAR SPECIES The flowers of Cedar Elm have 6–9 hairy sepals, and its trunk lacks Chinese Elm's mottled bark. The samaras of Winged Elm are lance-shaped to narrowly elliptic.

ENGLISH ELM *Ulmus procera* Salisb.
A.K.A. ENGLISH CORK ELM

QUICK ID Recognized by the combination of alternate, simple, double-toothed leaves; flower with hairy reddish-purple or tan sepals; fruit a samara, the margins hairless except near the apex.

Deciduous tree, to about 40 m tall. Erect, single trunk; crown open, branches sometimes with corky ridges. **BARK** Grayish brown, deeply furrowed, flaking. **TWIG** Slender, reddish brown, hairy, often rough to the touch, sometimes with corky wings. **LEAF** Alternate, simple; broadly lanceolate, elliptic, or ovate; base strongly asymmetric; tip acute; margins coarsely toothed, the teeth of 2 sizes. Upper surface dark green, rough to the touch; lower surface hairy with tufts in the vein axils. Blade 3–10 cm long, usually 4–6 cm broad; petiole 3–12 mm long, hairy, often rough to the touch. **FLOWER** Sepals 5–8, green, reddish purple, or tan; hairy. Spring. **FRUIT** Nearly circular, winged, light brown samara, 9–18 mm long; essentially hairless except near the apex; matures spring.

HABITAT/RANGE Introduced from Europe. Sparsely established in the East, 0–400 m; Ont., Conn., Mass., N.Y., R.I., Ill., and Mo.

SIMILAR SPECIES The samaras of Slippery Elm are hairy on the body, while those of Wych Elm are hairy along the central vein of the wing.

Wych Elm

twig

flower

flowers

fruit

Chinese Elm

twig

fruit

fruit

English Elm

flower

flowers

fruit

VERBENACEAE: VERVAIN FAMILY

As treated here, the vervain family includes about 35 genera and 1,000 species found in tropical and subtropical regions. Recent molecular genetic evidence suggests a close relationship between the Verbenaceae and Lamiaceae (mints), leading some authorities to include the genera *Petitia*, *Premna*, *Vitex*, and others (not treated here) within the mints rather than the vervains. The prized hardwood teak (*Tectona*), long allied with the vervains, is now also included within the mint family by many experts.

Several colorful ornamentals come from the vervain family, such as lantana (*Lantana*), and a few species provide herbal teas. The family is composed of herbs, lianas, shrubs, and trees. **TWIG** At least the young twigs are 4-sided and square in cross section. **LEAF** Opposite or whorled, simple or compound, the margins entire, toothed, or deeply lobed. **FLOWER** Borne in racemes, spikes, or heads. The calyx has 5 joined sepals, and the corolla has 5 joined petals that form a tube with 5 spreading lobes; the corolla is more or less bilateral, the 2 upper lobes sometimes nearly fused and appearing as one. There are usually 4 stamens, and a superior ovary with usually 4 chambers; the stigma has 2 lobes. **FRUIT** Drupe with 2 or 4 stones, or a dry fruit that splits into 2 or 4 nutlets.

SPINY FIDDLEWOOD *Citharexylum spinosum* L.
A.K.A. FLORIDA FIDDLEWOOD

QUICKID Easily recognized by the opposite simple leaves with an orange midvein and petiole.

Evergreen shrub or small, slender tree to about 12 m tall, 30 cm diam. Erect, single straight trunk; crown narrow, irregular. **BARK** Smooth, light reddish brown or gray, becoming scaly. **TWIG** Square in cross section. **LEAF** Opposite, simple, elliptic to obovate, leathery, thick; margins entire, rarely toothed on young branches. Upper surface lustrous green; lower surface yellow-green, dull, hairy, midvein tinted orange. Blade 5–17 cm long, 1–6 cm broad; petiole 1.5–2 cm long, orange or pinkish. **FLOWER** 9–12 mm long, white, tubular; petals 5, finely hairy;

borne in an elongated raceme to 30 cm long. Year-round. **FRUIT** Rounded red-brown or blackish drupe, 8–12 mm diam.; matures year-round.

HABITAT/RANGE Native. Hammocks, pinelands, 0–10 m; s. peninsular Fla. and Fla. Keys.

GOLDEN DEWDROPS *Duranta erecta* L.

QUICKID Sky-blue flowers and bright yellow fruit distinguish this species.

Evergreen, usually a shrub, occasionally vinelike, rarely a small tree to about 6 m tall, 8 cm diam. **BARK** Gray, becoming roughened and fissured with age. **LEAF** Opposite, simple, egg-shaped or elliptic, tapering to a short point at the tip; margins entire or toothed above the middle. Upper and lower surfaces dull green, essentially hairless. Blade 1.5–7.5 cm long, to about 2.5 cm broad; petiole to about 3 mm long. **FLOWER** About 1 cm diam.; petals 5, light blue; borne in an elongated raceme 5–15 cm long. Year-round. **FRUIT** Round yellow drupe, about 1.3 cm diam.; matures year-round.

HABITAT/RANGE Introduced from the West Indies. Escaped from cultivation; hammocks, pinelands, disturbed sites, 0–100 m; naturalized from s. Fla. to ec. Tex.

SPINY FIDDLEWOOD

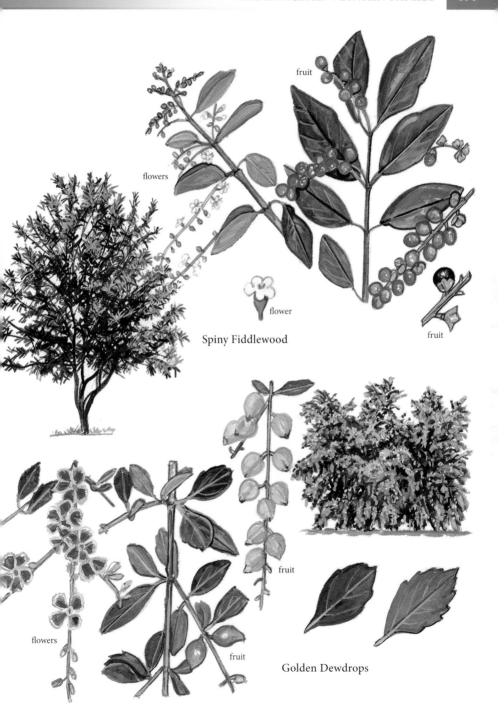

fruit

flowers

flower

Spiny Fiddlewood

fruit

fruit

flowers

fruit

fruit

Golden Dewdrops

■ *VITEX*: CHASTETREES

There are more than 250 species of chastetrees widely distributed in mostly tropical or subtropical regions of the world. Several species are grown as ornamentals; others are valued for lumber. At least 4 have naturalized in the East.

Deciduous or evergreen trees and shrubs. **LEAF** Opposite, palmately compound, divided into 3–9 leaflets with margins entire, toothed, or lobed. **FLOWER** Usually bisexual, more or less bilateral, small, white, blue, or yellowish, borne in loose to dense racemes or spikes; sepals 5, joined into a 5-toothed cup or tube; petals joined into a tube that extends beyond the calyx, flared into 5 lobes; stamens 4; ovary superior, 4-chambered, stigma 2-lobed. **FRUIT** Drupe.

LILAC CHASTETREE *Vitex agnus-castus* L.
A.K.A. COMMON CHASTETREE

QUICK ID Distinguished by the combination of palmately compound, 5-parted leaves, showy terminal racemes of lavender flowers, and strongly aromatic foliage.

Deciduous, strongly aromatic shrub or small tree to about 7 m tall, 10 cm diam. Erect, single trunk or multiple; crown rounded, dense. **BARK** Reddish brown or brown, smooth on young trunks, becoming finely fissured and scaly. **TWIG** Square in cross section, densely hairy. **LEAF** Opposite, palmately compound; petiole 1.5–7.5 cm long. Leaflets 3–9, usually 5, to about 10 cm long, to 3 cm broad; lanceolate, tapering to a sharp tip, margins entire or rarely toothed. Upper surface dull green, hairless, moderately lustrous; lower surface grayish green, finely hairy. **FLOWER** About 1 cm long; petals 5, lavender, blue, or white; borne in erect terminal clusters 12–18 cm long. Summer. **FRUIT** Round, dry, hard drupe containing a 4-parted stone; matures late summer to autumn.

HABITAT/RANGE Introduced from Eurasia. Cultivated, escaped, and sporadically naturalized throughout the Southeast, Pa. and Ky. south to s. Fla., west to Calif.

SIMILAR SPECIES The leaves of other naturalized species of *Vitex* have 3 or fewer leaflets.

CHINESE CHASTETREE *Vitex negundo* L.

Deciduous, usually a large shrub, rarely a small tree to 5 m tall. **LEAF** Opposite, palmately compound; leaflets 3–5, usually 3, lanceolate, to 11 cm long, to about 4 cm broad, margins toothed. **FLOWER** To about 3 mm long, 7 mm diam., violet, purple, or bluish; inflorescence to 42 cm long, 15 cm wide. **HABITAT/RANGE** Introduced from Asia; sporadically escaped from cultivation, chiefly in Fla., La., and Tex.

SIMPLELEAF CHASTETREE *Vitex trifolia* L.

Deciduous, typically a shrub. **LEAF** Palmately compound, distinguished by having 3 leaflets that are whitish and densely hairy on the lower surface. **FLOWER** Blue, borne in an upright terminal inflorescence. **HABITAT/RANGE** Introduced from Asia; escaped from cultivation, c. and s. Fla.

Lilac Chastetree

flower

flowers

fruit

Chinese Chastetree

flowers

fruit

underside

flower

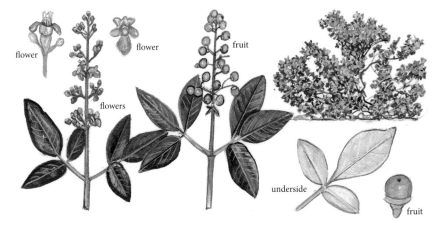

Simpleleaf Chastetree

flower

flower

flowers

fruit

underside

fruit

BASTARD STOPPER *Petitia domingensis* Jacq.

Evergreen shrub or small tree, 6–22 m tall, to 30 cm diam. Erect, single trunk. **BARK** Grayish, roughened, separating into scaly strips. **TWIG** Square in cross section. **LEAF** Opposite, simple, elliptic or oval, margins entire. Upper surface green, rough to the touch; lower surface yellowish green. Blade 7–16 cm long, to 8 cm broad; petiole 1.5–7 cm long. **FLOWER** Small, white, tubular, borne in branched clusters from the leaf axils. Year-round. **FRUIT** Round, 1-seeded blackish drupe, about 5 mm long. Year-round. **HABITAT/RANGE** Introduced from the West Indies; restricted in the U.S. to s. Fla.

FRAGRANT PREMNA *Premna odorata* Blanco

Evergreen large shrub or small tree, 3–8 m tall. **LEAF** Opposite, simple, egg-shaped or oblong, heart-shaped at the base, acute at the tip; margins entire or finely toothed. Upper surface lustrous, dark green; lower surface paler. Blade 10–20 cm long, 6–7 cm broad. **FLOWER** About 5 mm diam.; petals 4, white. **FRUIT** Round, dark purple drupe, to about 5 mm diam. **HABITAT/RANGE** Introduced from Asia; restricted in the U.S. to s. Fla.

XIMENIACEAE: XIMENIA FAMILY

This small family includes 4 genera and about 13 species distributed in tropical and warm temperate regions; 1 species is native to North America and is restricted to s. Fla. The family was formerly treated within Olacaceae, an artificial collection that has now been separated into several related families. Species of *Ximenia* are known parasites with haustorial roots (roots with parasitic outgrowths called haustoria) that intertwine with and parasitize the roots of other species. Some experts believe that this family may represent the first occurrence of root parasites in the order Santalales.

TALLOW WOOD *Ximenia americana* L.

QUICK ID Distinguished by the combination of elliptic leaves with an apical tooth, spiny branches, and orange fruit.

Evergreen shrub or small tree, usually 2–4 m tall, potentially to about 9 m. Erect, rambling, or scraggly, usually densely low-branched or with multiple trunks; crown irregular, with sprawling branches, the twigs often spine-tipped. **BARK** Grayish brown or reddish brown, smooth, often with visible lenticels. **LEAF** Alternate, simple, somewhat stiff and leathery; elliptic, ovate, oblanceolate, or nearly circular, often reflexed upward from the midrib; base broadly wedge-shaped or rounded; tip bluntly pointed or narrowly rounded, commonly with a tiny toothlike projection at the tip; margins entire. Upper surface dull or lustrous yellow-green, hairless. Blade 2.5–5 cm long, 1.2–3 cm broad; petiole 3–10 mm long, grooved. **FLOWER** Bisexual, fragrant, about 12 mm diam.; petals 4 or 5, greenish white, linear, 5–10 mm long, reflexed, densely hairy inside; produced in a several-flowered cluster. Predominantly spring to autumn, potentially year-round. **FRUIT** Ellipsoid, rounded, or egg-shaped drupe, 1.5–3 cm long; green at first, becoming orange. Year-round.

HABITAT/RANGE Native. Hammocks, scrub, pinelands, 0–10 m; s. Fla.

TALLOW WOOD

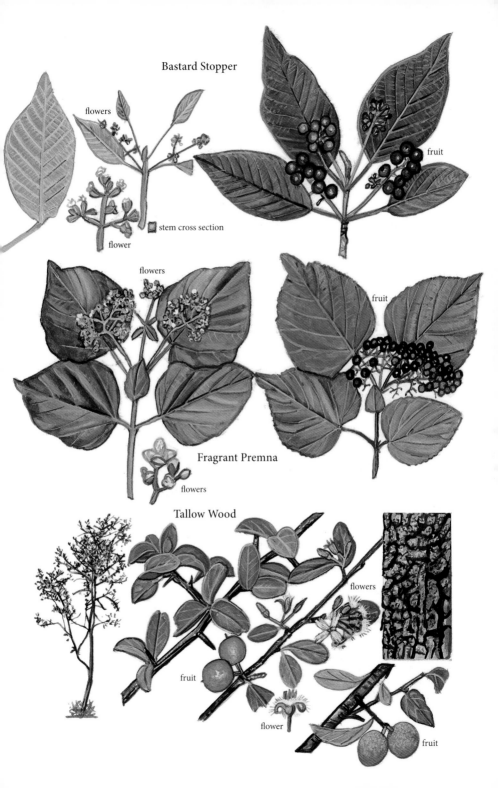

Bastard Stopper

flowers

flower

stem cross section

fruit

flowers

fruit

Fragrant Premna

flowers

Tallow Wood

flowers

fruit

flower

fruit

ZYGOPHYLLACEAE: CALTROP FAMILY

The caltrop family is a comparatively small family of about 26 genera and nearly 300 species of shrubs, herbs, annuals, and a few trees distributed in temperate, tropical, and subtropical regions of Africa, the Americas, Asia, Australia, and Europe. About 7 genera and 18 species occur in North America, at least 12 of which are native. The family is represented by 2 trees in the East, 1 native.

LEAF Opposite (rarely alternate), compound, the leaflets usually paired. **FLOWER** Bisexual, radial; petals and sepals 4–6; stamens 10–15; ovary superior. **FRUIT** Lobed or winged capsule, splitting to reveal seeds or separating into 5–10 indehiscent sections.

HOLYWOOD LIGNUMVITAE
Guaiacum sanctum L.
A.K.A. LIGNUMVITAE

QUICK ID Recognized by the combination of opposite compound leaves with 6–10 obovate leaflets, each tipped with a tiny projection; blue flowers; and red-coated seeds.

Evergreen large shrub or small tree to about 10 m tall, 20–45 cm diam. Young trees often strictly erect, with a single more or less straight trunk; older trees often produce multiple stems and low lateral branches, becoming irregular, diffuse, and somewhat gnarled; crown dense, spreading, usually rounded, often as wide or wider than the plant is tall; branch tips often drooping. **BARK** Pale gray or chalky white, deeply furrowed. **TWIG** Light gray, swollen at the nodes. **LEAF** Opposite, pinnately compound, blade 6–10 cm long, to about 6 cm broad; petiole to about 1 cm long. Leaflets 6–10, in 3–5 pairs, 2.5–3 cm long, less than 2 cm broad, leathery, oblong to obovate or oblanceolate; base narrowly wedge-shaped, asymmetric; tip rounded, tipped with a short projection; margins entire. Upper surface dark green; lower surface paler, hairless or with appressed, finely silky hairs. **FLOWER** Bisexual, radial; sepals 5, usually broadest near the tip, 5–7 mm long; petals 5, 7–12 mm long, blue, twisted, obovate with a rounded apex; produced singly or in clusters on hairy stalks. Spring. **FRUIT** Five-parted capsule, green at first and remaining so for some time, eventually turning brown; splits at maturity in autumn to reveal 5 seeds, each enclosed within a bright red covering.

HABITAT/RANGE Native, subtropical hammocks in Fla. Keys; cultivated and established on s. Fla. peninsula. Treated as endangered in Fla.

SIMILAR SPECIES The non-native **Common Lignumvitae** (*G. officinale* L.) is cultivated and established in s. Fla., especially in Miami-Dade County. It is distinguished by its leaves, which have only 4 leaflets, but is otherwise similar to the present species.

Notes: This plant's wood is hard, heavy, durable, and self-lubricating from internal resin, which has led to its use in the fabrication of bushings, propeller shafts, pulleys, and other similar applications. The resin was formerly used for medicinal purposes, especially in the treatment of syphilis. This genus of about 6 species is distributed in the Caribbean and w. Mexico.

HOLYWOOD LIGNUMVITAE

flower

split fruit

fruit

Holywood Lignumvitae

flower

Common Lignumvitae

flower

flowers

fruit

■ CREDITS

Figure of Evolution of the Carpel on p. 9 redrawn from P. H. Raven, R. F. Evert, S. E. Eichhorn, *Biology of Plants*, 4th ed. (New York: Worth Pub., Inc., 1986), Fig. 29–10, p. 591.

AUTHORS' ACKNOWLEDGMENTS

This project was originally conceived and presented to Princeton University Press by our editor, Amy K. Hughes. It has been a privilege and delight to work with her. Her ability to coordinate three authors and an artist, interact with the press and production crews, all the while maintaining good humor and patience, has been remarkable and is deeply appreciated. Robert Kirk of Princeton University Press saw the merit in our proposal and from that moment facilitated our efforts at every turn. Kathleen Cioffi, production editor, steady in the background, was always helpful when needed. David and Namrita Price-Goodfellow and their team at D & N Publishing produced the attractive and useful design of the book, and efficiently pushed the project through final production. Susi Bailey skillfully smoothed the rough edges with her copyediting expertise. Finally, Ken Womble, of Florida State University created the range maps, always with a cooperative "can-do" approach. To all these people, we extend deep gratitude for a job well done.

A number of botanists graciously supplied information that appears in the book; to each and every one of them we extend sincere thanks. Alphabetically, they are: Dr. George Argus, retired from the Canada Museum of Nature, Ottawa, for his help with the difficult willow (*Salix*) genus; Dr. Dan Austin, University of Arizona, provided valuable comment on soapberries (*Sapindus*); Dr. Luc Brouillet, University of Montreal, suggested authors from upcoming volumes of *Flora of North America* who might assist us; Keith Bradley, Institute for Regional Conservation, Miami, for assistance with range and species information for trees of southern Florida; Dr. Walter Judd, University of Florida, Gainesville, shared his knowledge and views of leaf morphology in the plant family Sapindaceae; Ron Lance of Asheville, North Carolina, provided assistance with several groups of southeastern trees, especially *Crataegus*; Dr. Austin Mast, Florida State University, Tallahassee, for unfettered access to the Robert K. Godfrey Herbarium; Dr. Guy Nesom, writer, botanist, and publisher of *Phytoneuron*,

Fort Worth, Texas, discussed with us problems in the ashes (*Fraxinus*); Dr. James Phipps, University of Western Ontario, helped with the hawthorns (*Crataegus*), including range maps and illustrative reference images; Dr. Joseph Rohrer, University of Wisconsin at Eau Claire, provided his manuscript for *Flora of North America* on the genus *Prunus*; and Dr. James Zarucchi, Missouri Botanical Garden, St. Louis, suggested authors from upcoming volumes of *Flora of North America* who might assist us.

In a project as diverse as this, hundreds of references were required, from the traditional technical taxonomic treatments of certain genera to reviews of plants occurring within a well-defined region. We thank those authors, many now deceased, who contributed so much to our understanding of North American trees. We further thank the online community for such excellent resources as Gymnosperm Database and its many contributors, USDA Plants, Angiosperm Phylogeny website, the Biota of North American Program, USGS tree species maps, Atlas of Florida Plants, Fairchild Tropical Garden Virtual Herbarium, Harvard University Herbaria, the University of North Carolina Herbarium, including Alan Weakley's online flora and the NCU Flora of the Southeastern United States, and numerous other websites; all were used extensively and have proved invaluable sources of information. And finally, to those who we might have inadvertently omitted, we sincerely thank them, noting that their aid, along with that of those above, has contributed to a thorough, concise, and informative gathering of information on trees of North America north of Mexico.

ILLUSTRATOR'S ACKNOWLEDGMENTS

The illustrator wishes to thank Myles Archibald, Julia Koppitz, and staff at Harper Collins, UK, and wishes to thank the following individuals and institutions for their help and support in providing references for the artwork: Marcel Blondeau, Keith Bradley, Judy Gibson of the Botany Department at the San Diego Natural History Museum, Richard R. Halse of the Oregon State Education Department, Roger Hammer, Neal Jackson and Martin Kelsen for technological and moral support, Ron Lance, Jim Phipps, Lulu Rico of the Herbarium Kew Gardens, Adele Smith of the Royal Botanic Gardens, and staff at Sul Ross State University of Texas.

STATE AND PROVINCE ABBREVIATIONS

United States	
State	*Abbreviation*
Alabama	Ala.
Alaska	Alaska
Arizona	Ariz.
Arkansas	Ark.
California	Calif.
Colorado	Colo.
Connecticut	Conn.
Delaware	Del.
Florida	Fla.
Georgia	Ga.
Hawaii	Hawaii
Idaho	Idaho
Illinois	Ill.
Indiana	Ind.
Iowa	Iowa
Kansas	Kans.
Kentucky	Ky.
Louisiana	La.
Maine	Maine
Maryland	Md.
Massachusetts	Mass.
Michigan	Mich.
Minnesota	Minn.
Mississippi	Miss.
Missouri	Mo.
Montana	Mont.
Nebraska	Nebr.
Nevada	Nev.
New Hampshire	N.H.
New Jersey	N.J.
New Mexico	N.M.
New York	N.Y.
North Carolina	N.C.

United States	
North Dakota	N.D.
Ohio	Ohio
Oklahoma	Okla.
Oregon	Ore.
Pennsylvania	Pa.
Rhode Island	R.I.
South Carolina	S.C.
South Dakota	S.D.
Tennessee	Tenn.
Texas	Tex.
Utah	Utah
Vermont	Vt.
Virginia	Va.
Washington	Wash.
West Virginia	W.Va.
Wisconsin	Wis.
Wyoming	Wyo.

Canada	
Province/Territory	*Abbreviation*
Alberta	Alta.
British Columbia	B.C.
Labrador	Lab.
Manitoba	Man.
New Brunswick	N.B.
Newfoundland	Nfld.
Northwest Territories	N.W.T.
Nova Scotia	N.S.
Nunavut	Nunavut
Ontario	Ont.
Prince Edward Island	P.E.I.
Quebec	Que.
Saskatchewan	Sask.
Yukon	Y.T.

METRIC–IMPERIAL EQUIVALENTS

25.4 millimeters (mm) = 1 inch
2.54 centimeters (cm) = 1 inch
0.3 meters (m) = 1 foot
1.6 kilometers (km) = 1 mile
0.4 hectares (ha) = 1 acre

Celsius to Fahrenheit:
$°F = 9/5 × °C + 32$

Centimeters
Inches

achene A tiny, one-seeded, dry, indehiscent fruit with a hard outer layer.

acuminate Abruptly tapered to a slender point, each side concave and often appearing as if pinched together.

adventitious Arising from a site that is more or less unusual, such as roots sprouting from a stem, or branches from the trunk.

aggregate fruit A fruit formed of the adjacent ovaries of a single flower, such as a blackberry.

alluvial Refers to deposits of sand, silt, gravel, and similar material formed by flowing water.

alternate Refers to a leaf arrangement in which only one leaf arises from each stem node. Compare *opposite*.

ament An elongated, scaly inflorescence of unisexual flowers; a catkin.

angiosperm A member of the flowering plants, a group of seed plants that develop seeds within an enclosed ovary.

anther The pollen-bearing structure at the tip of a stamen.

anthesis The time of expansion or opening of a flower; also the period during which the flower is in full bloom.

anthocarp A tiny one-seeded fruit enclosed in a fleshy, leathery, or woody covering derived at least in part from the perianth or receptacle.

apex The tip or distal end of a structure, farthest from the base (adj., *apical*).

apical meristem A small patch of cells at the tip of a stem or root that repeatedly divide, producing cells that differentiate into various cell types of the plant mostly behind the meristem, adding length to the structure.

apophysis The exposed, often thickened portion of a pinecone scale when the cone is closed.

appressed Pressed close to, lying flat against.

arborescent Having a tree form.

aril An outer covering on some seeds, commonly fleshy, sometimes brightly colored, often derived from the small stalk that connects the seed to the placenta.

ascending In plant habit, oriented upward or forward at an angle, often curving from the base, as in a coconut palm.

axil The angle formed by adjoining vegetative structures such as that between a leaf and the twig from which it grows.

axillary Located in, or arising from, an axil, or angle, usually between a twig and a leaf.

berry A fleshy fruit containing few to many seeds within.

bipinnate Refers to a compound leaf that is twice divided, with its primary segments branching from an axis, and each segment divided into separate leaflets along a secondary axis.

bole Tree trunk.

bract A scale or modified leaflike structure, associated with the seed-bearing cone scales of conifers; also found below the bases of some flowers, fruits, and flower and fruiting clusters.

bristle A minute, usually straight and stiff, hairlike extension, often at the tip of a leaf lobe or tooth (also called *awn*).

bud-scale scar A mark left on a twig when the scales surrounding a bud fall away.

bundle scar A mark within a leaf scar where a vascular bundle from the leaf entered the twig.

calyx The outermost of the four whorls of parts that make up a flower, formed by the sepals.

carpel The fundamental unit of the pistil, the pollen-receiving, seed-producing part of the flower.

capsule A dry, dehiscent fruit derived from a compound pistil; may have one or several chambers.

catkin A small, usually elongate cluster of highly reduced unisexual flowers, often deciduous as a unit.

chaparral An ecological community of shrubs adapted to dry summers and moist winters, mainly of s. Calif.

compound leaf A leaf with a blade that is divided to the midrib or to the tip of the petiole, thereby separated into smaller individual leaflets, each arising from an axis or central point. Contrast *simple leaf*.

conifer A cone-bearing plant of the gymnosperms order Coniferales, which includes the Cupressaceae and Pinaceae.

cordate In the shape of a heart; with regard to the base of a leaf blade, having two more or less rounded lobes, one on each side of the petiole (resembling the top of a Valentine heart).

corolla The whorl of parts formed by the petals of a flower.

corymb A flat-topped inflorescence in which the flowers mature from the outer edge inward (adj., *corymbose*).

costapalmate A leaf, such as a palm frond, that appears palmate (with the leaflets arising from a single point at the tip of the petiole), but actually has a very short midrib extending beyond the tip of the petiole.

crown The portion of a tree above the trunk formed by the branches and leaves.

crownshaft A portion of the stem in many palm trees, above the trunk and below the crown of leaves, composed of the bases of the leaves.

cyathium An inflorescence shaped like a small cup and resembling a tiny flower, containing a female flower and several male flowers, the flowers lacking sepals and petals and assumed to be evolutionarily reduced; several *cyathia* (pl.) may be aggregated and surrounded by brightly colored leaves, as in the Poinsettia.

cyme A terminal cluster of successive three-flowered units, the terminal flower of each cluster opening first and arresting further elongation of the cluster's axis, the two successive flowers at ends of branches originating below the terminal flower, the pattern repeated many times, often producing a flat-topped or convex flower cluster (adj., *cymose*).

cypsela An achene-like fruit that develops from an inferior ovary in plants of the Asteraceae.

dehiscent Regarding a dry fruit, splitting or otherwise opening at maturity.

dicotyledon, dicot A member of a group within the flowering plants that usually has two nutrient-storing leaves in the embryo within the seed, netlike leaf venation, and flower parts in multiples of four or five.

dioecious Having the male and female reproductive parts on separate plants.

drupe A fruit, such as a plum, with a three-layered ovary wall consisting of an outer skin over a fleshy layer and an innermost hard, bony layer forming one or more stones, each surrounding one seed.

ellipsoid Referring to a solid (three-dimensional) structure that is oval in outline as viewed from the side.

elliptic In the shape of an oval, the widest part across the middle.

endosperm Nutritive tissue formed around the embryo within a seed.

entire In describing margins of leaves (or sepals or petals), indicates that the margin is uninterrupted, as by teeth or lobes.

epicormic Refers to adventitious branches growing from a dormant bud.

exocarp The outermost layer of the ripened ovary walls of a fruit.

exserted Projecting beyond.

falcate Cutlass-shaped.

false terminal bud A lateral bud toward the tip of a twig that appears to be a terminal bud.

fascicle A small, closely held bundle or cluster (adj., *fasciculate*).

fastigiate Having a narrow, erect form of dense, upright, more or less parallel branches.

filament The stalk of a stamen.

follicetum An aggregation of follicles, as in the fruiting cluster of magnolias.

follicle A dry, podlike fruit derived from a single carpel that splits along one seam to release the seeds.

glabrous Without hairs, usually implying the surface to be smooth.

glaucous Having an impermanent powdery or waxy covering that often imparts a bluish tint, usually easily rubbed off.

gymnosperm A member of the group of seed plants in which the seeds do not develop within a closed ovary; includes the conifers.

habit A plant's growth form.

hairs Usually slender unicellular or multicellular structures growing from the epidermis of a plant; technically *trichomes*.

halophyte A plant adapted to soil high in salt content.

haustorium A parasitic outgrowth from a plant part, such as a root, that absorbs nutrients from a host plant; plural *haustoria*.

hesperidium A berry with a leathery rind, such as an orange.

heterophyllous Having more than one form of leaf.

hypanthium An often cuplike structure surrounding the ovary formed by the fused bases of the sepals, petals, and stamens; may be either free or fused to the ovary.

imbricate Overlapping, often forming a pattern like shingles on a roof.

indehiscent Remaining closed at maturity.

inflorescence The flower-bearing portion of a plant, usually referring to a cluster or arrangement.

infructescence The fruit-bearing portion of a plant; the inflorescence in a fruiting stage.

introduced Not native.

involucre A whorl of bracts subtending a flower or flowers, sometimes forming an enclosing structure.

krummholz A forest of subarctic or alpine zones in which the trees are stunted and contorted by climate conditions.

lanceolate A narrow shape much longer than wide, widest below the middle and tapering to a pointed tip, like the head of a spear.

lateral bud A bud that arises along a twig rather than at the growing tip.

lateral vein A side vein that branches from the midvein of a leaf.

leaf scar A mark left on a twig after a leaf drops.

legume The fruit of the Fabaceae, or bean family; a dry pod derived from a simple pistil that splits along two seams.

lenticel A patch of loose, usually pale, corky cells, varying from small dots to short dashes or even long lines, on a twig's surface, allowing the passage of gases into and out of the twig.

locule A chamber within a plant's ovary.

marcescent Withering but not falling off.

mesic Requiring or receiving a moderate amount of moisture; neither excessively wet nor dry.

mesocarp The middle layer of the part of a ripe fruit formed from the ovary wall.

microsporophyll A tiny spore-bearing structure.

midvein, midrib A vein that runs down the center of a pinnately veined leaf.

monocotyledon, monocot A member of a group within the flowering plants usually with one nutrient-storing leaf in the embryo within the seed, parallel leaf veins, and flower parts in multiples of three.

monoecious Having the male and female reproductive parts on the same plant.

mucro A tiny, sharp point extending beyond the margin, as at the tip of a leaf (adj., *mucronate*).

multiple fruit A fruit cluster formed of individual fruits of adjacent flowers joined together as a unit, as in the mulberry. Also called a *syncarp*.

native Originating from a given region.

naturalized Not native to a region but reproducing and persisting there as a population without the aid of horticultural practice.

nectary The gland of a flower that secretes the nectar; also called *nectar gland*.

net-veined Having a fine network of veins.

node Where a leaf or leaves attach to a stem.

nut An indehiscent one-seeded fruit with a hard outer wall.

nutlet See *pyrene*.

obovate Inversely ovate, with the broader end away from the base and toward the tip.

ocrea A tubelike sheath around the base of a petiole in some plants.

opposite Refers to a leaf arrangement in which two leaves are attached on either side of a stem node. Compare *alternate, whorled*.

ovate In the outline of an egg, with the broader end at the base, tapering toward the tip.

ovoid An egg-shaped solid, ovate in side view.

ovule A structure within a plant ovary that develops into a seed.

palmate In the shape of a hand or a fan, with lobes or veins radiating from a common point.

panicle A large multibranched inflorescence, the secondary branches of which are often racemes (adj., *paniculate*)

papilionaceous Of the Papilionoideae subfamily of the bean family (Fabaceae); often refers to the typical "pea-flower" form.

pedicel The stalk of a flower.

peduncle The stalk of an inflorescence.

peltate Having the stalk attached to the lower surface, rather than the margin, producing a form similar to a thumbtack or mushroom.

perianth The portions of a flower outside the stamens and pistil or pistils, usually consisting of the calyx and corolla, sometimes only the calyx. In some small, often wind-pollinated flowers, the perianth may be absent.

petal A unit of the corolla, the second whorl of the parts that make up a flower.

petaloid Resembling a petal in shape, texture, and color.

petiolate Having a petiole, or leaf stalk.

petiole The stalk of a leaf.

phyllode A leaflike structure formed of a flattened, expanded petiole in the absence of leaf blade tissue, often resembling a narrow, curved blade.

pine-needle bundle A sheathed cluster of leaves borne by members of the genus *Pinus*.

pinnate With the pattern of a feather, with a central axis and secondary axes extending from it in a plane on either side; often describes a pinnately compound leaf.

pistil The part of a flower bearing ovules and in which the seeds are produced; consists of a stigma (the pollen-receiving part), style (the sperm-transmitting part), and ovary (containing the ovule).

pistillate Having pistils; the term *pistillate flowers* refers to female flowers.

pith The central tissue within a twig or root, usually soft and more or less spongy, originating from the apical meristem and consisting of thin-walled cells.

pocosin A type of swamp or marsh formed in an upland area of the southeastern coastal plains.

pollen Tiny spores of a seed plant that produce sperm or sperm cells that fertilize the ovule.

polygamodioecious Having both unisexual and bisexual flowers on the same individual.

pome A fruit, such as an apple, formed by the thickened, fleshy hypanthium joined to the inferior ovary.

prickle A small, sharp-pointed growth from the surface tissue of the plant.

protogynous Describes a flower in which the female reproductive structure matures before the male parts, inhibiting self-pollination.

punctate Having tiny depressions scattered across the surface.

pustular Having pustules, or blisterlike protrusions.

pyrene The seed-containing stone of a small drupe, such as that of a holly; also called a *nutlet*.

raceme A loose (as compared to a *spike*), narrow inflorescence with stalked flowers along an elongate axis (adj., *racemose*).

rachilla In a bipinnately compound leaf, the rachis-like axis of a primary segment holding the leaflets.

rachis In a compound leaf, the central axis along which the leaflets are arranged; begins where the petiole ends, at the first leaflet at the base of the pinnately divided blade.

radicle The root portion of a plant embryo.

remote toothing Teeth that are well separated, not close together, and usually sparse along the margin of a leaf.

reticulate Forming a network.

revolute Rolled downward or backward.

samara A hard, dry, indehiscent fruit with one or more wings, such as that of a maple.

schizocarp A dry fruit comprising multiple carpels that splits open along the partitions between chambers into one-seeded sections.

semideciduous Describes plants that lose most but not all of their leaves at the end of the growing season or during dry periods, and occasionally all leaves during particularly extreme conditions.

semievergreen Retaining leaves through the winter (or the dry season) in some circumstances but not in all, usually depending on climate, latitude, or elevation.

sepal A usually flat green unit of the outermost of the four whorls that form a flower, collectively forming the calyx, and usually providing protection to the interior when flowers are in bud.

In some plants sepals are colored and more like petals (*petaloid*).

serotinous Maturing late in the growing season; regarding cones, remaining closed until opened by heat (usually fire) or considerable age and only then releasing seeds.

sessile Lacking a stalk.

short shoots Lateral twigs that grow very slowly and are much shorter than the faster-growing main branch, sometimes appearing as woody stubs, sometimes thorn-tipped, and often bearing leaves, flowers, or fruits; also called *spur shoots*.

simple leaf A leaf with an undivided blade; the blade may be toothed or deeply lobed, but not divided to the midrib or tip of the petiole. Contrast *compound leaf*.

spatulate Spatula-shaped; a shape in which the basal portion is very narrow and elongate and the tip is wider and rounded.

spike A tight, long, narrow inflorescence in which the individual flowers lack stalks (adj., *spicate*).

spine A needlelike structure that is derived from a leaf or a portion of a leaf, such as a cactus spine or mesquite spine.

spur shoots See *short shoots*.

stamen The pollen-producing (male) reproductive structure of a flower.

staminate Having stamens; the term *staminate flowers* refers to male flowers.

staminode A sterile stamen.

stellate Starlike, with radiating branches from a common central point of attachment.

stigma In a flower, the tip of the pistil, which serves as the pollen receptor.

stipitate Born on a stipe, or stalk.

stipule One of a pair of structures at the base of the petiole of a leaf, which are usually small, green, and leaflike, but may be modified into scales, bristles, or spines (called *stipular spines*).

stoma A microscopic pore in the surface of a leaf that allows for the exchange of water vapor and other gases in and out of the leaf (plural, *stomata*).

style The often elongate portion of a pistil between the ovary at the base and the stigma at the tip.

subglobose Nearly globose or spherical.

sub-opposite Regarding leaf arrangement, technically alternate but so close together as to appear opposite.

subpalmate Not quite palmate but suggestive of a palmate pattern.

subspecies A taxonomic category below the species level designating subgroups of a species that are closely related and capable of interbreeding, but typically do not, usually because of geographic separation. Abbreviated *subsp*. Compare *variety*.

syconium A fruit, characterized by the fig, derived from a highly modified inflorescence that bears tiny unisexual flowers inside.

syncarp See *multiple fruit*.

tepals Refers to perianth parts that are poorly or not differentiated as sepals and petals.

terminal bud A bud that forms at a twig's tip.

thorn A sharp-pointed woody structure derived from, and tipping, a twig.

trifoliolate A compound leaf divided into three leaflets.

tripinnate Refers to a compound leaf that is thrice divided, with its primary segments divided into secondary segments, and each of those divided into individual leaflets.

trunk The main portion of a tree's stem between the roots and the crown; bole.

twig The portion of a young branch produced by the current year's growth.

umbel An often flat-topped inflorescence in which the stalks of the individual flowers originate from a common point (adj., *umbellate*).

unifoliolate A compound leaf reduced to, or expressed as, a single leaflet.

valvate Regarding bud scales, meeting at the edges without overlapping, like the halves of a clamshell.

variety A taxonomic category below the species level designating subgroups of a species that are closely related and capable of interbreeding, but typically do not, usually because of geographic separation. Variety is of lower rank than subspecies, but in plants when only one category below species is used, variety and subspecies are conceptually equivalent. Abbreviated *var*. Compare *subspecies*.

vascular bundle A strand of a plant's water- and nutrient-transport system that contains tissues of various kinds.

vascular cambium A layer of unspecialized cells in a plant's vascular tissue.

waif A stray; a plant that has been introduced and is occasionally found growing naturally, but has not become naturalized or established self-perpetuating populations.

whorled Refers to a leaf arrangement in which three or more leaves are attached at a stem node.